The American Critical Archives is a series o
resentative selections of contemporary rev
American authors. Specifically, each volume ....
excerpts from reviews that appeared in newspapers and weekly and monthly
periodicals, generally within a few months of the publication of the work concerned. There is an introductory historical overview by a volume editor, as well
as checklists of additional reviews located but not quoted.

T. S. Eliot is widely regarded as one of the most important and influential
poets of the twentieth century. He was also extremely prolific. *T. S. Eliot: The
Contemporary Reviews* is a testament to both of these aspects of Eliot's work.
In it, Jewel Spears Brooker presents the most comprehensive gathering of newspaper and magazine reviews of Eliot's work ever assembled. It includes reviews
from both American and British journals. Brooker expands on the major themes
of the reviews and shows how the reviews themselves influenced not only Eliot,
but also literary history in the twentieth century.

AMERICAN CRITICAL ARCHIVES 10
T. S. Eliot: The Contemporary Reviews

The American Critical Archives

GENERAL EDITOR: M. Thomas Inge, Randolph-Macon College

T. S. Eliot

The Contemporary Reviews

Edited by
Jewel Spears Brooker

Eckerd College

CAMBRIDGE UNIVERSITY PRESS
Cambridge, New York, Melbourne, Madrid, Cape Town, Singapore, São Paulo, Delhi

Cambridge University Press
The Edinburgh Building, Cambridge CB2 8RU, UK

Published in the United States of America by Cambridge University Press, New York

www.cambridge.org
Information on this title: www.cambridge.org/9780521118989

First published 2004
Reprinted 2006
This digitally printed version 2009

A catalogue record for this publication is available from the British Library

Library of Congress Cataloguing in Publication data
T. S. Eliot: The Contemporary Reviews / edited by Jewel Spears Brooker.
p. cm. – (The American Critical Archives; 14)
Includes bibliographical references and index.
ISBN 0 521 38277 7
1. Eliot, T. S. (Thomas Stearns), 1888–1965—Criticism and interpretation.   I. Brooker,
Jewel Spears, 1940–   II. Series.
PS3509.L43Z87317   2004
821'.912—dc22   2003055755

ISBN 978-0-521-38277-9 hardback
ISBN 978-0-521-11898-9 paperback

For Ralph,
Rebecca, Allison, Jennifer, Caroline, Erika, and Amy
with love and gratitude

Contents

Series Editor's Preface

The American Critical Archives series documents a part of a writer's career that is usually difficult to examine, that is, the immediate response to each work as it was made public by reviewers in contemporary newspapers and journals. Although it would not be feasible to reprint every review, each volume in the series reprints a selection of reviews designed to provide the reader with a proportionate sense of the critical response, whether it was positive, negative, or mixed. Checklists of other known reviews are also included to complete the documentary record and allow access for those who wish to do further reading and research.

The editor of each volume has provided an introduction that surveys the career of the author in the context of the contemporary critical response. Ideally, the introduction will inform the reader in brief of what is to be learned by a reading of the full volume. The reader then can go as deeply as necessary in terms of the kind of information desired—be it about a single work, a period in the author's life, or the author's entire career. The intent is to provide quick and easy access to the material for students, scholars, librarians, and general readers.

When completed, the American Critical Archives should constitute a comprehensive history of critical practice in America, and in some cases the United Kingdom, as the writers' careers were in progress. The volumes open a window on the patterns and forces that have shaped the history of American writing and the reputations of the writers. These are primary documents in the literary and cultural life of the nation.

M. THOMAS INGE

Introduction

When T. S. Eliot died in London in 1965, he was widely regarded as the most important poet to have written in English in the twentieth century. His obituary in the London *Times* was entitled "The Most Influential English Poet of His Time" and in *Life* magazine, a memorial essay ended with "Our age beyond any doubt has been, and will continue to be, the Age of Eliot."[1] Although vociferously challenged, such assessments were still in place at the end of the century. In June 1998, *Time* magazine published a special issue on artists and entertainers of the past one hundred years. Picasso was named the artist of the century, Stravinsky the composer, Joyce the novelist, and Eliot the poet.[2] This list is a reminder that Eliot is part of a watershed in the history of Western art, and that *The Waste Land* (1922), his early showpiece, is the century's signature poem. Eliot was also a formidable literary critic, and his "Tradition and the Individual Talent" is perhaps the century's most noted essay in criticism. In the 1930s and 1940s, he turned to verse drama and social and religious criticism and made significant contributions to those genres as well. In the 1950s and 1960s, he became the focal point for a reaction against Modernism, and for several decades after his death, it became as fashionable to vilify him as it had once been to praise him. By century's end, the reaction against Modernism had itself become part of the ebb and flow of cultural history, and as suggested by the *Time* special issue, Eliot and his fellow modernists had settled down among the classics.

One of the most valuable perspectives on Eliot's career can be discovered by tracking the contemporary reviews of his work. These reviews provide a moving mirror reflecting the curve of his reputation as he was accepted as a man of letters, first in the United Kingdom, but rapidly thereafter in America, and also as he became a polarizing figure in post-Second World War literary politics. In retrospect, one can see that a few brief reviews of *Prufrock and Other Observations* were crucial in shaping the reception of Eliot's poetry; they created a place for it and generated the sort of discussion that made reviewers eager to see more of his work. The reviews of *The Sacred Wood*, his first collection of literary journalism, were also important, for they quickly confirmed his authority as a critic, and this authority underpinned his reputation as a poet and prepared the way for the reception of *The Waste Land*. Conversely, in the 1930s, the reviews of *After Strange Gods* and other religious and cultural essays complicated his authority and clouded judgments about his poetry and plays. These early reviews do more, however, than document the contemporary reception of Eliot's work. They anticipated to a remarkable extent the issues that would be raised in future criticism of his poetry and in future accounts of literary Modernism.

Eliot's first volume, *Prufrock and Other Observations*, was published in London in June 1917 by the Egoist Press, but it was preceded by the publication in 1915 of several major poems, including "Preludes" and "Rhapsody on a Windy Night" (in the short-lived Vorticist magazine *Blast*), "Portrait of a Lady"(in two different collections, *Catholic Anthology* and *Others*), and "The Love Song of J. Alfred Prufrock" (in *Catholic Anthology* and in Chicago-based *Poetry* magazine). The general response to Eliot's first poems was that they represented something "new" in English poetry, something uniquely "Modern," and the first readers struggled to name the quality that accounted for the newness. Two of the first reviewers, Conrad Aiken and Ezra Pound, were especially heartening, and their brief comments anticipated two persistent strains of Eliot criticism, the first emphasizing subjectivity, the second, objectivity. Both of these reviewers were Americans, both were poets, both were to prove consequential in Eliot's reception, and both were to remain Eliot's friends for life. Aiken was Eliot's Harvard classmate and one of his first literary confidants. They had worked together on Harvard's literary magazine, the *Harvard Advocate*, and when Eliot went to Paris for a year at the Sorbonne in the fall of 1910, Aiken arranged to visit him. In August 1911, Aiken arrived in Paris, and when shown a draft of "Prufrock," he was immensely enthusiastic. A couple of months later, both young poets were back at Harvard, and during the academic year of 1911–12, they met regularly for dinner and discussion of their work.

The second early reviewer was Ezra Pound, who came to the attention of Eliot and Aiken through his writings in *Poetry*. In the January 1913 issue, Pound maintained that the best poetry being written was by Yeats and the "*Imagistes*."[3] Aiken wrote a letter to the editor protesting Pound's "high-handed" and "propagandistic" views. He accused "the Editor and Mr. Pound" of caring more about self-promotion than about nurturing poetry and scolded them for using the magazine "too egotistically, . . . to give expression . . . to their own personalities." He insisted that Pound's poetry, while interesting enough, was not the touchstone by which all poetry should be measured. Harriet Monroe, the editor of *Poetry*, was unimpressed and chose not to print this mild complaint (it is preserved, however, in Aiken's published letters).[4]

In June 1914, Aiken went to London to try to make literary connections, not only for himself, but for Eliot. He took a typescript of "Prufrock" and "La Figlia che Piange," neither of which he was "able to sell," but he did succeed in having tea with Pound and telling him about Eliot's poetry.[5] Eliot himself arrived in London on 21 August 1914, and on 22 September, with an introduction from Aiken, he called on Pound in Kensington and showed him the typescript of "Prufrock." Pound, like Aiken, was impressed, and he immediately began a campaign to publicize Eliot's talent. He arranged for the publication of "Prufrock" in the June 1915 issue of *Poetry* and included it and several other Eliot poems in his *Catholic Anthology* (1915). In a review written a few months later, Aiken claimed that Pound's *Catholic Anthology* "blows the horn of revolution in poetry." With Eliot's poems in mind, he called his review "Esoteric Catholicity," and singled out "Prufrock" and "Portrait of a Lady" as two poems that exemplify both universality and idiosyncrasy (foreshadowing, perhaps, Eliot's "tradition" and "individual talent"): "Mr. Eliot . . . with a minimum of sacrifice to form conveys a maximum of atmosphere. Both poems are psychological character-studies, subtle to the point of insoluble idiosyncrasy, introspective, self-gnawing."[6] Aiken understood the early Eliot better than most readers, including Pound, and here, in miniature, is a brilliant bit of literary analysis. In describing Eliot's work as "psychological character-studies . . . introspective, self-gnawing," Aiken was associating these early poems with the great tradition that includes Shakespeare's soliloquies and Browning's dramatic monologues. Eliot's peculiar way of turning his portraits inside out is what makes him so modern, what gives him his "insoluble idiosyncrasy," and at the same time, what accounts for his universality and deep humanity. Aiken's account of Eliot's poems as portraits of interior states suggests that he was thinking in terms of modern painting, particularly in terms of the mood pieces of the Expressionists. Like the canvases of Edvard Munch, poems such as "Rhapsody on a Windy Night" objectify moods, such as melancholy, or feelings, such as disgust or alienation. What Munch accomplished with color and line, Eliot accomplished with music and image.

Pound's *Catholic Anthology* also attracted the attention of mainstream critic Arthur Waugh, who considered Pound's poets as anarchists, "literary Cubists" bent on destroying English tradition. Writing in October 1916, with the Battle of the Somme still raging just across the English Channel, Waugh had reason to be alarmed about revolutionaries and the survival of the United Kingdom. He pointed to "Prufrock" as especially dangerous because especially subversive of authority. Waugh concluded with a parable comparing Eliot to the drunken slaves that wealthy men used to bring out as negative examples for the benefit of their own sons.

Waugh's review was a godsend for Pound, for it gave him an excuse to join in the public discussion of his own book, increasing its notoriety and visibility. In June 1917, in the *Egoist*, he responded to Waugh with "Drunken Helots and Mr. Eliot." Pound's strategy was to embrace Waugh's barbs and proclaim them the hallmark of the new poetry. He loved being called a "literary Cubist," and characterized the contrast between Waugh and Eliot as an archetypal struggle between old and young, stodgy and imaginative, Victorian and modern. By the time *Prufrock and Other Observations* appeared in June 1917, Pound had a review ready to go, and it was published in the August issue of *Poetry*. Enlarging on his position from "Drunken Helots and Mr. Eliot," he goes into detail about Eliot's tradition—the Elizabethans and the French, with a dash of Browning—and his modernity. Pound praises Eliot's realism, saying that "all good art is realism of one sort or another," and his ability to observe and capture the objective world in language.

A few months later, in November 1917, Aiken followed up with a review in the *Dial*. He too lauds Eliot's "realism," but with a difference. In an extension of his comments of the previous year, he claims that Eliot's strength lies in the precision with which he maps mental and moral landscapes: "This is psychological realism, but in a highly subjective or introspective vein; . . . Mr. Eliot gives us . . . the reactions of an individual to a situation for which to a large extent his own character is responsible." Here in this brief first review of *Prufrock and Other Observations*, Aiken reveals a deeply disturbing quality of Eliot's poetry, one never really caught by Pound and by many Modernist critics. Aiken goes on to characterize these poems as "purely autobiographic," but "bafflingly peculiar" because they objectify something essentially private. He describes Eliot's temperament as "hyper-aesthetic . . . with a good deal of introspective curiosity."

Aiken's Eliot is modern (Anglo-American, personal, subjective, psychological, Expressionistic), whereas Pound's is Modernist (European, impersonal, objective, realistic, Post-Impressionistic, Cubistic, avant-garde). Both perspectives are valuable, so much so that entire schools of commentary have formed themselves around this basic polarity. (Eliot himself, one of the most self-reflexive and self-ironizing of poets, dealt with this binary in his criticism, most notably in his commentary on the English metaphysical poets).[7]

By the time the Prufrock volume appeared, then, it was already the topic *du jour* in literary circles. In struggling to describe Eliot's style, a number of reviewers followed Pound and Aiken in drawing on analogies with the visual arts. May Sinclair, for example, writing in the December 1917 *Little Review*, focused on Eliot's realism, particularly in "Preludes" and "Rhapsody on a Windy Night." Defending him against the charge that his images are ugly, she insisted on his integrity in forcing the reader to see urban reality as it is. He does in words, she claimed, what Hogarth did in painting, and, as in Hogarth, there is in his juxtapositions a mixture of irony and social criticism.

Reality stripped of all rhetoric, of all ornament, . . . is what he is after. His reality may be a modern street or a modern drawing-room; it may be an ordinary human mind suddenly and fatally aware of what is happening to it; Mr. Eliot is careful to present his street and his drawing-room as they are, and Prufrock's thoughts as they are: live thoughts, kicking, running about and jumping, nervily, in a live brain.

Sinclair praised his ability to convey the thoughts of an exceptionally intelligent character without resorting to abstractions. She noted the political undercurrent in the assessment that Eliot is dangerous. "Mr. Eliot is associated with an unpopular movement and with unpopular people. His 'Preludes' and 'Rhapsody' appeared in *Blast* . . . That circumstance alone was disturbing to the comfortable respectability of Mr. Waugh."

If May Sinclair is closer to Pound in her reading of the Prufrock volume, the American reviewer, Babette Deutsch, is closer to Aiken. Focusing on Eliot's technical achievement, she argues in the *New Republic* that it has the "hallmarks of impressionism."

> Impressions are strung along on a tenuous thread of sense . . . of dirty London streets, crowded with laborers, dilettantes, prostitutes; of polite stupidities in country houses; of satiric fencings; of the stale aroma of familiar things. Mostly they are impressions of a weary mind, looking out upon a crowded personal experience with impartial irony.

Marianne Moore also compared the poems with paintings, and like Pound, she saw an Eliot who is a true friend of the object. His poems are like Whistler's Post-Impressionistic English canvases, but just as Eliot's portraits are an improvement on Browning, his city scenes are an improvement on Whistler, for Eliot refuses to hide his objects "under shadows and the haze of distance."

Another enduring debate about Eliot's poetry was initiated by Edgar Jepson and William Carlos Williams. In the *English Review*, Jepson distinguished English poetry from "United States poetry," and added, "Mr. Eliot is United States of the United States; and his poetry is securely rooted in its native soil." Williams, who had already conceived of himself as the quintessential American poet and of Eliot as his opposite, responded in the *Little Review* by labeling Eliot a "subtle conformist." He too compared Eliot with Whistler, not (as Moore did) to praise him, but to show that he was a Europeanized American. Williams's review of Eliot's first volume did not appear until May 1919, and by that time, most of the poems that were to comprise Eliot's second volume, *Poems* (1919), had appeared. Williams must have seen them, for like his own comments on "Prufrock," they were published in the *Little Review*, and he must have felt that the quatrain poems confirmed his low opinion of Eliot. Williams's view, which was to gather steam after the Second World War, was entangled with resentment of Eliot and of critics who praised his poetry, including Pound.

The next cluster of Eliot reviews, coming in 1920 and 1921, had two *foci*, poetry and criticism. His second group of poems was published in 1919/1920 in three overlapping books—*Poems, Ara Vos Prec,* and *Poems* (1920). His first book of criticism—*The Sacred Wood*—appeared at the same time. The combination of opaque and avant-garde poetry with translucent and authoritative prose puzzled some readers and dazzled others. From this time forward, Eliot's reception as poet and his authority as critic would be indissolubly linked.

The publication of Eliot's new work was to follow the pattern of the publication of the *Prufrock* poems. Individual pieces were published separately in periodicals and discussed in previews. By the time they appeared in book form, they had already become objects of interest and controversy. Between 1917 and 1919, Eliot wrote a great deal of literary journalism—not only book reviews, but substantial essays including "Tradition and the Individual Talent." These pieces, published in little magazines and respected journals, were increasingly noticed and admired. He continued to write poetry during this period too, with most of the new poems appearing in the *Little Review*. In May 1919, Leonard and Virginia Woolf published his *Poems*, a slender volume of recent work (four quatrain poems and three poems in French). In February 1920, this collection was enlarged to include the already published *Prufrock* volume and a few new poems (notably, "Gerontion") and published as *Ara Vos Prec* in London and as *Poems (1920)* in New York. A few months later, in November 1920 (London) and February 1921 (New York), the best of his literary journalism appeared under the title *The Sacred Wood*. This flurry of publication was related in part to Eliot's need to justify to his parents his decision to live abroad, but in part to a shrewd sense of timing in regard to his career.

The reviewers of the new poems, like the reviewers of *Prufrock*, groped for words to describe Eliot's work, and most used analogies from the visual arts. Robert Nichols compared the poems to canvases by Walter Sickert and Rembrandt, and Clive Bell compared Eliot to Matisse, Picasso, and Braque. Neither Aiken nor Pound reviewed these volumes, but their general points of view were evident. Aiken's psychological slant can be seen in the review of *Ara Vos Prec* by John Middleton Murry, who suspected that there was something deeply personal in these poems, that the poet was a chameleon moving against protective backgrounds and contexts. He saw this chameleon as Prufrockian—intelligent, subtle, and ironic, a "connoisseur in the discrepancy between intention and achievement." Desmond MacCarthy, similarly, praised Eliot's uncanny talent for projecting the modern mind, and he tried to describe the techniques through which Eliot simultaneously conceals and reveals the self. Pound's Modernist slant, on the other hand, can be seen in the review by Clive Bell, who emphasized impersonality and wit. Bell associated Eliot with such figures as Stravinsky, Joyce, and Picasso. Richard Aldington, similarly, underscored Eliot's place in a movement that included these same figures. Babette Deutsch, whose views resembled Aiken's, introduced Eliot's "weird and brilliant book" to American readers by praising "Prufrock" as "a piece of psychological analysis of extraordinary delicacy and brilliance" and by classifying the quatrain poems as stilted and strange.

The reception of Eliot's early poetry was greatly enhanced by his growing prestige as a critic. Robert Nichols's review of *Ara Vos Prec*, written seven months *before* the publication of *The Sacred Wood*, Eliot's first volume of criticism, began by assuring readers that the author of these unusual verses "is known to the world at large . . . as a widely erudite critic possessed of a natural distinction in style and such a mordant perspicacity as is hardly to be matched in British or North American letters today." Nichols was writing in April 1920, just after the March publication of *Three Critical Essays on Modern English Poetry*, a special edition of *Chapbook* containing essays by Eliot, Aldous Huxley, and F. S. Flint.[8] This special issue had been previewed in *Chapbook* in February by Douglas Goldring, who lamented criticism's loss of prestige and expressed the belief that a young American now settled in London might be able to make a difference.

> Mr. Eliot has a scientific, analytical brain, and approaches his task with . . . the detachment of the great surgeon who, knife in hand, advances towards the exposed flesh of the anaesthetized "case." He rarely makes a cut in the wrong place, he dissects with an unhurried precision, and remorselessly reveals the structure and the content of the book on which he operates. His learning is prodigious . . .; he has undoubtedly one of the most distinguished critical minds of our time.

Goldring's description of Eliot's criticism—detached, impersonal, scientific, analytical, surgical—was accepted by an increasing number of critics, including the anonymous reviewers of the *Times Literary Supplement*, who joined the chorus, praising Eliot's concept of criticism as "just and high."

When *The Sacred Wood* was published a few months later, Leonard Woolf was one of the first reviewers, and he reiterated the view that Eliot represented a post-war recovery of detachment. Writing in the *Athenaeum*, Woolf claimed that Eliot's work "seems to cry aloud, 'Back to Aristotle,' and . . . brings us up with a shock against the satisfying, if painful, hardness of the intellect." For Eliot, as for Aristotle, he insisted, "criticism is a science, and it must . . . rely upon the two great scientific instruments, comparison and analysis." Woolf, like Pound, stressed the virtue of impersonality, quoting with approval Eliot's statement that "it is in . . . depersonalization that art may be said to approach the condition of science." Aldington and other reviewers echoed Woolf's position.

But Aiken demurred. In "The Scientific Critic," a long and substantial review in the *Freeman*, he contended that criticism is not a science, but an art, and it does not begin with an analysis of aesthetics, but with an understanding of life. Aiken complimented Eliot, but tempered his praise by calling into question two central tenets celebrated in the reviews by Woolf and his friends. First, he rejected the notion that art can be impersonal and expressed dissatisfaction with Eliot's "vague" use of the word "impersonality." Second, he denied that a great poet or even a great critic could ever really be "scientific." Regarding Eliot's stated desire "to see the object as it really is," Aiken asks "Is poetry an object, or an experience?" Criticism, he claimed, must begin in the human sciences with an attempt to understand "the function of art, social[ly] and psychologically . . . in the community, in the life of the artist."

In 1922, Eliot's most famous poem, *The Waste Land*, was published, first in periodicals, and immediately thereafter in book form. In the United Kingdom, it appeared in October in the inaugural issue of the *Criterion*, and in America, it came out in November in the *Dial*, in both cases without the dedication to Pound and without the "Notes." It was published as a book on 15 December in New York by Boni and Liveright, and on 12 September 1923 in London by the Woolfs at Hogarth Press. The poem outraged some readers, baffled some, and dazzled still others. For the most part, the first group considered it to be either meaningless or dangerous, whereas the second and third groups welcomed it as either a mirror of modernity or a bold experiment. The tone in a good number of these reviews was urgent and polemical, as if something much bigger was at stake than the fate of a single poet and a single poem.

As was the case with Eliot's earlier publications, *The Waste Land* entered literary discussion in the United Kingdom and America many months before the poem itself appeared in print. The London literary establishment knew that Eliot was working on a "long poem." Several friends, notably Pound and Aiken, had seen drafts of the fragments that were to make up the poem. The Bloomsbury set also knew the poem before it was published. On 18 June 1922, Eliot read it aloud to Virginia and Leonard Woolf and their friend Mary Hutchinson.[9] In America, Gilbert Seldes, editor of the *Dial*, had become an admirer, and in September, he arranged for Eliot to receive the *Dial* award for literature.[10]

The Waste Land made its presence felt almost immediately. Within a couple of weeks of its appearance in the *Criterion*, it was hailed by the *Times Literary Supplement* as a "great poem," "its vision singularly complex," "its labyrinths utterly sincere." The anonymous reviewer added, "we know of no other modern poet who can more adequately and movingly reveal to us the inextricable tangle of the sordid and the beautiful that make up life." Such an introduction guaranteed serious reviews, and scores were forthcoming. Several raised issues and themes that were to exercise Eliot studies for the rest of the century. As was the case with Eliot's earlier work, the most powerful reviews were by his fellow Americans—Aiken, Seldes, and Edmund Wilson.

The first few reviews included several related directly or indirectly to the 1922 *Dial* award. The award was announced in the *New York Times* on 26 November and in *Dial* in the December issue. Seldes wrote a piece on Eliot for the 6 December issue of *Nation* and commissioned Edmund Wilson to write a review of *The Waste Land* to accompany the announcement of the award in *Dial*. Wilson's essay was his second on Eliot in less than a month; both were brilliant and both prophetic of the direction future discussions would take. Wilson's first review, "The Rag-Bag of the Soul," appeared 25 November in the *New York Evening Post*. Like other critics in the 1910s and 1920s, he was trying to pinpoint the distinguishing characteristic of modern art. A number of reviewers, citing Eliot's poetry and criticism, maintained that the modern element was a new objectivity, a new classicism. Wilson, on the other hand, argued that the modern element was a new subjectivity. Beginning in the late nineteenth century with Expressionism, painters and writers began to show more interest in the world within the self than in the world of objects or of society, and they developed new forms to project their thoughts and feelings. Wilson suggested that "The characteristic literary form today . . . is a cross-section of the . . . consciousness of a single specific human being, usually carried through a very limited period, such as a day or a week." For support, he pointed to such works as "Prufrock" and "Gerontion," Pound's *Eight Cantos*, Joyce's *Ulysses*, Woolf's *Mrs. Dalloway*, and O'Neill's *The Hairy Ape*. Several critics, in discussing modern literature, had used the image of a "stream of consciousness." In describing Eliot's achievement in *The Waste Land*, Wilson changes the metaphor from a stream to a rag-bag, a repository of scraps haphazardly saved for possible use. The fragments in this rag-bag are spiritual and mental— "chunks of human consciousness." Some are personal—particles of passion or pieces of self-knowledge; some are cultural—nursery rhymes or bits of Shakespeare; many are accidental—shards found in a particular place at a particular time. Wilson's image is helpful, for whereas a stream suggests time, a rag-bag suggests space. The first allows for narrative, for sequence and order, for beginnings and ends, but the second suggests only juxtaposition and chance. Wilson's review, interestingly, represents a synthesis of the approaches to Eliot's work by Aiken and Pound. Like Aiken, he insists that the poem is personal, taking its origin and its material from Eliot's "soul." And like Pound, he argues that the poem is impersonal, a reflection of post-war culture, of "our present condition of disruption."

Wilson's second review, "The Poetry of Drouth," appeared in December in the *Dial*. One of his objectives was to preempt the argument that *The Waste Land* is either unreadable or too obscure to make it worth the trouble. Using Eliot's own notes, he wrote a primer on the mythical method, with explanations of the myth of the waste land drawn from Frazer and Weston.[11] He suggested that, for Eliot, the arid land where almost nothing can grow is a symbol, a concrete image, of a "spiritual drouth." He insisted that one does not have to know Eliot's allusions. "For all its complicated correspondences and recondite references . . . , *The Waste Land* is intelligible at first reading. . . . the very images and sounds of the words—even when we do not know why he has chosen them—are charged with a strange poignancy." As in his previous review, Wilson argued convincingly that *The Waste Land* is at once personal and impersonal, local and universal, temporal and timeless. It is marked by "the hunger for beauty and the anguish at living which lie at the bottom of all his work." At the same time, the poet is speaking "not only for a personal distress, but for the starvation of a whole civilization. . . . a whole world of strained nerves and shattered institutions."

Wilson's two reviews anticipate much of the best criticism of *The Waste Land* of the next half century. He identified the themes that make the poem seem so universal and described the structure that makes it seem so formidable. Chaos, he insisted, was not in the poem, but in the poet and the culture. In explaining the monomyth as narrative and relating it to history and religion, he provided the paradigm that the New Critics and many others would use in interpreting the poem. A decade later, in *Axel's Castle*, Wilson expanded his discussion of Eliot as part of a now classic genealogy of Modernism, correctly placing Eliot, Yeats, and other Modernists as heirs of the French Symbolists.[12]

Seldes's piece on Eliot appeared in the 6 December issue of the *Nation*. His purpose was to introduce Eliot to Americans and, further, to call attention to the *Dial* award. He discussed Eliot's criticism, with emphasis on the "historical sense," "depersonalization," and allusiveness. Claiming that "it is from his critical utterances that we derive the clue to his poetry," Seldes proceeded to use these concepts to interpret *The Waste Land*. He conceded the poem's brokenness, but argued that it has a "hidden form," that "each piece falls into place" when the reader knows Eliot's criticism and understands the title metaphor of the waste land. "Every great and original writer," Wordsworth said in 1807, "in proportion as he is great or original, must himself create the taste by which he is to be relished."[13] Seldes's essay suggested that Eliot had succeeded in creating such a taste and, with the help of his well-placed friends, had fostered a climate in which his poem could be appreciated.

A couple of months after Wilson and Seldes had reviewed *The Waste Land*, Aiken published his review, "An Anatomy of Melancholy," in the *New Republic*. This piece, like the two reviews by Wilson, raised issues which would remain under discussion for the rest of the century. As a reader of *The Waste Land*, Aiken was an insider. He had been a confidant throughout the entire period of the poem's composition, and in the fall and winter of 1921–22, while living in London, he had lunched with Eliot several times a week. He knew of Eliot's health and marital problems, and he had seen some of the fragments that were to be incorporated into the finished poem. In a note to a 1958 reprinting of his review, Aiken said that although he knew the background of the poem, he felt that it would have been a betrayal to have used this knowledge in the review.[14]

In retrospect, the complexity of Aiken's relationship with Eliot can be detected as an undercurrent in his evaluation of the poem. Aiken was lavish in praising *The Waste Land*, describing it as "unquestionably important, unquestionably brilliant"; at the same time, he also considered it "pretentious." His main objection related to its self-reflexivity, its learning, its "Notes." It is literature made of literature, and moreover, many of the allusions are too obscure to be meaningful. If allusions are to be effective, he argued, they "must flower where they are transplanted." But in spite of his reservations about the allusions, Aiken had no doubts about the poem's overall power. That power, he suggested, derives from its origins in Eliot's personal life, and he tried to say so obliquely by applauding its "emotional value." He contended that the poem has unity, not because it is built on some literary sub-structure, but because it is supported by a "dim unity of personality." It consists (as Wilson had also said) of fragments of consciousness, memories, and desires. It invites the reader "into a mind, a world, which is a 'broken bundle of mirrors,' a 'heap of broken images.'" Picking up on Prufrock's metaphor, Aiken maintained that in *The Waste Land*, Eliot had succeeded in throwing his nerves in patterns on the screen of the poem. He acknowledged a certain incoherence, if judged by standards of logic or narrative, but suggested that such standards are not relevant in modern poetry. *The Waste Land* "succeeds by virtue of its incoherence, not of its plan." Aiken also emphasized the poem's tonal qualities. Understanding the poem's structure, he claimed, is less dependent upon knowing the monomyth than upon having a good ear. It is "an emotional ensemble," "a melancholy tone poem," and its coherence is musical. He also used a visual analogy—*The Waste Land* is a "brilliant and kaleidoscopic confusion . . . a series of sharp, discrete, slightly related perceptions and feelings, dramatically and lyrically presented and violently juxtaposed."

The reviews of *The Waste Land* by Wilson and Aiken are the best of the sixty or more considered for this collection, but numerous others are also insightful. Burton Rascoe, who considered it the "finest poem of a generation" and wrote several good reviews, was amused to be considered part of a dark conspiracy to palm off "an unintelligible work by an obscure scribbler as the great poetic work of the year"; Elinor Wylie and Edgell Rickword, like Aiken, read the poem as the projection of a uniquely modern sensibility. Rickword, again like Aiken, used Prufrock's image of a magic lantern show in which the poet's nerves are thrown in patterns on a screen.

The negative reviewers of *The Waste Land* objected mainly to its allusiveness (its learning), its tone (its negativity), and its form (its incoherence and fragmentation). Louis Untermeyer took up all three points in a withering review, "Disillusion vs. Dogma," published 17 January 1923 in *Freeman*. Untermeyer had appreciated the *Prufrock* poems for their combination of irony and "poetic color," but he had been disappointed in the quatrain poems, with their "epigrammatic velleities" and "crackling" tone.[15] He was appalled by *The Waste Land*, which he saw as an attempt to combine these two styles, with disastrous consequences. Impatient with the allusions, he dismissed them as forming "a pompous parade of erudition," "cryptic in intention and dismal in effect." He was distressed by the lack of decorum shown by mixing high and low culture, combining genres and styles, "mingling . . . willful obscurity and weak vaudeville." Untermeyer maintained that the tone, though "an extension of

[Eliot's] early disillusion," was too pessimistic, too colored by "contemporary despair." And finally, he objected to the form of the poem. While accepting the notion that the chaos in the poem was a reflection of the chaos in contemporary culture, he insisted that the duty of an artist is "to give form to formlessness," not simply to reproduce it. This critique would later be christened the "fallacy of imitative form" by Yvor Winters. Other reviewers—F. L. Lucas, J. C. Squire, even John Crowe Ransom—were offended by various aspects of the poem. Still, by the time the cycle of reviews had run its course, Eliot had acquired an impressive reputation, with such knowledgeable critics as Clive Bell and Leonard Woolf calling him the best of modern English poets.

In 1925, Eliot published his second cumulative collection, *Poems 1909–1925*. It included the Prufrock poems, the 1920 poems, *The Waste Land*, and one important new work, "The Hollow Men." The reviews of this volume reveal a growing consensus regarding his work, and that consensus is overwhelmingly positive. There were dissenters, of course, but they were no match for Eliot's energetic admirers. His earlier reviewers picked up their pens again, and they were joined by the critic and psychologist, I. A. Richards. On the American side, the best reviews are by Edmund Wilson, Conrad Aiken, and Allen Tate; on the British, by Leonard Woolf, John Middleton Murry, and I. A. Richards. Wilson's review, like his brief pieces on *The Waste Land*, is brilliant, and he adds a new insight: Eliot can be seen as one of the American writers shaped by the Puritan mind. Aiken resumed his sometimes cantankerous but always insightful commentary, asserting that Eliot's theme was the "paralyzing effect of self-consciousness." Tate argued that Eliot is a poet of ideas. Among the British critics, Woolf and Murry resumed the discussion begun in their earlier reviews. Woolf maintained that Eliot perfectly represents the "spirit of 1922," and Murry argued that Romanticism and idealism died on the Somme, and that writers such as Eliot and Virginia Woolf reflect a "new classicism," a new realism and cynicism born of having weathered personal and national catastrophe.

Richards wrote a brief but impressive review for the *New Statesman*, and, a few months later, he included it as an appendix to the second edition of *Principles of Literary Criticism* (1926). Like Wilson and Aiken, Richards argued that the modern element in Eliot's poetry is a special subjectivity that controls structure, imagery, and mood. The structure is based on the coalescence and contrast of emotional effects; the central technique is "conjunction of feeling." The symbols are psychological, not mystical; the topic is not culture but sex, "the problem of our generation as religion was the problem of the last." The allusions are not important in themselves, but for the "emotional aura which they bring." Richards suggested that Eliot had marked his work with a "personal stamp, which is a certain sign of authenticity" in art.

By the middle 1920s, Eliot had achieved distinction as a man of letters; as an individual human being, however, he was close to collapse from a decade of stress and overwork. He had arrived in England in August 1914, the very month in which the Great War began, and for three years from September 1915, he suffered the hardships of life in a city under aerial bombardment. His closest friend was killed at Gallipoli, and many of his English friends were slaughtered or maimed. His marriage in June 1915 brought more grief than bliss, and, by the early 1920s, it had crumbled. His wife was ceaselessly ill, and the personal and financial strain of supporting her contributed to his own breakdown in 1921. All of this and more reached a climax in the mid-1920s, and in June 1927, as part of an attempt to reclaim his life, he entered the English Church. Both his crisis and his recovery can be traced in his writings. In 1928, he published a new collection of essays, *For Lancelot Andrewes*, with a preface stating that his "general point of view" could now "be described as classicist in literature, royalist in politics, and anglo-catholic in religion."[16] In the months that followed, he published in pamphlet form his great essay on Dante (1929) and his poetic sequence *Ash-Wednesday* (1930). In addition, he contributed several Christmas poems, including "Journey of the Magi," to Faber's *Ariel* series. Both the essays and the poems reflect his new commitment to Christianity.

The new Eliot was greeted with respect by a few, with astonishment by many more, and with a strange combination of admiration and disdain by others. When *For Lancelot Andrewes* appeared in November 1928, Jacob Bronowski wrote a review bemoaning Eliot's attack on humanism and challenging his connection of classicism and Christianity. In what would become a refrain in subsequent criticism, the *Times Literary Supplement* reviewer noted a contradiction between Eliot the critic and Eliot the poet, the first shaped by classical ideals and the second by romantic longing. The anonymous reviewer found the profession of Christianity "from the author of *The Waste Land* . . . astonishing, to say the least," and although he found much to praise in Eliot's new work, he clearly found much to regret. He also felt a sense of betrayal, for the most modern of all poets had "abdicated from his high position; he rejects Modernism for medievalism."

One of the most powerful voices emerging from the reviews of *For Lancelot Andrewes* was that of F. R. Leavis. In a rebuke to condescending reviewers, he reminded critics that Eliot was a poet of profound originality and a critic of immense intelligence. Wilson concurred, calling Eliot "the most important literary critic in the English-speaking world." Wilson said that he understood Eliot's disenchantment with modern materialism and substitute religions; at the same time, he argued that the turn to "medieval theology" was not one that modern intellectuals could follow. The most striking review of *For Lancelot Andrewes* was written by Eliot's old friend Conrad Aiken. Entitled "Retreat," it was published in the *Dial*, the very periodical that had done so much to launch *The Waste Land*. Aiken suggested that while it is impossible to read Eliot without respect, it is also impossible to read him without "misgivings."

Accusing Eliot of being "in retreat from the present and all that it implies," he concluded with comments that must have been painful for Eliot to have read. Aiken claimed that Eliot's new position represented "a complete abdication of intelligence. And with this abdication goes a striking change in Mr. Eliot's whole outlook and style. A note of withered dogmatism sounds repeatedly in these pages." Aiken expressed hope that Eliot would return to the present and resume his role as an "intrepid explorer" of modern life.

Aiken did not review *Ash-Wednesday* (1930), but later, somewhat surprisingly, he called it Eliot's "most beautiful" poem.[17] Most readers were struck by the discontinuity between it and Eliot's earlier poetry, but several of the poet's more astute critics noted that the surface discontinuity concealed a deeper continuity. Morton Zabel, for example, maintained that, in hindsight, Eliot's conversion was predictable and that it should be understood at least partially in terms of his deep identification with Dante. Anticipating a number of later critics, Zabel saw *The Waste Land* as a modern *Inferno* and *Ash-Wednesday* as a modern *Purgatorio*. The best of the *Ash-Wednesday* reviews are by two seasoned American reviewers of Eliot's work, Edmund Wilson and Allen Tate. Emphasizing continuity between *The Waste Land* and *Ash-Wednesday*, Wilson conceded that the poem is brilliant and a worthy successor to Eliot's earlier work. He saw the poem as a masterpiece of Symbolism and praised its musical values, its infinitely suggestive images, its appropriation of ritual, and most of all, the peculiar honesty it brought to the representation of the human soul. More formalist in orientation, Tate insisted that Eliot's poetry should be read as poetry and not as a commentary on Eliot's conversion. He did not argue that content and feeling are irrelevant, but simply that they should be sought in the poem and not in the poet. In a particularly valuable insight, he noted that the irony in the early poems is transfigured as humility in *Ash-Wednesday*.

The next cluster of reviews can be associated with Eliot's return to America in 1932. He had left the United States in 1914, and except for a brief trip home immediately after his marriage in 1915, he had not been back. This was due, in the first instance, to the war, but after the war, to a variety of economic and personal circumstances. When he sailed for Europe in the summer of 1914, he was a student; when he returned in 1932, he was one of the most distinguished men in the English-speaking world. The occasion for his return was an invitation to give the Charles Eliot Norton lectures at Harvard University for 1932–33. While in the United States, he was showered with awards and feted in glittering settings. In the spring of 1933, he gave the Page-Barbour lectures at the University of Virginia.

Three major publications, all in prose, can be associated with Eliot's homecoming. The first, *Selected Essays*, was a collection of his early journalism. Published in September 1932, it was timed to coincide with his arrival in the United States. The second, *The Use of Poetry and the Use of Criticism*, consisting of the Norton lectures, was published by Harvard University Press in

1933. The third, *After Strange Gods*, consisting of the Page-Barbour lectures, appeared in 1934. The cumulative effect of the reviews of these books was negative, with even the most admiring readers expressing concerns about Eliot's views on religious and cultural subjects.

For American readers, *Selected Essays* provided both a reminder of Eliot's eminence and an occasion to reassess his importance in modern literary culture. The London *Sunday Times* published a cordial review by R. A. Scott-James praising Eliot's "cool sanity," "analytical judgment," "fastidiousness," and his scrupulous attention to the object. In America, the *New York Times* joined the long list of papers paying homage to Eliot. Peter Monro Jack's review, "The Cream of T. S. Eliot's Literary Criticism," while not original, was upbeat and positive. R. P. Blackmur suggested in *Poetry* that Eliot was a valuable model, because "without insulting our intelligence or diminishing his own, he supplies us with something different from ourselves."

Many reviewers, however, seemed perplexed by *Selected Essays*. Their primary concern was the long-perceived discontinuity between Eliot's poetry and his prose, further complicated by his inclusion in *Selected Essays* of non-literary writings. In a generally positive piece in the *Saturday Review*, Paul Elmer More tried to come to terms with the "cleft Eliot." Edgell Rickword, one of Eliot's earliest and best reviewers, lamented the discontinuity between the poet's literary and moral imaginations. He maintained that when Eliot writes about literature, he has no equal, but when he writes about humanism, he becomes less interesting, less valuable. Some critics argued that there were at least "three Eliots"—a modern poet, a classic critic, and a mediocre thinker. Henry Hazlitt suggested in the *Nation* that it was almost unthinkable that these three could be the same person. Even Eliot's most admiring reviewers were forced to acknowledge the dissociation. Bonamy Dobrée, on the defensive for Eliot's sake, insisted that the poetry and criticism should be seen as the reflection of one mind, one sensibility. But even while praising Eliot's urbanity, clarity, and strength, he admitted that the essays on humanism diluted Eliot's greatness. Robert Hillyer, writing in the *New England Quarterly*, was less charitable. He saw the split in Eliot's prose collection as the reflection of a man divided against himself, and submitted that "Mr. Eliot's vogue" was due to the fact that his admirers were "similarly disorganized." Hillyer questioned Eliot's expatriation, seeing it as "a symbol of that homelessness which has obsessed his mind for so long" and has caused him to seek sanctuary in the Church.

The mixed reviews of *Selected Essays* modulated into the largely negative ones of the Harvard lectures, published in 1933 as *The Use of Poetry and the Use of Criticism*. A handful of reviews were positive, including that by Peter Monro Jack in the *New York Times*, and, more substantially, by Cleanth Brooks in the *Southwest Review*. Brooks, a pioneer of the New Criticism, was at the beginning of his distinguished career. Considering Eliot's work as a whole, he argued that it represented an attempt, largely successful, to reassess and reorder English poetry. But most reviewers demurred. The tenor is caught in the opening sentences of Richmond Lattimore's review in the *Journal of English and Germanic Philology*. *The Use of Poetry*, he suggested, "is on the whole disappointing, not so much because of its defects as because of the false hopes that may be raised in the reader's mind by the association of Mr. Eliot's known abilities with . . . his title. Mr. Eliot does not tell us what the use of poetry is, and he almost manages to convey a certain feeling of contempt for anyone who expects to be told." The expectations raised by Eliot's distinction were too high, and as Lattimore's comment indicates, his "known abilities" worked against him.

Lattimore identified three main criticisms of Eliot's new book. First, as noted by both American and British reviewers, the book seemed to have no thesis. *The Sacred Wood* and *Selected Essays* had been presented as collections of separate essays, but *The Use of Poetry* was advertised as a book, a series of interconnected lectures. A number of powerful reviewers, including John Crowe Ransom, Montgomery Belgion, and D. G. Bridson, in addition to Lattimore, pointed out that Eliot had failed to say what the use of poetry is or should be. Second, the book had an unfortunate tone, a feature pointed out by several reviewers, including Stephen Spender. And third, Eliot's habit of negative definition, of saying what a thing is not, rather than what it is, irritated some reviewers. Joseph Wood Krutch, for example, remarked that this habit is more provocative than helpful, more destructive than constructive.

Admirers of Eliot's early work expressed special unhappiness with *The Use of Poetry*. Some of these reviewers, notably Aiken and Pound, were compromised by their ideological divergence—Aiken by his distaste for religion and Pound by his obsession with economics. Still their reviews are telling and worth noting. Writing in the *Yale Review*, Aiken focused on Eliot's disagreement with I. A. Richards on the value of psychological readings of poetry and on the value of poetry as a modern religion. Aiken confessed that he himself "agrees entirely with Mr. Richards," especially in the view "that mankind, having shed religious dogma and arbitrary faith, will find through poetry a sufficient communication with the world and a sufficient source for belief." Pound, writing in the *New English Weekly*, was much harsher, sarcastically referring to his old friend as the "Dean of English Criticism" and the "Editor of Britain's Brightest Quarterly." He insisted that Eliot "shows no perception whatever" of the "obfuscation of literary perceptions" caused by "economic putridity." The reader of *The Use of Poetry*, he maintained, "would do well to read the first part [introduction and first chapter] and chuck the rest into the waste basket."

Reviews of *After Strange Gods*, the third book associated with Eliot's homecoming, mark the low point in his reception. In these essays, written as the Page-Barbour lectures for the University of Virginia, Eliot revisits his notion of tradition and tries to integrate his insights regarding culture and religion into his understanding of modern literature. The response was overwhelmingly negative. Reviewers chastised him for changing his notion of tradition, for mixing religion and literature, for a prejudicial reference to Jews, and for harsh judgments about contemporary writers. Neither of the American books (*The Use of Poetry* and *After Strange Gods*), cried Leavis, was worthy of the author. They contain much of value, he conceded, but at the same time, much that is "painfully bad, disablingly inadequate, often irrelevant and sometimes disingenuous." S. I. Hayakawa expressed a similar view: "To one who has sat unashamed at Mr. Eliot's feet for years, his latest volume is perplexing and distressing." He affirmed his admiration, insisting that "Mr. Eliot is a great writer . . . it is not without reason that everything he . . . writes commands the immediate and respectful attention of the entire English-speaking world"; at the same time, he lamented Eliot's negativity, especially his preoccupation with the darker aspects of religion, such as sin and damnation. Hayakawa voiced the fear "that [Eliot] will grow narrower and more disapproving in tone as he grows older." Pound, predictably, deplored Eliot's religious turn, and William Troy, writing in the *Nation*, was brutally negative. In "T. S. Eliot: Grand Inquisitor," Troy argued that Eliot was self-deceived and "morally reprehensible." He associated Eliot's earlier comment about royalism with fascism and the sentence about "free-thinking Jews" in *After Strange Gods* with anti-Semitism. A mild attempt at compromise was offered by Horace Gregory in the *New Republic*. He suggested that the real split in Eliot is not between the poet and the critic, but between the poet and the public figure. The first Eliot is real, but the second is bogus, an accidental result of the first.

In 1936, to the relief of most reviewers, the "real Eliot" resurfaced. *Collected Poems 1909–1935* brought together his work from 1920 and 1925 and added significant new poems, including "Journey of the Magi," "Marina," *Ash-Wednesday*, and "Burnt Norton." This volume, the first collection after his conversion and concurrent stylistic turn, provided an opportunity to assess his development. In both the United Kingdom and America, the reviews were largely positive, most confirming Eliot's centrality in modern poetry. Reviewers speculated on his poetic forebears, some discussing his descent from the Elizabethans, some his kinship with the French Symbolists, and some his similarities to the Decadents. Cyril Connolly, writing in the *Sunday Times*, asked the reader to imagine what English poetry would have been like in 1935 if T. S. Eliot had never existed. He suggested that it would have been far less prestigious and claimed that its future was brighter because Eliot was still writing. In one of the most interesting British assessments, D. W. Harding, in *Scrutiny*, asked why Eliot's early work was considered more *chic* than his later work. His response was that the early poetry lends itself more easily to protest, to readers who feel themselves victims of history, while the later poetry suggests that suffering arises from one's own choices. American reviews by Marianne Moore, Babette Deutsch, Morton Zabel, and Peter Monro Jack ranked Eliot as the most influential poet of his generation. Jack, writing in the *New York*

Times, described the poet's stylistic change from, say, *The Waste Land* to "Burnt Norton" as a welcome move toward greater accessibility, a move from being a "poet's poet" to being a "people's poet." The Marxist critic Rolfe Humphries, writing in *New Masses* and echoing D. S. Mirsky, praised Eliot for bringing his rare gifts to social themes (alienation, poverty, urban decay) of real significance. While admitting that Eliot himself never urges a classless society, he suggested that Eliot "has written, with poetic authority too great to be questioned, the elegy of an age that is passing."

Eliot's main creative energy in the 1930s, however, was not devoted to poetry. When he returned to England after the American tour, he turned to poetic drama, a genre that had interested him for two decades. Several of his early poems, including "The Love Song of J. Alfred Prufrock," consist of interior dialogues, and *The Waste Land*, as suggested by its working title ("He Do the Police in Different Voices"), is an arrangement of various voices. Eliot's early criticism, similarly, shows a keen interest in drama, and some of his well-known critical formulations, including the "objective correlative," arose from his reflections on Renaissance plays.[18] His first attempt to write a play resulted in *Sweeney Agonistes*, a fragment published in 1932 and intended as a dark comedy of contemporary life. His second effort, *The Rock*, published in 1934, was a pageant for several voices, written to raise money for church-building in London. His third dramatic endeavor was a fully realized play, *Murder in the Cathedral*, written by invitation and first performed in Canterbury Cathedral in 1935. His fourth, *The Family Reunion*, published in 1939, was his first venture for the secular stage. The response to these works followed a trajectory from negative to mixed to positive, followed by a retreat to mixed.

Sweeney Agonistes received few reviews, and most were negative. Reviewers felt that the characters and plot were dull; at the same time, some noted with interest Eliot's experimentation with music-hall and jazz rhythms. In regard to *The Rock*, reviewers were divided between an inclination to give due regard to Eliot the poet and a reluctance to define as art a work written to raise money for churches. Conrad Aiken, to mention one of the poet's earliest admirers, liked the choruses, but felt uncomfortable with the idea that art was being used as a handmaiden to religion. Some commentators upgraded their evaluation after seeing *Murder in the Cathedral*, deciding in retrospect that the pageant had been a warm-up for a landmark play.

The reception of *Murder in the Cathedral* was positive in both the United Kingdom and America. The *Times Literary Supplement*, which often set the tone for response to Eliot's new work, said that the play was the culmination of his experiments in dramatic style. I. M. Parsons, writing in the *Spectator*, claimed that Mr. Eliot "has reanimated a literary form which in England has been dead or dormant for nearly three hundred years, and in so doing he has found himself anew as a poet, only with an added ease, lucidity, and objectiveness." Edwin Muir emphasized the play's "intellectual scheme," and James

Laughlin commented on Eliot's evolution as an artist. The American reviews were substantial and lavish. Even Aiken, writing (hiding?) in the *New Yorker* under the pseudonym of Samuel Jeake, Jr., was enthusiastic.

> It is a triumph of poetic genius that out of such actionless material—the mere conflict of a mind with itself—a play so deeply moving, and so exciting, should have been written; and so rich, moreover, in the various language of *humanity*. . . . in the play Eliot has become human, and tender, with a tenderness and a humanity which have nowhere else in our time found such beauty of form.

Mark Van Doren, writing in the *Nation*, remarked that Eliot "has written no better poem than this." The title of Peter Monro Jack's review in the *New York Times* sums up his response: "T. S. Eliot's Drama of Beauty and Momentous Decision." Philip Rahv, in the *Partisan Review*, praised the play and commented on the "crudeness" of those who dismiss Eliot's poetry because they cannot share his religious beliefs. Reviews of the first New York performance were also positive.

Fortified by his success with *Murder in the Cathedral*, Eliot returned to the idea of doing a play about contemporary life for a secular audience. In *The Family Reunion*, published in 1939 and set in a drawing room in northern England, he revisited several of his old themes—the divided self, alienation, family and community, and perhaps most of all, the nature of evil/sin. Once again, the *Times Literary Supplement* set the tone. The anonymous reviewer lamented that Eliot had retreated to the naturalism he had earlier abandoned. Several British reviewers focused on Eliot's use of the *Oresteia* as a backdrop for the play, and most felt that the experiment was not successful. Desmond MacCarthy, writing in the *New Statesman*, opined that the Greek myth was implausible in a modern drawing room. Maud Bodkin, on the other hand, defended Eliot's use of Aeschylus, maintaining in *Adelphi* that he used the Furies to convey what he could not have conveyed through ordinary techniques. American reviewers were similarly divided on the use of the myth. Some, such as John Crowe Ransom, writing in *Poetry*, insisted that Eliot's Eumenides are "too 'literary' to express the metaphysical realities" he is struggling to convey and predicted that modern audiences would not accept them. Horace Gregory, in *Life and Letters*, called the play one of Eliot's "successful failures." He applauded the theme and the will to experiment with myth, but claimed that the use of the Eumenides was not satisfactorily realized. Other American reviewers focused on characterization and theme. In the *Kenyon Review*, Philip Horton argued that the characters were inadequately motivated, and the theme of "sin and expiation" was unintelligible. The problem of characterization was also taken up by Desmond Hawkins who, writing in the *New English Weekly*, related it to Eliot's much earlier discussion of *Hamlet*. Eliot's Harry, like Shakespeare's

Hamlet, is dominated by an emotion "in excess of the facts," by an "all-pervasive and universally diffused disgust . . . which overwhelms everything else in the play." To use the language of Eliot's essay on Hamlet: Harry's emotion lacks an objective correlative. Hawkins concluded that Harry is Eliot's Hamlet, "a Mona Lisa of literature." Many American reviewers, conversely, admired the play. Cleanth Brooks, writing in the *Partisan Review*, commented on its effective symbolism and its continuities with Eliot's earlier work. George Anthony, writing in the *Sewanee Review*, called it "far and away the best dramatic work Eliot has given us," and Frederick Pottle said in the *Yale Review* that it was a technical triumph.

Eliot's main concern during the 1930s, however, was not with dramas for Broadway or London's West End, but with the conflict shaping itself in the European political theatre. By the end of the decade, he knew that he and his generation were lost in the middle of the dark wood, "having had twenty years—/ Twenty years largely wasted, the years of *l'entre deux guerres*" ("East Coker"). In January 1939, in deep despair, he published his last issue of *The Criterion*. Prevented by the war from writing another play, he returned to the solitary work of writing poems and completed *Four Quartets*, an ambitious sequence of four poems. The first quartet, "Burnt Norton," grew from a passage cut from *Murder in the Cathedral*. Written in 1935 as a single poem, it was the primary new piece in *Collected Poems 1909–1935*. The remaining three quartets appeared during the Second World War. "East Coker," written on the "Burnt Norton" model, appeared in 1940. While working on "East Coker," Eliot conceived of a musical sequence of four poems, based on the four seasons and the four elements. "Burnt Norton" was republished as a separate work in 1941 and the third quartet, "The Dry Salvages," appeared in the same year; the fourth, "Little Gidding," in 1942; and the four together under the title *Four Quartets* in 1943.

Because the quartets were published over a period of several years, reviews appeared over an extended period, culminating in overviews of the sequence as a whole, the "complete consort dancing together" ("Little Gidding," V). As reviews go, the pieces on *Four Quartets* are unusually substantial. One reason is that they reflect the cumulative understanding of scattered reviewers in the process of coming to understand Eliot's larger scheme. Another is that they include an awareness of Eliot's earlier work, including the *Prufrock* poems, *The Waste Land*, "Ash-Wednesday," *Murder in the Cathedral*, the critical essays, and most significantly, the first three quartets. A final reason for the richness of these reviews is that they show a consciousness of the bleak and serious context, which included not only the war in Europe, but the deaths of Joyce and Yeats. Ian Jack, in a "review of reviews" for the *New York Times*, remarked that no poem "in many years has been so completely, exhaustively, and earnestly reviewed." "Now that Yeats is no longer writing," there is no poet to compare with Eliot and no poem to compare with *Four Quartets*. Jack noted the "almost unanimous decision in favor of the *Quartets*. One might think the critics had held a caucus and emerged with their separate opinions clearly coordinated."

The reviews of "Burnt Norton" are imbedded in reviews of *Collected Poems 1909–1935*. One of the most perceptive, written by D. W. Harding, appeared in *Scrutiny*. Harding admired Eliot's ability to create concepts at once religious and philosophic. Several reviewers of the wartime quartets, as the last three are sometimes called, referred back to Harding's fine review. For example, F. R. Leavis, writing six years later in *Scrutiny*, began his review of "The Dry Salvages" with Harding's insights on the religious nature of Eliot's later work. The second and third quartets, "East Coker" and "The Dry Salvages," were published only in the United Kingdom, and most of the reviews are British. The reviewers of "East Coker," including G. W. Stonier in the *New Statesman*, James Kirkup in *Poetry* [London], and Stephen Spender in *Horizon*, noted the recurrence of themes from the first two quartets, including the problem of time and the process of aging. Spender's review pointed to the poem's self-reflexivity, a theme that has become central in Eliot studies.

The reviewers of "The Dry Salvages" continued the discussion begun in the reviews of "East Coker." In a long essay in *Scrutiny*, F. R. Leavis used the publication of the third quartet as an occasion for reflecting on the first three and for speculating on the fourth and culminating poem that was on the way. Commenting retrospectively on much of Eliot's later poetry, he included substantial commentary on "Ash-Wednesday" and "Marina." He concluded by remarking that "it should by now be impossible to doubt that Eliot is among the greatest poets of the English language." "The Dry Salvages" appeared in 1941, and several reviewers, Muriel Bradbrook, for example, noted that it was in important ways a war poem. The third quartet sparked a debate between George Orwell and Kathleen Raine, both writing in *Poetry* [London]. Orwell claimed that Eliot's poetic sequence represents a "deterioration in [his] subject matter." Whereas the early poems reflect "a glowing despair," the *Quartets* reflect "a melancholy faith." The despair, Orwell suggested, seems more genuine, for it is the response of a civilized intellectual to the "ugliness and spiritual emptiness of the machine age." Raine chided Orwell, a Marxist, for expecting the *Quartets* to serve the interests of politics. She focused on the poetry's Modernist techniques, notably the blurring of material and psychological boundaries.[19]

By the time *Four Quartets* appeared in 1943, then, a body of reviews had prepared the way, and several of the new reviews deepened the evolving public discussion of the poem. Muriel Bradbrook, in *Theology*, and D. W. Harding, in *Scrutiny*, emphasized the religious significance of the sequence. Harding explained the levels of meaning at work in the poem and discussed Eliot's uneasiness with humanism. Malcolm Cowley, in the *New Republic*, associated the poem with the mystical tradition. Several emerging New Critics reviewed the poem. F. O. Matthiessen noted in the *Kenyon Review* the formal and thematic importance of puzzles, paradoxes, and the reconciliation of opposites.

In *Poetry: A Magazine of Verse*, James Johnson Sweeney analyzed the form of the poems and related form to the theme of theodicy that culminates in "Little Gidding." Louis Untermeyer, in the *Yale Review*, claimed that *Four Quartets* was at once simpler and more complex than Eliot's early work, simpler in form, but more subtle in meaning. Some critics disliked the sequence, dismissing it as "poetry of direct statement." As Delmore Schwartz put it in the *Nation*, the poem contains long passages that are simply boring, passages representing a failure of the poet's ear and a relaxation of his sensitivity.

Eliot's war poems, including the *Quartets*, were framed by two prose works in which he attempted to come to terms with the social, political, and religious implications of the resumption of war in Europe. On the eve of the war, at Corpus Christi College, Cambridge, he gave the "Boutwood Lectures," published in 1939 as *The Idea of a Christian Society*. After the war, he surveyed the ruins in *Notes Towards the Definition of Culture*, published in 1948. Fully aware in 1939 that the United Kingdom and other nations were again on a collision course with Germany, Eliot tried to imagine a way to understand and to counter Nazi values. One of his central points, based in part on his analysis of the Munich Crisis of September 1938, was that "neutrality" would not lead to "peace in our time," but to disaster. He maintained that pagan values could only be successfully countered with positive values, and wondered if democracy, as then conceived, had enough positive content to stand against dictatorship. In an attempt to imagine an alternative more likely to secure peace, he articulated an "idea" of a Christian society, not a society in which everyone would be Christian but one that would have an ethics and public policy grounded in Christian values. His arguments reached a broad audience, in part because they were summarized by most reviewers. The *Times Literary Supplement*, a bellwether for so much of his work, expressed admiration for Eliot's courage in addressing real problems in a real world. Other reviewers, even those who had reservations about Eliot's religion, were also appreciative. Malcolm Cowley, writing in the *New Republic*, said that "you find, even when you are hostile to the main trend of [Eliot's book], that it is full of moderation and worldly wisdom."

In 1948, Eliot offered a post-war analysis of culture in *Notes Towards the Definition of Culture*. The critical reaction was mixed. A number of reviewers complained that Eliot was excessively tentative, noting that although he said many interesting things about "culture," he never got around to defining it. Some critics, including E. M. Forster in the *Listener* and W. H. Auden in the *New Yorker*, resurrected the old line that there were three Eliots. For Forster, there was the poet, the literary critic, and the social analyst. The poet and the literary critic were brilliant, but the social critic was mediocre. For Auden, the three Eliots were an archdeacon with cool manners, a violent and passionate old man who had witnessed the horrors of history, and a young boy who liked to play practical jokes. Auden suggested that the value of Eliot's book was not the conclusions he reached but the issues he raised. Several critics, including George

Orwell in the *Observer* and R. P. Blackmur in the *Nation*, focused on Eliot's attitudes about class. In an illuminating review, Blackmur examined the poet's continuing concern for "the recovery of individual life from mass or collective life." He also stressed the importance of "prestige" in Eliot's appreciation of individual life, and the importance of religion as the source of all prestige.

A comprehensive understanding of Eliot's post-war reception should include an awareness of his own prestige, both as poet and as spokesman for values. For nearly a decade, since the deaths in quick succession of Yeats and Joyce, he had been considered the most distinguished writer in the English language. After the war, his prestige was officially acknowledged by a string of public honors, including in 1947 an honorary degree from Harvard and in 1948 both the Order of Merit and the Nobel Prize for Literature. Eliot's prestige was solidly anchored in decades of achievement as a man of letters, but in the post-war period, his prestige bred a less attractive stepchild—stardom. Although he was by nature modest and reserved, Eliot suddenly found himself lionized by an international public, and most of them knew little to nothing about his poetry. His fame became a major issue in the reception of his post-war work, consisting mainly of three comedies. In 1949, he published *The Cocktail Party*; in 1954, *The Confidential Clerk*; and in 1959, his valedictory, *The Elder Statesman*.

Eliot's "star" status is particularly evident in the response to *The Cocktail Party*. In a season that included *South Pacific* and Carson McCullers's *The Member of the Wedding*, *The Cocktail Party* was a genuine hit. It was the topic *du jour* at the best cocktail parties in Edinburgh, New York, and London, and was reviewed all over Europe and the English-speaking world. When it opened in New York for the first of its 409 performances, the sold-out audience included Ethel Barrymore and the Duke and Duchess of Windsor. In New York, it won the Drama Critics Circle award and three Tony awards, and Eliot made the cover of *Time* magazine (22 December 1952). In London, the play ran for 325 performances to capacity audiences and won the *Sunday Times* literary prize for best play. All told, according to the *Times* (21 December 1952), it was seen by a million and a half spectators. There were innumerable reviews, with most combining commentary on a specific performance with an assessment of the play as theatre. Of the several hundred examined for the present volume, only the 165 or so appearing between the first performance in August 1949 and the end of 1950 have been included or itemized in the checklist of additional reviews.

The prestige/stardom issue can be seen in most reviews of *The Cocktail Party*, with attitudes ranging from celebration to resentment. Some reviewers, such as Bonamy Dobrée, made a thoughtful case for the play, analyzing its accomplished layering of meanings; Robert Speaight, who had played Becket in *Murder in the Cathedral*, argued convincingly that *The Cocktail Party* was "profound and subtle" and "among the rare masterpieces of the modern stage." Many reviewers, on the other hand, embraced the play uncritically, showering it with unsupported superlatives. Still others, often as a preface to dissent, fore-grounded the issue, asking how far it is possible to separate one's response to the play from Eliot's fame. Writing in the *Partisan Review*, William Barrett suggested that Eliot, once a dragon-slayer, had become the dragon that must be slain. He noted that many of the reviewers were self-congratulatory, pleased to have liked what they *ought* to have liked. Preferring the early, more existential, Eliot, Barrett went on to say that by the standard of his earlier work, *The Cocktail Party* is "the weakest poetry that Eliot has yet written." Several reviewers, Stephen Spender, for example, joined Barrett in comparing the verse in the play to Eliot's earlier poetry and concurred that there had been a falling off in quality. On the other hand, a few reviewers, most notably William Carlos Williams, suggested that *The Cocktail Party* was better than the early work. For more than three decades, Williams had been denouncing Eliot's work, including *The Waste Land*, as a disaster for modern poetry, repeatedly claiming that the early Eliot had missed the pulse of common life. In a review for the *New York Post*, "It's About Your Life and Mine, Darling," Williams praised *The Cocktail Party*, saying that Eliot had finally "come down to his audience with humility . . . and success."[20]

The troubling issues that had emerged in reviews of *The Cocktail Party* were taken up with greater intensity when Eliot's next play, *The Confidential Clerk*, was first performed in 1953. There was the usual adulation, but, overall, there were fewer reviews, fewer defenders, more grumblers. A few praised the poet for being so down to earth, so accessible. Some puzzled over the question of genre, others rehearsed Eliot's dramatic theories, and still others dwelt on his themes. Russell Kirk, in a generally sympathetic review for *Month*, saw the play as a reworking of Eliot's old existential themes of alienation, loneliness, and identity, but predicted that *The Confidential Clerk* would not be remembered as one of the poet's "principal works." Richard Findlater, writing in *Twentieth Century*, dubbed it another "brilliant failure" for Eliot, adding that his "failure is of considerably greater importance to the future of English drama than the easier successes of other, luckier dramatists." Many reviewers insisted that *The Confidential Clerk* was boring and would have been ignored had it not been for the marque value of Eliot's name. In a mixed review in the *New Statesman*, T. C. Worsley expressed a concern that Eliot's public authority was skewing audience response. Similarly, but with a hint of sarcasm missing in Worsley's review, Burke Wilkinson noted in the *New York Times* that audiences came "in droves" to pay homage to the "pontiff of modern poets."[21] The issue of Eliot's authority was underscored in the fall of 1954 by a debate that erupted in the *Times Literary Supplement*. The debate was sparked by a review of Richard Aldington's *Ezra Pound and T. S. Eliot* (10 September) that suggested Eliot/Pound Modernism was dead. Robert Graves wrote letters to the editor attacking Eliot (1 October, 29 October) and Pound (19 November), and several critics rushed to defend him (15 October, 12 November). In retrospect, one can see that the writing was on the wall in regard to literary Modernism.

Eliot's final play, *The Elder Statesman*, appeared in 1958. Following what had become a familiar pattern, it opened in Edinburgh in August to warm reviews. In contrast to his earlier comedies, *The Elder Statesman* had a short run (92 performances) in London and was not even produced in New York. (*The Cocktail Party* had run for 325 performances in London and 409 in New York.) A few reviewers resumed their attacks on Eliot's authority, but most responded less harshly and quite a few displayed affectionate appreciation. The softer tone, however, seems not to have reflected a surge in enthusiasm. Two other factors were obviously at play in these reviews. The first was Eliot's May–December marriage, and the second was the awareness that *The Elder Statesman* would probably be Eliot's valedictory. In January 1957, he had married his longtime secretary Valerie Fletcher, and in a surprisingly personal poem, he dedicated the play to her. Many critics were intrigued with the transformation of Eliot's attitude toward marital love. The titles of reviews are revealing; for example, the title in *Time* is "Love and Mr. Eliot"; in the London *Times*, "Mr. Eliot's Most Human Play"; and in the *New Leader*, "Affirmation and Love in Eliot." The play opened in London on 25 September 1958, a day before Eliot's seventieth birthday, an occasion that reminded reviewers that the end of an era was at hand.[22] The end of the "Age of Eliot" was greeted with relief by some, but with nostalgia by others. Eliot, after all, was the elder statesman of literary Modernism. A number of reviews incorporated birthday conversations with the poet, and virtually all of the interviewers conveyed astonishment at Eliot's marital bliss and nostalgia for the age that was passing into history. Henry Hewes, for example, begins his review/interview by remarking that those who think of Eliot as cynical and despairing are going to be surprised by *The Elder Statesman*. In response to Hewes's observation that he seemed heartier than he had for years, Eliot replied that the change in both his work and his health was due to his marriage and added, "Love reciprocated is always rejuvenating." Hewes asked about Eliot's early masterpieces, by this time among the signature pieces of high Modernism. Helen Gardner's interview/review for the *Sunday Times*, "The 'Aged Eagle' Spreads His Wings," also combined appreciation of the love motif with respect for the now aged poet. Hugh Kenner's review in *Poetry* used the love motif to connect life and art, arguing that there is a mimetic relationship between Eliot's joy in his marriage and the new language of intimacy in *The Elder Statesman*. Eliot published a few essay collections during the 1950s, but for the most part, they were retrospective and thus contributed to the sense of closure at the end of his life's work.[23] In the same vein, he published his "complete" poems and plays (1953). The few reviews that appeared contain little that had not been said before and thus are not included in the present volume.

This volume is the most comprehensive collection of contemporary reviews of T. S. Eliot's work as it appeared. It includes reviews of all of his work except a few brief pamphlets, *Old Possum's Book of Practical Cats*, and late collections of previously published work. Since Eliot's work was published first in London, this collection includes British and Irish reviews; they are identified by an asterisk (*). Reviews published in both the United States and the United Kingdom are identified by two asterisks (**). Spelling and punctuation have been changed to American style throughout, but there has been no other attempt to impose uniformity on the original reviews. With rare exceptions, the collection does not include reviews from Australia, New Zealand, and Canada; nor does it reprint reviews in languages other than English. Regrettably, I have had to exclude some review essays, particularly on *Four Quartets*, simply because of length. These longer pieces, often twenty pages or more, are included in the "Checklist of Additional Reviews."

Each section of this volume includes the reviews of a single book, arranged in chronological order of original publication and followed by a checklist of additional reviews. Many of the reprinted reviews have been edited, with all omissions indicated by ellipses. The primary omissions are long quotations of the poetry, plot summaries of the plays, and obvious redundancies. Redundancies abound in the unedited reviews, in part because as Eliot's work became fashionable in the 1920s, and similarly, as it lost some of its glamour in the 1940s and 1950s, reviewers tended to imitate each other and even to compete with each other, first, in praise, and second, in carping. I have included the most original and provocative reviews and have included excerpts of others, where special insights so warranted. In some cases, I have included reviews because the reviewer was especially important in Eliot's career (for example, Ezra Pound, Conrad Aiken), especially astute in anticipating subsequent opinion (Edmund Wilson, Gilbert Seldes), or important in scholarly assessment of Eliot's work (Cleanth Brooks, Helen Gardner).

Scattered reviews of Eliot's poetry, particularly his earlier work, can be found in numerous casebooks and, more comprehensively, in *T. S. Eliot: The Critical Heritage*, edited by Michael Grant (1982), and *T. S. Eliot: Critical Assessments*, edited by Graham Clarke (1990). The first is a collection of reviews, and the second, a selection of memoirs, interviews, and early responses; both are valuable resources for Eliot studies.

Notes

1. "The Most Influential English Poet of His Time," *Times* (London), 5 January 1965; Conrad Aiken, "T. S. Eliot," *Life*, 15 January 1965, p. 93.
2. "Artists and Entertainers of the 20th Century," *Time* (June 1998).
3. Ezra Pound, "Status Rerum (I)," *Poetry* 1. no. 4 (January 1913), 123, 126.
4. *Selected Letters of Conrad Aiken*, ed. Joseph Killorin (New Haven: Yale University Press, 1978), 21–23.

5. Aiken, *Selected Letters*, p. 38.

6. Quotations from reviews contained in this volume are not separately documented.

7. Eliot, "The Metaphysical Poets," *Selected Essays* (1932) (New York: Harcourt Brace, 1950), 241–50.

8. The reviews of *Three Critical Essays* are included in this volume with the reviews of *The Sacred Wood*, pp. 51–73.

9. *The Diary of Virginia Woolf* (New York: Harcourt Brace, 1978), II.178.

10. For an account of the history behind the publication of the poem, see "Introduction," *The Waste Land: A Facsimile and Transcript of the Original Drafts Including the Annotations of Ezra Pound*, ed. Valerie Eliot (New York: Harcourt Brace, 1971), ix–xxx; and Lawrence Rainey, "The Price of Modernism: Publishing *The Waste Land*," *Institutions of Modernism* (Cambridge University Press, 1998), 77–106.

11. James G. Frazer, *The Golden Bough*, 3rd edn. 3 vols. (London: Macmillan, 1911–15); Jessie L. Weston, *From Ritual to Romance* (Cambridge University Press, 1920).

12. Edmund Wilson, "T. S. Eliot," *Axel's Castle: A Study in the Imaginative Literature of 1870–1930* (1931) (New York: Scribner's, 1959), 93–131.

13. Letter to Lady Beaumont, 21 May 1807, in *Letters of William Wordsworth*, ed. Philip Wayne (London: Oxford University Press, 1954), 94.

14. Aiken, "Prefatory Note to 'An Anatomy of Melancholy,'" in *A Reviewer's ABC* (New York: Meridian Books, 1958), 176.

15. See "Irony de Luxe," Untermeyer's review of *Poems 1920* in *Freeman* 1 (30 June 1920), 381–82, reprinted in this volume, pp. 44–46.

16. *For Lancelot Andrewes* (London: Faber & Gwyer, 1928), ix.

17. See Aiken's review of Eliot's *The Rock*, reprinted in this volume, pp. 312–14.

18. For a discussion of the "objective correlative," see Eliot's "Hamlet and His Problems," *Selected Essays*, new edn. (New York: Harcourt Brace, 1950), 121–26.

19. For an attempt to mediate between Orwell and Raine, see the letter to the editor from Irene Brown, "Mr. Eliot, Mr. Orwell and Miss Raine," *Poetry* [London] 2, no. 9 (February–March 1943), 61.

20. William Arrowsmith, in an essay published in the *Hudson Review* in 1950, offered the most substantial commentary on the play. His analysis, informed by impressive knowledge of classical literature and modern theatre, addresses most of the issues raised by Barrett and other critics. Arrowsmith's essay is too long to be reprinted in this volume, but it is listed in the "Checklist of Additional Reviews," p. 543, and highly recommended to anyone interested in the play.

21. Bonamy Dobrée has an excellent essay on *The Confidential Clerk*, published in the *Sewanee Review* in 1954. It is too long for reprinting here, but is included in the "Checklist of Additional Reviews," p. 562.

22. Several collections of tributes were published to mark the occasion, notably *T. S. Eliot: A Symposium for His Seventieth Birthday*, ed. Neville Braybrooke (London: Rupert Hart-Davis, 1958). This volume, which included tributes from old friends and enthusiastic scholars, was timed to coincide with his birthday, 26 September 1958.

23. Denis Donoghue's fine essay, "Eliot in Fair Colonus," in *Studies: An Irish Quarterly Review* 48 (Spring 1959), 49–58, is too long for reprinting here. See "Checklist of Additional Reviews," p. 583.

Acknowledgments

I am especially indebted to the work of Michael Grant, ed., whose *T. S. Eliot: The Critical Heritage* (1982) provided a model for my own: and also to Graham Clarke, ed., *T. S. Eliot.* Like all Eliot scholars, I am indebted to Donald Gallup's invaluable *T. S. Eliot: A Bibliography* (rev. edn., 1969), and to two bibliographies of secondary materials, Mildred Martin's *A Half-Century of Eliot Criticism* (1973) and Beatrice Ricks's *T. S. Eliot: A Bibliography of Secondary Works* (1980). In regard to the plays, I am most indebted to Randy Malamud's *T. S. Eliot's Drama: A Research and Production Sourcebook* (1992). In a more general way, I am grateful to Ronald Schuchard, Cyrena Pondrom, Paul Sonnenburg, and Carolyn Johnston for helpful conversations about my work.

Work on this volume has stretched over a number of years, and during this time, I have employed a number of fine research assistants. Jennifer LaRocco, Caroline Maun, Erika McVoy, Allison Payne, Amy Robinson, Rebecca Root, and Mariann Starkey have contributed at various stages, and I am grateful to each of them. I am also grateful to M. Thomas Inge, who invited me to do this project and who bore patiently with several missed deadlines. I appreciate his advice and his work as series editor. I am also grateful to a number of librarians, especially in the newspaper and microfilm departments of the Library of Congress, the Widener Library at Harvard University, the British Library (London), the University of South Florida Library, and the Eckerd College Library. I am very grateful to the National Endowment for the Humanities and the Pew Charitable Trust, from both of which I have received research fellowships, and to Eckerd College and the Colorado School of Mines, from which I received financial assistance. Finally, and principally, I am grateful to my husband, Hampton Ralph Brooker, and my children Emily and Mark, for their assistance and goodwill in what seemed at times to be a never-ending project.

The editor wishes to thank the following newspapers, journals, and individuals for permission to reprint reviews:

The Christian Century, v. 49 (12 October 1932), "Humanism Criticizes Itself" by W. E. Garrison; v. 52 (18 December 1935), "*Murder in the Cathedral*" by Edward Shillito.

Christian Science Monitor (14 November 1934), "A Classical Contemporary Pageant from Mr. Eliot" by Robert Peel.

The Hudson Review, v. 3 (Summer 1950), "Notes on the Theatre" by Frederick Morgan.

New England Quarterly, v. 6 (June 1933), "Book Reviews" by Robert Hillyer.

New Republic, v. 33 (7 February 1923), "An Anatomy of Melancholy" by Conrad Aiken; v. 41 (7 January 1925), "T. S. Eliot and the Seventeenth Century" by Edmund Wilson; v. 46 (10 March 1926), "Stravinsky and Others" by Edmund Wilson; v. 47 (30 June 1926), "A Poetry of Ideas" by Allen Tate; v. 58 (24 April 1929), "T. S. Eliot and the Church of England" by Edmund Wilson; v. 64 (20 August 1930) [untitled review] by Edmund Wilson; v. 72 (26 October 1932), "The 'Universe' of T. S. Eliot" by Waldo Frank; v. 79 (16 May 1934), "The Man of Feeling" by Horace Gregory; v. 98 (3 May 1939), "Original Sin" by Louis MacNeice; v. 102 (17 June 1940), "Tract for the Times" by Malcolm Cowley; v. 108 (7 June 1943), "Beyond Poetry" by Malcolm Cowley; v. 129 (21 September 1953), "*The Confidential Clerk*" by Philip Mairet.

New Statesman, for *Nation & Athenaeum*, v. 33 (22 September 1923), "T. S. Eliot" by Clive Bell; v. 38 (5 December 1925), "'Jug Jug' to Dirty Ears" by Leonard Woolf; v. 47 (31 May 1930), "Mr. T. S. Eliot" by Francis Birrell.

New Statesman, v. 22 (3 November 1923), "*The Waste Land*" by F. L. Lucas; v. 26 (20 February 1926), "Mr. Eliot's Poems" by I. A. Richards; v. 32 (29 December 1928), "For Mr. T. S. Eliot"; v. 36 (8 November 1930), "Mr. Eliot's Poetry" by Brian Howard; v. 4 (1 October 1932), "T. S. Eliot the Critic" by Peter Quennell; v. 6 (18 November 1933), "The Use of Poetry" by Stephen Spender; v. 11 (18 April 1936), "Mr. T. S. Eliot" by Peter Quennell; v. 17 (25 March 1939), "Some Notes on Mr. Eliot's New Play" by Desmond MacCarthy; v. 20 (14 September 1940), "Mr. Eliot's New Poem" by G. W. Stonier; v. 25 (20 February 1943), "Little Gidding" by Edwin Muir; v. 38 (3 September 1949), "The Edinburgh Festival–I" by Desmond Shaw-Taylor; v. 46 (5 September 1953), "*The Confidential Clerk*" by T. C. Worsley; v. 47 (20 March 1954), [untitled review] by Helen Gardner.

New York Times (29 January 1933), "The Cream of T. S. Eliot's Literary Criticism" by Peter Monro Jack; (3 December 1933), "Mr. Eliot's New Essays in the Field of Poetry" by Peter Monro Jack; (27 October 1935), "T. S. Eliot's Drama of Beauty and Momentous Decision" by Peter Monro Jack; (29 March 1936), "Strange Images of Death" by Brooks Atkinson; (14 June 1936), "T. S. Eliot: Poet of Our Time" by Peter Monro Jack; (16 May 1943), "Fare Forward Voyagers" by Horace Gregory; (29 January 1950), "Mr. Eliot's Party" by Brooks Atkinson; (19 March 1950), "After *The Cocktail Party*" by Stephen Spender; (7 February 1954), "A Most Serious Comedy by Eliot" by Burke Wilkinson.

Partisan Review (Summer 1939), "Sin and Expiation" by Cleanth Brooks.

Punch Ltd (5 October 1932), "A Critic of Poets."

Sewanee Review, v. 57 (Autumn 1949), "Culture and Reconstruction" by Richard M. Weaver; v. 67 (Winter 1959), "The London Stage" by Bonamy Dobrée.

Southwest Review, v. 19 (January 1934), "Eliot's Harvard Lectures" by Cleanth Brooks.

Time (3 March 1923), "*Shantih, Shantih, Shantih*"; (8 September 1958), "Love and Mr. Eliot."

Times Literary Supplement (20 September 1923), "A Fragmentary Poem" by [Edgell Rickword]; (6 December 1928), "Mr. Eliot's New Essays"; (13 October 1932), "Mr. T. S. Eliot"; (7 June 1934), "Mr. Eliot's Pageant Play"; (13 June 1935), "Mr. Eliot's New Play"; (25 March 1939), "Mr. Eliot in Search of the Present"; (4 November 1939), "A Christian Society: Mr. Eliot on Ideals and Methods"; (31 March 1950), "Entertainment and Reality."

PRUFROCK AND OTHER OBSERVATIONS
1917

PRUFROCK

AND

OTHER OBSERVATIONS

BY

T. S. ELIOT

THE EGOIST LTD
OAKLEY HOUSE, BLOOMSBURY STREET
LONDON
1917

Conrad Aiken.
"Esoteric Catholicity."
Poetry Journal 5
(April 1916),
127–29.

[Review of *Catholic Anthology*]

As anthologies go nowadays, Mr. Pound's *Catholic Anthology* is an interesting one.

[. . .]

Dull things there are, of course,—each critic will find his own—but for the present critic the *Catholic Anthology* seems worth while if only for the inclusion of "The Love Song of J. Alfred Prufrock" and the "Portrait of a Lady" by T. S. Eliot. These are remarkable. They are individual to a degree. Mr. Eliot uses free rhyme very effectively, often musically; and with the minimum of sacrifice to form conveys a maximum of atmosphere. Both poems are psychological character-studies, subtle to the verge of insoluble idiosyncrasy, introspective, self-gnawing. Those who are constitutionally afraid to analyze themselves, who do not think, who are not psychologically imaginative, will distrust and perhaps dislike them.

[. . .]

[A]ny anthology, which, like this, blows the horn of revolution in poetry, whether sound or unsound, is at the least certain to interest all poets, even the most conservative; and will, perhaps, be of value to them.

*Arthur Waugh.
"The New Poetry."
Quarterly Review 226
(October 1916), 386.

[Review of *Catholic Anthology*]

Cleverness is, indeed, the pitfall of the New Poetry. There is no question about the ingenuity with which its varying moods are exploited, its elaborate symbolism evolved, and its sudden, disconcerting effects exploded upon the imagination. Swift, brilliant images break into the field of vision, scatter like rockets, and leave a trail of flying fire behind. But the general impression is momentary; there are moods and emotions, but no steady current of ideas behind them. Further, in their determination to surprise and even to puzzle at all costs, these young poets are continually forgetting that the first essence of poetry is beauty.

[. . .]

[T]he *Catholic Anthology* . . . apparently represents the very newest of all the new poetic movements of the day. This strange little volume bears upon its cover a geometrical device, suggesting that the material within holds the same relation to the art of poetry as the work of the Cubist school holds to the art of painting and design. The product of the volume is mainly American in origin, only one or two of the contributors being of indisputably English birth.

[. . .]

The reader will not have penetrated far . . . before he finds himself in the very stronghold of literary rebellion, if not of anarchy. Mr. Orrick Johns may be allowed to speak for his colleagues, as well as for himself:

> This is a song of youth,
> This is the cause of myself;
> I knew my father well and he was a
> fool . . .

> [. . .]

And Mr. Ezra Pound takes up the parable in turn, in the same wooden prose, cut into battens:

> Come, my songs, let us express our
> baser passions.
> Let us express our envy for the man
> with a steady job and no worry
> about the future.
> You are very idle, my songs . . .
> You will come to a very bad end.
> And I? I have gone half cracked.

It is not for his audience to contradict the poet, who for once may be allowed to pronounce his own literary epitaph. But this, it is to be noted, is the "poetry" that was to say nothing that might not be said "actually in life—under emotion," the sort of emotion that settles down into the banality of a premature decrepitude:

> I grow old . . . I grow old . . .
> I shall wear the bottoms of my
> trousers rolled.
> Shall I part my hair behind? Do I dare
> to eat a peach?
> I shall wear white flannel trousers, and
> walk upon the beach.
> I have heard the mermaids singing,
> each to each.

> I do not think that they will sing to me.

Here, surely, is the reduction to absurdity of that school of literary license which, beginning with the declaration, "I knew my father well and he was a fool," naturally proceeds to the convenient assumption that everything which seemed wise and true to the father must inevitably be false and foolish to the son. Yet if the fruits of emancipation are to be recognized in the unmetrical, incoherent banalities of these literary "Cubists," the state of Poetry is indeed threatened with anarchy which will end in something worse even than "red ruin and the breaking up of laws." . . . [A] hint of warning may not be altogether out of place. It was a classic custom in the family hall, when the feast was at its height, to display a drunken slave among the sons of the household, to the end that they, being ashamed at the ignominious folly of his gesticulations, might determine never to be tempted into such a pitiable condition themselves. The custom had its advantages; for the wisdom of the younger generation was found to be fostered more surely by a single example than by a world of homily and precept.

---

*Ezra Pound. "Drunken Helots and Mr. Eliot." *Egoist* 4, no. 5 (June 1917), 72–74.

Genius has I know not what peculiar property, its manifestations are various, but however diverse and dissimilar they may be, they have at least one property in common. It makes no difference in what art, in what mode, whether the most conservative, or the most ribald-revolutionary, or the most diffident; if in any land, or upon any floating deck over the ocean, or upon some newly contrapted craft in the aether, genius manifests itself, at once some elderly gentleman has a flux of bile from his liver; at once from the throne or the easy Cowperian sofa, or from the gutter, or from the economical press room there bursts a torrent of elderly words, splenetic, irrelevant, they form themselves instinctively into large phrases denouncing the inordinate product.

This peculiar kind of *rabbia* might almost be taken as the test of a work of art, mere talent seems incapable of exciting it. "You can't fool me, sir, you're a scoundrel," bawls the testy old gentleman.

Fortunately the days when "that very fiery particle" could be crushed out by the *Quarterly* are over, but it interests me, as an archaeologist, to note that the firm which no longer produces Byron, but rather memoirs, letters of the late Queen, etc., is still running a review, and that this review is still where it was in 1812, or whatever the year was; and that, not having an uneducated Keats to condemn, a certain Mr. Waugh is scolding about Mr. Eliot.

All I can find out, by asking questions concerning Mr. Waugh, is that he is "a very old chap," "a reviewer." From internal evidence we deduce that he is, like the rest of his generation of English *gens-de-lettres*, ignorant of Laforgue; of De Régnier's *Odelettes*; of his French contemporaries generally . . . This is by no means surprising. We are used to it from his "b'ilin'."

However, he outdoes himself, he calls Mr. Eliot a "drunken helot." So called they Anacreon in the days of his predecessors, but from the context in the *Quarterly* article I judge that Mr. Waugh does not intend the phrase as a compliment, he is trying to be abusive, and moreover, he in his limited way has succeeded.

Let us sample the works of the last "Drunken Helot." I shall call my next anthology "Drunken Helots" if I can find a dozen poems written half so well as the following: [quotation in full of "Conversation Galante."]

Our helot has a marvelous neatness. There is a comparable finesse in Laforgue's "Votre âme est affaire d'oculiste," but hardly in English verse.

Let us reconsider this drunkenness: [quotation in full of "La Figlia che Piange."]

And since when have helots taken to reading Dante and Marlowe? Since when have helots made a new music, a new refinement, a new method of turning old phrases into new by their aptness? However, the *Quarterly*, the century old, the venerable, the praeclarus, the voice of Gehova and Co., Sinai and 51A Albemarle Street, London, W.1, has pronounced this author a helot. They are all for an aristocracy made up of, possibly, Tennyson, Southey and Wordsworth, the flunkey, the dull and the duller. Let us sup with the helots. Or perhaps the good Waugh is a wag, perhaps he hears with the haspirate and wishes to pun on Mr. Heliot's name: a bright bit of syzygy.

I confess his type of mind puzzles me, there is no telling what he is up to.

I do not wish to misjudge him, this theory may be the correct one. You never can tell when old gentlemen grow facetious. He does not mention Mr. Eliot's name; he merely takes his lines and abuses them. The artful dodger, he didn't (*sotto voce* "he didn't want 'people' to know that Mr. Eliot was a poet").

The poem he chooses for malediction is the title poem, "Prufrock."

[Quotation of lines 49–72]

Let us leave the silly old Waugh. Mr. Eliot has made an advance on Browning. He has also made his dramatis personae contemporary and convincing. He has been an individual in his poems. I have read the contents of this book over and over, and with continued joy in the freshness, the humanity, the deep quiet culture. "I have tried to write of a few things that really have moved me" is so far as I know, the sum of Mr. Eliot's "poetic theory." His practice has been a distinctive cadence, a personal modus of arrangement, remote origins in Elizabethan English and in the modern French masters, neither origin being sufficiently apparent to affect the personal quality. It is writing without pretense. Mr. Eliot at once takes rank with the five or six living poets whose English one can read with enjoyment.

[. . .]

The poetic mind leaps the gulf from the exterior world, the trivialities of Mr. Prufrock, diffident, ridiculous, in the drawing-room; Mr. Apollinax's laughter "submarine and profound" transports him from the desiccated new-statesmanly atmosphere of Professor Channing-Cheetah's. Mr. Eliot's melody rushes out like the thought of Fragilion "among the birch-trees." Mr Waugh is my "bitten macaroon" at this festival.

*Times Literary
Supplement 805
(21 June 1917), 299.

Mr. Eliot's notion of poetry—he calls the "observations" poems—seems to be a purely analytical treatment, verging sometimes on the catalogue, of personal relations and environments, uninspired by any glimpse beyond them and untouched by any genuine rush of feeling. As, even on this basis, he remains frequently inarticulate, his "poems" will hardly be read by many with enjoyment. For the catalogue manner we may commend "Rhapsody on a Windy Night."

[. . .]

Among other reminiscences which pass through the rhapsodist's mind and which he thinks the public should know about, are "dust in crevices, / Smells of chestnuts in the streets, / And female smells in shuttered rooms, / And cigarettes in corridors / And cocktail smells in bars."

The fact that these things occurred to the mind of Mr. Eliot is surely of the very smallest importance to anyone—even to himself. They certainly have no relation to "poetry," and we only give an example because some of the pieces, he states, have appeared in a periodical which claims that word as its title.

*"Recent Verse."
Literary World 83
(5 July 1917), 107.

Mr. Eliot is one of those clever young men who find it amusing to pull the leg of a sober reviewer. We can imagine his saying to his friends: "See me have a lark out of the old fogies who don't know a poem from a pea-shooter. I'll just put down the first thing that comes into my head, and call it 'The Love Song of J. Alfred Prufrock.' Of course it will be idiotic; but the fogies are sure to praise it, because when they don't understand a thing and yet cannot hold their tongues they find safety in praise." We once knew a clever musician who found a boisterous delight in playing that pathetic melody "Only a Jew" in two keys at once. At first the effect was amusing in its complete idiocy, but we cannot imagine that our friend would have been so foolish as to print the score. Among a few friends the man of genius is privileged to make a fool of himself. He is usually careful not to do so outside an intimate circle. Mr. Eliot has not the wisdom of youth. If the "Love Song" is neither witty nor amusing, the other poems are interesting experiments in the bizarre and violent. The subjects of the poems, the imagery, the rhythms have the willful outlandishness of the young revolutionary idea. We do not wish to appear patronizing, but we are certain that Mr. Eliot could do finer work on traditional lines. With him it seems to be a case of missing the effect by too much cleverness. All beauty has in it an element of strangeness, but here the strangeness overbalances the beauty.

E. P. [Ezra Pound].
"T. S. Eliot."
Poetry: A Magazine of Verse 10 (August 1917), 264–71.

[. . .]

After much contemporary work that is merely factitious, much that is good in intention but impotently unfinished and incomplete, much whose flaws are due to sheer ignorance which a year's study or thought might have remedied, it is a comfort to come upon complete art, naive despite its intellectual subtlety, lacking all pretense.

It is quite safe to compare Mr. Eliot's work with anything written in French, English or American since the death of Jules Laforgue. The reader will find nothing better, and he will be extremely fortunate if he finds much half as good.

[. . .]

I should like the reader to note how complete is Mr. Eliot's depiction of our contemporary condition. He has not confined himself to genre nor to society portraiture. His "lonely men in shirt-sleeves, leaning out of windows" are as real as his ladies who "come and go / Talking of Michelangelo." His "one-night cheap hotels" are as much "there" as are his "four wax candles in the darkened room, / Four rings of light upon the ceiling overhead, / An atmosphere of Juliet's tomb." And, above all, there is no rhetoric, although there is Elizabethan reading in the background. Were I a French critic, skilled in their elaborate art of writing books about books, I should probably go to some length discussing Mr. Eliot's two sorts of metaphor: his wholly unrealizable, always apt, half ironic suggestion, and his precise realizable picture. It would be possible to point out his method of conveying a whole situation and half a character by three words of a quoted phrase; his constant aliveness, his mingling of very subtle observation with the unexpectedness of a backhanded cliché. It is, however, extremely dangerous to point out such devices. The method is Mr. Eliot's own, but as soon as one has reduced even a fragment of it to formula, someone else, not Mr. Eliot, someone else wholly lacking in his aptitudes, will at once try to make poetry by mimicking his external procedure. And this indefinite "someone" will, needless to say, make a botch of it.

For what the statement is worth, Mr. Eliot's work interests me more than that of any other poet now writing in English. The most interesting poems in Victorian English are Browning's *Men and Women*, or, if that statement is too absolute, let me contend that the form of these poems is the most vital form of that period of English, and that the poems written in that form are the least like each other in content. Antiquity gave us Ovid's *Heroides* and Theocritus' woman using magic. The form of Browning's *Men and Women* is more alive than the epistolary form of the *Heroides*. Browning included a certain amount of ratiocination and of purely intellectual comment, and in just that proportion he lost intensity. Since Browning there have been very few good poems of this sort. Mr. Eliot has made two notable additions to the list. And he has placed his people in contemporary settings, which is much more difficult than to render them with mediaeval romantic trappings. If it is permitted to make comparison with a different art, let me say that he has used contemporary detail very much as Velázquez used contemporary detail in *Las Meninas*; the cold gray-green tones of the Spanish painter have, it seems to me, an emotional value not unlike the emotional value of Mr. Eliot's rhythms, and of his vocabulary.

James Joyce has written the best novel of my decade, and perhaps the best criticism of it has come from a Belgian who said, "All this is as true of my country as of Ireland." Eliot has a like ubiquity of application. Art does not avoid universals, it strikes at them all the harder in that it strikes through particulars. Eliot's work rests apart from that of the many new writers who have used the present freedoms to no advantage, who have gained no new precisions of language, and no variety in their cadence. His men in shirt-sleeves, and his society ladies, are not a local manifestation; they are the stuff of our modern world, and true of more countries than one. I would praise the work for its fine tone, its humanity, and its realism; for all good art is realism of one sort or another.

It is complained that Eliot is lacking in emotion. "La Figlia che Piange" is sufficient refutation to that rubbish.

If the reader wishes mastery of "regular form," the "Conversation Galante" is sufficient to show that symmetrical form is within Mr. Eliot's grasp. You will hardly find such neatness save in France; such modern neatness, save in Laforgue.

[. . .] [T]he supreme test of a book is that we should feel some unusual intelligence working behind the words. By this test various other new books, that I have, or might have, beside me, go to pieces. The barrels of sham poetry that every decade and school and fashion produce, go to pieces. It is sometimes extremely difficult to find any other particular reason for their being so unsatisfactory. I have expressly written here not "intellect" but "intelligence." There is no intelligence without emotion. The emotion may be anterior or concurrent. There may be emotion without much intelligence, but this does not concern us.

Versification:

A conviction as to the rightness or wrongness of *vers libre* is no guarantee of a poet. I doubt if there is much use trying to classify the various kinds of *vers libre*, but there is an anarchy which may be vastly overdone; and there is a monotony of bad usage as tiresome as any typical eighteenth- or nineteenth-century flatness.

In a recent article Mr. Eliot contended [. . .] that good *vers libre* was little more than a skillful evasion of the better known English meters. [. . .] But he came nearer the fact when he wrote elsewhere: "No *vers* is *libre* for the man who wants to do a good job."

[. . .]

On the other hand, I do not believe Chopin wrote to a metronome. There is undoubtedly a sense of music that takes count of the "shape" of the rhythm in a melody rather than of bar divisions, which came rather late in the history of written music and were certainly not the first or most important thing that musicians tried to record. The creation of such shapes is part of thematic invention. Some musicians have the faculty of invention, rhythmic, melodic. Likewise some poets.

[. . .]

Unless a man can put some thematic invention into *vers libre*, he would perhaps do well to stick to "regular" meters, which have certain chances of being musical from their form, and certain other chances of being musical through his failure in fitting the form. In *vers libre* his sole musical chance lies in invention.

Mr. Eliot is one of the very few who have brought in a personal rhythm, an identifiable quality of sound as well as of style. And at any rate, his book is the best thing in poetry since . . . (for the sake of peace I will leave that date to the imagination). I have read most of the poems many times; I last read the whole book at breakfast time and from flimsy and grimy proof-sheets: I believe these are "test conditions." Confound it, the fellow can write—we may as well sit up and take notice.

*"Shorter Notices." *New Statesman* 9 (18 August 1917), 477.

Mr. Eliot may possibly give us the quintessence of twenty-first-century poetry. Certainly much of what he writes is unrecognizable as poetry at present, but it is all decidedly amusing; and it is only fair to say that he does not call these pieces poems. He calls them "observations," and the description seems exact; for he has a keen eye as well as a sharp pen, and draws wittily whatever his capricious glance descends on. We do not pretend to follow the drift of "The Love Song of J. Alfred Prufrock," and therefore, instead of quoting from it, we present our readers with the following piece: [quotation in full of "The *Boston Evening Transcript*"]. This is Mr. Eliot's highest flight, and we shall treasure it.

Conrad Aiken. "Divers Realists." *Dial* 63 (8 November 1917), 453–55.

Mr. T. S. Eliot, whose book *Prufrock and Other Observations* is really hardly more than a pamphlet, is also a realist, but of a different sort. Like Mr. Gibson, Mr. Eliot is a psychologist; but his intuitions are keener; his technique subtler. For the two semi-narrative psychological portraits which form the greater and better part of his book, "The Love Song of J. Alfred Prufrock" and the "Portrait of a Lady," one can have little but praise. This is psychological realism, but in a highly subjective or introspective vein; whereas Mr. Gibson, for example, gives us, in the third person, the reactions of an individual to a situation which is largely external (an accident, let us say), Mr. Eliot gives us, in the first person, the reactions of an individual to a situation for which to a large extent his own character is responsible. Such work is more purely autobiographic than the other—the field is narrowed, and the terms are idiosyncratic (sometimes almost blindly so). The dangers of such work are obvious: one must be certain that one's mental character and idiom are sufficiently close to the norm to be comprehensible or significant. In this respect, Mr. Eliot is near the border-line. His temperament is peculiar, it is sometimes, as remarked heretofore, almost bafflingly peculiar, but on the whole it is the average hyper-aesthetic one with a good deal of introspective curiosity; it will puzzle many, it will delight a few. Mr. Eliot writes pungently and sharply, with an eye for unexpected and vivid details, and, particularly in the two longer poems and in the "Rhapsody on a Windy Night," he shows himself to be an exceptionally acute technician. Such free rhyme as this, with irregular line lengths, is difficult to write well, and Mr. Eliot does it well enough to make one wonder whether such a form is not what the adorers of free verse will eventually have to come to. In the rest of Mr. Eliot's volume one finds the piquant and the trivial in about equal proportions.

May Sinclair. "*Prufrock and Other Observations*: A Criticism." *Little Review* 4, no. 8 (December 1917), 8–14.

So far I have seen two and only two reviews of Mr. Eliot's poems: one by Ezra Pound in the *Egoist*, one by an anonymous writer in the *New Statesman*. I learn from Mr. Pound's review that there is a third, by Mr. Arthur Waugh, in the *Quarterly*.

To Mr. Ezra Pound Mr. Eliot is a poet with genius as incontestable as the genius of Browning. To the anonymous one he is an insignificant phenomenon that may be appropriately disposed of among the "Shorter Notices." To Mr. Waugh, quoted by Mr. Pound, he is a "drunken Helot." I do not know what Mr. Pound would say to the anonymous one, but I can imagine. Anyhow, to him the *Quarterly* reviewer is "the silly old Waugh." And that is enough for Mr. Pound.

It ought to be enough for me. Of course I know that genius does inevitably provoke these outbursts of silliness. I know that Mr. Waugh is simply keeping up the good old manly traditions of the *Quarterly*, "so savage and tartarly," with its war-cry:

" 'Ere's a stranger, let's 'eave 'arf a brick at 'im!" And though the behavior of the *New Statesman* puzzles me, since it has an editor who sometimes knows better, and really ought to have known better this time, still the *New Statesman* can also plead precedent. But when Mr. Waugh calls Mr. Eliot a "drunken Helot," it is clear that he thinks he is on the track of a tendency and is making a public example of Mr. Eliot. And when the anonymous one with every appearance of deliberation picks out his "*Boston Evening Transcript*," the one insignificant, the one negligible and trivial thing in a very serious volume, and assures us that it represents Mr. Eliot at his finest and his best, it is equally clear that we have to do with something more than mere journalistic misadventure. And I think it is something more than Mr. Eliot's genius that has terrified the *Quarterly* into exposing him in the full glare of publicity and the *New Statesman* into shoving him and his masterpieces away out of the public sight.

For "The Love Song of J. Alfred Prufrock," and the "Portrait of a Lady" are masterpieces in the same sense and in the same degree as Browning's *Romances* and *Men and Women*; the "Preludes" and "Rhapsody on a Windy Night" are masterpieces in a profounder sense and a greater degree than Henley's *London Voluntaries*; "La Figlia che Piange" is a masterpiece in its own sense and in its own degree. It is a unique masterpiece.

But Mr. Eliot is dangerous. Mr. Eliot is associated with an unpopular movement and with unpopular people. His "Preludes" and his "Rhapsody" appeared in *Blast*. They stood out from the experimental violences of *Blast* with an air of tranquil and triumphant achievement; but, no matter; it was in *Blast* that they appeared. That circumstance alone was disturbing to the comfortable respectability of Mr. Waugh and the *New Statesman*.

And apart from this purely extraneous happening, Mr. Eliot's genius is in itself disturbing. It is elusive; it is difficult; it demands a distinct effort of attention. Comfortable and respectable people could see, in the first moment after dinner, what Mr. Henley and Mr. Robert Louis Stevenson and Mr. Rudyard Kipling would be at; for the genius of these three traveled, comfortably and fairly respectably, along the great high roads. They could even, with a little boosting, follow Francis Thompson's flight in mid-air, partly because it was signaled to them by the sound and shining of his wings, partly because Thompson had hitched himself securely to some well-known starry team. He was in the poetic tradition all right. People knew where they were with him, just as they know now where they are with Mr. Davies and his fields and flowers and birds.

But Mr. Eliot is not in any tradition at all, not even in Browning's and Henley's tradition. His resemblances to Browning and Henley are superficial. His difference is two-fold; a difference of method and technique; a difference of sight and aim. He does not see anything between him and reality, and he makes straight for the reality he sees; he cuts all his corners and his curves; and this directness of method is startling and upsetting to comfortable, respectable people accustomed to going superfluously in and out of corners and carefully round curves. Unless you are prepared to follow with the same nimbleness and straightness you will never arrive with Mr. Eliot at his meaning. Therefore the only comfortable thing is to sit down and pretend, either that Mr. Eliot is a "Helot" too drunk to have any meaning, or that his *Boston Evening Transcript* which you do understand is greater than his "Love Song of Prufrock" which you do not understand. In both instances you have successfully obscured the issue.

Again, the comfortable and respectable mind loves conventional beauty, and some of the realities that Mr. Eliot sees are not beautiful. He insists on your seeing very vividly, as he sees them, the streets of his "Preludes" and "Rhapsody." He insists on your smelling them.

> "Regard that woman
> Who hesitates toward you in the light
>   of the door
> Which opens on her like a grin.
> You see the border of her dress
> Is torn and stained with sand,
> And you see the corner of her eye
> Twists like a crooked pin."

[Quotation of lines 23–37 of "Rhapsody on a Windy Night"]

He is "aware of the damp souls of housemaids / Sprouting despondently at area gates."

And these things are ugly. The comfortable mind turns away from them in disgust. It identifies Mr. Eliot with a modern tendency; it labels him securely "Stark Realist," so that lovers of "true poetry" may beware.

It is nothing to the comfortable mind that Mr. Eliot is

> . . . moved by fancies that are curled
> Around these images, and cling:
> The notion of some infinitely gentle
> Infinitely suffering thing.

It is nothing to it that the emotion he disengages from his ugliest image is unbearably poignant. His poignancy is as unpleasant as his ugliness, disturbing to comfort.

We are to observe that Mr. Eliot's "Observations" are ugly and unpleasant and obscure.

Now there is no earthly reason why Mr. Eliot should not be ugly and unpleasant if he pleases, no reason why he should not do in words what Hogarth did in painting, provided that he does it well enough. Only, the comfortable mind that prefers So and So and So and So to Mr. Eliot ought to prefer Hogarth's *Paul Before Felix* to his *Harlot's Progress*. Obscurity, if he were really obscure, would be another matter. But there was a time when the transparent Tennyson was judged obscure; when people wondered what under heaven the young man was after; they couldn't tell for the life of them whether it was his "dreary gleams" or his "curlews" that were flying over Locksley Hall. Obscurity may come from defective syntax, from a bad style, from confusion of ideas, from involved thinking, from irrelevant association, from sheer piling on of ornament. Mr. Eliot is not obscure in any of these senses.

There is also an obscurity of remote or unusual objects, or of familiar objects moving very rapidly. And Mr. Eliot's trick of cutting his corners and his curves makes him seem obscure when he is clear as daylight. His thoughts move very rapidly and by astounding cuts. They move not by logical stages and majestic roundings of the full literary curve, but as live thoughts move in live brains.

[Quotation in full of "La Figlia che Piange"]

I suppose there are minds so comfortable that they would rather not be disturbed by new beauty and by new magic like this. I do not know how much Mr. Eliot's beauty and magic is due to sheer imagination, how much to dexterity of technique, how much to stern and sacred attention to reality; but I do know that without such technique and such attention the finest imagination is futile, and that if Mr. Eliot had written nothing but ["La Figlia che Piange"] he would rank as a poet by right of its perfection.

But Mr. Eliot is not a poet of one poem; and if there is anything more astounding

and more assured than his performance it is his promise. He knows what he is after. Reality, stripped naked of all rhetoric, of all ornament, of all confusing and obscuring association, is what he is after. His reality may be a modern street or a modern drawing-room; it may be an ordinary human mind suddenly and fatally aware of what is happening to it; Mr. Eliot is careful to present his street and his drawing-room as they are, and Prufrock's thoughts as they are: live thoughts, kicking, running about and jumping, nervily, in a live brain.

Prufrock, stung by a longing for reality, escapes from respectability into the street and the October fog.

[. . .]

His soul can only assert itself in protests and memories. He would have had more chance in the primeval slime. "I should have been a pair of ragged claws / Scuttling across the floors of silent seas."

As he goes downstairs he is aware of his futility, aware that the noticeable thing about him is the "bald spot in the middle of my hair." He has an idea; an idea that he can put into action: "I shall wear the bottoms of my trousers rolled." He is incapable, he knows that he is incapable of any action more momentous, more disturbing.

And yet—and yet—

I have heard the mermaids singing,
  each to each.

I do not think that they will sing to me.

I have seen them riding seaward on
  the waves
Combing the white hair of the waves
  blown back
When the wind blows the water white
  and black.

We have lingered in the chambers of
  the sea

By sea-girls wreathed with seaweed
red and brown

Till human voices wake us, and we
drown.

Observe the method. Instead of writing round and round about Prufrock, explaining that his tragedy is the tragedy of submerged passion, Mr. Eliot simply removes the covering from Prufrock's mind: Prufrock's mind, jumping quickly from actuality to memory and back again, like an animal, hunted, tormented, terribly and poignantly alive. "The Love Song of Prufrock" is a song that Balzac might have sung if he had been as great a poet as he was a novelist.

It is nothing to the *Quarterly* and to the *New Statesman* that Mr. Eliot should have done this thing. But it is a great deal to the few people who care for poetry and insist that it should concern itself with reality. With ideas, if you like, but ideas that are realities and not abstractions.

Conrad Aiken. "New Curiosity Shop—and a Poet." *Dial* 64 (31 January 1918), 112.

[Review of *Others* anthology]

Who it was that started the current poetic fad for curio-collecting is a question not hard to answer: Ezra Pound is the man, let the Imagists and others deny it as loudly as they will. Pound has from the outset, both as poet and as critic, been a curio-collector—a lover of trinkets, *bijoux* of phrase, ideographic *objets*

de vertu, carved oddities from the pawn-shops of the past, aromatic grave-relics, bizarre importations from the Remote and Strange. There is no denying, either, that it is a delightful vein in verse. No great exertion is demanded of the reader; he is invited merely to pause before the display-window and to glance, if only for a moment, at the many intriguing minutiæ there arranged for him in trays.

[. . .]

This method in the writing of poetry is to be seen at its purest in the *Others* anthologies, the second of which Mr. Alfred Kreymborg has now edited, apparently undeterred by the success of the first . . . There is much here, of course, that is merely trivial, and a measurable quantity of the proudly absurd and naively preposterous; but if there are no such outstandingly good things here as "The Portrait of a Lady" by T. S. Eliot in the earlier issue, or Wallace Stevens's "Peter Quince at the Clavier," . . . [we can] pause with admiration and delight before the "Preludes" and "Rhapsody of a Windy Night" by T. S. Eliot, and "Thirteen Ways of Looking at a Blackbird" by Wallace Stevens. It is not that one is at all indifferent to the frequent charm and delicious originality (at least regards sensibility) of the *Others* poets, but that one finds in the two last mentioned not only this delicate originality of mind but also a clearer sense of symmetry as regards both form and ideas: their poems are more apparently, and more really, works of art. In comparison, most of the other work in this volume looks like happy improvisation. It is significant in this connection that Mr. Eliot uses rhyme and meter, a telling demonstration that the use of these ingredients may add power and finish and speed to poetry without in any way dulling the poet's tactile organs or clouding his consciousness—provided he has the requisite skill. Mr. Eliot's "Preludes" and "Rhapsody" are, in a very minor way, masterpieces of black-and-white impressionism. Personality, time, and environment—three attributes of the dramatic—are set sharply before us by means of a rapid and concise report of the seemingly irrelevant and tangential, but really centrally significant, observations of a shadowy protagonist.

[. . .]

B. D. [Babette Deutsch]. "Another Impressionist." *New Republic* 14 (16 February 1918), 89.

A slim little book, bound in pale yellow wrapping paper, *Prufrock* invites inspection, as much by the novelty of its appearance as the queer syllables of its title. The individual note which these suggest is even more emphatically pronounced in the poems between its covers.

The initial one, which gives its name to the volume, is "The Love Song of J. Alfred Prufrock." Mr. Prufrock, as he explains in his amorous discursions, is no longer young; his hair has perceptibly thinned, his figure has lost what Apollonian contours it may have possessed. He is self-conscious, introspective, timid. In a-metrical but fluent lines, embroidered with unique metaphor, he draws himself: his desires, his memories, his fears. "Do I dare," he asks, "Disturb the universe?"

[Quotation of lines 47–51]

In the end, he does not presume.

The method used in this poem is typical of Mr. Eliot's work. Impressions are strung along on a tenuous thread of sense. A familiar situation: the hesitating amours of the middle-aged, the failure of a certain man to establish the expected relation with a certain woman, is given in poetic monologue. The language has the extraordinary quality of common words uncommonly used. Less formal than prose, more nervous than metrical verse, the rhythms are suggestive of program music of an intimate sort. This effect is emphasized by the use of rhyme. It recurs, often internally, with an echoing charm that is heightened by its irregularity. But Mr. Eliot, like M. Géraldy, of whom he is vaguely reminiscent, is so clever a technician that the rhymes are subordinated to afford an unconsidered pleasure.

In these "observations" there is a glimpse of many slight but memorable things: of dirty London streets, crowded with laborers, dilettantes, prostitutes; of polite stupidities in country houses; of satiric fencings; of the stale aroma of familiar things. Mostly they are impressions of a weary mind, looking out upon a crowded personal experience with impartial irony. They have the hall-marks of impressionism: remoteness from vulgar ethics and aesthetics, indifference to the strife of nations and classes, an esoteric humor thrown out in peculiar phrases. Something of Eliot's quality may be got from "The *Boston Evening Transcript*," whimsically suggestive of that fragment of Sappho's: "Evening, thou that bringest all that bright morning scattered; thou bringest the sheep, the goat, the child back to her mother." [. . .]

When evening quickens faintly in the
    street,
Wakening the appetites of life in some
And to others bringing the *Boston
    Evening Transcript*,
I mount the steps and ring the bell,
    turning

Wearily, as one would turn to nod
    good-bye to Rochefoucauld,
If the street were time and he at the
    end of the street,
And I say, "Cousin Harriet, here is the
    Boston Evening Transcript."

M. M. [Marianne Moore]. "A Note on T. S. Eliot's Book." *Poetry: A Magazine of Verse* 12 (April 1918), 36–37.

It might be advisable for Mr. Eliot to pub-lish a fangless edition of *Prufrock and Other Observations* for the gentle reader who likes his literature, like breakfast coffee or grapefruit, sweetened. A mere change in the arrangement of the poems would help a little. It might begin with "La Figlia che Piange," followed perhaps by "Portrait of a Lady"; for the gentle reader, in his eagerness for the custom-ary bit of sweets, can be trusted to over-look the ungallantry, the youthful cruelty, of the substance of the "Portrait." It may as well be admitted that this hardened reviewer cursed the poet in his mind for this cruelty while reading the poem; and just when he was ready to find extenuating circumstances—the usual excuses about realism—out came this "drunken helot" (one can hardly blame the good English reviewer whom Ezra Pound quotes!) with that ending. It is hard to get over this end-ing with a few moments of thought; it wrenches a piece of life at the roots.

As for the gentle reader, this poem could be followed by the lighter ironies of "Cousin Nancy," "The *Boston Evening*

Transcript," etc. One would hardly know what to do with the two London pieces. Whistler in his post-impressionistic Eng-lish studies—and these poems are not entirely unlike Whistler's studies—had the advantage of his more static medium, of a somewhat more romantic temperament, and of the fact that the objects he painted half-hid their ugliness under shadows and the haze of distance. But Eliot deals with life, with beings and things who live and move almost nakedly before his individual mind's eye—in the darkness, in the early sunlight, and in the fog. Whatever one may feel about sweetness in literature, there is also the word honesty, and this man is a faithful friend of the objects he portrays; altogether unlike the sentimen-talist who really stabs them treacherously in the back while pretending affection.

---

*Edgar Jepson. "Recent United States Poetry." *English Review* 26 (May 1918), 419–28.

There is in the United States today a new school of poetry—United States Poetry; and its seat is fittingly Chicago, the typ-ical city. It is claimed for its poets that they are "securely rooted in their native soil"; that their poetry is "so much con-cerned with United States life and so much a part of it that it may be said to be becom-ing genuinely national"; that it is "creat-ing a new diction, a new idiom, and it is going to be a much more fluid thing than English critics have any idea of"; that it has "unique features"; and that "unless one realizes the new, autochthonic note" in United States poetry today—in the most distinctive United States poetry, that is—one realizes nothing of the subtle impulses and forces that are at work to create a new poetic environment for the coming generation.

[. . .]

[T]he school has its accredited masters, stamped authentic by the award of prizes for poems by the school itself. They are its chief representatives; their poetry is the fine flower of its growth—Messrs. Vachel Lindsay, Edgar Lee Masters, and Robert Frost.

[Discussion of representative lines by Lindsay, Masters, and Frost]

[T]his poor music is common to the great bulk of all the recent United States poetry I have read.

[. . .]

But the queer and delightful thing is that in the scores of yards of pleasant verse and wamblings and yawpings which have been recently published in the Great Pure Republic I have found a poet, a real poet, who possesses in the highest degree the qualities the new school demands. Western-born of Eastern stock, Mr. T. S. Eliot is United States of the United States; and his poetry is securely rooted in its native soil; it has a new poetic diction; it is as autochthonic as Theocritus. It is new in form, as all genuine poetry is new in form; it is musical with a new music, and that without any straining after newness. The form and music are a natural, integral part of the poet's amazingly fine presentation of his vision of the world.

Could anything be more United States, more of the soul of that modern land, than "The Love Song of J. Alfred Prufrock"? It is the very wailing testament of that soul with its cruel clarity of sophisticated vision, its thin, sophisticated emotions, its sophisticated appreciation of a beauty, and

its sophisticated yearning for a beauty it cannot dare to make its own and so, at last, to live.

[Quotation of lines 35–40, 45–54, 123–30 of "The Love Song of J. Alfred Prufrock"]

Never has the shrinking of the modern spirit from life been expressed so exquisitely and with such truth.

Consider, again, that lovely poem, "La Figlia che Piange": [quotation in full]. How delicate and beautiful is the emotion! How exquisite and beautiful the music! This is the very fine flower of the finest spirit of the United States . . . It seems incredible that this lovely poem should have been published in *Poetry* in the year in which the school awarded the prize to that lumbering fakement [by Masters], "All Life in a Life."

William Carlos Williams. "Prologue." *Little Review* 6 (May 1919), 76–78.

[Response to Jepson's "Recent United States Poetry"]

[. . .]

[A]ll U.S. verse is not bad according to Mr. J[epson]: there is "The Love Song of J. Alfred Prufrock."

It is convenient to have fixed standards of comparison: all antiquity! And there is always some everlasting Polonius of Kensington forever to rate highly his eternal Eliot. It is because Eliot is a subtle conformist. It tickles the palate of this archbishop of procurers to a lecherous

16

antiquity to hold up Prufrock as a New World type. Prufrock the nibbler at sophistication, endemic in every capital, the not-quite (because he refuses to turn his back) is "the soul of that modern land" the United States!

[. . .]

As Prufrock longed for his silly lady so Kensington longs for its Hardanger dairymaid. By a mere twist of the imagination, if Prufrock only knew it, the whole world can be inverted (why else are there wars?) and the mermaids be set warbling to whoever will listen to them. Seesaw and blind-man's-bluff converted into a sort of football.

But the summit of the United States achievement, according to Mr. J[epson]— who can discourse on Catullus—is that very beautiful poem of Eliot's, "La Figlia che Piange:" just the right amount of everything drained through, etc., etc., etc., etc., the rhythm delicately studied out and—IT CONFORMS! *ergo*, here we have "the very fine flower of the finest spirit of the United States."

Examined closely this poem reveals a highly refined distillation. Added to the already "faithless" formula of yesterday we have a conscious simplicity: "Simple and faithless as a smile and shake of the hand."

The perfection of that line is beyond cavil. Yet, in the last stanza, this paradigm, this very fine flower of U.S. art, is warped out of alignment, obscured in meaning even to the point of an absolute unintelligibility by the inevitable straining after a rhyme!—the very cleverness with which this straining is covered being a sinister token in itself. "And I wonder how they should have been together!"

So we have no choice but to accept the work of this fumbling conjurer.

Upon the Jepson filet Eliot balances his mushroom. It is the latest touch from the literary cuisine, it adds to the pleasant outlook from the club window. If to do this, if to be a Whistler at best, in the art of poetry, is to reach the height of poetic expression, then Ezra [Pound] and Eliot have approached it and *tant pis* for the rest of us.

[. . .]

Checklist of Additional Reviews

Little Review 4, no. 4 (August 1917), 24–25. [Unsigned letter]

Ezra Pound. "A Letter from Rémy de Gourmont." *Little Review* 4, no. 8 (December 1917), 6–7.

Edgar Jepson. "That International Episode." *Little Review* 5, nos. 10–11 (February–March 1919), 62–64.

POEMS
1919
ARA VOS PREC
1920
POEMS
1920

POEMS

BY

T. S. ELIOT

Printed & published by L. & V. Woolf
at THE HOGARTH PRESS, *Hogarth House, Richmond*
1919

*"Not Here, O Apollo." *Times Literary Supplement* 908 (12 June 1919), 322.

[. . .]

Mr. Eliot . . . is fastidiously on his guard against echoes. There shall not be a cadence in his few verses that will remind anyone of anything. His composition is an incessant process of refusing all that offers itself, for fear that it should not be his own. The consequence is that his verse, novel and ingenious, original as it is, is fatally impoverished of subject matter. For he is as fastidious of emotions as of cadences. He seems to have a "phobia" of sentimentality, like a small schoolboy who would die rather than kiss his sister in public. Still, since he is writing verses he must say something, and his remarkable talent exercises itself in saying always, from line to line and word to word, what no one would expect. Each epithet, even, must be a surprise, each verb must shock the reader with unexpected associations; and the result is this:

> Polyphiloprogenitive
> The sapient sutlers of the Lord
> Drift across the window-panes.
> In the beginning was the Word.
>
> In the beginning was the Word.
> Superfetation of τὸ ἔν,
> And at the mensual turn of time
> Produced enervate Origen.

Mr. Eliot, like Browning, likes to display out-of-the-way learning, he likes to surprise you by every trick he can think of. He has forgotten his emotions, his values, his sense of beauty, even his common-sense, in that one desire to surprise, to get farther away from the obvious than any writer on record, be he Donne or Browning . . . We say he has forgotten all these things, because there is no doubt of his talents. They are evident in "The Hippopotamus" and even in "Sweeney Among the Nightingales," where he carries the game of perversity as far at least as anyone has ever carried it. But poetry is a serious art, too serious for this game. Mr. Eliot is fatally handicapping himself with his own inhibitions; he is in danger of becoming silly; and what will he do then? Or else he is in danger of writing nothing at all, but merely thinking of all the poems he has refused to write: a state which would be for a poet, if not hell, at least limbo.

[. . .]

*"Is This Poetry?" *Athenaeum* 4651 (20 June 1919), 491.

[. . .]

The "ordinary man," the ghostly master or terror of most writers, would certainly ask the . . . question ["Is this poetry?"] about Mr. Eliot, and answer it with a decided negative.

> Polyphiloprogenitive
> The sapient sutlers of the Lord
> Drift across the window-panes.
> In the beginning was the Word.

Thus begins one of Mr. Eliot's poems, provocative of the question and of the jeering laugh which is the easy reaction to anything strange, whether it be a "damned foreigner" or a Post-Impressionist picture. Mr. Eliot is certainly damned by his newness and strangeness; but those two qualities, which in most art are completely unimportant, because ephemeral, in his claim the attention of even the serious critic. For they are part of the fabric of his poetry. Mr. Eliot is always quite consciously "trying for" something, and something which has grown out of and developed beyond all the poems of all the dead poets. Poetry to him seems to be not so much an art as a science, a vast and noble and amusing body of communal feeling upon which the contemporary poet must take a firm stand and then launch himself into the unknown in search of new discoveries. That is the attitude not of the conventional poet, but of the scientist who with the help of working hypotheses hopes to add something, a theory perhaps or a new microbe, to the corpus of human knowledge. If we accept, provisionally, Mr. Eliot's attitude, we must admit that he comes well equipped to his task. The poetry of the dead is in his bones and at the tips of his fingers: he has the rare gift of being able to weave, delicately and delightfully, an echo or even a line of the past into the pattern of his own poem. And at the same time he is always trying for something new, something which has evolved— one drops instinctively into the scientific terminology—out of the echo or the line, out of the last poem of the last dead poet, something subtly intellectual and spiritual, produced by the careful juxtaposition of words and the even more careful juxtaposition of ideas. The cautious critic . . . might avoid answering the question: "And is this poetry?" by asking to see a little more of Mr. Eliot than is shown in these seven short poems and even "Prufrock." But, to tell the truth, seven poems reveal a great deal of any poet. There is poetry in Mr. Eliot, as, for instance, in the stanzas:

The host with someone indistinct
Converses at the door apart,
The nightingales are singing near
The Convent of the Sacred Heart,

And sang within the bloody wood
When Agamemnon cried aloud
And let their liquid siftings fall
To stain the stiff dishonoured shroud.

Yet the poetry often seems to come in precisely at the moment when the scientist and the science, the method and the newness, go out. A poem like "The Hippopotamus," for all its charm and cleverness and artistry, is perilously near the pit of the *jeu d'esprit*. And so scientific and scholarly a writer as Mr. Eliot might with advantage consider whether his method was not the method of that "terrible warning," P. Papinius Statius. We hope that Mr. Eliot will quickly give us more and remove our melancholy suspicion that he is the product of a Silver Age.

Checklist of Additional Reviews

Marsden Hartley. "Breakfast Resumé." *Little Review* 5, no. 7 (November 1918), 46–50.

*"Experiments in Poetry." *Times Literary Supplement* 905 (22 May 1919), 274.

"Some Recent Verse." *Oakland Tribune* [California], 4 April 1920, p. 7. [not located]

"*Poems* by T. S. Eliot." *Sun and New York Herald*, 11 April 1920, sec. 3, p. 9. [not located]

W. S. B. [William Stanley Braithwaite]. "A Scorner of the Ordinary Substance of Human Nature." *Boston Evening Transcript*, 14 April 1920, pt. 2, p. 6. [not located]

S. T. C. [Samuel T. Clover]. *Richmond Evening Journal* [Virginia], 17 April 1920, p. 7.

Baltimore Evening Sun, 15 May 1920. [Clipping so dated, but incorrectly, in the Eliot Collection in the Houghton Library]

"Literature." *Booklist* 16 (June 1920), 305.

*Ford Madox Hueffer. "Thus to Revisit . . . Some Reminiscences." *English Review* 31 (September 1920), 209–17.

Babette Deutsch. "Orchestral Poetry." *Dial* 70 (March 1921), 343–46. [Review of Conrad Aiken's *House of Dust*, with Eliot considered the "assisting artist"]

Ara Vus Prec

by

T.S.Eliot

THE OVID PRESS

*John Middleton Murry. "The Eternal Footman." *Athenaeum* 4686 (20 February 1920), 239.

Here is Mr. T. S. Eliot, and here once again is the question: What are we to make of him? It is not a question that even the most assiduous (assiduity is demanded) and interested (interest is inevitable) of his readers would care to answer with any accent of finality. For Mr. Eliot, who is a connoisseur in discrepancy between intention and achievement, is likely to be himself an example of it. Nothing so sharpens one's sensitiveness to false notes in life at large as experience of them in oneself; so that there is more than a remote chance that even in regard to *Ara Vos Prec* and while we hold it in our hands Mr. Eliot may whisper deprecatingly: "That is not it at all. / That is not what I meant, at all."

Yes, it seems to us sometimes that the inmost vital core of Mr. Eliot's poetry, the paradoxical impulse of his expression, is his determination to be free to whisper that refrain in our ear; it seems that he is like the chameleon who changes color infinitely, and every change is protective. True, the range of variation is not truly infinite; there are colors which the chameleon cannot compass. But the chameleon, if he were an artist, would make it an essential of his art not to be lured against a background which he could not imitate.

The question for the critic is to determine whether Mr. Eliot—a conscious artist if ever there was one—has at any moment allowed himself to stray beyond his functional limit. That limit is set in the case of Mr. Eliot at the point where discrepancy ceases between intention and achievement, between soul and body, man and the Universe. At a crucial moment in his beautiful—we insist, precisely beautiful—"Love Song of J. Alfred Prufrock"—"the eternal Footman . . . snicker[s]." Since that day Mr. Eliot has fallen deeper and deeper into the clutches of the Footman, who has come to preside over his goings out and his comings in. The Footman has grown into a monstrous Moloch. All that Mr. Eliot most deeply feels is cast into his burning belly—or almost all.

Yet consider the case of men, and of their more perfect exemplars who are poets. It is only when the eternal Footman has given notice, when no longer "Human voices wake us and we drown," when we pass out of the limbo of discordant futility, that there comes to us all the crash, the collapse, the ecstasy, the peace of surrender. Mr. Eliot is like us, terribly like us, for all that he is much more clever; the difference is that the Footman clings to his service longer. With the truly aristocratic, as we know, the Footman will stay for fifteen shillings when he would leave Mr. Bleistein and fifteen guineas; and we admit the implication that Mr. Eliot is truly distinguished. Another implication is that it is difficult for Mr. Eliot to talk to us, and difficult (as the present essay proves) for us to talk to him.

The further question arises—we continue to speak in parables on a matter hardly susceptible of discussion otherwise—whether we are to accept that Footman or not. Is it polite of us, have we a right, to seek an interview with Mr. Eliot when the Footman is not there? The rightness of an action is fortunately not measured by its ease of execution, but neither can we accept the dogma that the difficult is necessarily the virtuous path. Have we a right to say in our turn: "That is not it, at all," to insist that the Footman in the long run makes everything impossible for us also, to gather up tell-tale accents that have escaped, bubble-clear and bubble-frail, from under the Footman's all-regarding eye? May we, for instance, perpend "The notion of some infinitely gentle / Infinitely suffering thing" and seek in it a solvent to the icy brilliance of an all but inexpugnable society manner? May we proceed thence, following a tenuous and evanescent clue, and ask not whether "Gerontion" is solidly and definitely anything, but what it was that brought him to his premature old age? Is there anything other than that which we found (if indeed we found it) cowering beneath the strange notion, which would be apt "To lose beauty in terror, terror in inquisition"?

The Footman snickers audibly. But do we care? Rather, do we care now? We, who have lost with the capability the desire to be respectable, can stop our ears to him when there is a chance of hearing something that is all important for us to know, whose sub-terrene tremor is not wholly lost. "Think at last / I have not made this show purposelessly" [quotation of these two and five subsequent lines of "Gerontion"]. Assuredly we are not tempted to think it was purposelessly made. The conviction of purpose remains whether we accept the Footman or reject him. True, we should prefer that he were dismissed, partly because his going (or our sense that he is gone) makes elucidation (or what we think elucidation) easier, but also in part because he can never be wholly abolished. The sense of the Footman belongs to a generation; he is our *datum*, our constant. But by an effort of imaginative will he can be compressed within the circle of our vision to less than a bogey-size. Mr. Eliot, more ably than ourselves, can stand apart from the Footman and his victim both. Is it necessary that he should turn himself into a bigger Footman still, and yet a bigger when that one too has been compressed, and a bigger *ad infinitum*?

Nowadays it is consciousness that makes cowards of us all. The complexity of our enemy is indicated by the fact of Mr. Eliot's determination that it shall make a brave man of him. But is it possible really? At least, Mr. Eliot would admit that it is a super-cowardice; he would claim that, indeed, as his exact intention. To make virtues of our vices is a good way of disarming them; but is it the best? Surely it cannot be unless with it is preserved the instinct that it must be abandoned when it begins to prey upon the vitals. *Impavidum ferient ruinæ.* We do not doubt it for one moment with Mr. Eliot; but we have a notion that in the last resort the ruins will count for more than the impavidity that marks his unflinching diagnosis.

> After such knowledge, what
>   forgiveness? Think now
> History has many cunning passages,
>   contrived corridors
> And issues, deceives with whispering
>   ambitions,
> Guides us by vanities. Think now . . .
> Neither fear nor courage saves us.
>   Unnatural vices
> Are fathered by our heroism. Virtues
> Are forced upon us by our impudent
>   crimes.

---

*"A New Byronism." *Times Literary Supplement* 948 (18 March 1920), 184.

The death of Swinburne marked the end of an age in English poetry, the age which began with Blake. It was impossible for any poet after Swinburne to continue the romantic tradition: he carried his own kind of versification and the romantic attitude as far as they could be carried, and both died with him. Now our poets have to make another beginning, to find a method of expression suited to their different attitude; and of this fact they are almost over-conscious. They have indeed often been led into an obvious error by that over-consciousness; because they must find new ways of expression and because they react differently to the great facts of life, some of them appear to think that the very subject matter of their verse must be different. This was the error of the eighteenth century; it sought for a new subject matter and chose one more suitable for prose than poetry, with the result that it developed a style suited for neither . . .

The romantic movement itself was at first a return to the proper subject matter of poetry and to a proper poetical technique. In its decline it narrowed the subject matter of poetry to themes which seemed obviously and easily poetical, and its technique also became obvious and too easily poetical. So the young poets of today are apt to insist that they will make poetry of what they choose; but their choice is not always so free as they think. It is conditioned by reaction, disgust, *ennui*; they want no more of "La Belle Dame sans Merci," or of King Arthur or Pan or Proserpine, just as they want no more of rhythms such as "By the tideless, dolorous, midland sea"—so they choose themes and rhythms the very opposite of these. Often they seem in their poetry to be telling us merely how they refuse to write poems and not how they wish to write them . . .

Mr. Eliot is an extreme example of this process. His cleverness, which is also extreme, expresses itself almost entirely in rejections; his verse is full of derisive reminiscences of poets who have wearied him. As for subject matter, that also is all refusal; it can be expressed in one phrase; again and again he tells us that he is "fed up" with art, with life, with people, with things. Everyone for him seems to be a parody of exhausted and out-of-date emotions. To read his verse is to be thrown deliberately into that mood which sometimes overcomes one in the streets of a crowded town when one is tired and bewildered, the mood in which all passers-by look like over-expressive marionettes pretending to be alive and all the more mechanical for their pretense. In such a mood one is morbidly aware of town squalor; everything seems to have been used and re-used again and again; the symbol of all life is cigarette ends and stale cigarette smoke; the very conversation is like that, it has been said a thousand times and is repeated mechanically; in fact all things are done from habit, which has mastered life and turned it into an endlessly recurring squalor.

[Quotation of lines 71–83 of "Portrait of a Lady"]

"Recalling things that other people have desired"—Mr. Eliot's verse is always doing that; and, like jesting Pilate, he will not wait for an answer to his own question—"Are these ideas right or wrong?" He asks it and goes on to something else with a hope, that is too like despair, that something may come of it. But nothing does come—

And I must borrow every changing
   shape
To find expression . . . dance, dance
Like a dancing bear,
Cry like a parrot, chatter like an ape.
Let us take the air, in a tobacco
   trance—

That may be satire on someone else, but it does exactly express the effect of his own verse, not once or twice but all the time. The habit of those whom he describes has got into his own technique, into his very way of experiencing; he, like the lesser romantics, has found too easy a way of functioning, and he functions and functions just as narrowly as if he were still writing about the Holy Grail.

[Quotation in full of "Preludes" II]

This might be a prelude to something, some passion or reality that would suddenly spring out of it, but with Mr. Eliot [it] is not. Near the end, after an enumeration of all the squalors he can think of, he says:—

> I am moved by fancies that are curled
> Around these images, and cling:
> The notion of some infinitely gentle
> Infinitely suffering thing.

That being so, why does he not tell us about it? It might be interesting; but no. After this momentary relenting, this flicker of natural feeling, he ends:

> Wipe your hand across your mouth,
>   and laugh;
> The worlds revolve like ancient
>   women
> Gathering fuel in vacant lots.

But if that is so, why write verse about it; why not commit suicide? Art presumes that life is worth living, and must not, except dramatically or in a moment of exasperation or irony, say that it isn't. But Mr. Eliot writes only to say that it isn't; and he does not do it so well as the author of *Ecclesiastes*, who at least keeps the momentum and gusto of all the experiences he pretends to have exhausted. For Mr. Eliot—"Midnight shakes the memory / As a madman shakes a dead geranium." There we are reminded a little of his countryman Poe, and "The Love Song of J. Alfred Prufrock" is like Poe even in its curious and over-conscious metrical effects. They seem to be, as so often in Poe, independent of the poem itself, as if the writer could not attain to a congruity between the tune beating in his head and

any subject matter. In this poem he is really, with the poet part of him, questing for beauty, but the other part refuses it with a kind of nausea.

[Quotation of lines 121–30 of "The Love Song of J. Alfred Prufrock"]

So it ends. Human voices for Mr. Eliot drown everything; he cannot get away from his disgust with them; he is "fed up" with them, with their volubility and lack of meaning. "Words, words, words" might be his motto; for in his verse he seems to hate them and to be always expressing his hatred of them, in words. If he could, he would write songs without words; blindly he seeks for a medium free of associations, not only for a tune but also for notes that no one has sung before. But all this is mere habit; art means the acceptance of a medium as of life; and Mr. Eliot does not convince us that his weariness is anything but a habit, an anti-romantic reaction, a new Byronism which he must throw off if he is not to become a recurring decimal in his fear of being a mere vulgar fraction.

---

*Robert Nichols. "An Ironist." *Observer*, 18 April 1920, p. 7.

Mr. Eliot is known to the world at large through the columns of the *Athenaeum* as a widely erudite critic possessed of a natural distinction in style and such a mordant perspicacity as is hardly to be matched in British or North American letters today. To some few else he is known also as the poet of *Prufrock*. The Ovid Press has now gathered up *Prufrock* and the later

Poems, and displays them to the world in one of the most beautiful productions of the modern press. The paper and printing (with initials and colophon by Mr. E. A. Wadsworth) are superb.

Let me say it at once: Mr. Eliot is, more especially in his later work, emphatically not an "easy poet." Nor is the reason far to seek. Mr. Eliot mostly does not deal with what are popularly considered the main streams of emotion. Not for him the generalized joys or sorrows of a Whitman or a Shelley, nor such rhythms as roll the consenting reader he scarcely knows whither upon the bosom of the flood. No; Mr. Eliot is not going to appear to lose his head or suffer the reader to lose his. Mr. Eliot, like the poet in *Candide*, muses to himself and the world overhears him; but not before he wished it to; no, not by a long chalk. For, you see, the stuff of his musing is complicated, and Mr. Eliot does not pretend it is easy. "The primrose by the river's brim" is for Mr. Eliot most emphatically neither a simple primrose nor a possible ingredient in a Disraelian salad. It is primarily something that someone else has written about, and which has thus become invested with such associations as can but destroy the innocence of Mr. Eliot's eye and apprehension. The pity is, he seems to hint, that there have been so many poems and, yes, it must be confessed, so few really satisfactory salads:

[Quotation of lines 55–69 of "The Love Song of J. Alfred Prufrock"]

It is, perhaps, this sense of everything having happened a trifle earlier in the day that gives me an impression of there being a preponderance of afternoons in Mr. Eliot's poetry:

[Quotation of lines 1–7 of "Portrait of a Lady"]

Or, if not of afternoons, of early evenings:

Let us go then, you and I,
When the evening is spread out
    against the sky
Like a patient etherised upon a
    table[.]

Ah, that patient etherized upon the table! It is not the evening only lying there in such lassitude; it is Mr. Eliot's perpetual spectator; it is the wistful and ironic evocation of all super-sophisticated persons; it is, alas! our cultured selves at this late and almost, it would sometimes seem, deliquescent stage of civilization. Under the spell of Mr. Eliot's gentle and wavering rhythms we become slightly etherized, and when the spell has sufficiently o'ercrowed our animal spirits we proceed, at once investigator and investigated, to inspect our emotions "as if a magic lantern threw the nerves in patterns on a screen"; a doleful piece of introspective dissection, a lamentable appraisement. Our scientific precision but informs us the nature of our trouble:

You will see me any morning in the
    park
Reading the comics and the sporting
    page.
Particularly I remark
An English countess goes upon the
    stage. . . .
I keep my countenance,
I remain self-possessed
Except when a street-piano,
    mechanical and tired
Reiterates some worn-out common
    song
With the smell of hyacinths across the
    garden
Recalling things that other people
    have desired.

And when the scientist has done, the artist steps in with his comedian melancholy to draw this conclusion:

Though I have seen my head (grown
    slightly bald) brought in upon a
    platter,
I am no prophet—and here's no great
    matter;
I have seen the moment of my
    greatness flicker,
And I have seen the eternal Footman
    hold my coat, and snicker,
And in short, I was afraid.

The irony of things-as-they-are haunts the poet as it haunted his forerunner Laforgue and levies board-wages upon all his emotions. Yet the poet has his moments:

I am moved by fancies that are curled
Around these images, and cling:
The notion of some infinitely gentle
Infinitely suffering thing.

The moment, however, will not last, and I cannot but puzzle whether it is not that capacity for enjoying the quintessential emotions precipitated from the still of literature which Mr. Eliot so superabundantly possesses and cultivates, that has vitiated his taste for those distractingly heterogeneous emotions which are the material offered him as an artist by Life itself. Irony is a good servant, but a bad master; the Footman, however eternal, should be kept in his place even if one is only the perennially passing visitor to the earthly mansion. Mr. Eliot has a taste for the more terrible realities—if he would only indulge it. He has the power of evoking "the still, sad music of humanity" from the most quotidian, sordid, and apparently unpromising materials. Here is an interior—as unqualified in statement as a Sickert, but in addition informed with something of the understanding and compassion of a Rembrandt:

[Quotation in full of "Preludes" III]

It is a pity, I feel, that Mr. Eliot seems in his later poems to have acquired a habit of steering away from so immediate and poignant a reality in order to make remote and somewhat generalized fun about the *Boston Evening Transcript*, the visit of a Cambridge intellectual to New England, the editor of the *Spectator*, and the Established Church.

---

*Desmond MacCarthy. "New Poets, T. S. Eliot." New Statesman 16 (8 January 1921), 418–20.

When two people are discussing modern poetry together the name of T. S. Eliot is sure to crop up. If one of them is old-fashioned, and refuses to see merit in the young poets who attempt to do more than retail "the ancient divinations of the Muse," the other is sure to say sooner or later: "But what about Eliot? You may dislike *vers libre* [. . .] and [other] attempts to manipulate in verse the emotional coefficients of modern experience, still what do you think of Eliot? You cannot dismiss him." And the other (I do not think I am attributing to him an unusual amount of sensibility or judgment) will reply: "Well . . . yes . . . Eliot . . . I grant you there seems to be something in him." I wish to try to find out here what that "something" is which recommends the poems of Mr. Eliot, if not to the taste, at least to the literary judgment of even those who think the young poets are, for the most part, on the wrong path.

Mr. Eliot, like Mr. Ezra Pound, is an American. This is not a very important fact about him, still it has its importance. Both poets resemble each other in two respects, one of which I will deal with at once, in connection with their nationality. When either of them publishes a book, they publish at the same time that they are scholars, who have at least five languages at command, and considerable out-of-the-way erudition. The allusions in their poems are learned, oblique, and obscure; the mottoes they choose for their poems are polyglot, the names that occur to them as symbolic of this or that are known only to book-minded people. In short, they both share the national love of bric-à-brac. A half-forgotten name, an echo from a totally forgotten author, a mossy scrap of old philosophy exercise over their imaginations the charm that the patina of time upon a warming-pan or piece of worm-eaten furniture does upon their more frivolous compatriots. Both poets are illegitimate descendants of the poet Browning, in whom the instinct of the collector was equally strong—with a difference I shall presently mark. Both share with Browning a passion for adapting the vivid colloquialism of contemporary speech to poetic purposes. [. . .] Mr. Eliot has woven a very remarkable literary style, composed in almost equal parts of literary and erudite allusions and crisp colloquialisms, in which to clothe the emotions he wishes to express. Let me make here at once the most adverse comment I have to make on his work, namely, that he is always in danger of becoming a pedant, a pedant being one who assumes that his own reading, wide or narrow, is common property or ought to be, so that any reference he makes is of general validity and bound to wake the same echoes in his reader's mind as it does in his own. Collector of bric-à-brac, mystificator, mandarin, loving to exclude as well as to touch intimately and quickly his readers, he would be lost as a poet were it not for his cautious and very remarkable sincerity. [. . .] Certainly he is a poet whom to admire at all fervently marks one down as among those who are certainly not a prey to the obvious.

Fitzgerald did not like Browning (partly because he knew Tennyson very well perhaps), and in one of his letters he throws out a phrase about "that old Jew's curiosity shop." Now Browning's curiosity shop is a huge rambling place, cobwebby, crammed, Rembrandtesque, while Mr. Eliot's reminds one rather of those modern curiosity shops in which a few choice objects, a white Chinese rhinoceros, a pair of Queen Anne candlesticks, an enamelled box, a Renaissance trinket or two, a small ebony idol are set out at carefully calculated distances on a net cloth in the window (one sees at a glance they are very expensive—no bargains here); but there is behind no vast limbo of armor, cabinets, costumes, death-masks . . . and boxes, containing pell-mell, watch-keys, miniatures, lockets, snuffers, and tongue-scrapers. The man who keeps the shop is not a creature with a Rabelaisian gusto for acquisition, whose hand shakes with excitement as he holds up the candle, expatiating volubly, but a sedate, slightly quizzical, aloof individual—a selector, perhaps, rather than a collector to whose maw the most indigestible treasures are delicious nutriment. Such is the difference between Browning's and Mr. Eliot's attitude towards the harvest of erudition.

I have compared them so far only to differentiate them; moreover Mr. Eliot's subject is always the ingredients of the modern mind and never, as was often the case with Browning, of the minds and souls of men and women who lived long ago. But it is instructive to compare them also at points in which they resemble each other, always remembering that the temperament of the elder poet is hot, responsive, ebullient, and simple, while that of the younger is subtle, tender, disillusioned, complicated, and cool. Both are possessed by the passion of curiosity to a greater degree than is common with poets; in both the analytical interest is extremely strong. Consequently, Mr. Eliot, too, loves to exploit that borderland between prose and poetry which yields as much delight to the intellect as to emotions—if not more. Most of his work is done in that region, and the most obvious thing to say about it as a whole is that even when it is not poetry it is always good literature. Re-read "The Love Song of J. Alfred Prufrock" or "Portrait of a Lady"; it will be obvious that he not only owes much to the diction and rhythm of Browning, but that he is doing the same thing as Browning for a more queasy, uneasy, diffident, complex generation. Here is the opening of the "Portrait": [quotation of lines 1–9 of "Portrait of a Lady"]. "The latest Pole / Transmit the Preludes, through his hair and fingertips"—is not that pure Browning? Like Browning, too, Mr. Eliot's favorite form is a soliloquy of the spirit or monologue. Many of his poems thus fall between the lyrical and the dramatic form; they are little mental monodramas, broken now and then after the manner of Browning by a line or two of dialogue or by exclamations . . . or by asides to the reader; but these asides never have the argumentative, buttonholing quality of Browning's. There is nothing of the impassioned advocate, so characteristic in Browning, in Mr. Eliot. He is rather a scrupulous, cool analyst of extremely personal and elusive modes of feeling, and his method (this is his most distinctive characteristic as a writer) is to convey an elusive shade of feeling, or a curious, and usually languid, drift of emotion, by means of the rapid evocation of vivid objects and scenes. He does not care whether or not there is a logical or even a casual association between these objects he presents to us one after the other. He is like a dumb man who is trying to explain to us what he is feeling by taking up one object after another and showing it to us, not intending that we should infer that the object is the subject of his thoughts, but that we should feel the particular emotion appropriate to it. This makes his poems hard even when they are not (and they often are) too obscure. The reader is always liable to dwell too long on these scenes or objects which he evokes so skillfully, instead of just skimming swiftly off them, as it were, an emotion they suggest, and then passing on to the next. A poet who thinks in pictures and allusions, and expects us to understand his mood and thought by catching one after the other the gleams of light flashed off by his phrases, must often be obscure, because compact phrases (Mr. Eliot's are extraordinarily compact) are apt to scatter refracted gleams which point in different directions. Indeed, we are often expected to catch not one of these flashes but several. First, however, let me give an example of his method of thinking in pictures or symbols. Take one of his later poems, "Gerontion." The whole poem is a description at once of an old man's mind, and of a mood which recurs often in Mr. Eliot's poems, namely, that of one to whom life is largely a process of being stilted, slowly hemmed in and confused; to whom experience, truthfully apprehended, gives only tantalizingly rare excuses for the exercise of the lyrical faculty of joy within him. His (Mr. Eliot's) problem as a poet is the problem of the adjustment of his sense of beauty to these sorry facts. His weakness as a poet is that he seems rather to have felt the glory of life through literature; while his reflection of all that contrasts with it has the exciting precision of direct apprehension. "The contemplation of the horrid or sordid by the artist," he says in one of his criticisms, "is the necessary and negative aspect of the impulse towards beauty." In him this impulse in a negative direction is far the strongest of the two.

[Quotation of lines 1–16 of "Gerontion"]

Now, in the first verse of what proves later a dark intricate poem, the symbolism is obvious; yet it is an example of the characteristics which make Mr. Eliot obscure. When the old man says he has not fought in the salt marshes, etc., we know that he means that he has not tasted the violent romance of life. We must not dwell too literally on the phrases by which he builds up the impression of sinister dilapidation and decay—"Blistered in Brussels, patched and peeled in London," etc. In reading Mr. Eliot an undue literalness must at all cost be avoided.

> I that was near your heart was
> removed therefrom
> To lose beauty in terror, terror in
> inquisition.
> I have lost my passion: why should I
> need to keep it
> Since what is kept must be
> adulterated?

These lines, which occur in the same poem, are perhaps the most personal he has published. Mr. Eliot has something of the self-protective pride, reserve, and sensibility of the dandy—like Laforgue. His impulse is not to express himself in poetry, but to express some mood, some aspect of life which needs expression. He sets about it coolly, like a man making up a prescription, taking down now this bottle, now that from the shelf, adding an acid from one and a glowing tincture from another. He belongs to that class of poets whose interest is in making a work of art, not in expressing themselves; and the fact that his subject matter . . . is psychological and intimate makes the result particularly piquant. But even the works of the most detached poet, if he is not imitating old poems, have an affinity to each other which has its roots in temperament.

The temperament, as in Laforgue's work, which shows itself in Mr. Eliot's is that of the ironic sentimentalist. "But where is the penny world I bought / To eat with Pipit behind the screen?" he asks, after concluding that he will not want Pipit in Heaven.

> Where are the eagles and the
> trumpets?
> Buried beneath some snow-deep
> Alps.
> Over buttered scones and crumpets
> Weeping, weeping multitudes
> Droop in a hundred A.B.C.'s.

The contrast between peeps into glory and the sordidness of life is never far from his mind. (It is in literature that he himself has seen the eagles and heard the trumpets—not in life.) His style has two other marked characteristics. His phrases are frequently echoes, yet he is the reverse of an imitative poet. They are echoes tuned to a new context which changes their subtlety. He does not steal phrases; he borrows their aroma.

> Defunctive music under sea
> Passed seaward with the passing bell
> Slowly: the God Hercules
> Had left him, that had loved him
> well.

> The horses, under the axletree
> Beat up the dawn from Istria
> With even feet. Her shuttered barge
> Burned on the water all the day.

Just as "weeping, weeping multitudes" in the other poem quoted above is an echo from Blake, so "Defunctive music" comes from "The Phoenix and the Turtle" and "Her . . . barge / Burned on the water," of course, from *Antony and Cleopatra*. But the point is that the poet means to draw a subtle whiff of Cleopatra and poetic passion across our minds, in order that we may feel a peculiar emotion towards the sordid little siren in the poem itself, just as he also uses later a broken phrase or two from *The Merchant of Venice* for the sake of reminding us of Shakespeare's Jew, compared with the "Bleistein" of the poem. His other characteristic is the poetic one of intensity; it is the exciting concision of his phrasing which appeals especially to his contemporaries: "I should have been a pair of ragged claws / Scuttling across the floors of silent seas . . ." He is master of the witty phrase, too, "My smile falls heavily among the bric-à-brac" and is, to my mind, the most interesting of "the new poets."

Clive Bell.
"Plus de Jazz."
New Republic 28
(21 September 1921), 94.

[. . .]

The Jazz movement is a ripple on a wave; the wave—the large movement which began at the end of the nineteenth century in reaction against realism and scientific paganism—still goes forward. This wave is essentially the movement which one tends to associate, not very accurately perhaps, with the name of Cézanne: it has nothing to do with Jazz: its most characteristic manifestation is the modern painting which, be it noted, Jazz has left almost untouched. The great modern painters—Derain, Matisse, Picasso, Bonnard, Friesz, Braque, etc.—were firmly settled on their own lines of development before ever Jazz was heard of . . .

The movement bounced back into the world somewhere about the year 1911 . . . Impudence is its essence—impudence in quite natural and legitimate revolt against Nobility and Beauty: impudence which finds its technical equivalent in syncopation: impudence which rags. "The Ragtime movement" would have been the better style, but the word "Jazz" has passed into at least two languages and now we must make the best of it. After impudence comes the determination to surprise: you shall not be gradually moved to the depths, you shall be given such a start as makes you jigger all over. And from this determination issues the grateful corollary—thou shalt not be tedious. The best Jazz artists are never long-winded . . . An accomplished Jazz artist, whether in notes or words, will contrive as a rule to stop just where you expected him to begin. Themes and ideas are not to be developed; to say all that one has to say smells of the school, and may be a bore . . . Lastly, it must be admitted, there is a typically modern craving for small profits and quick returns. Jazz art is soon created, soon liked, and soon forgotten. It is the movement of masters of eighteen; and these masterpieces created by boys barely escaped from college can be appreciated by the youngest Argentine beauty at the Ritz. Jazz is very young: like short skirts, it suits thin, girlish legs, but has a slightly humiliating effect on gray hairs. Its fears and dislikes—for instance its horror of the Noble and the Beautiful—are childish; and so is its way of expressing them. Not by irony and sarcasm, but by jeers and grimaces does Jazz mark its antipathies. Irony and wit are for the grown-ups. Jazz dislikes them as much as it dislikes Nobility and Beauty. They are products of the cultivated intellect, and Jazz cannot away with intellect or culture . . . [T]o bring intellect into art is to invite home a guest who is apt to be inquisitive and even impartial . . . Nobility, Beauty and intellectual subtlety are alike ruled out; the two first are held up to ridicule, the last is simply abused. What Jazz wants are romps and fun and to make fun; that is why, as I have said, its original name Rag-time was better. At its best, Jazz rags everything.

[. . .]

Though on painting its effect has been negligible, Jazz, during the last ten years, has dominated music and colored literature. It is easy to say that the genius of Stravinsky—a musician, unless I mistake, of the first order and in the great line—rises superior to movements. To be sure it does: so does the genius of Molière. But just as the genius of Molière found its appropriate food in one kind of civilization so does the genius of Stravinsky in another; and with that civilization his art must inevitably be associated . . . He has composed rag-times. So, if it is inexact to say that Stravinsky writes Jazz, it is true to say that his genius has been nourished by it . . . Far from seeking small profits and quick returns, he casts his bread upon the waters with a finely reckless gesture. In fact, Stravinsky is too big to be covered by a label; but I think the Jazz movement has as much right to claim him for its own as any movement has a right to claim any first-rate artist.

Similarly, it may claim Mr. T. S. Eliot—a poet of uncommon merit and unmistakably in the great line . . . Apparently it is only by adopting a demurely irreverent attitude, by being primly insolent, and by playing the devil with the instrument of Shakespeare and Milton, that Mr. Eliot is able occasionally to deliver himself of one of those complicated and remarkable imaginings of his: apparently it is only in language of an exquisite purity so far as material goes, but twisted and ragged out of easy recognition that these nurslings can be swathed. As for surprise, that, presumably, is an emotion which the author of *Ara Vos Prec* is not unwilling to provoke. Be that as it may, Mr. Eliot is about the best of our living poets, and, like Stravinsky, he is as much a product of the Jazz movement as so good an artist can be of any.

In literature Jazz manifests itself both formally and in content. Formally its distinctive characteristic is the familiar one—syncopation. It has given us a ragtime literature which flouts traditional rhythms and sequences and grammar and logic. In verse its products—rhythms which are often indistinguishable from prose rhythms, and collocations of words to which sometimes is assignable no exact intellectual significance—are by now familiar to all who read. Eliot is too personal to be typical of anything, and the student who would get a fair idea of Jazz poetry would do better to spend half an hour with a volume of Cocteau or Cendrars. In prose I think Mr. Joyce will serve as a perhaps not very good example . . . In his later publications Mr. Joyce does deliberately go to work to break up the traditional sentence, throwing overboard sequence, syntax, and, indeed, most of those conventions which men habitually employ for the exchange of precise ideas. Effectually and with a will he rags the literary instrument: unluckily, this will has at its service talents which are only moderate.

Contempt for accepted ideas of what prose and verse should be and what they should be about, nervous dislike of traditional valuations, of scholarship, culture and intellectualism, above all an emphatic protest against the notion that one idea or emotion can be more important or significant than another, are, I take it, amongst the leading tenets of this school, whose grand object it is to present, as surprisingly as possible, the chaos of any mind at any given moment. Like most theories of art it sounds stupid enough. What matters, however, are not theories but works: so what of the works of Jazz? If Stravinsky is to be claimed for the movement, it has its master: it has also its *petits maîtres*—Eliot, Cendrars, Picabia and Joyce . . . [S]uch talents are not to be disposed of simply by the present of a bad name. It is not enough to call an artist "extremist" or "reactionary," "cubist" or "impressionist," and condemn or approve him as such . . . It is the critic's business to inquire not so much whether an artist is "advanced" or "cubist" or "jazz" as whether he is good, bad, or "interesting"; and that is what most critics fail to do.

[. . .]

*Richard Aldington. "The Poetry of T. S. Eliot." *Outlook* 49 (7 January 1922), 12–13.

To define twentieth-century literature when it is only beginning to emerge is a feat one may be excused from attempting. But one may note a certain homogeneity in the writings of M. Marcel Proust and Mr. James Joyce, of Miss Sitwell and Mr. Huxley, of Miss Moore and H. D., of Jean Cocteau and Paul Morand and T. S. Eliot. They are intellectually contemporaries; they are post-war; they are sufficiently unlike each other to reward curiosity and sufficiently similar to show the first outline of a period. The typical modern poet whose affinities are chiefly with the writers above mentioned is something extremely unlike the conventional idea of a poet.

[. . .]

This (hypothetical) modern poet is not amiable or romantic or tender or tranquil; but neither is the age in which he lives. And as irreverence and indocility are qualities of this decade, so are they of this decade's poets. The platoons of poets "going through the motions" of verse in unison at the word of some invisible commander are superannuated for ever. The new poet is the "*poète contumace*" of Laforgue. His indocility is extreme and nearly as disturbing to the godly as his determination to accept none of the official wax effigies as realities, to take nothing seriously until it has been proved worthy of seriousness. His thought is pessimistic and disillusioned; his modes of expression sarcastic and his chief weapon an acrid wit. He is psychologically subtle and intellectually acute; his culture is extensive. He is not a democrat though he observes popular habits. He is a cosmopolitan, but he enjoys the flavor of nationality. He writes for an audience equipped to understand him, and is indifferent to popular success. His mind is exceedingly complex and moves with a rapidity incomprehensible to sluggish wits. He is perilously balanced among the rude forces of a turbulent mechanical age; he walks the tightrope over an abyss and he knows it. His work has the gusto of peril.

[. . .]

The reader will almost certainly have noticed that when the syllables "T. S. Eliot" are pronounced, the reply "Laforgue" is elicited as invariably as an automatic machine produces a very small piece of chocolate when pressed with a penny. Now it is certainly true that Mr. Eliot's poetry has some affinity with Laforgue's poetry; but is it not a perfect example of muddled thinking to deduce imitation from affinity of mind, just as the same muddled thought deduces affinity of mind from imitation? Is it not certain that such people have never worked out even this simple distinction? And yet, with so faulty an equipment, they will undertake to analyze a work as profound and complex as *Ara Vos Prec*. To say that Mr. Eliot imitates Laforgue because they have a common faculty for unexpected juxtapositions of ideas expressed with ironic wit is as foolish as it would be to say that Mr. Eliot imitates Ausonius because both frequently quote other poets in their verse. Moreover, Mr. Eliot has quite as much affinity with Rimbaud and Corbière. Mr. Eliot's "Mélange Adultère de Tout" depends for its full effect upon the reader's comprehending the reference to Corbière's "Epave Mort-Né." But Mr. Eliot has completely purged out Corbière's querulous romanticism and self-pity; he is hard on himself.

[. . .]

Mr. Eliot's English poetry is often attacked as incomprehensible and heartless, which is simply another way of saying that it is subtle and not sentimental. His desire for perfection is misrepresented as puritan and joyless, whereas it is plain he discriminates in order to increase his enjoyment. But, of course, refinement will not be applauded by those who cannot perceive it, nor will intelligence be appreciated by those who cannot understand it; literary criticism is not the only human activity wherein ignorance is made a standard. Mr. Eliot's poetry makes very high demands on a reader's intelligence and knowledge. It is caviare to the general. And yet this poetry can at once be assimilated into tradition, may be placed at once as the last development of two currents of thought, one French and the other English . . . [O]ne side of Mr. Eliot's poetry is a development of the secular tradition of "*poètes contumaces*" or "*poètes libertins*," which runs from the poets of today to Laforgue and Verlaine, to Rimbaud and Corbière . . . back to Villon, and beyond him to a shadowy host of mediaeval "*pinces-sans-rire*," "*goliards*" and satiric "*goguenards*," whose sharp tongues spared neither the Church nor the rich nor the pretty ladies. That tradition

of poignant, witty, derisive verse has survived many centuries and passed through many transformations; it has been stifled underground for a generation or more, but has always sprung up in some new form— that sharp French mind whose watchword is "*ne pas être dupe.*"

[. . .]

When this aspect of Mr. Eliot's poetry is explained, there remains the more serious and difficult problem of his so-called obscurity . . . [T]he obscurity of Mr. Eliot is as much a myth of lazy people as the obscurity of Browning. Indeed, Mr. Eliot's verse never makes the heavy demands on a reader that were made by "Sordello." But this subtlety of mind which makes necessary an effort for full comprehension is not something invented by Browning, but goes far beyond him to the so-called metaphysical poets, to Donne and Davies and Chapman.

[. . .]

Does not the modern poet speak with the accents of his great predecessors, though the matter of his speech be remote from theirs? Is it not certain that this feigned obscurity is no obscurity, but simply density of thought?

[. . .]

It is a long step from the dense thought of Mr. Eliot's "Gerontion" and the somber horrors of his "Whispers of Immortality" to the pleasant little rhymes now current. Between these rhymes, however pretty and melodious, and the intellectual poetry of Mr. Eliot, there is a wide gulf. Few will contest the originality of the mind expressed in his poetry, and yet the comparisons instituted show that Mr. Eliot's poetry is traditional, linking up on the one hand with the ironic French poets and, on the other, with the stately, subtle-minded Englishmen of the Renaissance. The poetry of Mr. T. S. Eliot is a healthy reaction against the merely pretty and agreeable, against shallowness and against that affectation of simplicity which verged on dotage. Mr. Eliot is to be honored as a poet who has brought new vigor to the intellectual tradition of English poetry.

Checklist of Additional Reviews

W. S. T. "An Irritable Intelligence." *Boston Herald*, 14 April 1920. [not located]

POEMS

by T. S. ELIOT

NEW YORK
ALFRED · A · KNOPF
1920

Babette Deutsch.
"The Season for Song—A Page on the Poets—T. S. Eliot's Weird and Brilliant Book."
New York Evening Post, 29 May 1920.

"You can not expect much from me anymore. I am now middle-aged," said Pound, at thirty-two. T. S. Eliot is at the same point of maturity, whence the only road is along the declivity. Whether or not he feels with Pound in this matter, one can only guess. Certainly there is an affinity of a sort between these two men; both Americans who have retired to England to pursue, far from the madding crowd, the art dearest to them; both scholars not a little proud of their philosophical erudition; both sensitive to curious rhythms, and dedicated to Verlaine's exhortation: "*Pas la Couleur, rien que la nuance!*"

Eliot is probably best known in his native land by "The Love Song of J. Alfred Prufrock," a piece of psychological analysis of extraordinary delicacy and brilliance. This work was included in a small volume published in England, which contained his fine "Portrait of a Lady," together with several minor pieces marked by keen percipience and a strong irony . . .

These poems, with an equal number of later experiments, were recently published by the Ovid Press, in a sumptuous if slender volume, on a heavy paper with wide margins, elaborate initials and colophon, in a limited edition.

[. . .]

It is this volume, in a cheap edition, its binding reminiscent of the ugly text books of our early youth, that Knopf has reprinted for the American public. But if the American edition is not likely to be kept for the paper and the printing, it is likely to interest those people who are engaged with the stuff of poetry rather than with any external aids to its enjoyment.

The *Prufrock* collection in itself is worth the whole volume. There is something fascinating in the manner in which Eliot skirts the edges of prose and yet keeps his excursions on the plane of poetry. His vocabulary is the vocabulary of prose. His rhythms, his repetitions, the emotional *au delà* which seems present almost in spite of him, are the elements of poetry. The new school of British fiction is attempting something of the same sort. And the drawing of hard and fast lines between the various branches of literature is a game scarcely worth the candle. In Eliot's work the flame burns as a fire that gives light rather than heat. It has the illuminating quality of prose, and yet one cannot search the secret places of a man's soul as he does without feeling the radiance that clings like a nimbus.

This is true of "Morning at the Window," it is true of "Preludes," as it is of the more difficult and analytical pieces. The titles of these poems are deceiving. They have none of the fluttering birds and leaves that one associates with such evocations. They are drab, sullen, malodorous. And penetrating as the sour smell of the tenements.

It is in Eliot's later work that one detects the amateur ironist, dismissing too lightly the serious artist . . . Eliot seems to have become an amateur of satire. And satire is an effective weapon against poetry, as well as against some other things. One would not easily resign such religious discourse as "The Hippopotamus," which begins thus: [quotation of lines 1–12 of "The Hippopotamus"]. [His satire] can be equally amusing in the Romance languages, as witness his picture in "Le Directeur" of a certain well-known British weekly: [quotation of lines 7–13 of "Le Directeur"]. But when one places these things against ... "Prufrock" ... one measures the difference between the poet and the jester.

[Quotation of lines 15–22 of "The Love Song of J. Alfred Prufrock"]

More than ever Eliot is preoccupied with the distasteful necessities of the animal man. More than ever he chooses words striking for their rarity rather than for their exactness with which to describe the details of a disgusting domesticity. More than ever he injects into his poetry a scholarship the less fascinating for being so strident. Even in these poems, however, there are impeccable passages: "Vacant shuttles / Weave the wind." He is a man in arms against the romantic cliché. But in his fury he neglects to make those unique and arresting things which would themselves put out the light of the things he hates. He is, unlike the True Church, flesh and blood, and he is thirty-two. *"Cependant, ce fut jadis un bel homme, de haute taille."*

Marion Strobel. "Perilous Leaping." *Poetry: A Magazine of Verse* 16 (June 1920), 157–59.

Mr. Eliot evidently believes that a view from a mountain cannot be appreciated unless the ascent is a perilous leaping from crag to crag. At least the first pages of his latest book (an American reprint, with a few additions, of *Prufrock and Other Observations*, published in 1917 by the London *Egoist*) are filled with intellectual curios—curios that form a prodigious array of hazards leading up to the big poems. Lovers of exercise will find their minds flexed, if not inert, after following the allusions and ellipses of "Gerontion." It is as though, in this initial poem, Mr. Eliot went through his morning calisthenics saying: "This, my good people, is a small part of what I do to give you a poem"; or more accurately perhaps: "Come—work with me—show you deserve true beauty." And with a "Whoopla"—for he is in beautiful condition—he swings from romance to realism, to religion, to history, to philosophy, to science, while you and I climb pantingly, wearily, after him, clinging to a few familiar words, and looking from time to time at sign-posts along the way to reassure ourselves of the fact that this does lead us to true beauty.

The poems guaranteed-to-produce-white-blood-corpuscles-in-any-brain come before page 37 (a specific hint for the faint-hearted). Fortified by a dictionary, an encyclopedia, an imagination, and a martyr's spirit, even these may be enjoyed. They are certainly remarkable for their mystifying titles, their coy complexities of content, and their line-consuming words. What, for instance, could be more naive than the introduction to Sweeney in "Sweeney Erect": [quotation of lines 1–12 and 21 of "Sweeney Erect"].

However, in among these stepping-stones to the poems that are worth a great deal of trouble to get—though one resents being reminded of the fact by Mr. Eliot himself—are one or two resting-places, such as the whimsical pathos of "A Cooking Egg," the gentle crudity of "Sweeney Among the Nightingales," and the sophisticated humor of "The Hippopotamus." And I must further acknowledge that Mr. Eliot's humor is the cultivated progeny of a teasing spirit of fun and a keen audacity—the mixture of the Zoo and the True Church in "The Hippopotamus" will tickle the palate of the most blasé epicurean.

And now, feeling that the ascent has been long and hard, we reach the summit, and are repaid by reading "The Love Song of J. Alfred Prufrock" and "Portrait of a Lady." These two poems are so far superior to the gymnastics that precede, and to the interesting versatilities that follow them, that they must be classed alone.

"Prufrock," which was first published by *Poetry* in 1915, is a psychological study of that rather piteous figure, the faded philandering middle-aged cosmopolite; a scrupulous psychological study, for the pervasive beauty of the imagery, the rhythms used, and the nice repetitions, all emphasize the sympathetic accuracy of the context. . . .

In "Portrait of a Lady" we find a like startling acuteness for details, with a dramatic ending which is a fitting example for the definition, "*L'art est un étonnement heureux.*"

And possibly—possibly—it is wise to work up to "J. Alfred Prufrock" and "Portrait of a Lady," and to slide pleasantly down again on the humor and ironies of the poems following; for we might become dizzy if we found ourselves on a mountain without the customary foundations.

---

e. e. cummings.
"T. S. Eliot."
Dial 68, no. 6 (June 1920), 781–84.

The somewhat recently published *Poems* is an accurate and uncorpulent collection of instupidities. Between the negative and flabby and ponderous and little bellowings of those multitudinous contemporaries who are obstinately always "unconventional" or else "modern" at the expense of being (what is most difficult) alive, Mr. T. S. Eliot inserts the positive and deep beauty of his skillful and immediate violins . . . the result is at least thrilling.

He has done the trick for us before. In one of the was it two *Blasts* skillfully occurred, more than successfully framed by much soundless noise, the "Rhapsody" and "Preludes." In one of the God knows nobody knows how many there will be Others, startlingly enshrined in a good deal of noiseless sound "Prufrock" and "Portrait of a Lady" carefully happened. But "this slim little volume" as a reviewer might say achieves a far more forceful presentation, since it competes with and defeats not mere blasters and differentists but τὸ ἕν's and origens and all that is Windily and Otherwise enervate and talkative.

"Some Notes on the Blank Verse of Christopher Marlowe" are, to a student of Mr. T. S., unnecessarily illuminating:

> . . . this style which secures its emphasis by always hesitating on the edge of caricature at the right moment . . . this intense and serious and indubitably great poetry, which, like some great painting and sculpture, attains its effects by something not unlike caricature.

Even without this somewhat mighty hint, this something which for all its slipperyness is after all a door-knob to be grasped by anyone who wishes to enter the "some great" Art-Parlors, ourselves might have constructed a possibly logical development from "Preludes" and "Rhapsody on a Windy Night" along "J. Alfred" and "Portrait" up the two Sweeneys to let us say "The Hippopotamus." We might have been disgracefully inspired to the extent of projecting as arithmetical, not to say dull, a classification of Eliot as that of Picasso by the author of certain rudimentary and not even ecclesiastical nonsense entitled *The Caliph's Design*. But (it is an enormous but) our so doing necessarily would have proved worthless, precisely for the reason that before an Eliot we become alive or intense as we become intense or alive before a Cézanne or a Lachaise: or since, as always in the case of superficial because vertical analysis, to attempt the boxing and labeling of genius is to involve in something inescapably rectilinear—a formula, for example—not the artist but the "critic."

However, we have a better reason. The last word on caricature was spoken as far back as 1913. "My dear it's all so perfectly ridiculous" remarked to an elderly Boston woman an elderly woman of Boston, as the twain made their noticeably irrevocable exeunt from that most colossal of all circuses, the (then in Boston) International. "My dear if some of the pictures didn't look like something it wouldn't be so amusing" observed, on the threshold, the e.B.w., adding "I should hate to have my portrait painted by any of those 'artists'!" "They'll never make a statue of *me*" stated with polyphiloprogenitive the e.w.o.B. "Sway in the wind like a field of ripe corn," says Mr. Eliot.

In the case of *Poems*, to state frankly and briefly what we like may be as good a way as another of exhibiting our numerous "critical" incapacities. We like, first, to speak from an altogether personal standpoint, that any and all attempts to lassoo Mr. Eliot with the Vorticist emblem have signally failed.

[. . .]

[A]t no moment do "T. S. Eliot" and "E. P. propaganda" simultaneously inhabit our consciousness.

Second, we like that not any of *Poems'* fifty-one pages fails to impress us with an overwhelming sense of technique . . . By technique we do not mean one thing: the alert hatred of normality which, through the lips of a tactile and cohesive adventure, asserts that nobody in general and some one in particular is incorrigibly and actually alive. This some one is, it would seem, the extremely great artist: or, he who prefers above everything and within everything the unique dimension of intensity, which it amuses him to substitute in us for the comforting and comfortable furniture of reality. If we examine the means through which this substitution is allowed by Mr. Eliot to happen in his reader, we find that they include: a vocabulary almost brutally tuned to attain distinctness; an extraordinarily tight orchestration of the shapes of sound; the delicate and careful murderings—almost invariably interpreted, internally as well as terminally, through near-rhyme and rhyme—of established tempos by oral rhythms.

[. . .]

To come to our final like, which it must be admitted is also our largest—we like that no however cautiously attempted dissection of Mr. T. S.'s sensitivity begins to touch a few certain lines whereby become big and blundering and totally unskillful our altogether unnecessary fingers:

The lamp hummed:
"Regard the moon,
La lune ne garde aucune rancune,
She winks a feeble eye,
She smiles into corners.
She smooths the hair of the grass.
The moon has lost her memory.
A washed-out smallpox cracks her
    face,
Her hand twists a paper rose . . ."

43

At risk of being jeered for an "uncritical" remark we mention that this is one of the few huge fragilities before which comment is disgusting.

Mark Van Doren.
"Anglo-Saxon Adventures in Verse."
Nation 110, no. 2869 (26 June 1920), 856a–57a.

T. S. Eliot's first formally collected volume, long awaited by those who think they recognize downright, diabolical genius when they see it, is distinctly and preciously an event. It is not known how long the author of "The Hippopotamus," "Sweeney Among the Nightingales," "The Love Song of J. Alfred Prufrock," "Rhapsody on a Windy Night," and "The *Boston Evening Transcript*" will remain in England, whither he went two years ago to set up as a critic. Whatever happens, it is hoped that he keeps somehow to poetry. For he is the most proficient satirist now writing in verse, the uncanniest clown, the devoutest monkey, the most picturesque ironist; and aesthetically considered, he is one of the profoundest symbolists. His sympathy and his vision travel together, striking like bitter lightning here, flowering damply and suddenly like mushrooms there. Three extracts from the twenty-four poems are not enough but must do: [quotation of lines 15–22 of "The Love Song of J. Alfred Prufrock"; lines 33–45 of "Rhapsody on a Windy Night"; "Morning at the Window" in full].

Louis Untermeyer.
"Irony de Luxe."
Freeman 1 (30 June 1920), 381–82.

For two or three years the poetry of T. S. Eliot has been championed warmly by a few protagonists and condemned even more heatedly by many who suspected the young author of all things from charlatanry to literary anarchism. Those who have read it have talked of this product, not as poetry, but as a precipitant, a touchstone; they pronounced "Eliot" as though the name were either a shibboleth or a red flag. Controversy was difficult. For, with the exception of two longish poems and half a dozen scattered verses, this native of St. Louis continued to publish his occasional pieces in England and threatened at the age of thirty-one to take on the proportions of a myth. This volume, then, is doubly welcome, for it enables one not only to estimate Eliot's actual achievement but to appraise his influence.

This influence, although exceedingly limited, is indisputable. And it is even more remarkable when one perceives that the present volume, including all of Eliot's poetical works, contains just twenty-four examples, four of them being in French. In these two dozen pieces there can be heard, beneath muffled brilliancies, two distinct and distinctive idioms. The first embodies the larger curve, the more flexible music; in it are held the shifting delicacies and strange nuances of "The Love Song of J. Alfred Prufrock" and the sensitized "Portrait of a Lady." It is the idiom which Conrad Aiken has exploited (and amplified) in "The Jig of Forslin," "Senlin," and "Nocturne of Remembered Spring." The second accent is sharper, swifter, more obviously sparkling. A far more definite tone of voice, it lends itself so easily to imitation that it has quickly captivated most of the younger British insurgents. Osbert Sitwell, whose anti-war verses are still remembered, frankly models his new quatrains on the plan of "Sweeney Among the Nightingales" and gives us (in part) such experiments in satiric futurism as:

> The dusky king of Malabar
> Is chief of Eastern potentates;
> Yet he wears no clothes, except
> The jewels that decency dictates . . . .
>
> But Mrs. Freudenthal, in furs,
> From Brioche dreams to mild surprise
> Awakes; the music throbs and purrs.
> The 'cellist with albino eyes
>
> Rivets attention; is, in fact,
> The very climax; pink eyes flash
> Whenever, nervous and pain-racked,
> He hears the drums and cymbals clash.

$$[\ldots]$$

It is but a step to the more acerb original. Here are two illustrative segments from ["Sweeney Erect" and "Whispers of Immortality"]:

> Apeneck Sweeney spreads his knees
> Letting his arms hang down to laugh,
> The zebra stripes along his jaw
> Swelling to maculate giraffe . . .
>
> Grishkin is nice: her Russian eye
> Is underlined for emphasis;
> Uncorseted, her friendly bust
> Gives promise of pneumatic bliss.

It is this vein that tempts him most—and is his undoing. For irony, no matter how agile and erudite—and Eliot's is both—must contain heat if it is to burn. And heat is one of the few things that can not be juggled by this acrobatic satirist. With amazing virtuosity, he balances and tosses fragments of philosophy, history, science,

tea-table gossip, carelessly screened velleities. There are times when he discards his flashing properties, changes his vocabulary of rare words for a more direct irony which is not only amusing but incisive. "The Hippopotamus," that audacious whimsicality, is an example . . .

[Quotation of lines 1–12 and 21–24]

But at least two-thirds of Eliot's sixty-three pages attain no higher eminence than extraordinarily clever—and eminently uncomfortable—verse. The exaltation which is the very breath of poetry—that combination of tenderness and toughness—is scarcely ever present in Eliot's lines. Scarcely ever, I reiterate, for a certain perverse exultation takes its place; an unearthly light without warmth which has the sparkle if not the strength of fire. It flickers mockingly through certain of the unrhymed pictures and shines with a bright pallor out of the two major poems.

These two are the book's main exhibit, its jeweled medallion. Medallion, too, in the sense that both of them complement each other, obverse and reverse. The "Portrait of a Lady," the franker and more easily communicable, is a half-sympathetic, half-scornful study in the impressionist manner of the feminine dilettante, the slightly-faded *précieuse* hovering tremulously on the verge of an abortive "affair."

[Quotation of lines 1–14 of "Portrait of a Lady"]

"The Love Song of J. Alfred Prufrock" is even more adroit though less outspoken. Sensitive to the pitch of concealment, this is an analysis of the lady's sexual opposite—an inhibited, young–old philanderer, tired of talk and the eternal tea-tables; a prey to boredom that breeds its own revulsion, a victim too sunk in himself to escape it. For him, eternally, it seems that "In the room the women come and go / Talking of Michelangelo." Prufrock would shatter the small talk, pierce the whispered inanities, cry out!

But he can neither discharge his protest not find words for it. He listens politely; he accepts the proffered cup; he chatters on aimlessly. It is the quiet tragedy of frustration, the *revolté* buried in the gentleman.

[Quotation of lines 114–25 of "The Love Song of J. Alfred Prufrock]

Yet Prufrock is not all psychology. Eliot can be delicately fantastic and purely pictorial when the mood is on him. [In "Morning at the Window,"] he can speak of . . . "the damp souls of housemaids / Sprouting despondently at area gates." He hears the laughter of Mr. Apollinax (who sounds suspiciously like Bertrand Russell) "tinkling among the teacups" and he thinks of ". . . Priapus in the shrubbery / Gaping at the lady in the swing." He watches the fog rubbing its back upon the windowpanes.

[Quotation of lines 16–22 of "The Love Song of J. Alfred Prufrock"]

But these are the exceptional moments. For the most part, Eliot cares less for his art than he does for his attitudes. Disdaining the usual poetic cant, he falls into another tradition; he leans towards a kind of versifying which, masquerading under the title of "occasional" or "social" verse, may be found in many a *Lyra Elegantiarum*. Pliny had in mind this type when he wrote: "These pieces commonly go under the title of poetical amusements; but these amusements have sometimes gained as much reputation to their authors as works of a far more serious nature." And some two thousand years later, Locker-Lampson described their qualities again:

"The tone should be pitched too high; it should be terse and rather in the conversational key; the rhythm should be crisp and sparkling, the rhyme frequent and never forced . . ." Both Pliny and Locker-Lampson might have been reviewing Eliot's conversational ironies. For Eliot's gift is seldom the poet's. His contribution is related to poetry only at rare intervals. His lines, for the most part, are written in a new *genre* or, to be more accurate, in a modernization of a surprisingly old one. They are, primarily, a species of mordant light verse; complex and disillusioned *vers de société*.

---

*Raymond M. Weaver. "What Ails Pegasus?" Bookman 52 (September 1920), 57–66.

[. . .]

We have it on the authority of a long line of poets and critics, reaching back to its *locus classicus* in Plato, that there is a mystery about creative art deeper than intellect or will, descending to the poet as by the theological mystery of grace. The great artist does not sit with grim deliberation in his study and proclaim: "Go to! I shall write a masterpiece!" The creation is done as by obsessional madness: a madness which after its enactment offers a test for the sanity of critics.

As society becomes intricate, sophisticated, and critical, it tends to discipline its creative spontaneity, the artist becoming a critic with a theory to exemplify; art degenerates into artifice, architecture into upholstering. Poetry comes to be a specialized vice fostered by "Societies" and "Schools"—a sickly ornament for an ugly existence, not a smile on the face of society, an overflowing of genuine happiness and power. The celestial madness of the heavenly bards finds sorry caricature in some of our half-demented versifiers. The prosaic dullness of the "divine average," immaculately ignorant of great poetry, is flattered by the Platonic contention that poets are mad—diverting neurotics to be viewed with the most complacent patronage.

Yet the classical poetic madness [. . .] is not, as our democratic civilization is so obligingly eager to believe, a sign of weakness or degeneration, but rather of perfected power. All authentic poetry is born of the conflict between irrational nature and rational desire . . . For the achievement of pleasure, relaxation, sanity of mind and body, these tensions must find some relief. In inferior beings, this tension may result in pathological derangement; in superior souls, however, relief—or purgation—from this stress is ideally achieved in religion or noble art. The "divine madness" of the poets—"*le rêve par lequel l'homme aspire à une vie superieure*"—is the bursting forth, from depths unplumbed by cold practical reason, of powers of lofty insight and heaven-born desire.

[. . .]

The *Poems*—ironically so-called—of T. S. Eliot, if not heavy and pedantic parodies of the "new poetry," are documents that would find sympathetic readers in the waiting-room of a private sanatorium. Clinically analyzed they suggest in conclusion one of Mr. Eliot's lines: "After such knowledge, what forgiveness?" As a parodist, Mr. Eliot is lacking in good taste, invention, and wit. Compared with Rudyard Kipling, Thackeray,

and Phoebe Cary (among the most accomplished parodists in the language) Mr. Eliot is prodigiously labored and dull. General incomprehensibility and sordidness of detail (defects not difficult to imitate, but excessively difficult to parody) are Mr. Eliot's distinguishing traits. He is usually intelligible only when he is nasty. His similes are without humor and without point:

> He laughed like an irresponsible
> foetus.
> ["Mr. Apollinax"]

> Midnight shakes the memory
> As a madman shakes a dead geranium.
> ["Rhapsody on a Windy Night"]

> The worlds revolve like ancient
> women
> Gathering fuel in vacant lots.
> ["Preludes"]

Mr. Eliot may cynically have perpetrated this slim volume in order to glean from the tributes of his admirers material for a new "Dunciad."

[. . .]

Padraic Colum. "Studies in the Sophisticated." *New Republic* 25 (8 December 1920), 52, 54.

[Discussion of *The Instigations of Ezra Pound*]

To give prose the precedence of verse in a review that deals with both is possibly wrong, but there is an excuse for it in the present case. *The Instigations of Ezra Pound* deal in many places with the poems of T. S. Eliot. Some of these passages make the best introduction that could be written for the poems. They are eulogistic, and at least in one passage, possibly extravagantly eulogistic. Mr. Eliot's form is compared to Ovid's form in the *Heroides*, and to Browning's form in *Men and Women.* "The form of *Men and Women* is more alive than the epistolary form of the *Heroides*," Mr. Pound says, and then he goes on to suggest that the present-day poet has made a certain advance on Browning's form— "Browning included a certain amount of ratiocination and of purely intellectual comment, and in just that proportion he lost intensity." Mr. Eliot has stripped away the ratiocination and the intellectual comment.

His first volume has been published in the present year—a small collection of twenty-four pieces, four being in French. Had Mr. Eliot excluded such pieces as "The *Boston Evening Transcript*," "Hysteria," "Cousin Nancy," one would be able to judge his poetry without making a reference to The Smart Set. That he has included these is evidence that he is not amongst the super-sophisticated.

I do not know if these poems mark the beginning of a cycle in poetry, but I am sure that they mark the end of one. Twenty years ago Mr. Yeats published *The Wind Among the Reeds*. He brought a new set of symbols into poetry. He heard "the Shadowy Horses, their long manes a-shake, their hoofs heavy with tumult." Today Mr. Eliot sees that "The red-eyed scavengers are creeping from Kentish Town and Golder's Green." The cycle is complete: the vague and visionary territory has become defined as points on a subway, and municipal employees have taken the place of creatures out of a myth.

And the truth is that our imaginations are put at no loss by the change in symbols. Mr. Eliot, like the Mr. Yeats of *The Wind Among the Reeds*, is a symbolist. He, too, has his Aedh, his Hanrahan, his Michael Robartes. But he calls them Sweeney, J. Alfred Prufrock, Mr. Apollinax. "The Hippopotamus" . . . takes the place of the boar with bristles and the deer with no horns. The change, of course, would not be real if there were no poetry transmitted through the symbols. Poetry is transmitted. In such poems as "Gerontion," "The Love Song of J. Alfred Prufrock," "Portrait of a Lady," "Cooking Egg," we get a glimpse of the visions and tragedies that are in the soul—it does not matter that the soul in these situations has to look out on restaurants instead of on temples, and on "rocks, moss, stonecrop, iron, merds," instead of on the mountains and the sea.

Mr. Eliot has learned from Jules Laforgue how to make modern settings as well as how to parade a mockery of the literary allusion. This by itself would serve to put him with the Modernists. But he is modern in a way that is more significant. He has the modern approach to the soul, or, let us say, to the psyche—to the soul that is not an entity but a collection of complexes—the soul that is at once positive and reticent, obscured and clairvoyant. The poet is well aware of the tragedy that is marked by a yawn, and the dreadful dismissal that is in a cliché repeated. His art is indeed achieved when he can give us such revelations in the medium of verse.

For a generation there have been attempts to do this kind of thing in English, and verse in which *ennui* turns upon disillusion has gone the rounds. But now that Mr. Eliot has published we see that in this verse there were only approaches. Mr. Eliot's work is complete; he has adapted a modern technique, and his personae are stabilized into types . . . Romantic poetry, in its spent stages, will encounter Sweeney and Prufrock and will not know what has happened to it. But that comparison is wrong: the poetry of Mr. Eliot, in spite of its being so well exercised and so well disinfected, belongs after all to Byzantium; the shadows of a long decay are upon it all.

[. . .]

THE SACRED WOOD:
ESSAYS ON POETRY AND CRITICISM
1920, 1921

THE SACRED WOOD

ESSAYS ON POETRY AND CRITICISM

BY

T. S. ELIOT

METHUEN & CO. LTD.
36 ESSEX STREET W.C.
LONDON

*Douglas Goldring.
"Modern Critical
Prose."
Chapbook 2, no. 8
(February 1920), 7–14.

[Review of *Three Critical Essays on Modern English Poetry* (by T. S. Eliot, Aldous Huxley, and F. S. Flint) 1920]

Wars, perhaps inevitably, have a bad effect on the critical spirit. They make the necessary detachment difficult or impossible, play havoc with our standards of values, and leave us often with an after-taste of commercialism which it takes years to eradicate. After a war such as the one from which we have just emerged, nothing is more necessary than the restoration of criticism to its old prestige, and it is one of the hopeful signs of the times that attempts in this direction are beginning to be made.

[Discussion of various British critics]

Among the few younger critics who show an entirely disinterested love for their art, perhaps the most interesting figures are Mr. T. S. Eliot and Mr. Aldous Huxley. Mr. Eliot has a scientific, analytical brain, and approaches his task with some of the detachment of the great surgeon who, knife in hand, advances towards the exposed flesh of the anesthetized "case." He rarely makes a cut in the wrong place, he dissects with an unhurried precision, and remorselessly reveals the structure and the content of the book on which he "operates." His learning is prodigious, and kept carefully under the counter until it is required. If some of the elusive essences of an author's heart and mind occasionally escape him, we have no right to object. Every critic has his limitations; Mr. Eliot fewer than most. Within these limitations, such as they are, he has undoubtedly one of the most distinguished critical minds of our time. He has a standard of values, and he is honest in applying it.

[. . .]

For the man who really has a standard of values can refer to it almost any kind of artistic expression with some degree of safety. The question he asks himself is not so much whether such and such a thing is or is not "high art," but rather is it good of its kind, and does it at least express a distinct personality?

[. . .]

It is high time a new note was struck in our criticism; high time it became impatient of shams and pretensions, indifferent to social influences and to the vagaries of fashion. Real criticism is, of course, a difficult job. It is a combination of an exact science and a delicate art, which demands a certain asceticism of the intellect for which the disorderly modern mind is perhaps little fitted. But there seems no reason why our reviewers should not begin once more to take an interest in the arts they write about, and to express opinions, independently arrived at, with frankness and honesty. It is to be hoped that they will once again find courage to utter those "truth-speaking things" which "shame the angel's veiling wings," things which "make the gods shake, they know not why." Our literary heaven is too comfortably asleep, and the return of Uriel is overdue.

*F. G. Bettany.
"The Bookshelf."
Arts Gazette 2 (3 April
1920), 741–42.

[Review of *Three Critical Essays
on Modern English Poetry*
(by T. S. Eliot, Aldous Huxley,
and F. S. Flint) 1920]

[. . .]

The *Three Critical Essays on Modern English Poetry* which constitute the current number of the *Chapbook*, are at once a challenge and a manifesto. Here we have dominant spirits of the new generation plying the rod upon the reviewer and advocating something like a new aesthetic ideal . . .

Each age likes to invent its own catchwords, so no one need be surprised over the discovery that neither Mr. T. S. Eliot nor his associates, Mr. Aldous Huxley and Mr. F. S. Flint, makes any mention of the "renascence of wonder." In point of fact even Mr. Eliot, whose province more particularly is the "criticism of poetry," scarcely troubles to offer a passing definition of poetry, so concerned is he to set up a lofty standard for the critic and to denounce the "disease of contemporary reviewing." "Poetry," he tells us, "is primarily an art, that is to say, a means of communicating those direct feelings peculiar to art, which range from amusement to ecstasy" and there he leaves it, taken for granted, while he passes on to inform us what criticism is not and what it should be. He declares roundly that "to the poet only the criticism of poets is useful" and adds

The critic is interested in technique—technique in the widest sense. You cannot understand a book on mathematics unless you are actively, not merely passively, a mathematician, unless you can perform operations, not merely follow them. And you cannot understand the technique of poetry unless you are to some extent capable of performing this operation.

But to what extent? There is the rub. Are we to set minor poets to judge major poets? Are we so sure that even a major poet, such as Swinburne, was the most judicious critic of literature? Is technique all that has to be considered in poetry? What about passion or freshness of observation or "fundamental brainwork"? And has the critic no duty to the public as well as to the poet, no duty to art of the past as well as of the present? Is not poetry primarily addressed to the public, and unless it can make good its appeal to that audience in the long run, must it not be stillborn, no matter what heralding it may obtain from your poet–critic? Are there not poets' poets and are not these, though masters of technique, the men who fail to strike a response from the heart of average humanity? Mr. Eliot writes too much from the standpoint of the executant or composer (whichever metaphor may be allowed me) and a craftsman himself, looks at criticism too much through the craftsman's eyes. Incidentally he limits the critic's range. He distinguishes between the critic and the historian or philosopher as though poetry could be stripped of its content of feeling and thought and so he comes very near the heresy that the expert's, that is the poet's, judgment is alone worth listening to about poetry.

[. . .]

*"The Function of Criticism."
Times Literary Supplement 956 (13 May 1920), 289.

[Review of *Three Critical Essays on Modern English Poetry* (by T. S. Eliot, Aldous Huxley, and F. S. Flint) 1920]

It is curious and interesting to find our younger men of letters actively concerned with the present condition of literary criticism.

[. . .]

[T]he excellent *London Mercury*, after whetting our appetite by announcing that it proposed to restore the standards of authoritative criticism, still leaves us a little in the dark as to what these standards are. Mr. T. S. Eliot deals more kindly, if more frigidly, with us in the monthly *Chapbook*. There are, he says, three kinds of criticism—the historical, the philosophic, and the purely literary. "Every form of genuine criticism is directed towards creation. The historical or philosophic critic of poetry is criticizing poetry in order to create a history or a philosophy; the poetic critic is criticizing poetry in order to create poetry." These separate and distinct kinds, he considers, are but rarely found today, even in a fragmentary form; where they do exist, they are almost invariably mingled in an inextricable confusion.

Whether we agree or not with the general condemnation of reviewing implicit in this survey of the situation, or with the division of criticism itself, we have every reason to be grateful to Mr. Eliot for disentangling the problem for us. The question of criticism has become rather like Glaucus the sea-god, encrusted with shells and hung with weed till his lineaments are hardly discernible.

[There follows a lengthy analysis of Eliot's classification of critics as historical, philosophical, and purely literary.]

"Poetry and Criticism."
Times Literary Supplement 985 (2 December 1920), 795.

Mr. Eliot is a critic with principles which have not been assumed hastily for the purpose of writing but which have grown out of his experience of literature. These he expresses calmly and with precision; he does not try to write prose-poetry about poetry, to make his criticism the poor relation of poetry. Criticism for him is an important and independent activity with its own procedure; it ought, he thinks, to be without caprice, raptures or tantrums, or egotism. It is science rather than art—though we are apt to make too sharp a division between these—and ought to have the manners of science. Since he has an experience of literature perhaps more wide than intense, a keen intelligence and the power of expressing it precisely in language, his criticism is always worth reading and often of great value. But it has also certain perversities, instinctive rather than rational, of which one gradually becomes aware, concealed though they be even from himself by the air of reason which he consciously and rightly maintains. Against these one must be warned so that one may profit by his wisdom.

The central essay of the book, that most concerned with principle, is the essay on "Tradition and the Individual Talent." Mr. Eliot says, ". . . [We are apt] to insist, when we praise a poet, upon those aspects of his work in which he least resembles anyone else . . . Whereas if we approach a poet without this prejudice we shall often find that not only the best, but the most individual parts of his work may be those in which the dead poets, his ancestors, assert their immortality most vigorously." This is true, not only of poets who like Milton and Keats revere tradition, but also of those who, like Wordsworth and Whitman, consciously rebel against some portion of it. These express themselves most richly and happily when tradition comes to their aid, like the forgiving father to the prodigal son. In their rebellion against it they are apt to be thin, restless, more conscious of themselves than of their theme. But Mr. Eliot proceeds to tell us what tradition is for the poet. It is the feeling that "the whole literature of Europe from Homer and within it the whole of the literature of his own country has a simultaneous existence and composes a simultaneous order."

It is not a sense of the past and of progress from it so much as a sense of eternity which yet, as he points out, is continually being modified by the new work of art. "What happens when a new work of art is created is something that happens simultaneously to all the works of art which preceded it . . . the relations, proportions, values of each work of art towards the whole are readjusted; and this is conformity between the old and the new." This, we believe, is true, novel, and well expressed; it provokes us to further thought on the subject. What is the use which the poet makes of tradition

when he conforms to it yet says something new both in substance and in forms? Is it not this, that he continues the exploration both of what is to be said in terms of poetry, and in the manner of saying it beyond the point to which that exploration had been carried before? He conquers for poetry what had hitherto been part of the prose of life; but this conquest is possible only because of the conquests of former poets. We, because we have a long tradition, a long effort of poetry, can in our poetry go deeper into the human mind than nations with little or no tradition. Each new poet can assume what has been poetized in the past, and starting from that assumption, can proceed further; in fact the new poet is he who subdues to poetry what it never occurred to any former poet to subdue; but this would not occur to him, but for the achievements of the former poets. And, as poetry is what it is trying to become, so it seems even to change a little in character or direction with each new conquest. But this happens, of course, only when the tradition is alive and unbroken. If poets either repeat or rebel blindly, tradition no longer helps them because it is not theirs.

[. . .]

Mr. Eliot would insist that what matters . . . is not the new thing said, but the poetizing of it—in fact, he seems to us to insist on this perhaps a little too much. He says truly that one error of eccentricity in poetry is to search for new human emotions to express, that the business of the poet is not to find new emotions, but to use the ordinary ones; but the fact remains that the new poet does poetize, not emotions perhaps but complex experiences that have not been poetized before, at least in his own literature; and that, in doing so, he does enrich the medium itself. Finally, however, Mr. Eliot makes the right distinction when he says that significant emotion is that which has its life in the poem, not in the history of the poet, that the emotion of art is impersonal.

One other passage we will quote [this one from "The Perfect Critic"] to show how just and high is his conception of criticism:

> A precept, such as Horace, or Boileau gives us, is merely an unfinished analysis . . . Such statements may often be justifiable as a saving of time; but in matters of great importance the critic must not coerce, and he must not make judgements of worse and better. He must simply elucidate: the reader will form the correct judgements for himself.

That, again, is true and well put; but we wish Mr. Eliot's practice always conformed to this high theory. Unfortunately, it is sometimes perverted by malice the more insidious because unconscious. We can see that there are some people whom he wishes to annoy, as, for instance, the people who like Meredith; and he tries to annoy them by slipping in contemptuous remarks about Meredith which cannot be refuted because they say nothing except that Mr. Eliot despises Meredith and those who admire him. This . . . is a judgment not even of worse or better, but merely a sentence . . . uttered, we are sure, only to annoy. And this malice betrays itself again in the essay on Swinburne as poet. He begins by admitting that Swinburne "did make a contribution"; but all that he quotes from Swinburne is to illustrate his defects; it is what no one would quote who wished to give an idea of his genius.

In fact Mr. Eliot is more grudging of praise than blame; often, indeed, he seems to grudge us our enjoyment, as if he took a pleasure in rubbing the gilt off the gingerbread, when really it is not gilt at all or mere gingerbread. And because of this we are tempted to read him with resentment, to resist even the many good things which he says. That he should provoke this resistance, that he should so often resemble the wind rather than the sun, is, we think, a proof that he is malicious without knowing it, and that this malice leads him sometimes into a practice contrary to those excellent principles which he states so well.

Robert Lynd. "Buried Alive." *Nation* 18 (4 December 1920), supplement 359–60.

Mr. Eliot, in his critical essays, is an undertaker rather than a critic. He comes to bury Hamlet, not to praise him. He has an essay on "Hamlet and His Problems," in which he assures us that "[s]o far from being Shakespeare's masterpiece, the play is most certainly an artistic failure." Now, there are several things about *Hamlet* that call for explanation. But there is one thing that needs no explanation, and that is its "artistic failure." One might well set out to explain why the mid-Atlantic is shallow, why Mont Blanc is lower than Parliament Hill, why Cleopatra was unattractive, why roses have an offensive smell. It might be possible for a writer of paradoxes to amuse himself and us on any of these themes. But Mr. Eliot is no dealer in paradoxes. He is a serious censor of literature, who lives in the gloom of a basement, and cannot believe in the golden pomp of the sun outside. It might be unfair to say that what he is suffering from is literary atheism. He has undoubtedly gods of his own. But he worships them in the dark spirit of the sectarian, and his interest in them is theological rather than religious in kind. He is like the traditional Plymouth Brother whose belief in God is hardly so strong as his belief that there are "only a few of us"—perhaps "only one of us"—saved. We see the Plymouth-Brother mood in his reference to "the few people who talk intelligently about Stendhal and Flaubert and James." This expresses an attitude which is intolerable in a critic of literature, and should be left to the *précieuses ridicules*.

Mr. Eliot, however, does not merely say that *Hamlet* is an artistic failure and leave it at that. He goes on to explain what he means. He believes that: ". . . Shakespeare's *Hamlet*, so far as it is Shakespeare's, is a play dealing with the effect of a mother's guilt upon her son, and that Shakespeare was unable to impose this motive successfully upon the 'intractable' material of the old play."

. . . Shakespeare's finished *Hamlet* is a play dealing with many things besides the effect of a mother's guilt on her son. It is a play dealing with the effect of a whole circle of ruinous events closing in on a man of princely nature, who was a foreigner amid the baseness that surrounded him. Shakespeare showed in *Hamlet* that it was possible, contrary to all the rules, to write a play which combined the largeness of a biography with essential dramatic unity. Mr. Eliot, however, clings to the idea that Shakespeare failed in *Hamlet* because he was divided in interest between the theme of the guilty mother and other intractable stuff "that the writer could not drag to light, contemplate, or manipulate into art." Now every great work of art is like the visible part of an iceberg; it reveals less than it leaves hidden. The greatest poem in the world is no more than a page from that inspired volume that exists in the secret places of the poet's soul. There is no need to explain the mysteries that crowd

about us as we read *Hamlet* by a theory of Shakespeare's failure. To summon these mysteries into the narrow compass of a play is the surest evidence of a poet's triumph. Let us see, however, how Mr. Eliot, holding to his guilty-mother theme, attempts to explain the quality of Shakespeare's failure.

[Quotation from "Hamlet and His Problems,"*The Sacred Wood* 100 and 101]

"Hamlet (the man)," he adds, "is dominated by an emotion which is inexpressible, because it is in *excess* of the facts as they appear." Mr. Eliot has a curious view of the things that justify violent emotion. I should have thought that the murder of a father by his usurping brother, the infidelity of a mother and a mistress, the use of former companions to spy on him, the failure of all that had once seemed honest and fair, plots to murder him, the suicide of his beloved, might have caused considerable perturbation even in the soul of a fish. If ever there was a play in which the emotion is not in excess of the facts as they appear, that play is *Hamlet*.

[. . .]

Mr. Eliot is like a man dissecting—and dissecting with desperate earnestness—a corpse that isn't there.

And his essays in praise have scarcely more of that vitality which is a prerequisite of good criticism than his essays in blame. He obviously admires Blake and Ben Jonson, but he leaves them as rigid and cold as though he were measuring them for their coffins. The good critic communicates his delight in genius. His memorable sentences are the mirrors of memorable works of art. Like the poet, he is something of a philosopher, but his philosophy is for the most part implicit. He is a light-bringer by means of quotation and aphorism. He may destroy, but only in order to let in the light . . . He knows that literature is not the game of a coterie, but is a fruit of the tree of life, hanging from the same boughs as the achievements of lovers and statesmen and heroes. There is so little truth in Mr. Eliot's statement that "a literary critic should have no emotions except those immediately provoked by a work of art—and these . . . are, when valid, perhaps not to be called emotions at all," that one would be bound to tell ten times more truth merely by contradicting it. The ideal critic would always be able to disentangle relevant from irrelevant emotions as he studied a work of art; but in practice all critics, save a few makers of abstract laws, are human, and the rich personal experience of the critic enters into his work for good as well as evil.

Mr. Eliot fails as a critic because he brings us neither light nor delight. But this does not mean that he will always fail. He has some of the qualities that go to the making of a critic. He has learning, and he enjoys intellectual exercise. His essay on "Tradition and the Individual Talent" shows that he is capable of ideas, though he is not yet capable of expressing them clearly and interestingly. Besides, as one reads him, one is conscious of the presence of a serious talent, as yet largely inarticulate, and wasting itself on the splitting of hairs and metaphysical word-spinning. His failure at present is partly a failure of generosity. If a critic is lacking in generous responsiveness, it is in vain for him to write about the poets . . . Let Mr. Eliot for the next ten years take as his patron saint the woman in the New Testament who found the piece of silver, instead of Johannes Agricola in joyless meditation. He will find her not only better company, but a wiser counselor. He may even find his sentences infected with her cheerful excitement, for want of which as yet they can break neither into a phrase nor into a smile.

*L. W. [Leonard Woolf].
"Back to Aristotle."
Athenaeum 4729 (17
December 1920), 834–35.

[. . .]

Mr. Eliot several times in the course of [*The Sacred Wood*] asserts or implies that there is today no such thing as English criticism. And, as we read on through his book—a book which you can only push your way through slowly, sometimes even laboriously—we became more and more convinced that Mr. Eliot means by criticism what Aristotle meant by criticism. When on page 33 we read that the tools of the critic are "comparison and analysis," we could no longer resist the impulse to go to the neglected shelf and take down that dusty volume of *The Poetics*, and we think it is a compliment to Mr. Eliot that we read through the remainder of his book with Aristotle open on our knees. This happy collocation of Athens and America showed us why there is no criticism today in the Aristotelian sense: "I propose to treat of Poetry in itself and of its various kinds, noting the essential quality of each; to inquire into the structure of the plot as requisite to a good poem; into the number and nature of the parts of which a poem is composed; and similarly into whatever else falls within the same inquiry."

[Quotation from "Imperfect Critics," *The Sacred Wood* 35]

These two quotations will perhaps explain why Mr. Eliot seems to cry aloud to us, "Back to Aristotle," and why . . . he brings us up with a shock against the satisfying, if painful, hardness of the intellect. For Mr. Eliot, as for Aristotle, criticism is not concerned with the personal psychology or psychological experiences of either author, character, or reader nor is the critic right when he attempts to interpret a poem or a play in the way in which, unfortunately, most performers conceive it to be their duty to interpret music, i.e., by rewriting it. For both these literary critics criticism is a science, the science of literary works of art, and it must therefore primarily rely upon the two great scientific instruments, comparison and analysis. It is important to note the effect of this attitude upon the work not only of Mr. Eliot the critic, but of Mr. Eliot the poet. We have sometimes thought, in reading his poems, that he was treating the writing of poetry as a science, as if it were possible for the poet, working upon the achievements of all his predecessors, to discover some entirely new poem in his own mind much as a scientist discovers a new spirochæte or trypanosome. The idea is now shown to be not so fantastic as at first sight it may have appeared. In an essay on "Tradition and the Individual Talent" he develops a theory with regard to the nature of poetic creation which it would be unfair to him for us to attempt to explain in the narrow confines of a review. The theory postulates, however, a kind of absorption of the poetic past by the poet of today and a process of depersonalization in the poet. "It is in this depersonalization," says Mr. Eliot, "that art may be said to approach the condition of science."

It is impossible here to deal adequately either with Mr. Eliot's theory or practice of criticism. The two things are not, of course, the same, though Mr. Eliot's conception of each emerges clearly, if gradually, in this book. Criticism is a science in its practice; in its theory it is rather a part of philosophy. In both branches Mr. Eliot seems to us, even when we strongly disagree with his theories, judgments, or analysis, to contribute something solid, something which can serve as a foundation for knowledge, a keener or juster appreciation, and even creation. And those, we agree with Mr. Eliot, are the objects of true criticism.

Marianne Moore. "*The Sacred Wood*." *Dial* 70 (March 1921), 336–39.

The Sacred Wood is a thoughtful book; its well-knit architecture recalls Trollope's comment upon Castle Richmond. It has "no appearance of having been thrown out of its own windows." As a revival of enjoyment it has value, but in what it reveals as a definition of criticism it is especially rich. The connection between criticism and creation is close; criticism naturally deals with creation but it is equally true that criticism inspires creation. A genuine achievement in criticism is an achievement in creation; as Mr. Eliot says, "It is to be expected that the critic and the creative artist should frequently be the same person." Much light is thrown on the problems of art in Mr. Eliot's citing of Aristotle as an example of the perfect critic—perfect by reason of his having the scientific mind. Too much cannot be said for the necessity in the artist of exact science.

[. . .]

One of the chief charms . . . of Mr. Eliot's criticism is that in his withholding of praise, an author would feel no pain. But when his praise is unmixed, the effect is completely brilliant as in the opening paragraphs of the essay on Ben Jonson. In his profound appreciation of the genius of Jonson, Mr. Eliot is perhaps more revealing than in any other of the studies in this volume and is entirely convincing in his statement that Ben Jonson is not merely the "man of letters" but is the "literary artist," who if played now, would attract thousands.

[. . .]

One recognizes the truth of the statement that Jonson's "skill is not so much skill in plot as skill in doing without a plot" and that "what holds the play together is a unity of inspiration that radiates into plot and personages alike." The distinction made in Ben Jonson's case between brilliance of surface and mere superficiality, is well made. As Mr. Eliot notes, the liveliness of Fletcher and Massinger covers a vacuum, whereas the superficies of Jonson is solid; "the superficies *is* the world."

[. . .]

In these studies it is interesting to note that truth is to the author a fundamental attraction. He defines the strangeness of Blake as "merely a peculiar honesty, which in a world too frightened to be honest, is peculiarly terrifying."

[. . .]

Blake's humanly personal approach to any subject that he treated, preserves him to us; he is a greener figure to the eye than Dante. It is not personal transcendence; it is, as Mr. Eliot observes, the combination of philosophy, theology, and poetry, which makes Dante strong and symmetrical. A conclusion with regard to Dante which has been largely held no doubt by many, is accurately expressed by Mr. Eliot when he says that "Dante, more than any other poet, has succeeded in dealing with his philosophy in terms of something *perceived*." We enjoy, furthermore, the critic's ability to separate the specious from the sound when he says apropos of Landor's failure to understand Francesca: "Francesca is neither stupefied nor reformed; she is merely damned; and it is a part of damnation to experience desires that we can no longer gratify. For in Dante's Hell souls are not deadened, as they mostly are in life; they are actually in the greatest torment of which each is capable."

. . . In his poetry, [Mr. Eliot] seems to move troutlike through a multiplicity of foreign objects and in his instinctiveness and care as a critic, he appears as a complement to the sheen upon his poetry. In his opening a door upon the past and indicating what is there, he recalls the comment made by Swinburne upon Hugo: "Art knows nothing of death; . . . all that ever had life in it, has life in it forever; those themes only are dead which never were other than dead. No form is obsolete, no subject out of date, if the right man be there to rehandle it."

Conrad Aiken. "The Scientific Critic." *Freeman* 2 (2 March 1921), 593–94.

Mr. T. S. Eliot has, as we know, an eye for the odd, and yet that is not to do him complete justice: his eye is for what is significant in the odd; and thus it is that we find him quoting, opposite the first page of his small, delightful book of criticism, *The Sacred Wood*, the cryptic line: "I also like to dine on becaficas." Becaficas? If one is not expert in sixteenth- and seventeenth-century literature one learns from the dictionary that becaficas are "small birds" or "warblers" or "golden orioles": what the Italian peasant would indiscriminately term *uccellini*. Mr. Eliot, that is, likes to dine on song-birds; and he apprizes us, with a gleaming and slightly sinister politeness, that he is about to do so. Would Mr. Eliot have us suppose that there is a trace of ferocity in this attitude? Does he wish to appear as something of a monster, perhaps in contrast to the sentimentality and idolatry which too often masquerade as criticism of poetry? One need not take the point too seriously. Yet it does afford, no doubt, a glimpse of motive. We are aware that Mr. Eliot intends, very deliberately intends, to be analytic and severe—severe even to the point of destructiveness.

Nor is one, in this regard, disappointed. His book is severe and analytic, and one can think of no two qualities in criticism which are at the moment more desirable. We should like to see every one of the thousand poets in this country with a copy of *The Sacred Wood* in his hands. It would perhaps restore to some that wholesome sense of the responsibility of the poet which, in America, has been weakened throughout our entire literary history by our proneness, as a young nation, to a maternal tenderness toward the local product. Mr. Eliot insists upon the value of tradition: it is a value which cannot, just now, be too much insisted upon. He insists, again, on the elimination, as far as possible, of irrelevant emotional factors which may interfere with the best judgment of art: there is no country, which pretends to any interest in art, where that doctrine is needed as America needs it.

But if to say these things is to praise Mr. Eliot's book on general grounds, is to praise, in a general sense, his temper and his attitude, it is not our intention to praise his temper and attitude unreservedly. It is, perhaps, rather what Mr. Eliot intends, in temper and attitude, than what he achieves, that we like. It is a good thing, at this moment, to have a young critic who so deliberately, even contemptuously, turns his back on the contemporary, and who endeavors to see afresh such poets as Massinger, Jonson, Blake, Dante,

even Shakespeare. Mr. Eliot is not timid, nor is he without learning; he speaks with confidence. One admires also, if one be in sympathy with that sort of thing, his tendency toward what might properly be termed the scientific method in criticism. But it is precisely here that one begins to qualify praise; for although one may agree with Mr. Eliot that criticism might profitably be more scientific, one is by no means convinced that *The Sacred Wood* takes criticism very far in that direction, nor, indeed, that Mr. Eliot *sees* very far in that direction. It is clear enough that for scientific criticism a very definite *point d'appui* will be indispensable, even if the *point d'appui* be only that aesthetic values are relative. The critic should apprize us at the outset what his attitude will be, thus enabling us to discount it. He must, therefore, be clear as to his attitude, must know thoroughly and easily the world of values in which he moves, must decide in advance what terms he will use. His terms should be expressly defined. If he intends, for example, to use the word "feeling" in the modern psychological sense, as distinct from "emotion," he should say so in advance, lest his reader be confused; or else substitute for it the less equivocal word "affect."

Mr. Eliot is not, in these matters, precise. He has been infected by modern psychology, and he uses the terms of it not infrequently; but the basis from which he employs it shifts, and one is not sure that he is aware of the shift. Not with impunity can one mix the James–Lange set of terms with the terms of Freud: nor again the terms of de Gourmont (who was an amateur psychologist, and often a misleading one) with those of Kostyleff. Poetry, says Mr. Eliot on one occasion, "is not the expression of personality, but an escape from personality." On another occasion he says: "Massinger had not the personality to create great farce." Again, he quotes with approval de Gourmont (*"Problème* du Style"): "*Le but de l'activité propre de l'homme est de nettoyer sa personnalité, de la laver de toutes les souillures qu'y dépose l'education . . .*" Of Massinger again: "His personality hardly exists." Now perhaps Mr. Eliot has something definite in mind when he speaks of personality, and perhaps he has some theory of the manner in which the personality of the poet relates to his work, but he fails to make either thing clear. To what extent, when he thinks of personality, is he thinking of sensibility? If sensibility be called *a* and experience *b*, then is personality *ab*? And would this make de Gourmont's advice meaningless? And, in the upshot, do we not make it clear that "personality" is so vague a word as to be useless, even dangerous if it is our intention to be scientific? Mr. Eliot perceives keenly the need for definition: love of definition is one of his most obvious characteristics. He performs an admirable service in this sort when, in his essay on "Poetic Drama," he opens a coroner's inquest on the word "rhetoric." But his sense of the definite is intermittent; it abandons him often at the most critical moment, and in consequence Mr. Eliot himself is forever abandoning *us* on the very doorstep of the illuminating. One has again and again the feeling that he is working, as it were, too close to the object. He is meticulous without being clear; he passes quickly from one detail of analysis to another; he is aggressively aware that he is "thinking," his brow is knit; but he appears to believe that mere fineness of analysis will constitute, in the sequence of his comments, a direction. What happens is that he achieves a kind of filigree without pattern. He does not always know in advance where he is going, and it often occurs, therefore, that he takes the wrong train of thought. That his talk continues to be of extraordinary interest does not avail: he is rapidly borne out of earshot. "*On pense mal quand on sait que l'on pense.*" Mr. Eliot is so intent

on being intelligent at every point, in every sentence, in every syllable, that many of his pages become mere incoherences of cleverness; the evidence of thought is weighty, but the value of it is vague.

If Mr. Eliot is only intermittently and at times sciolistically a psychologist in his efforts toward a scientific method, one must observe also that at the very basis of his attitude, where it is most explicit, in the essay called "The Perfect Critic," he is least scientific. The ignorant reader (I quote a passage in that essay) "is unable to distinguish the poetry from an emotional state aroused in himself by the poetry, a state which may be merely an indulgence of his own emotions . . . The end of the enjoyment of poetry is a pure contemplation from which all the accidents of personal emotion are removed; thus we aim to see the object as it really is . . ." Is this "pure contemplation" perhaps a chimera? Is poetry an object, or an experience, a relation to an object, a relation between ourselves and a set of stimuli which the artist has "arranged"? If the latter, which of the emotions aroused in us are "accidental"? The artist alone can tell us. I do not know, here, whether I agree or disagree with Mr. Eliot: I wish merely to point out that in what is obviously meant to be an important passage he falls far short of being clear. Supplement, moreover, the passage just quoted with this, from the essay on *Hamlet* (a play which Mr. Eliot terms an "artistic failure"): "And probably more people have thought *Hamlet* a work of art because they found it interesting, than have found it interesting because it is a work of art. It is the *Mona Lisa* of literature." This statement is quite logical in its contexts. It is here significant because it arouses a suspicion that Mr. Eliot is distrustful of the artist who uses "interesting" material, that he prefers the work of art which is a triumph over material of which the direct "emotional" interest is less obvious (the plays of Massinger and Jonson, for example). But surely a work of art is no less a work of art for dealing with an emotional experience which interests or charms us than for dealing with one that repels or leaves us indifferent? Let us again have recourse to algebra: let x represent a theme which "interests" us, y a theme which does not, z the utmost possible skill of arrangement of theme. It will be clear that xz will delight us more than yz. And it is quite proper, is it not, that this should be so? Mr. Eliot desires, of course, to make a distinction between the "emotional" appeal which a work of art may make, and the "aesthetic" appeal. The distinction is worth making, but not if it leads the critic to condemn the former in order to exalt the latter, or if it leads him to attempt to isolate the latter, for "pure contemplation."

All of this is confusing because it is part of an attempt to make a beginning of scientific criticism on what is really a secondary plane. It is useless, or nearly useless, to attempt an estimate of the "skill" of a work of art, because, as long as we do not know what the work of art is for, we cannot hope to know precisely what will constitute skill. If criticism is to be a science, then we must begin with an attempt to understand what is the function of art, socially and psychologically. What is the function of art in the community? In the life of the artist? This must be the starting-point, and the inquiry will deal very largely, at the outset, precisely with the question of "theme" as distinguishable from "arrangement." Analysis of the "aesthetic" values will come later.

Mr. Eliot's perplexity and obscurity and lack of coherence result from the fact that he is on this secondary plane and does not know it. It would be extremely unjust, however, to leave it at that. His observations are acute, his temperateness is refreshing. It is a testimonial to the range and ingenuity of his mind that as one puts down his book one thinks of so many points about which one would like to quarrel with him, and quarrel, moreover, respectfully. *Is Hamlet* a failure as a work of art? *Does* Mr. Eliot find, in his essay on that play, the "objective correlative" of his conviction? *Was* a suitable mythological or philosophical framework, provided by tradition, lacking for Blake? With questions like these Mr. Eliot invites us to a meditation prolonged and delicious . . . Nor would one forget to abuse him for his clever but insufficient theory of the prose style of Mr. Arthur Symons.

---

*"The Sacred Wood." New Statesman 16 (26 March 1921), 733–34.

Most bookish persons, and some who are not bookish, are artists *manqués*. Hence the perennial fascination of literary criticism: to read about works of art, to be helped to dissect the creative act, is to dissolve the pangs of thwarted creation into a soothing dream. Literary criticism can do that precisely because it is an impure activity. Mr. Eliot, indeed, tries to define for it a legitimate field, but on the whole without success, and yet both when he discusses what criticism ought and ought not to be, and when he applies his doctrine practically to literature, in some respects he satisfies our needs more completely than some even justly famous critics. The impulse that carries us palpitating through his book is the feeling: "What an ass I have been!"— the cry of the stifled creative spirit finding a semblance of liberation in the perception that it has been stifled.

The method by which Mr. Eliot produces this effect is, for all the complications of his discourse (he makes high demands on his reader's intelligence: that is another attraction), extremely simple at bottom. He assumes that art, in the sense of work of "eternal intensity," is something rare, exquisite, requiring intelligence for its apprehension, and indeed never understood save by a select minority. Because his grasp of this central assumption never falters, and is carried through with the coolness of a dandy and the air of a man of science, he is able to go straight to the heart of that starved, lonely creature, the artist in the reader. With Mr. Eliot for a guide the starveling sees, or thinks he sees, that, if he cannot create, he can at least appreciate in a way that is almost as much worth while. He had fancied, perhaps, that the cause of his failure to create was something wrong with his emotions, some lack of sincerity or intensity. But no. "It is not the 'greatness,' the intensity, of the emotions, the components, but the intensity of the artistic process, the pressure, so to speak, under which the fusion takes place, that counts." Whether a man can exert this pressure, whether his mind is like the shred of platinum (that is one of Mr. Eliot's most impressive metaphors) in presence of which two gases combine to form a third, that is clearly more or less an accident beyond his control; but it always remains open to him, by exerting his intelligence, to understand the creations of minds that have that property. And (who knows?) if he take enough trouble to be intelligent, to distinguish between the poetry and the emotional states aroused in him by the poetry, he may even develop the structure of his sensibility into a capacity for creation. In any case, with Mr. Eliot to help, there seems good hope of attaining and holding fast that impersonal attitude, that exorcism of the personal accidents of emotion, which is necessary for the systematic enjoyment of poetry. And even that will be an enormous improvement. The stimulating quality of Mr. Eliot's critical writing consists, we are inclined to think, in our susceptibility at the present moment to some such chain of ideas and feelings as that, rather than in the direct compulsive force of its judgments or in the fact that it brings intellect once more to bear on the problems of art. The book is one of those that gives impetus and direction to a tide caught on the turn. Those who are not carried away by that tide will entertain two main doubts: whether the depersonalized, scientific attitude towards art that Mr. Eliot professes is not more apparent than real, and whether the cogency of his judgments does not partly depend on the strategic advantage which that attitude gives him, rather than on the soundness or delicacy of his sensibility. We can see that on some themes he is better than on others, and that he is best when he applies his method to accepted reputations, such as those of Ben Jonson or Blake, about which, however, fundamental misconceptions have clustered. Ben Jonson is congenial to Mr. Eliot as the creator of a world which, unlike that of Shakespeare, is not what he calls three-dimensional, but which he nevertheless has no difficulty in presenting to us as a world of eternal intensity. Among the worlds which, although two-dimensional, are great poetry, and which, because they are mere surfaces with no tentacles striking down to our personal passions and desires, are apt to be misapprehended by an age that has lost the sense of "pure" art, Mr. Eliot moves with assured steps. His whole analysis of the distinction between the two kinds of art worlds—an analysis which, more than anything else, helps him to suggest the nature of that eternal intensity which both share—is work of abiding value. We feel this despite some evidence (witness the too sophisticated paper on *Hamlet*) that he is not at home with Shakespeare. Again, he succeeds with Blake for kindred reasons, and chiefly because Blake is one of the rare English examples of the "pure" artist. Blake, unhampered by education or social ambitions, "knew what interested him, and he therefore presents only the essential, only, in fact, what can be presented, and need not be explained. And because he was not distracted, or frightened, or occupied in anything but exact statement, he understood. He was naked, and saw man naked, and from the centre of his own crystal." From this angle Mr. Eliot is able to correct a number of misapprehensions closely connected with those that engage him when dealing with the Elizabethans, and within this sphere his work seems to us to deserve the highest praise. At the same time closer examination suggests that, for all our enjoyment of the wit and distinction of his writing, his sphere as a critic has disquieting limitations.

Everything in the last resort depends on the critic's sensibility, on the sureness with which he recognizes, whatever its period, work of eternal intensity when he sees it. By all means let us accept Mr. Eliot's doctrine that salvation lies in keeping our eye on the poetry and not on the poet; but what if we seem to see that his own eye on the poetry is sometimes, as it were, a glass eye, an ingenious contrivance of mirrors and strings? That need not, perhaps, shake our confidence in the doctrine, but it will make us think twice before abandoning ourselves altogether to the fascination of the exposition. And when we think twice we become aware of a curious element of bluff. Take, for instance, his analysis of Dante: the scientific apparatus is paraded, but in the end nothing convincing emerges, and we are left with an uneasy feeling that Mr. Eliot has no objection to mystifying us, that indeed he rather enjoys the process. We hardly like to ask whether in such cases he is trying to palm off on us some substitute for direct apprehen-

sion, and whether he has really perceived with absolute certainty the difference of intensity between, say, Mr. Ezra Pound and Dante or Marlowe; for Mr. Eliot has the gift of touching some spring in us—is it intellectual snobbery?—that makes us diffident about putting such questions. But, if we do, there is some evidence that he is not, in respect of native sensibility, so sure a critic as his learning and intelligence at first incline us to believe. Certainly, if he is sometimes in the dark, and knows it, he is not one of those who frankly invite the reader to grope with him; he prefers to rely on the suggestive force of his *fiat lux*. It would be interesting, had we space, to probe the reasons for this preference, and to ask what lies behind his instinct for the technique of suggestion—an instinct which never fails him and which teaches him the value of a hypnotic pass at the very opening. His very title is such a pass: *The Sacred Wood*, combined with the quotations before the title-page! One of those quotations is from Petronius; the other is: "I also like to dine on becaficas"—the reverential reader has already closed blissful eyes—and perhaps opened his modest mouth, ready for the spoon.

---

*"Detachment." *Saturday Review* 131 (2 April 1921), 281–82.

A desiccation of the emotions and a studied reliance on the intellect rob Mr. Eliot's essays on poetry and criticism of that which gives criticism its greatest value. He flatters his readers by not "writing down" to them, but his inability to communicate the pleasure he has derived from literature and his refusal to reveal to his readers the mysteries he himself has penetrated become, in the end, an irritation, an offense. His voice is level. He has no gesture. Scholarship, acuteness of mind, delicacy of perception and many ideas are his; but though he writes of poetry, he is coldly detached from it, and though life is the stuff of literature, we cannot feel that he has ever lived. It is a disembodied voice that speaks. The result is an extraordinary brittleness, even when truth is spoken; the moment a conclusion, after much, painful groping, is reached, it dissolves into dust.

This separation of the writer from the matter he criticizes is, in Mr. Eliot's case, both self-conscious and self-imposed. Erudition, he points out, "is useless unless it enables us to see literature all round, to detach it from ourselves, to reach a state of pure contemplation," and he praises two American writers because they "have endeavoured to establish a criticism which should be independent of temperament." But he goes farther than this. In his extraordinarily clever and provocative essay, "Tradition and the Individual Talent," he asserts that "the progress of an artist is a continual self-sacrifice, a continual extinction of personality." This, on the face of it, is so demonstrably untrue that Mr. Eliot is driven to adopt a theory, for the discovery of which we are willing to give him sole credit, that the poet has not a "personality" to express, but "a particular medium, which is only a medium and not a personality, in which impressions and experiences combine in peculiar and unexpected ways." The obvious retort, of course, is "If a poet has no personality, why does his progress depend on the extinction of that which he does not possess?" Mr. Eliot, it appears to us, is merely begging the question. His "particular medium" is but another term for personality; but things are not altered by giving them different names. He foresees this objection and, in attempting to defeat it, loses himself in a jungle of words. For example: "The business of the poet is not to find new emotions, but to use the ordinary ones and, in working them up into poetry, to express feelings which are not in actual emotions at all." Here is chaos. When Mr. Eliot states that emotions never experienced by a poet will "serve his turn as well as those familiar to him," he seems to suggest that emotion, *per se*, is of no value to the imaginative writer. That is, we are warmed by a man with an ice-cold heart. But we know from the statements of the poets themselves that this is not so. Emotion must precede and feed poetry, though at the moment of creation the writer may have all the "tranquility" that has been ascribed to him. One of the essentials that go to the making of a great poet is that he shall feel greatly, diversely: he must have universality of emotion. Imagination is the key to all the emotions that are not inherent in the psychology of the individual.

[. . .]

It is clear from Mr. Eliot's rather congested style, so closely packed with thought, that we have in this book a mind laboriously and honestly at work to discover principles of criticism free from the weakening and distorting influences of temperament . . . Yet his writing is not always laborious, and . . . he sometimes helps us to an understanding by a graphic metaphor, or a vivid presentation of the core of his thesis. He says of Swinburne's critical work: "One is in risk of becoming fatigued by a hubbub that does not march; the drum is beaten, but the procession does not advance." In writing of George Wyndham, he very aptly declares that "[t]he Arts insist that a man shall dispose of all he has, even of his family tree, and follow art alone." . . . This epigrammatic manner is only occasional, and we are far from saying that in it Mr. Eliot's great ability is most fully disclosed. It is in the least lucid of his pages that we become most aware of original and distinctive gifts striving to discover a mode of utterance, a vehicle, for his crowding thoughts.

John Middleton Murry. *"The Sacred Wood." New Republic* 26 (13 April 1921), 194–95.

It is unlikely that Mr. T. S. Eliot's book of criticism will impress any large section of the public; for one thing, it chiefly deals with a period of English literature of which—in spite of a general profession of acquaintance—very few nowadays have a real and active knowledge: the Elizabethan period; another, more important reason is that Mr. Eliot has made a serious tactical error in not doing his utmost to eliminate the traces of a superior attitude. This is the more to be deplored because there are people prepared to read criticism of literature about which they know nothing, sometimes with the vague idea that an essay will save them the trouble of reading anything more, sometimes, more laudably, with the intention of sampling work to which the first approach is difficult for them. They will be either frightened or offended by Mr. Eliot's manner. It is a pity.

What is more curious, and much more reprehensible, is that the people who ought to take Mr. Eliot's criticism seriously— above all, the English literary critics,— have also behaved as though they were frightened or offended. They have given no sign that they appreciated the important fact that Mr. Eliot possesses a critical intelligence of a high order and a sensibility of an unusual kind; instead of attempting to elucidate a critical attitude that is as surely individual as any of our time, they

have abused, misrepresented or ignored him. True, his manner is often unfortunate, portentous and disdainful; his actual writing often stiff and hidebound. But critics who know anything of their real business should be quick to forgive the second of these shortcomings when they realize that it is the direct result of an attempt to express some very subtle perceptions and expound some unfamiliar doctrines. That they have had no inkling—I speak, of course, only of English critics—of what Mr. Eliot is really trying to say; that they have praised him (in the few cases where he has been praised) even more ignorantly than they have blamed him is the most damning evidence I know of the general incompetence of English criticism at the present day.

Before making any attempt to criticize Mr. Eliot's criticism, I must endeavor to present—however inadequately—the main outlines of his thought. He begins with the assumption that a work of literary art is an object which arouses in an educated sensibility a peculiar emotion; but this emotion is not indescribable, as some theorists of the plastic arts hold, nor is it always the same. The main work of the critic is to elucidate the particular emotion aroused by a literary work, by an effort of comparison and analysis; his function is not to expound his own emotions, which may often be, quite legitimately, compounded of a hundred non-aesthetic responses, but to disengage and distinguish the precise emotion evoked by the object as a whole. As a corollary to this, but now regarding the work of literature from the angle of the artist, Mr. Eliot holds—following Rémy de Gourmont— that the construction of the object essentially involves a depersonalization of emotion; in other words, a poem of the highest order is not in any ordinary sense of the phrase an expression of personal emotion, but something arranged, built and created in such a way that it must impress in its unique and determined fashion any unbiased sensibility exposed to it. We must conceive of the writer less as one who speaks to us than as the carver of a solid thing which will compel us to react towards it in a certain way. An artist's seriousness—and this is a word which Mr. Eliot uses often in a sense that (in default of a definition) must be gleaned from his book as a whole—is measured by the degree to which he sacrifices all desire for immediate and unrestrained expression, all personal idiosyncrasy, to the impersonal task of building the solid object which is the work of literary art.

[. . .]

A fairly clear consequence of the theory is that pure works of literature, or the pure portions of impure works, may produce in us emotional responses of a very varied kind; for though our judgment that a work is pure must in the last resort depend upon the reactions of our sensibility, our sensibility may reasonably be expected to discriminate between a reaction to a general coherence and impersonal solidity and a reaction to particular kinds of coherence and solidity. One solid work of literature may arouse and satisfy far more complex emotional needs in ourselves than another equally solid. The aim of criticism should therefore be twofold: first, to inquire and establish the degree of artistic perfection in a given work, the extent to which the author's personal emotion has been transformed and depersonalized; second, to elucidate and describe the peculiar quality of the work in so far as it is perfect.

[. . .]

[Mr. Eliot's] criticism is *positive*; he not only conceives but exercises it as an adjunct and an aid to creation. I do not mean that it is what is commonly called "creative criticism," the activity by which a writer gives a loose rein to all the irrelevant emotions aroused in him by a work of literature, and—in Mr. Eliot's illuminating and rather contemptuous phrase— "indulges a suppressed creative wish." It is rather the opposite of this; a criticism which is directed towards a complete exploration of the work of literature with a view to mastering its mechanism.

[. . .]

Mr. Eliot . . . has been attacked by his critical colleagues in England in ways which only show that they are completely unable to grasp his conceptions or his methods. It is easy to make cheap fun of a man who is taking extreme pains to elucidate a subtle thought; it is much harder to understand him.

[. . .]

Mark Van Doren. "England's Critical Compass." *Nation* 112, no. 2913 (4 May 1921), 669–70.

[. . .]

Mr. Symons's *Baudelaire* belongs to a critical kind that is probably dying. It represents impressionism without character, Paterism withered beyond seed.

[. . .]

If Mr. Eliot has read Mr. Symons's book he has been outraged, no doubt; for he is leading what might be termed the school of the younger responsibles, and he has set himself unalterably against impressionistic criticism. His *Sacred Wood* shelters the best essays and reviews that he has contributed to the *Athenaeum* and other periodicals during the past few years, and represents in a way the most conscientious critical effort now being made in England. Those knife-sharp faculties of his which year in and year out have been trimming and clipping poems from the devil's own brain have also been busy at criticism, which, Mr. Eliot insists, is not an art, or a hobby, or even a business, but an exact science. Above all it is not creation. The trouble with Mr. Symons as a critic, says Mr. Eliot, is that he is trying to produce something more than criticism and only producing something less than creation. The real creator—and it is a pity that in England where critics are so few, so many creators must turn off into criticism—has no such difficulty when he discusses literature, since he has already satisfied his nature and is not the victim of a suppressed creative wish. Mr. Eliot is all for analysis, and for keeping the categories straight. He chastises emotion from the critical scene—the emotion which is concealed behind the abstract jargon of the pseudo-scientist no less than that which is displayed in the languorous synonyms of the impressionist—with the sobriety of an ascetic. His remedy for England's critical anemia is exercise in ideas, for which the teachers should be a Frenchman, Rémy de Gourmont, and a Greek, Aristotle—two men at least who see straight. Mr. Babbitt and Mr. More in America, says Mr. Eliot, powerfully possess ideas, but their vision suffers from ethical refraction. The perfect critic will be as cold as steel and as free from color as plate glass. Eliot is not a perfect critic, because he does not write well enough in prose; but in the course of his essays on Tradition, Rhetoric, Euripides, Marlowe, *Hamlet*, and Ben Jonson, he has drawn permanently valuable distinctions, and he has vindicated with rare

intelligence the right, indeed the necessity, of the critic to think and to go on thinking.

[. . .]

Richard Aldington. "*The Sacred Wood.*" *Today* 8, no. 4 (September 1921), 191–93.

The publication of Mr. T. S. Eliot's book of literary essays, *The Sacred Wood*, is an event of considerable intellectual importance. Many of these essays, it is true, were already known to those alert readers intelligent enough to follow Mr. Eliot's writings in the obscure or widely-known periodicals he favors with such impartial coldness; but their publication in book form makes a more cumulative effect, and creates a greater admiration than was possible when they were scattered about. The purpose of this note is simply to persuade, to a close reading of this book, all those potential readers who will certainly enjoy it, but who have been diverted from it by journalistic calumny or not even allowed to hear of it.

The Sacred Wood is the most stimulating, the most intelligent, and the most original contribution to our critical literature during the last decade—at least I cannot think of any book which combines in so eminent a degree these three qualities of stimulus, intelligence and originality. If for no other cause than its "revival of enjoyment" (to quote an interesting American writer, Miss Marianne Moore), *The Sacred Wood* deserves the approbation of all who can appreciate literature; for Mr. Eliot is a critic who is not tired, not bored, not petulant, not pretentious, not superficial, not ignorant, but—to be positive—alert and sensitive, profound and reasonable, above all one who has read the authors he criticizes with sympathy, enjoyment and discrimination. But this book is a great deal more than a merely intelligent "revival of enjoyment"; our admiration goes not so much to Mr. Eliot's gusto, his enthusiastic sense for what is good in literature, but to other and more important gifts in him, other and more important qualities in his writing.

The mind which exercises itself in *The Sacred Wood* has both distinction and fascination: the fascination of great natural gifts, the distinction of natural gifts used rightly. To distinguish between the qualities which are purely "natural" and those which are acquired is probably impossible, for it is often simply by stimulation and training that many valuable intellectual qualities are even discovered. All I am trying to bring out is the harmony between the presumably inherent gifts of this exquisite mind and their subsequent strengthening by right discipline. To say that the spirit animating these essays is the spirit of intelligence and right reason looks like saying rather little; but, reflect how rare are true intelligence and right reason (especially in literary criticism) and you will see that these two qualities alone set *The Sacred Wood* above all books of similar pretensions but dissimilar achievements. And two qualities, which everyone theoretically admires and so many small writers practically dislike and always attack when they manifest themselves, are intelligence and right reason. Now *The Sacred Wood* is intelligent to a very high degree and deserves (for that alone) our admiration and respect; it is intelligent because it is always cogent, always vital, always putting aside what is accidental and irrelevant to fix our attention on what

is essential and permanent. And its appeal is never to prejudice, never to ignorance, never to any of the myriad forms of sentimentality and mental laziness, but always to right reason. This last is a virtue not only intellectual but ethical; it is what the French mean by being "*loyale*"; it is, never being petty or perverse or partisan, or merely obstinate, but always trying to "*regarder les choses telles qu'elles sont en elles-mêmes*"—"to see the object as in itself it really is."

[. . .]

It is a very great pleasure to read a new book which is primarily a "disinterested play of the intelligence" upon a "flow of fresh ideas." For though the subjects Mr. Eliot chooses for his reflections are either the poetry of authors like Ben Jonson or Dante or Swinburne (all extremely familiar as topics), or abstractions like "Tradition and the Individual Talent," "The Perfect Critic," and so on, he has invariably a fresh point of view to enunciate and a remarkable number of new stimulating thoughts to throw off by the way. It is incredible that any serious student of literature can read *The Sacred Wood* without receiving that delightful shock we experience at the first contact with a fresh original mind; it is quite incredible that any reader—even if he disagrees with every sentence in the book—can fail to perceive the profound intellectual qualities displayed, the dispassionate search for truth inherent in Mr. Eliot's method. It *is* credible that readers and writers should disagree with what Mr. Eliot says, but it is perfectly incredible that any person above the ranks of the ignorant should affect to believe that Mr. Eliot's criticism is negligible, or that he is (to quote a newspaper critic) a *précieux ridicule*! That is an expression of human malignity or human stupidity for which not even my pessimism was prepared.

Checklist of Additional Reviews

* "*The Sacred Wood.*" *Common Sense*, [later incorporated into the *Manchester Guardian Commercial*] 12 April 1920. [clipping in Houghton Library]

* "The Criticism of Poetry." *Times Literary Supplement* 952 (15 April 1920), 236. [Review of *Three Critical Essays on Modern English Poetry* (by T. S. Eliot, Aldous Huxley, and F. S. Flint) 1920]

F. G. Bettany. *Arts Gazette* 3 (29 May 1920), 93. [not located]

* A. H. Hannay. "The Perfect Critic." *Athenaeum* 4709 (30 July 1920), 156. [Letter regarding Eliot's essay in *Three Critical Essays on Modern English Poetry*, by T. S. Eliot, Aldous Huxley, and F. S. Flint, 1920] [See Eliot's reply: *Athenaeum*, 6 August 1920]

Everyman 16 (7 August 1920), 356. [not located]

* A. de S. *Manchester Guardian*, 22 November 1920, p. 5.

* H. T. "The Bookshelf." *Star*, 23 November 1920, p. 10. [not located]

* *Liverpool Post*, 24 November 1920. [not located]

* Edgell Rickword. "Weed Killing." *Daily Herald*, 24 November 1920, p. 7.

* "A Wooden Rod." *Observer*, 28 November 1920. [not located]

* George Sampson. *Daily News*, 16 December 1920, p. 7. [not located]

"The Week's Books." *Near East* 18 (23 December 1920), 860. [not located]

* Robert McAlmon. "Modern Artiques." *Contact*, January 1921, unpaged.

* Thomas Moult. "On Following One's Own Taste." *English Review* 32 (January 1921), 87–89.

* E. B. Osborn. "Books of the Day." *Illustrated London News* 158 (8 January 1921), 48. [not located]

* "Books of the Day." *Morning Post*, 14 January 1921, p. 3. [not located]

* *Scotsman*, 17 January 1921, p. 2. [not located]

* E. S. *London Mercury* 3 (February 1921), 447–50. [Review of *The Sacred Wood* and three other books]

* "Critics and Criticism." *Weekly Westminster Gazette* 57 (5 February 1921), 16–17. [not located]

Keith Preston. "Respecting the Handy Man." *Chicago Daily News*, 9 February 1921, p. 12. [not located]

Richard Aldington. "A Critic of Poetry." *Poetry: A Magazine of Verse* 17 (March 1921), 345–48.

* W. J. A. "The Will to Value." *New Age* 29 (12 May 1921), 21.

* John Middleton Murry. "A Matter of Form." *Nation and Athenaeum* 29 (28 May 1921), 328–29. [Review of *Poetry in Prose: Three Essays* (by T. S. Eliot, Frederic Manning, and Richard Aldington) 1921]

* "The Razor of Croce." *Times Literary Supplement* 1014 (23 June 1921), 393–94.

* Herbert Read. "Readers and Writers." *New Age* 29 (8 September 1921), 222. [Review of *Poetry in Prose: Three Essays* (by T. S. Eliot, Frederic Manning, and Richard Aldington) 1921]

* Augustine Birrell. "Lord Rosebery as Essayist." *Bookman* 61 (November 1921), 80–82. [Review of Lord

Rosebery's *Miscellanies*. Eliot's *Sacred Wood* also discussed]

*Arthur Clutton-Brock. "The Case against *Hamlet*." *Shakespeare's 'Hamlet'* (London: Methuen, 1922), 14–32. [Lengthy rebuttal of Eliot's statement in *The Sacred Wood* that *Hamlet* is an "artistic failure"]

*W. V. D. [William Van Doorn]. *English Studies* 4 (1922), 42–43.

"The New Books." *New York Evening Post Literary Review*, 18 February 1922, p. 435. [not located]

*H. J. M. "The World of Books." *Athenaeum* 31, no. 4804 (27 May 1922), 309. [Review of Clutton-Brock's refutation of Eliot's *Hamlet* essay in *The Sacred Wood*]

*"Medallions III. Mr. T. S. Eliot. The Exact Critic." *Times*, 13 June 1922, p. 14. [not located]

*"Justifying *Hamlet*." *Outlook* 50 (2 September 1922), 196. [Review of Clutton-Brock's refutation of Eliot's *Hamlet* essay in *The Sacred Wood*]

Walter Cornelius Blum. "Journalistic Critics." *Dial* 76 (June 1924), 554–58. [Review of *Criticism in America*, with essays by Eliot and others]

*Orlo Williams. "Scientific Critics." *Contemporary Criticism of Literature* (London: Leonard Parsons, 1924), 132–65. [Pages 134–54 a discussion of *The Sacred Wood*]

THE WASTE LAND
1922

THE WASTE LAND

BY

T. S. ELIOT

"NAM Sibyllam quidem Cumis ego ipse oculis meis
vidi in ampulla pendere, et cum illi pueri dicerent:
Σίβυλλα τί θέλεις; respondebat illa: ἀποθανεῖν θέλω."

NEW YORK
BONI AND LIVERIGHT
1922

*Times Literary
Supplement 1084
(26 October 1922), 690.

[Review of *The Waste Land* and inaugural issue of the *Criterion*]

If we are to judge by its first number, the *Criterion* is not only that rare thing amongst English periodicals, a purely literary review, but it is of a quality not inferior to that of any review published either here or abroad. Of the seven items which make up this number there are at least five that we should like to see preserved in a "permanent" form. And of these five there are two, the long poem by Mr. T. S. Eliot called *The Waste Land* and Dostoevski's "Plan of a Novel," now first translated into English, that are of exceptional importance. We cannot imagine a more untidy plan for a novel or anything else than this one by Dostoevski, and yet, even on a first reading, one has a confused impression of having passed through an exciting and significant experience.

[...]

Mr. Eliot's poem is also a collection of flashes, but there is no effect of heterogeneity, since all these flashes are relevant to the same thing and together give what seems to be a complete expression of this poet's vision of modern life. We have here range, depth, and beautiful expression. What more is necessary to a great poem? This vision is singularly complex and in all its labyrinths utterly sincere. It is the mystery of life that it shows two faces, and we know of no other modern poet who can more adequately and movingly reveal to us the inextricable tangle of the sordid and the beautiful that make up life.

Life is neither hellish nor heavenly; it has a purgatorial quality. And since it is purgatory, deliverance is possible. Students of Mr. Eliot's work will find a new note, and a profoundly interesting one in the latter part of this poem.

Of the other items in this number we may single out an excellent short story by May Sinclair, an interesting literary study by Sturge Moore, and a maliciously urbane and delightful article on "Dullness," by George Saintsbury. What literary school, then, does this new quarterly represent? It is a school which includes Saintsbury, Sturge Moore, and T. S. Eliot. There is no such school, obviously. It becomes apparent that the only school represented is the school of those who are genuinely interested in good literature.

Edmund Wilson, Jr.
"The Rag-Bag of
the Soul."
*New York Evening Post
Literary Review*, 25
November 1922,
pp. 237–38.

To the eyes of many, even of the wisest of those who came to maturity in the nineteenth century, the last few years have seen what looks like the complete disintegration of literature. The dykes of the mind have been broken and are flooded by a furious sea—in which the order which so many centuries have labored to impose on human thought, the harmony which uncounted hands have molded for the imagination, are awash as dishonored fragments among the ordures and detritus of the world. Our elders can but pace the shrinking shore and lament the engulfment of their city; they have despaired of the integrity of art with the wreck of the shapes they have known. Yet if they would only row out a little way and fix their eyes on that turbulent ocean, they might observe that their familiar city had been reorganized below the tide and they might even, when they had got used to the new element, come to find themselves at home there again. One considerable structure, at least, they could hardly fail to make out— or, in other words, there is one new literary form which has conspicuously established itself since the war and which has now become as susceptible of description as any of the older ones.

I speak of "since the war," but it really goes back much further. The war was only one of the factors which have given literature its present shape. It is at the junction of many storms that we behold these shattered fixtures of our landscape, boiling in the nozzle of the whirlwind—fused and crushed together at its point. In the December of 1908 there appeared before a literary club in Moscow a man named Nikolai Yevreynov, who read a manifesto on "Monodrama." It was already [. . .] Expressionism full blown—a drama in which the external world was to be seen exclusively through the consciousness of the central character.

> What I call Monodrama (wrote Yevreynov) is a kind of dramatic representation which endeavors with the greatest fulness to communicate to the spectator the soul state of the acting character, and presents on the stage the world surrounding him as he conceives it at any moment in his stage experience. [. . .] Only with him do I identify myself, only from his point of view do I perceive the world surrounding him, the people surrounding him. [. . .]

It is easy to see that such a play as *From Morn to Midnight*, or even *The Hairy Ape*, conforms more or less closely to this description. And not only the newer drama but the newer poetry and fiction, too: T. S. Eliot's *The Waste Land* and Ezra Pound's *Eight Cantos*; James Joyce's *Ulysses*, and the short stories of such writers as Virginia Woolf and Sherwood Anderson (the latter in "Out of Nowhere into Nothing"). The characteristic literary form today, almost everywhere where the old formulas are being discarded, is a cross-section of the human consciousness of a single specific human being, usually carried through a very limited period—only a day or an hour—of his career. It is the whole world sunk in the subjective life of a single human soul—beyond whose vague and impassable walls there is nothing solid or clear, there is nothing which exists in itself as part of an objective order. [. . .] So the clear, heroic figures of Racine moving small upon a spacious stage, where the forces of society and religion rise above them and dominate them, contrast directly with the modern Expressionist play in which the personages form no part of a structure, but in which such traces as still remain of a structure, serve merely to clutter the mind of a single personage.

"But this is all an old story," you will say. "It is only Classicism and Romanticism over again. What you are describing is merely the old ideal, which dates from the beginning of the last century—when against the ideal of Church or State, of the individual as conforming to an institution, there arose the new ideal of the individual as supremely important in himself. The process of submerging the whole world in the subjectivity of a single person began when it came to be believed that emotions were valuable for their own sake— that de Musset's tears and Byron's storms and Chateaubriand's somber *malaises*— though they contributed neither to the City of God nor to the Republic of the Age of Reason, obeying no ancient rule and guided by no classic example—were justified by their own urgency, and interesting in themselves. Your Expressionist or your Dadaist is merely saying in uglier language what Don César de Bazan says when he suddenly enters through the chimney: '*Tant pis! c'est moi!*'"

Well, in the first place, what we are having just now is a reaction not against Classicism but against Naturalism. [. . .]

Expressionism was the furious repudiation of the Naturalistic ideal. Even the Impressionism to which it specifically opposed itself gave too much importance to the external world: with Impressionism it had always been a question of external things imposing themselves on *you*: henceforward it was to be a question of *your* imposing yourself upon *them*. One had had enough of copying things even in the vague, sketchy fashion of the Impressionists. What mattered was not what the thing was like, but what emotion it aroused in you. All the better if you had never seen the thing. [. . .] Take the external world and wring its neck, distort it, break it to pieces! In the reassembling of its fragments we shall make what it really means to us.

Towards the breaking up of things, furthermore, all the forces of the time seemed to drive: life itself was marching confused; even the unity of capitalism had collapsed. As the *Divina Commedia* reflects the unity and system of the Middle Ages, so James Joyce and T. S. Eliot reflect our present condition of disruption. We are all tumultuous fragments, cages of unreconciled monkeys; like the ogres in Western pictures, our souls are impossible monsters [. . .].

And if these [. . .] chunks of spiritual matter be examined a little more closely, it will be seen that they differ in kind as well as condition from the emotions of the Romantics. They are the fragments, not of mighty passions only partially comprehended, but of intimate and ironic self-knowledge. This is partly science, of course. The transforming of introspective art, "Psychology," and especially, above all, the discovery of the subconscious self, which, appearing to widen the field, to deepen the sea of the subjective, really made man feel a certain finality in his knowledge of himself, as if now that a false bottom had been removed from his soul, there were no hope of making it any larger. But another cause certainly contributed to his ironic knowledge of himself. The revelations of Dr. Freud were reinforced by other revelations. In the hardship, abasement, and despair of the war, the Western world found itself out. Seeing all established society in flux, all institutions imperilled, the gentlemen among the gallipots and the underling on the throne, man discovered how untrustworthy he was and how rankly an animal. Nor did he have any longer the illusion of superior beings to uphold him: the governors and kings and *savants* whom he had looked to as a higher race, as the guardians of a genuine knowledge and power which directed the destinies of life, seemed to turn out as ignorant, as incompetent, and as selfish as himself. No more ideal figures then— no more heroic giants! Only harsh self-mockery and self-knowledge—the human soul as a mess. A combination of nervous interest in the complexity of one's distastes and desires with a wry and unpleasant laughter at having found oneself out—and at having found out that no one else was very different from oneself.

And no one makes any attempt to pick up the scattered pieces. That is the final characteristic of post-war literature. [. . .] [T]he products of a great many [. . .] involve no belief in any sort of order— either moral or aesthetic. The human consciousness is a rag-bag, a rubbish heap— there is nothing more to be done with it. You cannot build with fragments like these. What if the limbs of divine broken statues are mingled with the old tin cans and dung? All attempts to bring a palace from this chaos have ludicrously failed. We are content to note the jarring elements which make up the consciousness of man without ever subduing them to a system or even forming a hypothesis about them. It is no longer a question, as it once was, of man in relation to God, or man in relation to society, or man in relation to his neighbor. Let us merely explore a single human consciousness and make a record of what we find there without venturing even the most rudimentary ideas as to what their significance may be or as to which of them may be considered the most valuable:

> What are the roots that clutch, what
>   branches grow
> Out of this stony rubbish? Son of man,
> You cannot say, or guess, for you
>   know only
> A heap of broken images, where the
>   sun beats,
> And the dead tree gives no shelter, the
>   cricket no relief,
> And the dry stone no sound of water.

T. S. Eliot's lines in *The Waste Land* furnish an apt description of the situation, and a quotation from a more conventional author who has yet caught something of the spirit of the time puts it even more clearly and briefly. "I know myself but that is all," cries one of Scott Fitzgerald's heroes, who has "grown up to find all gods dead, all wars fought, all faiths in men shaken." And that is precisely the point of view of the modern novelist or poet: "I know myself but that is all."

All the works which pursue this method do not, of course, so completely lack structure—or even ideas. I have rather described the type towards which modern expression seems to *tend*. This form has

its masterpieces, like another. In *Ulysses*, for example, though we have a section of the typical stream of consciousness in all its brokenness and triviality, its aimlessness and confusion, we have it organized within itself and brought into relation with the rest of the world. It is, in fact, a sort of *Divine Comedy* of the twentieth century. Mr. Joyce has no theological, philosophical, or political system, but he at least manipulates his hero's reactions in obedience to a precise technical plan—in such a way as to make them cover in a day the whole of average human experience. Mr. Bloom has his two supplemental figures present a sort of compendium of all that man is and knows about himself at present. Joyce has done the rag-bag of the mind on an exhaustive scale; it is the mind not merely of three obscure people over a period of twenty hours; it is the mind of a whole society.

The trouble with pure Expressionism is not only that it tends to throw structure overboard, depending for the direction it is to take on the velleity of the guideless mind, but also that the further inside himself the artist has withdrawn the more remote his images become from the images of the actual world, the more difficult is he to understand. The common language has been abandoned; he is sunk in an unfathomable sea. The old convenient agreement by which certain sense-impressions are to be known as a chair and certain others as a pair of shoes has been completely abrogated. [. . .]

Perhaps, then, there was, after all, a sound instinct behind the cries of dismay with which our fathers have seen the stream of consciousness engulfing the arts. Remembering the costly pains of great artists to save harmony from the hubbub of life and the long hard hours of philosophers to win logic from the vagaries of that very stream, to impose upon the aimless disorder of the world the discipline of meaning and of form, they are naturally alarmed and cry out that we are sinking in chaos. It is partially, of course, that they do not understand the new forms—which will doubtless appear to our children as simple as, say, Verlaine does to us; but it is also, I believe, that the anarchy of our art reflects the anarchy of our ideals, and that men who are used to a more orderly world shrink from it as from something sinister. And in some degree they are probably right. We are very proud nowadays of admitting everything, of having put on record the whole scale of our tiniest and most ignoble desires. And we really deserve to be proud: it is the proof of our honesty and research. But may it not be that in the future, when the age of bewilderment has passed, we shall find that our present conviction of knowing ourselves so thoroughly that we have come to the end of our rope was based upon an illusion? We are rather inclined to be contemptuous of the literature of the past because it seems at one time or another to have suppressed so many obvious facts—at one period "realistic detail," at another the sexual passions. Yet our fathers were ignoring or denying in the interests of some particular plan. They were doing their best to make the world live up to some definitely conceived ideal. And almost every page of their literature shows the mark of that ideal or plan—whether Augustan or Mediæval, Christian or Humanitarian. By pretending that the world was so and so, they actually succeeded in transforming it; by suppressing certain sets of phenomena they did to some degree abolish them. [. . .] But we have no pervasive plan and no dominating ideal. Even capitalistic progress, shabby as it was, can no longer lend its support to the intelligent. Nor is the Communist–Humanitarian idea making very much headway just at present. Its credit, like that of every other political ideal, was shaken by the war. But when we do become capable again of believing in something, we shall probably begin to censor the record of our consciousness in the interests of our faith. [. . .] I haven't, in fact, the slightest idea which set of phenomena would be censored. But I do believe that in a genuinely vigorous society some selection will have to be made among the instincts which make a menagerie of every human being—that certain impulses and ideas will have consistently to be suppressed while certain others are cultivated with a superlative intensity—if man is to have even the illusion of controlling his own fate.

"Comment."
Dial 73 (December 1922), 685–87.

The editors have the pleasure of announcing that for the year of 1922 the Dial's award goes to Mr. T. S. Eliot.

Mr. Eliot has himself done so much to make clear the relation of critic to creative artist that we hope not to be asked whether it is his criticism or his poetry which constitutes that service to letters which the award is intended to acknowledge. Indeed it is our fancy that those who know one or the other will recognize the propriety of the occasion; those who know both will recognize further in Mr. Eliot an exceedingly active influence on contemporary letters.

[. . .] Few American writers have published so little, and fewer have published so much which was worth publication. We do not for a moment suspect Mr. Eliot of unheard-of capacities; it is possible that he neither has been pressed to nor can write a popular novel. But the temptation not to arrive at excellence is very great, and he is one of the rare artists who has resisted it. A service to letters peculiarly acceptable now is the proof that one can arrive at eminence with the help of nothing except genius.

Elsewhere in this issue will be found a discussion of Mr. Eliot's poetry [by Edmund Wilson], with special reference to his long work, *The Waste Land*, which appeared in the *Dial* of a month ago; in reviewing *The Sacred Wood*, and elsewhere, we have had much to say of his critical work, and may have more. At this moment it pleases us to remember how much at variance Mr. Eliot is with those writers who having themselves sacrificed all interest in letters, are calling upon criticism to do likewise in the name of the particular science which they fancy can redeem the world from every ill but themselves. As a critic of letters Mr. Eliot has always had preeminently one of the qualifications which he requires of the good critic: "a creative interest, a focus upon the immediate future. The important critic is the person who is absorbed in the present problems of art, and who wishes to bring the forces of the past to bear upon the solution of these problems." This is precisely what Mr. Eliot has wished, and accomplished, in his function as critic of criticism.

[. . .]

There is another, quite different sense, in which Mr. Eliot's work is of exceptional service to American letters. He is one of a small number of Americans who can be judged by the standards of the past [. . .]. Mr. Eliot is almost the only young American critic who is neither ignorant of nor terrified by the classics, that he knows them (one includes Massinger as well as Euripides) and understands their relation to the work which went before and came after them. There are in his poems certain characters, certain scenes, and even certain attitudes of mind, which one recognizes as peculiarly American; yet there is nowhere in his work that "localism" which at once takes so much of American writing out of the field of comparison with European letters and (it is often beneficial to their reputations) requires for American writers a special standard of judgment.

[. . .]

When *Prufrock* in paper covers first appeared, to become immediately one of the rarest of rare books (somebody stole ours as early as 1919), Mr. Eliot was already redoubtable. Since then, poet with true invention, whom lassitude has not led to repeat himself, critic again with invention and with enough metaphysics to draw the line at the metaphysical, his legend has increased. We do not fancy that we are putting a last touch on this climax; we express gratitude for pleasure received and assured.

[. . .]

Mr. Eliot's command of publicity is not exceptional, and we feel it necessary to put down, for those who care for information, these hardly gleaned facts of his biography. In 1888 he was born in St. Louis; in 1909 and 1910 he received, respectively, the degrees of Bachelor and of Master of Arts at Harvard; subsequently he studied at the Sorbonne, the Harvard Graduate School, and Merton College, Oxford. He has been a lecturer under both the Oxford and the London University Extension Systems, and from 1917 to 1919 he was assistant editor of the *Egoist*. We have heard it rumored that he is still "*À Londres, un peu banquier*"; those who can persuade themselves that facts are facts will find much more of importance in the "Mélange Adultère de Tout," from which the quotation comes; as that poem was written several years ago it omits the names of Mr. Eliot's books: *The Sacred Wood*, *Poems* [1920], and *The Waste Land* (not to speak of the several volumes later incorporated into *Poems*) and omits also the fact that Mr. Eliot is now editor of the *Criterion* [. . .]. The most active and, we are told, the most influential editor–critic in London found nothing to say of one of the contributions to the first number except that it was "an obscure, but amusing poem" by the editor [*The Waste Land*] . . . [O]ur readers can judge of the state of criticism in England by turning to the first page of our November issue and reading the same poem there.

Edmund Wilson, Jr. "The Poetry of Drouth." *Dial* 73 (December 1922), 611–16.

Mr. T. S. Eliot's first meager volume of twenty-four poems was dropped into the waters of contemporary verse without stirring more than a few ripples. But when two or three years had passed, it was found to stain the whole sea. Or, to change the metaphor a little, it became evident that Mr. Eliot had fished a murex up. His productions, which had originally been received as a sort of glorified *vers de société*, turned out to be unforgettable poems, which everyone was trying to rewrite. There might not be very much of him, but what there was had come somehow to seem precious and now the publication of his long poem, *The Waste Land*, confirms the opinion which we had begun gradually to cherish, that Mr. Eliot, with all his limitations, is one of our only authentic poets. For this new poem—which presents itself as so far his most considerable claim to eminence—not only recapitulates all his earlier and already familiar motifs, but it sounds for the first time in all their intensity, untempered by irony or disguise, the hunger for beauty and the anguish at living which lie at the bottom of all his work.

Perhaps the best point of departure for a discussion of *The Waste Land* is an explanation of its title. Mr. Eliot asserts that he derived this title, as well as the plan of the poem "and much of the incidental symbolism," from a book by Miss Jessie L. Weston called *From Ritual to Romance*. The Waste Land, it appears, is one of the many mysterious elements which have made of the Holy Grail legend a perennial puzzle of folk-lore; it is a desolate and sterile country, ruled over by an impotent king, in which not only have the crops ceased to grow and the animals to reproduce their kind, but the very human inhabitants have become unable to bear children. The renewal of the Waste Land and the healing of the "Fisher King's" wound depend somehow upon the success of the Knight who has come to find the Holy Grail.

Miss Weston, who has spent her whole life in the study of the Arthurian legends, has at last propounded a new solution for the problems presented by this strange tale. Stimulated by Frazer's *Golden Bough*—of which this extraordinarily interesting book is a sort of offshoot—she has attempted to explain the Fisher King as a primitive vegetable god—one of those creatures who, like Attis and Adonis, is identified with Nature herself and in the temporary loss of whose virility the drouth or inclemency of the season is symbolized; and whose mock burial is a sort of earnest of his coming to life again. Such a cult, Miss Weston contends, became attached to the popular Persian religion of Mithraism and was brought north to Gaul and Britain by the Roman legionaries. When Christianity finally prevailed, Attis was driven underground and survived only as a secret cult, like the

Venus of the Venusberg. The Grail legend, according to Miss Weston, had its origin in such a cult; the Lance and Grail are the sexual symbols appropriate to a fertility rite and the eerie adventure of the Chapel Perilous is the description of an initiation.

Now Mr. Eliot uses the Waste Land as the concrete image of a spiritual drouth. His poem takes place half in the real world—the world of contemporary London, and half in a haunted wilderness—the Waste Land of the mediaeval legend; but the Waste Land is only the hero's arid soul and the intolerable world about him. The water which he longs for in the twilit desert is to quench the thirst which torments him in the London dusk. And he exists not only upon these two planes, but as if throughout the whole of human history. Miss Weston's interpretation of the Grail legend lent itself with peculiar aptness to Mr. Eliot's extraordinarily complex mind (which always finds itself looking out upon the present with the prouder eyes of the past and which loves to make its oracles as deep as the experience of the race itself by piling up stratum upon stratum of reference, as the Italian painters used to paint over one another); because she took pains to trace the Buried God not only to Attis and Adonis, but further back to the recently revealed Tammuz of the Sumerian–Babylonian civilization and to the god invited to loosen the waters in the abysmally ancient Vedic Hymns. So Mr. Eliot hears in his own parched cry the voices of all the thirsty men of the past—of the author of Ecclesiastes in majestic bitterness at life's futility, of the Children of Israel weeping for Zion by the unrefreshing rivers of Babylon, of the disciples after the Crucifixion meeting the phantom of Christ on their journey; of Buddha's renunciation of life and Dante's astonishment at the weary hordes of Hell, and of the

sinister dirge with which Webster blessed the "friendless bodies of unburied men." In the center of his poem he places the weary figure of the blind immortal prophet Tiresias, who, having been woman as well as man, has exhausted all human experience and, having "sat by Thebes below the wall / And walked among the lowest of the dead," knows exactly what will happen in the London flat between the typist and the house-agent's clerk; and at its beginning the almost identical figure of the Cumæan Sibyl mentioned in Petronius, who—gifted also with extreme longevity and preserved as a sort of living mummy—when asked by little boys what she wanted, replied only "I want to die." Not only is life sterile and futile, but men have tasted its sterility and futility a thousand times before. T. S. Eliot, walking the desert of London, feels profoundly that the desert has always been there. Like Tiresias, he has sat below the wall of Thebes; like Buddha, he has seen the world as an arid conflagration; like the Sibyl, he has known everything and known everything in vain.

Yet something else, too, reaches him from the past: as he wanders among the vulgarities which surround him, his soul is haunted by heroic strains of an unfading music. Sometimes it turns suddenly and shockingly into the jazz of the music-halls, sometimes it breaks in the middle of a bar and leaves its hearer with dry ears again, but still it sounds like the divine rumor of some high destiny from which he has fallen, like indestructible pride in the citizenship of some world which he never can reach. In a London boudoir, where the air is stifling with a dust of futility, he hears, as he approaches his hostess, an echo of Antony and Cleopatra and of Aeneas coming to the house of Dido—and a painted panel above the mantel gives his mind a moment's swift release by reminding him of Milton's Paradise and of the nightingale that sang there. Yet though it is most often things from books which refresh him, he has also a slight spring of memory. He remembers someone who came to him with wet hair and with hyacinths in her arms, and before her he was stricken senseless and dumb—"Looking into the heart of light, the silence." There were rain and flowers growing then. Nothing ever grows during the action of the poem and no rain ever falls. The thunder of the final vision is "dry sterile thunder without rain." But as Gerontion in his dry rented house thinks wistfully of the young men who fought in the rain, as Prufrock longs to ride green waves and linger in the chambers of the sea, as Mr. Apollinax is imagined drawing strength from the deep sea-caves of coral islands, so in this new poem Mr. Eliot identifies water with all freedom and illumination of the soul. He drinks the rain that once fell on his youth as—to use an analogy in Mr. Eliot's own manner—Dante drank at the river of Eunoë that the old joys he had known might be remembered. But—to note also the tragic discrepancy, as Mr. Eliot always does—the draught, so far from renewing his soul and leaving him pure to rise to the stars, is only a drop absorbed in the desert; to think of it is to register its death. The memory is the dead god whom—as Hyacinth—he buries at the beginning of the poem and which—unlike his ancient prototype—is never to come to life again. Hereafter, fertility will fail; we shall see women deliberately making themselves sterile; we shall find that love has lost its life-giving power and can bring nothing but an asceticism of disgust. He is traveling in a country cracked by drouth in which he can only dream feverishly of drowning or of hearing the song of the hermit-thrush which has at least the music of water. The only reappearance of the god is as a phantom which walks beside him, the delirious hallucination of a man who is dying of thirst. In the end the dry-rotted world is crumbling about him—his own soul is falling apart. There is nothing left to prop it up but some dry stoic Sanskrit maxims and the broken sighs from the past, of singers exiled or oppressed. Like de Nerval, he is disinherited; like the poet of the "*Pervigilium Veneris*," he is dumb; like Arnaut Daniel in Purgatory, he begs the world to raise a prayer for his torment, as he disappears in the fire.

It will be seen from this brief description that the poem is complicated; and it is actually even more complicated than I have made it appear. It is sure to be objected that Mr. Eliot has written a puzzle rather than a poem and that his work can possess no higher interest than a full-rigged ship built in a bottle. It will be said that he depends too much on books and borrows too much from other men and that there can be no room for original quality in a poem of little more than four hundred lines which contains allusions to, parodies of, or quotations from, the Vedic Hymns, Buddha, the *Psalms*, *Ezekiel*, *Ecclesiastes*, *Luke*, Sappho, Virgil, Ovid, Petronius, the "*Pervigilium Veneris*," St. Augustine, Dante, the Grail legends, early English poetry, Kyd, Spenser, Shakespeare, John Day, Webster, Middleton, Milton, Goldsmith, Gérard de Nerval, Froude, Baudelaire, Verlaine, Swinburne, Wagner, *The Golden Bough*, Miss Weston's book, various popular ballads, and the author's own earlier poems. It has already been charged against Mr. Eliot that he does not feel enough to be a poet and that the emotions of longing and disgust which he does have belong essentially to a delayed adolescence. It has already been suggested that his distaste for the celebrated Sweeney shows a superficial mind and that if he only looked more closely into poor Sweeney he would find Eugene O'Neill's Hairy Ape; and I suppose it will be felt in connection with this new poem that if his vulgar London girls had only been studied by Sherwood Anderson they would have presented a very different appearance. At bottom, it is sure to be said, Mr. Eliot is timid and prosaic like Mr. Prufrock; he has no capacity for life, and nothing which happens to Mr. Prufrock can be important.

Well, all these objections are founded on realities, but they are outweighed by one major fact—the fact that Mr. Eliot is a poet. It is true his poems seem the products of a constricted emotional experience and that he appears to have drawn rather heavily on books for the heat he could not derive from life. There is a certain grudging margin, to be sure, about all that Mr. Eliot writes—as if he were compensating himself for his limitations by a peevish assumption of superiority. But it is the very acuteness of his suffering from this starvation which gives such poignancy to his art. And, as I say, Mr. Eliot is a poet—that is, he feels intensely and with distinction and speaks naturally in beautiful verse—so that, no matter within what walls he lives, he belongs to the divine company. His verse is sometimes much too scrappy—he does not dwell long enough upon one idea to give it its proportionate value before passing on to the next—but these drops, though they be wrung from flint, are none the less authentic crystals. They are broken and sometimes infinitely tiny, but they are worth all the rhinestones on the market. I doubt whether there is a single other poem of equal length by a contemporary American which displays so high and so varied a mastery of English verse. The poem is—in spite of its lack of structural unity—simply one triumph after another—from the white April light of the opening and the sweet wistfulness of the nightingale passage—one of the only successful pieces of contemporary blank verse—to the shabby sadness of the Thames Maidens, the cruel irony of Tiresias' vision, and the dry grim stony style of the descriptions of the Waste Land itself.

That is why Mr. Eliot's trivialities are more valuable than other people's epics— why Mr. Eliot's detestation of Sweeney is more precious than Mr. Sandburg's sympathy for him, and Mr. Prufrock's tea-table tragedy more important than all the passions of the New Adam—sincere and carefully expressed as these latter emotions indubitably are. That is also why, for all its complicated correspondences and its recondite references and quotations, *The Waste Land* is intelligible at first reading. It is not necessary to know anything about the Grail legend or any but the most obvious of Mr. Eliot's allusions to feel the force of the intense emotion which the poem is intended to convey—as one cannot do, for example, with the extremely ill-focused *Eight Cantos* of his imitator Mr. Ezra Pound, who presents only a bewildering mosaic with no central emotion to provide a key. In Eliot the very images and the sound of the words—even when we do not know precisely why he has chosen them—are charged with a strange poignancy which seems to bring us into the heart of the singer. And sometimes we feel that he is speaking not only for a personal distress, but for the starvation of a whole civilization—for people grinding at barren office-routine in the cells of gigantic cities, drying up their souls in eternal toil whose products never bring them profit, where their pleasures are so vulgar and so feeble that they are almost sadder than their pains. It is our whole world of strained nerves and shattered institutions, in which "some infinitely gentle, infinitely suffering thing" is somehow being done to death—in which the maiden Philomel "by the barbarous king so rudely forced" can no longer fill the desert "with inviolable voice." It is the world in which the pursuit of grace and beauty is something which is felt to be obsolete—the reflections which reach us from the past cannot illumine so dingy a scene; that heroic prelude has ironic echoes among the streets and the drawing-rooms where we live. Yet the race of the poets—though grown rarer—is not yet quite dead: there is at least one who, as Mr. Pound says, has brought a new personal rhythm into the language and who has lent even to the words of his great predecessors a new music and a new meaning.

Gilbert Seldes.
"T. S. Eliot."
Nation 115 (6 December 1922), 614–16.

The poems and critical essays of T. S. Eliot have been known to a number of readers for six or seven years; small presses in England have issued one or two pamphlet-like books of poetry; in America the *Little Review* and the *Dial* have published both prose and verse. In 1920 he issued his collected *Poems*, a volume of some sixty pages, through Knopf, and the following year the same publisher put forth *The Sacred Wood*, a collection of fourteen essays devoted to two subjects, criticism and poetry. This year a volume no larger than the first, containing one long poem, is issued. The position, approaching eminence, which Mr. Eliot holds is obviously not to be explained in terms of bulk.

[. . .] The secret of his power (I will not say influence) as a critic is that he is interested in criticism and in the object of criticism, as a poet that he understands and practices the art of poetry. In the first of these he is exceptional, almost alone; in both, his work lies in the living tradition and outside the willfulness of the moment [. . .].

At the present moment criticism of literature is almost entirely criticism of the ideas expressed in literature; it is interested chiefly in morals, economics, sociology, or science. We can imagine a critic *circa* 1840 declaring that *Othello* is a bad play because men should not kill their wives; and the progress is not very great to 1922 when we are likely as not to hear that it is a bad play because Desdemona is an outmoded kind of woman. [. . .] [The critics'] creative interest is in something apart from the art they are discussing; and what Mr. Eliot has done, with an attractive air of finality, is to indicate how irrelevant that interest is to the art of letters. He respects these imperfect critics in so far as they are good philosophers, moralists, or scientists, but he knows that in connection with letters they are the victims of impure desires (the poet *manqué* as critic) or of impure interests (the fanatical "single-taxer" as critic). "But Aristotle," he says, "had none of these impure desires to satisfy; in whatever sphere of interest, he looked solely and steadfastly at the object; in his short and broken treatise he provides an eternal example—not of laws, or even of method, for there is no method except to be very intelligent, but of intelligence itself swiftly operating the analysis of sensation to the point of principle and definition." Again, more specifically, "The important critic is the person who is absorbed in the present problems of art, and who wishes to bring the forces of the past to bear upon the solution of these problems . . ." Criticism, for

Mr. Eliot, is the statement of the structures in which our perceptions, when we face a work of art, form themselves. He quotes Rémy de Gourmont: "To erect his personal impressions into laws is the great effort of man if he is sincere."

The good critic, as I understand Mr. Eliot, will be concerned with the aesthetic problem of any given work of art; he will (I should add) not despise ideas, but if he is intelligent he will recognize their place in a work of art and he will certainly not dismiss as paradoxical nonsense Mr. Eliot's contention that his baffling escape from ideas made Henry James the most intelligent man of his time. It is not an easy task to discover in each case what the aesthetic problem is; but that is the task, precisely, which every good critic . . . is always compelled to attempt. . . . Mr. Eliot has accomplished the task several times, notably in his essay on *Hamlet*, about which essay a small literature has already been produced. I have not space here to condense the substance of that or of the other critical essays . . . nor to do more than say that they are written with an extraordinary distinction in which clarity, precision, and nobility almost always escaping magniloquence, are the elements.

In turning to Mr. Eliot as a poet I do not leave the critic behind since it is from his critical utterances that we derive the clue to his poetry. He says that the historical sense is indispensable to anyone who would continue to be a poet after the age of twenty-five, and follows this with a statement that cannot be too closely pondered by those who misunderstand tradition and by those who imagine that American letters stand outside of European letters and are to be judged by other standards: "the historical sense compels a man to write not merely with his own generation in his bones, but with a feeling that the whole of the literature of Europe from Homer and

within it the whole of the literature of his own country has a simultaneous existence and composes a simultaneous order."

This is only the beginning of "depersonalization." It continues: "What happens is a continual surrender of himself [the poet] as he is at the moment to something which is more valuable. The progress of an artist is a continual self-sacrifice, a continual extinction of personality" [and concludes] "the more perfect the artist, the more completely separate in him will be the man who suffers and the mind which creates . . ."

[. . .]

"Poetry is not a turning loose of emotion, but an escape from emotion; it is not the expression of personality, but an escape from personality. But, of course, only those who have personality and emotions know what it means to want to escape from these things."

The significant emotion has its life in the poem and not in the history of the poet; and recognition of this, Mr. Eliot indicates, is the true appreciation of poetry. Fortunately for the critic he has written one poem, *The Waste Land*, to which one can apply his own standards. It develops, carries to conclusions, many things in his remarkable earlier work, in method and in thought. I have not that familiarity with the intricacies of French verse which could make it possible for me to affirm or deny the statement that technically he derives much from Jules Laforgue; if Rémy de Gourmont's estimate of the latter be correct one can see definite points of similarity in the minds of the two poets: "His natural genius was made up of sensibility, irony, imagination, and clairvoyance; he chose to nourish it with positive knowledge (*connaissances positives*), with all philosophies and all literatures, with all the images of nature and of art; even the latest views of science seem to have been known to him . . ."

A series of sardonic portraits—of people, places, things—each the distillation of a refined emotion, make up Mr. Eliot's *Poems* [1920]. The deceptive simplicity of these poems in form and in style is exactly at the opposite extreme from false *naiveté*; they are unpretentiously sophisticated, wicked, malicious, humorous, and with the distillation of emotion has gone a condensation of expression. In *The Waste Land* the seriousness of the theme is matched with an intensity of expression in which all the earlier qualities are sublimated.

In essence *The Waste Land* says something which is not new: that life has become barren and sterile, that man is withering, impotent, and without assurance that the waters which made the land fruitful will ever rise again. (I need not say that "thoughtful" as the poem is, it does not "express an idea"; it deals with emotions, and ends precisely in that significant emotion, inherent in the poem, which Mr. Eliot has described.) The title, the plan, and much of the symbolism of the poem, the author tells us in his "Notes," were suggested by Miss Weston's remarkable book on the Grail legend, *From Ritual to Romance*; it is only indispensable to know that there exists the legend of a king rendered impotent, and his country sterile, both awaiting deliverance by a knight on his way to seek the Grail; it is interesting to know further that this is part of the Life or Fertility mysteries; but the poem is self-contained. It seems at first sight remarkably disconnected, confused, the emotion seems to disengage itself in spite of the objects and events chosen by the poet as their vehicle. The poem begins with the memory of summer showers, gaiety, joyful and perilous escapades; a moment later someone else is saying "I will show you fear in a handful of dust," and this is followed by the first lines of *Tristan und Isolde*, and then again by a fleeting recollection of loveliness. The symbolism of the poem is introduced by means of the Tarot pack of cards; quotations, precise or dislocated, occur; gradually one discovers a rhythm of alternation between the visionary (so to name the memories of the past) and the actual, between the spoken and the unspoken thought. There are scraps, fragments; then sustained episodes; the poem culminates with the juxtaposition of the highest types of Eastern and Western asceticism, by means of allusions to St. Augustine and Buddha; and ends with a sour commentary on the injunctions "Give, sympathize, control" of the *Upanishads*, a commentary which reaches its conclusion in a pastiche recalling all that is despairing and disinherited in the memory of man.

A closer view of the poem does more than illuminate the difficulties; it reveals a hidden form of the work, indicates how each thing falls into place, and to the reader's surprise shows that the emotion which at first seemed to come in spite of the framework and the detail could not otherwise have been communicated. For the theme is not a distaste for life, nor is it a disillusion, a romantic pessimism of any kind. It is specifically concerned with the idea of the Waste Land—that the land *was* fruitful and now is not, that life had been rich, beautiful, assured, organized, lofty, and now is dragging itself out in a poverty-stricken and disrupted and ugly tedium, without health, and with no consolation in morality; there may remain for the poet the labor of poetry, but in the poem there remain only "[t]hese fragments I have shored against my ruins"—the broken glimpses of what was. The poem is not an argument and I can only add, to be fair, that it contains no romantic idealization of the past; one feels simply that even in the cruelty and madness which have left their record in history and in art, there was an intensity of life, a germination and fruitfulness, which are now gone, and that even the creative imagination, even hallucination and vision have atrophied, so that water shall never again be struck from a rock in the desert. Mr. Bertrand Russell has recently said that since the Renaissance the clock of Europe has been running down; without the feeling that it was once wound up, without the contrasting emotions as one looks at the past and at the present, *The Waste Land* would be a different poem, and the problem of the poem would have been solved in another way.

The present solution is in part by juxtaposition of opposites. We have a passage seemingly spoken by a slut, ending "Goonight Bill. Goonight Lou. Goonight May. Goonight / Ta ta. Goonight. Goonight," and then the ineffable "Good night, ladies, good night, sweet ladies, good night, good night." . . . And in the long passage where Tiresias, the central character of the poem, appears, the method is at its height, for here is the coldest and unhappiest revelation of the assault of lust made in the terms of beauty.

> [Quotation of lines 215–48 (episode of the typist and the clerk) of *The Waste Land*]

It will be interesting for those who have knowledge of another great work of our time, Mr. Joyce's *Ulysses*, to think of the two together. That *The Waste Land* is, in a sense, the inversion and complement of *Ulysses* is at least tenable. We have in *Ulysses* the poet defeated, turning outward, savoring the ugliness which is no longer transmutable into beauty, and, in the end, homeless. We have in *The Waste Land* some indication of the inner life of such a poet . . . [I]n each, the theme, once it is comprehended, is seen to have dictated the form. More important still, I fancy, is that each has expressed something of

supreme relevance to our present life in the everlasting terms of art.

A. T. [Allen Tate]. "Whose Ox." *Fugitive* 1 (December 1922), 99–100.

[. . .]

It is agreed, we assume, that the aesthetic problem confronting the poet is eminently practical—versification, diction, composition, in a word, mechanics being the elusive enemy to capture and subdue . . . And it is pretty well decided beforehand that his finished product must *represent* some phase of life as ordinarily perceived, and that he must look for his effects in new combinations of images representing only the constituted material world. It is possible that his notion, unlike the question of technique, is somewhat gratuitous and inadequate; and I believe that the unique virtue of the contemporary revolt is its break, in a positive direction, with the tyranny of representation.

Mr. Clive Bell has ably shown that Modern Art has to its credit worthwhile things quite outside the untoward perversion of seeing life whole. It is patent, for instance, that the art of Duncan Grant and of Picasso has no objective validity and *represents* nothing; but perhaps the world as it is doesn't afford accurate correlatives of all the emotional complexes and attitudes; and so the painter and, it may be, the poet are justified in not only rearranging (witness entire English Tradition) but remaking, remolding, in a subjective order, the stuff they must necessarily work with—the material world. It is inevitable that there should be excesses, that the logical consequences of such a theory should lead many into an arid and fantastic subjectivism remote from the forms in which life presents itself to us. But surely the one extreme is not more undesirable than the other . . .

The problem of representation is of equal concern to the poet, for his solution of it will largely determine his diction and, especially, his prosody. Concede the banality that form and content are one, and it is then clear that the apparently inexplicable framework of T. S. Eliot's *The Waste Land* is inevitable and final; for to imagine that poem in another music would be very much like thinking of *The Iliad* as written in a sequence, say, of triplets or cinquains. I think for all time—so important is *The Waste Land*—Mr. Eliot has demonstrated the necessity, in special cases, of an aberrant versification, for doubtless none assails the authenticity of his impersonal and increasingly abstract art, though some may not care for it. . . .

Perhaps T. S. Eliot has already pointed the way for this and the next generation, as Mr. Seldes says. But there are and will be many still faithful to the older, if not more authentic, tradition: for the old modes are not yet sapped. However, the Moderns have adequately arrived, and their claims are by no means specious . . .

Burton Rascoe.
"In Defense of T. S. Eliot."
Herald-Tribune [New York], 7 January 1923, sec. 6, p. 22.

To lunch with Gilbert Seldes and Edmund Wilson, Jr., and we were all in a happy frame of mind over the imminence of Gilbert's departure for Europe. We drew up a telegram to Lee Wilson Dodd suggesting that he write a parody of *The Waste Land* [. . .].

We made merry over the fact that here were gathered together three critics looked upon as arch-conspirators in the effort to palm off on the public an unintelligible poem by an obscure scribbler as the great poetic work of the year.

Eliot, of course, is about as obscure among the literate as Rudolph Valentino is among movie fans; Clive Bell, the English critic, went so far as to say recently that Eliot is the most considerable poet writing in English, being not unmindful of the fact that William Butler Yeats, John Masefield, and Thomas Hardy are still alive; and although the bulk of Eliot's work is very small, he has had the greatest influence perhaps of any one poet living upon the work of younger men.

And *The Waste Land* is not unintelligible. It is, naturally enough, unintelligible to people who read it as carelessly as, say, Keith Preston does. Keith quotes

O the moon shone bright on Mrs.
   Porter
And on her daughter
They wash their feet in soda water

and then he comments: "As persiflage it has its points. The phantasy of moonlit damsels washing their feet in ice cream soda water has a sort of Kubla Khandy store flavor that we find refreshing." The poem says nothing about "ice cream soda water"; it says plain soda water, a not uncommon bath for tired and swollen feet. To comprehend the mood and meaning of these few lines is to comprehend the mood and meaning of the whole poem. The poem is, as I have said before, tragic in mood; it is akin to a dirge or lament, but it differs from the usual tragic poem in that it is keyed sardonically, not romantically, as for instance, is "The Lament for

Bion," or prophetically, as for instance, are the lamentations of the Old Testament, or wrathfully, as is "The Revolt of Islam," or philosophically, as is Goethe's *Faust*. Its sardonic quality is peculiarly modern.

Eliot sings, to put the matter quite simply, the diminution of the energy of the world. "Faith," says Elie Faure, "is the religious name we give energy"; it is the decline of faith, of energy, that Eliot in this poem laments. Modern life, he says, is arid, without a driving faith, lacking in the great dreams and illusions which sent men in quest of the Holy Grail, impelled Columbus to cross the Atlantic and made possible all the great epochs in history we call progress. To emphasize this he selects lines from great poets, from Sappho, from Ovid, from Virgil, from Shakespeare, from Spenser, from Dante, who celebrated beauty with a great faith, and revises their sentiments in consonance with the arid drabness of modern life.

One has but to compare the nuptial passages in the *Æneid* with its modern counterpart (as Eliot sees it) in the expeditious, listless affair Eliot relates between the typist and the young house agent's clerk to see the similarity and the violent contrast. Virgil's celebration of Dido's love for Æneas is the finest flight of his poetic fancy. Everything is lovely; everything is perfect; Aphrodite and Juno unite in making things nice for the lovers. Eliot, in contrast, pictures a modern love scene in a great city, London: a young typist, tired out from a day's work, returns to her hall bedroom for her meal hastily prepared from cheap canned goods. There is a bed that serves her as a divan, piled with articles of dress. Her lover is a brisk, self-satisfied animal without sentiment or delicacy who expedites matters, "bestows one final patronising kiss" and descends the stairs. Meanwhile how does this modern Dido of the tenements regard her encounter with her Æneas? Goldsmith has written:

> When lovely lady stoops to folly
>   And finds too late that men betray,
> What charm can soothe her
>   melancholy?
> What art can wash her guilt away?

And Virgil had voiced that sentiment when he makes Dido soothe her melancholy in suicide. But, sings Eliot:

> She turns and looks a moment in the
>   glass,
> Hardly aware of her departed lover;
> Her brain allows one half-formed
>   thought to pass:
> "Well now that's done: and I'm glad
>   it's over."
> When lovely woman stoops to folly
>   and
> Paces about her room again, alone,
> She smoothes her hair with automatic
>   hand,
> And puts a record on the gramophone.

The modern Dido of the tenements, says Eliot, is too fatigued, too disillusioned, too cynical, to take love seriously, to make it a purposeful, energizing thing. She says "That's that" and thinks no more about it.

Again, the poet Day sings:

> A noise of horns and hunting, which
>   shall bring
> Actæon to Diana in the spring.

While Eliot paraphrases it with a bitter twist:

> The sound of horns and motors,
>   which shall bring
> Sweeney to Mrs. Porter in the spring.
> O the moon shone bright on Mrs.
>   Porter
> And on her daughter
> They wash their feet in soda water

*Et O ces voix d'enfants, chantant dans
la coupole!*

There is "ape-necked Sweeney" of a former comic poem by Eliot playing Actæon to Mrs. Porter's Diana. There is the reminiscent parody of the once popular ballad, "The Moon Shines Bright on Pretty Red Wing," a quick juxtaposition of an anti-climax in the image of Mrs. Porter and her daughter bathing their swollen feet in soda water, and a sardonic employment of the loveliest line from one of the loveliest of Verlaine's religious poems, "Parsifal."

Throughout *The Waste Land* this method of contrasts by parodies, alterations, and distorted images is pursued by Eliot with a result in perhaps the most sardonic poem in the language. To say that the poem lacks beauty is to delimit the word beauty to such qualities as "sweetness," "prettiness," "exalted sentiment," etc., which have, strictly, little to do with beauty, even though a beautiful poem may be at the same time sweet and pretty and exalted. *The Waste Land* is as rich in poetic fallacy as any poem by Marlowe or Keats, but it is poetic fallacy of a different sort.

To say that life is not as bad as it is depicted in this poem is silly and irrelevant; of course it isn't; neither is it as good as life is depicted in the *Eclogues* of Virgil.

Louis Untermeyer. "Disillusion vs. Dogma." *Freeman* 6 (17 January 1923), 453.

The *Dial*'s award to Mr. T. S. Eliot and the subsequent book-publication of his *The Waste Land* have occasioned a display of some of the most enthusiastically naïve superlatives that have ever issued from publicly sophisticated iconoclasts. A group, in attempting to do for Mr. Eliot what *Ulysses* did for Mr. Joyce, has, through its emphatic reiterations, driven more than one reader to a study rather than a celebration of the qualities that characterize Mr. Eliot's work and endear him to the younger cerebralists. These qualities, apparent even in his earlier verses, are an elaborate irony, a twitching disillusion, a persistent though muffled hyperaesthesia. In "The Love Song of J. Alfred Prufrock" and the extraordinarily sensitized "Portrait of a Lady," Mr. Eliot fused these qualities in a flexible music, in the shifting nuances of a speech that wavered dexterously between poetic color and casual conversation. In the greater part of *Poems* [1920], however, Mr. Eliot employed a harder and more crackling tone of voice; he delighted in virtuosity for its own sake, in epigrammatic velleities, in an incongruously mordant and disillusioned *vers de société*.

In *The Waste Land*, Mr. Eliot has attempted to combine these two contradictory idioms with a new complexity. The result—although, as I am aware, this conclusion is completely at variance with the judgment of its frenetic admirers—is a pompous parade of erudition, a lengthy extension of the earlier disillusion, a kaleidoscopic movement in which the bright-colored pieces fail to atone for the absence of an integrated design. As an echo of contemporary despair, as a picture of dissolution of the breaking-down of the very structures on which life has modeled itself, *The Waste Land* has a definite authenticity. But an artist, is, by the very nature of creation, pledged to give form to formlessness; even the process of disintegration must be held within a pattern. This pattern is distorted and broken by Mr. Eliot's jumble and narratives, nursery-rhymes, criticism, jazz-rhythms, *Dictionary of Favorite Phrases* and a few lyrical moments. Possibly the disruption of our ideals may be reproduced through such a *mélange*, but it is doubtful whether it is crystallized or even clarified by a series of severed narratives—tales from which the connecting tissue has been carefully cut—and familiar quotations with their necks twisted, all imbedded in that formless plasma which Mr. Ezra Pound likes to call a Sordello-form. Some of the intrusions are more irritating than incomprehensible. The unseen sailor in the first act of *Tristan und Isolde* is dragged in (without point or preparation) to repeat his "*Frisch weht der Wind*"; in the midst of a metaphysical dialogue, we are assured

O O O O that Shakespeherian Rag—
It's so elegant
So intelligent

Falling back on his earlier *métier*, a species of sardonic light verse, Mr. Eliot does not disdain to sink to doggerel that would be refused admission to the cheapest of daily columns:

When lovely woman stoops to folly
    and
Paces about her room again, alone,
She smoothes her hair with automatic
    hand,
And puts a record on the gramophone.

Elsewhere, the juxtaposition of Andrew Marvell, Paul Dreiser and others equally incongruous is more cryptic in intention and even more dismal in effect:

But at my back from time to time I
    hear
The sound of horns and motors,
    which shall bring

Sweeney to Mrs. Porter in the spring.
O the moon shone bright on Mrs.
    Porter
And on her daughter
They wash their feet in soda water
*Et O ces voix d'enfants, chantant dans
    la coupole!*

It is difficult to understand the presence of such cheap tricks in what Mr. Burton Rascoe has publicly informed us is "the finest poem of this generation." The mingling of willful obscurity and weak vaudeville compels us to believe that the pleasure which many admirers derive from *The Waste Land* is the same sort of gratification attained through having solved a puzzle, a form of self-congratulation. The absence of any verbal acrobatics from Mr. Eliot's prose, a prose that represents not the slightest departure from a sort of intensive academicism, makes one suspect that, were it not for the Laforgue mechanism, Mr. Eliot's poetic variations on the theme of a super-refined futility would be increasingly thin and incredibly second rate.

As an analyst of desiccated sensations, as a recorder of the nostalgia of this age, Mr. Eliot has created something whose value is, at least, documentary. Yet, granting even its occasional felicities, *The Waste Land* is a misleading document. The world distrusts the illusions which the last few years have destroyed. One grants this latter-day truism. But it is groping among new ones: the power of the unconscious, an astringent scepticism, a mystical renaissance—these are some of the current illusions to which the Western World is turning for assurance of their, and its, reality. Man may be desperately insecure, but he has not yet lost the greatest of his emotional needs, the need to believe in something—even in his disbelief. For an ideal-demanding race there is always one more God, and Mr. Eliot is not his prophet.

Elinor Wylie.
"Mr. Eliot's Slug Horn."
New York Evening Post Literary Review, 20 January 1923, p. 396.

The reviewer who must essay, within the limits of a few hundred temperate and well-chosen words, to lead even a willing reader into the ensorcelled mazes of Mr. T. S. Eliot's *Waste Land* perceives, as the public prints have it, no easy task before him. [. . .]

Amazing comparisons have been drawn between Mr. Eliot and certain celebrated poets; his admirers do not couple him with Pound nor his detractors with Dante, and both are justified in any annoyance which they may feel when others do so. His detractors say that he is obscure; his friends reply that he is no more cryptic than Donne and Yeats; his detractors shift their ground and point out with perfect truth that he has not the one's incomparable wit nor the other's incomparable magic; his friends, if they are wise, acquiesce. It is stated that he is not so universal a genius as Joyce; the proposition appears self-evident to anyone who believes with the present reviewer, that Joyce is the sea from whose profundity Eliot has fished up that very Tyrian murex with which Mr. Wilson rightly credits him. Some comparisons, indeed, suggest the lunatic asylums where gentlemen imagine themselves to be the authors of Caesar's Commentaries and the *Code Napoléon*.

But when we begin to inquire what Mr. Eliot is, instead of what he is not—then if we fail to respond to his accusing cry of "*Mon semblable,—mon frère!*" I am inclined to think that we are really either hypocrite readers or stubborn ones closing deliberate eyes against beauty and passion still pitifully alive in the midst of horror. I confess that once upon a time I believed Mr. Eliot to be a brutal person: this was when I first read the "Portrait of a Lady." I now recognize my error, but my sense of the hopeless sadness and humiliation of the poor lady was perfectly sound. I felt that Mr. Eliot had torn the shrinking creature's clothes from her back and pulled the drawing-room curtains aside with a click to admit a flood of shameful sunlight, and I hated him for his cruelty. Only now that I know he is Tiresias have I lost my desire to strike him blind as Peeping Tom.

This power of suggesting intolerable tragedy at the heart of the trivial or the sordid is used with a skill little less than miraculous in *The Waste Land*, and the power is the more moving because of the attendant conviction, that this terrible resembling contrast between nobility and baseness is an agony in the mind of Mr. Eliot of which only a portion is transferred to that of the reader. He is a cadaver, dissecting himself in our sight; he is the god . . . who was buried in Stetson's garden and who now arises to give us the benefit of an anatomy lesson. Of course it hurts him more than it does us, and yet it hurts some of us a great deal at that. If this is a trick, it is an inspired one. I do not believe that it is a trick; I think that Mr. Eliot conceived *The Waste Land* out of an extremity of tragic emotion and expressed it in his own voice and in the voices of other unhappy men not carefully and elaborately trained in close harmony, but coming as a confused and frightening and beautiful murmur out of the bowels of the earth. "I did not know death had undone so many." If it were merely a piece of virtuosity it would remain astonishing; it would be a work of art like a fine choir of various singers or a rose window executed in bright fragments of glass. But it is far more than this; it is infused with spirit and passion and despair, and it shoots up into stars of brilliance or flows down dying falls of music which nothing can obscure or silence. These things, rather than other men's outcries, are shored against any ruin which may overtake Mr. Eliot at the hands of Fate or the critics.

As for the frequently reiterated statement that Mr. Eliot is a dry intellectual, without depth or sincerity of feeling, it is difficult for me to refute an idea which I am totally at a loss to understand; to me he seems almost inexcusably sensitive and sympathetic and quite inexcusably poignant, since he forces me to employ this horrid word to describe certain qualities which perhaps deserve a nobler tag in mingling pity with terror. That he expresses the emotion of an intellectual is perfectly true, but of the intensity of that emotion there is, to my mind, no question, nor do I recognize any reason for such a question. A very simple mind expresses emotion by action: a kiss or a murder will not make a song until they have passed through the mind of a poet, and a subtle mind may make a simple song about a murder because the murder was a simple one. But the simplicity of the song will be most apparent to the subtlest minds; it will be like a queer masquerading as a dairy maid. But as for Mr. Eliot, he has discarded all disguises; nothing could be more personal and direct than his method of presenting his weariness and despair by means of a stream of memories and images the like of which, a little dulled and narrowed, runs through the brain of any educated and imaginative man whose thoughts are sharpened by suffering. [. . .] [T]hough Mr. Eliot may speak with the seven tongues of men and of angels, he has not become as sounding brass and tinkling cymbal. His gifts, whatever they are, profit him much; his charity, like Tiresias, has suffered and foresuffered all. If he is intellectually arrogant and detached—and I cannot for the life of me believe that he is—he is not spiritually either the one or the other; I could sooner accuse him of being sentimental. Indeed, in his tortured pity for ugly and ignoble things he sometimes comes near to losing his hardness of outline along with his hardness of heart; his is not a kindly tolerance for weakness and misery, but an obsessed and agonized sense of kinship with it which occasionally leads him into excesses of speech, ejaculations whose flippancy is the expression of profound despair.

Were I unable to feel this passion shaking the dry bones of *The Waste Land* like a great wind, I would not give a penny for all the thoughts and riddles of the poem; the fact that Mr. Eliot has failed to convince many readers that he has a soul must be laid as a black mark against him. Either you see him as a parlor prestidigitator, a character in which I am personally unable to visualize him, or else you see him as a disenchanted wizard, a disinherited prince. When he says *Shantih* three times as he emerges from *The Waste Land* you may not think he means it: my own impulse to write *Amen* at the end of a poem has been too often and too hardly curbed to leave any doubt in my mind as to Mr. Eliot's absorbed seriousness; he is fanatically in earnest. His *Waste Land* is Childe Roland's evil ground, the names of all the lost adventurers his peers toll in his mind increasing like a bell. He has set the slug horn to his lips and blown it once and twice: the squat, round tower, blind as the fool's heart, is watching him, but he will blow the horn again.

Burton Rascoe.
"*The Waste Land* Controversy."
New York Herald Tribune, 21 January 1923, sec. 6, p. 27.

To Edmund Wilson, Jr.'s after the theater, and thence to Elinor Wylie's, where we talked of this and that, and Wilson told me that Louis Untermeyer had an attack on *The Waste Land* in the current *Freeman*, wherein he, too, voiced the notion that a group of us are conspiring to mislead the public. [. . .]

On the way home I got the magazine and read Louis's article. He is plainly on the defensive throughout and he resorts to cheap epithets directed not against Eliot or his poem, but against the people who like it. His opening sentence is a disingenuous distortion of fact to score an irrelevant point: "The *Dial*'s award to Mr. T. S. Eliot and the subsequent book-publication of his *The Waste Land* have occasioned a display of some of the most enthusiastically naïve superlatives that have ever issued from publicity-sophisticated enthusiasts." The implication is that the enthusiasm is consequent to the *Dial*'s award. The facts are these: I read the poem in galley proofs from Boni and Liveright's office and wrote about it in an article for *Shadowland* a week or so before the *Dial* had even tried to get *The Waste Land* for magazine publication. Wilson had read the poem in manuscript and written a magazine article about it before the poem's publication in the *Dial* or in book form. The *Dial*'s award was not decided upon until weeks after we had all had our separate say on the poem's merit. And what is more, none of us had

ever talked with the other about the poem until after we had had our say about it. Wilson called me up one night and said he had just been reading "Eliot's new long narrative poem; you want to get hold of it. It's a very extraordinary piece of work." That is all. And if Louis will recall, after the poem's publication in the *Dial*, I called him up one night under a similar impulse only to find that Louis had read the poem and did not like it.

If Louis had judged the poem on aesthetic grounds and had found it wanting, his critique might have been salutary. He makes but one point that is not irrelevant—"the absence of an integrated design"—a point which all of us have made with reference to Eliot's too frequent use of ellipsis and disdain for "wadding," or, as Louis says, "connecting tissue." "Man," Louis winds up grandly, "may be desperately insecure, but he has not yet lost the greatest of his emotional needs, the need to believe in something—even in his disbelief." That is a noble thought, Louis, but what in the world has it to with Eliot's poem?

*Harold Monro.
"Notes for a Study of *The Waste Land*: An Imaginary Dialogue with T. S. Eliot."
Chapbook 34 (February 1923), 20–24.

[Part 1 consists of an imaginary dialogue with Eliot]

2.

Most poems of any significance leave one definite impression on the mind. This poem makes a variety of impressions, many of them so contradictory that a large majority of minds will never be able to reconcile them, or conceive of it as an entity. Those minds will not go beyond wondering why it so often breaks itself up violently, changes its tone and apparently its subject. It will remain for them a *potpourri* of descriptions and episodes, and while deprecating the lack of *style*, those people will console themselves with soft laughter. That influential London Editor–critic who dismissed it as "an obscure but amusing poem" is an instance.

Obscure it is, and amusing it can be too; but neither quite in the way he seems to have meant. They who have only one definition for the word poem may gnash their teeth, or smile. One definition will not be applicable to *The Waste Land*. Of course, most poets write of *dreaming*, [. . .] but this poem actually is a dream presented without any poetic boast, bluff, or padding; and it lingers in the mind more like a dream than a poem, which is one of the reasons why it is both obscure and amusing. It is not possible to see it whole except in the manner that one may watch a cloud which, though remaining the same cloud, changes its form repeatedly as one looks. Or to others it may appear like a drawing that is so crowded with apparently unrelated details that the design or meaning (if there be one) cannot be grasped until those details have been absorbed into the mind, and assembled and related to each other.

3.

A friend came to me with the discovery that he and I could not hope to understand Mr. Eliot's poems; we had not the necessary culture: impossible for us to recognize the allusions. I asked him whether the culture could be grown in a bottle or under a frame, or in the open. Mr. Edmund Wilson, Jr. tells us, on the other hand, that "it is not necessary to know . . . any but the most obvious of Mr. Eliot's allusions to feel the force of the intense emotion which the poem is intended to convey." I was inclined to side with Mr. Wilson, so we confined ourselves to discussing the permissibility of introducing, as Mr. Eliot does, into the body of a poem, wholly or partly, or in a distorted form, quotations of other poems. "In the absence of inverted commas," said my friend, "the ignorant, when they are French quotations (seeing that Mr. Eliot has written several French poems) or German even, might mistake them for lines belonging to the poem itself. It is simple cribbing. The distortions are more serious still. For instance:

> When lovely woman stoops to folly
>   and
> Paces about her room again, alone,
> She smoothes her hair with automatic
>   hand,
> And puts a record on the gramophone.

is an outrage, and a joke worthier of *Punch*, than of a serious poet. Also I much prefer the Bible, Spenser, Shakespeare, Marvell, and Byron to Eliot. Marvell wrote: 'But at my back I always hear / Time's wingèd chariot hurrying near.' Eliot writes: 'But at my back in a cold blast I hear / The rattle of the bones, and chuckle spread from ear to ear.' Well, that is simply a meretricious travesty of one of the most beautiful couplets in English poetry. It is wicked."

I answered: "[. . .] What we have to find out is whether T. S. Eliot is a sufficiently constructive or imaginative, or ingenious poet to justify this freedom that he exercises."

He answered: "Yes, but . . . 'But at my back I always hear / Eliot's intellectual sneer.' Now I'm doing it myself."

4.

This poem is at the same time a representation, a criticism, and the disgusted outcry of a heart turned cynical. It is calm, fierce, and horrible: the poetry of despair itself become desperate. [. . .] Our epoch sprawls, a desert, between an unrealized past and an unimaginable future. *The Waste Land* is one metaphor with a multiplicity of interpretations.

5.

[Quotation of lines 1–7 of *The Waste Land*]

Conrad Aiken. "An Anatomy of Melancholy." *New Republic* 33 (7 February 1923), 294–95.

Mr. T. S. Eliot is one of the most individual of contemporary poets, and at the same time, anomalously, one the most "traditional." By individual I mean that he can be, and often is (distressingly, to some) aware in his own way; as when he observes of a woman (in "Rhapsody on a Windy Night") that the door "opens on her like a grin" and that the corner of her eye "Twists like a crooked pin." Everywhere, in the very small body of his work, is similar evidence of a delicate sensibility, somewhat shrinking, somewhat injured, and almost always sharply itself. But also, with this capacity or necessity for being aware in his own way, Mr. Eliot has a haunting, a tyrannous awareness that there have been many other awarenesses before; and that the extent of his own awareness, and perhaps even the nature of it, is a consequence of these. He is, more than most poets, conscious of his roots. If this consciousness had not become acute in "Prufrock" or "Portrait of a Lady," it was nevertheless probably there: and the roots were quite conspicuously French, and dated, say, 1870–1900. A little later, as if his sense of the past had become more pressing, it seemed that he was positively redirecting his roots—urging them to draw a morbid dramatic sharpness from Webster and Donne, a faded dry gilt of cynicism and formality from the Restoration. This search of the tomb produced "Sweeney" and "Whispers of Immortality." And finally, in *The Waste Land*, Mr. Eliot's sense of the literary past has become so overmastering as almost to constitute the motive of the work. It is as if, in conjunction with Mr. Pound of the *Cantos*, he wanted to make a "literature of literature"—a poetry not more actuated by life itself than by poetry; as if he had concluded that the characteristic awareness of a poet of the 20th century must inevitably, or ideally, be a very complex and very literary awareness able to speak only, or best, in terms of the literary past, the terms which had molded its tongue. This involves a kind of idolatry of literature with which it is a little difficult to sympathize. In positing, as it seems to, that there is nothing left for literature to do but become a kind of parasitic growth on literature, a sort of mistletoe, it involves, I think, a definite astigmatism—a distortion. But the theory is interesting if only because it has colored an important and brilliant piece of work.

The Waste Land is unquestionably important, unquestionably brilliant. It is important partly because its 433 lines summarize Mr. Eliot, for the moment, and demonstrate that he is an even better poet than most had thought; and partly because it embodies the theory just touched upon, the theory of the "allusive" method in poetry. *The Waste Land* is, indeed, a poem of allusion all compact. It purports to be symbolical; most of its symbols are drawn from literature or legend; and Mr. Eliot has thought it necessary to supply, in "Notes," a list of the many quotations, references, and translations with which it bristles. He observes candidly that the poem presents "difficulties," and requires "elucidation." This serves to raise at once, the question whether these difficulties, in which perhaps Mr. Eliot takes a little pride, are not so much the result of complexity, a fine elaborateness, as of confusion. The poem has been compared, by one reviewer, to a "full-rigged ship built in a bottle," the suggestion being that it is a perfect piece of construction. But *is* it a perfect piece of construction? Is the complex material mastered, and made coherent? Or, if the poem is not successful in that way, in what way is it successful? Has it the formal and intellectual complex unity of a microscopic *Divine Comedy*; or is its unity—supposing it to have one—of another sort?

If we leave aside for the moment all other considerations, and read the poem solely with the intention of understanding, with the aid of the "Notes," the symbolism, of making out what it is that is symbolized, and how these symbolized feelings are brought into relation with each other and with the other matters in the poem; I think we must, with reservations, and with no invidiousness, conclude that the poem is not, in any formal sense, coherent. We cannot feel that all the symbolisms belong quite inevitably where they have been put; that the order of the parts is an inevitable order; that there is anything more than a rudimentary progress from one theme to another; nor that the relation between the more symbolic parts and the less is always as definite as it should be. What we feel is that Mr. Eliot has not wholly annealed the allusive matter, has left it unabsorbed, lodged in gleaming fragments amid material alien to it. Again, there is a distinct weakness consequent on the use of allusion which may have both intellectual and emotional value for Mr. Eliot, but (even with the "Notes") none for us. The "Waste Land" of the Grail legend, might be a good symbol, if it were something with which we were sufficiently familiar. But it can never, even when explained, be a good symbol, simply because it has no immediate associations for us. It might, of course, be a good *theme*. In that case it would be *given* us. But Mr. Eliot uses it for purposes of overtone; he refers to it; and as overtone it quite clearly fails. He gives us, superbly, a waste land—not *the* Waste Land. Why, then, refer to the latter at all—if he is not, in the poem, really going to use it? Hyacinth fails in the same way. So does the Fisher King. So does the Hanged Man, which Mr. Eliot tells us he associates with Frazer's Hanged God—we take his word for it. But if the precise association is worth anything, it is worth *putting into the poem*; otherwise there can be no purpose in mentioning it. Why, again, "*Datta, Dayadhvam, Damyata*"? Or "*Shantih.*" Do they not say a good deal less for us than "Give: sympathize: control" or "Peace"? Of course; but Mr. Eliot replies that he wants them not merely to mean those particular things, but also to mean them in a particular way—that is, to be remembered in connection with an *Upanishad*. Unfortunately, we have none of us this memory, nor can he give it to us; and in the upshot he gives us only a series of agreeable sounds which might as well have been nonsense. What we get at, and I think it is important, is that in none of these particular cases does the reference, the allusion, justify itself intrinsically, make itself felt.

When we are aware of these references at all (sometimes they are unidentifiable) we are aware of them simply as something unintelligible but suggestive. When they have been explained, we are aware of the material referred to, the fact, (for instance, a vegetation ceremony) as something useless for our enjoyment or understanding of the poem, something distinctly "dragged in," and only, perhaps, of interest as having suggested a pleasantly ambiguous line. For unless an allusion is made to live identifiably, to flower, where transplanted, it is otiose. We admit the beauty of the implicational or allusive method; but the key to an implication should be in the implication itself, not outside of it. We admit the value of esoteric pattern: but the pattern should itself disclose its secret, should not be dependent on a cipher. Mr. Eliot assumes for his allusions, and for the fact that they actually allude to something, an importance which the allusions themselves do not, as expressed, aesthetically command, nor, as explained, logically command; which is pretentious. He is a little pretentious, too, in his "plan,"—"*qui pourtant n'existe pas.*" If it is a plan, then its principle is oddly akin to planlessness. Here and there, in the wilderness, a broken finger-post.

I enumerate these objections not, I must emphasize, in a derogation of the poem, but to dispel, if possible, an illusion as to its nature. It is perhaps important to note that Mr. Eliot, with his comment on the "plan," and several critics, with their admiration of the poem's woven complexity, minister to the idea that *The Waste Land* is, precisely, a kind of epic in a walnut shell: elaborate, ordered, unfolded with a logic at every joint discernible; but it is also important to note that this idea is false. With or without the notes the poem belongs rather to that symbolical order in which one may justly say that the "meaning" is not explicitly, or exactly, worked out. Mr. Eliot's net is wide, its meshes are small; and he catches a good deal more—thank heaven—than he pretends to. If space permitted one could pick out many lines and passages and parodies and quotations which do not demonstrably, in any "logical" sense, carry forward the theme, passages which unjustifiably, but happily, "expand" beyond its purpose. Thus the poem has an emotional value far clearer and richer than its arbitrary and rather unworkable logical value. One might assume that it originally consisted of a number of separate poems which have been telescoped—given a kind of forced unity. The Waste Land conception offered itself as a generous net which would, if not unify, at any rate contain these varied elements. We are aware of a superficial "binding"—we observe the anticipation and repetition of themes, motifs; "Fear death by water" anticipates the episode of Phlebas, the cry of the nightingale is repeated, but these are pretty flimsy links, and do not genuinely bind because they do not reappear naturally, but arbitrarily. This suggests, indeed, that Mr. Eliot is perhaps attempting a kind of program music in words, endeavoring to rule out "emotional accidents" by supplying his readers, in notes, with only those associations which are correct. He himself hints at the musical analogy when he observes that "In the first part of Part V three themes are employed."

I think, therefore, that the poem must be taken,—most invitingly offers itself,— as a brilliant and kaleidoscopic confusion; as a series of sharp, discrete, slightly related perceptions and feelings, dramatically and lyrically presented, and violently juxtaposed (for effect of dissonance) so as to give us an impression of an intensely modern, intensely literary consciousness which perceives itself to be not a unit by a chance correlation or conglomerate of mutually discolorative fragments. We are invited into a mind, a world, which is a "broken bundle of mirrors"; a "heap of broken images." Isn't it that Mr. Eliot, finding it "impossible to say just what he means,"—to recapitulate, to enumerate all the events and discoveries and memories that make a consciousness,—has emulated the "magic lantern" that throws "the nerves in patterns on a screen"? If we perceive the poem in this light, as a series of brilliant, brief, unrelated or dimly related pictures by which a consciousness empties itself of its characteristic contents, then we also perceive that, anomalously, though the dropping out of any one picture would not in the least affect the logic or "meaning" of the whole, it would seriously detract from the value of the portrait. The "plan" of the poem would not greatly suffer, one makes bold to assert, by the elimination of "April is the cruellest month," or Phlebas, or the Thames daughters, or Sosostris or "You gave me hyacinths" or "A woman drew her long black hair out tight"; nor would it matter if it did. These things are not important parts of an important or careful intellectual pattern; but they are important parts of an important emotional ensemble. The relations between Tiresias (who is said to unify the poem, in a sense, as spectator) and the Waste Land, or Mr. Eugenides, or Hyacinth, or any other fragment, is a dim and tonal one, not exact. It will not bear analysis, it is not always operating, nor can one with assurance, at any given point, say how much it is operating. In this sense *The Waste Land* is a series of separate poems or passages, not perhaps all written at one time or with one aim, to which a spurious but happy sequence has been given. This spurious sequence has a value—it creates the necessary superficial formal unity; but it

need not be stressed, as the "Notes" stress it. Could one not wholly rely for one's unity,—as Mr. Eliot *has* largely relied—simply on the dim unity of "personality" which would underlie the retailed contents of a single consciousness? Unless one is going to carry unification very far, weave and interweave very closely, it would perhaps be as well not to unify at all; to dispense, for example, with arbitrary repetitions.

We reach thus the conclusion that the poem succeeds—as it brilliantly does—by virtue of its incoherence, not of its plan; by virtue of its ambiguities, not of its explanations. Its incoherence is a virtue because its "donnée" is incoherence. Its rich, vivid, crowded use of implication is a virtue, as implication is *always* a virtue;—it shimmers, it suggests, it gives the desired strangeness. But when, as often, Mr. Eliot uses an implication beautifully—conveys by means of a picture-symbol or action-symbol a feeling—we do not require to be told that he had in mind a passage in the Encyclopedia, or the color of his nursery wall; the information is disquieting, has a sour air of pedantry. We "accept" the poem as we would accept a powerful, melancholy tone-poem. We do not want to be told what occurs; nor is it more than mildly amusing to know what passages are, in the Straussian manner, echoes or parodies. We cannot believe that every syllable has an algebraic inevitability, nor would we wish it so. We could dispense with the French, Italian, Latin and Hindu phrases—they are irritating. But when our reservations have all been made, we accept *The Waste Land* as one of the most moving and original poems of our time. It captures us. And we sigh, with a dubious eye on the "notes" and "plan," our bewilderment that after so fine a performance Mr. Eliot should have thought it an occasion for calling "Tullias's ape a marmosyte." Tullias's ape is good enough.

Harriet Monroe. "A Contrast." *Poetry: A Magazine of Verse* 21 (March 1923), 325–30.

[Review of *The Waste Land* and Lew Sarett's *The Box of God*, also published in 1922]

[. . .]

In the important title-poems of the two [poets] we have an adequate modern presentation of the two immemorial human types. One might call these types briefly the indoor and the outdoor man, but that would be incomplete; they are also the man who affirms and the man who denies; the simple-hearted and the sophisticated man; the doer, the believer, and the observant and intellectual questioner. These two types have faced each other since time began and they will accuse each other till quarrels are no more. Both, in their highest development, are dreamers, men commanded by imagination; seers who are aware of their age, who know their world. Yet always they are led by separating paths to opposite instincts and conclusions.

Mr. Eliot's poem—kaleidoscopic, profuse, a rattle and rain of colors that fall somehow into place—gives us the malaise of our time, its agony, its conviction of futility, its wild dance on an ash-heap before a clouded and distorted mirror. "I will show you fear in a handful of dust," he cries, and he shows us confusion and dismay and disintegration, the world crumbling to pieces before our eyes and patching itself with desperate gaiety into new and strangely irregular forms. He gives us, with consummate distinction, what many an indoor thinker thinks about life today, what whole groups of impassioned intellectuals are saying to each other as the great ball spins.

Yet all the time there are large areas of mankind to whom this thinking does not apply; large groups of another kind of intellectual whose faith is as vital and constructive as ever was the faith of their crusading forefathers. To the men of science, the inventors, the engineers, who are performing today's miracles, the miasma which afflicts Mr. Eliot is as remote a speculative conceit, as futile a fritter of mental confectionery, as Lyly's euphemism must have been to Elizabethan sailors. And these men are thinkers too, dreamers of larger dreams than any groups of city-closeted artists may evoke out of the circling pipe-smoke of their scented talk. These men are creating that modern world which the half-aware and over-informed poets of London and Montmartre so darkly doom.

[. . .]

We live in a period of swift and tremendous change: if Mr. Eliot feels it as chaos and disintegration, and a kind of wild impudent dance-of-death joy, Mr. Sarett feels it as a new and larger summons to faith in life and art. [. . .]

But I would not be understood as belittling the importance of Mr. Eliot's glistening, swiftly flowing poem of human and personal agony because it does not say the whole thing about the age we live in. Mr. Eliot would be the first to disclaim such an intention—he would probably say that *The Waste Land* is the reaction of a suffering valetudinarian to the present after-the-war chaos in Europe, with its tumbling-down of old customs and sanctities. It is a condition, not a theory, which confronts him; and he meets the condition with an artist's invocation of beauty. One would expect a certain deliberateness in Mr. Eliot's art, but this poem surprises with an effect of unstudied spontaneity. While stating nothing, it suggests everything that is in his rapidly moving mind, in a series of shifting scenes which fade in and out of each other like the cinema. The form, with its play of many-colored lights on words that flash from everywhere in the poet's dream, is a perfect expression of the shifting tortures in his soul. If one calls *The Waste Land* a masterpiece of decadent art, the words must be taken as praise, for decadent art, while always incomplete, only half-interpretive, is pitifully beautiful and tragically sincere. The agony and bitter splendor of modern life are in this poem, or that part of it which dies of despair while the world is building its next age.

[. . .]

J. F.
"*Shantih, Shantih, Shantih*: Has the Reader Any Rights Before the Bar of Literature?"
Time 1 (3 March 1923), 12.

There is a new kind of literature abroad in the land, whose only obvious fault is that no one can understand it. Last year there appeared a gigantic volume entitled *Ulysses*, by James Joyce. To the uninitiated it appeared that Mr. Joyce had taken some half million assorted words—many such as are not ordinarily heard in reputable circles—shaken them up in a colossal hat, laid them end to end. To those in on the secret the result represented the greatest achievement of modern letters—a new idea in novels.

The *Dial* has awarded its $2,000 prize for the best poem of 1922 to an opus entitled *The Waste Land*, by T. S. Eliot. Burton Rascoe, of *The New York Tribune*, hails it as incomparably great. Edmund Wilson, Jr., of *Vanity Fair*, is no less enthusiastic in praise of it. So is J. Middleton Murry, British critic.

Here are the last eight lines of *The Waste Land*:

London Bridge is falling down falling
  down falling down
Poi s'ascose nel foco che gli affina
Quando fiam uti chelidon—O
  swallow swallow
Le Prince d'Aquitaine à la tour abolie
These fragments I have shored against
  my ruins
Why then Ile fit you. Hieronymo's
  mad againe.
Datta. Dayadhvam. Damyata.
                Shantih shantih shantih

The case for the defense, as presented by the admirers of Messrs. Eliot, Joyce, et al., runs something like this:

Literature is self-expression. It is up to the reader to extract the meaning, not up to the writer to offer it. If the author writes everything that pops into his head—or that is supposed to pop into the head of a given character—that is all that should be asked. Lucidity is no part of the auctorial task.

It is rumored that *The Waste Land* was written as a hoax. Several of its supporters explain that that is immaterial, literature

J. M.
Double Dealer 5 (May 1923), 173–74.

being concerned not with intentions but results.

[. . .]

The Waste Land is, it seems to me, the agonized outcry of a sensitive romanticist drowning in a sea of jazz. When Mr. Burton Rascoe calls it "perhaps the finest poem of this generation," one is compelled to challenge the verdict because comparisons in the arts are unjust in the first place and *The Waste Land* is not as a whole superb. But one would be very foolish indeed who would deny that it contains magnificent elements and supremely beautiful lines.

This medley of catch-phrases, allusions, innuendoes, paraphrase and quotation gives unmistakable evidence of rare poetic genius. One is certain that, read by Mr. Eliot, to whom every allusion is clear, for whom every catchword has a ghostly portent, for whom every quotation has an emotional and intellectual connotation of intense significance, *The Waste Land* is a great poem. To us who cannot read with Mr. Eliot's spectacles, colored as they are by Mr. Eliot's experience, it must remain a hodgepodge of grandeur and jargon. It cannot, from the standpoint of the average reader or of the average writer of verse, be appraised as a complete success.

Mr. Eliot, an immortal by instinct, finds himself submerged—a "drowned Phoenician Sailor"—in the garish and to him not charming swirl of animalistic, illiterate human life, now seething on both sides of the Atlantic. Caught in this maelstrom, he catches glimpses of the world of drama and romance and stable beauty which he would prefer and which, no question, he has found in books. From that ideal world come floating ghostly cadences, images and reminders. To these straws he clings, as a sort of salvation.

> O swallow swallow
> *Le Prince d'Aquitaine à la tour abolie*
> These fragments I have shored against
>   my ruins

The fragments from the other world which Mr. Eliot clings to in *The Waste Land*, like the fragments which he quotes in *The Sacred Wood*, are of the very heart of poetry: "Those are pearls that were his eyes" echoes throughout.

Taking the poem as a whole, the average reader will object that many passages, as pure art, are not satisfactory. I venture to repeat that Mr. Eliot's own intellectual or emotional associations give to some of the language used in *The Waste Land* a significance which it does not and cannot have for another individual. The discords, in Mr. Eliot's opinion and in that of certain readers, no doubt, have their place in the pattern, adding a beauty of contrast, heightening the effect of the harmonies. To me the discords seem unsatisfactory discords. *The Waste Land* is a poem containing passages of extreme beauty, but I believe there are few persons who can read it all with sustained delight.

[Quotations of passages from "The Burial of the Dead," "A Game of Chess," and "Death by Water"]

Many of us have contended for a long time that T. S. Eliot is one of the most exceptional men of letters of his epoch. *The Waste Land* confirms that belief. How much of it or of his previous work is

105

indelible I would not venture to estimate. That that work reveals a genius and a personality extremely rare, I am certain. And that Mr. Eliot, as poet or as critic or as scholar, eminently deserved such an award as the *Dial* prize, seems to be incontrovertible.

John Crowe Ransom. "Waste Lands." *New York Evening Post Literary Review* 3 (14 July 1923), 825–26.

[. . .]

The field of literature in our day—perhaps beyond all other days—is an unweeded garden, in which the flowers and weeds are allowed to grow side by side because the gardeners, who are the critics, do not know their botany. The commonest and fatalest error in the riot of our letters is the fundamental failure of the creative imagination, and it ought always to be exposed.

[. . .]

[C]riticism should be prepared to make an example of bad artists for the sake of the good artists and the future of art.

But what a congenial exercise is furnished the critic by that strange poem, *The Waste Land*. In the first place, everybody agrees beforehand that its author is possessed of uncommon literary powers, and it is certain that, whatever credit the critic may try to take from him, a flattering residue will remain. And then his poem won a spectacular triumph over a certain public and is entitled to an extra quantity of review. Best of all, Mr. Eliot's performance is the apotheosis of modernity, and seems to bring to a head all the specifically modern errors, and to cry for critic's ink of a volume quite disproportionate to its merits as a poem.

The most notable surface fact about *The Waste Land* is of course its extreme disconnection. I do not know just how many parts the poem is supposed to have, but to me there are something like fifty parts which offer no bridges the one to the other and which are quite distinct in time, place, action, persons, tone, and nearly all the unities to which art is accustomed. This discreteness reaches also to the inside of the parts, where it is indicated by a frequent want of grammatical joints and marks of punctuation; as if it were the function of art to break down the usual singleness of the artistic image, and then to attack the integrity of the individual fragments. I presume that poetry has already gone further in this direction. It is a species of the same error which modern writers of fiction practice when they laboriously disconnect the stream of consciousness and present items which do not enter into wholes. Evidently they think with Hume that reality is facts and pluralism, not compounds and systems. But Mr. Eliot is more enterprising than they, because almost in so many words he assails the philosophical or cosmical principles under which we form the usual images of reality, naming the whole phantasmagoria "Waste Land" almost as plainly as if he were naming cosmos "Chaos." His intention is evidently to present a wilderness in which both he and the reader may be bewildered, in which one is never to see the wood for the trees.

Against this philosophy—or negation of philosophy—the critic must stand fast. It is good for some purposes, but not for art. The mind of the artist is an integer, and the imaginative vision is a single act which fuses its elements. It is to be suspected that the author who holds his elements apart is not using his imagination, but using a formula, like a scientist anxious to make out a "case"; at any rate, for art such a procedure suggests far too much strain and tension. For the imagination things cohere; pluralism cannot exist when we relax our obsessions and allow such testimony as is in us to come out. Even the most refractory elements in experience, like the powerful opposing wills in a tragedy, arrive automatically at their "higher synthesis" if the imagination is allowed to treat them.

There is a reason besides philosophical bias which makes the disconnection in the poem. The fragments could not be joined on any principle and remain what they are. And that is because they are at different stages of fertilization; they are not the children of a single act of birth. Among their disparities one notes that scraps from many tongues are juxtaposed; and yet one knows well that we are in different "ages of intelligence" when we take the different languages on our lips; we do not quote Greek tragedy and modern cockney with the same breath or with the same kinds of mind. We cannot pass, in *The Waste Land*, without a convulsion of the mind from "O O O O that Shakespeherian Rag," to "Shantih shantih shantih." And likewise, the fragments are in many meters, from the comparatively formal meter which we know as the medium of romantic experiences in the English thesaurus to an extremely free verse which we know as the medium of a half-hearted and disillusioned art. But, above all, some fragments are emotions recollected in tranquility and others are emotions kept raw and bleeding, like sores we continue to pick. In other words, the fragments vary through almost every stage, from pure realism to some point just short of complete fertilization by the romantic imagination, and this is a material which is incapable of synthesis.

A consequence of this inequality of material is a certain novelty of Mr. Eliot's which is not fundamentally different from parody. To parody is to borrow a phrase whose meaning lies on one plane of intelligence and to insert it into the context of a lower plane; an attempt to compound two incommensurable imaginative creations. Mr. Eliot inserts beautiful quotations into ugly contexts. For example:

When lovely woman stoops to folly
    and
Paces about her room again, alone,
She smoothes her hair with automatic
    hand,
And puts a record on the gramophone.

A considerable affront against aesthetic sensibilities. Using these lovely borrowed lines for his own peculiar purposes, Mr. Eliot debases them every time; there is not, I believe, a single occasion when his context is as mature as the quotation which he inserts into it; he does not invent such phrases for himself, nor, evidently, does his understanding quite appreciate them, for they require an organization of experience which is yet beyond him.

[. . .]

But it may be put to the credit of Mr. Eliot that he is a man of better parts generally than most of the new poets, as in the fact that he certainly bears no animus against the old poetry except as it is taken as a model by the new poets; he is sufficiently sensitive to its beauties at least to have held on with his memory to some of its ripest texts and to have introduced them rather wistfully into the forbidding context in his own poems, where they are thoroughly ill at ease.

The criticism does not complete itself till it has compared *The Waste Land* with the earlier work of its author . . . *Poems*, which appeared a year previously, hardly presaged the disordered work that was to follow. The discrepancy is astonishing. Sweeney and Prufrock, those heroes who bid so gaily for immortality in their own right, seem to come out of a fairly mature and at any rate an equal art. They are elegant and precious creations rather than substantial, with a very reduced emotional background, like the art of a man of the world rather than of a man of frankly poetic susceptibilities . . . I presume that *The Waste Land* with its burden of unregenerate fury, was disheartening to such critics as Mr. Aldington, who had found in the *Poems* the voice of a completely articulate soul; I presume that for these critics the *Poems* [1920] are automatically voided and recalled by the later testament; they were diabolically specious, and the true heart of the author was to be revealed by a very different gesture. But I prefer to think that they were merely precocious. They pretended to an intellectual synthesis of which the author was only intellectually aware, but which proved quite too fragile to contain the ferment of experience. One prefers *The Waste Land* after all, for of the two kinds it bears the better witness to its own sincerity.

The Waste Land is one of the most insubordinate poems in the language, and perhaps it is the most unequal. But I do not mean in saying this to indicate that it is permanently a part of the language; I do not entertain it as a probability. The genius of our language is notoriously given to feats of hospitality: but it seems to me it will be hard pressed to find accommodations at the same time for two such incompatibles as Mr. Wordsworth and the present Mr. Eliot; and any realist must admit that what happens to be the prior tenure of the mansion in this case is likely to be stubbornly defended.

Helen McAfee. "The Literature of Disillusion." *Atlantic* 132 (August 1923), 227.

Under pressure of war emotion, we did undoubtedly idealize one another (at least, all those on one side), and we sometimes forgot to judge men's motives on the basis of our accumulated knowledge of human nature. The rebound to self-criticism and cynicism had to come. But another element has entered in during these last five years. "Happy is he who suffers and knows why," says one of Claudel's dying heroines. With the spectacle of the peace before them, and its aftermath in Europe, some men no longer see why they suffered.

Certainly the most striking dramatization of this depth of confusion and bitterness is Mr. Eliot's *The Waste Land*. As if by flashes of lightning it reveals the wreck of the storm. For this effect it is clear that the author has consciously striven—indeed he refers to his work as "my ruins." The poem is written in what is called the Expressionist manner—a manner peculiarly adapted to the present temper. It does not present the social order in a series of concentric circles, as in Dante, with the individual passing from one to the other in mathematical succession; or as a wall against which the individual dashes himself, usually in vain, as in Tolstoy or Ibsen. It rather presents his mind, or his mood, as the center around which the world gyrates wildly, and with which it makes few contacts, and those chiefly enigmatic. To students of psychology, the method of procedure in *The Waste Land* must be highly significant. Impressions, fragments of experience, memories of other men's writings, drift through the author's consciousness at the bidding of the subconscious. There is little attempt at completion of any one pattern out of the mass of details and allusions, or at logical climax. But the parts move with a certain rhythm—the rhythm of daydreams—and, dream-fashion, resolve one into another and so achieve a whole. It is mood more than idea that gives the poem its unity. And that mood is black. It is as bitter as gall; not only with a personal bitterness, but also with the bitterness of a man facing a world devastated by war for a peace without ideals. The humor—for it has humor—is sordid, grotesque. Yet even in the barren ugliness of *The Waste Land* there is redeeming grace. After quoting a bit from that most delightful of all spring poems, the "*Pervigilium Veneris*," and two other lines equally fine, Mr. Eliot seems content to rest his case—"These fragments," he writes, "I have shored against my ruins."

Allen Tate.
"Waste Lands."
New York Evening Post Literary Review 3 (4 August 1923), 886.

John Crowe Ransom's article, "Waste Lands," in the [*New York Evening Post*] *Literary Review* of July 14 [see this volume, pp. 106–08], [. . .] does such scant justice to the school of so-called philosophic criticism, to which one supposes he belongs, that it may be of interest to your readers to consider [. . .] a few of the errors into which it leads him.

[. . .] Mr. Ransom rightly says that the critic "should be prepared to make an example of bad artists for the sake of the good artists"; but this example cannot be made by exorcizing pluralism to the advantage of a gentler but equally irrelevant ghost: "For the imagination things cohere; pluralism cannot exist when we relax our obsessions and allow such testimony as is in us to come out." In other words, no honest man can be a pluralist—which is not only palpably untenable but quite outside the course of his argument.

[. . .]

The real trouble with Mr. Ransom's article comes out when he proceeds to comment on specific aspects of *The Waste Land*. Mr. Eliot is a pluralist; he has not "achieved" a philosophy; *ergo*, he is immature, and his poem is inconsiderable. I take it that Anatole France is immature. But Mr. Ransom's worry on this point really is his inability to discover the form of the poem, for, says he, it presents meters so varied and such lack of grammar and punctuation and such bewildering array of discrete themes, that he is at a loss to see the poem as one poem at all. Whatever form may be, it is not, I dare say, regularity of meter. Artistic forms are ultimately attitudes, and when Mr. Ransom fails to understand Mr. Eliot's purpose in using lines from other poets, like "When lovely woman stoops to folly," calling it parody, we are aware of a *naïveté* somewhat grosser than that which he ascribes elsewhere in his essay to modern experimentation generally. He makes his point by a highly imaginative *petitio principii*: the fragments are at different stages of "fertilization" and represent different levels of intelligence; and then, too, Eliot inserts these quotations into a context

109

never so rich as their proper abode. Is it possible that Mr. Ransom thinks that these beautiful fragments were put into *The Waste Land* simply to lend it a "beauty" which its author could not achieve for himself? And is he confusing parody with irony? His definition of parody, without the dogmatic implication that one plane of consciousness is "higher" than another, is really a definition of irony: the incongruous is not always the deformed or ludicrous. And it is probably true that meters are never more than an organic scaffolding upon which the poet hangs an attitude; the "form" of *The Waste Land* is this ironic attitude which Mr. Ransom relegates to the circus of Carolyn Wells. My remarks here are excessive; at this point in Mr. Ransom's argument we suspect that he should not be taken seriously.

It is to be regretted also that T. S. Eliot repudiates his first volume *ipso facto* by writing *The Waste Land*. The only discoverable difference between *Poems* and *The Waste Land* is certainly not one of central attitude. Mr. Eliot, an intellectual romanticist, need not commit himself to the same intuition of the world today as yesterday; he must shift all the time, for his motive is curiosity, not prepossession, even though he is driven always by the same thirst. The free intelligence cannot harbor a closed system.

And if tradition means sameness, then Mr. Eliot cannot survive with Wordsworth. But Mr. Ransom doesn't say just where it is that poems survive. However, it is likely that the value of *The Waste Land* as art is historical rather than intrinsic, but the point of my objection to John Crowe Ransom's essay is that the method he employs is not likely to give T. S. Eliot much concern. And my excuse for this extended objection is that Mr. Ransom is not alone. He is a *genre*.

[Edgell Rickword]. "A Fragmentary Poem." Times Literary Supplement 1131 (20 September 1923), 616.

Between the emotion from which a poem rises and the reader, there is always a cultural layer of more or less density from which the images or characters in which it is expressed may be drawn. In the ballad "I wish I were where Helen lies" this middle ground is but faintly indicated. The ballad, we say, is *simpler* than the "Ode to the Nightingale"; it evokes very directly an emotional response. In the ode the emotion gains resonance from the atmosphere of legendary association through which it passes before reaching us. It cannot be called better art, but it is certainly more sophisticated and to some minds less poignant. From time to time there appear poets and a poetic audience to whom this refractory haze of allusion must be very dense; without it the meanings of the words strike them so rapidly as to be inappreciable, just as, without the air, we could not detect the vibration of light. We may remember with what elaboration Addison, among others, was obliged to undertake the defense of the old ballads before it was recognized that their bare style might be admired by gentlemen familiar with the classics.

The poetic personality of Mr. Eliot is extremely sophisticated. His emotions hardly ever reach us without traversing a zig-zag of allusion. In the course of his four hundred lines, he quotes from a score of authors and in three foreign languages, though his artistry has reached that point at which it knows the wisdom of sometimes concealing itself. There is in general in his work a disinclination to awake in us a direct emotional response. It is only, the reader feels, out of regard for someone else that he has been induced to mount the platform at all. From there he conducts a magic-lantern show; but being too reserved to expose in public the impressions stamped on his own soul by the journey through the Waste Land, he employs the slides made by others, indicating with a touch the difference between his reaction and theirs. So the familiar stanza of Goldsmith becomes

> When lovely woman stoops to folly
> and
> Paces about her room again, alone,
> She smoothes her hair with automatic
> hand,
> And puts a record on the gramophone.

To help us to elucidate the poem Mr. Eliot has provided some notes which will be of more interest to the pedantic than the poetic critic. Certainly they warn us to be prepared to recognize some references to vegetation ceremonies. This is the cultural or middle layer, which, whilst it helps us to perceive the underlying emotion, is of no poetic value in itself. We desire to touch the inspiration itself, and if the apparatus of reserve is too strongly constructed, it will defeat the poet's end. The theme is announced frankly enough in the title, *The Waste Land*; and in the concluding confession, "These fragments I have shored against my ruins," we receive a direct communication which throws light on much which had preceded it. From the opening part, "The Burial of the Dead," to the final one we seem to see a world, or a mind, in disaster and mocking its despair. We are aware of the toppling of aspirations, the swift disintegration of accepted stability, the crash of an ideal. Set at a distance by a poetic method which is reticence itself, we can only judge of the strength of the emotion by the visible violence of the reaction.

Here is Mr. Eliot, a dandy of the choicest phrase, permitting himself blatancies like "the young man carbuncular." Here is a poet capable of a style more refined than that of any of his generation parodying without taste or skill—and of this the example from Goldsmith is not the most astonishing. Here is a writer to whom originality is almost an inspiration borrowing the greater number of his best lines, creating hardly any himself. It seems to us as if *The Waste Land* exists in the greater part in the state of notes. This quotation is a particularly obvious instance:

> London Bridge is falling down falling
> down falling down
> *Poi s'ascose nel foco che gli affina*
> *Quando fiam uti chelidon*—O
> swallow swallow
> *Le Prince d'Aquitaine à la tour abolie.*

The method has a number of theoretical justifications. Mr. Eliot himself has employed it discreetly with delicious effect. It suits well the disillusioned smile which he had in common with Laforgue; but we do sometimes wish to hear the poet's full voice. Perhaps if the reader were sufficiently sophisticated he would find these echoes suggestive hints, as rich in significance as the sonorous amplifications of the romantic poets. None the less, we do not derive from this poem as a whole the satisfaction we ask from poetry. Numerous passages are finely written; there is an amusing dialogue in the vernacular, and the fifth part is nearly wholly admirable. The section beginning "What is that sound high in the air" has a nervous strength which perfectly suits the theme; but he declines to a mere notation, the result of an indolence of the imagination.

Mr. Eliot, always evasive of the grand manner, has reached a stage at which he can no longer refuse to recognize the limitations of his medium; he is sometimes walking very near the limits of coherency.

But it is the finest horses which have the most tender mouths, and some unsympathetic tug has sent Mr. Eliot's gift awry. When he recovers control, we shall expect his poetry to have gained in variety and strength from this ambitious experiment.

*Clive Bell.
"T. S. Eliot."
Nation & Athenaeum 33
(22 September 1923),
772–73.

To be amongst the first to think, say, or do anything, is one of the silliest and most harmless of human ambitions: I was one of the first in England to sing the praises of Eliot. I shall not forget going down to a country house for the Easter of 1916—or was it '17?—with *Prufrock* in my pocket, and hearing it read aloud to a circle of guests with whose names I am too modest to bribe your good opinion. Only this I will say, no poet could ask for a better send off. "The Love Song of J. Alfred Prufrock" was read aloud two or three times and discussed at intervals; it was generally admired or, at any rate, allowed to be better than anything of the sort that had been published for some time: and it pleases me to remember that its two most ardent admirers were a distinguished mathematician (not Bertrand Russell) and an exquisite lady of fashion.

To me "Prufrock" seemed a minor masterpiece which raised immense and permissible hopes: my opinion has not changed, but my hopes have dwindled slightly. For, as yet, Eliot has written nothing better than "Prufrock," which seems less surprising when we discover that, in a sense, he

has written nothing else; for the last seven years, I mean, he has been more or less repeating himself. He has lost none of the qualitites which made me then describe him as "about the best of our younger poets"; his intelligence and wit are as sharp as ever, and his phrasing is still superior to that of any of his contemporaries: but he has not improved.

Eliot, it seems to me, has written nothing wittier, more brilliantly evocative of a subtle impression, than "Mr. Apollinax"; and that, I believe, he wrote before he came to England. It is proper to add that if in this style he has not improved on himself, neither has anyone, in the interval, improved upon him. As for phrasing—a term which in his case I prefer to "diction" (musicians will understand why)—it is his great accomplishment; and if you will open *Prufrock* at the very first page you will come upon the following passage:

> Let us go, through certain
>   half-deserted streets,
> The muttering retreats
> Of restless nights in one-night cheap
>   hotels
> And sawdust restaurants with
>   oyster-shells:
> Streets that follow like a tedious
>   argument
> Of insidious intent
> To lead you to an overwhelming
>   question . . .

than which, in my opinion, he has done nothing better. Before contradicting me let the reader count at least ten, and give his memory a jog. In Mr. Eliot's later poems he will find, to be sure, better phrases than any of these; but is he sure they are by Mr. Eliot? The poet has a disconcerting habit of omitting inverted commas. "Defunctive music," for instance, is from Shakespeare; and not only the Elizabethans are laid under contribution. The other day a rather intemperate admirer quoted at me the line [from "Cousin Nancy"], "The army of unalterable law," and declared that no modern could match it. You know it is by Meredith.

If you will read carefully Eliot's three longer poems—"Prufrock," "Gerontion," and *The Waste Land*—I think you will see what I mean (even if you do not agree with me) in saying that he has been more or less repeating himself. And here we come at Eliot's essential defect. He lacks imagination; Dryden would have said "invention," and so will I if you think it would sweeten my discourse. Eliot belongs to that anything but contemptible class of artists whose mills are perfect engines in perpetual want of grist. He cannot write in the great manner out of the heart of his subject; his verse cannot gush as a stream from the rock: birdlike he must pile up wisps and straws of recollection round the tenuous twig of a central idea. And for these wisps and straws he must go generally to books. His invention, it would seem, cannot be eked out with experience, because his experience, too, is limited. His is not a receptive nature to experience greatly. Delicate and sensitive admirers have found, I know, the key to lifelong internal tragedy in those lines [from "Gerontion"] with their choice Elizabethan tang:

I that was near your heart was
    removed therefrom
To lose beauty in terror, terror in
    inquisition.
I have lost my passion: why should I
    need to keep it
Since what is kept must be
    adulterated?

But for my part, I cannot believe they are wrung from the heart of tragic experience. The despairing tone which pervades Eliot's poetry is not, it seems to me, so much the despair of disillusionment as the morbidity of *The Yellow Book*.

But how the man can write! And the experience, if it be small, is perfectly digested and assimilated; it has gone into the blood and bones of his work. Admit that the butter is spread unconscionably thin; at least the poet may claim, with the mad hatter, that it was the best butter. By his choice of words, by his forging of phrases, by his twisting, stretching, and snapping of rhythms—manipulations possible only to an artist with an exact ear—Eliot can make out of his narrow vision and meager reaction things of perpetual beauty, [as in following lines from "The Fire Sermon"]:

At the violet hour, the evening hour
    that strives
Homeward, and brings the sailor
    home from sea,
The typist home at teatime, clears her
    breakfast, lights
Her stove, and lays out food in tins.

Mark the transition—the technical one I mean—the stress and scarcely adumbrated stress—"HOMEward, and brings the sailor *home* from sea, / The typist *home* at teatime," so as to run on in a breath "clears her breakfast." A less dextrous artist would have had to break the flow with a full stop to show that he had changed the subject. The line, "Her drying combinations touched by the sun's last rays," is a piece of obvious comic-weekly humor, unworthy of so fastidious a writer. But try a line or two lower down:

He, the young man carbuncular,
    arrives,
A small house agent's clerk, with one
    bold stare,
One of the low on whom assurance
    sits
As a silk hat on a Bradford millionaire.

In its own modern way it is as neat as Pope, and one can almost see Mr. Arnold Bennett going to the races. I should be surprised if

Eliot were ever to write a great poem; but he might easily write three or four which would take their places among the most perfect in our language.

Eliot reminds me of Landor: I believe he will not disdain the comparison. Landor wrote half-a-dozen of the most perfect poems in English, and reams of impeccable dullness. Like Eliot he had very little imagination or invention; a narrow vision and, as a rule, tepid reactions; unlike Eliot he was incontinent. Spiritually, he looked out of the window of a suburban villa on the furniture of a suburban garden: the classical statue he set up in the middle of the grass plot was more often than not a cast. No, it was something more spacious than a villa garden; but it bore a horrid likeness to a public park. Yet, on the rare occasions when Landor could apprehend the humdrum world he inhabited with something like passion, his art enabled him to create a masterpiece. [. . .]

Eliot is said to be obscure; and certainly *The Waste Land* does not make easy reading. This I deplore, holding, with the best of English critics, that "wit is most to be admired when a great thought comes dressed in words so commonly received that it is understood by the meanest apprehensions." Only let us not forget that "Prufrock," which at first seemed almost unintelligible, now seems almost plain sailing, and that "Sweeney Erect," which was described as "gibberish," turns out to be a simple and touching story; so when we cudgel our brains over his latest work let us hesitate to suppose that we cudgel in vain. It was decided, remember, that Gray's odes were quite incomprehensible; so were *In Memoriam* and [George Meredith's] *The Egoist*; and the instrumentalists—those practical experts—assured the conductor that no orchestra ever would play Beethoven's symphonies, for the very simple reason that they were unplayable. I respect the man who admits that he finds Eliot's poetry stiff; he who from its obscurity argues insincerity and mystification I take for an ass.

Turn to Eliot's criticism (*The Sacred Wood*) if you want proof of his sincerity, and of one or two more qualities of his. Here he gives you some of the most interesting criticism and quite the silliest conclusions going. Here is a highly conscious artist, blessed with an unusually capable intellect and abnormal honesty, whose analysis of poetical methods is, therefore, bound to be masterly; who is never flabby, and who never uses well-sounding and little-meaning phrases to describe a quality in a work of art or a state in his own mind. Eliot is an exceptional critic. Unluckily, he is a Cubist. Like the Cubists, he is intent upon certain important and neglected qualities in art; these he detects unerringly, and he has no eyes for any others. His vision, you remember, was said to be narrow. He has an *a priori* theory, which is no sillier than any other *a priori* theory, and he applies it unmercifully. It leads him into telling us that *Coriolanus* is better than *Hamlet* and *The Faithful Shepherdess* than *Lycidas*—it leads him into absurdity. His conclusions are worthless; the argument and analysis by which he arrives at them are extraordinarily valuable. As in his poetry, in criticism his powerful but uncapacious mind can grasp but one thing at a time; that he grasps firmly. He disentangles with the utmost skill an important, hardly come at, and too often neglected quality in poetry; and if it were the only quality in poetry he would be almost the pontiff his disciples take him for. Not quite—for no aesthetic theory can explain his indiscreet boosting of the insignificant Miss Sinclair and the lamentable Ezra Pound. These predilections can be explained only by a less intelligent, though still perfectly honorable, misconception.

*J. C. Squire. "Poetry." *London Mercury* 8 (October 1923), 655–56.

I read Mr. Eliot's poem [*The Waste Land*] several times when it first appeared; I have now read it several times more; I am still unable to make head or tail of it. Passages might easily be extracted from it which would make it look like one of those wantonly affected productions which are written by persons whose one hope of imposing on the credulous lies in the cultivation of a deliberate singularity. It is impossible to feel that when one reads the whole thing: it may bewilder and annoy, but it must leave the impression on any open-minded person that Mr. Eliot does mean something by it, has been at great pains to express himself, and believes himself to be exploring a new avenue (though we may think it a dark cul-de-sac) of poetic treatment. The work is now furnished with an extensive apparatus of notes. There are references to *Ezekiel*, Marvell, *The Inferno*, Ovid, Wagner, St. Augustine, Sir James Frazer, and the Grail legend. But though these will tell those who do not know where Mr. Eliot got his quotations and symbolism from, they do not explain what these allusions are here for. The legend about the Cumæan Sibyl, which Rossetti paraphrased in verse, combined with the title and one casual reference, suggest that Mr. Eliot believes the poem to be about the decay of Western civilization and his own utter sickness with life. But even with this knowledge I confess that I do not see where it comes in. There is a vagrant string of drab pictures which abruptly change, and these are interspersed with memories of literature, lines from old poets, and disconnected ejaculations. This is a fair specimen of the poem's progress:

[Quotation of lines 189–206 from "The Fire Sermon"]

After which we proceed to the Smyrna currant merchant who asked Mr. Eliot (or somebody else perhaps) to tea at the Cannon Street Hotel, and we conclude with "Shantih shantih shantih," which, we are told, is "a formal ending to an *Upanishad*." Conceivably, what is attempted here is a faithful transcript, after Mr. Joyce's obscurer manner, of the poet's wandering thoughts when in a state of erudite depression. A grunt would serve equally well; what is language but communication, or art but selection and arrangement? I give it up; but it is a pity that a man who can write as well as Mr. Eliot writes in this poem should be so bored (not passionately disgusted) with existence that he doesn't mind what comes next, or who understands it. If I were to write a similar poem about this poem the first line from another work which would stray into the medley would be Mr. Chesterton's emphatic refrain "Will someone take me to a pub?" The printing of the book is scarcely worthy of the Hogarth Press.

*F. L. Lucas. "*The Waste Land.*" *New Statesman* 22 (3 November 1923), 116–18.

"*Solitudinem faciunt, poëma appellant.*"

Among the maggots that breed in the corruption of poetry one of the commonest is the bookworm. When Athens had decayed and Alexandria sprawled [. . .]; when the Greek world was filling with libraries and emptying of poets, growing in erudition as its genius expired, then first appeared [. . .] that *Professorenpoesie* which finds in literature the inspiration that life gives no more, which replaces depth by muddiness, beauty by echoes, passion by necrophily. The fashionable verse of Alexandria grew out of the polite leisure of its librarians, its Homeric scholars, its literary critics. Indeed, the learned of that age had solved the economic problem of living by taking in each other's dirty washing, and "Alexandra" of Lycophron, which its learned author made so obscure that other learned authors could make their fortunes by explaining what it meant, still survives for the curious as the first case of this disease [. . .]. The malady reappears at Rome [. . .] in the gloomy pedantry that mars so much of Propertius; it has recurred at intervals ever since. [. . .]

Readers of *The Waste Land* are referred at the outset, if they wish to understand the poem or even its title, to a work on the ritual origins of the legends of the Holy Grail by Miss J. L. Weston, a disciple of Frazer, and to *The Golden Bough* itself. Those who conscientiously plunge into the two hundred pages of the former interesting, though credulous, work, will learn that the basis of the Grail story is the restoration of the virility of a Fisher King (who is an incarnation, like so many others in Frazer, of the Life-Spirit), and thereby of the fertility of a Waste Land, the Lance and the Grail itself being phallic symbols. While maintaining due caution and remembering how "Diodorus Siculus / Made himself ridiculous, / By thinking thimbles / Were phallic symbols," one may admit that Miss Weston makes a very good case. [. . .] The sick king and the waste land symbolize, we gather, the sick soul and the desolation of this material life.

But even when thus instructed and with a feeling of virtuous research the reader returns to the attack, the difficulties are but begun. To attempt here an interpretation, even an intelligible summary of the poem, is to risk making oneself ridiculous; but those who lack the common modern gift of judging poetry without knowing what it means, must risk that. *The Waste Land* is headed by an allusion from Petronius to the Sibyl of Cumae, shrunk so small by her incredible age that she was hung up in a bottle and could only squeak, "I want to die." She typifies, I suppose, the timeworn soul's desire to escape from the "Wheel" of things. The first of the five sections opens in spring with one of the snatches of poetry that occur scattered about the poem:

> April is the cruellest month, breeding
> Lilacs out of the dead land, mixing
> Memory and desire, stirring
> Dull roots with spring rain.

The next moment comes a spasm of futile, society conversation from a Swiss resort, followed by a passionate outburst at the sterile barrenness of life, though not without hope of its redemption.

> [Quotation and brief description of representative passages from all five sections of *The Waste Land*]

[T]he gist of the poem is apparently a wild revolt from the abomination of desolation which is human life, combined with a belief in salvation by the usual catchwords of renunciation—this salvation being also the esoteric significance of the savage fertility-rituals found in *The Golden Bough*, a watering, as it were, of the desert of the suffering soul.

116

About the philosophy of the poem, if such it be, it would be vain to argue; but it is hard not to regret the way in which modern writers of real creative power abandon themselves to the fond illusion that they have philosophic gifts and a weighty message to deliver to the world, as well. In all periods creative artists have been apt to think they could think, though in all periods they have been frequently harebrained and sometimes mad; just as great rulers and warriors have cared only to be flattered for the way they fiddled or their flatulent tragedies. But now, in particular, we have the spectacle of Mr. Lawrence, Miss May Sinclair, and Mr. Eliot, all sacrificing their artistic powers on the altar of some fantastic Mumbo-Jumbo, all trying to get children on mandrake roots instead of bearing their natural offspring.

Perhaps this unhappy composition should have been left to sink itself: but it is not easy to dismiss in three lines what is being written about as a new masterpiece. For at present it is particularly easy to win the applause of the *blasé* and the young, of the coteries and the eccentricities. The Victorian "Spasmodics" likewise had their day. But a poem that has to be explained in notes is not unlike a picture with "This is a dog" inscribed beneath. Not, indeed, that Mr. Eliot's "Notes" succeed in explaining anything, being as muddled as incomplete. What is the use of explaining "laquearia" by quoting two lines of Latin containing the word, which will convey nothing to those who do not know that language, and nothing new to those who do? What is the use of giving a quotation from Ovid which begins in the middle of the sentence, without either subject or verb, and fails to add even the reference? And when one person hails another on London Bridge as having been with him "at Mylae," how is the non-classical reader to guess that this is the name of a Punic sea-fight in which as Phoenician sailor, presumably, the speaker has taken part? The main function of the "Notes" is, indeed, to give the references to the innumerable authors whose lines the poet embodies, like a mediaeval writer making a life of Christ out of lines of Virgil. But the borrowed jewels he has set in its head do not make Mr. Eliot's toad the more prepossessing.

In brief, in *The Waste Land* Mr. Eliot has shown that he can at moments write real blank verse; but that is all. For the rest he has quoted a great deal, he has parodied and imitated. But the parodies are cheap and the imitations inferior. Among so many other sources Mr. Eliot may have thought, as he wrote, of Rossetti's "Card-Dealer," of [Browning's] "Childe Roland to the Dark Tower Came," of [Tennyson's] "Vision of Sin" with its same question: "To which an answer peal'd from that high land, / But in a tongue no man could understand." But the trouble is that for the reader who thinks of them the comparison is crushing. *The Waste Land* adds nothing to a literature which contains things like these. And in our own day, though Professor Santayana be an inferior poet, no one has better reaffirmed the everlasting "No" of criticism to this recurrent malady of tired ages, "the fantastic and lacking in sanity":

Never will they dig deep or build for
  time
Who of unreason weave a maze of
  rhyme,
Worship a weakness, nurse a whim,
  and bind
Wreaths about temples tenantless of
  mind,
Forsake the path the seeing Muses
  trod,
And shatter Nature to discover God.

*Humbert Wolfe. "Waste Land and Waste Paper." Weekly Westminster 1 (17 November 1923), 94.

I begin by admitting that I do not understand Mr. Eliot's poem in the sense that I could not pass an examination upon it. If, for example, I were set the following three questions (two compulsory),

(1) What relation does the expressed desire of the Cumæan Sibyl to die bear to the poem that it prefaces?
(2) How far does each part of the poem carry on the meaning of its predecessor and point on to the conclusion?
(3) Is it really necessary, in order to understand the poem, to make a detailed study of the literature of anthropology? Illustrate your reply by reference to Miss Jessie L. Weston's book *From Ritual to Romance*, *Handbook of Birds of Eastern North America*, and Bradley's *Appearance and Reality*.

I should be prepared to give answers, and I am certain that they would be quite unlike the answers that others who, equally with me, admire the poem, would give, and, like all the answers, would be unsatisfactory to Mr. Eliot. But that doesn't bother me in the least. Part of the truth about poetry is its beautiful and essential unintelligibility, just as obscurity is its most fatal defect. Unintelligibility, in my use of the word here, conveys that rushing sense of suggestion hiding behind the actual written word that almost stuns the receptive mind, as might a too-bright light projected upon a sensitive eye. All poetry worthy of the name shakes just perceptibly beyond the ordinary power of the mind, but it shakes in brightness not in darkness. It is not that the poet can't make himself clear to us, but it is that true poetry is always reaching out beyond itself to the thoughts and feelings for which no words have yet been found. There is about it always an unprospected land, no-man's because it is trodden, in default of fools, by angels. From all of which it follows that everybody who cares for poetry must always fail in an examination of a strict kind. To confess, therefore, that I don't understand Mr. Eliot's poem seems to me to be no more a criticism of it than to say that (in the same sense) I don't understand Shakespeare's sonnets. Neither needs in that sense to be understood.

But that is not to say that I don't get from *The Waste Land* just those thrills that I associate with what I believe to be poetry. I do emphatically, and if they come by unusual channels, that after all is the best tribute that could be paid to any work of art.

[. . .]

[W]hat are we to suppose is hidden under these excursions from the Starnbergersee by way of a hyacinth garden and fortune-telling by cards to the "brown fog of a winter dawn" in London? Is it the soul sprawling from mountains out of spring past a viscous summer into the drabbest of winters? I don't interpret, because even as I attempt interpretation Mr. Eliot assaults me with "You! hypocrite lecteur!—mon semblable,—mon frère!"

Well, if I am his brother, I shall proceed by saying that the next movement, "The Game of Chess," is the symbol of the nightingale of beauty singing in the ears of all of us, choked with the dirt of the common burdens of mortality. Ending how? Why thus: "Good night, ladies, good night, sweet ladies, good night, good night." (That line hits me between the eyes. It is, to me, poetry's closing-time.)

As to the third movement, "The Fire Sermon," the nightingale sings again: "Twit twit twit / Jug jug jug jug jug jug / So rudely forc'd. / Tereu" between the rats in the slime, the wanton typist in her sodden attic, and "where the walls / Of Magnus Martyr hold / Inexplicable splendour of Ionian white and gold." Rats, lust, inexplicable splendor all in one tumbled heap: "la la / To Carthage then I came."

So then the fourth movement, "Death by Water," and how things lovely endure by dying before loveliness decays, and here no nightingale need sing. [In the] fifth movement and last, "What the Thunder Said," here are the "falling towers," the black end when:

A woman drew her long black hair
   out tight
And fiddled whisper music on those
   strings
And bats with baby faces in violet
   light.

Thus we have progressed through every form of ruin and despair over the Waste Land to where: "London Bridge is falling down falling down falling down."

As I began by saying, I don't pretend to understand, but end with the sense that the five movements are knit together by some invulnerable strand. There remains in my mind a sound of high and desolate music. So poetry should end.

[. . .]

Checklist of Additional Reviews

Burton Rascoe. "A Bookman's Daybook." *New York Herald Tribune*, 26 October 1922. [So dated in the Eliot Collection in the Houghton Library, but not found in the paper for this date]

Burton Rascoe. "A Bookman's Daybook." *New York Herald Tribune*, 5 November 1922, sec. 5, p. 8.

"The Sporting Spirit." *New York Evening Post Literary Review*, 11 November 1922, p. 1. [not located]

"Books and Authors." *New York Times Book Review*, 26 November 1922, p. 12.

Burton Rascoe. "A Bookman's Daybook." *New York Herald Tribune*, 3 December 1922, sec. 6, p. 18. [not located]

Gorham B. Munson. "Congratulations and More 'Ill-Mannered References.'" *Secession* 4 (January 1923), 31–32.

Mary M. Colum. "Modernists." *Literary Review* 3 (6 January 1923), 361–62.

Christopher Morley. "Apollo and Apollinaris." *New York Evening Post*, 9 January 1923, p. 349.

Burton Rascoe. "A Passage in *The Waste Land*." *New York Herald Tribune*, 14 January 1923, sec. 6, p. 23. [Reprinted in *Bookman's Daybook* (New York: Horace Liveright, 1929), 71–72]

"The *Dial*'s Prize." *Boston Herald*, 27 January 1923, p. 6.

Burton Rascoe. "Personal Letters Which All May Read." *New York Herald Tribune*, 28 January 1923, sec. 6, pp. 21, 26. [not located]

F. Van de Water. "Books and so Forth." *New York Tribune*, 28 January 1923, p. 19. [not located]

Fanny Butcher. "Help, Help." *Chicago Tribune*, 4 February 1923, pt. 7, p. 23. [not located]

Oregonian [Portland], 11 February 1923, sec. 5, p. 3. [not located]

John Dury. "World's Greatest Poem." *Chicago Daily News*, 14 February 1923, p. 15. [not located]

119

Otto Heller. "T. S. Eliot Awarded $2,000 Prize for *The Waste Land.*" *St. Louis Post Dispatch*, 24 February 1923, p. 10. [not located]

Robert L. Duffus. "Genius and the Guffaws of the Crowd." *New York Globe and Commercial Advertiser*, 28 February 1923, p. 16. [not located]

N. P. Dawson. "Enjoying Poor Literature." *Forum* 69 (March 1923), 1371–77. [Reprinted in *Critical Essays on T. S. Eliot's The Waste Land*, ed. Lois Cuddy and David Hirsch (Boston: G. K. Hall, 1991), 37–41]

*Desmond MacCarthy ["Affable Hawk"]. "Books in General." *New Statesman* 20 (10 March 1923), 660. [not located]

Christian Science Monitor, 23 March 1923, p. 18. [not located]

Herbert S. Gorman. "The Waste Land of the Younger Generation." *Literary Digest International Book Review* 1 (April 1923), 46, 48, 64.

Henry G. Hart. "New Plays and Poems." *Philadelphia Record*, 1 April 1923, sec. T, p. 6. [not located]

N. P. Dawson. "Theodoro, the Sage." *New York Globe and Commercial Advertiser*, 12 April 1923, p. 17. [not located]

Clement Wood. "If There Were a Pillory for Poets. *The Waste Land.*" *New York Herald*, 15 April 1923, pp. 3, 6. [not located]

N. P. Dawson. "Books in Particular." *New York Globe and Commercial Advertiser*, 17 April 1923, p. 14. [not located]

Burton Rascoe. "More About Eliot." Reprinted with a date of 18 April 1923 in *Bookman's Daybook*, pp. 96–97.

"A Group of Poems by T. S. Eliot." *Vanity Fair* 20 (June 1923), 67.

Clement Wood. "The Tower of Drivel." *Call Magazine* [New York], 20 June 1923, p. 11. [not located]

*Elsa Gidlow. "A Waste Land, Indeed." *New Pearson's* 49 (July 1923), 57. [not located]

William Rose Benét. "Among the New Books, Poetry Ad Lib." *Yale Review* 13 (October 1923), 161–62.

*Edward Shanks. "Books and Authors—New Poets." *Daily News*, 8 October 1923, p. 9. [not located]

*C. P. [Charles Powell]. *Manchester Guardian*, 31 October 1923, p. 7.

*J. M. H. "Poetry: Old and New." *Freeman* [Dublin], 9 February 1924, p. 9. [not located]

*N. T. [Netta Thompson]. "Modern American Poetry." *Aberdeen Press*, 26 May 1924, p. 3. [not located]

Gorham B. Munson. "The Esotericism of T. S. Eliot." *1924* 1 (1 July 1924), 3–10.

Edwin Muir. "T. S. Eliot." *Nation* 121 (5 August 1925), 162–64. [Reprinted in *Nation & Athenaeum*, 29 August 1925, pp. 644–46 and in *Transition* (New York: Viking, 1926)]

"Life's Brass Medal." *Life* 85 (12 March 1926), 24.

HOMAGE TO JOHN DRYDEN
1924

HOMAGE TO JOHN DRYDEN

THREE ESSAYS ON POETRY OF THE SEVENTEENTH CENTURY

T. S. ELIOT

PUBLISHED BY LEONARD AND VIRGINIA WOOLF
AT THE HOGARTH PRESS, TAVISTOCK SQUARE
LONDON, W.C.1
1924

Edmund Wilson, Jr. "T. S. Eliot and the Seventeenth Century." *New Republic* 41 (7 January 1925), 177–78.

This small volume contains three essays on seventeenth-century poetry in Mr. Eliot's best vein. The discussion of English literature has suffered peculiarly from a lack of well-informed and independent criticism outside its official historians, who as a rule accept the same scheme of rankings and hand the same phrases on to one another. It was the great merit of George Moore's imaginary conversations with Edmund Gosse that they attempted to disturb this system. Mr. Moore, reading many celebrated English novels for the first time rather late in life, complained, as a novelist, that the actual artistic qualities of these works did not fit the conventional accounts of them; and Mr. Gosse, who had come to guard the treasures of English culture with almost as little over-exercise of the critical sense as the Beefeater who watches the Crown Jewels in the Tower of London, was represented as rather hard put to it to make a satisfactory defense. So Mr. Eliot, who has the advantage over Mr. Moore of having studied his subject as thoroughly as any compiler of textbooks, becomes bored with the cliché reputations of the English poets: he is tired of hearing about Ben Jonson's "comedy of humors" and the "quaint conceits" of the "metaphysical" poets and the superlative lyric excellence of Wordsworth and Shelley. And he sets out to find what artistic realities are laid away in these parroted phrases.

One of the features of Mr. Eliot's revaluation is a dissatisfaction with the nineteenth century and a corresponding enthusiasm for the Elizabethans and the seventeenth century. I am not sure that, in his reaction against the vulgar conception of English poetry as coming to its fullest growth in the Romantics and Victorians, with Milton and Shakespeare as lonely oaks out-topping the barbarous undergrowth of earlier periods, he has not sometimes fallen over into paradox in urging the claims of the comparatively neglected. Does he not, for example, exaggerate a little when he says that Dryden's "powers were, we believe, wider but no greater, than Milton's," as if implying that they were as great, and when he describes Marlowe—with all his merits—as "a man of prodigious intelligence"? And I should also like to protest against his use of a certain passage from Dryden's *Secular Masque*—which has already been used by Mrs. Colum in an essay of her own for the same purpose—as a proof of Dryden's poetic genius; this passage when taken by itself may be made to sound quite exciting, rather like something in Mr. W. B. Yeats, but it seems to me difficult to continue to regard it as impressive when one has looked it up and found out what it actually means in the essentially interesting form in which it occurs. Mr. Eliot has a curious weakness—in his own poetry it appears as a gift—for finding in isolated passages of this sort effects which they were evidently never intended to convey. Another example in this book is to be found in the turn he gives to certain lines in Bishop King's "Exequy on His Dead Wife": here, he says, "there is that effect of terror which is several times attained by one of Bishop King's admirers, Edgar Poe." It certainly is possible by quoting these lines separately to lend them an effect of terror; but I doubt whether anything of the kind was intended by King or that any one but Eliot would have thought of it. It is the poet Eliot and not the poet King or the poet Dryden who expressed his temperament in these selected passages—the poet who has already given a new color and meaning to lines taken out of their context from his predecessors by embodying them in his own poems.

These minor exaggerations do not, however, impair the force of Mr. Eliot's excellent case for the superior artistic seriousness and success of the seventeenth-century poets over their eighteenth- and nineteenth-century successors.

[Quotation from "The Metaphysical Poets," *Selected Essays* 46–47]

Perhaps the most interesting discovery in the book is the resemblance which Mr. Eliot finds between the seventeenth-century poets and the Elizabethans on the one hand, and Baudelaire and the French Symbolists, on the other. A "telescoping of images" and "multiplied association" is characteristic of both. They both possess "a mechanism of sensibility" which can "devour any kind of experience" and their poems are equally complex. They perform the function of the poet indicated by Mr. Eliot in the first of the passages quoted above—that of "amalgamating disparate experience." That is why Webster and Donne have come back into fashion in America and England simultaneously with the belated English symbolistic movement which derives its original inspiration from Rimbaud and Laforgue. Young people no longer object, like William Archer, to the absurdity of Webster's plots nor, like Bernard Shaw, scoff at his intelligence. They know that he is a poet trying to convey special effects of feverishness and apprehension rather than a dramatist like Sir Arthur Pinero, and that he succeeds where a modern symbolistic dramatist like Maeterlinck fails. Mr. Eliot has profited in his own practice as a poet by the discovery which he here expounds and this is one of the facts which has given him his importance in contemporary literature. He has carried on the French tradition of Symbolism in English—unlike many other English-writing Symbolists—by working from the English tradition of "wit" and "metaphysical poetry" which came to an end in the seventeenth century.

---

*Edwin Muir. "Mr. Eliot's Criticism." *Calendar of Modern Letters* 1 (May 1925), 242–44.

The title of this volume is misleading, for the two more important of the three essays included are devoted to the metaphysical poetry of the seventeenth century. Though short, these essays contain probably the most penetrating body of observation on the metaphysical poets that has yet appeared in English, and it is nothing less than a calamity for literature that Mr. Eliot should have been compelled to discontinue the book, "beginning with Chapman and Donne, and ending with Johnson," which, he tells us in the preface, he once projected. He was admirably fitted for the work both by his gifts and his predilections; and the book, had it been completed, would not only have enriched the literature of criticism, but would also have stimulated, by making it more conscious of its aims, the poetry of today.

Mr. Eliot's diagnosis of the increasing psychological debility of English poetry since the time of the Elizabethans and their immediate successors is sufficiently well known, but here it may be briefly stated again. The poets of these eras, he says, "possessed a mechanism of sensibility which could devour any kind of experience." Afterwards—Mr. Eliot attributes the evil to Milton and Dryden—"a dissociation of sensibility set in." Poetry occupied itself only with certain classes of "experience." Of the verse of the eighteenth-century poets—Pope, Collins, Gray, Johnson, and that of the Romantic poets—Shelley, Keats, Wordsworth, Tennyson—this was equally true. From this poverty of the poetic spirit, this failure of poetry to deal completely with experience, sentimentality, among many other evils, arose. The main problem of the poet now is to reintegrate this poetic consciousness which for two centuries has been split up, and to deal with experience completely again. But this he will do successfully only if, among other things, he knows and steeps himself in, and does not imitate, the poetry in the English tradition in which this has already been done.

This bald summary does small justice to a very notable analysis of English poetry, but it may serve to indicate what a wealth of application, not only to the poetry of the past, but to that of our day, would have flowed from analysis had Mr. Eliot written his projected survey. That this analysis is accepted as a truism by intelligent people today is due chiefly to Mr. Eliot; the trouble is that it is very loosely accepted, too loosely to be of effectual use to the poet. Mr. Eliot has always striven to make as exact as possible the implication of this theory. He has tried to show the necessary connection with a sensibility capable of devouring any kind of experience, of a habit of mind in a certain sense philosophical—or, at least, intellectually curious—and of that with a poetry which will be at need "simple, artificial, difficult, or fantastic." He has reiterated that "the possible interests of a poet are unlimited; the more intelligent he is

the better"; and this, as he is careful to demonstrate, is not merely a pious opinion, but a fact which may be deduced from a study of great poetry. He has shown admirably that poetry which dispenses with these qualities—with what might be called psychology—is bound sooner or later to become sentimental. But, best of all, he has not demonstrated all this on the plane of general ideas; he has been interested rather in the actual ways in which this more complete poetic sensibility works and can work, showing how and in what terms the unlimited interests of the poet have been and may be again translated into poetry, and what have been the uses and possibilities for the poet of the "simple, artificial, difficult, and fantastic." Were the body of Mr. Eliot's criticism larger—three or four times larger—than it is, its influence on contemporary poetry would perhaps be decisive. It is, one feels, a misfortune that it has not been decisive.

The danger of criticism such as this, which has its eye disinterestedly on possibilities of the English poetic tradition which have been overlooked or unfulfilled, is that it tends to exalt poets, however small, who have expressed some of those possibilities, at the expense of others, however great, who have not. Mr. Eliot's criterion of poetry becomes insensibly a pragmatic one, and the poet who is more stimulating than another to this age becomes to him not only stimulating but sometimes, one feels, great. This fault is more injurious than it seems: it gives an effect of derangement of values. For example, the excellent essay on Marvell in this volume would be calculably more important if it did not contain a depreciatory reference to Milton. Such things throw a critical judgment out of proportion, the last thing, one imagines, that Mr. Eliot desired. But after one has encountered in all of the three essays in this volume an exasperated sentence on Milton, one begins to wonder if Mr. Eliot is in reality capable of appreciating the greatness of Milton's poetry, and although the doubt is dismissed as unjust, a certain feeling of insecurity has been given. It is bound to be intensified when one reads, "I have long felt that the poetry of the seventeenth and eighteenth centuries, even much of that of inferior inspiration, possesses an elegance and a dignity absent from the popular and pretentious verse of the Romantic Poets and their successors." Wordsworth, the greatest of the Romantic poets, is neither popular nor pretentious, and at his best has a dignity far less assailable, because his own, than that of Johnson or Gray, even if in his case it is incompatible with elegance. Mr. Eliot's failure—perhaps through impatience—to acknowledge things such as these, lessens the weight of his judgments, and lessens it needlessly. His criticism is more comprehensive and more sound than that of any other writer of this generation, but it would be infinitely better if it were compatible with an appreciation of the importance of Milton as well as Marlowe, of Wordsworth as well as Dryden, in the English poetic tradition. Until it is, it will have a faint but damaging, and altogether misleading, resemblance to the criticism of a school.

Checklist of Additional Reviews

*Edwin Muir. "Recent Criticism." *Nation & Athenaeum* 36 (December 1924), 370, 372.

Mark Van Doren. "First Glance." *Nation* 119 (31 December 1924), 732–33.

*Raymond Mortimer. "New Books from the Morning Room Table." *Vogue* [British edition], January 1925.

*John Freeman. "Literary History and Criticism-II." *London Mercury* 11 (April 1925), 662–64.

"Comment." *Dial* 80 (February 1926), 176–78.

POEMS 1909–1925
1925

POEMS

1909—1925

By T. S. ELIOT

FABER & GWYER LTD

LONDON MCMXXV

*Edgell Rickword. "The Modern Poet." *Calendar of Modern Letters* 2 (December 1925), 278–81.

If there were to be held a Congress of Younger Poets, and it were desired to make some kind of show of recognition to the poet who has the most effectively upheld the reality of the art in an age of preposterous poeticizing, it is impossible to think of any serious rival to the name T. S. Eliot.

[. . .]

The impression we have always had of Mr. Eliot's work, reinforced by this commodious collection in one volume, may be analyzed into two coincident but not quite simultaneous impressions. The first is the urgency of the personality, which seems sometimes oppressive, and comes near to breaking through the so finely-spun aesthetic fabric; the second is the technique which spins this fabric and to which this slender volume owes its curious ascendency over the bulky monsters of our time. For it is by his struggle with technique that Mr. Eliot has been able to get closer than any other poet to the physiology of our sensations (a poet does not speak merely for himself) to explore and make palpable the more intimate distresses of a generation for whom all the romantic escapes had been blocked. And, though this may seem a heavy burden to lay on the back of technique, we can watch with the deepening of consciousness, a much finer realization of language, reaching its height in passages in *The Waste Land* until it sinks under the strain and in

"The Hollow Men" becomes gnomically disarticulate.

The interval is filled with steady achievement, and though the seeds of dissolution are apparent rather early, there is a middle period in which certain things are done which make it impossible for the poet who has read them to regard his own particular problems of expression in the same way again; though he may refuse the path opened, a new field of force has come into being which exerts an influence, creates a tendency, even in despite of antipathy. [. . .]

Let us take three main stages in this development of technique, [. . .] "The Love Song of J. Alfred Prufrock," "Gerontion" and *The Waste Land*. (The neo-satiric quatrains do not raise any fundamental queries; they are the most easily appreciated of Mr. Eliot's poems, after "La Figlia che Piange." The French poems remind us of Dryden's prefaces [*vide* Swift], and there are half-a-dozen other mere *jeux d'esprit*.)

"Gerontion" is much nearer to *The Waste Land* than "The Love Song" is to "Gerontion." The exquisite's witty drawing-room manner and the deliberate sentimental rhythms give way to more mysterious, further-reaching symbols, and simpler, not blatantly poetic rhythms. As an instance, we have in "The Love Song":

> For I have known them all already,
>   known them all—
> Have known the evenings, mornings,
>   afternoons,
> I have measured out my life with
>   coffee spoons;

But in *The Waste Land*:

> And I Tiresias have foresuffered all
> Enacted on this same divan or bed;
> I who have sat by Thebes below the
>   wall
> And walked among the lowest of the
>   dead.

The relation and the difference of these passages hardly need stressing, but, though I had not intended to enter into an examination of the psychological content of these poems, I find that this subject of fore-knowledge is cardinal to the matter. Fore-knowledge is fatal to the Active Man, for whom impulse must not seem alien to the end, as it is to the vegetative life of the poets, whose ends are obscured in the means. The passage in "Gerontion" beginning: "After such knowledge, what forgiveness?" and the remainder of the poem are such profound commentary on the consequent annihilation of the will and desire that they must be left to more intimate consideration. The passage is a dramatic monologue, an adaptation one might hazard of the later Elizabethan soliloquy, down even to the senecal:

> Think
> Neither fear nor courage saves us.
> Unnatural vices
> Are fathered by our heroism. Virtues
> Are forced upon us by our impudent
> crimes.

"Gerontion" is a poem which runs pretty close to *The Waste Land*, and it is free from the more mechanical devices of the later poem, but lacks its fine original verse-movements. In the Sweeney quatrains, especially in the last stanzas of "Among the Nightingales," the noble and the base, the foul and the fine, are brought together with a shock; the form has little elasticity, and tends to become, like the couplet, stereotyped antithesis. In the fluid medium of *The Waste Land* the contrast may be brought about just as violently, or it may be diffused. This contrast is not, of course, the whole content of the poem, but Mr. Eliot has most singularly solved by its means the problem of revoking that differentiation between poetic and real values which has so sterilized our recent poetry.

His success is intermittent; after a short passage of exquisite verse he may bilk us with a foreign quotation, an anthropological ghost, or a mutilated quotation. We may appreciate his intention in these matters, the contrast, the parody, enriches the emotional aura surrounding an original passage, but each instance must be judged on its own merits; whether the parody, for instance, is apposite. On this score Mr. Eliot cannot be acquitted of an occasional cheapness, nor of a somewhat complacent pedantry, and since we cannot believe that these deviations are intrinsic to the poetic mind, we must look for their explanation elsewhere. We find it in the intermittent working of Mr. Eliot's verbal imagination. He has the art of words, the skill which springs from sensitiveness, and an unmatched literary apprehension which enables him to create exquisite passages largely at second-hand (lines 60–77). It is when this faculty fails of imaginative support, as it must at times, that certain devices are called in; the intellect is asked to fill in gaps (possibly by reference to the notes, when they are, as they rarely are, helpful) which previous poets have filled in with rhetoric, perhaps, but at any rate by a verbal creation which stimulates the sensibility. The object of this verbal effort is not merely to stimulate the sensibility, since disjunctive syllables can do that, but to limit, control, and direct it towards a more intense apprehension of the whole poem. That is where a failure in verbal inventiveness is a definite poetic lapse. In a traditional poet it would result in a patch of dull verse, in Mr. Eliot's technique we get something like this:

> To Carthage then I came
>
> Burning burning burning burning
> O Lord thou pluckest me out
> O Lord thou pluckest
>
> burning

130

Whether this is better of worse than dull verse I need not decide; that it is a failure, or the aesthetic scheme which would justify it is wrong, can I think be fairly upheld.

Though we may grasp the references to Buddha's Fire Sermon and Augustine's *Confessions*, and though Mr. Eliot may tell us that "the collocation of these two representatives of eastern and western asceticism, as the culmination of this part of the poem, is not an accident," we find it difficult to be impressed. It is the danger of the aesthetic of *The Waste Land* that it tempts the poet to think the undeveloped theme a positive triumph and obscurity more precious than commonplace. The collocation of Buddha and Augustine is interesting enough, when known, but it is not poetically effective because the range of their association is [. . .] limited by widely dispersed elements in the poem, and the essential of poetry is the presence of concepts in mutual irritation.

This criticism might be extended to the general consideration of the technique of construction used in *The Waste Land*; it is still exploited as a method, rather than mastered. The apparently free, or subconsciously motivated, association of the elements of the poem allows that complexity of reaction which is essential to the poet now, when a stable emotional attitude seems a memory of historical grandeur. The freedom from metrical conformity, though not essential, as *Don Juan* shows, is yet an added and important emancipation, when the regular meters languish with hardly an exception in the hands of mechanicians who are competent enough, but have no means of making their consciousness speak through and by the rhythm. Mr. Eliot's sense of rhythm will, perhaps, in the end, be found his most lasting innovation, as it is the quality which strikes from the reader the most immediate response.

*Leonard Woolf.
"'Jug Jug' to Dirty Ears."
Nation & Athenaeum 38
(5 December 1925), 354.

To the Victorian and to most of his ancestors the poet was a nightingale. The bird and the man did but sing because they must, and, though the song might be sad, it must also be sweet—indeed the sweetest songs are those which tell of saddest thought. We have changed all that: Mr. Eliot, who is a long way the best of the modern poets, makes his nightingales sing "'Jug Jug' to dirty ears" and tells us how

> The nightingales are singing near
> The Convent of the Sacred Heart,
>
> And sang within the bloody wood
> When Agamemnon cried aloud
> And let their liquid siftings fall
> To stain the still dishonoured shroud.

The dirty ears and the liquid siftings are now as essential a part of the nightingale's song as the magic casements, the perilous seas, the verdurous glooms, and the winding mossy ways . . .

There are many who will welcome this collected edition of Mr. Eliot's poems. Personally I *like* Mr. Eliot's poems so much that I am afraid of appearing exaggerated in criticizing them. When I get a book of his into my hands, I become fascinated; I simply cannot stop rereading the poems until something physical from outside forces me to shut the book. Naturally I think that there is something rare in the book itself to cause so rare a reaction. In the first place I believe it to be poetry, for real poetry is very rare. Mr. Eliot is a real poet. That he is difficult to understand, I admit; and this difficulty will cause many people to miss the poetry. But if anyone will read the opening of *The Waste Land*, and the whole of "Gerontion," without fussing very much about whether or not he is understanding exactly what the author means, he will suddenly be amazed and delighted by the mere beauty of the poetry:

[Quotation of lines 1 to 6 of "Gerontion."]

Secondly, Mr. Eliot has not only got the poetry, but he has found the instrument, the tune, the measure, the method which exactly fit the singing of "Jug Jug" to dirty ears. I feel the spirit of 1922 moving in *The Waste Land* more violently and potently than in any other contemporary poem: the spirit of the age is breathed into it much as the spirit of 1850 was breathed into *In Memoriam*.

I have admitted that Mr. Eliot's poetry is difficult to understand, but I admit it with so many qualifications that the admission is valueless. I am sure that I understand every poem which Mr. Eliot has written; I could not tell you what every word and line mean, but that is not necessary for an understanding and appreciation of the poems. In fact, the real criticism of Mr. Eliot is that he is too easy to understand, because he is always saying the same thing in different ways. His method, which alone involves obscurity, consists in keeping two tunes going at the same time, often one against the other. First, he works persistently through allusions: in the simplest case four words, lifted from Shakespeare and inserted in a poem called "Burbank with a Baedeker: Bleistein with a Cigar," evoke the image of Cleopatra and how her barge burned on the water, an image which is flung in the face of the Princess Volupine, the "Chicago Semite Viennese" Bleistein, and Sir Ferdinand Klein. Secondly, he attempts to communicate rather subtle emotions by the crude and violent juxtaposition of discordant scenes, thoughts, emotions. My only criticism of him is that the theme which he plays on these subtle strings is always the same and is very old. The splendor and romance of our desires and imaginations, the sordidness of reality—that is the theme of "Prufrock," of "Sweeney," of "Burbank," of *The Waste Land*, of "The Hollow Men." The nightingale never sings anything but "Jug Jug" to dirty ears. The mind is eternally "aware of the damp souls of housemaids / Sprouting despondently at area gates," while eternally looking for the barge of Cleopatra burning all day upon the water. The end of life is "an old man driven by the Trades / To a sleepy corner," with "Thoughts of a dry brain in a dry season," and the world, when it ends, will end "*Not with a bang but a whimper.*"

---

*John Middleton Murry. "The 'Classical' Revival." *Adelphi* 3 (February 1926), 585–95, and (March 1926), 648–53.

One reads not seldom nowadays of a "classical" revival in modern literature. There is a certain justification for the term. A fairly definite tendency can be observed among modern writers since the publication of Mr. Lytton Strachey's *Eminent Victorians*. [. . .]

There is no reason why this large and general movement of the public taste should not be called a "classical" revival, save that the phrase suggests much more than the reality. It suggests, moreover, that the new wave of classicism succeeds a previous romanticism. Actually this is not the case. What went before the new classical movement was not anything that could be usefully called romanticism: but rather a literature of social optimism and religious nullity.[1] [. . .]

[. . .] The classical revival belongs to the after-war period. It is an expression of a universal skepticism. In so conscious a practitioner as Mr. Strachey it is the manifestation of a certain amused contempt for Victorian equivocations [. . .]. On the still more popular levels—represented by *The Beggar's Opera*—there is a corresponding weariness of social problems and seriousness, and an inarticulate conviction that idealism and high-falutin' did not save us from disaster, but rather took us into it. The universal desire is to be amused without *arrière-pensée*. The "classical" revival is an expression or a satisfaction of this universal desire.

Therefore it is far better to call it an Augustan than a "classical" revival, since classicism stands for a good deal more than skepticism and amusement. The Augustan revival represents the reaction from a collapsed, and consequently a false, idealism; and probably the impulse would, in times of greater energy, have produced a movement of realism. But precisely at this moment the chaos of consciousness is so extreme that the effort necessary to deal with modern life realistically would be prodigious; on the other hand, the general lassitude among men of ability is such that even a moderate effort of the kind would be refused. More than this, the skepticism of the *intelligentsia* is so complete that it involves the art of literature itself. [. . .] Idealism, even the writer's idealism for his craft, in other than a superficial sense, is the enemy. It is not to be required of literature that it should aim at discerning and expressing some beauty which is the truth in the welter of contemporary life. Hence the vogue of the eighteenth century, wherein human beings can be contemplated, as it were, in a condition of paradisal ignorance of the complexities

which now assail them: and, to correspond with this, in the writers who affect to give some picture of the contemporary life, a complete cynicism and detachment. The human beings they depict are mere talking machines: intellectual marionettes. They are not given, and they are not intended to have, any creative truth: their purpose is not to reveal, but to amuse.

[. . .]

The "classical" revival, in so far as it is homogenous, is based upon an absolute skepticism, and is, like the hedonistic philosophy with which it is allied, impervious to criticism. [. . .]

But the "classical" revival is not really homogenous, not wholly Augustan. It has a "serious" wing. The cynical and the serious classicists are lumped together by a perfunctory criticism. Nothing is more remarkable in the utterances of journalists who affect the classical revival than an indiscriminate juxtaposition of the names of Mr. Lytton Strachey, Mrs. Virginia Woolf, Mr. Aldous Huxley, Mr. David Garnett, and Mr. T. S. Eliot. Mr. Strachey, Mr. Garnett, and Mr. Huxley do indeed belong together, though there are signs of incipient *malaise* in Mr. Huxley: but Mrs. Virginia Woolf and Mr. Eliot are of another kind. They are serious, while the others are cynical, "classicists."

We shall have later most sharply to distinguish between Mrs. Woolf and Mr. Eliot, for their seriousness has important points of difference. Mrs. Woolf, being a woman, is serious as Falstaff was a coward, on instinct; Mr. Eliot rather by premeditation. But a similar seriousness finds a similar manifestation in both of them: each desires to be loyal to what we can only call the modern consciousness—a complex state of mind, a spiritual "atmosphere" which exists now, and has never existed before. Each endeavors to create something adequate to the welter of dissatisfactions and desires which has invaded the sensitive mind during and since the war. Mrs. Woolf's *Jacob's Room* and Mr. Eliot's *The Waste Land* belong essentially to the same order. [. . .]

[T]he immediate effect of these two works is the same: the exercise of a prodigious intellectual subtlety to produce the effect of a final futility. The word is just, however harsh it may appear to those who are aware of the gifts of the authors. Both are unusually fine critics; both are tormented by the longing to create. But their creations, despite the approval of the *quid-nuncs* and the *claqueurs*, are futile. Fifty, ten years hence no one will take the trouble (no small one) to read either of these works, unless there should be some revolutionary happening in their authors—some liberation into a real spontaneity—which will cause these records of their former struggle in the wilderness to be studied with the sympathy and curiosity which a contemporary now bestows upon them.

These two writers are indeed interesting. The contradiction between so much serious intention, so much proved ability, and so paradoxical an outcome—*parturiunt montes; nascetur ridiculus mus*—is at first sight scarcely less than portentous; so is the contrast between the failure, intrinsic and external, of these serious classicists and the twofold success of the cynical classicists with whom they are so indiscriminately confused.

Yet the contradiction and the contrast are easy to explain. It is precisely because Mrs. Woolf and Mr. Eliot *are* more serious than their fellow classicists that they fail. For to be serious is not to be cynical; and not to be cynical is to be lacking in the attitude which gives the possibility of perfection to contemporary classicism. The attitude must be congruous with the method. In the cynical classicists it is: a technique of detachment for an attitude of detachment. With the complexities and heart-searchings of modern life they are ostentatiously unconcerned; they turn their backs upon it and seek their relaxation in the trim *parterres* of the Augustans. By these same complexities and heart-searchings, the serious classicists are deeply perturbed. [. . .] They strive to grapple with the modern consciousness: they become experimental, alembicated, obscure. They achieve nothing.

Yet why not? [. . .]

Actually the reason for their failure is simple. Their works are over-intellectualized; they lack spontaneity; they are overladen with calculated subtleties (which are quite different from the instinctive subtleties of the writer who is master of his purpose, his instrument and himself); and they fail to produce any unity of impression. The reader is compelled, in the mere effort to understand, to adopt an attitude of intellectual suspicion, which makes impossible the communication of feeling. The works offend against the most elementary canon of good writing: that the immediate effect should be unambiguous.

But why, being classicists, should they offend in this most unclassical way? The answer to that is that they are *not* classicists. As critical intelligences, they have, and have not given utterance to, pro-classical velleities—for order and clarity and decorum; as creative writers they are, in spite of all the restraint they impose upon themselves, disordered, obscure, indecorous. It is not their fault, they are children of the age against which they rebel. Above all, they are serious. They wish to express their real experience. And it happens that their real experience is such that it gives rise to classical velleities and defies classical expression.

For there is no *order* in modern experience, because there is no accepted principle of order. The obvious paradox of Mr. Eliot the classicist writing *The Waste Land* is a mere trifle compared to the inward contradiction between the profession of classical principles such as his and the *content* of that poem. The poem expresses a self-torturing and utter nihilism: there is nothing, nothing: nothing to say, nothing to do, nothing to believe, save to wait without belief for the miracle. Once its armor of incomprehensibility is penetrated the poem is found to be a cry of grinding and empty desolation. Nothing could conceivably be more remote from the complacent skepticism of the cynical Augustans. This is a voice from the Dark Night of the Soul of a St. John of the Cross—the barren and dry land where no water is.

To order such an experience on classical principles is almost beyond human powers. In might conceivably be done, by an act of violence, by joining the Catholic Church. St. John of the Cross *was* a Catholic. But the stupendous difference is that St. John of the Cross was born a Catholic, who thought and felt instinctively in the categories of the Church. Mr. Eliot was not; he was born into the same tormenting fluidity as the rest of us. And it is not likely that he will sell his equivocal birthright; like the rest of us, sooner or later he will be forced to crystallize his miracle out of himself.[2]

But what in the name of all incomprehensibles has such a man, in such a condition, to do with classicism? What can classicism mean for him? A spiritual technique he envies and cannot use; a certainty he longs for and cannot embrace—it could mean either of these things. But to envy classicism is not to be a classicist; it is to be, most unenviably, a romantic: a romantic who is conscious of sin in being what he is, and cannot take the plunge into the unknown; whose being knows that there is but one way, but whose mind, fascinated by ancient certitudes, can discern only nothingness along the only way.

The Waste Land, with a vengeance: but surely Mr. Eliot must know that no classicist ever got there. That is a station on the mystic path. The only classicism that knows anything about it is the classicism of the Catholic Church: and its knowledge derives from the fact that it has managed to include most romanticisms. If he requires a nearer precedent, it is to the romantics that he must go.

This profound and absolute contradiction lies beneath all Mr. Eliot's professions of classicism. He is, essentially, an unregenerate and incomplete romantic; and he must remain unregenerate and incomplete so long as he professes classicism: for so long will his professions and his reality remain utterly divorced.

The overcoming of this divorce between his understanding and his being is precisely the miracle he asks for in *The Waste Land*. It will not happen: such miracles never do happen.[3] A man has to create his own miracles, by paying for them, outwardly in the eyes of men and inwardly in his own soul's eye. The outward price Mr. Eliot is called upon to pay is a public recantation of his "classicism." It is unfortunate for him that his recantation must be public; but, since his profession was public, it is inevitable.

We have pressed home the analysis of Mr. Eliot's condition because he is the most striking example of the self-stultification involved in the profession of a serious classicism today. "Classicism" is all very well; but to be coherent, to be viable, it must not be serious. A serious classicism is a contradiction in terms for a modern mind; and since, when one is serious, errors of thought have their direct consequences upon the whole of the inward man, no criticism of Mr. Eliot can be serious unless it follows home the visible contradiction of his professions and his practice to their source in an internecine conflict between his understanding and his being.

That conflict will never be resolved, can never be resolved, save at the cost of a sacrifice. There is a moment, in life and in letters, when a man must lose his life to save it.

[. . .]

Notes

1. I am not unmindful of the fact that critics of repute—Babbitt, Seillière, Lasserre—French, or of French inspiration, maintain that precisely this *is* "romanticism." But romanticism and religious nullity are, in my judgment, mutually exclusive. [. . .] Similarly, I refuse the name of "classical" to a movement based on a religious nullity. Ultimately, I hold that classicism assumes the existence of God, and strives to understand Him; in other words, it keeps firmly before it the problem of good and evil and seeks demonstrably to justify the ways of God to men, as in classical Greek drama and Dante: whereas romanticism seeks to discover the existence of God, and is content ineffably to know Him, and in the act of knowledge transcends the distinction between good and evil, as in the high drama of Shakespeare—*Lear* and *Antony*. For a true classicism the existence of God is a real intellectual postulate; for a true romanticism a real spiritual experience.

[. . .]

2. Of course, not out of himself *alone*: the miracle—regeneration—is precisely the knowledge that he is not alone.
3. [. . .] [The] new complete edition of Mr. Eliot's poems [. . .] contains one poem written later than *The Waste Land*: "The Hollow Men" (1925). Nothing could more painfully confirm my statement that the miracle will not happen. This is a more absolutely *barren* poem than *The Waste Land*. The utterance is more naked, as though Mr. Eliot had no longer the energy to cover himself.

   [Quotation of lines 83–89 of "The Hollow Men" V]

*Louise Morgan. "The Poetry of Mr. Eliot." Outlook 57 (20 February 1926), 135–36.

No poet of the present generation has been more violently attacked or more passionately admired, and more perfectly misunderstood than Mr. T. S. Eliot. Over and over again the critics, some of them poets, "new poets," themselves, have repeated that he is merely clever, very very clever, that he is an erudite charlatan, often incomprehensible and obscure, that he has a brain and no heart. Since the publication of his collected poems the same criticisms have reappeared in the reviews; once more we are told that he is a cerebralist only, and a disillusioned one besides. Indeed, a facile but grotesquely irrelevant analogy which originated two years ago with Mr. Louis Untermeyer in his [. . .] *American Poetry* is employed again in the current quarterlies by two critics, both poets—the comparison of *The Waste Land* to a cross-word puzzle.

[It is] incredible that any reader sensitive to poetry should not be aware of the profound emotional quality in Mr. Eliot's work. To have emerged untouched from "Preludes," or "Rhapsody on a Windy Night," or "Morning at the Window," or "The Love Song of J. Alfred Prufrock," or *The Waste Land*, is a feat comparable with strolling in full evening dress through a tropical tornado or an arctic blizzard unscathed. There are various reasons for this strange insensibility. One is the popular fallacy that feeling and thought are incompatible, that when a man begins to use his brain he must cease to feel. As if, when the blood goes racing to the brain, the heart is not obliged to beat faster!

The peculiar emotional force in Mr. Eliot's poetry is mainly due to the mental control he constantly exercises over his feelings, giving the effect so to speak of the hounds of feeling straining at the taut leash of the mind. Or to vary the figure, the source of his poetry is deep in his heart as the source of the spring is deep in the bowels of the mountain, but as it issues it is filtered and purified by the active sunlight of his brain. Another current fallacy allied to the one just mentioned is that poetry does not flourish on disillusion. But what did *Hamlet*, which is stuffed full of the world's finest poetry, spring from! The chiefest reason, however, is that this poet is as uncompromisingly and as self-awarely new as were Wordsworth and Coleridge in the last decade of the eighteenth century.

In Mr. Eliot we have evidence of one of those renewals of poetry which happen roughly once in a century, and which spring from direct and deliberately made contact with the common life and speech of the moment. That actual life and speech which gives poetry a fresh vitality becomes in its turn literesque and sterile, until another contact creates another renewal. The test of Mr. Eliot's power is that he gives the sense of his own time in no local or provincial way, but as a part of all the time that has gone before it, implying inevitably the timeless in time. With a kind of dramatic tenderness he isolates the essential human thing from all its infinite varieties of manifestations. Actaeon and Diana are but different symbols for Sweeney and Mrs. Porter. The poor little typist, torpidly seduced by the carbuncular clerk, is lovely woman that stoops to folly. It is as if he had opened all the tight little bundles into which we parcel up our consciousness—parchment and seals for our knowledge of history, white tissue and ribbon for our aesthetic functions, brown paper and string with double knots for our physiological—had opened them and

strewn their contents flat under the midday sun, Leicester's velvet cloak near the typist's drying combinations, the singing mermaids from the chambers of the sea next to Prufrock's trousers with the bottoms rolled. An important peculiarity of his method in procuring this effect of the life of all time expressing itself in the particular disguise of the moment, is the use of literary quotations. He is the first poet to set echoing in his lines the overtones of an experience which is often richer and sharper than our direct encounter with life and nature—our experience with literature.

We have alluded to his dramatic quality; no other poet since Shakespeare has put dauntlessly cheek by jowl the sublime and the commonplace. In a minor way, and necessarily much more condensed form, the same intensely dramatic effect of reality is achieved by the setting together in Prufrock's mind of his white flannel trousers and the siren beauty of the sea, as by the juxtaposition of the drunken porter and Macbeth's terribly ecstasy. It is by his daring to make use of this dualism which is so integral a part of all life but which has only rarely before been considered the proper material for poetry, that Mr. Eliot secures his most deeply moving effects, sincere and simple effects which, because [. . .] not understood [. . .], are labeled "obscure" and "merely clever" by the worldly-wise critics. His instrumentation, to mention only one other detail of his technique, is constantly varied, as often as not from line to line; apparently willful, it is carefully and subtly calculated. He rhymes or does not rhyme, uses assonance, repetition, the latter with singular beauty, or ignores all the accepted mechanical means of conjuring up the poetic mood, entirely to suit his own turn. He contrives to cap a tragic stanza powerfully with the doggerel rhyme of "visit" with "is it?"; he succeeds with such novel experiments as making rhymes out of a grammatical ending, as in the opening lines of *The Waste Land*; he employs the refrain to help achieve a deeply exciting sound pattern in Lil's friend's monologue in the same poem. [. . .]

Without doubt for many and lamentable decades still we shall have variations on the familiar themes, on sentimental, old, unhappy, far-off things and romantic peaks in Darien, just as couplets in the prescribed eighteenth-century manner persisted far down into the nineteenth. But in the meantime the generation of 1925 has as clear and deliberate a statement of a new order of poetic values in the *Poems* of Mr. T. S. Eliot as had the generation of 1798 when Wordsworth and Coleridge challenged the old order of that day with the *Lyrical Ballads*.

---

*I. A. Richards. "Mr. Eliot's Poems." *New Statesman* 26 (20 February 1926), 584–85.

[. . .]

Mr. Eliot's poetry has occasioned an unusual amount of irritated or enthusiastic bewilderment. The bewilderment has several sources. The most formidable is the unobtrusiveness, in some cases the absence, of any coherent intellectual thread upon which the items of the poem are strung. A reader of "Gerontion," of "Preludes," or of *The Waste Land* may, if he will, after repeated readings, introduce such a thread. Another reader after much effort may fail to contrive one. But in either case energy will have been misapplied. For the items are united by the accord,

contrast, and interaction of their emotional effects, not by an intellectual scheme that analysis must work out. The only intellectual activity required takes place in the realization of the separate items. We can, of course, make a "rationalization" of the whole experience, as we can of any experience. If we do we are adding something which does not belong to the poem. Such a logical scheme is, at best, a scaffolding which vanishes when the poem is constructed. But we have so built into our nervous systems a demand for intellectual coherence, even in poetry, that we find a difficulty in doing without it.

This point may be misunderstood, for the charge most unusually brought against Mr. Eliot's poetry is that it is over-intellectualized. One reason for this is his use of allusion. A reader who in one short poem picks up allusions to: *The Aspern Papers*, *Othello*, "A Toccata of Galuppi's," Marston, "The Phoenix and the Turtle," *Antony and Cleopatra* (twice), "The Extasie," *Macbeth*, *The Merchant of Venice*, and Ruskin feels that his wits are being unusually well exercised. He may easily leap to the conclusion that the basis of the poem is in wit also. But this would be a mistake. These things come in, not that the reader may be ingenious or admire the writer's erudition (this last accusation has tempted several critics to disgrace themselves) but for the sake of the emotional aura which they bring. Allusion in Mr. Eliot's hands is a technical device for compression. *The Waste Land* is the equivalent in content to an epic. Without this device twelve books would have been needed. But these allusions and the notes in which some of them are elucidated have made many a petulant reader turn down his thumb at once.

This objection is connected with another, that of obscurity. To quote a recent pronouncement upon *The Waste Land* from Mr. Middleton Murry: "The reader is compelled, in the mere effort to understand, to adopt an attitude of intellectual suspicion, which makes impossible the communication of feeling. The works offend against the most elementary canon of good writing: that the immediate effect should be unambiguous." [See "The 'Classical' Revival" (1926) in this volume, pp. 132–36.] Consider first this "canon." What would happen, if we pressed it, to Shakespeare's greatest sonnets or to *Hamlet*? The truth is that very much of the best poetry is necessarily ambiguous in its immediate effect. Even the most careful and responsive reader must re-read and do hard work before the poem forms itself clearly and unambiguously in his mind. An original poem, as much as a new branch of mathematics, compels the mind which receives it to grow, and this takes time. [...]

The critical question in all cases is whether the poem is worth the trouble it entails. For *The Waste Land* this is considerable. There is Miss Weston's *From Ritual to Romance* to read, and its "astral" trimmings to be discarded—they have nothing to do with Mr. Eliot's poem. There is Canto XXVI of the *Purgatorio* to be studied—the relevance of the close of that Canto to the whole of Mr. Eliot's work must be insisted upon. It illuminates his persistent concern with sex, the problem of our generation as religion was the problem of the last. There is the central position of Tiresias in the poem to be puzzled out—the cryptic form of the note which Mr. Eliot writes on this point is just a little tiresome. It is a way of underlining the fact that the poem is concerned with many aspects of the one fact of sex, a hint that is perhaps neither indispensable nor entirely successful.

When all this has been done by the reader, when the materials with which the words are to clothe themselves have been collected, the poem still remains to be read. And it is easy to fail in this undertaking. An "attitude of intellectual suspicion" must certainly be abandoned. But this is not difficult to those who still know how to give their feelings precedence to their thoughts, who can accept and unify an experience without trying to catch it in an intellectual net or to squeeze out a doctrine. One form of this attempt must be mentioned. Some, misled no doubt by its origin in a Mystery, have endeavored to give the poem a symbolical reading. But its symbols are not mystical but emotional. They stand, that is, not for ineffable objects but for normal human experience. The poem, in fact, is radically naturalistic; only its compression makes it appear otherwise. And in this it probably comes nearer to the original Mystery which it perpetuates than transcendentalism does.

If it were desired to label in three words the most characteristic feature of Mr. Eliot's technique this might be done by calling his poetry a "music of ideas." The ideas are of all kinds, abstract and concrete, general and particular, and, like the musician's phrases, they are arranged, not that they may tell us something but that their effects in us may combine into a coherent whole of feeling and produce a peculiar liberation of the will. They are there to be responded to, not to be pondered or worked out. This is, of course, a method used intermittently in very much poetry, and only an accentuation and isolation of one of its normal resources. The peculiarity of Mr. Eliot's later, more puzzling, work is his deliberate and almost exclusive employment of it. In the earlier poems this logical freedom only appears occasionally. In "The Love Song of J. Alfred Prufrock," for example, there is a patch at the beginning and another at the end, but the rest of the poem is quite straightforward. In "Gerontion," the first long poem in this manner, the air of monologue, of a stream of associations, is a kind of disguise and the last two lines— "Tenants of the house, / Thoughts of a dry brain in a dry season"—are almost an excuse. The close of "A Cooking Egg" is perhaps the passage in which the technique shows itself most clearly. The reader who appreciates the emotional relevance of the title has the key to the later poems in his hand. *The Waste Land* and "The Hollow Men" (the most beautiful of Mr. Eliot's poems, if we reserve a doubt as to the last section, astonishing though it is) are purely a "music of ideas," and the pretense of a continuous thread of associations is dropped.

How this technique lends itself to misunderstandings we have seen. But many readers who have failed in the end to escape bewilderment have begun by finding on almost every line that Mr. Eliot has written [. . .] that personal stamp which is the hardest thing for the craftsman to imitate and perhaps the most certain sign that the experience, good or bad, rendered in the poem is authentic. Only those unfortunate persons who are incapable of reading poetry can resist Mr. Eliot's rhythms. The poem as a whole may elude us while every fragment, as a fragment, comes victoriously home. It is difficult to believe that this is Mr. Eliot's fault rather than his reader's, because a parallel case of a poet who so constantly achieves the hardest part of his task and yet fails in the easier is not to be found. It is much more likely that we have been trying to put the fragments together on a wrong principle.

Another doubt has been expressed. Mr. Eliot repeats himself in two ways. The nightingale, Cleopatra's barge, the rats and the smoky candle-end recur and recur. Is this a sign of a poverty of inspiration? A more plausible explanation is that this repetition is in part a consequence of the technique above described, and in part something which many writers who are not accused of poverty also show. Shelley, with his rivers, towers, and stars, Conrad, Hardy, Walt Whitman, and Dostoevsky spring to mind. When a writer has found a theme or image which fixes a point of relative stability in the drift of experience, it is not to be expected that he will avoid it. Such themes are a means of orientation. And it is quite true that the central process in all Mr. Eliot's best poems is the same: the conjunction of feelings which, though superficially opposed—as squalor, for example, is opposed to grandeur—yet tend as they develop to change places and even to unite. If they do not develop far enough the intention of the poem is missed. Mr. Eliot is neither sighing after vanished glories nor holding contemporary experience up to scorn. Both bitterness and desolation are superficial aspects of his poetry. There are those who think he merely takes his readers into the waste land and leaves them there, that in his last poem he confesses his impotence to release the healing waters. The reply is that some readers find in his poetry not only a clearer, fuller realization of their plight, the plight of a whole generation, than they find elsewhere, but also through the very energies set free in that realization, [they find] a return of the saving passion.

---

*J. C. S[quire].
"Poems."
London Mercury 13
(March 1926), 547–48.

Mr. Eliot's work is mainly an elaborate expression of disgust. He ends his volume with these lines:

> *This is the way the world ends*
> *This is the way the world ends*
> *This is the way the world ends*
> *Not with a bang but a whimper.*

140

And he calls his longest poem *The Waste Land*, its apparent object being to reflect in a vagrant and fatigued sequence of images the exhaustion of our civilization. The mood is familiar enough: it is what thirty years ago they used to call "*fin-de-siècle*": Baudelaire without his guts. It is a dyspeptic mood, the mood of a man of low vitality, a man feeling "below par." The diagnosis on which it is nominally founded seems to me unsound. Our civilization appears at least as vigorous as it was a century ago, and the urban ugliness and the emptiness of the lives of many people, rich and poor, is no new thing; neither is the exaggeration of it from outside. And what new complexion has recently come over our situation versus the universe I do not make out. Nevertheless a poet must be granted his opinions and his mood, though an obstinate pessimism or fierce despair is more likely to produce moving literature than the muted dejection which appears habitual with Mr. Eliot, who seems unable to love anything or, by the same token, to hate. In the last resort we have to ask ourselves what are the qualities of his work and what pleasure does it give us.

Certain powers of intellect and craftsmanship he obviously possesses. There is an acute, if perverse, mind in these poems, and a faculty, too seldom employed, for a faint individual music: Mr. Eliot observes closely, and he has a vocabulary which will do anything he wants, a vocabulary which, perhaps, might be richer if it were poorer, for it is stuffed with terms drawn from obscure *penetralia* of learning which are no assistance to his toiling reader. Unhappily Mr. Eliot has very little regard for his reader. In one of the poems of his earliest period, when his poems were weary, and comparatively lucid, reveries over the vacuity of daily life in general and cultivated tea parties in particular, he depicted himself as mounting his aunt's doorstep and "turning / Wearily, as one would turn to nod good-bye to La Rochefoucauld, / If the street were time and he at the end of the street." The lucidity, of late, has vanished, but whenever there is an opening in the mists which surround the later Mr. Eliot, he is still to be observed nodding good-bye to Rochefoucauld—who stands at the end of a street sparsely populated with pale typists, cats, barrel-organs, and footmen going out for a drink. It is not a very infectious attitude; nor does it generate the simple, sensuous, and passionate. In the later poems Mr. Eliot has reinforced his detachment by a further detachment of speech. Now and again he is comprehensible and strong (as in the stanzas about Webster and Donne) or comprehensible and melodious (as in the first lines of *The Waste Land* and the last stanza of "Sweeney Among the Nightingales"); usually he is obscure, so inconsequent, that the kindest thing one can suppose is that he is experimenting with automatic writing. Why on earth he bothers to write at all is difficult to conceive; why, since he must write, he writes page after page from which no human being could derive any more meaning (much less edification or pleasure) than if they were written in Double-Dutch (which parts of them possibly are) is to me beyond conjecture. Why to the Waste Land add a Valley of peculiarly Dry Bones?

Edmund Wilson, Jr. "Stravinsky and Others." *New Republic* 46 (10 March 1926), 73–74.

[. . .]

This is perhaps not an appropriate place to speak of the collected edition of

T. S. Eliot's poems which has just been published in England. This volume contains nothing new except a set of poems called "The Hollow Men," which represents an even more advanced stage of the condition of demoralization already given expression in *The Waste Land*; the last of these poems—the disconnected thoughts of a man lying awake at night—consists merely of the barest statement of a melancholy self-analysis mixed with a fragment of the Lord's Prayer and a morose parody of "Here We Go Round the Mulberry Bush." "*This is the way the world ends,*" the poet concludes, "*Not with a bang but a whimper.*"

No artist has felt more keenly than Mr. Eliot the desperate condition of Europe since the War nor written about it more poignantly. Yet, as we find this mood of hopelessness and impotence eating into his poetry so deeply, we begin to wonder whether it is really the problems of European civilization which are keeping him awake nights. Mr. Eliot has lived abroad so long that we rarely think of him as an American and he is never written about from the point of view of his relation to other American authors. Yet one suspects that his real significance is less that of a prophet of European disintegration than of a poet of the American Puritan temperament. Compare him with Hawthorne, Henry James, E. A. Robinson, and Edith Wharton: all these writers have their Waste Land, which is the aesthetic and emotional waste land of the Puritan character and their chief force lies in the intensity with which they communicate emotions of deprivation and chagrin. The young men of Eliot's earlier poems, with their prudence and their inability to let themselves go, are like the young men of Henry James's early novels and like the Hawthorne of the *Notebooks*; and the later creations of Eliot, with their regrets for having dared too little, correspond

exactly to the middle-aged men of the later Henry James, of *The Ambassadors* and "The Beast in the Jungle." What is most important about Mr. Eliot, however, is that even in his deepest dejections and tending, as he seems to do here, to give his emotions a false significance, he remains a poet of the first order. One is struck, in going through this new edition, by the fact that he survives re-reading better than almost any of his contemporaries, American or English.

[. . .]

Allen Tate. "A Poetry of Ideas." *New Republic* 47 (30 June 1926), 172–73.

Poems: 1909–1925 by Mr. T. S. Eliot is a spiritual epilogue to *The Education of Henry Adams*. It represents a return of the Anglo-French colonial idea to its home. A pervasive sense of public duty led Adams into morally and politically active life, but it was not strong enough to submerge the "finer grain," with which his hereditary European culture had endowed him. The conflict was disastrous; he repudiated the American adventure too late. But in Mr. Eliot, Puritan obligation withdraws into private conscience; a system of conduct becomes a pattern of sensibility; his meager romanticism, like the artificially constructed ruin of the eighteenth century, is strictly an affair of the past; it has nothing whatever in common with a creed of practical romanticism like that of William James. Going home to Europe, Mr. Eliot has had to understand Europe; he could not quite sufficiently be the European simply to feel that he was there; he has been forced to envisage it with a reminiscent philosophy. And it is not insignificant that the quarterly of which he is the editor is the first British journal which has attempted to relate the British mind to the total European mind; that has attempted a rational synthesis of the traditions of Roman culture; that has, in a word, contemplated order. Mr. Eliot's position in this scheme of recapitulation, of arranging the past when the future seems to him only vaguely to exist, is in some respects particularly fortunate. It has enabled him to bring to England, in his poetry, the sense of a contemporary spiritual crisis, which shell-shock had already rendered acute, but of which the English Channel had perhaps kept out the verbally conscious signification. The essays of Maurras, Valéry, Massis, the philosophy of Spengler, all may variously attest to the reality of European disorder. It is nevertheless the special poetical creation of Mr. Eliot's cultural disinheritance and gloom.

It has not, I believe, been pointed out that Mr. Eliot's poetry is principally a poetry of ideas, that these ideas have steadily anticipated the attitude of a later essay [. . .] "The Function of Criticism." *The Sacred Wood* was written in the years of this anticipatory verse, but this volume is singularly devoid of its chief issues. For the early essays presuppose a static society and the orderly procession of letters: "Tradition and the Individual Talent" presupposes a continuity of traditional culture as literature. The baroque agony of the poetry in the corresponding period was preoccupied, however, with the anarchy which he has subsequently rationalized and for which he has proposed as remedy the *régime* of a critical dictatorship, in "The Function of Criticism."

The critical idea of disorder began, in the poetry, as the desperate atmosphere of isolation. It was obviously conviction prior to reflection, but to one in Mr. Eliot's spiritual unrest it speedily becomes a protective idea; it ceases to be emotion, personal attitude; one ceases reiterating it as such. This rationalization of attitude puts in a new light the progressive sterilization of his poetry. It partly explains the slenderness of his production: a poetry with the tendency to ideas betrays itself into criticism, as it did in Arnold, when it becomes too explicit, too full. His collected *Poems* is the preparation for a critical philosophy of the present state of European literature. As this criticism becomes articulate, the poetry becomes incoherent. The intellectual conception is now so complete that he suddenly finds there is no symbolism, no expressive correspondence, no poetry, for it. An emotional poetry uncensored by reason would be intolerable to his neo-classical predilections. For Mr. Eliot apprehends his reality with the intellect, and the reality does not yield a coherent theme. This is evidently the formula of *The Waste Land* (1922), where the traditional mythologies are no longer forms of expression, but quite simply an inexplicable burden the meaning of which the vulgar brutality of modern life will not permit the poem to remember. The mythologies disappear altogether in "The Hollow Men" (1925), for this series of lyrics stands at the end of his work as the inevitable reduction to chaos of a poetry of the idea of chaos:

> *Here we go round the prickly pear*
> [. . . . .]
> *This is the way the world ends*
> *Not with a bang but a whimper.*

The series is substantially an essay on contemporary Europe.

Throughout Mr. Eliot's poetry two principle devices advance the presentation of spiritual disorder. [. . .] The first is the device of shifted movement, or of logically irrelevant but emotionally significant conclusion, used with typical success at the end of the "Preludes" [. . .]. [T]he second device [is] that of projecting simultaneously events which are separated in time, destroying the commonplace categorical perception of time and space and erecting the illusion of chaos—a device of tremendous effect in the Tiresias passage and the Sweeney poems. [. . .] [Such] is the rhythm of Sweeney, Grishkin, Burbank; also a system of imagery too specific in its properties to have been learned directly from Laforgue, supposedly Mr. Eliot's chief French influence.

While he has all along been under the influence of Laforgue and Corbière, it has not given him his two major effects. From these poets he has borrowed, not tricks of construction so much as attitudes and particular lines; for example, Mr. Eliot's beautiful line "Simple and faithless as a smile and shake of the hand" is a paraphrase, in which the metaphor is made a definite image, of "*Simple et sans foi comme un bonjour.*" The line was Laforgue's, but now because Eliot has improved it, it is his. And the Elizabethan element is impure. Webster's varied complexity of pattern, its fusion of heterogeneous sensations, breaks down under Mr. Eliot's treatment. It has undoubtedly served him as a model of diction, but the physical presentation of psychological terror and the sense of formal beauty, fused in Webster, are in Eliot, as Mr. Edwin Muir has pointed out, simply mixed, alternately recurring. His Elizabethanism has indubitably been too ingenuously appraised by some critics, and it has thus been objected that such a formula is inadequate to contemporary "problems"; but even were the formula of most of Eliot's poetry what these critics suppose it to be, criticism might as well assert that Dryden was not the poet of his age because he did not permit the lately "discovered" law of gravitation to alter the quality of sensitivity of his verse. Mr. Eliot's poetry has attempted with considerable success to bring back the total sensibility

as a constantly available material, deeper and richer in connotations than any substance yielded by the main course of English poetry since the seventeenth century.

He has borrowed intelligently from a great many sources; it is only because of an interested romantic criticism that the privilege has fallen into dishonor. Those aspects of recent French poetry which reappear in Eliot have been impugned as echo and faddism; it is forgotten that some of Massinger's best lines are revisions of Tourneur, are unoriginal. And it is not merely as a skillful borrower that Mr. Eliot is the most traditional poet of the age. For him and for all sound criticism down to Pater, the body of literature in the Greco-Roman culture lives as an organism; he has deliberately employed such of its properties as extend, living, into the creative impulse of his age. His attention in both criticism and poetry has been to the poetry, not to the poet; to the essence and not the momentary vicar of the essence. The attitude is self-contained, impersonal, classical, and the critics of opportunity and private obsession have regretted the lack of personal exploitation; his unfamiliar system of metaphor has offered a great deal for a vulgar age to misunderstand. His conviction that the traditional inspiration, in immediately inherited forms, is exhausted produced the transition poem, *The Waste Land*: it exhibits this inspiration as it now exists in decay, and it looks by implication toward a new world-order the framework of which Mr. Eliot lacked the excessive divination to supply. He is traditional, but in defining tradition as life, as a living cultural memory, instead of a classical dictionary stocked with literary *dei ex machina*, he is also the type of contemporary poet.

Mr. Eliot's is a scrupulous, economic mind. It is possible that he has nothing more to say in poetry. "The Hollow Men" ends at least a phase. Whether the difficulty is the personal quality of his Puritan culture, as Mr. Edmund Wilson seems to believe, or lies in the tangle of contemporary spiritual forces, it would be hazardous just now to say.

[. . .]

Conrad Aiken. "The Poetic Dilemma." *Dial* 82 (May 1927), 420–23.

It has been often enough, perhaps too often, said of late, that the almost fatal difficulty which confronts the poet nowadays is the difficulty of finding a theme which might be worth his power. If he be potentially a "major" poet, this difficulty is thought to be particularly formidable, if not actually crippling; but for even the "minor" poet (to use minor in no pejorative sense), it is considered serious. Mr. T. S. Eliot, whose *Poems* have been reprinted by Mr. Knopf, has himself contributed something to this theory. In his admirable note on Blake, in *The Sacred Wood*, he suggests that Blake was potentially a major poet who was robbed of his birthright by the mere accident of there not being, at the moment, a prepared or traditional cosmology or mythology of sufficient wealth to engage, or disengage, his great imaginative power. He was compelled, in the absence of such a frame, to invent a frame for himself; and in this was, perhaps inevitably, doomed to failure. Had he been born to a belief as rich and profound as that which Dante inherited, might he not have been as great a poet? . . .

This is an ingenious idea; but it is possible to take it too seriously. It is obvious enough that some sort of tradition is a very great help to a poet—it floats him and sustains him, it carries him more swiftly and easily than he could carry himself, and it indicates a direction for him. But a fact too often lost sight of, at the present time, is that the great poet may be, precisely, one who has a capacity to find, at *any* given moment, a theme sufficient for the proper exercise of his strength. There were contemporaries of Dante who were excellent poets, but for whom the cosmology which enchanted Dante was not evocative. If Blake scanned his horizon in vain for "huge cloudy symbols," Goethe, scanning the same horizon, was not so unsuccessful. It is true enough that, with the decay of religion as a force in human life, poetry must be robbed of that particular *kind* of conviction, as has been noted by Mr. I. A. Richards; but to assume from this that the poetry of the future must inevitably be a poetry of skepticism or negation is perhaps to oversimplify the issue. Poetry has always shown itself able to keep step easily and naturally with the utmost that man can do in extending his knowledge, no matter how destructive of existing beliefs that knowledge may be. Each accretion of knowledge becomes, by degrees, a part of man's emotional attitude to the world, takes on affective values or overtones, and is then ready for use in poetry. The universe does not become each year simpler or less disturbing, nor is there any reason to suppose that it ever will. The individual who is born into it will continue to be surprised or delighted by it, or surprised and injured; and in direct ratio with this surprise and delight or surprise and injury, he will continue to be a poet.

The wail of contemporary criticism, therefore, to the effect that poetry can find nothing to cling to, leaves one a little skeptical, though it is easy enough to sympathize with the individual poets who, suffering from that delusion, have for the moment lost themselves in self-distrust. Mr. Pound and Mr. Eliot are perhaps very typical victims of this kind. But whereas Mr. Pound has evaded the issue, seeking asylum in a sense of the past (rather half-heartedly held), Mr. Eliot has made a poetry of the predicament itself. His poetry has been from the outset a poetry of self-consciousness; of instinct at war with doubt, and sensibility at odds with reason; an air of precocious cynicism has hung over it; and his development as a poet has not been so much a widening of his field—though at first sight *The Waste Land* might suggest this—as a deepening of his awareness of it. Prufrock, who antedated by a decade the later poem, could not give himself to his emotions or his instincts because he could not bring himself, *sub specie aeternitatis*, quite to believe in them: he was inhibited, and preferred to remain a despairing spectator, but at the same time he wished that he might have been a simpler organism, "a pair of ragged claws." The theme of "Gerontion," a good many years later, is the same: it is again the paralyzing effect of consciousness, the "After such knowledge, what forgiveness?" And *The Waste Land* is again a recapitulation, reaching once more the same point of acute agony of doubt, the same distrust of decision or action, with its "awful daring of a moment's surrender / Which an age of prudence can never retract."

The reissue of *Poems* is not the occasion for a detailed review of Mr. Eliot's early work, however; for our present purpose it is sufficient to note that Mr. Eliot has conspicuously shared the contemporary feeling that there are no "large" themes for the poet, and that he has had the courage and the perspicacity to take as his theme precisely this themelessness. Why not—he says in effect—make a bitter sort of joke of one's own nihilism and impotence? And in making his bitter joke, he has written some of the most searchingly unhappy and vivid and individual of contemporary poetry. One feels that his future is secure, by virtue of his honesty quite as much as by virtue of his genius.

Checklist of Additional Reviews

*William Van Doorn. "How It Strikes a Contemporary, New Series I. T. S. Eliot." *English Studies* 8, no. 5 (1926), 138–42.
**Arthur Hood. "Delicate Spirits and a Hunchback." *Poetry Review* 17 (January–February 1926), 53–54.
*C. Henry Warren. "Three Poets." *Bookman* 69 (February 1926), 263–64.
*A. L. Morton. "Notes on the Poetry of Mr. Eliot." *Decachord* 2 (March–April 1927), 209–18.

FOR LANCELOT ANDREWES:
ESSAYS ON STYLE AND ORDER
1928, 1929

FOR LANCELOT ANDREWES

ESSAYS ON STYLE AND ORDER

BY

T. S. ELIOT

'*Thou, Lord, Who walkest in the midst of the golden candlesticks, remove not, we pray Thee, our candlestick out its place; but set in order the things which are wanting among us, and strengthen those which remain, and are ready to die.*'

LONDON

Faber & Gwyer

*J[acob] Bronowski.
Cambridge Review 49
(30 November 1928), 176.

Mr. Eliot asserts himself. He is no longer the intelligent layman; there are moments when he is near becoming the intolerant cleric. This religious preoccupation is as irritating as that of M. Maurras, and as irrelevant. Dogma is an integral part of classicism; but it is a part only; and when Mr. Eliot underlines it so insistently, he endangers the whole perspective of his attitude. The essay on the humanism of Prof. Babbitt shows to what falsification this must lead, and cannot be passed over without challenge.

Mr. Eliot, in attacking American humanism, suggests that humanism is ancillary to religion; and develops a picture of Christianity as continuous in contrast to a sporadic humanism. This is patently false. If there has always been a remnant of religious tradition in the High Church—and such passages as Tractarian humanism make even this doubtful—there has certainly been no such tradition in the English Church proper. Neither have the European races an "actual tradition of Christianity"; but, as T. E. Hulme showed, European culture since the Renaissance has been almost continuously humanist. The confessions of Rousseau, the table-talk of Queen Victoria, or the sermons of Archbishop Fénelon, are ample illustration. The humanist attitude is in fact quite tenable in an age sufficiently self-satisfied; and it is only Prof. Babbitt's classical contacts which make him uncertain. America as a whole is not uncertain; the danger of its attitude is not, as Mr. Eliot suggests, collapse, but the danger of a culture out of contact with Europe, and without tradition. That is why it is a danger to Europe as well as to America.

It is superfluous to say that all these essays, with the exception perhaps of those on Middleton and Baudelaire, are important; that on Machiavelli particularly so. We can only hope that by the time Mr. Eliot finishes *The School of Donne*, he will have become less self-conscious of his faith.

*"Mr. Eliot's New Essays."
*Times Literary
Supplement* 1401
(6 December 1928), 953.

Mr. Eliot owes his eminence in the world of modern literature to something more than his possession of a critical and poetic mind of a high and original order; even those who have never been able to accept his point of view have always recognized and paid tribute to the seriousness and integrity displayed in his unremitting quest for a philosophy, or at least a mental attitude, which might square with the complexities, the realities and, in particular, the skepticisms of contemporary living. None could attribute to him a merely facile classicism, and yet it has sometimes seemed to us that he rather desired to be than indubitably was a classicist. The pages of his early book, *The Sacred Wood*, reiterate the desirability—indeed the necessity—for a living tradition of which the artist might fully avail himself. "It is part of the business of the critic to preserve tradition—where a good tradition exists." But what if it does not exist? *The Sacred Wood* makes clear enough its author's desire for a cultural tradition, but are we not entitled to assert that it does nothing to show such a tradition as existing or even possible today. Again, if his poems can be called classical at all it is only in the most superficial and negligible sense, in their debts, their borrowings. In every essential, just in so far as they do most truly express Mr. Eliot in his singularity, they are unrestrainedly romantic. That, lost in the deserts of the Waste Land, amid "the mountains of rock without water," he should cry aloud for the security of an established tradition and all that it implies need surprise no one. But such a refuge, so viewed, must surely have seemed more than ever afar off!

It is now some years since it was first suggested by an acute critic that Mr. Eliot would find it possible to reconcile his principles with his practice only "by an act of violence, by joining the Catholic Church." [See John Middleton Murry, "The 'Classical' Revival" (1926), in this volume, pp. 132–36.] A drawing near to Anglo-Catholicism is the step his new book announces. For it is not, he declares, simply a collection of literary essays. In that case it "would have been much bigger." These eight articles have been carefully selected and arranged "to indicate certain lines of development, and to disassociate myself from certain conclusions which have been drawn from my volume of essays, *The Sacred Wood* . . . The general point of view may be described as classicist in literature, royalist in politics and anglo-catholic in religion." The first of these two quoted sentences contains an ambiguity unusual in Mr. Eliot's writing, leaving it not clear whether he thinks the "certain conclusions" justifiably or erroneously drawn. In view of his new preface to the second (1928) edition of the earlier book, we must presume the latter, but in that case, without further specification, the comment is not very helpful. Certainly, as we read the two books it would seem that the later Mr. Eliot has little to regret or

revise, for we find in these new pages just the same "scrupulous respect for words, that their meaning should be neither vague nor exaggerated," the same preference for the direct above the "fine" phrase, the same fastidious striving towards a prose too perfectly "welded with the matter" to startle by sudden exultation in purple passages. Even more peremptorily than before does he reject "personality" as the source of any "ultimate value" in the arts, seeking to reduce the distortion of objective truth by the writer's individuality to a minimum. "Andrewes's emotion," he writes, summing up his ideal in a sentence, "is purely contemplative; it is not personal, it is wholly evoked by the object of contemplation, to which it is adequate; his emotions wholly contained in and explained by its object." He follows his precepts with, on the whole, admirable precision. The essay on Andrewes reveals him almost at his very best. He sets that Anglican Bishop clearly in his place in the English Church of the seventeenth century, dissects the peculiar excellences of his style as revealed in his sermons, and finally isolates his unique quality in the course of an illuminating comparison with Donne. The form of the essay is perfect, the expression (but for one or two harsher outbursts) almost exquisite in its unemotional purity. "John Bramhall" follows similar lines. "Niccolo Machiavelli" is directed to show the author of *The Prince* as an exceptionally honest, a "pure" and "intense" observer of human nature. F. H. Bradley appears not least as a great stylist who brought "British philosophy closer to the Greek tradition," Baudelaire—not wholly familiarly—as "essentially a Christian born out of his due time; and a classicist, born out of his due time." The essay on Thomas Middleton is excellent in its penetrative deliberation; that upon Crashaw contains some surprising comparisons with Keats and Shelley, and is less good. The concluding essay, "The Humanism of Irving Babbitt," calls for more detailed comment.

So far one has read these pages with pleasure and admiration, if with occasional and increasing perturbation. More and more one finds Mr. Eliot expressing controversial sentiments which he makes little or no effort to support, and growing, too, more and more uncompromising. In the essay on Bradley he is by no means the pure critic; he deals with his subject as defending a point of view in which they both concur. It is difficult to say whose views, if not of both, are being presented in such a passage as the following: "Morality and religion are not the same thing, but they cannot beyond a certain point be treated separately. A system of ethics, if thorough, is explicitly or implicitly a system of theology." Such questionable sentences are frequent. Bramhall, he says, "implies the profounder objection to Hobbes when he says simply that Hobbes makes praise and blame meaningless. 'If a man be born blind or with one eye, we do not blame him for it; but if a man have lost his sight by his intemperance, we blame him justly.' This objection is finally unanswerable." But is it? Have we really any right to go beyond the position of those who urge both free will and predestination as equally indisputable though incompatible facts? Admittedly we take free will for granted, but are we entitled to hold it as more than a working belief? Undeniably the modern tendency is not to blame a man for his failings and failures— but Mr. Eliot has already in "Lancelot Andrewes" declared for medieval against modern. He denies the ability of the individual to stand alone; destroy communion with God, he asserts, and the most enlightened humanism can yield only disappointment. All these issues are brought to a head in the final essay, which is in purpose a questioning of Mr. Babbitt's philosophy of secular humanism from the viewpoint of one accepting a religion of revelation and dogma. Can such humanism, he asks, ever provide an alternative to Christianity—save perhaps temporarily and on a basis of Christian culture? Is not the humanist, suppressing the divine, "left with a human element which may quickly descend again to the animal"? Has humanism ever achieved more than a sporadic accompaniment to a continuous Christianity? Can it, in short, be more than parasitical, secondary to religion? And he replies: "To my mind, it always flourishes most when religion has been strong; and if you find examples of humanism which are anti-religious, or at least in opposition to the religious faith of the place and time, then such humanism is purely destructive, for it has never found anything to replace what it destroyed." The characteristic modern refusal to receive anything upon an authority exterior and anterior to the individual he rejects decisively: "[U]nless by civilization you mean material progress, cleanliness, etc.—which is not what Mr. Babbitt means; if you mean a spiritual and intellectual coordination on a high level, then it is doubtful whether civilization can endure without religion, and religion without a church." The essay in its parts and as a whole leads "to the conclusion that the humanistic point of view is auxiliary to and dependent upon the religious point of view. For us, religion is Christianity; and Christianity implies, I think, the conception of the Church."

Here, certainly, is nothing new, but from the author of *The Waste Land* it is at first sight astonishing, to say the least. We ourselves can only conceive of Mr. Eliot's "act of violence" as consequent upon a dynamic fusion of the need for an object of belief with the desire—the increasing desire—for a universal and continuous rather than a living tradition. He has discovered at once a respite and a continuity.

But it is our view that by accepting a higher spiritual authority based not upon the deepest personal experience (for that we must still turn to the poems), but upon the anterior and exterior authority of revealed religion, he has abdicated from his high position. Specifically he rejects Modernism for medievalism. But most of us, like Mr. Babbitt, have gone too far to draw back. It is to the country beyond the Waste Land that we are compelled to look, and many will consider it the emptier that they are not likely to find Mr. Eliot there. Recently he recorded his conviction that Dante's poetry represents a saner attitude towards "the mystery of life" than Shakespeare's. Not a saner, we would say, but simply a different attitude, and to the majority, the great majority, today no longer a vital one.

*"For Mr. T. S. Eliot." *New Statesman* 32 (29 December 1928), 387–88.

[. . .]

[W]e prefer to deal with this little book as what it appears to be: a collection of essays on miscellaneous subjects to which the author has not succeeded in giving that coherent force which is the quality of a very determined character—the kind of force, for instance, which Dr. Saintsbury, whose predilections are very much what Mr. Eliot asserts his own to be, gives to all his writings. Mr. Eliot's great reputation with the young is due to two facts: that, of the men who practice and criticize the more recent fashions in literature, he has some acquaintance with the past—an acquaintance that strikes with awe the

young men whose reading begins with the Edwardians; that he holds very distinct and reasonably dogmatic opinions, and evidently writes from his mind rather than from his "dark inwards" or "the red pavilion of his heart."

[. . .]

*F. R. Leavis. "T. S. Eliot—A Reply to the Condescending." *Cambridge Review* 50 (8 February 1929), 254–56.

Under the title "For Mr. T. S. Eliot," there appeared in a recent number of the *New Statesman* a review of Mr. Eliot's last book.

"Mr. Eliot's great reputation with the young," pronounced the reviewer, "is due to two facts: that, of the men who practice and criticize the more recent fashions in literature, he has some acquaintance with the past—an acquaintance that strikes with awe the young men whose reading begins with the Edwardians; that he holds very distinct and reasonably dogmatic opinions, and evidently writes from his mind rather than from his 'dark inwards' or 'the red pavilion of his heart.'" [See excerpt of review on this page.] One recognized the note. It tends to recur when the consciously adult, especially in the academic world, speak and write of Mr. Eliot. [. . .] Those of us who are aware of our debt to Mr. Eliot have learnt not to be too provoked by this kind of condescension. It offsets the snobism attendant, inevitably, upon the vogue that Mr. Eliot enjoys, and suffers from. But the challenge

152

quoted above does seem to give one who still counts himself among the young, and who discusses literature a good deal with others of the young, a fair opportunity to acknowledge the debt and to define its nature.

First of all, we recognize in Mr. Eliot a poet of profound originality, and of especial significance to all who are concerned for the future of English poetry. To describe him as "practicing the more recent fashions" is misleading, and betrays ignorance and prejudice. It suggests that he is one of a herd of "Modernist" poetasters. But there is no other poetry in the least like Mr. Eliot's: he is an originator, and if he has his mimics, he could be confused with them only by the malicious or the incompetent. Nor is it his fault if he is included in the Sitwellian "we." "Profound originality" were considered words. Mr. Eliot says in *The Sacred Wood* that the historical sense is "nearly indispensable to anyone who would continue to be a poet beyond his twenty-fifth year; and the historical sense involves a perception, not only of the pastness of the past, but of its presence [. . .]. This historical sense, which is a sense of the timeless as well as of the temporal and of the timeless and of the temporal together, is what makes a writer traditional. And it is at the same time what makes a writer most acutely conscious of his place in time, of his own contemporaneity." Mr. Eliot is now well beyond his twenty-fifth year, and his latest poetry has a new vitality. "Salutation," which appeared in the *Criterion* for January, last year, and "Perch' io non spero," which appeared in the last *Printemps* number of *Commerce*, have a power and a beauty that might, one would think, compel recognition even from an anthologist. The poet bears out the critic. His poetry is more conscious of the past than any other that is being written in English today. This most modern of the moderns is truly more traditional than the "traditionalists"—and he is a poet.

"By losing tradition," he says in *The Sacred Wood*, "we lose our hold on the present." It is because of his hold on the present that he has his great reputation among the young. Poetry tends recurrently to confine itself by conventions of "the poetic" which bar the poet from his most valuable material, the material that is most significant to sensitive and adequate minds in his own day; or else sensitive and adequate minds are barred out of poetry. Something of this kind has clearly been wrong with poetry in this century, and efforts at readjustment, those, for instance, of Mr. Masefield, Mr. Binyon, and Mr. Squire, have commonly served only to call attention to its plight. Mr. Eliot is so important because, with a mind of very rare sensitiveness and adequacy, he has, for himself, solved the problem, and so done more than solve the problem for himself. His influence will not be measured by the number of his imitators, but will manifest itself in indirect and subtle ways of which there can be no full account. In any case, the academic mind charting English poetry a century hence will not be tempted to condescend to Mr. Eliot.

His influence has made itself so profoundly and so widely felt in so short a time because he is a critic as well as a poet, and his poetry and his criticism reinforce each other. One would hardly guess from the description of him as "criticizing the more recent fashions in literature" that his criticism has been almost wholly confined to writers of the past. If Dryden and Donne are in fashion, Mr. Eliot may have had something to do with their being so; it is he alone who has made them more than fashions. "The important critic," he says in *The Sacred Wood*, "is the person who is absorbed in the present problems of art, and who wishes to bring the forces of the past to bear upon the solution of these problems." We who are aware of our debt to Mr. Eliot find his criticism so important because it has pursued this aim with such indubitable success. The present writer, having undertaken to lecture on contemporary poetry, looked through several years of the likely journals, and found that the helpful review or critique almost always showed the influence of *Homage to John Dryden.*

Mr. Eliot's acquaintance with the past, then, has impressed us so much because it has illuminated for us both the past and the present. We find commonly that the erudition of the constituted authorities does neither. His acquaintance with the past is profound enough to have reshaped the current effective idea of the English tradition. If no serious critic or poet now supposes that English poetry in the future must, or can, develop along the line running from the Romantics through Tennyson, this is mainly due to Mr. Eliot. But for him we certainly should not have had this clear awareness; and for this debt alone—it is a very great, though incalculable debt—that histories of English literature will give him an important place.

All this might suggest that Mr. Eliot's criticism is pervaded by the propagandist spirit. It is not so: "English criticism," he has remarked, "is inclined to argue or persuade rather than to state"; but his own is the last against which such a charge could be brought. It is so entirely controlled by the will to "see the object as in itself it really is" that some people reading it, and missing the non-critical that they expect to find in criticism, think (or so they report) that it contains nothing at all. It makes some of us feel that we never read criticism before. At any rate Mr. Eliot represents for us the essentially critical, and when, intimidated by the insinuation of priggishness, we are told that criticism is "any kind of writing about books," we are stiffened by the thought of him as by a vicarious conscience. Those of us who are giving a good part of our lives to the study of literature are especially grateful to him. For no one has set forth for us our justifying ideas so clearly and cogently, and no critic has served them in his practice with such austere integrity.

The critic, he concludes, in [. . .] "The Function of Criticism," must have "a very highly developed sense of fact." This suggests well enough where, in his account of criticism, the stress falls. The critic must cultivate this sense of fact in regions where there are no facts that can be handed round or brought into the laboratory. He must aim, in so far as he is a critic, to establish the work of art as a fact, an object existing outside of, and apart from, himself. Actually, of course, this cannot be done, and there is no one demonstrably right judgment. But a critic is a critic only in so far as he is controlled by these ideals. And their inaccessibility leads, not to arbitrariness, but to askesis, not to assertiveness, but to docility. He seeks help, confirmation, and check from as many qualified minds as possible. "For the kinds of critical work we have admitted," writes Mr. Eliot, "there is the possibility of cooperative activity, with the further possibility of arriving at something outside of ourselves, which may provisionally be called truth." All this may be both old and obvious to the adult, but we who admire Mr. Eliot had never before had it made obvious to us; and we are grateful to him for the clearness and force with which he has set forth the idea of criticism, and for the athletic rigor with which he has verified his principle with his practice.

We have learnt from Mr. Eliot what is meant by "an interest in art and life as problems which exist and can be handled apart from their relations to the critic's private temperament." And it seems to us the only kind of interest that can justify a prolonged study of literature. But there will always be people who find Mr. Middleton Murry's kind of interest more exciting (though we ourselves acknowledge a debt to Mr. Murry for stimulus, derived mainly from his early work). It is not, however, only those who prefer prophecy, exaltations, and the ardors of the private soul who find Mr. Eliot's criticism unrepaying. There are others, sober enough, who are baffled and repelled by the very purity of its devotion to literature, by its very rigor. For Mr. Eliot never forgets that poetry is made of words. His approach is commonly by way of technique, and his dealings with "content" are always rigorously controlled and disciplined. He is not (to adapt some words of his own) one of those who, in writing about Hamlet, forget that their first business is to study a work of art. So those who are accustomed to think of Hamlet as a man with a life antecedent to, and outside of, the play, a subject for psycho-analysis, feel Mr. Eliot induces cerebral corrugations to no end. "To the member of the Browning Study Circle," he says, "the discussion of poets about poetry may seem arid, technical, and limited. It is merely that the practitioners have clarified and reduced to a state of fact all the feelings that the member can only enjoy in the most nebulous form; the dry technique implies, for those who have mastered it, all that the member thrills to; only that has been made into something precise, tractable, under control. That, at all events, is one reason for the value of the practitioner's criticism—he is dealing with his facts, and he can help us do the same."

Although Mr. Eliot never forgets to see poetry as a texture of words, he is as much concerned with what lies behind as other critics, and more effectively. "Their words," he says, comparing Shakespeare, Donne, Webster, and Tourneur with Jonson, "have often a network of tentacular roots reaching down to the deepest terrors

and desires. Jonson's most certainly have not . . ." This suggests fairly well the manner of Mr. Eliot's approach to the more inward critical problems, and the kind of control he maintains. And with this continence he is, we find, as fertile in generalizations, explicit and implied, as any critic we know. "*Eriger en lois ses impressions personnelles, c'est le grand effort d'un homme s'il est sincère*": it is not for nothing that he set this sentence from Rémy de Gourmont at the head of the first essay in *The Sacred Wood*. For instances of his generalizing one may adduce his elucidation of impersonality, of the relation between the work of art and the personality of the artist, and the account which he gives in *Homage to John Dryden* of the relation between thought and emotion in poetry. Such things as these we find in the essential structure of our thinking about art. They seem to us to be among those ideas which, says Mr. Eliot, "stand forth luminous with an independent life of their own, so true that one forgets the author in the statement."

And among such ideas, for some of us, is Mr. Eliot's conception of order. The more we brood over the critic's problem of making his judgment something more than an assertion of personal like or dislike the more inevitable we find the conception of European literature as an organic whole, and within it, English literature as an organic whole, an order—an order in which each new thing must find a place, though the existing order is modified all through by the addition. Here we come to the wider implications of Mr. Eliot's "classicism," and about these there is, naturally, less certain agreement than about statements of principle that arise immediately out of considerations of technique. And, of course, the "classicism" involves things outside of literature.

These other things are to the fore in Mr. Eliot's last book. The "very distinct and reasonably dogmatic opinions" that he holds concerning these things, whether we agree with them or not, seem to us to give *For Lancelot Andrewes* the "coherent force" that we have always found in Mr. Eliot's work. The reviewer's judgment to the contrary seems to us so perverse as to call for something other than ordinary critical incompetence to explain it. In any case, to liken Mr. Eliot's "dogmatic opinions" to Dr. Saintsbury's "predilections" will not do. Dr. Saintsbury's high Toryism appears mainly as accidental to his writings on literature. And whoever found in the expressions of it anything more than traits of a personality, racy and assertive, a Character? Mr. Eliot's "predilections" are central to all his work; they are its structure and articulation, its organization, and if we leave them out we leave out everything. This is not to intend any disrespect to Dr. Saintsbury; we know the debt that we owe to scholarship. But the mention of his name serves to bring out the peculiar nature of the debt we owe to Mr. Eliot. It is because of Mr. Eliot that such erudition as Dr. Saintsbury's does not merely overwhelm us, and make us feel that life is not long enough to take literature seriously. For if Mr. Eliot has told us that erudition is "useless unless it enables us to see literature all round, to detach it from ourselves, to reach a state of pure contemplation," he has also given us inspiriting, if chastening, examples of erudition being used to such end. It is he who has heartened us and shown us the way to a study of literature that may hope to produce something other than mere accumulation.

In his latest utterances, now that he has passed on "to the problem of the relation of poetry to the spiritual and social life of its time and of other times," we may not always follow him, in either sense of the word. But we await eagerly the promised statements of his position. And we believe that, whatever this may be, it is compatible with the completest intellectual integrity. Meanwhile we are much impressed by his way of stating the problem—the problem of preserving civilization. At any rate, we feel that we must consider very seriously his view of civilization as depending upon a strenuously achieved and traditional normality, a trained and arduous common sense, a kind of athletic poise that cannot be maintained without a laborious and critical docility to traditional wisdom.

Even were the problems that Mr. Eliot is concerned with less urgent, to us he would be notable for the spare and sinewy scrupulousness of his writing. It is this that has enabled him to exert so much influence with a bulk of published work that would fill no more than a middling-sized book. "When there is so much to be known," he says, "when there are so many fields of knowledge in which the same words are used with different meanings, when everyone knows a little about a great many things, it becomes increasingly difficult for anyone to know whether he knows what he is talking about or not." There could be no more effective awakener of the intellectual conscience than Mr. Eliot: he has made it less easy to shirk.

[. . .]

Francis Fergusson. "Golden Candlesticks." *Hound and Horn* 2 (April–June 1929), 297–99.

In his Preface to the 1928 edition of *The Sacred Wood*, Mr. Eliot says that the views he expressed in that volume in 1920 he still substantially holds. He was, however, at that time concerned with the thing called poetry and not with its relation to society or ethics. One of course believes Mr. Eliot when he says this: no one is such a consummate master of the art of sticking to the point; indeed it is this humble concentration on the subject that makes his criticism the most authoritative now being written. At the same time he is unique in the extent to which he has also the complementary virtue: he always sees the object in its context. [. . .] [A]lthough his method is to talk always about a particular thing (e.g., Symons's translation of Baudelaire), still everything he says implies the larger pattern which he holds in his mind's eye. [. . .] [O]f the essays in *Lancelot Andrewes* Mr. Eliot says, "I have made bold to unite these occasional essays merely as an indication of what may be expected, and to refute any accusation of playing 'possum. The general point of view may be described as classicist in literature, royalist in politics, and anglo-catholic in religion."

This is of course far more explicit than anything in *The Sacred Wood*, where all the questions not strictly relevant to poetry were shelved or referred to Tradition. Unless one was sure one knew what he meant by Tradition, it was easy to infer from that volume a doctrine of art for art's sake. In the present volume he does not talk about Tradition very much, but he discusses a political thinker (Machiavelli); a metaphysician (Bradley); a humanist (Irving Babbitt); and two bishops (Lancelot Andrewes and John Bramhall), as well as three poets. He is interested in each of them from several points of view. He is interested in their styles, their worldly wisdom, or lack of it, and in whether they have religious understanding. He permits himself in other words to bring a larger part of his pattern into focus; and we see

that what he called Tradition in *The Sacred Wood* he now calls God, or one manifestation of God, depending on whether one thinks his vision has remained fairly constant and only his exposition broadened, or his vision continuously broadened and deepened. Probably he has simply been waiting to speak until his vision should have become set and clarified. He is so self-conscious that he knows when he is ready to speak. Moreover he has an acute sense of what might be called the politics of spirituality, which determines the way he speaks when he has once made up his mind, as well as a sense of himself as an important actor on the world's stage. By *Lancelot Andrewes* he seems to have settled most of these questions of emotion, conscience and tact, and to be ready to announce a position. He has passed a certain point and mastered his development, which begins to seem steady and consistent.

This development might have begun (speaking diagrammatically and on the basis of hints which he himself has given) with the revelation of Henry James, whose piety toward the English social organism, though more solemn and credulous than Eliot's, seems to have been the latter's inspiration. Eliot also learned a great deal, from the point of view of method, from James's intelligence. ("He had a mind so fine that no mere idea could violate it.") Bradley's logic came to confirm and justify this type of intelligence, Bradley also having been humble before concrete, while insisting upon the unity of the whole picture. [. . .] With these guides he then acquired an enormous erudition, especially [. . .] in the Elizabethan period and the Mediterranean classics. He developed a loyalty to the best in the European tradition—classicism and Christianity— as well as a loyalty to English culture. His conversion to anglo-catholicism now comes as the keystone of this structure. He

157

says of Hooker and Andrewes: "They were fathers of a national Church and they were Europeans."

One already sees this creation as extremely impressive, meeting as it does the needs of an extraordinary sensibility, an extraordinary intelligence, and an extraordinarily intense emotion. Some of Mr. Eliot's audience may wonder in what proportions his sense of expediency, his religious need and his highly educated Puritan conscience, combined to produce the final movement of his conversion. Perhaps the clue is to be found in the quotation he places at the beginning of *Lancelot Andrewes*; "Thou, Lord, Who walkest in the midst of the golden candlesticks, remove not, we pray Thee, our candlestick out of its place; but set in order the things which are wanting among us, and strengthen those which remain, and are ready to die." We who have no golden candlestick must find his final position as unproductive of "manna and partridges" for us as Professor Babbitt's irreproachable individualism—Mr. Eliot's own lessons in "context" make that sufficiently clear; but he will take his place like Professor Babbitt as one of the guides that we will always need.

Edmund Wilson, Jr. "T. S. Eliot and the Church of England." *New Republic* 58 (24 April 1929), 283–84.

This volume of essays by T. S. Eliot contains papers on Lancelot Andrewes and John Bramhall, two seventeenth-century English divines, and on Machiavelli, F. H. Bradley, Baudelaire, Thomas Middleton, Crashaw, and Irving Babbitt. They are all distinguished by Eliot's unique combination of subtle and original thinking with simple and precise statement, and will be read by everybody interested in literature. T. S. Eliot has now become perhaps the most important literary critic in the English-speaking world. His writings have been brief and few, and it is almost incredible that they should have been enough to establish him as an intellectual leader; but when one tries to trace the causes of the change from the point of view of the English criticism of the period before the War to the point of view of the criticism of our own day, one can find no figure of comparable authority. And we must recognize that Eliot's opinions, so cool and even casual in appearance, yet sped with the force of so intense a seriousness and weighted with so wide a learning, have stuck oftener and sunk deeper in the minds of the postwar generation of both England and America than those of any other literary critic.

For Lancelot Andrewes, however, is not, like *The Sacred Wood*, a book merely of literary criticism. The essays which it contains have been selected by Eliot for the purpose of indicating a general point of view in literature, politics and religion. This point of view, he tells us in his preface, "may be described as classicist in literature, royalist in politics, and anglo-catholic in religion"; and it is to be further expounded in "three small books" called respectively *The School of Donne*, *The Outline of Royalism*, and *The Principles of Modern Heresy*.

Eliot's ideas, in *For Lancelot Andrewes*, appear chiefly by implication; and we run the risk of misrepresenting them in attempting to discuss them merely on the basis of this book. Still, Eliot has invited us to read this slender collection of essays as signifying classicism, royalism and anglo-catholicism, and it is difficult to know how else to write about it. The clearest and most explicit statement on the subject of religion which I can find is the following from the essay in which Eliot points out the deficiencies of Irving Babbitt's humanism: "[U]nless by civilization you mean material progress, cleanliness, etc. . . . if you mean a spiritual and intellectual coordination on a high level, then it is doubtful whether civilization can endure without religion, and religion without a church." One recognizes a point of view which is by way of becoming fashionable among certain sorts of literary people. Yet this usually presents itself merely as a feeling that it would be a good thing to believe rather than as a real and living belief. And, though Eliot lets us know that he does believe, his faith, as it appears both in these essays and in his recent poems, seems a faith entirely uninspired by hope, entirely unarmed with force—a faith which is merely, to quote his own epigraph, "ready to die."

Now, no one will dispute that the world, just at present, is badly in need of the sort of ideals which the Church was able formerly to supply; but it seems to me that the objection to Eliot's position is simply that the Church is now practically impossible as a solution to our present difficulties because it is so difficult to get educated people to believe in its fundamental doctrines—and that, even if a few first-rate men like Eliot manage to convince themselves that they do not accept them, one cannot see how they can honestly contemplate the possibility of a renaissance of faith general enough to make the Church intellectually important again. I agree that, without a church, you cannot have anything properly describable as religion; and I sympathize with Mr. Eliot's criticism of certain substitute religions, like that of H. G. Wells, which try to retain the benefits of faith while doing away with the necessity of believing. You cannot have real Christianity without a cult of Christ as the son of God. But since it is plainly becoming more and more difficult to accept Christ in this role, it seems that we must do without both the Church and religion. The answer to Mr. Eliot's assertion that "it is doubtful whether civilization can endure without religion" is that we have got to make it endure. Nobody will pretend that this is going to be easy; but it can hardly be any more difficult than trying to believe that the intellectual leadership of the future will be supplied by the Roman Catholic Church or by the Church of England, or by any church whatsoever.

Nothing seems to me more sadly symptomatic of the feeble condition of modern literary people, of their unwillingness or incapacity to confront the realities about them, than the movement back to Thomas Aquinas—or, as in Eliot's case, back to Bishop Andrewes. It is not a question of the wisdom or the authority of Bishop Andrewes or Aquinas in their own day, when it was still possible for a first-rate mind to accept the supernatural basis of religion. But to argue, as, in the literary world, one sometimes finds people doing, that, because society is badly off without religion, we should make an effort to swallow medieval theology, seems peculiarly futile. If the salvation of civilization depends on such religious fervor as the present literary generation is capable of kindling—if it depends on the edifying example of the conversion of Jean Cocteau and the low blue flame of the later Eliot—then I fear that we must give up hope.

I was writing last week of John Dos Passos and his mirage of social revolution.

It seems to me that T. S. Eliot is a case of much the same kind: T. S. Eliot, like Dos Passos, is a highly cultivated American who finds it difficult to accept contemporary America; but, instead of escaping from the American situation by way of Greenwich Village radicalism and the myth of a serious-minded and clear-eyed proletariat, as Dos Passos tends to do, Eliot has gone to England and evolved for himself an aristocratic myth out of English literature and history. Eliot's classicism, royalism, and anglo-catholicism, from the notion I get of them in his recent writings, seems to me as literary and lacking in plausibility as Dos Passos' class-conscious proletariat: it seems as difficult to imagine royalty and the Church becoming more, instead of less, important even in England as it does to imagine the American employees becoming less, instead of more middle-class. Most Americans of the type of Eliot and Dos Passos— that is, sensitive and widely read literary people—have some such agreeable fantasy in which they allow their minds to take refuge from the oppression and perplexities about them. In the case of Mencken, it is a sort of German university town, where people drink a great deal of beer and read a great many books, and where they respect the local nobility—if only the Germany of the Empire had not been destroyed by the War! [. . .] With Ezra Pound, it is a medieval Provence, where poor but accomplished troubadours enjoy the favors of noble ladies—if only that world were not as dead as Provençal! With John Dos Passos, it is a society of workers, disinterested, industrious, and sturdy, but full of the gaiety, good-fellowship, and frankness in which the Webster Hall balls nowadays are usually so disappointingly lacking—if only the American workers were not preoccupied with buying radios and Ford cars, instead of organizing themselves to overthrow the civilization of the bourgeoisie! And with T. S. Eliot, it is a world of seventeenth-century English churchmen, who combine scrupulous consciences with good prose—if it were only not so difficult nowadays for men capable of becoming good writers to believe in the Apostolic Succession!

Among these, writers like Dos Passos and Mencken stay at home and denounce America, while writers like Eliot and Pound go abroad and try to forget it. It is peculiarly hard for such men to get an intellectual foothold in our world: New York, particularly, at the present time, is like the great glass mountain of the Arabian Nights, against which the barques of countless young writers are continually coming to grief. And this is true not of the United States only, but more or less of the whole western world. Europe, industrially, politically, and socially, is becoming more and more like America every day; and the European catastrophe of the War has left America demoralized, too. It is up to the young American writers to make some sense of their American world—for their world is not everybody's world, and, if they fail to find a way to make possible in it "a spiritual and intellectual coordination on a high level," it may be that no one else will be able to do it for them. That world is a world of many religions, but without the leadership of any church— and it is a world where, whatever reorganization one may prophesy for a democratic state, it is difficult to imagine the restoration of monarchy. It is a world in which T. S. Eliot's positive programs would not, therefore, seem particularly helpful. We shall, I fear, not be able to lean upon the authority of either Church or King, but shall have to depend for our new social and moral ideals on a resolute study of contemporary reality, and upon our own imaginations.

Arthur Colton.
"A Significant Direction."
Saturday Review 5
(27 April 1929), 947.

I once asked a French scholar to explain the high estimate placed on Bossuet by French critics, even the worldly minded; and he replied: "His magnificent logic." Some such epithets, magnificence and logic, we make use of in our estimate of Burke, but it is no doubt more inveterate with the French to insist on the aesthetic values of logic. At a time when we are feeling that habit and emphasis are rather conspicuously absent from the contemporary program, it is significant that Mr. Eliot's very significant mind turns to the seventeenth century—to the sermons of Bishop Andrewes and to Bishop Bramhall's *Just Vindication of the English Church*—for his initial examples of style, and of order as the first principle of style. Literary criticism of sermons is not often met with now. One's memory has to go back to Coleridge and Johnson in search of it, and notes that their admiration, too, was for the seventeenth-century preachers. In so thinking of the subject from a literary standpoint, one notes further that the old-fashioned sermon had very distinct structural form. Divinity students must have been taught how to build them, and taught a principle like that imposed on the drama. As for the plot, so for the argument; nothing belongs there which does not move it forward. The formal divisions and subdivisions were devices to force average preachers—who as average men would tend to wander from coherence—to force them into clarity and consecutive precision in spite of themselves.

Mr. Eliot finds that Andrewes's sermons are models of absorption in the subject, whereas Donne's sermons are interfused and interrupted by Donne's personality. It was a strange personality, and strange personalities interest us; but Mr. Eliot prefers personality behind rather than in front. In the same way he finds the almost forgotten Bramhall a sounder and more logical thinker than Hobbes. The two bishops are important men historically, because the Church of England was formulated under Elizabeth, and these and their like gave it its intellectual background and substance. Andrewes's prose "is not inferior to that of any sermons in the language, unless it be some of Newman's. [. . .] [And his] place second to none in the history of the formation of the English Church." Bramhall's prose "is great prose only in the sense that it is good prose of a great epoch."

Mr. Eliot defends Machiavelli as a realistic and logical thinker whose reputation has been falsified ever since his time by a persistent romanticism which was shocked by his "cynicism." But he was neither a cynic nor a prophet.

> [H]e was concerned first of all with truth, not with persuasion, which is one reason why his prose is great prose, [. . .] a model of style for any language. [. . .] What makes him a great writer, and for ever a solitary figure, is the purity and single-mindedness of his passion. [. . .] Only the pure in heart can blow the gaff on human nature as Machiavelli has done. [. . .] The cynic is always impure and sentimental.

One may object that cynicism is not always that, while admitting it the wrong word to apply to Machiavelli. One may object that neither is romanticism, in Mr. Eliot's derogatory sense, the right word to describe the feeling that has always been repelled by the logical, but unscrupulous, politics of *The Prince*. It is not exactly romanticism which rejects the doctrine that a sufficient end justifies any means. It is perhaps an instinct more realistic than any logic. But a defense of Machiavelli, like a defense of Fascism, must start from the situation and alternative of the time. Whether it justifies or not, it explains. And if Mr. Eliot, in his apotheosis of Machiavelli, goes further than most of us would go, the essay is nevertheless in line with the two preceding, and indicative of the general direction in which his mind is moving. It is seeking the path from an era of romance and roundabout thinking out into an era of straight thinking applied to undisguised realities.

So, too, with the essay on F. H. Bradley. He prefers Bradley to Arnold, as Bramhall to Hobbes and Andrewes to Donne, because he finds him a more realistic thinker, more secure on his feet, and less subject to hallucination. Again, in the essay on Baudelaire, he points out that Mr. Symons mistranslates Baudelaire into the faded dialect of the "decadent 'nineties." But Baudelaire was more substantial than that, more like Racine than like Swinburne, for whose childish disciples "evil was very good fun." To Baudelaire it was a reality. Again, in the essay on Thomas Middleton, a name associated as collaborator in a number of long-winded plays, it is shown that in each of two of these plays, *The Changeling* and *The Roaring Girl*, there is a woman character of extraordinary vitality and permanent truth to human nature, independent of the conventions of any epoch. Again, in the essay on Crashaw, the constant "brain work" in Crashaw is contrasted with the absence of that "brain work" in passages quoted from Shelley. Shelley seems to be Mr. Eliot's favorite hunting ground for samples of an age gone astray after unsubstantial things. To an ex-romanticist, not entirely repentant, it seems that the Shelley verse somehow sings, like a Shakespearean lyric, and the pace is swift; whereas the Crashaw verse does not sing but only meditates and the pace is slow. Mr. Eliot may say that "somehow sings" may stand for that very kind of day dreaming from nowhere to nowhere, which enclosed the whole romantic era in its violet fog. Still I suspect that, if no value is to be seen except where the thing is thought through to its outcome—no "mutations," nothing translunary and inexplicable—then something with reality in it is going to be missed.

The final essay is on "The Humanism of Irving Babbitt." I had always thought of Professor Babbitt and Mr. Eliot (companioned by M. Julien Benda) as moving in the same direction; and as regards purely literary criticism they do. Mr. Eliot acknowledges his relations to Professor Babbitt in terms of the utmost respect. But here is a question of ethical theory, where Professor Babbitt is an individualist, and is complained of as "trying to build a Catholic platform out of Protestant planks." His "inner check" is found as insufficient a substitute in feasible ethics for the solidities of the older faith, as F. H. Bradley found Arnold's "best self," or "culture," or "the stream of tendency" that on the whole "makes for righteousness." The criticism in both cases is sufficiently cogent, but one might think it only fair of Mr. Eliot to submit his own position. Perhaps it is not so much a position as a direction, and perhaps that is the best kind of position to take in times like these. The direction seems headed back to the seventeenth century, in so far that, however much or little he may accept their premises, he finds satisfaction in the reasoning of the seventeenth-century divines; just as he finds satisfactory "brain work" in the seventeenth-century poets and a correspondence to the realities of life.

It is his direction, as well as his force and scholarship, that leads me to think

Mr. Eliot among the most indicative of modern critics, indicative of the way things will possibly be tending a generation ahead, when the elders among us have gone away with our recollections and our surmises.

Mark Van Doren. "The Letter Giveth Life." *Nation* 128 (15 May 1929), 590.

I have heard this book abused as sterile by persons who had not got past the already famous preface wherein Mr. Eliot states that his general point of view is "classicist in literature, royalist in politics, and anglo-catholic in religion." Mr. Eliot, so the legend goes, has withered into a triple faith, hardened into a three-headed dogma—turned a fastidious, tired back upon our glorious confusion and gone the easy, empty way of absolutism. The author of *The Waste Land*, people say, has repudiated even his vision of our contemporary intellectual desert—a vision which was useful at least in that it showed us what we are—in honor of meaningless formulas from old time which he alone mumbles, thinking thereby to achieve impossible certitudes.

But Mr. Eliot announces in the same preface that he has in preparation three volumes explaining his classicism, his royalism, and his anglo-catholicism; and after several readings of the present volume I am inclined to suggest that his detractors wait until the publication of that trilogy—when quite possibly, there will be nothing to say. For all of Mr. Eliot's very fine and strong intelligence is here; he has in no sense lost footing, though his steps may take him where most of us never dream of walking these days. And I have every reason to believe that, far from being at the end of his critical career, he is only at the beginning of it. This in spite of the fact that he is seriously interested in religion and enormously concerned about the meaning of words. There is a connection between the two for Mr. Eliot, who approaches the problem of Grace through nothing less than the intellect. I fancy, indeed, the meaning of his book to be that almost no one else approaches it thus today. "Of course Mr. Shaw and Mr. Wells are also much occupied with religion and *Ersatz-Religion*. But they are concerned with the spirit, not the letter. And the spirit killeth, but the letter giveth life." Anyone who cannot guess what Mr. Eliot intends in the pregnant paradox had better read *For Lancelot Andrewes*. At least he will have read one of the most deliberate, precise, and fruitful of contemporary books.

[. . .] In an age of slovenly thought and blowzy discourse Mr. Eliot is a great relief. Whether or not the letter leadeth into salvation, may he follow it in peace.

Conrad Aiken. "Retreat." *Dial* 86 (July 1929), 628–30.

If it is impossible to read Mr. T. S. Eliot's criticism without respect, it is also becoming increasingly impossible to read it without misgivings. In *The Sacred Wood*, and again in *Homage to John Dryden*, Mr. Eliot provided his immediate generation with a group of literary essays which were an admirable corrective for many of the intellectual and aesthetic disorders of the time. They were compact, precise, astringent; they brought the past to bear on the present, the present into a visible relation with the past; in short, they helped materially to restore, for a literary generation which had lost its bearings, a sense of tradition as a living and fruitful thing. If one had any complaint to make, with regard to these essays, it was not of their main tendency, which was wholesome; nor had one any fault to find with Mr. Eliot's intelligence and aesthetic tact, which were acute; it was rather with regard to the plane on which Mr. Eliot chose to conduct his analysis—and the tone which he adopted—that one might have cavilled. In the matter of plane, one had to note that Mr. Eliot tended to be somewhat abstract, not to say academic. His analysis was more often analysis of the document itself than of the psychological dynamics of which the document was the sign; he seemed to regard literary forms as absolute and autonomous; and correspondingly, he seemed to minimize the merely functional, or social and psychological, elements in the creation of literature.

These restrictions made for simplicity and weight; but they also gave one an uncomfortable feeling that a great deal was being left out. In his very preoccupation with what was past and fixed, Mr. Eliot was perhaps already beginning to define himself, and his limitations, more candidly than he was quite aware. It was as if the immediate, the fluidly immediate, the here and now—whether it were to be seen in terms of personality, and the relation of personality to the work of art, or in terms of the relation of the work of art to its social "moment"—were positively frightening to him. Again and again he took elaborate pains to evade or minimize the problem of personality: even going so far as to maintain that the work of art is an *escape* from personality; a very revelatory

view. It may here be pertinently questioned whether it is not precisely in this curious *doctrine* that Mr. Eliot is seeking an "escape from personality." From the psychological chaos of the "I" and the "now," let us seek refuge in a world of canons, forms, and rituals.

But if one felt, now and then, a shiver from this quarter in *The Sacred Wood*, one is exposed to a merciless blast of it in Mr. Eliot's new book, *For Lancelot Andrewes*. In this, Mr. Eliot seems to be definitely and defeatedly in retreat from the present and all that it implies. A thin and vinegarish hostility towards the modern world is breathed from these pages. Seeking certainties, or at least a hope of certainties, Mr. Eliot sounds a quavering recall, and attempts to lead us back to classicism in literature, to royalism in politics, and to the anglo-catholic church in religion. Humanism he condemns as merely a "sporadic" ancillary of religion, a kind of parasite, unable to exist fruitfully in its own right. Reason is bankrupt. Of the human race, the less said the better. Of Machiavelli, he remarks in this new book: "[He] was no fanatic; he merely told the truth about humanity. The world of human motives which he depicts is true—that is to say, it is humanity without the addition of superhuman Grace. It is therefore tolerable only to persons who have also a definite religious belief; to the effort of the last three centuries to supply religious belief by belief in Humanity the creed of Machiavelli is insupportable. . . . What Machiavelli did not see about human nature is the myth of human goodness which for liberal thought replaces the belief in Divine Grace."

It is hard to describe this as anything but a complete abdication of intelligence. And *pari passu* with this abdication goes a striking change in Mr. Eliot's whole outlook and style. A note of withered dogmatism sounds repeatedly in these pages; the circle of Mr. Eliot's sympathies has narrowed and hardened; in his essays on Andrewes and Bramhall, he is even led, by his propagandist zeal, to write dully of dull subjects. Throughout the entire book—unless we except some excellent pages on Middleton and Baudelaire—we feel the presence of a spirit which is inimical to everything new or bold or generous. Cautiously, jejunely, with an air of puritan acerbity, it seeks a refuge from humanity in Grace, from personality in dogma, and from the present in the past. Turning its back on the living word, it retreats into a monastic chill; and denies the miracle and abundance of life. But can the miracle and abundance be denied in this fashion? Not, one suspects, so simply or so summarily. The moment is still with us, it is a world to be explored, and there are still intrepid explorers. Mr Eliot might have been one of these—as indeed in his verse at times he *has* been—and, but for the Grace of God, he might be yet. It is to be hoped that he will not continue to prefer a narrower and safer path.

Checklist of Additional Reviews

*D. W. B. "Book News and Reviews." *Oxford Magazine* 47 (24 January 1929), 318–19.
*Sherard Vines. "Intellectual Reaction." *Nation & Athenaeum* 44 (26 January 1929), 588, 590.
*Desmond MacCarthy. "The World of Books: Anglo-Catholic Criticism." *Sun Times*, 3 February 1929, p. 10.
*F. L. Lucas. "Criticism." *Life and Letters* 3 (November 1929), 448–55.
John Chamberlain. "New Volumes of Essays by Aldous Huxley and T. S. Eliot." *New York Times Book Review*, 24 November 1929, pp. 12–13.

DANTE
1929
ANIMULA
1929
MARINA
1930

DANTE

BY

T. S. ELIOT

'*In quella parte del libro de la mia memoria
dinanzi a la quale poco si potrebbe leggere
si trova una rubrica la quale dice:
INCIPIT VITA NOVA.*'

LONDON
FABER & FABER
24 RUSSELL SQUARE

T. S. Eliot

ANIMULA

Wood Engravings by

Gertrude Hermes

London:

Faber & Faber Ltd

1929

T. S. ELIOT

M A R I N A

With Drawings by

E. McKnight Kauffer

London

Faber and Faber Ltd

1930

Franklin Gary.
Symposium 1 (April
1930), 268–71.

[Review of *Dante*]

This little book on Dante may be considered from at least three points of view: as an introduction to Dante, as a discussion of poetry and belief, and as an amplification of what might be called Mr. Eliot's classical ideal. Mr. Eliot disclaims any intention of writing another brief introduction to the study of Dante and declares that he is incompetent to perform such a task; but he has written such an introduction, he has written the best we have, an important and exciting book; and so we can scarcely admit that he is incompetent. "A quotation, a critical remark, an enthusiastic essay," he writes, "may well be the accident that sets one to reading a particular author; but an elaborate preparation of historical and biographical knowledge has always been to me a barrier." Such knowledge is always a barrier in an *introduction*, and most of the introductions to Dante have too much of it. Mr. Eliot pursues a different method: he relates the process and stages of his own comprehension, his gradually growing awareness of the unity of Dante; and his whole endeavor seems to be to make us aware too.

The book is still more valuable because, while he was writing it, Mr. Eliot was preoccupied with a question that is urgent today, the question of poetic belief. Mr. I. A. Richards, in *Practical Criticism*, has shown how important this question is. Mr. Eliot is concerned with analyzing the question only to the extent of clearing the ground for an appreciation of Dante, but his theory has wider implications, and it is to be hoped that he will develop his point of view in more detail. His general conclusion may be indicated in a sentence: "I deny, in short, that the reader must share the beliefs of the poet in order to enjoy the poetry fully." His discussion is interesting, furthermore, because with this question he tackles an aspect of the larger problem formulated in the Preface to the 1928 edition of *The Sacred Wood*: "that of the relation of poetry to the spiritual and social life of its time and of other times," for poetry, he now believes, "certainly has something to do with morals, and with religion, and even with politics perhaps, though we cannot say what." It should be noted that in *Dante*, however, he is most concerned with what poetry has *not* to do with morals, religion, and politics, or, in other words, with reiterating that, to begin with, "we must consider it primarily as poetry and not another thing."

The best amplification of the classical ideal is approached by recalling, in a general way, the ideal put forward in *For Lancelot Andrewes*. Mr. Eliot would agree with M. Ramon Fernandez to this extent at least, that classicism is not "a certain manner of having been classic" which haunts the very style of the neo-classicists; he would agree further that it is "a sharply specific way of thinking and way of feeling"; but soon, if I understand the two positions, they would part company. Mr. Eliot's ideal, I believe, is to be found in his analysis of Andrewes:

When Andrewes begins his sermon, from beginning to end you are sure that he is wholly in his subject, unaware of anything else, that his emotion grows as he penetrates more deeply into his subject, that he is finally 'alone with the Alone,' with the mystery which he is seeking to grasp more and more firmly . . . Andrewes's emotion is purely contemplative; it is not personal, it is wholly evoked by the object of contemplation, to which it is adequate; his emotions wholly contained in and explained by its object.

If we omit Professor Babbitt, this is, in essentials, the ideal to which the other six men [discussed in *For Lancelot Andrewes*] approximate. Sometimes the very phrases are echoed, as when Mr. Eliot speaks of the "purity and single-mindedness" of the passion of Machiavelli, of Bradley's "purity and concentration of purpose," or of Middleton's observation about human nature, "without fear, without sentiment, without prejudice, without personality." This classical ideal may be summed up, perhaps, in the word "contemplation." The seven classicists are superficially quite different, living in different ages, aiming at different ends, but more profoundly they all resemble each other in this, that they are all men of contemplation. Superficially, also, their styles are different, for Mr. Eliot is not concerned with a certain manner of having been classic which haunts the style of the new-classicists, but with a certain manner of being classic which will always produce a fundamental similarity. He has no recipe for style, but traces it back to a "training of the soul."

This idea is put forward in a quotation at the very beginning of *Dante*: "*La sensibilité, sauvée d'elle-même et conduite dans l'ordre, est devenue un principe de perfection.*" M. Fernandez appears to omit the stage expressed in the clause "*sauvée d'elle-même*": he gives the impression that he wishes to order merely the same personal emotions which the romantics cultivated. Mr. Eliot, on the other hand, strikes at the very root of the romantic

metaphysic: he wishes to save sensibility from itself, he wishes intellect and sensibility to be in harmony, to make an identical effort towards perfection. The analysis of Mr. Eliot's ideal and the comparison of it with M. Fernandez's should be carried further, but here there is only space enough to suggest that, along with the question of poetic belief, this ideal was uppermost in Mr. Eliot's mind when he wrote *Dante*. It shines through the discussion of Dante's language, his use of allegory and simile. "The aim of the poet," Mr. Eliot wrote in his essay on Dante in *The Sacred Wood*, "is to state a vision"; and in this little book he goes on to analyze the devices which Dante used to state his vision. "Dante's is a *visual* imagination," he writes,

> . . . in the sense that he lived in an age in which men still saw visions . . .
>
> Dante's attempt is to make us see what he saw. He therefore employs very simple language, and very few metaphors, for allegory and metaphor do not get on well together. And there is a peculiarity about his *comparisons* which is worth noticing in passing.
>
> . . . The purpose of this type of simile is solely to make us *see more definitely* the scene which Dante has put before us in the preceding lines.

This classical ideal seems to have been instrumental in bringing about a change in Mr. Eliot's own poetry. The change, when we read his poems chronologically, is seen to be a gradual one; and to bring this out most clearly we must contrast his first and his last style. In the former we often get the impression that the poet is *searching* for "objective correlatives" which shall be the formula for his particular emotion:

And I must borrow every changing
  shape
To find expression . . .
            ["Portrait of a Lady"]

            Tenants of the house,
Thoughts of a dry brain in a dry
  season.
               ["Gerontion"]

In these quotations the search appears explicit; more important are the numerous places where it appears implicit. In his latest poetry Mr. Eliot seems to me to be doing something different. He no longer strives to find the formula for his disembodied emotion, but strives to be so wholly in his subject that the emotion will be evoked, will grow as he penetrates more deeply into it. Consequently, in "Animula," he has set himself a subject—"Issues from the hand of God, the simple soul"—and has explored it. It is hard to determine just how much this impression is due to the suggestion of Mr. Eliot's criticism, but one cannot help coming to the conclusion, in the end, that, though suggested by the criticism, one's impression is securely based in fact. It is instructive, for instance, to compare the earlier monologues, "Gerontion" and "The Love Song of J. Alfred Prufrock," with the later "Journey of the Magi" and "A Song for Simeon": in the first we are given the quotidian ague of our life, but in the second we are given that abstraction which comes from intense concentration. In my opinion Mr. Eliot has not yet surpassed certain poems written in his earlier style, but we are aware that he is doing something different. "Devotional poetry," he wrote in *For Lancelot Andrewes*, "is religious poetry which falls within an exact faith and has precise objects for contemplation." With "Perch' io non spero . . . ," "Som de l'escalina," "Animula," and the poems already mentioned, Mr. Eliot has emerged as a devotional poet.

Marianne Moore. "A Machinery of Satisfaction." *Poetry: A Magazine of Verse* 38 (September 1931), 337–39.

[Review of *Marina*]

What seas what shores what grey
  rocks and what islands
What water lapping the bow
And scent of pine and the woodthrush
  singing through the fog
What images return
O my daughter.

This inquiry, without question mark, is the setting of *Marina*. It is a decision that is to animal existence a query: death is not death. The theme is frustration and frustration is pain. To the eye of resolution

Those who sharpen the tooth of the
  dog, meaning
Death
Those who glitter with the glory of the
  hummingbird, meaning
Death
Those who sit in the sty of
  contentment, meaning
Death
Those who suffer the ecstasy of the
  animals, meaning
Death

Are become unsubstantial.

173

T. S. Eliot is occupied with essence and instrument, and his choice of imagery has been various. This time it is the ship, "granite islands" and "woodthrush calling through the fog." Not sumptuous grossness but a burnished hedonism is renounced. Those who naively proffer consolation put the author beyond their reach, in initiate solitude. Although solitude is to T. S. Eliot, we infer, not "a monarchy of death," each has his private desperations; a poem may mean one thing to the author and another to the reader. What matters here is that we have, for both author and reader, a machinery of satisfaction that is powerfully affecting, intrinsically and by association. The method is a main part of the pleasure: lean cartography; reiteration with compactness; emphasis by word pattern rather than by punctuation; the conjoining of opposites to produce irony; a counterfeiting verbally of the systole, diastole, of sensation—of what the eye sees and the mind feels; the movement within the movement of differentiated kindred sounds, recalling the transcendent beauty and ability, in *Ash-Wednesday*, of the lines:

One who moves in the time
between sleep and waking, wearing

White light folded, sheathed about
her, folded.
The new years walk, restoring
Through a bright cloud of tears, the
years, restoring
With a new verse the ancient
rhyme.

As part of the revising of conventionality in presentment there is the embedded rhyme, evincing dissatisfaction with bald rhyme. This hiding, qualifying, and emphasizing of rhyme to an adjusted tempo is acutely a pleasure besides being a clue to feeling that is the source, as in *Ash-Wednesday*, of harmonic contour like the sailing descent of the eagle.

Marina is not for those who read inquisitively, as a compliment to the author, or to find material for the lecture platform. Apocalyptic declaration is uncompliant to parody. If charged by chameleon logic and unstudious didacticism with creating a vogue for torment, Mr. Eliot can afford not to be incommoded, knowing that his work is the testament of one "having to construct something upon which to rejoice."

Checklist of Additional Reviews

Rebecca West. "The Weaker Image." *New York Herald Tribune Books*, 5 January 1930, p. 8.
**Federico Olivero. "An English Poet–Critic and an Italian Reviewer." *Poetry Review* 21 (January–February 1930), 68–69.
*R. Ellis Roberts. "Two Poets." *Bookman* 77 (March 1930), 359–60.
Lawrence Leighton. "Eliot on Dante." *Hound and Horn* 3 (April 1930), 442–44.

ASH-WEDNESDAY
1930

ASH-WEDNESDAY

BY

T. S. ELIOT

LONDON
FABER & FABER LTD.
1930

*Gerald Heard.
"T. S. Eliot."
Week-End Review 1
(3 May 1930), 268–69.

Mr. Eliot is so serious a poet that he deserves, like all who have escaped from the idle singing through an empty day, to be noted, not for the way he says things, but for the things themselves. His style is that most living style, a language distinctive because it is fitted so closely to a personal thought. It is a symptom and can only be justly criticized if an attempt is made to judge the thought from which it springs. So his poetry, though highly stylized, may be appreciated by the ordinary thinking man. Mr. Eliot's poems are not written as exercises in prosody or illustrations of new sound-patterns; they are his philosophy. What he says, he says because not otherwise could he give expression to his strong conviction. *The Waste Land* could only be understood if it was realized how deeply the poet had suffered because of the war's desolation.

The clue to these six poems called *Ash-Wednesday* seems to be that the poet has entered on a new stage of his life. *Adhesit pavimento* might still be written over them, but also *De profundis*, for the strongest feeling that they give is of a spirit's communing. They do not seem addressed to any public, still less to appreciators of verse.

This, of course, is not to say that they will not interest poetry lovers; but certainly such will be distracted from their love of pure expression by the way that philosophy will keep breaking in. Indeed, it does not seem that it is possible to appreciate this verse unless one can first discover to which of the traditions of English

religious verse Mr. Eliot really belongs. On the one side we have the broad organ notes of the main tradition, the expression of a people whose main characteristic is that they have cared for the word rather than the rite, for statement rather than symbol. It is the tradition which gave *The Authorized Version* and which speaks through Milton, and through Dryden, though a Catholic. Religion to it is not so much a mystery to be shown forth by symbols and ritual, but is rather "sanctified commonsense" to be set forth in the most stately language. On the other side is what may be called the iconographic tradition, the tradition which uses words, not for argument or for rhetoric, but to raise visual images, to create hard clear symbols, for it believes the infinite can only so be approached and words may only so be used to shadow it forth.

In English poetry, this tradition runs alongside our main canon. We can trace it back from Hopkins and Thompson, to Crashaw and Donne, back even to the author of *The Pearl*. Now to which of these two does Mr. Eliot belong? For some time he seemed to be attached to the visual school, but it is only possible to be a true visualizer if the main current is given a wide berth. In English it flows so strongly that for a poet to approach it is to be drawn into its tideway. Francis Thompson realized that. It seems to have been a deliberate attempt to free himself of the associative sound tradition that made him take for his greatest expression of the search for the strayed soul by the divine lover, not the perfect simile of the Good Shepherd, which has followed man for a hundred generations, but the violent, contradictory simile of the dog hunting down its prey.

It is therefore very remarkable that through these verses of Mr. Eliot, *The Authorized Version* breaks out on every hand. "And God said, / Shall these bones live?" "The burden of the grasshopper." "Redeem the time." "O my people, what have I done unto thee." "And let my cry come unto Thee." Who can say how these rhythms would sound to ears which have never echoed to the lectionary's cadences, and who can say that a poet who takes into his verse such phrases entire is not already passing into the main English tradition?

Such a symptom compels speculation as to the poet's spiritual bourne. The process of those who move in the direction of system and meaning is too often assumed to be Anglican, High Anglican, Roman, and probably the chances are in favor of such a solution for those who think visually and not orally. But it is really an accident that poets should so think—and even then the end is not certain. William Morris, a poet of the eye and not the ear, who called Milton a damned rhetorician, and a furious romantic to boot, did not charge into Catholicism from his unhistorical notion of the middle ages, but into Socialism. Taken as a whole, poets should be primarily artists of the ear, and if so they will tend to find their meaning and system in utterance rather than in rite, in prophecy rather than in symbol. Protestantism, because it suspects plastic art, must express its supreme feeling and intuition in poetry. [. . .] The nations to whom a rite and a sacrament are the supreme manifestations of reality must take to plastic expression to symbolize their religious feeling. The major poets must be poets of the ear, and they will always be prophetic, not priestly. That is why England is the home of Protestantism, supreme poetry, and of only a secondary sculpture and painting.

The future of Mr. Eliot's muse is therefore of interest to philosophy as well as to poetry. Will the main English tradition reassert itself with this returned New Englander? It seems to be doing so. If it does, when it wins him, his allegiance will mean more than a turn in poetic fashion.

---

*Francis Birrell. "Mr. T. S. Eliot." Nation & Athenaeum 47 (31 May 1930), 292–93.

When Mr. T. S. Eliot started out on a poetical career which was to astonish many and ravish some, he was primarily a satirist and a "wit," not merely in choice of subject, as in "Mr. Apollinax," but in the definite sardonic quality with which, by the arts of juxtaposition or abnormal stressing, he invested words that had not yet had such a significance:

> Princess Volupine extends
> A meagre, blue-nailed, phthisic
> hand
> To climb the waterstair. Lights, lights,
> She entertains Sir Ferdinand
> Klein.

The somber melody is intentionally out of key with the poet's ironic intention. [. . .] But in Ash-Wednesday—the ironic intent has completely vanished from the poems of Mr. Eliot, and with it perhaps the superficial qualitites that made him appeal to the younger generation. He is now out for what is known as "beauty," and "beauty" is less in request than wit. The six short poems that make up Ash-Wednesday are an elaborate study in pure form; and to my mind contain many passages of great loveliness:

> At the first turning of the second stair
> I turned and saw below
> The same shape twisted on the
> banister
> Under the vapour in the fetid air

Struggling with the devil of the stairs who wears
The deceitful face of hope and of despair.

[Quotation of lines 1–5 of *Ash-Wednesday* IV]

The main difficulty I have in facing this remarkable poem is that I do not understand what it is all about. What are the "three white leopards . . . under a juniper tree," what exactly are the three staircases, and the veiled sisters? Are they mystical or liturgical images with which I ought to be acquainted, or are they merely private associations in the sensibility of Mr. Eliot? On the second assumption, are they permissible? And on the first, how much information is an author justified in assuming his reader to possess? Does not such a great poet as Donne positively suffer in the extravagance of his sensibility? Though to be sure, Mr. Eliot would answer this last question with a violent negative. Then perhaps the difficulties will clear themselves up. When I first read *The Waste Land*, or even "Prufrock," I could hardly make head or tail of them, yet they now present no particular difficulty.

A short poem like *Ash-Wednesday* can only be appreciated by being read all through, and read more than once. Only thus will the reader be able to absorb the complexity of its texture, the elaboration of its prosody, the richness and violence of its internal rhymes, its liturgical somberness (for I suppose the liturgies of the Church dictate the form as well as the inspiration of the poem).

Mr. Eliot, very early in his career, developed a vocabulary. There was about his works, almost from the start, that authentic smell which enables one to tell them almost from a distance. No poet has "arrived" until he has developed his vocabulary, and some poets have not done so until late in life. But with the success comes the danger. The poet may rest content with his vocabulary and develop a manner and a mannerism. He becomes repetitive. Mr. Eliot is too inquisitive, emotionally as well as linguistically, for this to be a danger. On the other hand his temptation is to be too constantly on the move and keep the reader continually guessing. It is the best danger for a poet.

Eda Lou Walton. "Desire for Oblivion." *Nation* 131 (6 August 1930), 155.

That T. S. Eliot was in *The Waste Land* already bent toward a search into religious faith is, I believe, undeniable. In that picture of sterility he made his accusation against his age, stated his desire for perfection, and began his search for faith and for God. He could not continue to cry against drought; he must find the principle, for himself at least, of life. Nor would he be likely to find this in any adaptation to a scientific point of view. There is therefore no break between Eliot's earlier poems and his later. The difference is merely one of development. His passion was always for the past; it was therefore more or less to be expected that he would finally accept not only classicism in form but one of the oldest of religions, the Anglo-Catholic.

It is with the theme of the later poems that we are concerned. Has Eliot found in the acceptance of the Anglo-Catholic religion anything that has greatly altered his poetry? I do not believe so. The fundamental emotion, the emotion which is the source of the man's creative ability in poetry, remains the same. Every poem published since his pronouncement of his creed is upon the theme of death in life, life in death, and the sincere desire for oblivion. Life is a slow dying, death is a rebirth, and neither process is subject so much for ecstasy or rejoicing as it is for pain and denial. Whenever Eliot has developed his argument up to the point where a moment of vision might shatter doubt, he takes that last step toward faith not by vision, and not intellectually, but by a cry for the Word: "Lord, I am not worthy / but speak the word only."

[Quotation of fourth stanza of *Ash-Wednesday* I]

In *Journey of the Magi*, one of the several poems published in pamphlet form before *Ash-Wednesday*, Eliot speaks of Christ's birth as "Hard and bitter agony for us, like Death, our death." In another, *A Song for Simeon*, his theme is death. And, finally, in *Ash-Wednesday* we have a long ritualistic chant or prayer for the acceptance of faith. The poem is very difficult of interpretation because it relies upon no ecstatic penetration of the mysteries, but upon a symbolism not so much Catholic as it is personal. The poem opens with lines reminiscent of Dante and Shakespeare, but the poet does not resort thereafter to quotation:

Because I do not hope to turn again
Because I do not hope
Because I do not hope to turn
Desiring this man's gift and that man's
    scope.

The theme of the entire first part is renunciation of life, of life which cannot find its reason for being as do trees and plants. Part II then develops through a series of symbols—three leopards who feed on the flesh and the bones, the lady who may be the Church—the idea that the flesh and the spirit wish oblivion. The bones finding peace in oblivion, the spirit comes upon the symbol of unity: "The single Rose / Is now the Garden." Part III may be said

to recall Dante again. An ascent of three stairs toward paradise is described. On the first step one leaves behind the demons of hope and despair; on the second is a blankness (again the waste land), an "old man's mouth drivelling, beyond repair." The third stair affords a renewed consciousness of sensual living. Only after this memory which fades comes the cry:

Fading, fading; strength beyond hope
    and despair
Climbing the third stair.

Lord, I am not worthy
Lord, I am not worthy

            but speak the word only.

Part IV is difficult of exact interpretation. Here the forces of life and death are interwoven. Mary, the Virgin, spirit of life walking between the violet and the violet, renews all things. The years walk there too and take away the fiddles and the flutes; the new years cry "Redeem the time, redeem the dream." This is followed by Part V, where the answer as to the way of redemption is found in the Word:

And the light shone in darkness and
Against the Word the unstilled world
    still whirled
About the centre of the silent Word.

        O my people, what have I
    done to thee?

Part VI comes back to the refrain of Part I, "Although I do not hope to turn again," and to the statement that this is the time of tension between dying and birth, when the spirit is reborn.

[Quotation of lines 27–35 of *Ash-Wednesday* VI]

The poet never reaches, it seems, any overpowering certainty. The emotion never reaches great pitch. There is more intensity in those lines which state the poetic desire for oblivion than in any affirming religious faith. Throughout, the mood is almost desperately sad.

Edmund Wilson, Jr.
New Republic 64
(20 August 1930),
24–25.

The three short and pious poems which T. S. Eliot has brought out as Christmas cards, since "The Hollow Men" announced the nadir of the phase of despair and desolation given such effective expression in The Waste Land, seemed comparatively uninspired and mild—far below his earlier level. One felt that the humility of his new religious phase was having the effect of enfeebling his poetry. But his new poem, or group of poems, Ash-Wednesday, which follows a scheme somewhat similar to that of The Waste Land and makes a sort of sequel to it, is not an unworthy successor.

The poet begins with the confession of the bankruptcy of his former hopes and ambitions:

[Quotation of first and last stanzas of Ash-Wednesday I]

There follow passages in which the prayer is apparently being answered: the poet's humility and pious resignation are rewarded by a series of visions which first console, then lighten his heart. We find an imagery new for Eliot, a symbolism semi-ecclesiastical and not without a Pre-Raphaelite flavor: white leopards, a Lady gowned in white, junipers and yews, "The Rose" and "The Garden," and "jewelled unicorns draw[ing] by the gilded hearse": these are varied by an interlude which returns to the imagery and mood of The Waste Land—[quotation of first stanza of Ash-Wednesday III]—and a swirling, churning, anguished passage which suggests certain things of Gertrude Stein's—[quotation of first stanza of Ash-Wednesday V].

At last the themes of the first section recur: the impotent wings of the "agèd eagle" seem to revive, as,

From the wide window towards the
   granite shore
The white sails still fly seaward,
   seaward flying
Unbroken wings
[. . . . .]

The broken prayer ["Bless me father"], at once childlike and mystically subtle, with which the poem ends seems to imply that the poet has come closer to the strength and revelation he craves. Grace is about to descend.

[Quotation of last stanza of Ash-Wednesday VI]

The literary and conventional imagery upon which Ash-Wednesday so largely relies and which is less vivid, because more artificial, than that of Eliot's earlier poems, seems to be a definite feature of inferiority: the "devil of the stairs" and the "shape twisted on the banister," which are in Eliot's familiar and unmistakable personal vein, somehow come off better than the "jewelled unicorns" which incongruously suggests Yeats. And I am made a little tired of hearing Eliot, only in his early forties, present himself as an "agèd eagle" who asks why he should make the effort to stretch his wings. Yet Ash-Wednesday, though less brilliant and intense than Eliot at his very best, is distinguished by most of the qualities which made his other poems remarkable: the exquisite phrasing in which we feel that every word is in its place and that there is not a word too much; the metrical mastery which catches so naturally, yet with so true a modulation, the faltering accounts of the supplicant, blending the cadences of the liturgy with those of perplexed brooding thought; and, above all, that "peculiar honesty" in "exhibiting the essential sickness or strength of the human soul" of which Eliot has written in connection with Blake and which, in his own case, even at the moment when his psychological plight seems most depressing and his ways of rescuing himself from it least sympathetic, still gives him a place among those upon whose words we reflect with most interest and whose tones we remember longest.

Morton D. Zabel. "T. S. Eliot in Mid-Career." *Poetry: A Magazine of Verse* 36 (September 1930), 330–37.

If only because the history of Mr. Eliot's mind was for over a decade regarded as typical of the ordeal of the twentieth-century intelligence progressing down the *via obscura* of the modern world, his latest encounters must command the attention of every contemporary. The hand that produced "Sweeney," "Prufrock," and *The Waste Land* unquestionably left its thumbprint on the thought and art of a generation. However little Eliot's former disciples may be able to follow the recent submissions of the poet from whom they learned the final accents of disillusionment, his experience remains one of the few authentic records of intellectual recovery in our time. For five years, that is,

since his last appearance as a poet, he has perplexed his readers by a slow reversion (announced as fully achieved in the preface of *For Lancelot Andrewes*) to the moral absolutism of which "The Hippopotamus" was an inverted parody, "Mr. Eliot's Sunday Morning Service" a social indictment, "Gerontion" a broken and pathetic echo, and the chorus of "The Hollow Men" a derisive denial. What had long been implicit in his work was at length fully disclosed: Eliot had never succeeded in cutting the roots of native puritanism which bound him to the soil of Christianity. His nostalgia for the heroic and sanctified glories of the past, when man's role in the universe was less equivocal and his destiny mystically shrouded by the doctrine of redemption, had finally led him not to suicide but to the affirmations of faith. His explorations had never been conducted as far afield as those of a self-deluded des Esseintes or of Verlaine. His realism, though crossed with the subtle lineage of Donne, was in the more immediate line of Arnold, of [James Thomson] of "The City of Dreadful Night," of Housman, and Hardy. Yet his return to faith might have been forecast by the courageous a dozen years ago. His early poems implicitly forecast a conversion as imminent as the deathbed avowals of those *fin-de-siècle* apostates who ended by espousing the creeds whereof they had made at worst a travesty, at best a rich and sensuous symbolism for their emotional adventures. In their luxuriating intoxications Eliot took no share. If anything made his reaction surprising it was the clear-eyed confrontation of reality in *The Waste Land*, or the withering and totally unflattering self-portraiture, singularly unlike the elaborate conceit of the "aesthete," in "Prufrock." But the element of self-pity was not lacking, and with it went an assumption of premature senility, a Byronesque mockery of conventions, and the extraordinary imaginative audacity which are unmistakable vestiges of a romanticism always mistrusted and finally rejected by Eliot in his literary philosophy. The finality of his despairing self-scrutiny implied a reserve of idealism to which, escaping suicide, he must some day fly for recourse. "The eagles and the trumpets" might be "Buried beneath some snow-deep Alps," but the possibility of digging them out remained. The "old man in a dry month, / Being read to by a boy, waiting for rain" did not release his last hope of a reviving shower, even where, across the parched acres of the waste land, it failed to fall. The straw-stuffed men in their idiotic dance around the prickly pear, waiting for the world to end "*Not with a bang but a whimper*," could not forget the phrases of a liturgy promising the resurrection and the life.

This poem, "The Hollow Men" of 1925, serves as a link between the earlier poems and *Ash-Wednesday*. In its complete form it not only provides an endpiece to the age of desolation and emptiness, but contrives a plea for conciliation.

[Quotation of first stanza of "The Hollow Men" III]

Reality had claimed of its victim his last desire, but hope sent a persistent echo through his brain.

[Quotation of last stanza of "The Hollow Men" IV]

And

Between the desire
And the spasm
Between the potency
And the existence
Between the essence
And the descent
Falls the Shadow
For Thine is the Kingdom

Here were probably the final lines of Mr. Eliot's *Inferno*. His present volume,

along with the three pamphlet poems lately published, may be considered the opening cantos of his *Purgatorio*. These terms are not applied fortuitously. They are suggested both by Mr. Eliot's long and penetrating study of Dante, whereof his recent essay is a record, and by a symbolism which combines liturgical allusion with the properties of the *Commedia*: the "multifoliate rose," the turning staircases, the "blue of Mary's colour" which suffuses the prospects of the future. From Dante Mr. Eliot has endeavored to derive the profound and salient simplicity which, in his own early poems, baffled so many readers by its resemblance to the ineluctable precision of Laforgue and Corbière; he has likewise seen in Dante the triumph of the visual imagination upon which the poet must rely for his direct, unequivocal, and *symbolical* approach to truth: a method natural to Mr. Eliot's creative temperament and wholly at variance with the discursive expositions of new-classicism. "Gerontion," "Sweeney Among the Nightingales," and "Burbank with a Baedeker" employed that method on a miniature but precise scale, and *The Waste Land* cut cleanest to the core of its inner meaning when it found symbolical instruments of unqualified accuracy (for instance, the first twenty lines, lines 77–110 and 257–265, and the first half of Part V). In Mr. Eliot's mind Dante's stylistic splendor is indissoluble from his mediaeval inheritance, the condition and certitude of his religious avowals, and the immediate veracity of his imagery. Dante has provided not only a tutelage for Mr. Eliot's literary concepts, but a guide toward the conversion which has now capped his career.

It was likely that Mr. Eliot should find this guide, not among the exigencies of material life or through flaying his conscience with the rods of logic and dialectic, but in a great poem. One is not debating his sincerity when one recalls that his former despairs were tutored by tragic and decadent poets, whose thoughts and feelings were imposed on his mind as ineffaceably as their phrases were imposed on his poems. From the desolation into which Webster, Donne, de Nerval, and Baudelaire led him, Dante (not to mention the Bishops Bramhall and Andrewes) stood ready to conduct him back to safety. The cure was apparently as ready at hand as the torture. It remains to be seen if it was adopted out of as extreme and inevitable a necessity, and if it has yielded a poetry as distinguished by passion and clairvoyance, by discipline in phrase and outline, by those qualities of "equipoise, balance, and proportion of tones" which in the *Homage to John Dryden* won for Marvell Mr. Eliot's incisive praise.

Mr. Eliot's approach to the doctrine of the Incarnation is presented in "Journey of the Magi"; his persistent weariness in the face of the world's burden—a weariness and a failure in moral courage hitherto counterbalanced by the rigorous integrity of his craftsmanship—reappears in "A Song for Simeon," where, with his "eighty years and no to-morrow," the tyranny of age and rationality still oppresses him. In *Ash-Wednesday* the torment of confusion and of exhausting intellectual scruples alike begin to disappear.

[Quotation of lines 1–8 and 24–31 of *Ash-Wednesday* I]

The poem, which is in six brief parts, is constructed around a paradoxical petition: "Teach us to care and not to care." Thus, by several allegorical devices the rejection of material concerns is described. The bones of mortal curiosity, "scattered and shining," sing "We are glad to be scattered, we did little good to each other." The spirit, climbing three staircases to the cadence of "Lord, I am not worthy, / but speak the word only," leaves behind the deceitful demons of hope and despair. "Mary's colour" becomes the signal of promise as the poet reproaches himself with the memory of his gospel of desolation: "O my people, what have I done unto thee."

[Quotation of last stanza of *Ash-Wednesday* V]

The final phrases, rejecting again the desperate realism of disillusionment, almost capture peace, the *Shantih* of *The Waste Land*, in an evening of beatitude, charity, and exaltation, with "let my cry come unto Thee" on the poet's lips.

Mr. Eliot's religious experience has not thus far impressed one as conceived in intellectual necessity, or as imposed through other than aesthetic forces on a crowded and exhausted mind. He will never be capable of forming a slovenly concept or judgment: his present essay and poems are distinguished by lucid statement and well-reasoned concision. They contain passages of subtle beauty. But of the impact of profound conviction and the absolute creative certitude of which the early poems partook and which still remains for Mr. Eliot's study in [Donne's] "The Extasie," [in Marvell's] "To His Coy Mistress," in Baudelaire's "La Mort," [. . .] one finds little here. The facility of design that made "The Hollow Men" a flagging and dispirited declamation, devoid of organic fusion, has led to a desultory kind of allegory, subtle enough in itself, but unsharpened by wit or emotional intensity, undistinguished by the complete formal synthesis which Aquinas advocated as a moral property and Dante exemplified in his slightest allusion. As a consequence, the contour of the design, as well as the clean accuracy of reference and the pure aphoristic subtlety, which alone would sustain the key of exaltation demanded by this quest for illusion and transfiguration, is lacking. Eliot spoke with complete authority in his first phase. In his second he displays a conciliatory attitude which may persuade few of his contemporaries but which, as a worse consequence, deprives his art of his once incomparable distinction in style and tone. These brief poems, however, find their place in a remarkable personal document which already contains some of the finest poetry and some of the most significant entries in modern literature.

William Rose Benét. "Round about Parnassus." *Saturday Review of Literature* 7 (18 October 1930), 249–50.

[. . .]

The most distinguished volume of poetry that has come to us recently is T. S. Eliot's *Ash-Wednesday*, though it is a very brief series of flights. The second movement appeared originally in the *Saturday Review of Literature*. *Ash-Wednesday* is another distillation of Eliot's despair mixed with a rather hopeless appeal for aid from the Christian religion. "Teach us to sit still," he reiterates. Let us give up, let us sit still. If that is the most modern and refined interpretation of how we should feel since once God so loved the world, we can only say that we violently disagree with it. In fact, even a superficial perusal of the New Testament will reveal a Christ who was ever a source of action. This other attitude smacks of a new Pharisaism. The Church, indeed, as it has developed, is not exempt from snobbery, a spiritual snobbery that we particularly detest. That the religion of Jesus

Christ should ever be even faintly associated with this or with a dead-end philosophy is inconceivable. But the ascetics have always entirely misinterpreted him. Eliot is a modern anchorite. Also he strives with none, for none is worth his strife, partaking of Landor's high conceit of himself. But our old conception of a prophet from the desert was that the locust and wild honey had played the office of a burning coal of fire upon the tongue. Revelation was spoken upon the prophets' return. There was no injunction to sit still. Quite the opposite. There was a wrathful summons to get up and do something.

Of course, Mr. Eliot and ourself differ so fundamentally in our attitude towards life, especially in our approach to the mystic, that, though we may deeply admire the strange, moving music and majestic somberness of some of Mr. Eliot's verse, we cannot share at all his continuous vast disillusionment that approaches apathy. When we are feeling a particularly good health we feel like praising God, and usually do so. Also, we have encountered no little stark tragedy in the course of our life, but it has not led us to ask to be allowed to sit still. At that, we are not known as being notably active. No, as Mr. Dudley Fitts says, in a recent *Hound and Horn*, "What 'metaphysical measure' can relate . . . Eliot and W. R. Benét [. . .]?" The answer is, quite aside from other considerations, None at All. Which makes more remarkable the strong impress that the writing of T. S. Eliot leaves on our mind. We are leagues removed from his disciples, as we are from all the snobbish modern literary cliques, including the Proustian. We regard it as so-easy-that-it-is-not-worth-doing to write a parody of Eliot. But not one of the busy little boys who have gone around copying him has come anywhere near him. For a man's soul, whatever it is worth, is his own single possession. It is one thing that no one else, save perhaps the

Devil, can steal from him. What is left out of the imitations of Eliot is merely everything, because what is necessarily omitted is the evidence of the soul. He is one of few modern poets who truly present it.

*Brian Howard.
"Mr. Eliot's Poetry."
New Statesman 36
(8 November 1930), 146.

It has been the delightful, but exhausting, task of the writer of this article to collect during the past year an anthology of verse by the younger English poets; one of the most exhausting things about it has been the numberless variations, generally in the treble key, upon Mr. Eliot's renowned poem, *The Waste Land*. Most of these, of course, have had to be rejected. It became such a plague that the moment the eye encountered, in a newly arrived poem, the words "stone," "dust," or "dry," one reached for the waste-paper basket. But there were a number of poems that came, showing an equally marked influence, towards which one felt very differently. These authors had read their Eliot, but they had profited. It was not the stones, the dustiness, and the droughts that affected them so much as the thought that lies behind this passage from Mr. Eliot's latest poem:

> Because I know that time is always
>   time
> And place is always and only place
> And what is actual is actual only for
>   one time
> And only for one place
> [. . . . .]
> Because I cannot hope to turn again

Consequently I rejoice, having to
    construct something
Upon which to rejoice

This, perhaps, is the pith, not only of *Ash-Wednesday*, but of the whole of Mr. Eliot's poetic message. It is the fearless, the truly modern, thought behind it that is influencing many of our better young poets, and influencing them for their good.

It is now some ten years since *The Waste Land* appeared, like some austere and unfamiliar flower in that blown-up garden which was English poetry immediately after the war. The Georgian poets were busy planting hardy perennials where hardy perennials grew before. Not even Mr. Siegfried Sassoon, sedulously slipping weed-killer into their watering-cans, was successful in deterring their dreary reconstruction. *Wheels* [a six-volume anthology of verse, edited by Edith Sitwell, 1916–21] itself creaked in vain. The young poets, who because of their age had escaped alive, were dazedly trooping up to help. Suddenly—*The Waste Land*, and it may be said with small exaggeration that English poetry of the first half of the twentieth century began. It is a pity that it was written by an American, but there you are. We are not quite so original as we were.

It was Mr. Eliot who suggested to our young poets, more by his poetry than by his admirable critical work, that they should begin seriously to think of what poetry really was. Granted that the guns had stopped, and that it was possible to hear again the nightingale, and granted that to "get into a state" about nightingales is the poet's function, the time had undoubtedly come to consider the general nightingale situation, so to speak. Of course, there is no time at which a poet should not consider it, but poetry has a way of deciding about the nightingale situation, and then leaving it. In England, as it happened, it had been decided by the Romantics, and left for a hundred years. The result was Georgian poetry. The nightingale had become a mockingbird. What was to be done? It was largely Mr. Eliot who supplied the answer. One must begin again, he suggested, to *think* about the nightingale. To begin with, what is it? The poet who asks himself this question at once becomes, unlike Keats, a metaphysical poet. Keats, you will say, had no need to ask such a question. Being the particular sort of poet he was, living at his particular time, and being a genius into the bargain—you are quite right. But you are quite wrong if you think that it was not high time for all who confuse a partiality for bird songs with an apprehension of Nature to go into the question of what a nightingale is.

In short, at a time when it was long overdue, it was Mr. Eliot who introduced the present limited, but definite, metaphysical revival. It was he who reminded our young poets—taking them, as it were, by the lapel as they were yawningly replacing the bird baths—that the poetic transcription of natural history is all the better, occasionally, for a thought or two about the nature of reality.

This newest among Mr. Eliot's longer poems has, it must be admitted, a certain flamelessness. It rarely transports. But the level kept is a high one, and if one seldom crosses a peak, it is a mountain road. As a technician, no one today excels its author in the writing of free verse. The rhythms are held and broken with the control of a master, and the interior rhyming is as refreshing as it is beautiful. As an illustration of this, the following is perhaps the best example from *Ash-Wednesday*:

Where shall the word be found, where will the word
Resound? Not here, there is not enough silence

Not on the sea or on the islands, not
On the mainland, in the desert or the rain land,
For those who walk in darkness
Both in the day time and in the night time
The right time and the right place are not here
No place of grace for those who avoid the face
Not time to rejoice for those who walk among noise and deny the voice

The comparative absence of adjectives in the foregoing, and the inclination towards one-syllable words are both things to be noted. It is like seeing—feeling—one sound stone being placed exactly, firmly, and permanently upon another, and there are many of us who believe that it is with such stones as these that the seriously damaged temple of English poetry must be repaired.

Woven into the text are several liturgical fragments. "The Hail Mary," "Pray for us now and at the hour of our death." The priest's preparation for Holy Communion, "Lord, I am not worthy." Then from the Bible, *Ezekiel*, "And God said, / Shall these bones live?" And St. Paul, "Redeem the time."

No charge of plagiarism, however, could be brought against Mr. Eliot any more than it could against Gray. Mr. Eliot fulfills the one condition upon which the incorporation by a poet of the work of others is allowed. The total result is entirely his own.

We will not end without saying that *Ash-Wednesday* is, in the sum, an important and beautiful poem. That it is grave, that it is what is termed "intellectual," is true. But it is this very quietness, this very severity, which imparts to it that particular quality of beauty so gratefully devoured by the sensitive modern mind. The courage for fine frenzies is already, let us hope, returning. It is being given to us, a trifle savagely, by Mr. Roy Campbell. But it is Mr. Eliot—and you may see how in the first quotation in this article—who will have made these future frenzies possible and valuable again, if valuable they prove to be. Because, upon reflection, it was not the guns that had silenced the nightingale. It was the mockingbird.

Allen Tate.
"Irony and Humility."
Hound and Horn 4
(January–March 1931),
290–97.

Every age, as it sees itself, is the peculiarly distracted one: its chroniclers notoriously make too much of the variety before their own eyes. We are now inclined to see the variety of the past as mere turbulence within a fixed unity, and our own surface standardization as the sign of a profound disunity of impulse. We have discovered that the chief ideas that men lived by from about the twelfth to the eighteenth centuries were absolute and unquestionable, and that the social turmoil of European history was simply shortsighted disagreement as to the best ways of making these deep assumptions socially good. The temper of literary criticism in the past appears to bear out this belief. Although writers were judged morally, no critic expected the poet to give him a morality. The standard of judgment was largely unconscious; a poem was a piece of free and disinterested enjoyment for minds mature enough—that is, convinced enough of a satisfactory destiny—not to demand of every scribbler a way of life. Dante invented no formula for society

to run itself; he only used a ready-made one. [. . .]

To discuss the merits of such a critical outlook lies outside my argument. It would be equally pointless to attempt an appraisal of any of its more common guides to salvation, including the uncommon one of the *Thirty-Nine Articles*, which have been subscribed to by Mr. T. S. Eliot, whose six poems published under the title *Ash-Wednesday* are the occasion of this review. For it is my thesis that, in a discussion of Mr. Eliot's poetry, his doctrine has little to command interest in itself. Yet it appears that the poetry, notwithstanding the amount of space it gets in critical journals, receives less discussion each year. The moral and religious attitude behind it has been related to the *Thirty-Nine Articles*, to an intellectual position that Eliot has defended in prose. The poetry and the prose are taken together as evidence that the author has made a rather inefficient adaptation to the modern environment; or at least he doesn't say anything very helpful to the American critics in their struggles to adapt themselves. It is an astonishing fact that, in an atmosphere of "aesthetics," there is less discussion of poetry in a typical modern essay on that fine art than there is in Johnson's essay on Denham. Johnson's judgment is frankly moralistic, but he seldom capitulates to a moral sentiment because it flatters his own moral sense. He requires the qualities of generality, invention, and perspicuity. He hates Milton for a regicide, but his judgment of *Paradise Lost* is the most disinterested in English criticism. Mr. Eliot's critics are a little less able each year to see the poetry for Westminster Abbey; the wood is all trees.

I do not pretend to judge how far our social and philosophical needs justify this prejudice, which may be put somewhat summarily as follows: all forms of human action, economics, politics, even poetry, and certainly industry, are legitimate modes of salvation, but the more historical religious mode is illegitimate. It is sufficient here to point out that the man who expects to find salvation in the latest lyric or a well-managed factory will not only not find it there; he is not likely to find it anywhere else. If a young mind is incapable of moral philosophy, a mind without moral philosophy is incapable of understanding poetry. For poetry, of all the arts, demands a serenity of view and a settled temper of the mind, and most of all the power to detach one's own needs from the experience set forth in the poem. A moral sense so organized sets limits to the human enterprise, and is content to observe them. But if the reader lack this sense, the poem will be only a body of abstractions either useful or irrelevant to that body of abstractions already forming, but of uncertain direction, in the reader's mind. This reader will see the poem chiefly as biography, and he will proceed to deduce from it a history of the poet's case, to which he will attach himself if his own case resemble it; if it doesn't, he will reject it. Either way, the quality of the poem is ignored. But I will return to this in a moment.

The reasoning that is being brought to bear upon Mr. Eliot's recent verse is as follows: Anglo-Catholicism would not at all satisfy me; therefore, his poetry declines under its influence. Moreover, the poetry is not contemporaneous; it doesn't solve any labor problems; it is special, personal, and it can do us no good. Now the poetry *is* special and personal in quality, which is one of its merits, but what the critics are really saying is this—that his case-history is not special at all, that it is a general form of possible conduct that will not do for them. To accept the poetry seems to amount to accepting an invitation to join the Anglican Church. For the assumption is that the poetry and the religious position are identical. If this were so, why should not the excellence of the poetry induce them to join the Church, in the hope of writing as well, since the irrelevance of the Church to their own needs makes them reject the poetry? The answer is, of course, that both parts of this fallacy are common. There is an aesthetic Catholicism, and there is a Communist–economic rejection of art because it is involved with the tabooed mode of salvation.

The belief is that Mr. Eliot's poetry is a simple record of the relation of his personality to an environment, and it witnesses the powerful modern desire to judge an art scientifically, practically, industrially, according to how it works. The poetry is viewed as a pragmatic result, and it has no use. Now a different heredity–environment combination would give us, of mechanical necessity, a different result, a different quantity of power to do a different and perhaps better work. Doubtless this is true. But there is something disconcerting in this simple solution to the problem when it is looked at more closely. Two vastly different records or case-histories might give us, qualitatively speaking, very similar results: Baudelaire and Eliot have in common many qualities but *no history*. Their "results" have at least the common features of irony, humility, introspection, reverence—qualities fit only for contemplation and not for judgment according to their desirability in our own conduct.

It is in this, the qualitative sense, that Eliot's poetry has been, I believe, misunderstood. In this sense, the poetry is special, personal, of no use, and highly distinguished. But it is held to be a general formula, not distinct from the general formula that Eliot subscribed to when he went into the Church.

The form of the poems in *Ash-Wednesday* is lyrical and solitary, and there is almost none of the elaborate natural description and allusion which gave *The Waste Land* a partly realistic and partly symbolic character. These six poems are a brief moment of religious experience in an age that believes religion to be a kind of defeatism and puts its hope for man in finding the right secular order. The mixed realism and symbolism of *The Waste Land* issued in irony. The direct and lyrical method of the new poems creates the simpler aesthetic quality of humility. The latter quality comes directly out of the former, and there is a nice continuity in Mr. Eliot's work.

In *The Waste Land* the prestige of our secular faith gave to the style its peculiar character. This faith was the hard, coherent medium through which the discredited forms of the historic religions emerged only to be stifled; the poem is at once their vindication and defeat. They are defeated in fact, as a politician may be defeated by the popular vote, but their vindication consists in the withering irony that their subordinate position casts upon the modern world.

The typical scene is the seduction of the typist by the clerk in "The Fire Sermon." Perhaps Mr. J. W. Krutch has not discussed this scene, but a whole generation of critics have, and from a viewpoint that Mr. Krutch has recently made popular: the seduction betrays the romantic disillusion of the poet. The mechanical, brutal scene shows what love really is—that is to say, what it is scientifically, since science is Truth; it is only an act of practical necessity, for procreation. The telling of the story by the Greek seer, who is chosen from a past of illusion and ignorance, permits the scene to become a *satire on the foolish values of the past*. The values of the past were absurd and false; the scientific Truth is both true and bitter. This is the familiar romantic dilemma, and the critics have read it into the scene from their own romantic despair.

There is none in the scene itself. The critics, who being in the state of mind I have described are necessarily blind to an effect of irony, have mistaken the symbols of an ironic contrast for the terms of a philosophic dilemma. Mr. Eliot knows too much about classical irony to be overwhelmed by a doctrine in literary biology. For the seduction scene shows, not what man is, but what *for a moment* he thinks he is; in other words, the clerk stands for the secularization of the humane and qualitative values in the modern world. And the meaning of the contrast between Tiresias and the clerk is not disillusion but irony. The scene is a masterpiece; perhaps the most profound vision that we have of modern man.

The importance of this scene as a key to the intention of *Ash-Wednesday* lies in the moral identity of humility and irony and in an important difference between them artistically. Humility is subjective, a quality of the moral character, a habitual attitude. Irony is the particular and objective instance of humility—that is, it is an event or situation which induces humility in the mind of a spectator; it is that arrangement of experience, either premeditated by art or accidentally appearing in the affairs of men, which permits to the spectator an insight superior to that of the actor, and shows him that the practical formula, the special ambition, of the actor is bound to fail. Humility is thus the self-respect proceeding from a sense of the folly of men in their desire to dominate a natural force or situation. The seduction scene is the picture of the modern and dominating man. The cleverness and the pride of conquest of the "small house agent's clerk" are the badge of science, bumptious practicality, overweening secular faith. The very success of his conquest witnesses its aimless character; it succeeds as a wheel succeeds in turning; he can only do it over again.

His own failure to understand his position is irony, and the poet's insight into it is humility. This is essentially the poetic attitude, an attitude that Mr. Eliot has been approaching with increasing purity. It is not that his recent verse is better or more exciting than that of the period ending with *The Waste Land*. Actually it is less spectacular and less complex in subject-matter; for Eliot less frequently objectifies his leading emotion, humility, into irony. His form is simple, expressive, homogeneous, and direct, and without the usual elements of violent contrast.

There is a single ironic passage in *Ash-Wednesday*, and significantly enough it is the first stanza of the first poem. This passage represents objectively the poet *as he thinks himself for the moment to be*. It establishes that humility towards his own merit which sets the whole mood of the poems that follow. And the irony has been overlooked by the critics because they take the stanza as a literal exposition of the latest phase of the Eliot "case-history"—at a time when, in the words of Mr. Edmund Wilson, "his psychological plight seems most depressing." Thus, here is the pose of a Titan too young to be weary of strife, but weary of it nevertheless.

[Quotation of first stanza of
Ash-Wednesday I]

If the six poems are taken together as the focus of a specific religious emotion, the opening stanza, instead of being a naive personal "confession," becomes only a modest but highly effective technical performance. This stanza has two features that are necessary to the development of the unique imagery which distinguishes the religious emotion of *Ash-Wednesday* from any other religious poetry of our time and which, in fact, probably makes it the only valid religious poetry we have. The first feature is the regular yet halting rhythm, the smooth uncertainty of movement which may either proceed to greater regularity or fall away into improvisation. The second feature is the imagery

itself. It is trite; it echoes two familiar passages from English poetry. But the quality to be observed is this: it is secular imagery. It sets forth a special ironic emotion, but this emotion is not identified with any specific experience. The imagery is thus perfectly suited to the character of the rhythm. The stanza is a device for getting the poem under way, starting from a known and general emotion, in a monotonous rhythm, for a direction which to the reader is unknown. The ease, the absence of surprise, with which Mr. Eliot brings out the subject to be "discussed" is admirable. After some further and ironic deprecation of his worldly powers, he goes on:

> And pray to God to have mercy upon
>   us
> And I pray that I may forget
> These matters that with myself I too
>   much discuss
> Too much explain.

We are being told, of course, that there is to be some kind of discourse on God, or a meditation; yet the emotion is still general. The imagery is even flatter than before; it is imagery at all only in that special context; for it is the diction of prose. And yet, subtly and imperceptibly, the rhythm has changed; it is irregular and labored. We are being prepared for a new and sudden effect, and it comes in the first lines of the second poem:

> Lady, three white leopards sat under a
>   juniper-tree
> In the cool of the day, having fed to
>   satiety
> On my legs my heart my liver and that
>   which had been contained
> In the hollow round of my skull. And
>   God said
> Shall these bones live? shall these
> Bones live?

From here on, in all the poems, there is constant and sudden change of rhythm, and there is a corresponding alternation of two kinds of imagery—the visual and tactile imagery common to all poetry and without significance in itself for any kind of experience, and the traditional religious symbols. The two orders are inextricably fused.

It is evident that Mr. Eliot has hit upon the only method now available of using the conventional religious image in poetry. He has reduced it to metaphor, to the plane of sensation. And corresponding to this process, there are images of his own invention which he almost pushes over the boundary of sensation into abstractions, where they have the appearance of conventional symbols. The passage I have quoted above is an example of this: for the "Lady" may be a nun, or even the Virgin, or again she may be a beautiful woman; but she is presented, through the serious tone of the invocation, with all the solemnity of a religious figure. The fifth poem exhibits the reverse of the process; it begins with a series of plays on the *Logos*, which is the most rarified of all the Christian abstractions, and succeeds in creating an *illusion of sensation* by means of a broken and distracted rhythm:

> If the lost word is lost, if the spent word is spent
> If the unheard, unspoken
> Word is unspoken, unheard;
> Still is the unspoken word, the Word unheard,
> The Word without a word, the Word within
> The world and for the world . . .

Checklist of Additional Reviews

*Hugh MacDiarmid [pseudonym "A.L."]. Review of *Ash-Wednesday*. *Scottish Educational Journal*, 23 May 1930. Reprinted in Hugh MacDiarmid, *The Raucle Tongue: Hitherto Uncollected Prose*, ed. Angus Calder, Glen Murray, and Alan Riach (1997), 235–37. See also MacDiarmid's review of Eliot's translation of St. J. Perse, *Anabasis. Scottish Educational Journal*, 18 July 1930, reprinted in *The Raucle Tongue*, 237–40.

*Orgill McKenzie. "Recent Books." *New Adelphi* 3, no. 5 (June–August 1930), 336–38.

Eda Lou Walton. "T. S. Eliot Turns to Religious Verse." *New York Times Book Review*, 20 July 1930, p. 9. [Compare her review of Pound's *A Draft of XXX Cantos* in NYTBR, 2 April 1933, reprinted in *Ezra Pound: The Critical Heritage*, ed. Eric Homberger]

*Thomas Moult. "Contrasts in Current Poetry." *Bookman* 78 (September 1930), 354–55.

*E. G. Twitchett. *London Mercury* 22 (October 1930), 557.

William J. Gorman. "Eliot's *Ash-Wednesday*." *Inlander* 11, no. 1 (November 1930), 5–10.

Horace Gregory. "Eliot Inward." *New York Herald Tribune Books*, 25 January 1931, p. 14.

*"Book Reviews." *Dublin Magazine* 6 (April–June 1931), 73.

192

SELECTED ESSAYS 1917–1932
1932

T. S. ELIOT

Selected Essays

1917-1932

HARCOURT, BRACE AND COMPANY

NEW YORK

*V. Sackville-West.
"Books of the Week."
Listener 8 (28 September
1932), 461.

[...]

[T]o the fastidious reader I would now like to recommend the *Selected Essays* of T. S. Eliot. These essays are chosen by Mr. Eliot himself out of work done by him since the year 1917, and I recommend them not because I delude myself into the belief that Mr. Eliot will ever find appreciation among a very large number of people, but because I honestly believe him to stand among the most acute of contemporary critics, and certainly among the most notable of contemporary poets. I think, therefore, that I should be guilty of dishonesty towards myself and towards you if I failed to draw your attention to this book of essays, however stiff you may find it to read. I do not say that you will enjoy it; you certainly will not, unless you happen to have an austere and scholarly taste, akin to the taste of Mr. Eliot himself. You may find, indeed, that it leaves you feeling as though you had bitten into a sloe; and if you have ever bitten into a sloe you will know what I mean—as though your mouth were all dried up suddenly by a strangely astringent juice. Mr. Eliot's criticism has this astringent quality. It is severe and dry. It is restrained and unemotional; above all, it is not in the least picturesque. It makes no concessions to the popular taste. It stands at the very opposite pole to the popularization of literature—those snippets from the recognized great; those paths made easy for us to a nodding acquaintance with great minds, though not to any real comprehension of them; that cheapening; that skimming, superficial knowledge which enables us to talk of this thing or that; so shallow, so convenient, and so really contemptible. Mr. Eliot, thank heaven, is one of the few writers left to keep himself clean from all this smirch of a vulgar publicity; witness the very few essays that he has collected into this volume out of the many years that have elapsed between 1917 and 1932. Fifteen years—a long time to produce a smallish book at the end of it, even though that book takes in such various subjects as Christopher Marlowe, Dante, Euripides, Seneca, Shakespeare, Dryden, Blake, Swinburne, Baudelaire, Wilkie Collins, and Dickens. Mr. Eliot's range may be wide, but it is also deep. And it is also, as I said before, astringent. It screws one's standard of values up to the keenest pitch. Do you remember those lines of Andrew Marvell?

> He nothing common did, or mean,
> Upon that memorable scene,
> But with his keener eye,
> The axe's edge did try.

Those lines applied in Marvell's intention to the execution of Charles I; but, like all really great poetry, they have an application outside their actual subject. For instance, one can apply them to Mr. Eliot. He nothing common does, or mean; and with his keener eye he tries the axe of literary criticism all the time.

The axe of literary criticism may seem, to many, an axe not worth grinding. There are other, more active, things in life, you may say. But whatever one believes in is surely worth believing in with all one's heart, whether it be literature, or farming, or banking, or politics. And Mr. Eliot does believe in his own profession. He does believe in the power of the written word. That is a belief worthy of respect. And Mr. Eliot holds it. So, if you read his book of essays, and if you think it rather too dry and rather too scholarly, do, at least, realize that there is a real conviction behind it; the conviction that books matter, that intelligent thought matters, that literature matters, and is not a dead thing. For what is writing, after all—the best writing, the best books—but the best sifting-out of the best minds? Writing is the only record we can hope to have of such minds. It may put us into a severe school. Mr. Eliot, who has a severe taste, puts us into a very severe school indeed. It requires some effort on our part to follow him. But, truly, the effort is worthwhile.

*Peter Quennell. "T. S. Eliot the Critic." *New Statesman* 4 (1 October 1932), 377–78.

Mr. Eliot's volume of *Selected Essays*, just now published as he leaves us for America, represents in four hundred and fifty pages fifteen successive years of work. Here are essays from the early *Sacred Wood*, which first made its appearance in 1920; here, too, is a large part of *For Lancelot Andrewes*. The brilliant trilogy, entitled *Homage to John Dryden*, re-emerges next to the little book on Dante. *Thoughts after Lambeth* also recur. Two essays reproving Professor Babbitt, and generally setting about the neo-Humanists, are neighbored by a brief encomium on Marie Lloyd. A sympathetic portrait of Charles Whibley brings this various procession to a close.

The last choice was particularly apt. Mr. Eliot ends the survey of his own criticism by a study of a very different type of critic, precisely—even dramatically—opposed to himself. All that Whibley was not, Eliot is. All the qualities that the older critic possessed—and the modern writer is not behind-hand in appreciation; he pays a generous tribute to Whibley's talents—are qualities he himself has never displayed. How far this abstention has been deliberate is a problem both fascinating and hard to solve.

Whibley was a "man of the world" in literature. I do not suggest that Mr. Eliot's critical work shows any lack of worldly knowledge, but his knowledge is of a specialized and rarified kind, accumulated by a special sort of experience. He is analytical rather than discursive. It is the peculiar strength of such critics as Charles Whibley that the enthusiasm they have derived from their private reading should be reflected on the surface of their critical style, and that they should charm us by a warmth of reflected enjoyment. Pleasure is made the basis of understanding, while analysis provides a subsidiary means of approach.

Enjoy, begs the critic, as I enjoy! True, every critic worth the title must have appreciated before he can expound; but then appreciation may assume conflicting guises. Whibley's appreciation of English literature was that of a cultivated and scholarly man of the world, an epicurean in the purest and oldest sense, *honnête homme*, like Saint Evremond or Sir William Temple. His prose has a Cyrenaic smoothness; and Mr. Eliot practices literature as a form of asceticism. Though we read his critical work for our own pleasure, we can't help feeling that it was often written from a sense of duty.

Not that he seems to toil against the grain. No reader of *Homage to John Dryden* and the Elizabethan essays in *The Sacred Wood* can doubt that he is capable of deep enjoyment and thinks pedagogy a poor substitute for true delight. He has said as much himself in the former study. My point is that, since puritan and epicure are both preoccupied in the last resort by the pursuit of happiness, Mr. Eliot has chosen the puritanical method. He analyzes in order that we may enjoy; he sacrifices immediate charm to ultimate clarity.

And so one feature distinguishes all his criticism—an avoidance, carried to strict lengths, of what he considers vain and superfluous ornament. Let the critic, he implies, remain a critic. He has expressed his distrust of the common type of writer whose critical efforts are a secondary form of creation, a consolation-prize in the race he has failed to win. Hence a marked absence of phrases and redundant imagery. He never starts a campaign with a display of fireworks, never marches around a citadel to the blast of trumpets. It has become, one feels, a rigid code of honor to observe the courtesy of a scientific siege.

These preferences must be accepted by his readers: few phrases, no brilliant and lively discursions, a prose style intentionally cold and colorless which throws his subject into clear if chilly relief—a style, in short, consistently self-effacing. It is an impersonal style, and when prejudice emerges—as it is apt to do, even here, from time to time—and he speaks of the Arch-Fiend in *Paradise Lost* as "Milton's curly-headed Byronic hero," the effect is not infrequently a trifle awkward. Whether his rare phrases are awkward through want of interest, or whether he eschews them from lack of facility, we can only conjecture.

I mean facility of the pyrotechnic kind. At all events, they are unimportant in his critical essays where words for the sake of words seldom figure. Some writers begin by blindfolding us with verbal eloquence, lead us up a steep and difficult path, snatch off the bandage and show us the view. Eliot starts by removing the scales from our eyes. An operation for cataract is always painful; and many fellow critics confronted by an opening paragraph which states—oh, so simply and oh,

so coldly! albeit with a certain underlying benevolence—that if they admire *this* they are not likely to admire *that* and had much better return to their false gods, have been known to snort indignantly in the surgeon's face and argue that they prefer their original dimness.

Mr. F. L. Lucas is one of these.

[. . .]

Mr. Lucas once arrayed against the critic some of his more startling literary judgments—that *Hamlet* is unsuccessful as a work of art, that Crashaw is a finer poet than Shelley—and asked us to draw our own conclusions. Well, we don't go to a critic for absolute truth; that is to say, we can't measure a critic's usefulness by totting up a balance-sheet of right and wrong. Literary excellence is comparative at the best of times; and, whatever may be our opinion of Crashaw's merits—and he had some merits which to Shelley were quite unknown—there is little doubt that, as expressed by Mr. Eliot, the contrast was provocative and stimulating.

[. . .]

Objections, of course, can be raised. We are accustomed to envisage the perfect critic as being suspended in the void—preferably in the void of mild agnosticism—who surveys the world with disabused detachment. We are offended by any touch of *parti pris*. True, all criticism enshrines some prejudice; but we hate to think that such prejudice as we may encounter is imposed on us by an orthodox religious system. Mr. Eliot is now essentially orthodox. As long as the point of view, to which I have referred, continues to assimilate these beliefs—they are foreshadowed even in *The Waste Land*—it seems impertinent to quarrel with private convictions. Puritanism is a dominant mode in English literature, and Mr. Eliot is a Puritan of American ancestry.

It is a Puritan intelligence he brings to bear. Critics naturally less ascetic have proved less sensitive to the beauties of language and added less to our understanding of its spell. Mr. Eliot writes as a poet but not poetically. Looking through this volume of *Selected Essays*, it is very hard to find a chapter or a single line in which the desire to make an effect or round a paragraph predominates over a Spartan sense of fitness. No metaphor, flown with syllabic intoxication, breaks into the strenuous hush of the critic's dissecting-room.

There he labors, and on subjects very diverse. Mr. Eliot is not temperamentally expansive, but his interests are sympathetic and range wide. He treats of Swinburne as sensibly as of Andrew Marvell, of Blake, Jonson, Baudelaire and many others, always with an experienced and odd touch like an artist investigating a foreign studio. It is perhaps one of his greatest critical virtues that he should have done his best to redeem modern criticism from its tendency to slovenly picturesqueness. We may agree with him, or violently disagree. The austerity of his professional attitude commands respect.

---

*R. A. Scott-James. "A Critic's Critic." *Sunday Times*, 2 October 1932, p. 8.

Mr. Eliot among writers belongs to a rare species. He is preeminently a "critic's critic." We cannot think of him as a propagandist intent on converting a Philistine world to a true belief in literature. His mission, if mission it can be called, is to those who have already had some initiation in the sacred mysteries. Quiet, self-possessed, confident, he puts his analytical judgment at the service of the fastidious reader. He is one of the few living critics who have thought themselves into a consistent view about literature; and he brings carefully sharpened tools to each fresh task of literary judgment.

In this world, so uncertain for most of us, we have the feeling that Mr. Eliot at least always knows just where he stands, and is ready to explain, reasonably and urbanely, where we are, too, in relation to the ages. If all critics were of his kind they would be engaged together in "a simple and orderly field of beneficent activity"; there would be no need for the gently ironic words in which he regrets the rarity of the critic who endeavors to "compose his differences with as many of his fellows as possible, in the common pursuit of true judgment."

A Sound Classicism

No; it certainly is not quite like that, though we may observe that a number of his fellows have been together in acclaiming a classicist trend discernible in certain distinctively modern literature. But just because, in this surface movement, there has been so much that is artificial and finicky, we may be all the more grateful to Mr. Eliot for endeavoring to establish principles of a sound classicism catholic enough to allow for everything that has happened between the times, say, of Boileau and Mr. Aldous Huxley.

Mr. Eliot stands primarily for "order" in literature, and order implies authority— not that of Aristotle, or Boileau, or any other single law-giver, but not the less sure because it is distributed among the whole body of writers who have contributed to the great tradition of literature. By "tradition" he does not mean the handing down of old ways of doing things, which we are to imitate. Rather, just as Croce said that history is humanity's memory of its own past, so Mr. Eliot says "the conscious present is an awareness of the past." We know more than the "dead writers," but they are "that which we know." [. . .] Literature is conceived as a continuous process in which the present reabsorbs the past, and by renewed creation in terms of a changing world modifies the past and helps to complete it. The function of his critic is to relate literature to the main current of conscious creative effort. And so we find him constantly insisting on the need, not of narrowly defined rules of writing, but of a sort of training, or *askesis*—even, in some cases, a convention—so that the works of the artist will accord with, rather than defy, the inescapable destiny of tradition.

Tradition and Discipline

Thus, whilst he is not altogether successful in telling us what William Blake *was*, he can easily tell us what he was *not*—"his genius . . . lacked . . . a framework of accepted and traditional ideas which would have prevented him from indulging in a philosophy of his own"—a truth which might be put a little more baldly by saying "it is a pity Blake was not better educated." Or again—the Russian ballet, at its best, delighted us because it "seemed to be everything that we wanted in drama, except the poetry . . . It seemed to revive the more formal element in drama for which we craved." It rested upon a tradition and severe discipline. It was "a system of physical training, of traditional, symbolical and highly skilled movements."

And similarly in regard to the drama—he considers that the weakness of the Elizabethan plays, and also the weakness of the realistic plays which Mr. William Archer admired so much, lay in "the lack of a convention." He asks us to conceive what the Elizabethan drama might have been if it had been "formed within a conventional scheme—the convention of an individual dramatist, or of a number of dramatists working in the same form at the same time"—presumably in the same sense that the Greek tragedians worked within a certain form, or morality plays of the type of *Everyman* [. . .].

Two Opposite Tendencies

I cannot here pursue the arguments with which Mr. Eliot, in essay after essay, discussing Elizabethan, or Caroline, or modern writers, endeavors to show what has been or what might have been gained by precision, by formalism, by something akin to ritual, by that scrupulous absorption in the object which makes a work of art impersonal and universal. He is restating the claims of classicism in its demand for order, poise, and "right reason."

What is surprising in one so detached in his sympathies is that he should so definitely take sides between classicism and romanticism, and that he should follow—though in a broader spirit—the old prejudice which made men feel that if the one was right the other was all wrong. One would rather have expected him to recognize—as Pater did—that there are here two opposite tendencies which from time immemorial have asserted themselves in literature, each of which has its distinctive merits and defects, and requires correction the one by the other. But on the whole we in this country have at no time since the eighteenth century been in danger of a deficiency in Romanticism—not even in this neo-Georgian period. Rather the opposite—we stand always in need of the cool sanity, the analytical judgment, the fastidiousness which may be found exemplified in Mr. Eliot's severely intellectual criticism.

*"A Critic of Poets." *Punch* 183 (5 October 1932), 391.

It is rare to discover a critic to whom principles are more important and more sedulously to be cultivated than taste. Not that I deny the possession of a palate to Mr. T. S. Eliot—whose *Selected Essays, 1917–1932* [. . .] is the text of this meditation—but the endowment is subordinated to more excellent gifts. True, neither fiction nor theology is here Mr. Eliot's strong suit. His enjoyable "Lancelot Andrewes," for instance, ignores obvious derivatives from St. Augustine. He even quotes the whimsical African's jest about the Baby Word that could not speak as though it were pure Jacobean; and his "Thoughts after Lambeth" exhibits only a piecemeal coherence. It is as a critic of poets and, what is more to his purpose, poetry that Mr. Eliot excels. His manifesto [. . .] "Tradition and the Individual Talent" gives the key to his attitude; and a steady relentless war on the pretensions of the second-rate is implied throughout a really commanding exposition of the first-rate. He realizes the futility of a search for exotic emotions when new combinations of the old, fused under high pressure, are the sole condition of poetic output; and the results of his technical research are amazingly interesting, especially those scattered up and down a dozen studies of the Elizabethan dramatists. His appreciation of the levity that enhances seriousness—a capital issue in a delightful essay on Marvell—strikes me as one the finest concessions in a book which has enlarged as well as enriched my own pretty ample notion of the Muses' territory.

Henry Hazlitt. "The Mind of T. S. Eliot." *Nation* 135 (5 October 1932), 312–13.

T. S. Eliot has one of the most curious and interesting minds of the present age. It would doubtless be absurd to imply that he has a split personality, in any pathological sense, but one finds it difficult to discuss his work until one has divided him into three Eliots: the poet, the critic, and the philosopher. Eliot is a major poet if we have any major poets living. I do not intend to discuss him as a poet here, but merely as a critic and thinker: it is sufficient for our present purposes to observe that anyone who first comes to his prose after reading his poetry (I except *Ash-Wednesday*), or who first comes to his poetry after reading his prose, receives something like a shock of incredulity: they seem so violently contrasted in vocabulary and tone. If we could imagine each of them surviving, without signature, it seems to me highly improbable that posterity would have the wit to put them together again. The contrast almost makes one believe that the same man who wrote the prose of Bacon could have written the poetry of Shakespeare.

Yet among critics, Eliot's eminence is hardly less than among poets. His acute sensitiveness to literary values, his insights and fine incidental observations, the range and depth of his erudition, the boldness and independence of his judgment, and the dignity and closely woven texture of his prose, entitle him to rank with some of the greatest English critics; while the definiteness and self-assurance, one might almost say the arrogance, of his point of view, are much more a strength than a weakness. His tone and attitude toward his subjects outwardly resemble the tone and attitude of the scientist. He is a lecturer who puts his specimens under the microscope and tells us in great detail what he finds there. He is an analytical chemist who is not satisfied with mere qualitative analysis but only with exact quantitative analysis. Is he going to tell us something about Seneca's influence on the Elizabethan drama? Then you can be sure he will not rest in generalities: he will consider, first, the precise extent of Seneca's responsibility for the *Tragedy of Blood*; "second, his responsibility for *bombast* in Elizabethan diction; and third, his influence upon the *thought*, or what passes for thought, in the drama of Shakespeare and his contemporaries."

The two chief instruments in Eliot's criticism, then, are analysis and comparison. The analysis, as I have hinted, is almost chemical: it is the punctilious and rather thorough separation of a compound into its elements. The comparison is almost as thorough, and is not made, as by most critics, merely now and then, but systematically. [. . .] [W]e have come a long way from impressionism.

This straining for exactness in Eliot becomes almost an obsession. I have never read a critic more impatient with the individual statements of other critics, more eager to pounce upon one unfortunate word. He will quote Hazlitt on Dryden, so that he may write: "In one sentence Hazlitt has committed at least four crimes against taste." He will begin an essay on Marlowe by quoting Swinburne on Marlowe, merely that he may say: "In this sentence there are two misleading assumptions and two misleading conclusions." He will quote a paragraph from Norman Foerster's *American Criticism*, a book which he professes to regard as "brilliant," only to call the paragraph "a composition of ignorance, prejudice, confused thinking and bad writing." Matthew Arnold he finds distressingly vague: "Culture and Conduct are the first things, we are told; but what Culture and Conduct are, I feel that I know less well on every reading . . . Culture is a term which each man not only may interpret as he pleases, but must indeed interpret as he can."

One might suppose that a writer so harsh in dealing with the alleged looseness of others would be himself a paragon of definiteness and precision. But here is where my bewilderment begins. As soon as he departs from a description of the specific qualities of the author or work before him (where he is for the most part admirable), as soon as he begins to launch into general statements, either about literature, or science, or religion, or morals, Eliot seems to me to use words not only loosely, but recklessly, meaninglessly. What can he possibly mean when he tells us, for example, that "the business of the poet is . . . to express feelings which are not in actual emotions at all"? I have only a vague idea of what he is talking about, again, when he goes on to remark that "Poetry is not a turning loose of emotion, but an escape from emotion." Why should the poet—or his reader—want to escape from emotion? In what sense is poetry an escape from emotion? Is it a sublimation? a deflection? a katharsis? Well, one may have several guesses, but surely both "escape" and "emotion" in this context are words "which each man not only may interpret as he pleases, but must indeed interpret as he can." The reader's predicament is even worse when he encounters such a statement as, "Dryden, with all his intellect, had a commonplace mind." His dizziness is not lessened when he comes to the Johnsonian sentence immediately following: "His [Dryden's] powers were, we believe, wider, but no greater, than Milton's." Thus the poet with wider powers than Milton's had a commonplace mind. Words have lost all meaning; let us hold our heads in our hands and stagger out.

[. . .]

The truth is that philosophically Eliot is a very confused man. What chiefly disguises this fact, apart from the illusion of precision which his constant verbal distinctions and qualifying phrases create, is that he never condescends to argue a problem on its merits. One almost gathers that his real objection to certain views is not that they are logically untenable, but that their proponents are rather crude, and when he has pointed out the crudity of the supporters of an opinion, he sometimes forgets to ask whether the opinion may not after all be true. His superciliousness thus frequently protects him from exposing his own logical weakness. He almost invariably begs the question, and hardly pretends to do anything else. Thus in an essay which professes to be about a forgotten divine named John Bramhall, but immediately switches to his immensely more interesting opponent, that "extraordinary little upstart" (to quote Eliot's somewhat less than objective description), Thomas Hobbes. Eliot quotes the views of I. A. Richards and of Bertrand Russell, in which each seeks to show that value springs from desire and depends upon the harmonization of conflicting desires. "The difficulty with such theories," comments Eliot aloofly, "is that they merely remove the inherently valuable a further degree." And that is all he deigns to say about them: the reader is supposed to consider them disposed of. But the mere phrase "inherently valuable," in this context, reveals that Eliot himself is quite at sea in philosophy. To recognize that this is so it is not necessary to go to the length of Spinoza, who says boldly that we desire nothing because it is good, but it is good only because we desire it. It is merely necessary to recognize that no value—economic, aesthetic, or moral—can exist apart from some human appreciation of it, or some human preference for it.

[. . .] Personally I cannot feel that the total drift of his thought carries him to the destination where he pretends to be. As Edmund Wilson has shrewdly remarked: "We feel in contemporary writers like Eliot a desire to believe in religious revelation, a belief that it would be a good thing to believe, rather than a genuine belief." The truth of this observation is confirmed for me by, among other things, a phrase which Eliot allows to slip out in discussing Irving Babbitt's humanism. His own analysis leads, Eliot thinks, "to the conclusion that the humanistic point of view is auxiliary to and dependent upon the religious point of view. *For us*, religion is Christianity." The italics are mine. By "us" Eliot here means, I suppose, us Occidentals, those of us who have been *brought up* as Christians. But the remark implies that what is important is not the objective truth of the religion, not *which* religion, but the supposed functional value of "religious" belief itself. No real believer would let such a phrase escape him. It would not occur to Eliot to say: "For us, two and two make four." That would imply not belief, but skepticism; it would imply, at best, that the fourness of two and two was the most desirable or convenient assumption for the Western world. This is the serpent's doctrine of "As If," of necessary illusions; and it is more cynical at bottom than the crude beliefs of us poor naturalists, who feel, with Santayana, that illusion may be truly pleasing while we think it true, but that to cling to it knowing it to be an illusion is ignominious and well-nigh impossible.

202

W. E. Garrison.
"Humanism Criticizes Itself."
Christian Century 49
(12 October 1932), 1243.

Mr. Eliot has three reputations—as a poet, as a critic and interpreter of English literature, and as an exponent of one type of humanism. The greater part of the contents of this volume of collected essays has to do with the second of these fields of activity. Of the dozen or more essays on the Elizabethan dramatists and the poets of the seventeenth and eighteenth centuries, it is sufficient to say that they represent a high level of critical intelligence united with mature scholarship and a rare competence in the writing of criticism which is literature in its own right. The rather long essay on Dante is a worthy addition to the literature of that vast field.

As a humanist, Mr. Eliot gives striking proof of the heterogeneity of the humanist camp, for he expends most of his energy in pointing out the errors and inadequacies of such humanistic thinkers as Mr. Irving Babbitt, to whom he devotes one entire essay, and Mr. Norman Foerster, to whom he devotes most of another. If one begins this section with the reading of the paper entitled "Thoughts after Lambeth"—a critique of the Lambeth conference of 1931 and the encyclical issued by it—there will be a growing wonder, from the first page to the last, that this man should be called a humanist at all. Surely it must be a term to juggle with if it can be applied to one who considers the section on the Doctrine of God the most important part of that report, who insists that sound theological dogma supported by the corporate mind

of the church is basic to right conduct, and that the church ought to reverse the order of the "medical and spiritual advice" which it recommends in certain domestic emergencies and to make the latter (now become the former) mandatory rather than merely optional for its communicants.

Mr. Eliot partially defines his own position by saying that he began as a disciple of Mr. Babbitt and that he feels that he has rejected nothing that is positive in his teaching. Yet he has rejected *in toto* the idea that a humanistic view of the world and of man can stand on its own feet and make its own way apart from religion, or that there is any such thing as a vague and generalized religion which can exist and function without the church. The contrary notion is evidently rated— and wisely rated, I think—not as a positive contribution but as one of the negative implications of a humanism which, departing from the tolerant and genial attitude which is proper to it, has grown dogmatically anti-ecclesiastical and individualistically self-sufficient.

Humanism, as Mr. Eliot views it, is general culture; it is breadth and tolerance and sanity; it is critical rather than constructive; its business is neither to establish dogmas nor to refute anything; and it is valuable both "by itself, in the 'pure humanist,' who will not set up humanism as a substitute for philosophy and religion, and as a mediating and corrective ingredient in a positive civilization founded on definite belief." It is the tempering and civilizing influence without which on the one hand "we reap the whirlwind of pragmatism and behaviourism," and on the other incur the rigors of theological dogmatism and ecclesiastical tyranny.

His most important and heartening discovery is that the humanistic point of view is, if not actually a parasite upon religion, at least an auxiliary to it, meaningless and impotent without it. Mr. Babbitt, like any good classicist, is zealous for the maintenance of a system of absolutes, but he seems painfully vague as to what they are, where they can be found, by what criteria they are to be recognized and by what sanctions enforced. Mr. Eliot not only feels the need of absolutes and despises equally the Protestant liberalism and the Menckenite libertarianism which lack them, but he knows where to find them. He looks to the Christian tradition and to the church. But when it comes to the actual solution of the ancient antinomy between freedom and authority, one feels that he rather spins a web of fine words between the two than builds any substantial bridge or achieves any genuine reconciliation.

*"Mr. T. S. Eliot."
Times Literary
Supplement 1602
(13 October 1932), 728.

Mr. Eliot's *Selected Essays* contains his "choice among all the prose that he has written during the last fifteen years." The two essays which begin the volume— "Tradition and the Individual Talent" and "The Function of Criticism"—might be regarded as the definition of the general principles which are to be illustrated in the practical essays which follow. They are typical of the dialectic qualities peculiar to Mr. Eliot: the strict reduction and compression of his material to the limits necessary to the achievement of a carefully proposed objective, the elimination of side-issues, a dryness calculated to promote the utmost sobriety of mind in the reader.

In them he seeks to establish some sort of authority, some external touchstone of value, as opposed, "classically," to what he deprecates with much dry wit as the "Inner Voice" of romanticism. Literature is to be regarded as a continuously living whole. New art is to be measured against it and judged by its "conformity," its capacity to "fit in" and thereby extend the tradition, altering its entire perspective. Yet Mr. Eliot has to qualify this "test of value" in admitting that "we are none of us infallible judges of conformity"; and he is led time and again to the admission of the necessity of reliance on something not unlike the disparaged "Inner Voice." But if there is this tentativeness at the root of his formulae, he has still been able to achieve a unique constancy of direction in his criticism. His discipline has enabled him to reach conclusions of positive value, as in his brilliant disquisition on *Hamlet*; it is no less valuable as a corrective to the sort of criticism which he has described as "no better than a Sunday park of contending and contentious orators, who have not even arrived at the articulation of their differences." At his best, when he is writing of specific literary work—in his studies of the Elizabethans, of Dryden, of Dante— we find intelligence and sensibility in a rare combination. And there is more in these studies than fine appreciation. It is to Mr. Eliot that we owe the recognition of a tradition that can be used, the recovery of values that had seemed lost: it is largely to him that modern poetry owes its release from the oppression of the immediate past.

But some defects inherent in Mr. Eliot's qualities must be admitted; defects more apparent in the two essays we have discussed than elsewhere; and perhaps more irritating here because of a certain pontifical tone which lessens as the book advances. In practical criticism, focused on actual work, Mr. Eliot's method is successful and assured. But in general and abstract discussion it is apt to mislead, even to be dangerous. In "Tradition and the Individual Talent" we have a compression that moves the argument forcefully towards a chosen objective; but, it seems to us, at the expense of completeness, and by the exclusion of issues not always irrelevant:

> [T]he poet has, not a "personality" to express, but a particular medium, which is only a medium and not a personality . . . The business of the poet is not to find new emotions, but to use the ordinary ones and, in working them up into poetry, to express feelings which are not in actual emotions at all.

In this description of the poet "using" ordinary emotions and "working them up" into poetry we have an example of Mr. Eliot's dialectic hyperbole, opposed here by a statement implying that the genesis of poetry is fortuitous, "a concentration which does not happen consciously or of deliberation," though "there is a great deal, in the writing of poetry, which must be conscious and deliberate." Mr. Eliot does not specify when, at what times or places, the poet ought to be conscious and when unconscious. These statements are perhaps "facts" such as he writes of in "The Function of Criticism" when he refers to "the value of the practitioner's criticism—he is dealing with his facts, and he can help us do the same." Mr. Eliot is a "practitioner" and in a position to amplify his account of poetic practice. Here such amplification would have been far from irrelevant in clarifying the radical point about the poet's impersonality. But Mr. Eliot leaves us with these ambiguous counters and the remark that his essay has confined itself "to such practical conclusions as can be applied by the responsible person interested in poetry." Much later in the book, in a note to his fine essay on Dante, Mr. Eliot reaches conclusions which illustrate the inadequacy of narrow generalizations:

> . . . I can only conclude that I cannot, in practice, wholly separate my poetic appreciation from my personal beliefs . . . It would appear that "literary appreciation" is an abstraction, and pure poetry a phantom; and that both in creation and enjoyment much always enters which is, from the point of view of "Art," irrelevant.

The point also raised in this note, that something may be true for purposes of limited discussion but untrue if pushed to its conclusion, is itself capable of protracted argument.

[. . .]

---

*Bonamy Dobrée. "A Major Critic." *Listener* 8 (15 October 1932), supplement, ix.

There are many people who, when asked their opinion of Mr. Eliot's poetry, profess themselves baffled, and then hasten to take refuge in a declaration that they admire his criticism. This is, to say the least of it, odd, because the same mind, the same sensibility, are so patently working in both: if you really understand one, you will not be baffled by the other, and Mr. Eliot's criticism is at least as bold, as drastic, as his poetry. But, such questions apart, it is likely that if Mr. Eliot were not a poet he would not be the critic that he is; his criticism is so sure because he has handled the stuff himself; he is a workman discussing his craft; thus he knows what he is talking about, and what is more, he knows when he is not talking about the subject. He is indeed that surprisingly rare thing, a literary critic. There are very few who do not come to talk about their own emotions (for some reason this is called "creative criticism") or display their own personality, or again, leap over the bounds of literature into the realms of morals, metaphysics, or religion. For Mr. Eliot the first business of the critic is to subdue his own personality, so as to be free to discover general principles in the art he is discussing, and further, for him, "the function of criticism seems to be essentially a problem of order." But no one knows better than he does that literature cannot exist in the air; it is connected with life, and man's other intellectual and imaginative activities. The difficulty is to know where, in literary criticism, to stop, and for the most part Mr. Eliot prefers "to halt at the frontier of metaphysics." Poetry, he has said, "certainly has something to do with morals, and with religion, and even with politics perhaps, though we cannot say what . . . The best that we can hope to do is to agree upon a point from which to start." That was, in part, the subject of *The Sacred Wood*, as it is, in part, of this.

Thus Mr. Eliot discusses literature, and, except where he definitely departs from it, literature alone, but with a full realization of what it implies, so that to follow his criticism, and to test it, you have to bring not only your feelings towards literature, but also your experience of life. For, in common with all first-rate criticism, Mr. Eliot's leads you to discover things about yourself as well as about other people. And again, in common with all criticism which means anything, which leads anywhere, the discussions, the fascinating comparisons, the pointing out of certain aspects and effects, end in some admirable generalization, sometimes even startling,

but which will stand the test of knowledge. Mr. Eliot, though detached, is never aloof; feeling in his bones as he does the importance of literature, he could not be the latter; thus, though he makes us also detached, he kindles, or increases in us, the warmth of our love for the poems or prose works he discusses. His range is extraordinarily varied, from an abstract discussion of criticism to Marie Lloyd, from the metaphysical poets to Wilkie Collins, from Marlowe to Charles Whibley, while one section—the book is divided into seven sections according to subject—is devoted to his beautifully lucid introduction to Dante.

For me, at least, the first five sections, which are pure literary criticism, provide unadulterated delight. In prose which is a masterly example of the expository style, never appealing to the emotions alone, never falling to seduce with meretricious graces, always concentrated on his purpose, he opens up and solves literary questions with a result it is hard to oppose; and not a sentence but does some necessary work. No doubt you have to share, as most of us do nowadays, his views as to the weakness of the romantics, and the strength of, say, Dryden; but then, having followed his argument, so suave as hardly to seem an argument, his exposition, so cunningly illustrated by extracts, you will arrive at his *obiter dicta* with enormous pleasure. These sections contain the most valuable contributions to criticism of our day. The sixth, to which perhaps the essays on humanism in the last should be garnered, appears somewhat strangely in this collection. What, we ask, is "Thoughts after Lambeth" doing in this gallery? Literature is not the subject, and Mr. Eliot allows his prejudices to appear; it is, for instance, something foreign to his almost invariable good manners to refer to Hobbes as "one of those extraordinary little upstarts," as he does in his essay on John Bramhall, whom even Mr. Eliot cannot persuade us to be interesting from the literary point of view, however important he may be in the history of the Church. Now and again the Mr. Eliot who is so scrupulous to support his opinion in literary matters gives us a view sustained by nothing but his desires, or his religious beliefs. Not that we would wish Mr. Eliot to deny himself the expression of these in his criticism, but they should be fused, in a critical essay, with his literary beliefs and scales of value. This is, no doubt, a business of extreme difficulty, but that Mr. Eliot can overcome the difficulty he makes triumphantly plain in his essays on Baudelaire, and on Arnold and Pater. It is, nevertheless, a pity that he should have treated Pater purely from the moral point of view, however much he may lend himself to it; and though Pater may have lacked the religious sense and the religious intellect (if there is such a separate thing), he had a keen critical perception in many directions, and made some extremely valuable general observations: it is curious that Mr. Eliot should not have raised similar issues when discussing Dryden. The truth is that in his later work Mr. Eliot is departing a little from his previous restriction of not overstepping into the realm of metaphysics; he is, of course, at liberty to do so, and he knows when he is doing it, but the ground is not so sure, and we could wish that instead of "Thoughts after Lambeth" he had given us his essay on George Herbert and the preface to Johnson's poems, both of which contain purely literary matter of the first order. But though we may here and there cavil at Mr. Eliot, here is a book written with a profundity of knowledge, sensibility, and intellect, in a style which is (with rare exceptions) free from querulousness, and combines the virtues of urbanity, clarity, strength, and, not the least, of humor.

*Richard Sunne. "Men and Books." *Time and Tide* 13 (15 October 1932), 1010–11.

Consciously or not, Mr. T. S. Eliot has, I think, based his critical methods on Dr. Johnson's. His admiration for that great critic's *Lives of the Poets* no one can fail to recognize; but I do not know that the resemblance in approach has been noticed before. It is as evident in Mr. Eliot's faults, in the essay on *Hamlet* and that on the poetry of Swinburne, as in his virtues, most clearly seen, when we consider this volume of selected essays, in the essays on "Shakespeare and the Stoicism of Seneca," "A Dialogue on Dramatic Poetry," some of the essays on Elizabethan dramatists, the supremely good essay on Dante, and the essays on Humanism. Mr. Eliot fails just where and as Samuel Johnson fails. He is in insufficient sympathy with the purely poetic. The pure poet writes from imagination, not thought. There is a sense in which we may say that Shakespeare never thinks. That is the cause of Mr. Shaw's dissatisfaction with Shakespeare; for Mr. Shaw never, except in moods of comedy, stops thinking. The poet has no need of ratiocination. He knows: and others can only confirm his judgment by argument, or, failing to understand his process, use reason to confute what is not strictly amenable to that criterion. If a man, as a poet may, flies to a summit, it is no use confronting him with a map and pointing out to him the arduous route by which he should have ascended. He is there. And not all you say can dislodge him or make his foothold less secure. The penalty of the Johnsonian method is that he who uses it for unsuitable objects fails to make his point even by his own standards. Thus Johnson himself fails with *Lycidas*. Thus Addison fails in many of his criticisms of *Paradise Lost*. Thus Mr. Eliot fails in his criticism of one of Swinburne's best-known passages.

> Before the beginning of years
>   There came to the making of man
> Time with a gift of tears;
>   Grief with a glass that ran. . . .

This is not merely "music"; it is effective because it appears to be a tremendous statement, like statements made in our dreams; when we wake up we find that the "glass that ran" would do better for time than for grief, and that the gift of tears would be as appropriately bestowed by grief as by time.

That has the proper Johnsonian look of common sense; but its apparent reasonableness is a dream. First, the critic should have noticed that the poet has evidently changed the poetical commonplace of time's glass and grief's tears in order to surprise the reader into attention. He may think this device illegitimate, but he must not assume that we will agree that Swinburne did not know what he was doing. Secondly, he misses the real strength of the passage, if we look at it in the light of Swinburne's general philosophy. Man, the poet asserts, comes into a world where even misery has no permanence, into a world where even time fails to bring a surcease to sorrow.

[. . .]

[T]he remarkable essay on Dante [. . .] is Mr. Eliot's best essay. It is not only a most ably assembled and persuasive piece of prose: it has at once the assurance and the humility which make for great critical writing, and contains some of Mr. Eliot's most illuminating asides. He has a great gift for the aside, a gift of which he is too sparing. "Genuine poetry can communicate before it is understood." "We take it for granted that our dreams spring from below: possibly the quality of our dreams suffers in consequence." "Dante and Shakespeare divide the modern world between them; there is no third." Mr. Eliot then moves at liberty only in that world. It is at best arguable that there is no newer world than that world of Dante and of Shakespeare. Nay more, those of us who believe that the seers and the saints and the poets have the truth, are prepared to wager that this is alone the real world; and that those who journey elsewhere could not travel at all save from that country they afterwards consign to oblivion. It is Plato's world, and Sophocles's; the dear city of Zeus as well as the holy hill of Zion. Its springs are unfailing [. . .]. We have more names for more things; man insists that he is no longer the measure of all things, and, by demanding that we put faith in his insistence, restores himself to the position he has abandoned; there are more facts, and less vision—but we need vision to enable us to believe in the facts, and it is to his understanding of this truth that Mr. Eliot owes his position among his contemporaries.

<hr>

Waldo Frank. "The 'Universe' of T. S. Eliot." *New Republic* 72 (26 October 1932), 294–95.

<hr>

The collected essays of Mr. Eliot provide a portrait of a mind that for the past twelve years has prominently played on the American literary scene. [. . .] The book portrays a sensitive, finely endowed person. Itself an accumulation of comments on many matters, it suggests a review of like nature: one is tempted to pass from page to page detailing, comparing, dissenting. But the place of Mr. Eliot as a literary influence in our time, and the cultural crisis of our time, make this method inadvisable. It is important to employ the book as a means for seeing the man whole; and, having done so, to deduce a measure of his values as a leader and thereby a measure of the time which took him as a leader.

The first revelation is of a man with an exquisite, almost infallible, taste for the stuffs of literary art. Whether he touches a line of Dante or of Swinburne, a melodrama of Cyril Tourneur or of Wilkie Collins, the prosody of Baudelaire or Blake, Mr. Eliot evinces an aesthetic delight which implies true contact with his subject. This first trait is particularly distinguished in an age in which the field of literary discussion has been almost monopolized by writers who may know something of baseball or economics but who ignore the nature of literary art. The second trait of Mr. Eliot, not less pervasive but more subtly entextured in his book, his moral sense; and this, coupled with his first, is even more rare. We have had plenty of moralists—More, Mencken, Lewisohn, are examples—writing on literature and totally insensitive to literary aesthetics; we have had a few "aestheticians" disclaiming the moral sense (as if aesthetic form were some kind of insubstantial absolute and not an organic configuration of ordinary human experience and motive), and therefore writing with even worse futility on books. When Mr. Eliot compares lines in Massinger and Shakespeare, contrasts tropes in Dryden and Milton, draws a prosodic sequence from Donne to Shelley, he reveals, in his taste and judgment, the moral integer: he knows the *human nature* of aesthetics. This moral sense is organic in the man; it is no mere acceptance of rules,

it is not moralistic. Being the permeation, within his specific literary experience, of his general view of life, the moral quality in Mr. Eliot is religious. Everywhere, although he may be discussing merely a choice of verbs in Middleton, he reveals a general and definite attitude toward existence taken as a whole: and this attitude, when logically formed, becomes religion.

T. S. Eliot, then, is portrayed by this book as a man with a sense of the whole, with a conviction of his place in the whole, as a man engaged in an activity (literature) for which he is fitted and to which he gives his entire equipment. Such a crystallization comes close to what Nietzsche meant by a cultural act; and in an epoch whose literary critics have been insensitive and incompetent men, it makes Mr. Eliot an exceedingly welcome figure. If, however, we turn from those contemporaries in contrast with whose nullity he looms, and measure him rather by his own subjects and by the literary exigencies of our epoch, Mr. Eliot dwindles. No single major essay in this book, for instance, can be said to be organic either as a presentation of its subject or as a literary essay. Consider the "Dante" in whose study he is at his best: every observation is exact, many a phrase stands forth a luminous gem; but the observations merely mount arithmetically into so many pages of running comment. Dante and his work are never objectified, never dimensionally recreated either in the world of Dante or in the world of T. S. Eliot. Or consider the justly admired pages on the Elizabethans: they contain glimpses both precise and profound into the art of the theatre, into the poets and their world. But none of the plays, none of the dramatists, is made to stand whole, either in the epoch, in the drama, or in some total conception of the critic.

If, then, as I have stated, there is wholeness in Mr. Eliot, we are led to question what kind of wholeness it must be that can focus so superbly on details in a dozen poets and a dozen epochs, and yet fail to envelop any one of them. It is true that this failure is not always complete. In the "Baudelaire," for instance, or the "Swinburne," we obtain a kind of two-dimensional cross section, built from the prosodic study, which we can place for ourselves in the organic milieu of the nineteenth century. But in the essays on the more cosmic men there are no dimensions beyond mere points of light. And in the studies of dynamic but little-discussed figures, the failure is disastrous. The pages on Bradley, for example, proceed without the faintest evocation of the two ideological worlds— Hegelianism and English individualism— which Bradley sought to synthesize. The chapter on Lancelot Andrewes is a mere ringing of personal responses to the old priest's music, which become sentimental and pretentious, since there is no effort to place this music in the symphony of Roman Catholic, Jewish, and Arabic exegesis, from which it was never truly independent.

T. S. Eliot, it becomes plain, is a man of integrity in the real sense of the word; but his vision is such that it can never hold more than details; and his energy is too weak to give organic form either to his subjects or to his essays. Unlike most of his fellows, who suffer in chaos, he lives in a "universe." But this "universe" of Mr. Eliot's is evidently small and minor. It is achieved by huge and deliberate exclusions. It scarcely contacts with the modern world—the world whose radical transformations in physics, psychology, and economics have dissolved all the old formal values. Nor does it really embrace the past worlds with which Mr. Eliot is so sympathetic: Dantean Europe or Jacobean England. This failure of mastery even on Mr. Eliot's chosen ground is revealing. No

one can understand a living past who is not actively engaged in the living present. For any past age is an integer in the creating of today, and only by conscious sharing of this creation can the past, as part of it, be understood. Fundamentally, Mr. Eliot's subjective love of the anglo-catholic tradition leaves him as remote from what England really was as his distaste for modern problems leaves him remote from us—and for the same reason.

That reason brings us to the heart of our portrait. Any living world, whether it be Seneca's or Shakespeare's or our own, in so far as it lives, is dynamic; and Mr. Eliot's world is static. Wherefore, in confrontation with a chaos of dynamic forces like our modern era, a chaos which our dynamic will must meet, grapple with, and mold, Mr. Eliot can only ignore; and in confrontation with dynamic worlds of the past, he can only rather sentimentally adore. His own static vision picks out details, reflects them and variates them into a kind of series, like the stills of a cinema, whose total effect may be sensitive and delightful, but cannot be organic.

This same static quality explains Mr. Eliot's loyalty to a class and a class creed. A static universe does not evolve, cannot believe in evolving. It does, however, accumulate, and its "additions" make a quantitative change—the one kind of change and of cultural contribution which Mr. Eliot admits (see "Tradition and the Individual Talent" and "The Function of Criticism"). In a static universe, transfiguration and revelation, and the capacity for these, are all stratified in the past. And this is another way of saying that Mr. Eliot's spiritual experiences, from which issue his moral and aesthetic taste, although they are real, have the form not of life, but of an inherited convention. Thus Mr. Eliot, with a religious sense, conceives of no religion except the orthodox Christian; with a tragic sense, conceives of man's struggle exclusively in the cant meanings of Original Sin; with a sense of the spirit's need of discipline and order—both in society and in the person—dreams of no method but that of a moneyed class ruling through church and state.

Are such views valid, in the sense of having a relationship with reality? Is there a position from which the universe is static; in which transfiguration and revelation are past; in which good, evil, and the given political and economic forms are absolute? The answer is yes, in the sense that death, being real, is valid. The living world of the mind is as dynamic as the material world (they are one); there, too, the individual life must partake of the dynamism of the whole, and when it is severed from that dynamism we call it dead. The only difference is that in the world of the mind we do not commonly employ the term "death"; we prefer to say conventional, dogmatic, static. Mr. Eliot's position is that of a man who has withdrawn from growth—in our meaning, withdrawn from life. *He* is static, his soul's transfiguration is past, whatever progress he conceives must be a mere consolidation of himself into forms already uttered. His intellectual, spiritual, and poetic "life" is a rationalization of this death deep within him.

We hold now, I believe, the key to T. S. Eliot. He is a man who has abdicated; but since he has been deeply sensitized to life, the articulation of his experience remains an exquisite, lingering echo. Such abdicated men have always existed, and have never been vital: even in periods of cultural stability (like that of Dante, for example), the cultural whole had constantly to be re-created by dynamic men. But in our age, where stability has foundered into chaos, and where the need for spiritual growth has become absolutely identified with the bare struggle for survival, the discrepancy between a man like Mr. Eliot and adequate leadership becomes enormous.

What we have really defined in our portrait of T. S. Eliot is a type of minor poet. He is in the tradition, neither of our major poets—Poe, Whitman, Melville—nor of the great Victorians. He is close to a cultivated and popular figure like Thomas Gray; and his *Waste Land* is a poem as good, and of the same nature, as the "Elegy." Gray also was a technical innovator with an immense appeal because he foreshadowed, unconsciously, what was to become the dominant appetite of Europe: closeness to nature. From the energy of this appetite, Titans were to evolve the method for absorbing and controlling nature. But in Gray, the motion took a reactionary form: a sentimental harking back to the values of Puritanism (and to the language of Milton). The analogy with *The Waste Land* is complete. Here, too, is technical innovation together with a vague foreshadowing of what is *now* the dominant need of the world: the need of an organic, a livable Whole in which all men may function. This foreshadowed need gives to the poem its pathos, its unity, and its importance. But, as in Gray, it is negatively stated by an evocation of a sentimental memory and by the use of old materials—in Mr. Eliot's case, more diffused and catholic, since no strong Milton stands immediately behind him.

The questions remain: why has Mr. Eliot been a leader and what does his leadership reveal about our literary generation? The questions are swiftly answered. Even in an age of confused standards, there is recognition of literary merit. Mr. Eliot's clarity, it is true, is achieved not by integrating the chaos that has bewildered us, but by withdrawal. Yet to the men whom the cultural dissolution has frightened and weakened (the majority of men), these limitations make him only more acceptable. A long time ago, I wrote of what I called "the comfort of limit," and explained its appeal to many types of mind lost in our modern chaos. Only athletic souls can face a world that has become, perhaps more than in any other era, an overwhelmingly open and darkened future. The temptation to limit this world, either by rationalistically charting its future (a disguised reactionism) or by merely advocating its reform in an image of the past, is great and manifold.

All the dogmatisms of our day are really such "limits"—such simplifications of the real. There is the dogmatism of science (the comfort of limiting reality and its mastery to problems of mechanics and addition); there is the dogmatism of cynical despair (the comfort of giving up hope and therefore struggle); there is the dogmatism of a pseudo-Marxian dialectic (the comfort of explaining the human tragedy in terms solely of a simple, solvable class struggle). And, for the weakly poetic, there is the haven of an elegiac past, like Mr. Eliot's, in which great poets still sing and sure priests thunder.

The one way of life that has no limit and affords no comfort is the way ahead—into the bitter and dark and bloody dawn of a new world, wherein mankind shall integrate without loss the stormy elements that make the chaos of our day, and its promise.

*Michael Roberts. *Adelphi* 5 (November 1932), 141–44.

[. . .]

Of Mr. Eliot's virtue as a literary critic there can be no dispute; his style is capable of ordonnance, clarity, and economy; at its best—and it is frequently at its best—

it approaches the neatness and precision of geometry. In [. . .] "Tradition and the Individual Talent," Mr. Eliot sets up his rigorous method against the slap-dash criticism of the daily press. Then, in essays on the Elizabethan dramatists and the Metaphysical poets, he illustrates his method. In each essay, the general survey, the guarded generalization, and the definition of some essential quality, prepare the way for a final clear statement. In the hands of Mr. Eliot it is a method which, even when it does not intensify our appreciation of a poet, invariably clarifies our thinking. It is the classical method, and as such it possesses limitations which the classicist would neither deny nor regret.

It tends to keep the critic close to his text—the best of Mr. Eliot's criticism is technical and, in no disparaging sense, trivial—and it tends to discourage him from those romantic reinterpretations of the whole sense of a man's work which are often driveling, always arbitrary and personal, and sometimes (very rarely) of first rate importance. The second essay in this book, "The Function of Criticism," attacks this type of criticism. In it, we begin to see the inherent weakness of Mr. Eliot's position. True, he still appears to have the best of the argument, but his case is less closely reasoned and he is compelled to add that desperate weapon, ridicule, to his critical armory.

Both Mr. Eliot and his opponent Mr. Murry had taken up extreme positions, Mr. Eliot asserting that "Those of us who find ourselves supporting what Mr. Murry calls Classicism believe that men cannot get on without giving allegiance to something outside themselves" while Mr. Murry claimed that "The English writer, the English divine, the English statesman, inherit no rules from their forebears; they inherit only this: a sense that in the last resort they must depend upon the inner voice." Certainly, in making any particular judgment, one must choose between these processes, but it does not follow that there are two opposed positions. It is possible that both Mr. Murry and Mr. Eliot would agree that a critical hierarchy could be established which would be authoritative but not absolute. The question is: at what point are we to cease giving allegiance to something outside ourselves?

At this point, however, both Mr. Murry and Mr. Eliot desert pure literary criticism. In [Eliot's "A Dialogue on Dramatic Poetry"]:

You can never draw the line between aesthetic criticism and moral and social criticism; you cannot draw a line between criticism and metaphysics; you start with literary criticism, and however rigorous an aesthete you may be, you are over the frontier into something else sooner or later.

Further, the attempt to enunciate and coordinate our beliefs in any field must lead us in the end to the despised science of theology. Most Englishmen—including communists and those who profess and call themselves atheists, would, if they tidied their own minds, find themselves driven back to a Christian theology: a few, like Mr. Murry and perhaps Mr. Eliot, would discover themselves to be heretics willing or unwilling, as the case may be, to submit to the Holy Church.

But this analysis, this tidiness of mind, is not more popular now than it has ever been: in intellectual circles today respectability dictates a slovenly Unchristianity in place of the slovenly Christianity of a century ago. Consequently, Mr. Eliot is able to say of a reviewer of his book *For Lancelot Andrewes*: "In words of great seriousness and manifest sincerity, he pointed out that I had suddenly arrested my progress—whither he had supposed me to be moving I do not know—and that to his distress I was unmistakably making

off in the wrong direction. Somehow I had failed, and had admitted my failure; if not a lost leader, at least a lost sheep; what is more, I was a kind of traitor . . ." [*Selected Essays* 358].

Mr. Eliot is wholly unable to comprehend the reviewer's disappointment; but it was a disappointment that was widely shared. It was not that Mr. Eliot had discovered himself to be a Christian: that is a fate which might happen to any of us if we were sufficiently honest, patient, and intelligent, but that the implications of Mr. Eliot's Christianity were so much less than we had hoped. We admit that we are plodding the road from nowhere and we do not believe that the removal of suffering will make a better world. But we do believe that the removal of a cause of suffering is a good act, even though new causes may arise.

Mr. Eliot says in a casual footnote: "it is a public misfortune that Mr. Bertrand Russell did not have a classical education." That may well be true, but it is equally unfortunate that Mr. Eliot did not have a scientific education. The crudities of the "scientific" attitude will not be abolished by unsympathetic gibes at "scientific" radicals whose philosophy is "crude and raw and provincial" but by making the scientific view an integral part of humanist culture. It is not merely that Mr. Eliot sometimes spoils an excellent argument by the use of an inappropriate scientific simile and makes a howler in elementary chemistry, but rather that he over-emphasizes the value of the historical as against the scientific view of society, ignoring the fact that the progress of applied science has changed certain problems, such as the general provision of food and shelter, from historical to mere technical problems of distribution.

Within the last few years it has become possible to remove a vast amount of human misery, but there is a danger that when the impeding stupidity, self-interest, and timidity are at last overcome, the change will be controlled by men having no ideas beyond material aims which are now easily attainable. Against the disaster of a revolution managed by Big Business or by Trade Unions we have hoped, and still hope, for a revolution in which the "intellectuals" will again fulfill their proper social function. But in so far as Mr. Eliot is their representative, they and all good Churchmen stand aloof.

> The World is trying the experiment of attempting to form a civilized but non-Christian mentality. The experiment will fail; but we must be very patient in awaiting its collapse; meanwhile redeeming the time: so that the Faith may be preserved alive through the dark ages before us; to renew and rebuild civilization, and save the World from suicide. [*Selected Essays* 377]

That is fine rhetoric: and there are many of us who are very sure that the experiment of forming a morality based on "a naive doctrine of happiness" will fail, that every man of integrity must hold in balance an inner impulse, and an outer discipline, which is something more than self-control directed toward a known end.

But because the Church will not help us, the new moral hierarchy when it rises will be a church which, however Christian it may be in essence, will use no word of the discredited Christian theology and will have nothing but contempt for those Christians of Mr. Eliot's generation, who refused to cooperate with "radicals" whose philosophy lacked the wisdom which "consists largely of skepticism and uncynical disillusion." The value of that wisdom we do not doubt; it is our last protection in the face of immitigable misery. But its proper field has from time to time been restricted by those changes

we call progress. And the present is such a time, and to some of us the demeanor of Mr. Eliot is too urbane, too "calm and socialized." It is not that we resent his aloofness as artist—or critic—but that when he does find himself "over the frontier" into sociology and politics he is still aloof. Serenity is very remote from indifference, and we find in Mr. Eliot's later essays too much wisdom, too little human sympathy.

Paul Elmer More. "The Cleft Eliot." *Saturday Review* 9 (12 November 1932), 233, 235.

When T. S. Eliot came from London to Harvard as Professor of Poetry for the year on the Charles Eliot Norton Foundation, the selection was generally applauded, though a few may have asked cynically what Mr. Norton himself, with his kinship to the old preaching Eliots of Massachusetts and his uncompromising notions of art, would have thought of such an appointment. The significant fact is that the present scion of the family is perhaps the most distinguished man of letters today in the British-speaking world, and that his homecoming was the occasion of much comment, favorable and unfavorable, and of much searching of our critical principles. [. . .]

As for the distinguished position of Mr. Eliot, no one is likely to dispute the fact who is familiar with the English press and knows with what frequency and respect his name occurs. More significant even is his following among the younger thinking men of England, especially in the universities. Nor is this following confined to his adopted country. I can well remember the furor of enthusiasm aroused among the youthful intelligentsia of Princeton a few years ago when I proposed that he should be invited to lecture here. Whatever the more sober part of the world may think of him, his name acts, or certainly has acted, like a spell upon the forward pushing minds of two countries.

The fact of Mr. Eliot's reputation is indisputable. But if one asks the reason for it, the answer is not so quickly at hand. As a critic he stands high. For myself I have been going through the volume of his *Selected Essays* [. . .]. Undoubtedly the author comes well through this ordeal of continuous reading. There is capable scholarship in these essays, particularly in those that deal with the Elizabethan and Jacobean dramatists; there is a play of alert and penetrating thought, and above all a certain unassumed gravity of judgment, a certain note of authority, not readily defined but instinctively felt. The "metaphysical" poets, from whom Mr. Eliot rightly draws his spiritual lineage, will have a new value for anyone who has read his analysis of their method. Yet there are sides to his critical work which are not so easily reconciled with his reputation. His apparent blindness to the real greatness of Milton may be explained by the fact that Milton stands at the head of the line of development which to Mr. Eliot's disciples, if not to Mr. Eliot himself, has acted like a damper upon English poetry until the advent of the modern "metaphysicals"; but that cavalier judgment will not please many whose taste was formed in an older school, nor those younger advocates of a return to Milton of whom Professor Elliott, of Amherst, is a leader. And, on the other hand, the critic's pages are sprinkled with pungent sayings that must shock and sting the complacent enthusiasts of Modernism. Who then are the authenticators of this critical renown, the conservatives or the modernists?

But Mr. Eliot is a poet as well as a critic, or, more precisely, a poet primarily; and it might be presumed that the source of his great reputation could be found in his verse rather than his prose. And this in a sense is true. Yet here too difficulties arise, which perhaps may be best exhibited by relating a bit of personal experience. I am myself a staunch admirer of his *Ash-Wednesday*, though the poem has been pretty harshly judged by certain narrow champions of his earlier style. Well, I have read the poem aloud five or six times to variously composed groups of listeners (and reading aloud is about the final test of a poet), with invariably the same result. Without exception, whether their taste was of the older or the newer model, the auditors have been deeply impressed. For one thing they have felt the sonority of the lines and have been stirred by the cadences of a music which is extremely rare in our free verse. And this is not the melody of merely prettily selected and adroitly joined words, independent of their sense, but suggests the profounder harmony—if one could only find it—of an organically constructive genius behind the superficial disarray of the phrases. Yet without exception also the poem—and generally it was read aloud two or three times consecutively to the same group— failed to convey any clear meaning. Regularly the comment was the same: This is beautiful, this holds our attention; but we have the vaguest notion, if any notion, of what it is all about. Ordinarily the complaint was made by way of disparagement, whether of the poet's intelligence or the hearer's capacity. But not always. On one occasion the poem selected for reading was

"The Hippopotamus," which ends, as will be remembered, with this rather startling comparison:

He shall be washed as white as snow,
By all the martyr'd virgins kist,
While the True Church remains below
Wrapt in the old miasmal mist.

At the conclusion of the reading I turned to one of the most attentive authors, an enthusiast to whom Mr. Eliot is the sublimest poet since Milton (the concession to Milton being, I suspect, of the lips only), with the query: Now this has the ring of poetry; but what in the name of sense *is* the hippopotamus? "Does it make any difference?" cried he, almost jumping out of his chair at the indignity of such a question. And his answer, if it did not elucidate Mr. Eliot, explained several things to me in the taste of the younger generation. (I may add that on a later occasion the poet himself, with his sly ironic smile, put me off by intimating that possibly the writer could not—he meant would not—expound my riddle.)

Now all this points to a curious discrepancy in Mr. Eliot's position. I find a good many poetry lovers of the older tradition simply neglecting him as unintelligible and unimportant; and this indifference I can understand, though I do not share it. A few also of the ultra modern type repudiate him with equal finality, but with an added note of supercilious contempt which is rather characteristic of the fully emancipated mind. Miss Rebecca West, for instance, ridicules his "flustered search for coherence," and a preposterous contributor to the Boston *Transcript* ends a long diatribe with the complaint: "He still is lost in his Waste Land and, whether with malice or not, is still pointing out false roads to the oasis to those travelers who seek from him the way"—rather than from Mr. Calverton.

Other radicals distinguish for their own satisfaction between the poet of the past and the critic of the present. I once asked a young student of very advanced ideas about art and life how he, as an admirer of Mr. Eliot, reconciled *The Waste Land* with the program of classicism and royalism (i.e., the divine right of kings) and Anglo-Catholicism announced in a recent preface. His reply was quick and decisive: "I don't reconcile them; I take the one and leave the other." And to this rebuke I had nothing to say, since it pointed to a cleft in Mr. Eliot's career to which I am myself sensitive, though my young friend's order of values is the reverse of my own.

There it is, the dilemma that confronts those who recognize Mr. Eliot's great powers; somehow they must reconcile for themselves what appears to be an inconsequence between the older poet and the newer critic, or must adjust their admiration to what cannot be reconciled. It is not that we have to do with an author who is strong in one phase of his work and weak in another, but that this power is so differently directed here and there. The writer of *The Waste Land* and the other poems of that period appeals to us as one struck to the heart by the confusion and purposelessness and wastefulness of the world about him, and as dismayed by the impoverishment of our human emotions and imagination in a life so divested of meaning and so dull of conscience. And to that world his verse will be held up as a ruthlessly faithful mirror. The confusion of life will be reflected in the disorganized flux of images; its lack of clear meaning in the obscurity of language; its defiance of authoritative creeds in a license of metrical form; its dislocated connection with the past in the floating debris of allusion; while its flattened emotions will be reproduced realistically, without comment. If there be any salvation from such a whirligig of chance and time it is only into the peace of utter escape—"Shantih shantih shantih."

And now against this lyric prophet of chaos must be set the critic who will judge the world from the creed of the classicist, the royalist, and the anglo-catholic, who will see behind the clouds of illusion the steady decrees of a divine purpose, and who has gone so far at least in that program as to compose a long pamphlet (included in the *Selected Essays*) of *Thoughts after Lambeth*. And what has the young rebel who rejoices in the disillusion of *The Waste Land* to do with the Bishops of the Church assembled in solemn conclave to unravel the purposes of Deity? In one sense it would be easy to reconcile such a *volte face* by saying simply that the author has undergone a deep conversion; and that explanation is in a way true. But the embarrassing fact remains that somehow the poet contrives to carry on the old shop in the new market. I think, for instance, that a sensitive mind cannot read *Ash-Wednesday* without an uneasy perception of something fundamentally amiss in employing for an experience born of Anglo-Catholic faith a metrical form and a freakishness of punctuation suitable for the presentation of life regarded as without form and void. Such a discord manifestly was felt by those to whom I have read the poem, though one and all they responded to the mere magic of the language in itself. [. . .]

No, it is not the revolution in Mr. Eliot's views of life, his conversion if you prefer the word, that troubles his true admirers, but the fact that his change on one side is complicated and disrupted by lack of change on the other side. And here I would like to recall a bit of conversation with him, trusting that I may do so without any breach of confidence or betrayal of the intimacies of friendship (if Mr. Eliot will allow me the honor of calling myself a friend). It was in his London home; I was lauding the audacity of the critical conversion announced in the preface to *For Lancelot Andrewes*, then recently published, and I concluded with the query: "And now, when you have completed this heroic program and returned, as your intention is, to verse, will you cling to the old impossible (so I expressed it) manner of *The Waste Land*?" "No," he exclaimed, losing for a moment his armor of placid irony, and shaking a defiant fist in the air—"No; in that I am absolutely unconverted!"

I am not at all confident that I have interpreted Mr. Eliot correctly, or that, in particular, I have grasped his state of mind when he composed the earlier poems; his is an elusive, though an unmistakable, genius. But my perplexity over some unreconciled paradox, at once provocative and baffling, in his attitude towards life and letters has been confirmed by too many witnesses to leave me in doubt of its justification. Mr. Eliot, I am sure, would disavow any ambition to pose as a leader of men; but he is a leader, and a very influential leader. Our difficulty is that he seems to be leading us in two directions at once.

Samuel C. Chew. "Essays in Criticism." *Yale Review* 22 (December 1932), 386–90.

The publication of a representative selection of his prose writings has come at an appropriate time when Mr. Eliot is performing his new duties as visiting Professor of Poetry at Harvard University, Turnbull Lecturer at Johns Hopkins, and occasional lecturer at other American academic institutions. The collection opens with the celebrated and influential essay [. . .] "Tradition and the Individual Talent," which has already won such provisional immortality as may be attained by a place on the prescribed reading in courses for freshmen. Parts of *The Sacred Wood* reappear, notably in the studies in the Elizabethan drama. The brilliant and a little perverse *Homage to John Dryden* and the small book on Dante are reprinted entire. Two essays in which Mr. Eliot crosses swords with the neo-humanists reappear, not very necessarily perhaps, for this subject begins to grow stale. The critic's Anglo-Catholic opinions are represented by the paper on Andrewes and by the "Thoughts after Lambeth." And there are several minor pieces, including the essay in which he blames Arnold for Pater, the fine study of Baudelaire, and a delightful appreciation of a critic as different as can be imagined from Mr. Eliot— Charles Whibley.

This is an opportunity, then, to see Mr. Eliot's talents as a critic more widely displayed than in any of the four original slender volumes or in the scattered essays. His voice, always authoritative, sounds more than ever *ex cathedra*. The formidable strength with which he sets forth his opinions is grounded in quietness and confidence. There is no reliance upon brilliant imagery or clever divagation, no sacrifice of the subject for the sake of the style; and on the rare occasions on which Mr. Eliot lets himself go (as in the paragraph on the nearness of England to the Continent should Englishmen ever conceivably wish to avail themselves of the opportunity afforded them) he seems by the sudden irony to emphasize the cool dispassionateness of his usual style. In one of his papers he remarks that English criticism argues or persuades but does not state. Mr. Eliot states. No other transalpine voice speaks with such certitude of infallibility. Opinions are enunciated with such calm, dispassionate, and apparently disinterested confidence that even the wary reader must look sharp lest he accept as fact what is, after all, merely opinion. Some of these pronouncements from the chair have been widely quoted; it is hardly too much to say that they are on the way to revolutionize taste among young intellectuals. Take one example. On page 306 of [*Selected Essays*] Mr. Eliot prints two quotations, the one from Dryden, the other from Shelley. He believes one might "defy" anybody to show that the lines by Shelley are "superior on intrinsically poetic merit" to the passage from Dryden. Now, it is merely perverse to set some harsh, jog-trot, singularly uncouth lines of Dryden (by no means Dryden anywhere near his best) in comparison with the great final chorus of "Hellas"; and Mr. Eliot's smooth contempt for Shelley's image of the snake in this passage entirely misses the significance of the snake in Shelley's poetry. But the critic's "defiance" is so formidable and so cold that most readers are compelled against their will to think they must be wrong, Mr. Eliot must be right. So with a score of his assertions—on the comparative greatness of Milton and Dryden, of Shelley and Crashaw, and the famous remark about *Hamlet* being a failure as a work of art. But for those who while refusing to accept Mr. Eliot's words as inspired utterances can relish breadth of scholarship, a severely disciplined mind, a sense of order and decorum, a reverence for tradition, this volume is an intellectual feast.

[. . .]

Peter Monro Jack.
"The Cream of T. S. Eliot's Literary Criticism."
New York Times Book Review, 29 January 1933, p. 2.

The twentieth century is still the nineteenth, says Mr. Eliot, remarking (in his essay on Dryden) on the persistence of Victorian misjudgments, "although it may in time acquire its own character." What that character will be and what the correspondence in literature, we can only guess. It may strive to continue the romantic individualism of Mr. Middleton Murry, which Mr. Murry is finding it hard to continue himself. It may follow the classicism of Mr. Eliot. Or it may (what is difficult to believe) surprise us into a line of action for which we seem to have no preparation. Of one thing, however, we may be sure: that its poetry and criticism (if they are to persist) will be profoundly affected by the poetry and criticism of Mr. Eliot, and that this book is likely to be the chief document in whatever revaluation we make of our literary tradition and present aims. Indeed, readers of *The Sacred Wood*, or *For Lancelot Andrewes*, or of one essay and another in the London *Criterion*, may well be surprised at the vigorous challenge that the book in its totality comes to mean. The essay on Blake, for instance, sounds, in *The Sacred Wood*, thin, questionable, and perhaps even querulous; here, in this context, coming after the essays on Dante, Dryden, and Marvell, it seems right and reasonable; at the least, we can recognize that Eliot could take no other position. We recognize, too, that it needed courage and conviction as well as scholarship to defend this position—that if Blake had been educated to a better tradition he would have been a better poet.

It is a remarkable book, remarkable in the range of its interests and in the flexibility and stamina of Mr. Eliot's mind as he moves from theory to demonstration, from comment to elucidation—from "The Function of Criticism" to an elaborate introduction to the poetry of Dante, from an observation on Marie Lloyd of the old music hall to a brief analysis of the problem of *Hamlet*—an analysis that has reduced a literature on *Hamlet* to a Ptolemaic system. This variety is refreshing in a book of such sustained critical reasoning. It has a further value, however. It illuminates, from this point or that, the still more remarkable centrality of Mr. Eliot's thinking and the integrity of his mind.

The essays are more than a stimulation to enjoy the fruits of others' experience. They are essays in order, exercises in the discipline of facts and the precision of thinking and feeling. They are essays in conduct as well as essays in criticism. The center, as well as the range, of Mr. Eliot's mind is here. If he is right—and it is important for other writers to discover if he is right—his mind, as a reflecting instrument, should be close to the tradition of literature (and culture) on which we rely for the renewal of the principles of reality, coherence, and mental health. But first we should be clear about the primary service of these essays, which is to remove the confusion and impurities that prevent recognition of these principles. It is in this work that the charge might be made that Mr. Eliot makes over tradition to suit himself. His views seem new and radical. They are radical but not new. What may be new is not the criticism but the conduct that might follow. To say that "more can be learned about how to write poetry from Dante than from any English poet" is not to say anything new, for English poets from Spenser to Swinburne have defiantly writ a language that allowed no imitation. "The language of Dante is the perfection of a common language." But if English writers went to school with Dante instead of with Keats or Browning or Hopkins, that would be new. To say "I can see no reason for believing that either Dante or Shakespeare did any thinking on his own" may startle us for a moment, but would hardly startle Ben Jonson, who knew Shakespeare; whereas we can readily imagine how startled Jonson would be at the thought of Wyndham Lewis's Machiavellian Shakespeare, or Middleton Murry's messianic Shakespeare. If English critics were less concerned with their own image in the poet and more concerned with the fact of poetry, that would be new. This distinction between one's self and what is outside (the work of art and the tradition into which it fits) is the first critical distinction. The tradition, though Eliot understands it because it has made him what he is, must be clarified by a radical analysis and seen by its own light.

Mr. Eliot is better, or at least this book shows itself to be better, at demonstrating the vitality of tradition than at defining it. The essay on Dante is no doubt the best in the book; it is a much more confident essay than "The Function of Criticism." The theoretical essays, except where they are engaged in confuting romanticism or revelationism, are overcautious and hesitant. The fault probably lies outside the essays, in the confusion of our language and logic. But in commenting from page to page on the *Divine Comedy*, or in drawing a portrait of his friend, Charles Whibley, or in staging the dispute between Bramhall and Hobbes (and Bertrand Russell and I. A. Richards), or in the masterpiece of witty

polemic in the first half of "Thoughts after Lambeth," or in the too truthful predictions of a bad end for Mr. Babbitt's philosophy, or in the information that he gives us of the Elizabethans, Mr. Eliot is a master of critical exposition.

If the function of criticism is not exactly defined, or defined by terms of too many meanings whose meanings it is not Mr. Eliot's business to fix, it is clearly enough seen. Given the tradition—whose classicism Mr. Eliot has attempted to clarify in these essays—one may learn by the constant use of comparison and analysis to avoid the ordinary inflations and deflations of literary opinion and to prevent mere eccentricity from making a grotesque of the work of art. And it would be surprising if this ordering of our feelings about literature, achieved through tradition, training, askesis, were not to help in steadying the general tenor of life.

In the practical matter of reading and writing, at all events, Mr. Eliot's direction can do nothing but good. His classicism is healthy, supple, and, in the coarsest sense, tough; it can stand up to anything.

*Edgell Rickword.
Scrutiny 1 (March 1933), 390–93.

This substantial and comely volume contains the greater part of Mr. Eliot's influential criticism. There is about half of *The Sacred Wood*, the three essays from the crucial *Homage to John Dryden* pamphlet, and the Dante study entire. The additions on the literary side include essays on Middleton, Heywood, Tourneur, and Ford; two excellent studies of Senecan influence on Elizabethan drama, a rather discouraged dialogue on dramatic poetry, and an essay on Baudelaire.

The novelty in the essays on the dramatists and on Baudelaire is the appearance of Mr. Eliot as an appreciator of moral essences. In this encroachment on the domain of such verbose critics as Mr. Murry and Mr. Fausset, he is not, of course, trying to put across an individual conception of morality; tradition governs this as much as it does taste. Mr. Eliot's tradition of morality is the most respectable of all, and when he says that "the essence of the tragedy of *Macbeth* is the habituation to crime," one could do nothing but assent if it were not that the italics show that he is not referring to the man but to the play. Again, he tells us, "In poetry, in dramatic technique, *The Changeling* is inferior to the best plays of Webster. But in the moral essence of tragedy, it is safe to say that in this play Middleton is surpassed by one Elizabethan alone, and that is Shakespeare." But even if that is a safe thing to say, the way of saying it is not free from danger. For after subtracting the poetry and the dramatic technique what is there left by which the moral essence may be apprehended? Again, in the essay on Baudelaire he writes: "In his verse, he is now less a model to be imitated or a source to be drained than a reminder of the duty, the consecrated task, of sincerity." But is our sensation of the poet's sincerity anything more than one of the reactions attendant on the poem's successful communication? Is anything really clarified by talking of a technical as if it were a moral achievement? It seems a pity that an essay that at the outset affirms the importance of Baudelaire's prose works should not have given some consideration to *L'Art Romantique* and *Curiosités aesthétiques*, which illustrate Baudelaire's poetic much more than the diaries do. The "revelations" in the *Journaux Intimes*, written later than the majority of the poems,

are perhaps rather specious intellectualizations, the violent efforts of a man to whom convictions of that sort were a novelty, to create a "strong personality" for himself; their forthrightness is deceptive, I think. But Mr. Eliot "hazards" an illuminating conjecture when he suggests "that the care for perfection of form, among some of the romantic poets of the nineteenth century, was an effort to support, or to conceal from view, an inner disorder." And he goes on to say: "Now the true claim of Baudelaire as an artist is not that he found a superficial form, but that he was searching for a form of life." I quote this, firstly because it is a good saying in itself, and also because the form of expression is comparatively new in Mr. Eliot's work. As it stands it is paradoxical. Not quite so paradoxical as Mr. G. K. Chesterton methodically is, but surprisingly near it. It marks a cleavage between Mr. Eliot's earlier and later criticism. It oversteps the conscious limitations of his earlier method. It must be every ambitious critic's aim to resolve the dichotomy between life and art; and every superficial critic does it constantly with negligent ease. Whether Mr. Eliot has the philosophical stamina, as he certainly has the poetic sensitiveness, for such a task, remains to be seen.

The latter part of this volume is mainly occupied by essays on attitudes rather than works and here Mr. Eliot is heavily engaged with the Martin Marprelates of today and yesterday, some of them within the Church, like Viscount Brentford, and some outside it. The outsiders are, in general, those who believe that art, culture, reason, science, the inner-light or what-not, may constitute efficient substitutes for organized religion. Arnold, Pater, Aldous Huxley, Bertrand Russell, Middleton Murry, and some American humanists who loom more sinisterly in Mr. Eliot's consciousness than seems necessary over

221

here, provide a variety of scapegoats. His diagnosis of the disease that must ensure the ultimate instability of all such eclectic systems, built up from "the best that has been thought and done in the world," is devastatingly acute. The antidote is provided in "Thoughts after Lambeth."

This volume leaves us, then, except for tentative branchings-out, as far as literature is concerned, much where we were after the publication of *Dante*. One should not, perhaps, grumble at that; but the impression given by this heterogeneous mass is not so profound as that given by the slim volumes that found their way into the world more quietly. The essays on general subjects dilute that impression, for Mr. Eliot is not as outstanding as a "thinker" as he is as a literary critic. His thinking is adequate to his own emotional needs, as a good poet's always is, but it has not much extra-personal validity. [. . .]

I must try and say briefly why Mr. Eliot's earlier work seems to me more valuable than his later, or it may seem that I underrate it just because its conclusions are unsympathetic to me. The intelligence displayed in the later essays might be matched by several of his contemporaries; the literary sensibility of the earlier essays is not matched by any of them. "Literary sensibility" is a horrible phrase and it does not sound a very impressive faculty, but when one considers how very few people there are actually capable of responding to poetry or word-order generally without prompting from its prestige, or message, or because the objects named evoke a pleasant response, perhaps the possession of this gift may be appreciated at its proper value. It is only the beginning, of course, but its absence vitiates the other critical faculties. Sometimes, when it is present, there is an absence of the coordinating faculty and thus the response is deprived of any significance beyond that of a plea-

surable sensation. It was the presence of these faculties in unison which differentiated Mr. Eliot's earlier criticism from the "appreciative" convention in vogue at the time. The method at which he aimed, and which he practiced with such delicate skill, is perhaps best described by a quotation he used from Rémy de Gourmont—*ériger en lois ses impressions personnelles*. If Mr. Eliot has for the time being gone outside literature, the loss is very much to literature; no doubt there is a compensation somewhere. But literature, in spite of wireless and cinema, is still the life-blood of the time; we are not sots or sadists by accident and one should not be too fatalistic about the approaching dark ages. If literary criticism is not one of the means Mr. Eliot envisages of redeeming the time, nothing can obscure the value of his example. As our writings are, so are our feelings, and the finer the discrimination as to the value of those writings, the better chance there is of not being ashamed of being a human being.

R. P. Blackmur.
"T. S. Eliot in Prose."
Poetry: A Magazine of Verse 42 (April 1933), 44–49.

[Review of *John Dryden* and *Selected Essays*]

[. . .]

John Dryden is slight but characteristic. More nearly popular in intent and tone than most of Mr. Eliot's criticism, these lectures—I take them to have been delivered as such—ought both to arouse and accommodate, without terminating, an interest in Dryden. The unfortunate possibility is that the reader will be content with Mr. Eliot and go no further with Dryden than to give him a better place on his shelves. That is because Mr. Eliot has a knack—admirable in his larger pieces—of seeming to extract the best juice of his subject by quotation and qualification, and because the qualities to be admired in Dryden are those we prefer rather to name than to exemplify. "No writer in the next and more polished generation, not even Addison, has more urbanity. 'Elegance' and 'Urbanity': two words of commendation which have long been in disrepute; but which are always needed." Mr. Eliot, in his own pursuit of these qualities—or it may have been in the exigence of the smaller intent of popular lectures—has been content with a far lighter, more tentative contact with the substance of Dryden than satisfied him in his earlier, soberer essay *Homage to John Dryden*. Though it be only a glancing blow upon the armor of reputation, it would have been better had the present volume not been published. Yet there are relishes, for which much may be forgiven: as when we are reminded that Ben Jonson, "when he returned to the Anglican fold after temporary defection to Rome, showed his enthusiasm by seizing the chalice, at his first communion, and draining it to the last drop."

To turn to the *Selected Essays* is an act of pleasure and accomplishment. With every regard to their limitations, and most of all remembering that the quality of Mr. Eliot's mind cannot be the effective quality of many minds, these essays form the most useful criticism of our time. There is more to be got from them, and more to be acknowledged that has been got from them, than from the work of any living critic. It is not that Mr. Eliot has more resources in scholarship and insight than his colleagues, but that he has seen and maintained, what many have not, an integrity of interest. What he says of his dead friend Charles Whibley applies to himself:

> [T]he first condition of being interesting is to have the tact to choose only those subjects in which one is really interested, those which are germane to one's own temper . . . Whibley had this discretion, that of the *honnête homme* as critic, to select subjects suited to his own temperament.

Many critics, pitiably, choose what they can sell; others, contemptibly, because they can sell everything, choose everything: these augment a reputation for publishing frequently.

Real interest has the attractive force of passion. That is why those who are non-Christian, or who wear their religion placidly without a difference, yet find themselves disturbed, attracted, repelled by essays on Lancelot Andrewes, John Bramhall, or the report of the Lambeth Conference. Mr. Eliot, by the strength of his own interest, has seized [forced] to the light . . . the latent interest of others; and his virtue is as effective in studies of the English Church as in his examination of Dante or the metaphysical poets. If some have been led to read the *Divine Comedy* with greater understanding, others have run after Mr. Eliot into the more decorative and dramatic parts of his Church. A critic no more than a poet (remember those who, after *The Waste Land*, wrote poetry with less understanding than ever) is responsible for his victims. Influence, since it is more readily felt and less readily digested by the weak than the strong, is less obviously good than bad; as we have witness in the disciples of Irving Babbitt.

But the worst influence is perhaps upon those who deny it, those who, in Mr. Eliot's case, call out at the bar rather than the chancel rail, "Jesuit!" and "Renegade!" The fools do not matter so soon as they are named such; let them run. There remain those who have been disturbed, who have experienced by insight that there may be in the Church an "odd and rather exhilarating feeling of isolation," and who understand with Mr. Eliot that theology may be a masculine discipline. These, realizing that to be a Christian is today almost more of an adventure than it was to be an atheist a generation ago, will envy without being able to share the positive character of his experience.

There is a good deal of regret going about because paragraphs like that above can be written in description of a man who formerly aroused enthusiasm or antipathy only by his opinions on poetry. It is like regretting, because he loved God, that Dante wrote poetry. We ought rather to be thankful that a man of his talent should occasionally write about religion. The religious are few and are always outsiders, and it may be that what we value most in Mr. Eliot will be his Christianity. Only those who never discerned the devout and savage Christian in "The Hippopotamus," "Mr. Eliot's Sunday Morning Service," and *The Waste Land* have any cause to regret a change that never took place. Even the argument that his religion might interfere with the composition of poetry or honesty of criticism falls rather flat when we remember that there is no connection and no war between the autonomy of religion and the autonomy of poetry.

Mr. Eliot may be most useful because without insulting our intelligence or diminishing his own, he supplies us with something different from ourselves. Surely we need not fear a difference when it is worn so bravely.

Robert Hillyer.
"Book Reviews."
New England Quarterly 6 (June 1933), 402–04.

In Mr. Eliot's essays we note the evolution of the attitudes which he himself summarized as classicism, royalism, and anglo-catholicism. His poetry, in general, not only shows fewer traces of this development but because of its willfulness of style and its indulgent self-expression can most justly be described as decadent romanticism. The mind of the essayist and the mind of the poet are uncongenial to each other, and it may be surmised that this spectacle of a mind divided against itself, rather than the work it produces, is the cause of Mr. Eliot's vogue with a generation similarly disorganized.

The Waste Land shows us a spirit frustrated by the world it inhabits and beating in vain against the doors of the past into which it would escape. In the essays, the escape has been made, and now the spirit is at home among the mighty dead whom alone it considers worthy of regard. The uncertainty of the poem is displaced by an assurance which sometimes becomes dogmatism. Yet there is nothing here to cause dissension among contemporary writers. The controversial note is one, rather, to arouse the professional scholars. Whoever takes sides will be amid a battle of ghosts. The present reviewer delightedly agreed that "after the erection of the Chinese Wall of Milton, blank verse has suffered not only arrest but retrogression." He considered other *obiter dicta*—the attacks on Pater, for example—childish and in questionable taste. But except for the mental stimulation of alternative bravos and boos, which, were they to be expanded, would result merely in a series of learned articles, nothing happened. There is, in Mr. Eliot's criticism, a dignified refusal to run a channel through from the seas of the past to the angry flux of the present. Interesting and informed as are his enthusiasms and his hates, they might well be regarded as applying to some literature in a tongue no longer used.

Considering the essays on the Elizabethans, the manly and sensible tributes to Dryden and Marvell, one is regretful to withhold full praise. The essay on Blake provides one with a number of pleasant jolts; and an anti-Milton temperament is again titillated to read that "Milton's celestial and infernal regions are large but insufficiently furnished apartments filled by heavy conversation"; but as a whole, the essay succumbs to authoritarian thesis. Blake is an overrated poet, if you will, but one shudders to imagine his prophetic books rewritten in the terms of Catholic mythology. The essay on Swinburne is a large inflation of the familiar truth that Swinburne's world was a world of words. "Thoughts after Lambeth," with the almost pathetic earnestness of the convert, deals with points of doctrine less important, perhaps, to a world in agony than to one who has turned his back on the world. And finally we applaud in "The Function of Criticism" the insistence on tradition in the arts. But again, as the essay, which is admittedly rambling, continues, we are irritated to read that "the French in the year 1600 had already a more mature prose" (than the English). If the glories of the Elizabethan translations are merely the bloom of adolescence, one might wish that English prose had been spared the French influence that, in the eighteenth century, brought it to arid maturity.

But this review must close. It would be impudent, were it not largely significant, to speak of Mr. Eliot's expatriation. The geographical fact, however, is a symbol of that homelessness which obsessed his mind for so long and at last caused him to grip faiths which more natural minds may take for granted. All the writers whom he most admires elbowed their way eagerly through the hurly-burly of their time. Had they been of his cast of mind, Mr. Eliot would have had no subject-matter for his distinguished prose.

Checklist of Additional Reviews

*"From Humanism to Anglo-Catholicism." *Glasgow Herald*, 15 September 1932. [not located]

*Osbert Sitwell. "A Great Critic." *Week-End Review* 6 (17 September 1932), 318.

*Rebecca West. "What is Mr. T. S. Eliot's Authority as a Critic?" *Daily Morning Post and Telegraph*, 30 September 1932.

*Hugh Ross Williamson. "Notes at Random: Lawrence and Eliot." *Bookman* 83 (October 1932), 4, 6.

*"Poet and Critic." *Saturday Review* 154 (8 October 1932), 370.

*I. M. Parsons. "Mr. Eliot's Authority." *Spectator* 149, no. 5441 (8 October 1932), 450–52.

*"Ye Agéd Eagle." *Granta* 42 (14 October 1932), 18.

*N. A. M. L. *Isis* 854 (19 October 1932), 14.

George N. Shuster. "Mr. Eliot Returns." *Commonweal* 16 (19 October 1932), 581–83.

*E. R. T. "Mr. Eliot's Essays." *Manchester Guardian*, 24 October 1932, p. 5.

*Ezra Pound. "*Praefatio aut tumulus cimicium.*" *Active Anthology* (London: Faber and Faber, 1933), 9–27.

William Lyon Phelps. "As I Like It." *Scribner's Magazine* 93 (January 1933), 60–64.

Morris U. Schappes. "T. S. Eliot Moves Right." *Modern Monthly* 7 (August 1933), 405–08.

*Robert Strong. "The Critical Attitude of T. S. Eliot." *London Quarterly and Holborn Review* 158 (October 1933), 513–19.

SWEENEY AGONISTES
1932

SWEENEY AGONISTES

FRAGMENTS OF AN
ARISTOPHANIC MELODRAMA

BY

T. S. ELIOT

LONDON
FABER & FABER LIMITED
24 RUSSELL SQUARE

D. G. Bridson. "Views and Reviews: *Sweeney Agonistes.*" *New English Weekly* 2 (12 January 1933), 304.

It is difficult to criticize Mr. Eliot. It is difficult, in fact, to fix him "pinned and wriggling on the wall." His elusiveness [. . .] is invaluable to him. No sooner has a critic pronounced his later work a manifestation of his return to the fold, than a true disciple ups and denies the assertion flatly. The form is more regular, it seems, yet the implication is more subtle than ever. So let it be with Sweeney. But when Mr. Eliot labels his work "fragments of an Aristophanic melodrama," he gives us an axis of reference.

In the first place, then, we do not readily think of Mr. Eliot as the modern Aristophanes. Aristophanic his moods may be, but Aristophanic they have certainly never appeared. The belly-shaking laughter of many passages in *Ulysses* are as Aristophanic as we choose to call them. But an Aristophanic melodrama by Mr. Eliot . . . ! Sooner a parody of the Sermon on the Mount by St. Thomas Aquinas! And when a man of high seriousness (such we esteem Mr. Eliot) turns himself (as Mr. Eliot has done) to satiric melodrama or farce on the broad scale, we can hazard a guess at the result. [. . .]

A good deal might be said about the form of the fragments now published. [. . .] In the first place, their nature suggests that the whole is not conspicuous for what Frere called "the utter impossibility of the story." They appear to be rather fragments of a "melodrama" in which "an adherence to the probabilities of real life is an essential requisite." [. . .] Mr. Eliot's staging of nine characters simultaneously is defensible. His suppression of a separate chorus in favor of duets replete with tambo and bones is excusable. But Aristophanic or not, his melodrama has every appearance of being decidedly dull. His choice of epigraphs would suggest that he is not more in love with Sweeney today than he was in 1920. But the terseness and compression of the Sweeney poems was the most remarkable thing about them. Their tension was more interesting than their content. But Sweeney in melodrama is rather less impressive than Sweeney in lyric. Sweeney in melodrama [. . .] sprawls.

That the people he describes annoy Mr. Eliot intensely we can well believe. But it is less the people described than Mr. Eliot's description of them that annoys his reader. To describe dullness in an interesting, even in an amusing manner, is defensible as possible art. So Mr. Eliot has done in many of his earlier poems. But to describe dullness accurately and in detail, fully and at length, is a different matter.

[Quotation of lines 1 to 13 of *Sweeney Agonistes*]

Thus opens the "Fragments of a Prologue." It is all very clever, all very cutting, all very true, and all very futile, as Mr. Eliot, no doubt, intended it to be. In so far as he has achieved with it what he (apparently) intended to achieve, the technique of the passage may therefore be justified forthwith. But the value of the passage remains suspect. The best way to satirize dullness is not, necessarily, to record it dully.

Klipstein and Krumpacker, two Americans over in London on business, awake an expectancy (if only by their names)

229

for work of the Burbank and Bleistein order. But the following remark of Klipstein is not very reassuring: "Yes we did our bit, as you folks say, / I'll tell the world we got the Hun on the run." It is rather more obvious, as humor, than we might have desired. That Klipstein should be wearing music-hall horn-rimmed glasses and chewing music-hall gum seems inevitable.

Perhaps the easiest thing in the work to praise is its rhythm. This is pure barrel-organ, and with its constant repetition in music-hall crosstalk, makes no bad medium for the whole. The parodies of popular song are also well enough in their way, but again rather obvious. A mildly amusing feature of the dialogue, however, is its accurate recording of inflection. Snow remarks that he is "very interested" in a tale of Sweeney's. Loot Sam Wauchope is described as being "at *home* in London."

[. . .]

If *Sweeney Agonistes* were completed, no doubt the effect of the whole would be sufficient justification for every fault we can find in these fragments. But that is not sufficient justification for them in itself. That they give a fair picture of banality is the most that can be said for them. And this is not exactly the sort of criticism we should prefer to pass on a work of so peculiar a genius as Mr. Eliot's. There are not many living poets who could not have equaled the achievement, and we may suspect that there are a number who could have bettered it. Mr. Eliot has written no other work of which this could be said.

Morton D. Zabel. "A Modern *Purgatorio*." *Commonweal* 17 (19 April 1933), 696–97.

The quotation from Saint John of the Cross which Mr. Eliot prefixes to his latest book of verse goes farther than the hint of parody in his title or the apologetic compromise of his subtitle to explain his motive in republishing these two desultory fragments of satire from the *Criterion*. "Hence the soul cannot be possessed of the divine union, until it has divested itself of the love of created beings." Mr. Eliot's portrayal of "created beings" has in the past been sufficiently scathing; its purpose must be understood by anyone who wishes to grasp the nature and process of his spiritual experience. In the desolation and vacuity of "A Cooking Egg," "The Hippopotamus," "Gerontion," "Prufrock," and *The Waste Land*, he achieved that ruthless notation of reality without mastering which no knowledge of material fact may be gained and no renunciation of it justified. These were records of a self-scrutiny bordering on spiritual masochism. They explored with an ironic intensity unknown to most of Mr. Eliot's contemporaries the material ambition and depravity of his time. They found their climax in the empty monotony of "The Hollow Men" and their justification in the regenerative impulse of *Ash-Wednesday*. It is difficult to see how his new long poem (of which two sections have already appeared: *Triumphal March* and *Difficulties of a Statesman*) or the present operatic burlesque improves on the earlier presentation, or, indeed, justifies a repetition of what has already found its logical place in a remarkable personal and historical record.

The method of Eliot remains his own; his imitators cannot dispute that fact. A poet should also be granted his diversions. These facts do not, however, improve the dullness which *Sweeney Agonistes* offers in fully twenty of its thirty pages. The Aristophanic element is hardly authentic enough to enliven a kind of satire already over-exploited in recent years, whereas the use of "jazz as a medium for tragedy" attributed to these fragments by one critic is not only a dubious venture, but a venture at which Mr. Eliot, despite his mastery of topical accents and banality, has not conspicuously succeeded. The fact that he has already depicted that tragedy in classic terms renders this book a tactical error to any reader who has followed him into the beautiful and profound passages of *Ash-Wednesday*.

There is one purpose which may justify these poems, however. Most modern readers require a great quantity of repetition before an effect is achieved in their minds. If Mr. Eliot still thinks it possible to reach this audience, there can be no question that even an obtuse reader will leave these pages without admitting the emptiness, tedium, and depravity of the elements in contemporary life which they describe. The renunciation of "the love of created beings" is not only a painful process, but a slow one. Since the evidence guaranteeing Mr. Eliot's sincerity exists, he should doubtless be allowed not only the amusement but the thoroughness by which he will achieve that spiritual triumph. To those who cannot accept the sterile horrors here presented, he offers another quotation, this time from the *Oresteia*: "You don't see them, you don't—but *I* see them: they are hunting me down, I must move on." The last phrase here contains, of course, one of the most important declarations in modern poetry.

Marianne Moore. "Reviews, *Sweeney Agonistes*." *Poetry: A Magazine of Verse* 42 (May 1933), 106–09.

In *Sweeney Agonistes* Mr. Eliot comes to us as the men of the neighboring tribes came to Joshua under a camouflage of frayed garments, with moldy bread in the wallet. But the point is not camouflaged. Mortal and sardonic victims though we are in this conflict called experience, we may regard our victimage with calmness, the book says; not because we don't know that our limitations of correctness are tedious to a society which has its funny side to us, as we have our slightly morbid side to it, but because there is a moment for Orestes, for Ophelia, for Everyman, when the ego and the figure it cuts, the favors you get from it, the good cheer and customary encomium, are as the insulting wigwaggery of the music-halls.

Everyman is played by Pereira, an efficiently inconspicuous, decent, studious chap. Well, not so decent, since he pays the rent for Doris and Dusty, who are an unremarkable, balky, card-cutting pair of girls whose names symbolize society's exasperating unanimity of selfishness. Shakespeare's "lecherous as a monkey" is rather strong, but in a world of buncombe and the fidgets, where you love-a me, I love-a you, "One live as two / Two live as three"—and there is no privacy—under the bamboo tree, the pair of given names go well with the surnames of a [. . .] shallow set of heroes from America, London, Ireland, Canada, who become intimate at the time they "did" their "bit" and "got the Hun on the run." There is, as the author intended, an effect of Aristophanic melodrama about this London flat in which the visitors play with the idea of South Sea languor and luxury—work annihilated, personality negatived, and conscience suppressed; a monkey to milk the goat and pass the cocktails—woman in the cannibal-pot or at hand to serve.

It is correct and unnotorious for the race to perpetuate itself; committing adultery and disclaiming the obligation is the suicide of personality, and the spirit wearies of clarity in such matters. The Furies pursuing Orestes are abler casuists than the King of Clubs and Queen of Hearts of Dusty and Doris. "They are hunting me down," he said.

A stark crime would not be so difficult to commit as the mood of moral conflict is difficult to satisfy. One is dead in being born unless one's debts are forgiven; and equipoise makes an idiot of one. The automatic machinery of behavior undoes itself backwards, putting sinister emphasis on wrong things, and no emphasis on the right ones.

> If he was alive then the milkman
> wasn't and the rent-collector wasn't
> And if they were alive then he was
> dead.

[. . .]
> Death or life or life or death
> Death is life and life is death.

Is one to become a saint or go mad? – remain mad, we should say. "The soul cannot be possessed of the divine union until it has divested itself of the love of created beings," St. John of the Cross says; as all saints have said. If one chooses God as the friend of the spirit, does not the coffin become the most appropriate friend for the body? "Cheer him up?" [asks Dusty]. "Well here again that dont apply," says Sweeney. "But I've gotta use words when I talk to you." This plucky reproach has in it the core of the drama. In their graveyard of sick love which is no love, which is loneliness without solitude, the girls can't understand what Pereira has to do with it and that it is a lucky eclecticism which cuts him off from what the Krumpackers and Horsfalls call a good time. A man should not think himself a poor fish or go mad, Sweeney maintains, because two girls are blockheads. He should answer a question as often as they ask it and put in as good an evening as possible with them. If by saying, "I've gotta use words when I talk to you," he insults them and they don't know they've been insulted, they, not he, should go mad.

When the spirit expands and the animal part of one sinks, one is not sardonic, and the bleak lesson here set forth is not uncheerful to those who are serious in the desire to satisfy justice. The cheer resides in admitting that it is normal to be abnormal. When one is not the only one who thinks that, one is freed of a certain tension.

Mr. Eliot is not showy nor hard, and is capable at times of too much patience; but here the truculent commonplace of the vernacular obscures care of arrangement, and the deliberate concise rhythm that is characteristic of him seems less intentional than it is. Upon scrutiny, however, the effect of an unhoodwinked self-control is apparent. The high time half a dozen people of unfastidious personality can seem to be having together is juxtaposed with the successful flight of the pursued son of Agamemnon, and it is implied, perhaps, that "he who wanders shall have reign, he who reigns shall have rest." One is obliged to say "perhaps"—since Sweeney in conflict is not synonymous with Sweeney victorious.

Checklist of Additional Reviews

*George Barker. *Adelphi* 5 (January 1933), 310–11.
*Ivor Brown. "Criticism in Cameo. The State." *Sketch* 172 (9 October 1935), 84.
*D. W. "At the Play." *Punch* 189 (9 October 1935), 412.

THE USE OF POETRY AND THE USE OF CRITICISM
1933

THE USE OF POETRY
AND THE USE OF CRITICISM

STUDIES IN
THE RELATION OF CRITICISM
TO POETRY IN ENGLAND

BY

T. S. ELIOT

Charles Eliot Norton Professor of Poetry
in Harvard University
1932–1933

LONDON
FABER AND FABER LIMITED
24 RUSSELL SQUARE

*Edwin Muir.
"The Use of Poetry."
Spectator 151, no. 5499
(17 November 1933),
703.

This volume contains eight lectures given by Mr. Eliot at Harvard University during the term of his professorship. Their purpose is roughly defined by the title, and more particularly by a sentence in the introductory lecture. "Let me start," Mr. Eliot says, "with the supposition that we do not know what poetry is, or what it does or ought to do, or of what use it is; and try to find out, in examining the relation of poetry and criticism, what the use of both of them is." The examination is careful and penetrating, but the result of it is not something that can be shortly formulated in a review; it is rather a body of conviction which grows as the author deals with one period of poetry after another. He does not arrive finally at any hard and fast definition of the use of poetry and criticism, nor does he seem to have much faith in the use of such a definition. His way of giving us a lively impression of the use of these two activities is to show us what it is not; and though that may appear at first a purely negative method, it is hard to imagine a more suitable one for dealing with a problem which cannot be satisfactorily solved by a generalization. But if Mr. Eliot does not tell us what the use of poetry and criticism is, he tells us a great many things about it, and that, for the student of poetry and criticism, is probably a far more useful thing.

The introductory lecture is more or less a general statement of the problem; the others "treat of the various conceptions of the use of poetry during the last three centuries, as illustrated in criticism, and especially in the criticism provided by the poets themselves." Mr. Eliot examines in turn Sidney, Dryden, Wordsworth and Coleridge, Shelley and Keats, Matthew Arnold, and a few recent writers such as Mr. I. A. Richards and the Abbé Brémond, concluding with a discussion of some of the difficulties confronting poets and critics today. He considers first the great increase of self-consciousness in criticism which is evident in the period covered. This increase, he points out, is most striking in ages that witness the decay or breakdown of literary convention previously accepted; the necessity to write in a new way drives poets and critics to reconsider the nature of poetry, and this reconsideration is naturally expressed in a new interpretation of poetry which, whether truer than the former one or not, is more highly conscious. Thus Dryden, who appeared in such a period, is more aware of what the process of poetic creation consists in than Sidney was; and Coleridge, who came at a similar but later stage, shows a still more conscious awareness of it. The work of Mr. I. A. Richards in our own time represents yet another advance in this direction. Mr. Eliot says: "I have not wished to exhibit this 'progress in self-consciousness' as being necessarily *progress* with an association of higher value." But it is in any case the development along which most of what is valuable in criticism since Dryden has gone, and it has had such a deep influence on poets that their problem now is, if not fundamentally, yet in its practical aspects very different from that of poets in the Elizabethan age or in the age of Wordsworth. This intensification of self-consciousness is one of the things which most sharply distinguishes modern poets from their predecessors.

This is one of the changes which Mr. Eliot examines. Whether it has any connection with another change that he deals with is not very clear. This concerns more nearly the "use" of poetry, or rather the functions which poetry has been required to fulfill at different periods of our literature. "Sidney's assumption," Mr. Eliot says, "is that poetry gives at once delight and instruction, and is an adornment of social life and an honour to the nation." Such assumptions, he maintains, "for a long time . . . were never questioned or modified," and "during that time great poetry was written, and some criticism which just because of its assumptions has permanent instruction to give." Though Shakespeare's passage on imagination, for which Mr. Eliot professes admiration, claims more for poetry than this, no doubt this generalization may be accepted as roughly true. "My point here," Mr. Eliot goes on,

> is that a great change in the attitude towards poetry, in the expectations and demands made upon it, did come, we may say for convenience towards the end of the eighteenth century. Wordsworth and Coleridge are not merely demolishing a debased tradition, but revolting against a whole social order; and they begin to make claims for poetry which reach their highest point of exaggeration in Shelley's famous phrase, "poets are the unacknowledged legislators of mankind."

It is this change in the use demanded from poetry with which Mr. Eliot is really most concerned, and the greater part of the last two-thirds of the book is devoted to it. It is an attitude associated with the great romantic poets, but it survived them. Matthew Arnold, foreseeing the imminent collapse of dogmatic religion, perceived a substitute for religion in poetry; and Mr. Richards, who fears that the future will bring "a mental chaos such as man has never experienced," says: "Poetry is capable of saving us." Mr. Eliot does not believe in assumptions of this kind, and he refutes them sympathetically, wittily, and I think effectually, without diminishing in the least our sense of the true greatness of poetry, or of the importance of its uses. What he says in effect is that poetry cannot take the place of religion or philosophy. Stated in such simple terms, the truth of the thesis seems obvious; but in order to establish it a great number of counter assumptions, many of them still popular, have to be dislodged or otherwise disposed of; and it is there that Mr. Eliot is so penetrating and so effective. He has not tried to destroy the basis of romantic criticism; he is generously appreciative of it at its best; but he is merciless to its extravagances.

The best things in a book such as this are often the particular observations thrown off in the course of the argument. Mr. Eliot's originality of mind makes these interesting in themselves and can be felt even in his parenthetical judgments, as when he says: "I suspect Arnold of helping to fix the wholly mistaken notion of Burns as a singular untutored English dialect poet, instead of as a decadent representative of a great alien tradition." One can feel his independence of judgment even when one violently disagrees with him. Anyone who reads this volume attentively—and it is written with the most enticing clarity—will not get a new definition of poetry and criticism, but he will know a great deal more about them than he knew before. It is probably the most comprehensive and reasoned critical work that Mr. Eliot has yet written, and it should certainly be read by all readers of poetry.

*Stephen Spender. "The Use of Poetry." New Statesman 6 (18 November 1933), 637–38.

The subtitle of this book, "Studies in the Relation of Criticism to Poetry in England," explains what it is about. There is an introductory chapter in which Mr. Eliot discusses the functions of criticism and the nature of poetry. This is followed by an essay on the Countess of Pembroke and her circle, in which the relation of poetry to criticism is inquired into, and Mr. Eliot maintains in this and in other essays that the importance of the criticism contemporary even to Elizabethan poetry is greater than we suppose, and that a very critical period need not be an uncreative period: in fact, that the criticism may precede, and to some extent create, the poetry. This sort of argument will be familiar to the reader of *The Sacred Wood*, but is not maintained here with the same fervor as in the earlier book. There is also an interesting lecture on Wordsworth and Coleridge, in which Mr. Eliot discusses the relations of Wordsworth's philosophy to his poetry, and argues that Arnold and other critics have been over-anxious to prove that his philosophy is irrelevant to the greatness of his poetry.

However, there is no very strong thread of argument running through these lectures: the last lecture, called "Conclusion," may even be described as highly inconclusive. A preceding essay, "The Modern Mind," is a collection of different points of view, of Maritain, Mr. I. A. Richards, the Abbé Brémond, and Riviere. The positions of all of these writers are considered, given fairly high marks, and then quite finally dismissed. Mr. Eliot ends the lecture with some negative reflections on our inability to appreciate more than a limited range of poetry. We must admire this. I suppose that Mr. Eliot's aim was to make his audience think, not to make up their minds for them. He certainly does succeed in making us all think.

Where one may wish that Mr. Eliot were a little more positive is in his attitude to political morality, and in his occasional references to religion. He explains on the first page of his first lecture, "the present lectures will have no concern with politics." Yet frequent references to what I understand to be (in the widest sense) politics are made; indeed, if one discusses Trotsky's *Literature and Revolution*, and at the same time declares that one is not concerned with politics, it seems to me that one is striking a political attitude— an attitude of superiority. Mr. Eliot would perhaps feel less superior to those who are interested in politics if he saw that, in a time of partial revolution and partial chaos, a realistic interest in politics must imply an interest in morals. *The Revenger's Tragedy*, for example, is a play about politics and morals, at the point where they almost coincide.

In his references to religion Mr. Eliot is content always with innovations. We are told that Matthew Arnold is a "Philistine" in religion, and that he "was not a man of vast or exact scholarship, and he had neither walked in hell nor been rapt to heaven." I dare say that these judgments are just, but they are very serious judgments to make, because they are not only about a man's poetry, they are also about his life. Most of us would hesitate to assert definitely of anyone that he had not walked in hell, and one would certainly make no such assertions unless one were oneself religious and unless one had oneself walked through hell. Now I believe that Eliot is a true poet, and I believe that he has "walked through hell"; I think also that he is a writer of genuine humility, and often a writer of great frankness: there are plenty of examples of such writing in this book. Therefore it seems the more surprisingly inconsistent that he often gives the impression of being snobbish and superior. When he goes farther and rejects for the following reasons Arnold's famous definition "Poetry is at bottom a criticism of life," one begins to suspect that a process of distortion sometimes takes place in his mind. "At bottom," he says, "that is a great way down; the bottom is the bottom. At the bottom of the abyss is what few ever see, and what those cannot bear to look at for long; and it is not a 'criticism of life.'" So that in a few words he has twisted Arnold into meaning at the bottom of life. If he had omitted the unfortunate "at bottom" the distortion would not have occurred. Arnold's phrase may not deserve its fame, but it is not nonsense. Surely one of the reasons for the psychological importance of poetry is that the most profound criticism of life, revealed to the most everyday people in moments of tension or crisis, is a vision that could best be expressed in poetry.

One of Mr. Eliot's gambits is this habit of making a loosely expressed phrase, even where its meaning is clear, seem meaningless. But what are we to think when he himself speaks thus of Arnold: "It is a pleasure, certainly, after associating with the riff-raff of the early part of the century, to be in the company of a man *qui sait se conduire*"? Who are the riff-raff? we ask in the manner that he himself has taught us. If they are just riff-raff who were the riff-raff of that time, the sentence is meaningless, because there must have been as many, if not more, riff-raff amongst Arnold's contemporaries. Were they Shelley, Keats, and Byron? Or Blake? We are forced to assume that they were some of these, and if so, it seems that snobbishness could scarcely go farther in choosing the company which one is going to criticize.

---

*Joan Bennett. *Cambridge Review* 55 (24 November 1933), 132–33.

Mr. Eliot's criticism illuminates by flashes, his strength does not lie in sustained argument. It would be rash to expect from him, perhaps indeed from anyone, an answer to the large questions he raises in his introduction: "Let me start with the supposition that we do not know what poetry is, or what it does or ought to do, or of what use it is; and try to find out, in examining the relation of poetry and criticism, what the use of both of them is." If that is indeed what Mr. Eliot tried to do in these lectures, he did not succeed. Nor does the book supply an answer to that other question which concerns some of us even more nearly, and with which the introduction closes, the question "whether the attempt to teach students to *appreciate* English literature should be made at all; and with what restrictions the teaching of English literature can rightly be included in any academic curriculum, if at all." The solution of these problems will not be found in the ensuing pages. High hopes are raised and they are not fulfilled. But Mr. Eliot's failures are more illuminating than the successes of cruder minds. He feels his way, recalls with scrupulous fidelity his own adventures among poets and critics, confesses his own hopes and ambitions as a poet, even allows us a glimpse into his workshop. Anyone who has hitherto assumed that Mr. Eliot writes poetry for an intellectual minority will be much shaken by this book. On the contrary, he questions whether any poet even deliberately restricts his public:

> From one point of view, the poet aspires to the condition of the music-hall comedian. Being incapable of altering his wares to suit a prevailing taste, if there be any, he naturally desires a state of society in which they may become popular, and in which his own talents will be put to the best use.

Later on he tells us that "the worst fault a poet can commit is to be dull," and he notices of what great value it was to the Elizabethan dramatist that he had to earn his living by amusing "an alert, curious, semi-barbarous public, fond of beer and bawdry, including much the same sort of people whom one encounters in local outlying theatres to-day." His own preferred audience would be one "which could neither read or write." It is difficult to see how such an audience could deal with Mr. Eliot's intricate allusiveness, but at least we can now be sure that he is not deliberately writing for a cultivated minority.

Anyone who has felt the fascination of Mr. Eliot's poetry will inevitably turn greedily to such passages as these and others which throw light on its inception. But Mr. Eliot is modest: he has not written a book about himself, though it is above all a personal book, refreshing in its candor and in its fidelity to his own experience. For instance, "It is perhaps as well to warn you that Addison is a writer towards whom I feel something very like antipathy . . . the smugness and priggishness of the man," or of Shelley "I find his ideas repellent." This is as refreshing as meeting a friend at a dinner party. On these terms real opinions can be exchanged. Mr. Eliot takes his own taste as a basis and in its light considers his problem, the function of criticism in Queen Anne's day, or the effect upon poetry of a doctrine which the reader "rejects as childish and feeble." But if his critical opinions are personal, they are never perverse. He may sanction our distaste for Addison's complacency or for Shelley's lack of judgment; but he will not encourage the exclusion of Milton from the company of great poets, nor the elimination of whole centuries of poetic endeavor. "When a poet has done as big a job as Milton, is it helpful to suggest that he has just been up a blind alley?" he asks with reference to Mr. Herbert Read's assertion (*Form in Modern Poetry*) that Milton is outside the main English tradition; and, again, in connection with Mr. Read, "it is rather strong to suggest that the English mind has been deranged ever since the time of Shakespeare, and that only recently have a few fitful rays of reason penetrated its darkness. If the malady is as chronic as that, it is pretty well beyond cure."

In a modest preface to these lectures, Mr. Eliot writes that "such success as they had was largely dramatic, and they will be still more disappointing to those who heard them than they will be to those who did not." But it is hard to believe that they were in fact better heard than read. They lack the compelling form of good lectures; no conclusion is reached, no plan is fulfilled. Their value lies in those incidentals and asides which are likely to escape a listener; but to which a reader can return and over whose implications he will wish to linger.

"Poetry and Criticism." *Independent* 1 (25 November 1933), 21–22.

"I cannot help regretting," writes Mr. T. S. Eliot of the Elizabethan dramatists, "that some of their best plays are not better than they are." It would be difficult to invent a more unprofitable expenditure of energy, yet Mr. Eliot has shown himself capable of this too. He has devoted his unusually acute and sensitive mind to considering the use of "a mug's game," if we may borrow his elegant definition of poetry. His new volume of lectures, *The Use of Poetry and the Use of Criticism*, is remarkably uneven in quality: judgments of a most capricious kind jostle with unnecessary pedantries, which can hardly fail to distress a reader who is sympathetic enough to grant the brilliance and intelligence of the rest.

Mr. Eliot's criteria range from the art of the music-hall comedian to sound theology, and as few poets, and fewer critics, can survive these tests, none is allowed to pass his scrutiny unscathed. A writer who is pontifically correct in his condemnation of the sentences of Coleridge and Arnold should at least be free from obscurity or faultiness of expression himself. Yet Mr. Eliot is not, though he contrives to leave the impression that it is hard for him not to begin all his paragraphs of criticism with the words, "This is not a felicitous expression." On the next occasion that he is offended by what he terms "Arnold's irritating use of italicised words," let him, for the sake of justice, turn over the pages of his own composition. Perhaps he will be persuaded that there are better tasks to engage in than the enumeration of the minor deficiencies of others: the habit of italics, at any rate, will appear as much his own as it is Matthew Arnold's.

Apart from these superficial but annoying tricks, there is a great deal of wisdom in these eight lectures, of which the aim is to determine the relation of the critical currents of English literature to the general stream of creative activity. The virtues we have been led to expect in Mr. Eliot's writing, familiarity with a wide range of literature, an uncommon sensibility to the musical phrase, and the capacity to apply an acutely analytical mind to his material, are here in full. The sincerity of his judgments is not to be questioned. What is it, then, that leaves us with the sense that on the whole these pages do not represent their author at his best? It may not unreasonably be answered that they display two fundamental misapprehensions: first, they imply that it is better to occupy oneself with writings of the critics of poets rather than with that of the poets themselves; and, in the second place, they show no perception of the inequality of the terms of comparison that form the basis of the argument.

Mr. Eliot is perhaps unwise in attempting what is strictly the task of the scholar and neglecting in its favor the opportunity for that discussion of poetry and that exposition of the method by which it works that made his essays on Dante and Dryden, to take but two examples, of such unusual significance. When he moves from Sidney to Dryden he does not convince us that he is aware of the allowance that is to be made for the fact that, whereas Sidney's classical bias was adverse to the current of the whole creative activity of the next thirty years, Dryden's was sympathetic to the age of which he is taken as representative. A similar want of historical sense is revealed in his censure of Arnold for his deficiency in the exact use of language. He forgets that he has not vouchsafed this to Johnson or Coleridge, and that only in recent years has anything like a systematic approach to the problem of meaning in language been undertaken, which has yet scarcely borne fruit. In short, however stimulating to hear when they were delivered at Harvard, these discourses are only fitfully satisfactory in print: they would be the better for a careful and scrupulous revision, even to the removal of the persistent misspelling of the title of Coleridge's *Biographia Literaria*.

[. . .]

*Hugh Sykes Davies. "Criticism and Controversy." *Listener* (29 November 1933), supplement vii.

In this book Mr. Eliot deals for the first time with a large body of material already familiar to the average student of English literature. A study of the succession of our poet–critics—Sidney, Campion, Daniel, Dryden, Addison, Johnson, Wordsworth, Coleridge, Shelley, Keats, Arnold—is almost a standard curriculum for those who pursue an organized education in English literature beyond the slender rudiments acquired at school. [. . .]

In general, his known critical virtues become even plainer against a background new to them, but familiar to us—his grasp of the periods of English literature as wholes, and as parts of a coherent development: his feeling for part of any man's work in relation to his whole character and personality. His detailed comment never loses general significance, never becomes niggling, and he reduces the most troublesome stuff to order. For example, in the previous writings on the subject, the problem of the relation between Elizabethan critical and creative productions has been largely evaded—burked, almost. The notions which have been current concerning it have been rather shoddy makeshifts, pedagogic commonplaces. Mr. Eliot clears a way through this hedge, and at least demonstrates the possibility of a respectable approach to the matter.

We have become accustomed to expect from him exactly this new means of approach, a certain thrill of novelty, a fresh aspect of his subject. In the past, the uncharitable might say, this has not been difficult, because he has often chosen subjects unduly neglected, about which almost any statement would be novel and valuable. But even the uncharitable must admit that the same virtue is displayed in his handling of the present, by no means neglected, subject. A definite point is made about almost all the figures mentioned [. . .]. The essay on Wordsworth in particular is likely to be very helpful in the discussions which have gathered recently around him and his motives for writing poetry. It may be questioned whether the political interest, so much stressed by Mr. Eliot, is the only point of view—but probably it is not intended to be that, and certainly the stress is fully justified in consideration of the comparative neglect of Wordsworth's political feelings by serious students. And anyone who has read the notes written in 1835 on the new Poor Laws will welcome Mr. Eliot's defense of the poet against the too easily repeated charge of apostasy which clung to him since the rumor got about that he was "The Lost Leader."

For myself, the most disappointing part of the book is that which deals with Coleridge. I still prefer to believe that something can be made of those philosophical interests. Even if Coleridge understood wrongly the part which they played in his analysis of the poetic processes—of

243

his own processes and Wordsworth's—still they did play some part. [. . .]

In style and manner of exposition, these essays differ from most of Mr. Eliot's early critical work as one expects a book written to be delivered as lectures to differ from one written for simple publication. They are more discursive, and somewhat less remote than his previous criticism. The first and the last two chapters reveal a great deal more about his personal tastes, his lesser likes and dislikes, than has been vouchsafed before. Above all, he enters freely into controversies with other critics, and displays the gifts, of which we have not so far seen much from him, of a controversialist at once serious and witty. The examination of Dr. Richards's "theological ideas" is both excellent fun, and pointed criticism.

*D. W. Harding. "Mr. Eliot at Harvard." *Scrutiny* 2 (December 1933), 289–92.

It is clear, and Mr. Eliot insists that it shall be clear, that this book is dominated by its origin as a course of lectures of a not very technical kind. Inevitably therefore the writing is loose in texture. What is more regrettable is that the general plan of the course only partially succeeds in knitting together its parts, and some sections, as for instance that on Keats, seem to be little more than lecture making. [. . .]

The most accurate statement of his views is to be found in the brief remarks on communication.

> We have to communicate—if it is communication, for the word may beg the question—an experience which is not

an experience in the ordinary sense, for it may only exist, formed out of many personal experiences ordered in some way which may be very different from the way of valuation of practical life, in the expression of it. *If* poetry is a form of "communication," yet that which is to be communicated is the poem itself, and only incidentally the experience and the thought which have gone into it.

This sparse and accurate statement of observable fact contrasts strangely with the following, which the audience presumably preferred:

> What I call the "auditory imagination" is the feeling for syllable and rhythm, penetrating far below the conscious levels of thought and feeling, invigorating every word; sinking to the most primitive and forgotten, returning to the origin and bringing something back, seeking the beginning and the end.

In such a passage as this, looseness of texture becomes almost laxity.

On the important topic of the book, that of the significance of the poet's motives and beliefs, Mr. Eliot's formulated views are less acceptable than those on communication, although his contribution of obvious good sense to a confused problem is exceptionally welcome from such a writer. Combating the view of Dr. I. A. Richards, he asserts the inevitable importance for the reader of the poet's personal convictions. He supports this less by generalized arguments than by appealing to his own experience in the enjoyment of poetry, by far the most impressive method he could have adopted. But his statement of his own position is not altogether satisfactory. "When the doctrine, theory, belief, or 'view of life' presented in a poem is one which the mind of the reader can accept as coherent, mature, and founded on the facts of experience, it interposes no obstacle to the reader's enjoyment, whether it be one that he accept or deny, approve or deprecate." Although the general meaning of this—as one would grasp it in listening to the lecture—seems sound enough, its exact verbal form, if insisted on, leaves several difficulties unsolved. It must be observed first, of course, that the way is still open for Mr. Eliot to [admit] that "Actually, one probably has more pleasure in the poetry when one shares the beliefs of the poet." But if so, belief is an obstacle, or its absence a deprivation of a means, to the *full* enjoyment of the poem; and hence to say merely that a doctrine "interposes no obstacle to the reader's enjoyment" is to evade, at least verbally, the whole question, which hinges on the *degree* of enjoyment possible. The phrase "facts of experience" raises a further doubt. If it stands for "the more obvious facts of experience" the general sense of the passage remains clear. But if it means "*all* the facts of the reader's experience" then it is difficult to see how the reader could fail to *believe* a coherent and mature doctrine founded upon "the facts of experience." [. . .]

What from his wider context Mr. Eliot seems to suggest is that some views which we regard as heresies, nevertheless bring together enough of the facts of our experience for us to sympathize with them, and to realize that, given certain differences of experience, we could have accepted them as true doctrine. Other heresies are altogether too far removed from anything that might have appealed to us and we are therefore only repelled. This to the simple-minded would seem the natural consequence of the natural view that your like or dislike for a poem or a poet's work is affected by every aspect of his performance and all you know about him. [. . .]

In some ways the most valuable parts of the book and those that make it fascinating to read are its glimpses of Mr. Eliot's personal opinions on a great variety of topics—Marxist criticism, English literature in the school curriculum, the potential value of the theatre to the poet. Even more interesting are the fragments of personal history that he scatters through the lectures and the comments he makes from time to time upon his intentions and methods in his own poetry. [. . .]

The latter part of the book consists largely in attacks upon the view that poetry can be a substitute for religion. At this point the strength, perhaps, of Mr. Eliot's convictions, combined with the effect of a popular audience, seems to make his onslaught a little unfair. [. . .] [H]is merciless insistence on the literal meaning of Matthew Arnold's "criticism of life" is in striking contrast with his generous concern to make Dryden intelligible. As for the more positive final contributions, all, coming from him, are valuable and interesting, but, as Mr. Eliot would readily agree, a full and definite account of the use of poetry and the use of criticism is still far to seek, if, indeed, it is conceivable.

Peter Monro Jack. "Mr. Eliot's New Essays in the Field of Poetry." *New York Times Book Review*, 3 December 1933, p. 2.

Mr. Eliot's theme, which he develops historically in a résumé of English criticism, is the relation of the poet to his audience, his purpose being to show that as society alters, the function of poetry changes. The history of the criticism of poetry is the history of these readjustments between poetry and the world in and for which it is produced. And if we observe what changes, and how and why, we may observe what does not change. We may be better able to judge what is permanent in poetry and what is merely the expression of the spirit of the age. In any case, we may discover and possibly correct the limitations of our time and space.

The exposition of this theme—which Harvard students heard as the Charles Eliot Norton Lectures for 1932–1933— might well be thought a difficult and dangerous undertaking; how is one to escape the economic and sociological and psychological and even political dimensions which the word "use" inevitably starts, and which have been the chief contribution of our time to literary criticism? Mr. Eliot does not try to escape from his own position, which has always been in dispute and sometimes in disrepute. He has some very sensible words on his conception of the relation of poet, critic, and audience. He may be driven to the little magazines, or he may hope only—as Mr. Eliot hoped in an early essay written under the influence of Ezra Pound and now, we should suppose, repudiated—to interest an "intelligent drawing-room." But Mr. Eliot knows quite well, and says so here, that every poet wants a large and popular audience. It is the greatest pity if he cannot suit his poetry to the prevailing taste; but he will continue to hope for a society which will have a better taste for his poetry. He naturally wishes his talent "to be put to the best use." Mr. Eliot himself would prefer to reach his audience through the theatre. "There might, one fancies, be some fulfillment in exciting this communal pleasure, to give an immediate compensation for the pains of turning blood into ink"—a rather remarkable statement, coming from Mr. Eliot, and very much the point of view of Jean Cocteau's *Le Sang d'un Poète*.

We must not be tempted to discuss the relative merits of poetry and showmanship, and the chances of a writer having both. The important point is that poetry should wish to justify itself by being desired, it should be entertaining and popular, it should have "some direct social utility." But the dangerous implications of "social utility" are instantly quashed. Mr. Eliot does not mean that the poet "should meddle with the tasks of the theologian, the preacher, the economist, the sociologist or anybody else; that he should do anything but write poetry, poetry not defined in terms of something else." Of course the poet should not meddle with the tasks of the theologian or sociologist; but the poet—and the critic, too—possess religious belief or unbelief and sociological interests that will determine, if not the nature of his poetry, at the least its functioning in society; and it is there that confusion arises.

It would have taken Mr. Eliot more time than he had at his command to explore this confusion, but he can indicate how it came about. The real change which led to so many dilemmas for the modern poet is seen in the poetry and criticism of Wordsworth and Coleridge. Before 1800, in spite of differences of approach and conclusion, the critics knew they were dealing with poetry as poetry—something that, in its own way and under its own conditions, "delighted and instructed." Sidney was concerned with the laws of poetry and drama— chiefly the laws of the Unities—against a background of classical influences. Dryden was restating the matter against a background more favorably composed of native elements. Addison shows a further change, exactly reflecting the deterioration in society, in criticism, in poetry: the critic has become the "bourgeois literary dictator." Johnson is the last of the tradition of literary critics who keeps within his limitations: "When you know

what they are, you know where you are."
[. . .]

With Johnson the chapter on poetry as an art ends, though it ends without conclusion—but then poetry is not concluded; and with Wordsworth begins the new chapter of poets as priests and prophets. There is a "conscious change." Poetry has become infinitely more than a delight and instruction. It is the "breath and finer spirit of all knowledge." Poets are "the unacknowledged legislators of mankind." Poetry is little short of a religion. Keats might bring us back to some executive sense, but Shelley's phrase led the field. Arnold checked this extravagant romanticism, or rather he guided it into a temporary though false stability, tempering its ecstasy with the social conscience and the idea of culture, insisting that poetry shall be a substitute for religion, of uncertain spiritual conviction but impeccable demeanor. This moral valuation of poetry, with its great subjects and high seriousness, without religious values but as yet without the psychological values to give it authority, continues in Pater, Symons, Symonds, Stephens, Myers, and Saintsbury (we can see it in [Robert Bridges'] "The Necessity of Poetry," urging poets to replace the "unworthy" old Hebrew poetry). What is not in Arnold is in I. A. Richards, who represents the psychological approach, or in Trotsky, whose *Literature and Revolution* Mr. Eliot takes to be "the most sensible statement of a Communist attitude" that he has seen.

It is heartening to find Mr. Eliot again in direct controversy with Mr. Richards, though he is still nibbling cautiously and his careful "releases" of occasional judgments are miracles in the exaggeration of understatements, designed to correct the haste and carelessness of Richards. For these two, when they conflict, illuminate each other and the business of poetry and criticism with peculiar brilliance. As Wordsworth emphasized the social functions of poetry and Arnold brought the religious issue into the discussion of literature, so Mr. Richards may be said to think of sex as the persistent concern of our generation. Mr. Eliot dissents, believing that we are still with Arnold in trying to escape the religious issue, and playing Maritain and the Abbé Brémond against Richards: we still, he believes, ask poetry to do too much, and in trying to do more than it can—in trying to be a substitute for other things in a desperate effort to "save us" (as Richards said)—it falls into confusion. It is a confusion of our age, and poetry reflects it. Mr. Eliot cannot be expected to clear up the confusions of an age, but he does clear up some of the confusions of our poetry and criticism in this admirable little book, whose influence, we are sure, will be immediate and widespread, and without doubt to the benefit of our thinking about poetry.

Joseph Wood Krutch. "A Poem is a Poem." *Nation* 137 (13 December 1933), 679–80.

Mr. T. S. Eliot is, in part at least, the creation of his disciples. In their minds he stands for something which ought to exist and which, to be sure, he sometimes suggests. But I, at least, have always felt a certain disappointment when I have sought in his critical writings precisely what I had been assured one would find there and there only. At moments he is brilliantly suggestive. No other contemporary critic has more boldly and more successfully challenged the current platitudes about poetry, and none perhaps has provoked a more significant questioning of just these platitudes. But to me it seems that one will look in vain for something to which his more abject admirers seem to be always referring—namely, a complete, original, definite, and logically formulated body of doctrine.

Certainly one will not find it in the lectures which he delivered under the auspices of the Norton Professorship at Harvard. Perhaps he felt that something academic would be expected of him and perhaps for that reason he cast his discourse in the form of a commentary upon the various ideas of poetry expressed by the great English critics from Sir Philip Sidney to I. A. Richards. But whatever the reason, the result is a series of all too academic lectures punctuated here and there with arresting remarks which make the reader wish that almost any one of them had been made the theme of a chapter or a volume instead of being allowed merely to bob up here and there and then to be lost again under the flood of a far less interesting discourse. I found myself skimming rapidly over the commonplaces of literary history and marking in the margin all the author's expressions of his own opinion. Then I attempted to put these opinions together, and when I had done so, I found, still further, that they seemed far less revolutionary, uncompromising, and final than I had expected them to be.

[. . .]

I am distressed, nevertheless, for the simple reason that it seems dangerously close to an acquiescence in that relativism, that impressionism, and that slough of merely personal taste, and merely idiosyncratic reactions from which Mr. Eliot's disciples (though not, perhaps, Mr. Eliot himself) have suggested that he was born to save us. I find no standards, no ultimate objectivity, there. A good poem is a poem that seems good to a man of good taste. A good

critic is a critic who assumes the personality of the author criticized. The appreciation of "pure poetry"—poetry which is merely poetry and not interesting for some extraneous reason also—is "only an ideal" when it is "not merely a figment." "Each age demands different things from poetry . . . So our criticism from age to age, will reflect the things that the age demands." Mr. Eliot, to be sure, does add a warning: "Amongst all these demands from poetry and responses to it there is always some element in common, just as there are standards of good and bad writing independent of what any one of us happens to like and dislike." He does not, however, explain how in practice these standards are to be discovered or agreed upon, and if to believe no more than this is to become "classicist in literature," then I expect to discover than I am also "royalist in politics and anglo-catholic in religion."

By far the most interesting of the lectures is that devoted to the modern mind. In the course of it Mr. Eliot very suavely achieves the difficult task of expressing a contemptuous disagreement with I. A. Richards, while maintaining at the same time the polite fiction that he has for his antagonist a respect very near to awe. Mr. Richards, it will be remembered, has suggested that poetry can become a substitute for religion and as such "save mankind." To this Mr. Eliot protests in the names of both poetry and religion. Nothing is or can be a substitute for anything else. As Miss Stein (who is not cited) has said, "A rose is a rose is a rose." And this brings us back to the most original and significant of all Mr. Eliot's contentions, which is simply that a poem is a poem is a poem. You may define it as "communication" if you like, but you must remember that the thing communicated is not, as is sometimes rashly assumed, the experience which generated the poem but something quite different— namely, the poem itself.

Probably no contemporary critic has said anything more simply or richly suggestive than this. It cuts cleanly through a great deal of the dreadful nonsense of which all schools from the most decadently romantic to the most austerely Marxian are frequently guilty. But it does not, after all, take us very far; it does not answer the real question, which is simply this: How, then, does the experience of a poem differ from the experience afforded by a thought or an emotion; what are the characteristics of a genuinely aesthetic experience? Surely it is not quite enough, though it may be very useful, to say what a poem is not. Surely the function of criticism is not merely that of preventing the student from giving wrong answers to the questions it raises. And yet if it is actually to do more it must make some effort, however tentative, to say what a poem is as well as what it isn't. But perhaps Mr. Eliot intends as a theologian to devote himself more seriously to this problem. From Jacques Maritain he quotes the following sentence: "The unconcealed and palpable influence of the devil on an important part of contemporary literature is one of the most significant phenomena of the history of our time." To this Mr. Eliot adds a footnote (whether humorously or not I do not know): "With the influence of the devil on contemporary literature I shall be concerned in more detail in another book."

Babette Deutsch.
"Fine Insights."
New York Sun,
16 December 1933, p. 27.

At the conclusion of this short book Mr. Eliot confesses that he has "no general theory" of his own about the use of poetry. It is perhaps this want of a theory that is responsible for the lack that one feels in reading these extremely provocative but on the whole disappointing essays. He undertook here to review the changes in criticism from the Elizabethan period, on through the age of Dryden, the romantic revival, Matthew Arnold's effort to substitute poetry for faith, coming down to the attitude toward poetry of what he calls "the modern mind." This study of criticism "as a process of readjustment between poetry and the world in and for which it is produced" might, he believed, "help us to draw some conclusions as to what is permanent or eternal in poetry, and what is merely the expression of the spirit of an age." The attempt was certainly worth making. And Mr. Eliot would seem to be the man to make it. He has, as he says of Coleridge, the "authority due to his great reading," in addition to that of [being a] self-critical and influential poet.

His scholarship, his acute appreciation of widely various types of poetry, and, by the same token, of various types of mind, his interest in opinions, especially contemporary opinions with which he is out of sympathy, combine to make these papers rich in knowledge, in careful elucidation, and in suggestive observations. At the same time they contain not a few confusing, contradictory, or debatable statements, and repeatedly appear to be leading up to some overwhelming question that is not answered because it is never so much as broached. The writer keeps reminding one of his own timorous Prufrock, albeit a Prufrock possessed of a learning, a sensibility, a capacity for wit, far exceeding that of the prudent and unhappy gentleman in Mr. Eliot's poem.

In the end, without too much help from the essayist, with some doubt as to whether one has read him aright, one comes to the conclusion that he believes poetry to have not so much "a use" as many uses, but that its chief one is to make us "a little more aware of the deeper, unnamed feelings which form the substratum of our being, to which we rarely penetrate"; that it is, in effect, although Mr. Eliot might himself hesitate to describe it precisely in these terms, an extraordinary and superlatively delightful kind of psychotherapy. At all events, however unsatisfactory his developments of his theme, and however tentative his findings, his book contains so many fine insights into the varieties of both poetry and criticism, their interplay with each other and with the world beyond them, and their shift from age to age, as to reward the close attention of all students of these matters.

Mark Van Doren. "Shall We Be Saved by Poetry?" *New York Herald Tribune Books*, 17 December 1933, p. 5.

These eight lectures are the ones which Mr. Eliot has chosen to preserve out of the many he must have delivered in the United States last winter. They group themselves about a theme which interests him because of its bearing upon the contemporary critical situation. Indeed, they admit of even a narrower description. They are in effect an answer to, or at any rate a comment upon, the well known assertion of Mr. I. A. Richards that our civilization, which is rapidly sliding toward "a mental chaos such as man has never experienced," may yet—nay, must—be "saved" by poetry. For all the respect which Mr. Eliot insists he has for Mr. Richards, the assertion is to him nothing but nonsense. And his lectures as printed represent an attempt to say why it is nonsense.

Mr. Eliot, to be sure, does not say this in so many words. Part of his method, and part of his charm, is that he says nothing in so many words. His criticism is as indirect and circumambulatory as his poetry; he is something of a symbolist even in disputation. His book, then, is chiefly a collection of hints, a series of adroit and elaborate ways he has taken to suggest something that is very important to him. What the thing itself is might be very difficult to say—as difficult, for instance, as the thing which a good poem all but says and never quite says. But it is something like this. Poetry is one of those valuable commodities of which we shall never know the price, or, for that matter, the exact use. It has always existed, and presumably it will always exist; and it is eminently worth thinking and talking about—indeed, it demands that we talk about it. But we must never be too sure that we understand its secret. And we must never assume that we know its function.

In its happiest periods poetry has been accepted for what it is—whatever it is. But in its less happy periods it has been nervously examined for its value. Mr. Eliot's lectures are among other things a historical sketch of such nervous examinations in England. For after two chapters on the criticism of Sidney and Dryden—men who discussed poetry rather purely as an art—he leaps into the true center of his discourse by inquiring how Wordsworth and Shelley discussed it. He reminds us that they found it to be something which could be employed to regenerate mankind—as, he admits, it may be, since poetry can be almost anything, and since it has been a different thing in every age of man thus far, as has the criticism which inevitably accompanies it. But the next step is more distasteful to him. It is the step that Matthew Arnold took when he, anticipating Mr. Richards, called upon poetry to save us from despair. After that Mr. Eliot confines himself to Mr. Richards. Not that he argues with him. He merely, by placing him at the end of a line whose direction has been downhill—well, merely places him; though he pauses to ask him what he means, and pauses once more to protest that all this is asking too much of poetry. To ask too much of it is to do it as much harm as to ask too little, for it is to deny its limits and therefore its essence.

What its essence is Mr. Eliot nowhere attempts to state. In this he is wise, since it is so much better, if one can, to talk about poetry in such a way as to suggest its essence. Definitions of poetry are notoriously absurd, like definitions of love and death. They have a way of becoming either old fashioned or unintelligible almost as soon as they are uttered. Whereas discourse about poetry by a man who obviously knows it and lives by it and thinks exclusively about it is bound, if the man can write well, to survive the occasion of the discourse. The great critics have been of such a sort. We do not remember their definitions or their dogmas; but we remember how their voices sounded as they discussed the matter at hand, and we remember all kinds of things they said aside—smiling and interrupting themselves and explaining. Mr. Eliot has a style for criticism as he has a style for poetry, and it is an excellent style. In the course of this book he fails to say what poetry is; but he says perhaps a hundred things that make us realize how well he knows what it is. And he says these things with the wit, the learning, and the ease of one who has every right to be walking where he walks.

*D. G. Bridson.
"Poetry and Criticism."
New English Weekly 4
(28 December 1933),
256–57.

[. . .]

As I understand them, the lectures here printed set out rather to study criticism than poetry (or poetry *through* criticism) and to give a conspectus rather of what the use of poetry and criticism cannot possibly be, than what it actually is. This, no doubt, is all to the good. Instead of a carefully-worked-out sequence of conclusions, the book presents a readable collection of *obiter dicta*. And having read it through twice, I can say that the book reads better at the second sitting than the first, which is once more all to the good. At first reading, indeed, one is rather too concerned with what one fancies Mr. Eliot ought to be saying, to enjoy what he happens to be saying. The still small voice, as it were, fails to penetrate: the penny refuses to drop. And this I find to be the case with most of Mr. Eliot's critical work to date. If the tendency is eventually to agree with him all along the line—which it is— the tendency is primarily to miss what he may be driving at. Certainly, there is little enough to disagree with in the present volume. It is concerned very consistently with the opinions of critics not so much lost as gone before. Sidney, Campion, Jonson, Dryden, Johnson, Wordsworth, Coleridge, Shelley, Keats, and Arnold, in fact, provide the meat for Mr. Eliot's condiments, and as a survey of critical opinion, more properly a running commentary on it, the book is very good salt. Not even to Johnson's pork can Mr. Eliot be said to have served up applesauce.

The immediately significant fact about the critics chosen and considered, of course, is that each and every one of them was also a poet practicing in his own right. According to Ben Jonson, "to judge of poets is only the faculty of poets; and not of all poets, but the best." This I take to be the case. And Mr. Eliot has elsewhere explained, as it happens, that he considers a poet eminently suited to criticism of poetry on account of his sense of fact, coming out of the limbo of supposition into the circle of actual knowledge. He has also suggested that "the criticism employed by a trained and skilled writer on his own work is the most vital, the highest, kind of criticism"—a suggestion recently echoed by Mr. Pound. And this, I think, is true enough in its turn. But the *use* of criticism—whether written by poet or otherwise—remains to be decided. Mr. Eliot has stated that its end "appears to be the elucidation of works of art and the correction of taste." If such is its end, such—presumably—is its use. Mr. Pound's opinion of critics, however, is that:

> The best are those who actually cause an amelioration in the art which they criticize.
> The next best are those who most focus attention on the best that is written (or painted or composed or cut in stone).
> And the pestilential vermin are those who distract attention *from* the best, either to the second rate, or to hokum, or to their own critical writings.

By their fruits, in short, shall we know them. "The critic is either a parasite or he is concerned with the growth of the next paideuma"—which, needless to add, is Mr. Pound's also.

Whether or not a critic—acting *as* critic rather than as practicing poet—can "cause an amelioration" in poetry is distinctly open to question. Mr. Eliot has had his influence right enough, but it is doubtful whether he would have had it if he had written no more than his *Selected Essays*. What seems far more likely is that criticism, by *begetting* criticism, causes a gradual amelioration in criticism itself. Mr. I. A. Richards, says Mr. Eliot, is to be respected even if he *is* up a blind alley, insofar as he will probably act as a warning to others— he will, that is to say, "have done something in accelerating the exhaustion of the possibilities" of his blind alleys. Criticism invites criticism of itself; like the worthy Cronus, it has its little Zeus. And like the worthy Cronus, further, it can't always swallow what it gives rise to.

This being the case, the "use" of criticism would seem to be little more than a Phoenix-like self-snuffing out in self-adjustment and self-renewal. The taste which it is everlastingly "correcting" is the taste which itself established, and which itself, therefore, deprecates. This is very little less than saying that criticism has no use at all, which would seem to be Mr. Eliot's own opinion, seeing that he has not actually declared its use once throughout his lectures. After all, one cannot say that the use of men is to beget men and to get themselves killed off.

It would seem, then, that criticism is useful—if at all—merely for the light which it throws upon the critic. If the critic is anyway interesting—as a poet must be declared to be interesting—then the criticism will deserve attention as the autobiography of its writing mind. This is the reason, of course, why one cares far less what Messrs. Richards, Leavis, and Co., say about Messrs. Pound, Eliot, and Co., than one cares what Messrs. Pound, Eliot, and Co. say about Messrs. Richards, Leavis, and Co.

Whether criticism has any use for its writer, on the other hand, will depend upon whether the writer—creatively—draws upon "inner voice" or tradition. And as Mr. Eliot has considered this matter elsewhere, he cannot be blamed for not considering it in the present book. What he *might* possibly be blamed for is his failure to make perfectly clear what his opinion of the use of either poetry or criticism, to writer or reader, really is. As he would have been bound to fail—or at least disappoint—in any such attempts, however, he was probably well advised to save his breath rather than cool his porridge.

*Montgomery Belgion. *Dublin Review* 194 (January 1934), 151–53.

In the autumn of 1932 Mr. Eliot went to America. In the course of the following winter he delivered at Harvard eight lectures. Then, last spring, he gave a further series of lectures at the University of Virginia. This book contains the lectures he gave at Harvard. According to the dedication and the preface, he is not entirely pleased with them. He speaks in the preface of committing "another unnecessary book" solely because it was a condition of their being given orally that they should afterwards be published. That can only apply, however, to their appearance in America.

One would of course like to protest that his misgivings are unwarranted. Unfortunately, that is not with honesty altogether possible. In these lectures Mr. Eliot's prose, which has found so many admirers, retains its quality; needless to say, he has not failed to raise a number of questions that are certainly exciting and may be important, and he makes many passing remarks worth

noting; but what he apparently sets out to do he does not, I feel, achieve.

He would have it that criticism operates between two theoretical limits, "at one of which we attempt to answer the question 'what is poetry?' and at the other 'is this a good poem?'" Accepting this, I do not believe that anyone can discover from these lectures what Mr. Eliot understands by poetry or why he considers any particular poem to be good. On the whole, it is towards the former of his limits that he tends, and this seems a pity, for I incline to think that his real virtue as a critic lies in his ability to appraise both the parts and the whole of individual poems. As a theorist, he is apt to wander.

One instance is where he seeks to illuminate the problem of poetry and the poet's beliefs by analyzing his own discomfort in the presence of the "philosophies" of Wordsworth, Shelley, and Goethe. He might perhaps have taken advantage of the clue he himself supplies in relating in another lecture Johnson's poetic success to Johnson's "moral elevation," and have exploited the implications of his adolescent enthusiasm for Shelley in relation to his present indifference. Moral elevation is what Wordsworth, for all his earnestness—or, perhaps, solemnity—lacks. It is certainly absent from Shelley, as indeed Mr. Eliot says. As for Goethe, he posed, unconsciously, no doubt, but all the more so on that account. One feels, indeed, that Mr. Eliot's verdicts must usually be just, and he should give us more of them; it is when he is struggling to explain his taste that he fails us. He has always been prone to semi-oracular statements; one suspects him of having the wish to be helpful without the will to be clear. Here, for example, he would distinguish between beliefs as "held" and beliefs as "felt." It is to be guilty of a defect with which he charges Matthew Arnold, the defect of leaving a statement "in suspension." And the reader is left too—wondering how beliefs could be "felt" without in some sense also being "held."

Again Mr. Eliot appears to insist, with the aid of one of his favorite chemical formulas, that poetic appreciation can only be "subjective." Yet, earlier, he says that "the experience of enjoying a bad poem while thinking it is a good one is very different from that of enjoying a good poem"; and if appreciation is never more than "subjective," then the expressions "a bad poem" and "a good poem" in this context have no meaning. Although Mr. Eliot does not say so, he has taken the semi-oracular affirmation bodily from Mr. I. A. Richards. Presumably this is not acknowledged because throughout the lectures Mr. Richards is already referred to with a frequency which to some readers will seem excessive.

Altogether, one awaits with a mingled curiosity the Virginia lectures, which are also to be published.

Cleanth Brooks. "Eliot's Harvard Lectures." *Southwest Review* 19, supplements 1–2 (January 1934), 1–2.

"From time to time, every hundred years or so, it is desirable that some critic shall appear to review the past of our literature, and set the poets and the poems in a new order." Thus Eliot remarks in the course of this book. Without claiming to be this critic, Eliot has for the past several years been going about the task of reordering the poets of the English tradition. This most recent work of his, the Charles Eliot Norton Lectures for 1933, continues the reordering with special reference to the history of English criticism.

It is necessary to call attention to all this in giving any account of this work, for Eliot's criticism is all of a piece. These lectures can hardly be read profitably apart from his earlier criticism, *The Sacred Wood*, and *For Lancelot Andrewes*. It is particularly necessary to call attention to this in view of the prevailing conception of Eliot as the talented but finicky man of taste who is always taking delicate measurements of inflection and *nuance*, but is never able to relate his estimates under a total concept—never positive enough to come to a unified view. The reader who approaches this volume as a collection of charming critical tidbits, or as a group of interesting but unrelated evaluations, will find much to reward him, but he will certainly miss the chief value of the book. *The Use of Poetry* is, indeed, the antithesis of a work like Housman's recent *The Name and Nature of Poetry*, where all the familiar landmarks appear, and the journey through the tradition is noteworthy only because of the author's company and conversation.

Eliot's reordering of the tradition grows out of the problems of modern poetry. Eliot's own poetry, for instance, raises at once the question of the validity of intellectual poetry, the compatibility of wit and high seriousness, the relation of simplicity and sincerity, etc. Approval of such poetry will naturally require alterations in our estimates of our older poets. It has always been thus. Indeed, we may venture the following assertion: Our judgment of poetry and of passed poets is always essentially the judgment passed by the last group of radical poets. For example, up to the very recent past we have judged poetry largely in terms of the poetry of the Romantic revolt—not only the poetry written after 1800, but that prior to 1800 as well. It is the poets, of course, not the professors, who alter conceptions of poetry. And the poet can come to a decision as to what poetry essentially is only in terms of his problems as a contemporary poet. His judgment on that problem will naturally affect his judgment of the entire tradition. As often as we have had radical poets, therefore, we have had to rearrange the poets "in a new order." With Wordsworth and with Coleridge the rearrangement involved, among other things, giving a higher valuation to the folk-ballad and a lower to the poetry of Dryden and Pope. In the present case, one can already see that the reordering will have the effect of elevating the "School of Donne" and of lowering the importance of the Victorian poets and some of the Romantics.

Eliot has briefly sketched the historical aspects of his reassessment in his essay, "The Metaphysical Poets" (1922). His promised *School of Donne* will presumably develop this detail in so far as it concerns the metaphysical poets. The present volume is important as giving further ramifications of the general theory. Viewed in this light, it becomes an important critical document in an important critical movement.

Moreover, when the book is considered in this fashion as an attempt at a reassessment of the English poetic tradition, the plan of the lectures becomes evident. The various points are marshaled in good order. "The Apology for the Countess of Pembroke" turns out to be an apology for the importance of criticism in the making of poetry, a thesis enforced by Eliot's revelation of its importance in our most spontaneous and least critical period—the Elizabethan. "The Age of Dryden" restates and emphasizes the value of our still too lightly regarded neo-classic criticism. The lecture on "Wordsworth and Coleridge" relates intellectual poetry to the distinction

which these two poets drew between the fancy and the imagination.

One may remark here that Eliot needs to be read closely. The last-mentioned lecture, for instance, grows out of one sentence of an essay written in 1921: "The difference between imagination and fancy, in view of this poetry of wit [metaphysical poetry and that of Laforgue and Corbière], is a very narrow one." In the same way the lecture on Matthew Arnold requires a reading of Eliot's earlier essay on Arnold for fullest understanding. Such a comment as the following wins its own acceptance, of course: "He is not, on the one hand, quite a pure enough poet to have the sudden illumination which we find in the criticism of Wordsworth, Coleridge, and Keats; and on the other hand he lacked the mental discipline and continuity of reasoning which distinguishes the philosopher." But unless one has already read the earlier essay on Arnold, he will hardly understand Eliot's criticism of the ordering of the tradition which Arnold made or the conception of poetry which he held.

It is proper here to make a comment on Eliot's prose style. It is Eliot's "passion for exactness" which has irritated some of his readers. Edmund Wilson, for example, amusingly parodies Eliot's erudition and his habit of qualification in one of the chapters of *Axel's Castle*. Eliot has been criticized for being a connoisseur of velleities and *nuances*. But fineness of discrimination, choice of the exact word, careful qualification and exception do not necessarily betoken the preciosity of the aesthete—they may be merely the honest and accurate use of terms required of a major critic. Inability to see Eliot's general thesis, or to see that he has a general thesis at all, has thus led to confusion here.

Perhaps no single one of these lectures is so brilliant a piece of writing as the essay on Swinburne or so satisfactory as that on Andrew Marvell. The last lecture, and the most interesting, "The Modern Mind," is relatively inconclusive. That on Shelley and Keats can only be praised for putting succinctly and well what many modern critics have already come to feel. But the volume is important. It is a tribute to Eliot that any further development of his critical position is necessarily of interest to every serious student of poetry.

Francis Fergusson. "Eliot's Norton Lectures." *Hound and Horn* 7 (January–March 1934), 356–58.

Mr. Eliot's new book has a more general title than his others, but his methods are the same as before. In *The Sacred Wood* he told us what the critic should be, and he brought out a certain ideal of what poetry is in itself by a process of elimination. His essays on Seneca, taken together, have a far wider meaning than the title admits. His constant habit in fact is to put flesh on his grander ideas by focusing his taste and intelligence on particular texts.

These scrupulous ways gave occasion, last year, for one of the less intelligent attempts to "circumvent Mr. Eliot": that of Mr. Waldo Frank, who proclaimed [in a review of *Selected Essays*] in *The New Republic* that Mr. Eliot was incapable of making a "Synthesis." [See "The 'Universe' of T. S. Eliot" (1932) in this volume, pp. 208–12.] Mr. Eliot is incapable of heroically hoo-hooing into the windy spaces, like a loudspeaker on Union Square: but his quiet methods do not justify the belief that his thought lacks either consistency or depth. Nor does the fact that Mr. Eliot would probably hasten to agree with Mr. Frank. "Let me start with the supposition that we do not know what poetry is," he says, at the beginning of his new book,

> or what it does or ought to do, or of what use it is; and try to find out, in examining the relation of poetry and criticism, what the use of both of them is. We may even discover that we have no very clear idea of what *use* is; at any rate we had better not assume that we know.

[. . .] The modesty which assumes on the part of the reader at least some experience of the thing to be investigated, and also the inadequacy of any translation of this experience into foreign terms, is Socratic. It is easy to see why it should have misled Mr. Frank: there is in all of us if we don't watch out a strong strain of Frank, which therefore provides a good starting point for the attempt to appreciate Mr. Eliot's methods. What we should do is assume that we know as little as Mr. Eliot, and *not* assume that we have the whole meaning of his studies in our pocket.

One of the distinctions that Mr. Frank appears to be unaware of is between the problems Mr. Eliot studies and the particular examples he offers. In the essay called "Apology for the Countess of Pembroke," he seems to do hardly more than make a few judgments on specimens of Elizabethan poetry and criticism, connected by general remarks so quiet that you might pass them by as commonplaces. Yet they actually serve to illustrate a theory of the drama which he has warily approached before in "Shakespeare and the Stoicism of Seneca" and the essay on William Archer. So in "The Age of Dryden" he seems only to protest mildly against certain notions of the relative importance of Dryden, Addison, and Johnson, and in "Matthew Arnold" to correct and amplify his previous remarks on that critic. (Arnold "was apt to think of the greatness of poetry rather than of its genuineness.") In all of the essays he focuses the large problem and the particular figure together. If you do not see the large problem, or think you have solved it, you miss not only the unity of his thought, but the thought itself.

It is of course hard to see his problems as he does without a comparable experience of literature, and this makes it easy to refrain from trying to summarize or criticize his thought. His experience appears to be so wide that he can contemplate the history of literature itself, "the direction in which the mind is moving." One of the ways he acquired this experience was by resolutely reading the mediocrities of the last three centuries as well as the great authors and the authors whom he naturally liked.

> The exhaustive critic, armed with a powerful glass, will be able to sweep the distance and gain an acquaintance with minute objects in the landscape with which to compare minute objects close at hand; he will be able to gauge nicely the position and proportion of the objects surrounding us, in the whole of the vast panorama.

Mr. Eliot is not talking about himself in this passage, but it describes very well that deflated scholarly coldness and certainty which is the background for the exercise of his taste. There is something in Mr. Eliot, when he writes, that is carefully dead; but what he talks about is always alive. Perhaps the dogma so often felt in his work is only the dogma of the mysterious independence of the things he studies. [. . .]

There is another habit of Mr. Eliot's, also Socratic, which might also mislead those who would rather be misled than made uncomfortable. That is the habit of approaching a general idea [. . .] by attacking the general ideas and formulations of others. Much of "The Modern Mind" is

devoted to such a treatment of the ideas of Mr. I. A. Richards. His objections to Mr. Richards's theories stem from his objections to Mr. Richards's notions of religion and belief, and he quotes Mr. Jacques Maritain with approval in this connection. But he by no means identifies himself with Mr. Maritain's position, and his conclusion is all his own:

> Amongst all these demands from poetry and responses to it there is always some permanent element in common, just as there are standards of good and bad writing independent of what any one of us happens to like and dislike; but every effort to formulate the common element is limited by the limitations of particular men in particular places and at particular times; and these limitations become manifest in the perspective of history.

It would be very interesting to see an extended comment by Mr. Eliot on *Art et Scolastique*: there, if anywhere, one might hope to see him confess the purpose as well as the painfulness of his skepticism; there is an all-important hair's-breadth by which he differs from his nearest contemporary allies. He proposes however to connect his thought with Mr. Maritain's in a more characteristic way: through that "influence of the devil on contemporary literature" which he agrees with Mr. Maritain is "very palpable": he tells us in a footnote, "With the influence of the devil on contemporary literature I shall be concerned in more detail in another book." He is in fact still condemned or self-condemned to draw only the unhappy deductions from his beliefs. "Sometimes to be a ruined man is itself a vocation," he smiles; and he maintains the difficult and gloomy consistency of his attitude from the dedication ("To the Memory of Charles Whibley to whom I promised a better book") until his rather stagey exit, while the "sad ghost of

Coleridge ... beckons from the shadows." If he can be made happy by nothing less than both summits of Parnassus, that is his misfortune and our good fortune. It should not prevent us from drawing life-giving deductions which he never makes explicit, or from seeing (with or without the permission of Mr. Waldo Frank) that his freedom from the formulations of any time or place may be a gift to the spirit of our time and place.

Geoffrey Stone. "Indirect Affirmations." *Commonweal* 19 (9 February 1934), 418–19.

Most of T. S. Eliot's affirmations are made by indirection. When some while ago, in *For Lancelot Andrewes*, he came forth and spoke not at all obliquely, saying in religion he believed in Anglo-Catholicism, in politics, in royalism, and, in literature, in classicism, there were those who protested rather bitterly against this sort of thing: they had been approving of Mr. Eliot all along and he had been insidiously inoculating them with doctrines they simply could not abide. In the present book (which is composed of the Charles Eliot Norton Lectures for 1932–1933) Mr. Eliot does not so dogmatically state what the use of poetry is; on the use of criticism he is more forthright; and it is by examining the criticism of various periods, and what it demanded of poetry, that he contrives to give hints of the ends which poetry may serve.

I suggest, that we may learn a good deal about criticism and about poetry by examining the history of criticism, not merely as a catalogue of successive notions about poetry, but as a process of readjustment between poetry and the world in and for which it is produced.

Examination of the group which surrounded the Countess of Pembroke, the sister of Sir Philip Sidney, results in the conclusion that in their "simple assertions that poetry gives high delight and adorns society is some awareness of the problem of the relation of the poem to the reader and the place of poetry in society." In "The Age of Dryden" Mr. Eliot finds an increased subtlety in criticism, and makes more plain what Dryden wanted used in poetry than what use he wanted it put to—the implication of which may be that Dryden thought a poem sufficient reason for its own being. From this he goes on to say that "for Johnson poetry was still poetry, and not another thing"—which it had not been for Addison, who saw it as a substitute for expensive or criminal pleasures.

This latter tendency appears as further developed with Wordsworth and Coleridge; theirs being an age of change, and so of some confusion, "poetry was for them the expression of totality of unified interests."

"With Shelley we are struck from the beginning by the number of things poetry is expected to do." These things are bound up with Shelley's ideas, and "The ideas of Shelley," Mr. Eliot reveals, "seem to me always to be ideas of adolescence." Both the new function poetry is required to perform and poetry itself suffer in consequence. With Keats, on the contrary, ideas—and Keats's ideas are found to be of a better order than Shelley's—are used to make poetry; "he was occupied only with the highest use of poetry." The ultimate of the progressive misuse of poetry is arrived at in Matthew Arnold, who asks "of poetry that it give religious and philosophic satisfaction," a satisfaction found, to Mr. Eliot's way of thinking, better perhaps only, in religion and philosophy. Finally Mr. Eliot comes down to the present day and wittily disposes of I. A. Richards's contention that poetry is the way out of the modern dilemma.

Perhaps Mr. Eliot has not shown us what the use of poetry is; but he has made clear what its uses are not. And in the process of doing so he has given us the delight of watching a learned and tasteful mind ranging over four hundred years of verse and its criticism; he has thrown out epigrammatical suggestions that will probably be expanded into essays over other names; and he has done something which few critics succeed in doing—he has made us anxious to read many of the poets of whom he writes.

In this volume, as in a previous one, Mr. Eliot has been rather harsh in his judgment of Matthew Arnold; yet when one seeks a figure to whom to compare the author of *The Waste Land*, it is Matthew Arnold who comes to mind: there is the same felicity of expression, the later man has the "real taste" he grants the earlier one, and, though there may be some difference as to degree, they are both on the side of the angels.

Conrad Aiken.
"The Use of Poetry."
Yale Review 23 (March 1934), 643–46.

Mr. Eliot's new essays, which were delivered last year at Harvard from the Charles Eliot Norton chair, have all the virtues of the first-rate lecture: they move easily, they are lucid and orderly, they are infor-mative without being too much weighted with pedantry, and they do not forget to be entertaining. We are given a survey, excellently planned and simplified (and, on the whole, with very judicious omissions) of the linked progress, or evolution, side by side, of English poetry and criticism, from Elizabethan times to the present day. Mr. Eliot's method is that of the inquirer—he makes few assumptions, he has little recourse to dogma. He asks questions, very pertinently and gently; and answers them, generally, with a careful tentativeness. If at times he appears a little superficial, or sketchy, or if his transitions are occasionally somewhat meager and hurried, it is only fair to assume that at least a part of this arises from the normal difficulty of the lecturer. A style too packed or dense would have defeated his purpose.

What emerges from the book—of general "view," or conclusion—does so largely by implication: if Mr. Eliot lays down any emphatic dogma at all, it is simply that poetry can, and does, vary in its function at different times and in different places; and that along with it, *pari passu*, criticism alters its pace and direction. That criticism has gradually sharpened in technical analysis, in objectivity, in its ability and willingness to keep fresh a sense of the past, and in psychological and social awareness, Mr. Eliot seems to admit. This evolution he traces, very neatly and illuminatingly, all the way from Sidney to Mr. I. A. Richards. But that with this "progress" in the perceptiveness of criticism has developed any clearer or more precise idea of what poetry is, or what it is for, he does not appear altogether convinced. What his own views may be, of the nature and function of poetry, or of the nature and function of criticism, emerges, again, rather by implication or negation than by statement; and these, of course, are of particular interest, as coming from one of the most important poets of our time.

Implied, to begin with, in Mr. Eliot's whole attitude to his subject (the variability of poetry's social use or function), is a skepticism as to the existence of any universal, or essence, or "permanent," in poetry—or, at any rate, a doubt as to what it is. "The extreme of theorizing about the nature of poetry," he says, "the essence of poetry if there is any, belongs to the study of aesthetics." Perhaps he might better have said, to psychology and to sociology—for aesthetics, like poetry, changes its tone and temper with time and place. If there is any "permanent" or universal in poetry, it is its social function; and about this, modern psychologists have already had a good deal to say, and will have more. Sooner or later they will tell us what, at all times and in all places, poetry *does*. It is my own opinion that Mr. Richards, in his *Principles of Literary Criticism* especially, but in his other books as well, is making a very important step in this direction.

From Mr. Eliot's view of poetry as a thing of variable and indeterminate function, to his suggestion that it is not so much a "communication" as "itself a thing to be communicated" (a separate entity) is a natural step. This is again to cut away the psychological roots. It seems to me quite impossible to rule out communication. If language is communication, poetry is simply communication (or language) working at its highest pitch. Poetry cannot communicate itself alone, any more than language can communicate itself alone—Miss Stein to the contrary. What the writing of the poem does to the poet, the reading of it does to the reader; and whether we call it "organization," with Mr. Richards, or revelation, with the mystics, it is *au fond* a sharing, a making common, a communication. Criticism, here, will simply say how successful the communication is, and why, and of what; it will regard the poem not as an absolute but as a dynamic: and will trace its references backward to the

poet and forward to the reader. A poem as a completely separate entity would be a poem completely without reference, and therefore without meaning: an impossibility. This is not to say that criticism could not usefully discriminate between the thing communicated (the world) and the communication (the word). But analysis, pushed far enough, would discover them (one suspects) to be the same thing. In this regard, Mr. Eliot's remark that "meaning" may be simply the chief method of keeping the reader diverted "while the poem does its work upon him" seems to be the result of confused thinking. Remove the logical statement from a poem, an important part of the "meaning" would still remain—the affective. And it is precisely in this way that poetry makes the highest use of language, as it perhaps also represents the highest degree of consciousness of which man is capable: the most complete. It combines the logical or factual with the affective.

As will seem natural enough from the foregoing, Mr. Eliot shies at the notion of poetry as "revelation," and equally at Mr. Richards's suggestion that in poetry we can find a "substitute" for religion: he must have them separate. Is this our old friend the Ivory Tower? Perhaps Mr. Eliot's private religious predicament is answerable for it—in any case, he is at some pains, and with considerable sophistical disingenuousness, to ridicule Mr. Richards's idea that mankind, having shed religious dogma and arbitrary faith, will find through poetry a sufficient communication with the world and a sufficient source of "belief." I am myself in entire agreement with Mr. Richards about this—it seems to me not impossible that religion was simply a temporary form of poetry. And I cannot agree with Mr. Eliot that poetry cannot be philosophic, or can only *borrow* its thinking: poetry can think deeply and still be poetry; it has thought deeply in the past, and is learning to think again. Poetic "thinking" is real thinking. What about Zarathustra?

[. . .]

John Crowe Ransom. "T. S. Eliot on Criticism." *Saturday Review of Literature* 10 (24 March 1934), 574.

Mr. Eliot writes about critics as he has written about poets: with a citation, a precisely qualified approval or disapproval, perhaps an extended discussion going almost into the profession of principles. But he does not quite profess to principles; he is the most particularistic critic that English poetry and English criticism have met with.

He does not like to raise his head from the text. And it is the source of his strength; nobody else is so constant in his reference to the thing itself. A critic of this sort we may call intensive in his method. The other sort, whom we may call the extensive critic, but who will be more immediately recognized if we call him the dogmatic critic, is much more common with us. On the whole the dogmatic critic has done a great deal of damage to our understanding of poetry. Confronted with a poem, it is never certain that he can receive its effect; he has for his fatal equipment a handy body of critical doctrine to apply quickly; for it is part of his position that he must be prepared to do a large business, in fact to attend to all the business that comes, and therefore to act with the speed and the decision that a tax assessor exhibits. The tax assessor is within his rights, he has

only to find the market value of the object appraised; but the object of criticism has no automatic public status and in itself is infinitely various, suggesting an apparatus of appraisal which is delicate, laborious, provisional, and never dogmatic.

It is widely understood that Mr. Eliot, who here writes about critics, is himself a great critic. It is not an adjective I approve, being indeterminate in meaning and something less than adult, let us say collegiate, in its tone; but the public hungers for it, and Mr. Eliot himself fancies it, and uses it often of his poets, along with its degrees of greater and greatest. But let us at least apply it to Mr. Eliot with some connotation. When he says that Coleridge was perhaps the greatest of English critics, I should add, "of a certain sort"; feeling that among the rarer tribe of intensive critics Eliot himself is greatest.

[. . .]

Nevertheless it is likely that many readers have put down the present book with a slight feeling of grievance. Writing a whole book on criticism, Mr. Eliot was at last, we thought, going to offer a systematic critical theory; a bold big structure of principles accounting for the brilliance of his practice. It would be a "classical" theory, whatever that meant; for Mr. Eliot had once committed himself on that point, at the time when he announced himself as royalist in politics, anglo-catholic in religion, and classical in literature. But there is nothing about the classical in this book; and there is no adoption of doctrine whatever.

The classicism of Mr. Eliot must be interpreted as very much like his Aristotelianism, or his humanism, or his emphasis on intelligence, taste, and common sense. These are terms which he refuses to define, and uses constantly and almost interchangeably; and having come to this conclusion I think I can state at last

Mr. Eliot's critical Credo. He has written it, and its Articles are numbered in a hard consecutive style, though they will not be found to amount to quite so positive an expression of faith as we might desire. The passage occurs in an earlier essay, "Second Thoughts on Humanism." I take the liberty to substitute "criticism" for "humanism," and I quote loosely.

I. The function of criticism is not to provide dogmas or philosophical theories. Criticism is not concerned with philosophical foundations. When it proceeds to exact definitions, it is something other than itself.

II. Criticism makes for breadth, tolerance, equilibrium, and sanity. It operates against fanaticisms.

III. It is critical rather than constructive.

IV. Criticism is valuable (a) by itself, in the "pure critic," who will not set up poetry as a substitute for philosophy and religion, and (b) as a mediating and corrective ingredient in a civilization founded on definite belief.

Mr. Eliot in the present book praises the taste which Mr. I. A. Richards exhibits in his appreciation of actual poetry, and then indicates sufficiently, or at least to my satisfaction, that the general theory of literature which Mr. Richards constructs is not competent. He does much the same thing for Arnold and Coleridge. The implication is that it is a pity Richards and Arnold and Coleridge had not stuck to the exercise of taste and shunned the pursuit of theory; that taste is prior to theory and renders theory unnecessary; that in fact a theory of literature is not possible. But the evidence for this conclusion is only the fact that certain critics, or all critics if necessary, have found themselves unable to articulate theories big enough and precise enough

to accommodate their actual judgments. Now it makes a great deal of difference whether the theories are only insufficient in their scope or positively misguided.

But Mr. Eliot's nicety on this point is somewhat ridiculous. It probably has a temperamental basis, or a basis in personal history, which cannot be accepted. Criticism cannot really be independent of theory. It requires fresh and delicate perceptions, but what is perceived is constantly being judged, or brought under patterns which the mind has carefully acquired. Criticism is a science, and a science must know what it is doing. The Aristotle who dropped a few pertinent comments in the *Poetics* may be the Aristotle whom Mr. Eliot admires, but there was also an Aristotle who constructed vast systems.

[. . .]

So here is Mr. Eliot, an acute and versatile critic, a blaster of critical reputations wherever they rest on bad judgments, or on theoretical structures which are too slight. His influence is very large both in the positive and in the negative. He is able to say quite truly about the vast and muddy volume of literary criticism that we have inherited: "Few forms of intellectual activity seem to have less to show for themselves, in the course of history, in the way of books worth reading, than does criticism." What comes out of this assemblage of items when we survey it? Perhaps a prophecy.

By the year 2033, perhaps by the year 1983, if the continuity of our literary development is not broken in some collapse of the political or economic pattern, criticism will possess a degree both of precision and of substantiality incomparably beyond what we or the former generation have known. Theory will have been pushed much farther; critics will have become technically learned and dialectically expert; perception will have been reeducated to poetry. The event will owe much to the Mr. Eliot of the 1933 volume. Also, though this sounds contradictory, it will take place in spite of Mr. Eliot.

M[orton] D. Z[abel]. "The Use of the Poet." *Poetry: A Magazine of Verse* 44 (April 1934), 32–37.

The problems to which T. S. Eliot dedicated his lectures at Harvard in 1932–33—*The Use of Poetry and the Use of Criticism*—are far from slight, and for most people far from solved. It is disappointing to find the book in which his speculations are now printed (by the Harvard University Press) as slight and apologetic as it is. His own regrets extend from dedication-page to epilogue. Each chapter is scattered with cautions and hairsplittings that force one to deplore the loss of the "pontifical solemnity" and acuteness for which Mr. Eliot apologized in *The Sacred Wood*. But any carping over this book's discretion should not imply disgust that it leaves its problems unsolved. The uses of poetry and criticism are more easily practiced than stated. Eliot's poetry is among the little in our day that has made those uses real and imperative to the twentieth-century public. A man who writes poetry that demands to be read as his has been read, may be pardoned for finding the job of explaining its uses difficult and tedious. *The Use of Poetry* has been regarded by reviewers chiefly as an irritant. It has a greater value—as biography and provocation. Its worth lies in what it tells of Eliot's career and his importance to an age which his work has both enlightened and perplexed. A poet who covers this much ground has proved his usefulness. In a time when by turns everything or nothing is expected of poets, it is important to know what that service has been.

For readers of *The Waste Land* it still consists in expressing "the disillusionment of a generation," but this function Eliot has repudiated. And it is the basic assertion of these lectures that a poet who officially *expresses* any cause or mission, disillusionment or faith, or who makes his art the vehicle of the moment's convenience, is hardly worthy of his name. Critics who demand this service of poets are sponsors of aesthetic crime. Here belongs such a "bourgeois literary dictator" as Addison (used as foil to Dryden), and "the moralising critics of the nineteenth century, to which Landor makes a notable exception." Here belong the defective parts of Shelley and Goethe, who, with poetic gifts of "the first order," tried to philosophize on their "own *poetic* insight," and thus make one skull do the work of two. They had philosophy, but not the "philosophic mind" of the true poet, who does not state ideas but creates and actualizes them. Unlike Dante and Shakespeare, Keats and Coleridge, they were too often content when their poems stated passionate interests, moral and political, instead of embodying "a totality of unified interests." And here stands preeminently Matthew Arnold, on whom Eliot's irony and pity fasten. Arnold, the defender of tradition and taste, the priest of culture, and prophet of anarchy, gives Eliot his real clue to the misuses both poetry and criticism may suffer. He points toward "the modern mind" which Eliot dissects in his last chapter. Ironically, he also points more clearly than any past critic toward the ordeal and methods of the author of *The Waste Land*.

The misuses made of poetry today, as Eliot sees them, are already familiar to his readers. The value of his view of them lies in his aloofness to calling them errors merely because they are modern. They reduce to two fallacies. The first, sponsored earlier by Arnold and today by I. A. Richards, makes poetry a "criticism of life," a "powerful and beautiful application of ideas" to it, and thus a substitute for moral discipline and religion. The second lies in the demand made on poetry by causes external to it—in the past theological, today chiefly political and sociological. Here poetry usually becomes propaganda, the vehicle of philosophy rather than the sum and experience of it; it is debilitated, as Goethe's and Shelley's too often was, by confusion in serving two principles. In either case, the primary function of poetry suffers—and with it the ideas which poetry is called on to serve. [. . .]

The two men whom Eliot calls on to state his case for him come from the opposite extremes of modern thought—Maritain the Catholic, and Trotsky the Communist: Maritain because he refutes the "deadly error" of Arnold and Richards that "poetry is capable of saving us" by providing "the supernatural nourishment of man," and Trotsky because he says in *Literature and Revolution* that:

> Artistic creation is always a complicated turning inside out of old forms, under the influence of new stimuli which originate outside of art. In this large sense of the word, art is a handmaiden. It is not a disembodied element feeding on itself, but a function of social man indissolubly tied to his life and environment.

Thus he seems to Eliot "to draw the commonsense distinction between art and propaganda, and to be dimly aware that the material of the artist is not his beliefs as *held*, but his beliefs as *felt* [. . .]."

Propagandists, religious or political, must communicate. A poem is the sum of so much more than communicable thought that Eliot is put to the ingenuity of holding that the explicable part of a poem is there merely to catch the reader's attention while the poetic and vital reality—verbally incommunicable—is given to him. Where Coleridge held that "poetry gives most pleasure when only generally and not perfectly understood," Eliot would be satisfied (since every poet wants to have "some direct social utility") by having a part to play in society as worthy as that of the music-hall comedian. "I believe that the poet naturally prefers to write for as large and miscellaneous an audience as possible [. . .]." Thus—in addition to inspiring a revival of poetic drama on the side—he might make people "a little more aware of the deeper, unnamed feelings which form the substratum of our being, to which we rarely penetrate; for our lives are mostly a constant evasion of ourselves, and an evasion of the visible and sensible world."

It is not to be wondered that this doctrine strikes most people as rooted in a deep cynicism concerning human taste and culture. At the present moment, when religion and revolution are again demanding service of poetry (not as a substitute for old faiths but to preach new ones), any plea for poetry's independent way of functioning takes on the appearance of a sacrilegious denial of life. Eliot's music-hall comedian is hardly a happy figure. An age crying for prophets and light-bearers is not likely to stumble across the truth in a vaudeville house. [. . .]

Behind his caution and irony lies a respect for life and its principles too great to tolerate any threat or insult to them through bad art. Anyone who has ever thought seriously about the matter knows that a single Psalm has served Christianity better than a thousand psalm-books; [. . .] and that a single poem by Blok has struck the heart of revolutionary idealism better than all the hymns in *The New Masses*. [. . .] Beyond the roar of prophecy and revolution lie more fundamental experiences of life, and it is to be hoped that poetry will still be one way of realizing them. If it is, and if, in an age of cultural harmony which even Arnold could not imagine, we find ourselves enjoying it in a music-hall, we will at least know that we are neither in a church nor on a battlefield when the author of *The Waste Land* and *Ash-Wednesday* steps up to do his turn.

---

*Ezra Pound. "What Price the Muses Now." *New English Weekly* 5 (24 May 1934), 130–33.

[. . .]

[Eliot's] opening pages would [. . .] if properly used, serve to clear off a good many vermin, partly British and mostly longstanding, whereas the mentally alert sufferers in Cambridge, Mass., had hoped that the more immediate obstacles, cankers, barnacles on American literary life, would be scraped. They felt let down by the lecturer's dealing with faint and far away whiffs of Dryden and Mat. Arnold, very much as if you had tried to retreat. These youngsters having the weekly and monthly spew of Canby and Co., the *Atlantic*, a quarterly affair disrespectfully referred to as "Bitch and Bugle," and the old line demo-liberal tosh of the N.Y. weeklies, copied and dishwatered down from the very stale stink of the London literary weeklies, etc., had hoped that the Dean of English Criticism

and Editor of Britain's Brightest Quarterly would fire a few volleys at some of the more overshadowing pests.

As it is, indeed, a great pity that he shouldn't have done, even though it would have irritated his sponsors in baptism and perturbed the somnolence of the elms.

However, granting the opportunity missed, one may also regard the opportunity taken. Mr. Eliot adapted the motto of another of Harvard's presidential families: "*Aquila non captat muscas*"; he would probably defend himself on the ground that mere mention of these American local odors would have been beneath the dignity of the Norton professor, and would have conferred too much honor on the condemned. As a professing Christian, whether biblican or not, he would probably tell me that Adam named the beasts in the garden but did not confer separate cognomens on each heap of animal excrement.

For the sake of clarity I shall deal with some of the lectures seriatim.

Introduction: Carefully written, carefully considered, sound doctrine that can only do good to the reader (whoever he may be). The few minor divergences one might wish to indicate are of a personal nature and on the second plane. They do not affect the main statement. This is a sound essay and the suggestions it contains *could* be very useful if violently acted upon, to the general cleansing of cloacæ and sluicing out the streets of literary publicity, book reviewing, and professorial functions. The criticism of a book must concern itself with what the book is, and only in minor degree, if at all, with what the book is not, or with extenuations or aggravations of circumstance.

Second essay: Pawky humor in the title. Essay full of meat, acute observation, Mr. Eliot's own view with highly respectable knowledge of the matter. Possibly does not seem revolutionary to inexpert auditor or to the layman, but supposing an acquaintance with academic or professorial opinion of university specialists, the essay is full of startling divergences from the accepted opinions of this body of men, small in relation to the gross population at large, but enormous in proportion to the number of readers familiar with even the titles of some of the works which Mr. Eliot says cheerily "everyone has read."

[. . .]

From here on Mr. Eliot has dealt with inferior and in some cases vile matter. I don't know whether the subjects for particular lectures were imposed by the dead hand of the endowment. At any rate, if Mr. Eliot had a clear aim he seems to have lost his North. That is if his lectures were supposed to leave his students with a clearer perception of poetry and a more valid perception of values. [. . .]

The gravest charge against his rank as critic is that he ventures to label an essay "The Modern Mind," and to have found NONE of the more vigorous intellects of the past century worth even passing mention.

His high-water mark is an allusion to Lévy-Bruhl, who is at any rate a first-rate professor. Fabre, Fraser, Frobenius, Fenollosa would appear to mean nothing to him. Ben Jonson's best tip is not only neglected but Eliot swings round to a diametrically opposite course, and composes his list from obtuse and unqualified writers of tertiary or *n*th intensity, and from dabblers in minor theories.

He renders lip service to the idea that exactness in use of words is valuable but implies that this lack in Mat. Arnold disqualified him "*as philosopher.*" He prophesies *re* Mr. Richards on no base of offered evidence, but in the hope that Richards will kill off certain minor pests [. . .].

The nastiest blasphemy is quoted from the typical French religious faddist, and a racketeer on the borders of aesthetics. If this essay is a sign of anything save Eliot's boredom, or if one were to take it as serious indication of his maximum capacity one would have to conclude that his gross insensitivity to the history of the past 150 years, to the makers and recorders of that history, to the makers and perceivers of contemporary history, and to the inventors of ideas now *taking body* is so great as to disqualify him from any perception of poetry in relation to life or to any thought outside the interlocking cenacles of just such racketeer–aesthetes and theorists.

[. . .]

The introduction and first essay are well worth the price of the book. Unless the reader is a psychiatrist with special interest in "fatigue and unconscious responses," and with a mission for saving Mr. Eliot from the perils of long residence in low countries, he would do well to read the first part of the work and chuck the rest into his waste basket.

Eliot gives evidence of what every sufferer knew, namely, that we have about us a lot of muddling second-rate and seventh-rate writers. But he shows no perception whatever of the pestilence and confusion spread by the economic putridity, the gross drag of writing *committed* from economic pressure direct and indirect, and the endless perversion and dullness thereby protruded to the obfuscation of literary as well as all other preceptions of communications.

As long as careerist curés and careerist employees are diddled into writing neither what they THINK nor what they think is worth writing about, the first great categoric frontier in all contemporary work will be *between* that wherein a man has clarified his intentions, to the point of being sure that he writes what he thinks, and the 99 and more percent. of printed

266

manifestations caused directly, indirectly, or at *n*th remove by economic pressure, and the *various mental perversions* due at Ist and *n*th range by the pressure.

The fallacy of scarcity, the neo-malthusian derivatives, artificial fecundation, the fall of the church, in its failure to deal with evil when that evil menaces the comfort of its subsidized professors and professional racketeers, the dimming, in whatever order you like of theology, philosophy, language itself, the means of inter-communication *via* requirements of the ghoul press, the strangling of periodicals, *via* the banks, the strangling of newspaper value *via* the advertising control WITH all their minor derivatives and malarial seepage.

Mr. E not only fails to register any of this in his chapter on the modern mind, but he fails to include any man who has ever given it any attention, or who has had sufficient acumen to perceive it. He also fails to ascribe importance to anyone whose ideas have gone into contemporary CONSTRUCTION of any kind. Marx and Lenin do not exist in his survey, but he cites Trotsky's dilettante twaddle. Precisely what did NOT function in Moscow.

Supposing him to have agreed without much reflection to lecture on Dryden, etc., his final lectures were obviously his chance to show some awareness to life.

Perhaps he is not suffering from anemia but from under-nourishment. Perhaps he needs to read a few solid books. It is extremely easy for an editor to acquire the habit of reading mainly or exclusively the stuff submitted to him to edit, and so, gradually to circumscribe his horizon to what contending contributors think he is likely to publish, or to stuff boosted by snobs in their circles.

Mr. E once said to an etiolated epigon of the British Upper Middle reaches: "What you need is a plate of good buckwheat pancakes."

It is perhaps time to make a similar abrupt suggestion to the dean of English essayists: What you need is a bit of good solid reading matter.

The potter's hand and the clay! If a writer avoid, from whatever cause, the most vigorous and most deeply thought verbal manifestations of his time and of the decades immediately preceding it, his appreciation, etc., his essays, etc., are bound, in time, to show the effects of this avoidance, be he never so occasionally circumspect and occasionally so just in his formulation.

Richmond Lattimore. *Journal of English and Germanic Philology* 33 (July 1934), 482–84.

It may be said at once that this book is on the whole disappointing, not so much because of its defects as because of the false hopes that may be raised in the reader's mind by the association of Mr. Eliot's known abilities with the first part of the title. Mr. Eliot does not tell us what the use of poetry is, and he almost manages to convey a certain feeling of contempt for anyone who expects to be told. Perhaps such an expectation is in fact naive, yet one cannot help feeling that there is little good to be got out of raising a question without trying to answer it. What Mr. Eliot is really concerned with is the relation of the criticism of poetry to poetry; and in his opinion criticism is valuable, not because it gives definitions, but because the active practice of it enriches our experience of poetry.

The starting-point for the book is reached in a protest against the proposition which separates "ages of creation" and "ages of criticism" into antithetical and mutually exclusive entities. Hence we are led off upon an admittedly cursory survey of critics of poetry from Daniel and Campion to I. A. Richards. But the ostensible thesis (if it is such) is a clue to start with, not a thread running through the whole. The book has many excellent things in it, but it lacks structure. Even this might be pardonable enough if the sequences of thought were coherent, but this (for one reader at least) is usually not the case. And this fragmentary character seems to me to be essentially related to the quality of Mr. Eliot's critical talents. His excellence is in analysis rather than synthesis; more specifically (in case the foregoing appears rather worse than meaningless) he can take a man apart better than he can put him together again. It would take too long to work out an instance in full, but anyone who is particularly interested might read the constructive exposition of Dryden's account of the poetical process [in lecture III]. I cannot avoid the conclusion that one of these two things is true: either Dryden meant what he said, in which case he is not the critic Mr. Eliot seems to think him; or else, Dryden was incapable of saying what he meant. Nor, again, is the discussion of Campion's critical theories very illuminating. One gathers that he had some, and that, it seems, is the whole point, but it emerges bit by bit and never with much resolution. Mr. Eliot analyzes out Matthew Arnold's faults as a critic and as a poet—his lack of sensitiveness, his inconsistency, his confused values—with sure and merciless accuracy; yet he still thinks that Arnold is a reliable critic, and one is completely at a loss to see why. Arnold has his virtues, certainly, but this is no place to look for an account of them. And it seems to be even more violently the case, when Mr. Richards is under discussion, that an unre-solved feeling of approval survives its own contradiction in one detail after another. But when Mr. Eliot opens a discussion frankly with a confession of distaste for some writer—Addison, for instance, or Shelley—one may confidently expect to find him at his best in analysis; and his best is very good indeed.

It is this characteristic co-presence of clear and sensitive insight and confused structure that makes the book at once disappointing and stimulating. We come once more upon the peculiarly fugitive quality remembered in Mr. Eliot's poetry. "Prufrock" is the final exhibition of the apologetic man; and Mr. Eliot insists on apologizing for his best writing. The conclusion is marred by a half-answer to the question about use, suggesting that the theatre is the proper medium for the poet; and this, coming from Mr. Eliot (or, perhaps, from anyone) seems fantastic. But there is in the conclusion an analysis of the process of creating poetry, grounded in introspection and therefore presented with many apologies, which would be hard to beat anywhere; and a sudden calling up of images which tells us, what we must have been sure of long ago, that Mr. Eliot knows what poetry is even if he cannot tell us, even if he cannot always write it. There are other good things. The Note on the development of "Taste" (once more, "subjective") is excellent; and when I read, as a stricture upon Arnold, that he was "apt to think of the greatness of poetry rather than its genuineness" I hoped, if without expectation, that the audience at his lecture rose up and cheered. Yet the conclusion ends on a note of [. . .] apology, as if the author were aware of having got through a job, not well done but at least done somehow. And this is in a measure true, but I wonder why it should be necessary. If Mr. Eliot would only commit himself more often, we should be glad to forgive him for making many more mistakes than he does.

Checklist of Additional Reviews

*Basil de Sélincourt. "The Deity of Dryness—Mr. Eliot's Harvard Lectures." *Observer*, 12 November 1933, pp. 405–08.

*F. C. "The Use of Mr. Eliot." *Granta* 43 (15 November 1933), 103.

*"Christmas Books for Young and Old." *Schoolmaster*, 23 November 1933, supplement, p. iii.

*"Poetry and Criticism: Mr. Eliot's Harvard Lectures." *Scotsman*, 23 November 1933, p. 2.

*Hugh Kingsmill. "Goethe, Wordsworth, and Mr. Eliot." *English Review* 57 (December 1933), 667–70.

*Desmond MacCarthy. "Poetry as Criticism of Life." *Sun Times*, 3 December 1933, p. 8.

*Desmond Hawkins. "Mr. Eliot's Criticism." *Week-End Review* 8 (9 December 1933), 636.

*"The Use of Poetry." *Times Literary Supplement* 1663 (14 December 1933), 892.

*A. M. *Blackfriars* 15, no. 166 (January 1934), 70–72.

Herschel Brickell. "The Use of Poetry." *North American Review* 237 (February 1934), 192.

*Sean O'Casey. "Notes on the Way." *Time and Tide* 15 (10 February 1934), 168.

*Ashley Sampson. "In Pursuit of Psyche." *Saturday Review* 157 (17 February 1934), 190.

*Rayner Heppenstall. *Adelphi* 7 (March 1934), 460–62.

*Christopher V. Salmon. "Critics and Criticism." *Nineteenth Century* 115 (March 1934), 366–68.

Clarence Gohdes. "Poetry and Criticism." *South Atlantic Quarterly* 33 (April 1934), 205–07.

James Southall Wilson. "The Faculty of Poets." *Virginia Quarterly Review* 10 (July 1934), 477–78.

Margaret C. Meagher. *Catholic World* 140 (January 1935), 498–99.

A. E. Dodds. *Modern Language Notes* 51 (January 1936), 49–52.

AFTER STRANGE GODS:
A PRIMER OF MODERN HERESY
1934

After Strange Gods

A PRIMER OF MODERN HERESY

BY

T. S. ELIOT

THE PAGE-BARBOUR LECTURES
AT
THE UNIVERSITY OF VIRGINIA
1933

———

καὶ ταῦτ᾽ ἰὼν
εἴσω λογίζου· κἂν λάβῃς ἐψευσμένον,
φάσκειν ἔμ᾽ ἤδη μαντικῇ μηδὲν φρονεῖν.
—*Œdipus Rex*: l. 460-462.

———

HARCOURT, BRACE AND COMPANY

NEW YORK

R. P. Blackmur. "The Dangers of Authorship." *Hound and Horn* 7 (1934), 719–26.

Mr. Cowley [in *Exile's Return*] and Mr. Eliot [in *After Strange Gods*] are looking—but neither together nor in the same direction—for a living standard of approach to literature. Neither, in the books before us, is primarily a literary critic—as indeed their subtitles attest; neither attacks his problem from within the field of literature as an art that finds autonomy in its practice, and neither fortifies himself in any logic of aesthetics. Each, rather, regards literature as it interprets life rightly or wrongly, with reference to a general, complete view of life as distinguished from the free, uncontrolled, merely literary view. Each deeply realizes that literature does not ever in fact—at least in the degree that it is serious—escape into thin air without first influencing the moral and spiritual life of its readers; and each therefore requires that literature assent, for its own salvation, or at least to secure its best possibilities, to a definite intellectual and spiritual discipline. Mr. Eliot asserts the discipline of Christian orthodoxy and provides examples of the evils that result from ignoring it. Mr. Cowley suggests a discipline that rises from an honest recognition of the class-struggle and all its implications in economic and political life; and he provides us with a comparative history of recent literary futility as it resulted from a distorted emphasis upon the individual. It should be observed that neither Mr. Eliot nor Mr. Cowley is an absolutist; both allow for great art outside the fold, but not the greatest.

Here they have each a cause to serve; each wishes to correct the living author from the dangers of the unguided pursuit of his profession; they want to save him from confusion, from irrelevance, from dishonesty, and from the corruption of moral or social diabolism. Nobler, and rasher, intentions could not be conceived; their object is to solve the dilemma of those who lack convictions and faith but who feel increasingly the urgency of both. The rashness consists in what I take to be the tacit assumption of both men that any particular frame of faith, political, moral, or religious, can fit any large body of men at any one time, or even, what is more important, the abler minds among it. That is the risk the apologist must always take and upon which he is eventually defeated; his success lies elsewhere and in the interim, while men deceive themselves that the dogma in question is flexible, plastic, hierarchic, and universal.

Let us examine first the idea of Christian orthodoxy that Mr. Eliot brings forward. Here there is no proffered gambit. Mr. Eliot (I think because of the magic element which inheres in orthodoxy) assumes we are already initiate. He finds it necessary to presuppose that we know a good deal about Christianity and are able to distinguish roughly what in our experience, in our prejudices and prepared attitudes, is Christian in origin or direction and what is not; and this regardless of the presence or absence of specific faith; when the plain fact is that most of us—and I include atheists, Jews, and the multitude of the indifferent—merely have something of Christianity in our blood and no more know what it is than we do the fear and the animal hope which are also there. Other generations may have differed, may have possessed a general, pervasive sense of Christianity in which every sentiment and every event of the mind found its orderly—or its disorderly—place; our own generation I think has only analytic and separated notions, and therefore, since faith is whole or nothing, can only draw back cheated of understanding at what I take to be the critical sentence of the book:

> What I have been leading up to is the following assertion: that when morals cease to be a matter of tradition and orthodoxy—that is, of the habits of the community formulated, corrected, and elevated by the continuous thought and direction of the Church—and when each man is to elaborate his own, then *personality* becomes a thing of alarming importance.

That the Church is catholic, not Roman Catholic but the Church of England, and hence to a large part of the Christian world seems schismatic and heretical and to another part seems something worse, formalistic and idolatrous, and that in any case the same Church is known in America under the style of Protestant Episcopal—these considerations only contribute to the confusion with which the outsider must greet the word. We simply do not know what is meant by the Church in the crucial sense in which Mr. Eliot refers to it.

Two further sentences will specify the difficulty. "It should hardly be necessary to add that the 'classical' is just as unpredictable as the romantic, and that most of us would not recognise a classical writer if he appeared, so queer and horrifying he would seem even to those who clamour for him." Mr. Eliot has previously suggested, with the peculiar emphasis of understatement characteristic of his method, that there is an analogue between the orthodox and the classical, the heretical and the romantic; and I wish here tentatively to substitute the theological terms for the literary in Mr. Eliot's sentence. We would not know an orthodox writer if he appeared, nor, I think, could the writer know himself to be orthodox. The second sentence is Mr. Eliot's statement concerning the rift some critics have observed between his poetry and his essays. "I should say that in one's prose reflexions one may be legitimately occupied with ideals, whereas in the writing of verse one can deal only with actuality." The sentiment is admirable and as an antithesis it helps explain Mr. Eliot's verse, which indeed constantly requires explanation; but it seems, to an outsider, the opposite of the orthodox position. As orthodoxy it is at least startling and requires a development Mr. Eliot does not give it before it can be digested under the "continuous thought and direction of the Church."

[. . .]

The major predicament in which Mr. Eliot leaves us is this. With a seductive vigor of speech and a persuasive air of authority he sets up for our use in evaluating literature the criterion of an orthodox Christianity which the greater part of us have lost, surrendered, or denied—if indeed we ever had it. He then reminds us that all men are naturally impure, that most writers, even the most orthodox, are somewhat heretical, and that orthodoxy, which is a consensus of the living and the dead, unlike tradition exists whether there be any who know it or not. He further implies that in his own case orthodoxy appears in his verse only through the irony that its ideal form is absent. The predicament would hardly be worth formulating and we could safely leave Mr. Eliot to his private adventure, were it not that this very ineluctable orthodoxy again and again brings its apologist to the point of keen judgment and profound feeling. It is something to be able to judge for oneself of the good and evil in life and its mirror art, and it is a great deal to be able to affirm that judgment persuasively over others; and if it is the "continuous thought and direction of the Church" that has given Mr. Eliot his access of critical strength we must respect the mystery to which we cannot assent.

But it may be there is another explanation, which the outsider, in his own interest, cannot help suggesting. Perhaps it is not the orthodoxy witnessed by the Church which imbues Mr. Eliot's critical blood, so that his Christianity, as such, only lends a color of terminology to his thought without affecting its substance, as when he criticizes the sentimental melodrama of Thomas Hardy under the head of diabolism. As Mr. Eliot once observed in speaking of Wordsworth, "the difference between revolution and reaction may be by the breadth of a hair"; and the difference between the orthodoxy of Mr. Eliot's criticism and that of his Church may be even finer, and equally profound, by the mere split of a hair. He uses, or at least we may recognize in him when he avoids theology and handles the literature before him, an orthodoxy which flows merely on the application of the whole intelligence. His judgments of Yeats and Pound and Hopkins, Joyce and Mansfield and Lawrence, have a merit and a utility upon which the conviction of the Church only intrudes. The criteria he actually applies are not canonical; he measures his men rather by the degree of their honesty and the depth of their sensibility.

Mr. Eliot would deny this explanation and find its purview blind. "I doubt," he observes during his discussion of diabolism, "whether what I am saying can convey very much to anyone for whom the doctrine of Original Sin is not a very real and tremendous thing." Mr. Eliot may be right and if so it represents a grave loss for him as well as for ourselves. In other words, by insisting on his terms and

retreating upon his Church he limits our understanding of him and deforms his own approach. Mr. Eliot may be right, too, of course, in another sense: he may be speaking inspired and literal truth. But we can neither act upon nor controvert matters where there is no fundamental agreement. Few men have a capacity for religion, fewer still can find it animate in the arms of the Church; and this though all equally be saved or damned; these few must walk alone, or suffer the terrible punishment of being followed by the empty, the vain, and the foolish. But why should we put aside a man who can distinguish the peculiarity of great poetry as "merely a peculiar honesty, which, in a world too frightened to be honest, is peculiarly terrifying"; who can remark that "morals for the saint are only a preliminary matter; for the poet a secondary matter"; and who can describe thus the essential advantage for a poet: "it is to be able to see beneath both beauty and ugliness; to see the boredom, the horror, and the glory." Certainly not because he and a few others nourish their intelligence upon a Church which stultifies so many. Only, as we admire him, we cannot follow him.

[. . .]

---

*Christopher Dawson. "Mr. Eliot's Heresy Hunt." *Listener* 11 (7 March 1934), supplement, xi.

In the three lectures, delivered appropriately enough at the University of Virginia, Mr. T. S. Eliot comes forward as the defender of orthodoxy and tradition against the heresies of the modern man of letters: not his literary heresies, be it understood, but that lack of objective moral or spiritual standards which causes literature to transgress its proper limits and to become confused with religion or philosophy. The result of this state of things is that every successful man of letters tends to become the prophet or Messiah of the moment and imposes his personal view of life on his readers as a new gospel. And since his prestige rests on nothing but his personality and his literary powers, it is essentially fugitive and temporary and is entirely dependent on the changing tastes of the public. This situation is an uncomfortable one even for the favorite of the moment, and that is why our literary prophets are prophets of revolt against the existing order and why, like D. H. Lawrence, they struggle so desperately to escape from their own personalities and to achieve some contact with the powers that lie beneath the surface of life.

Unfortunately, as Mr. Eliot points out, these powers are not necessarily benign ones, and the free personality, released from the bonds of social tradition and moral obligation, is in danger of becoming the servant of dark and sinister forces. Hence, in Mr. Eliot's view, the vital need of our time is "to concentrate, not to dissipate, to renew our association with the traditional wisdom, to re-establish a vital connection between the individual and the race." Here he is at one with Irving Babbitt and the American humanists and with Charles Maurras and the French traditionalists. But he admits that traditionalism and humanism are not enough. They must be reinforced by orthodoxy, that is to say by the strenuous adhesion of the individual mind and will to the truths that are absolute and eternal. It is the loss of this conception—a loss which he illustrates by a characteristic passage from Professor Macmurray's *Philosophy of Communism*—which is the cause

both of the weakness and sentimentality of sheer traditionalism and of the anarchy and spiritual perversion of modernism.

These defects are, strictly speaking, religious defects, and the weakness of modern literature is a religious weakness. "The chief clue to the understanding of most contemporary Anglo-Saxon literature is to be found in the decay of Protestantism." That is to say, it is the result of the reaction from a religious tradition that had itself originated in a revolt and which had become progressively narrower and more impoverished. The attitude of such different men as Irving Babbitt and D. H. Lawrence towards Christianity was perhaps determined by the fact that they knew that religion only in a debased and uncultured form, and that is why each in his own way went "after strange gods," the one to the remote ethical idealism of Confucius and the other further still to the barbarism of ancient Mexico—to gods as dark and bloodthirsty as those of which the Hebrew prophet wrote. Thus the revolt against tradition and orthodoxy does not bring man spiritual freedom. It merely deprives him of chart and rudder and compass and leaves him adrift in an unknown sea at the mercy of every wind that blows.

---

*Ezra Pound. "Mr. Eliot's Mare's Nest." *New English Weekly* 4 (8 March 1934), 500.

Mr. Eliot's thesis, nowhere so clearly expressed in his text as in the jacket-announcement, is that: "The weakness of modern literature, indicative of the weakness of the modern world in general, is a religious weakness, and that all our social problems, including those of literature and criticism, begin and end in a religious problem."

As there is muddle and confusion even in this statement, one is not surprised that a verbatim reprint of lectures gives no solid ground for argument.

In the first place the main idea is neither true nor expressed with sufficient precision.

The fact is that "religion" long since resigned. Religion in the person of its greatest organized European institution resigned. The average man now thinks of religion either as a left-over or an irrelevance.

In the "Ages of Faith," meaning the Ages of Christian faith, religion in the person of the Church concerned itself with ethics. It concerned itself specifically with economic discrimination.

It concerned itself with a root dissociation of two ideas which the last filthy centuries have, to their damnation, lost.

In Dante's intellectual world certain financial activities are "against nature"; they are damned with sodomy. The Church was not abrogating her claim to judge between good and evil along one of the most vital and intimate lines of social relation.

Creative investment, productive exchange, sharing the profits of shared risk, were considered good. Destructive parasitism was forbidden. I am not arguing, I am stating historical fact. I am not saying that the detailed regulations of mediaeval business can to advantage be resurrected in the identical forms. I am not making a plea to return to the past.

I am asserting a known and established fact: when religion was real the church concerned itself with vital phenomena in ECONOMICS.

This is, perhaps, NOT the place to give the history of Protestant revolt, Leo X's desire for taxes, etc. In any case they fall outside a review of Mr. Eliot's brochure, which does not even concern itself with the history or the dogma he mentions (or asserts to be a personal reality to himself).

The weakness he is gunning for is NOT a *religious* weakness *in something else*, but an ethical weakness *in* organized Christianity. The sacerdos has been superseded by the (often subsidized) ecclesiastical bureaucrat.

This decline was not unexpected and the Middle Ages are full of propaganda and warning against this particular danger.

The battle was won by greed. The language of religion became imprecise, just as the language of all forms of modern flim flam, including popular and philological lectures, has become imprecise.

Mr. Eliot, in a moment of inattention, has interpreted part of his bargain with the Virginia institution literally. He was asked to lecture, and then apparently found he was expected to publish what he had said verbatim, or at least he so construed his contract, and as a result the pages of this book probably say both more or less *sic* than he means, and in any case are full of lacunae.

It is highly confusing to find half way through the book that what he means by "orthodoxy" is merely the extension of literary subject matter to certain ranges of human consciousness that inferior writers now neglect as have inferior writers in other times.

---

*"After Strange Gods." Life and Letters and the London Mercury and Bookman 10 (April 1934), 111–13.

There is a curious note of despair in Mr. T. S. Eliot's three lectures to the University of Virginia, which he has published with the subtitle of *A Primer of Modern Heresy*. It is as though he had become suddenly aware of isolation, of the degree of stubbornness with which his former followers were determined to prefer the chance manna of the waste land to any grape harvests from Canaan—"in our time, controversy seems to me, on really fundamental matters, to be futile."

A curious note, because the overwhelming importance of Mr. Eliot as a moralist, arises from the fact that he does not stand alone, that he has a Church behind him. Compared with that authority his kinship with his great American predecessors, Henry Adams and Henry James, is a small thing, though it may appeal to those who are readier to accept the dogmas of a critic than of a Church. These three writers have examined the decay of the religious tradition in the modern world with an equal integrity, but Mr. Eliot has been enabled to proceed further than his predecessors by not remaining outside the Church.

Henry Adams saw clearly enough: "Of all the conditions of his youth which afterwards puzzled the grown-up man, this disappearance of religion puzzled him most," but the sight helped him to nothing better than a peculiarly hopeless historical theory. Henry James reacted in the same direction as Mr. Eliot: "We had all the fun of licence, while the truth seemed really to be that fun in the religious connection closely depended upon bondage"; but he stopped short where Roland Mallet in *Roderick Hudson* stopped short, with the wonder "whether it be that one tacitly concedes to the Roman Church the monopoly of guarantee of immortality, so that if one is indisposed to bargain with her for the precious gift one must do without it altogether." It remained for Mr. Eliot to be explicit over the remedy:

The World is trying the experiment of attempting to form a civilized but non-Christian mentality. The experiment will fail; but we must be very patient in awaiting its collapse; meanwhile redeeming the time: so that the Faith may be preserved alive through the dark ages before us; to renew and rebuild civilization, and save the World from suicide. ("Thoughts After Lambeth," *Selected Essays*).

The three lectures in *After Strange Gods* are very short; indeed they are too short for Mr. Eliot to approach his subject, the effect on literature of this decay of religious tradition, with due caution. The very perfection of his critical prose (and we must go back to Dryden to find a style so exactly ordered and free from extraneous ornament) throws into relief the startling orthodoxy of his criticism: his discussion of heresy and diabolical influence in contemporary literature.

I am afraid that even if you can entertain the notion of a positive power for evil working through human agency, you may still have a very inaccurate notion of what Evil is, and will find it difficult to believe that it may operate through men of genius of the most excellent character. I doubt whether what I am saying can convey very much to anyone for whom the doctrine of Original Sin is not a very real and tremendous thing.

His first two lectures are little more than introductions to this theme. In his first he defines his use of the term tradition: "all those habitual actions, habits and customs, from the most significant religious rite to our conventional way of greeting a stranger, which represent the blood kinship of 'the same people living in the same place.'" Unity of religious background is needed for the proper development of a tradition, and to preserve what is valuable in tradition, to make it a dynamic and not a static way of life, he postulates continuous criticism under the supervision of orthodoxy, orthodoxy being a matter of the conscious intelligence, while tradition is a way of "feeling and acting." In his second lecture he deals with the crippling effect upon men of letters of not having been brought up in the environment of a living and central tradition, examining for this purpose the poetry of Mr. Yeats and Mr. Pound, and short stories by D. H. Lawrence and Katherine Mansfield. But it is when Mr. Eliot reaches in his last lecture the subject of diabolical influence, of the operations of the Evil Spirit, that one is aware among his audience of a shocked agnosticism. Mr. Eliot has never made any secret of his Faith. To be a Catholic (in Mr. Eliot's case an Anglo-Catholic) is to believe in the Devil, and why, if the Devil exists, he should not work through contemporary literature, it is hard to understand. It may be objected (with doubtful truth) that this is not aesthetic criticism, but Mr. Eliot writes, "I am uncertain of my ability to criticize my contemporaries as artists; I ascended the platform of these lectures only in the role of moralist." Moral criticism indeed, if one accepts the truth of Christianity at all, is of far greater importance than literary criticism, which is concerned only with refining the intellectual pleasures, while moral criticism is concerned with the saving of souls.

That statement is not likely to appeal to a large proportion of those concerned with literature; an appeal to humanitarianism, to the salvation of the body, will win more support. And that appeal is implicit too in Mr. Eliot's criticism of such writers as Lawrence who claim an Inner Light, who waken men to spiritual experience and then cram them with some religious concoction of their own making. "Most people are only very little alive; and to awaken them to the spiritual is a very great responsibility: it is only when they are so awakened that they are capable of real Good, but that at the same time they become first capable of Evil." It is too early to see the result of Lawrence's hysterical religious beliefs on his followers, and Mr. Eliot might have reinforced his case with the example of Laurence Oliphant, an earlier writer of talent, whose trust in the Inner Light broke up two lives and led to one suicide. Humanitarians are more nearly touched by a death than a damnation.

The elaboration of an individual morality, in place of a moral order directed and modified by a Church, the expression, in Mr. Eliot's phrase, of "seductive personalities," cannot be excused by sensibility of style. The greater the writer the more dangerous his uncontrolled personality becomes. Mr. Eliot has here dealt with two writers only, Lawrence and Hardy. To them might be added a poet who has perhaps passed the dangerous peak of his popularity, Mr. A. E. Housman, with his Roman morality and his cult of suicide and despair. But if these are cases of diabolic influence, the curious thing is that the devil is after all not given the best tunes. It is in Hardy's rather absurd short stories, in Lawrence's tedious cult of dark gods, in Mr. Housman's crude adjurations to "be a man stand up and end you," that we trace the expression of the unregenerate personality. Lawrence's lovely "Ship of Death," Hardy's "Surview" (to take one of a score of examples), the penultimate poem of Mr. Housman's *Last Poems* might all have been written under the supervision of the strictest orthodoxy. The unregenerate personality, "the hot breath and the roused passion" of James's story, "The Jolly Corner," is in James's phrase blatant, vulgar, and Mr. Eliot is not strictly orthodox when he writes in a criticism of Mr. Pound's *A Draft of XXX Cantos*: "a Hell altogether without dignity implies a Heaven without dignity also." The unregenerate personality, checked by no outside order and free from any but self-criticism, *is* without dignity and works, as in Marlowe's tragedies, with squibs and firecrackers. This Saving Grace (that once marked Cain's brow) almost eliminates the distinction between morals and aesthetics and makes it unnecessary for Mr. Eliot to disclaim in these lectures the role of literary critic.

---

*Montgomery Belgion. *Dublin Review* 194 (April 1934), 320–24.

[*After Strange Gods*] by Mr. Eliot contains the three lectures he delivered last spring at the University of Virginia. Their subject is of special interest to contemporary men and women in general and to Catholics in particular. It may be recollected that in a note at the beginning of *For Lancelot Andrewes* (1928) Mr. Eliot announced his intention of writing three further books, one of which was to be about heresy in our time. *After Strange Gods* is what he now offers as that book. I cannot help fearing that his most eager and discriminating readers will be disappointed.

In the first place, the volume is much too small for what is attempted in it. [. . .] [O]ne does not see why in this small space Mr. Eliot should so frequently pass by what he leads one to expect he will say. For instance, he begins by stating that he wishes to outline the subject of his essay, written fifteen years ago, "Tradition and the Individual Talent," as he now

conceives it. In passing, he remarks that in that essay are "some unsatisfactory phrasing and at least one more than doubtful analogy." One naturally looks for a reparation of these avowed blemishes. But in vain. And this trick of promising and not fulfilling he goes on to repeat. It seems to me at once a discourtesy to the reader and a failure in literary technique.

Then, in the second and main lecture, Mr. Eliot provides some notes on D. H. Lawrence, Irving Babbitt, Ezra Pound, W. B. Yeats, and Gerard Manley Hopkins. It will be admitted that what he says is often very good.

I have (he remarks) the highest respect for the Chinese mind and for Chinese civilisation; and I am willing to believe that Chinese civilisation at its highest has graces and excellences which may make Europe seem crude. But I do not believe that I, for one, could ever come to understand it well enough to make Confucius a mainstay.

He then recalls his own experience during two years devoted to the study of Sanskrit and a year "in the mazes of Patanjali's metaphysics," and concludes that his "only hope of really penetrating to the heart of that mystery would lie in forgetting how to think and feel as an American or a European." The point is, I think, important. [. . .] His central argument is that these writers—though Hopkins less than the others—have deliberately given rein to their "individuality," cultivating their differences from others, and that this is disastrous. Yet he relates the standpoints they have adopted to the decay of Protestantism. It does not seem to me that the writers in question have been as "individual" as he contends. I feel that they have in their way followed a tradition, only it is not the tradition Mr. Eliot relies on himself. And I think that in order to be fair to them and illuminating to his reader, Mr. Eliot should have considered them to some extent historically.

Furthermore, as he proceeds, Mr. Eliot comes to speak categorically of certain writers' "aberrations." This would be permissible in a Catholic, for everyone would be aware of the standpoint from which he spoke. But Mr. Eliot is not only not a Catholic, he expressly repudiates a purely religious attitude. He thus appears to exhibit some lack of charity. This is the more deplorable in that he is not always on firm ground. He speaks, for example, of George Eliot as a serious but eccentric moralist. The interesting thing about George Eliot, however, is that in professing, not, as Mr. Eliot says, her "individualistic morals," but the morals of Comte as apprehended through George Henry Lewes, she succeeded in being profoundly orthodox.

Finally, in the third lecture, Mr. Eliot has a shot at considering "the intrusion of the *diabolic* into modern literature." His examples are from the prose of D. H. Lawrence and Thomas Hardy. I have not read Hardy's story, "Barbara of the House of Grebe," but I gather that he detects diabolism in it because it is a story of cruelty. And so apparently is another specimen, Lawrence's "The Shadow in the Rose Garden." This notion of the diabolic strikes me as naive.

[. . .]

*Jack Common. *Adelphi* 8 (April 1934), 68–70.

Mr. Eliot seems unable to write nowadays except in mittens. He has got into a finicking habit of adjusting the aspidistras and making remarks over his shoulder all the time a question is being discussed. The general effect is that Auntie Eliot knows best, but she's too sly to be tempted on to the carpet. Here we have him compiling a primer of modern heresy, a far as it can be done in a few lectures. He is concerned to "develop a more critical spirit, or rather to apply to authors critical standards which are almost in desuetude." You can see at once the opportunity this enterprise offers for aspidistra-fiddling and remarks about the people next door. Call yourself orthodox in a country without an orthodoxy and you have all the advantages of the heretic without the onus of seriously explaining or seriously defending your position. You can be smoothly ironical about the leading figures of the contemporary literature of your country, but your irony is essentially flippant. When Chesterton spotted the advantage of this position, we applauded his perversity. Eliot also interests us as a Protestant heretic, and the role he is compelled to play on pain of losing our attention.

But the many heresies which accompany the decay of Protestantism and the collapse of its material basis, Capitalism, tend to collect under two main headings as time goes on. It begins to be seen that every Protestant or bourgeois heresy, however ingeniously devised, leads to one or other of two positions. These two positions used to appear in Eliot's pages under the terms Classicism or Romanticism. In this book he prefers to use Tradition or Orthodoxy *versus* Heterodoxy and Heresy. A change of wool, perhaps, but still mittens. Probably the plain bare fists of the matter is Reaction *versus* Revolution, and to those words Eliot would come if his creed ceased to be an intellectual freak flourishing on the decay of Protestantism, and became a vital matter for him and us. If they seem to smack too much of politics and need some stretching to fit the multiplicity of problems this sadly fissured world gives birth to, at least they belong to the street, to the ordinary man's vocabulary. Say "revolution," and most people have an approximate notion what you're after, but "heresy" means damn-all, or near it, except in fairly intimate gatherings such as, for instance, Marxist study-groups.

Conceived in these terms Eliot's primer would awake into denunciatory thunder. He would not say of revolutionaries, as he can of heretics: they have "an insight more important often than the inferences of those who are aware of more but less acutely aware of anything." This dilettante contemplation of the weeds corresponds to no real principle of good gardening. There must be a certain fervor in a man who proposes to enlighten us on what is our damnation. No fervor here.

There are, however, some good remarks. "The most ethically orthodox of the more eminent writers of my time is Mr. Joyce." "His work is penetrated with Christian feeling." One is reminded of these wise-cracks in reading Mr. Budgen's account of his friendship with Joyce. One night as Joyce was coming away from a performance of the St. Matthew Passion, he said of Bach, "I simply cannot understand how any man can mix the synoptic gospels with the gospel according to St. John." Eliot is right about Joyce, in a calamitous fashion. There is probably no writer of these times who is more conspicuously crucified on the cross of Christian dualism. No fear of him making the mistake of so many of our artists, and also Mr. Joad, who go "back to Bach" because his music has form and authority. Joyce knows at once that what we find attractive in Bach in his manifest faith, the man believed

in God, though not in the God of the Jesuits Joyce is occupied in unsuccessfully denying.

[. . .]

William Troy. "T. S. Eliot, Grand Inquisitor." *Nation* 138 (25 April 1934), 478–79.

In a curious preface in which he seems to apologize for putting these three lectures into print at all, Mr. Eliot announces that he has no desire to preach (this is the word he uses) to those whose views are fundamentally opposed to his own. Controversy, in our time at least, he believes to be entirely futile: there are not enough common assumptions, and the most important assumptions are, in any case, those that are felt rather then those that can be formulated. This should be properly discouraging to most readers—to all, in fact, except those whom Mr. Eliot designates as the "possibly convertible." It should probably serve as a sufficient warning to all others to absent themselves from Mr. Eliot's services, to leave him at peace among his candlesticks and prayer books. But there is a certain note of challenging arrogance in this reasoning. It consists not so much in the implication that the assumptions Mr. Eliot is going to make are the only right ones as in the implication that these assumptions are necessarily peculiar to the particular point of view which Mr. Eliot has expressed in all his recent criticism. The most fundamental of these assumptions is of course the importance for criticism, the primacy over all other kinds of problems, of the moral problem—"the conflict between Good and Evil." And in his preface to the present collection Mr. Eliot warns us quite fairly that it is once again in the role of moralist that he ascends the platform; the subtitle of his book is *A Primer of Modern Heresy*. He is perfectly right, therefore, in insisting that all those not interested in his subject should withdraw from the congregation. But it does not follow that anyone interested in morality in general, or in the particular question of the relations between morality and modern literature, should pay him the same courtesy. Morality is one of the broadest of the many broad terms that we are in the habit of using in criticism; and it is the right, indeed the duty, of anyone genuinely concerned about modern literature to examine a little into the application of the term that Mr. Eliot makes in his collection.

Tradition is again Mr. Eliot's principal subject in these lectures—that view of tradition which is the fruit of the grotesque misalliance in France at the beginning of the present century between American pragmatism and ultra-montane Catholicism. As a view of society and culture requiring a fundamental religious emotion at its base to give it any true validity for this or any time, it reveals its weakness through the inappropriate ardor with which it is usually expressed—an ardor that is much more distinctly of the mind than of the heart. Like his masters, Charles Maurras and Jacques Maritain, Mr. Eliot makes the mistake of protesting quite a little too much; his logic is much too fluent; and in such a passage as the following what we hear are the accents of a man trying hard to convince himself of something rather than those of a man who is completely—that is, emotionally as well as intellectually— persuaded of what he is talking about.

What we can do is to use our minds, remembering that a tradition without intelligence is not worth having, to discover what is the best life for us, not as a political abstraction, but as a particular people in a particular place; what in the past is worth preserving and what should be rejected; and what conditions, within our power to bring about, would foster the society that we desire.

Obviously in such a statement Mr. Eliot is more concerned with expressing a desire than with recognizing a reality. His confusion is a result of failing to distinguish between what is, at the present stage in the development of Western European culture, possible and what his sensibility sets up as desirable. Mr. Eliot is a poet, and since poets not infrequently fall into such confusions, he may be understood—if not altogether pardoned. For the danger of such a confusion becomes apparent a little later on the same page when the corollary that homogeneity is necessary for tradition leads Mr. Eliot to conclude that "reasons of race and religion combine to make any large number of free-thinking Jews undesirable." Using such a remark as a basis, we need not stumble over ourselves in the effort to prove that Mr. Eliot is a fascist. Theoretically, Mr. Eliot is for royalism rather than for fascism, which are not the same thing in theory, although in actuality they may be the same thing today. What the remark illustrates is the kind of inhuman and unrealistic conclusion to which Mr. Eliot's confused and sentimental view of tradition inevitably leads the moment that he touches a particular contemporary reality.

And this brings us back to the fundamental question of morality as it enters into Mr. Eliot's inquisition of modern letters. For it is possible to discover in the confusion just pointed out, in Mr. Eliot's persistent refusal to see the modern world as it is, a wilfulness that is at least as morally reprehensible as any of the sins of the several heretic modern writers whom he singles out for rebuke. D. H. Lawrence undoubtedly suffered from being cut off from a settled religious and social tradition; his work is tainted to a marked degree with modern vices of "sincerity" and "personality." It is even possible to agree that in many cases his influence has been more harmful than good. But what still gives to his work a moral justification, what cancels whatever incidental unmoral or "diabolic" elements may be found in it, is his effort, the essentially *moral* effort, to include all of the truth as he perceived it in the vision of the modern world that he left at his death. There was in him no sacrifice of honest perception for the sake of an intellectual structure which, however appealing it may be to the dialectic faculties, no longer has sufficient feasibility for our time. A distinction that may be made, therefore, is between the morality of the writer conceived as effort—the unrelenting effort to integrate his perceptions with his beliefs, to reconcile the actual with the ideal—and the morality of the artist conceived as conformity to a systematized body of beliefs deriving from the conditions of an earlier period of religion and culture. Of these two views of morality Mr. Eliot has chosen the second; and the unfortunate consequences of his choice are revealed not only in his verse, in the progressive weakness of everything that he has written since *The Waste Land*, but in his prose, in such a frank admission as this of the separation in the same personality between the artist and the critic: "I should say that in one's prose reflections one may be legitimately occupied with ideals, whereas in the writing of verse one can only deal with actuality." In psychological terms, this amounts to nothing less than a "schizoid" state of the personality;

and since one of the objects of morality is the unification of the personality, one can only conclude that there is something profoundly wrong with Mr. Eliot's view of morality. For the poet nothing could be more useless or infertile than a system of beliefs which cannot stand up under the pressure of the actuality with which he has to deal. And in the critic who, like Mr. Eliot, is also a poet nothing could be more indefensible than this blithe acceptance of the divorce between "ideals" and "actuality." Do we not have here an example of that *unregenerate* self-deception which, as everyone knows, is one of the ways in which Mr. Eliot's favorite antagonist, the devil, works in the modern world?

Horace Gregory. "The Man of Feeling." *New Republic* 79 (16 May 1934), 23–24.

[Review of *The Use of Poetry and The Use of Criticism* and *After Strange Gods*]

"It is the general notion of 'thinking' that I would challenge . . . We talk as if thought was precise and emotion was vague. In reality there is precise emotion. . . . What every poet starts from is his own emotions." I quote the above observations from T. S. Eliot's essay on Shakespeare for several reasons: first, because they are more acute than any that appear in the two books before me; second, because I think they reveal a premise on which all of Eliot's writing is based; and third, because I am certain now more than ever before, that the popular conception of him as an "intellectual" is largely false.

Perhaps no other poet since Baudelaire has thrived so well upon critical abuse as T. S. Eliot: from the very start of his career, each step that he has taken has been followed by quick dissent on the part of friends and enemies. Among the most frequent of the charges brought against him has been the charge of excessive "intellectuality," supposedly a fatal accusation against a poet, one that condemns him as a cold-blooded monster, or still worse as an actor incapable of arousing in himself the emotions that are genuinely his own. The real trouble, I think, has always been quite the opposite. The fine instrument, discernible in his poetry as well as in his prose and so often referred to as his "mind," is in reality that rare thing called "imagination." Behind it lies a surplus rather than a lack of undefined emotion. I believe that he, more than any other single figure in our time, deserves belated recognition as the twentieth-century Man of Feeling.

Today we have his two books: *After Strange Gods*, subtitled *A Primer of Modern Heresy*, a curious document that has already performed its services as a series of lectures at the University of Virginia; and *The Use of Poetry*, the Charles Eliot Norton lectures delivered at Harvard during the winter of 1932–33. If we are to trust the introductions to both books, Eliot is not unaware that the lectures are loosely phrased and written for the ear rather than the more careful analysis of the eye. They presuppose a number of beliefs held by one who lacks the time to explain his development toward a given point. This person is in the singular position of a man who invites a tabloid reporter to his home, offers the young man a chair and then proceeds to entertain him with intimate confidences. As the interview draws to a close, and the reporter is about to leave the room,

he is warned that the "story," interesting as it may be, is not for publication and this point only remains clear: that such a revelation would be a breach of verbal contract and the lecturer would be made the victim of a cad.

Apparently we are to hear these remarks as tentative proposals toward critical convictions, but the convictions themselves are to be taken for granted or withheld from public view; we are kept in suspense waiting for a final word and perhaps the entire set of lectures is dependent upon a *single* word, or a last moment of revelation before utter darkness. The whole world—shall I say?—is to be relaxed in some suspended flux of "feeling," where the precise emotion must be defined before the act and where the thought processes must be retarded until some distant moment after the event. This is, I think, the ideal world that Eliot attempts to realize as an environment for his public appearances.

Such a world is hinted at when he says in *After Strange Gods* that one's prose reflections "may be legitimately occupied with ideals, whereas in the writing of verse one can deal only with actuality." Meanwhile, in discussing the uses of poetry there is time for wit and incidental speculation, "time yet for a hundred indecisions." In his Harvard lectures, for example, there is a shrewd commentary on the uses of "comic relief" in dramatic poetry—and on one use in particular, which may be traced back to the nature of a human audience whose need for it always "springs from a lack of the capacity for concentration." This observation is put into practice by Eliot himself in discussing Coleridge; and note here the whiplash of wit that brings the statement to a close:

> . . . he was condemned to know that the little poetry he had written was worth more than all he could do with the rest

of his life. The author of *Biographia Literaria* was already a ruined man. Sometimes, however, to be a "ruined man" is itself a vocation.

In attacking Matthew Arnold on several sides at once, and principally because of "the deplorable moral and religious effects of confusing poetry and morals in the attempt to find a substitute for religious faith," Eliot approximates a definition of the particular kind of poetry he himself has written:

> We mean all sorts of things, I know, by Beauty. But the essential advantage for a poet is not, to have a beautiful world with which to deal: it is to be able to see beneath both beauty and ugliness; to see the boredom, and the horror, and the glory.

The acceptance of this definition rests upon an emotional response to the situation that is created here by Eliot; one begins to foresee again a need for "comic relief" and again the need is quietly satisfied by his farewell to Arnold: "Perhaps, looking inward and finding how little he had to support him, looking outward on a state of society and its tendencies, he was somewhat disturbed. He had no real serenity, only an impeccable demeanour."

At this point the public Eliot emerges; we recognize the so-called "split" in Eliot's literary personality which has led him to that extraordinary coupling of "prose" with "ideals" and "poetry" with "actuality." This inconsistency, which he so freely admits, is, I think, as unreal as the ideal environment that he conceives as a setting for his lectures. The actual "split," I think, springs from another source and has little to do with the obvious difference in the states of mind that precede the writing of a poem on one occasion, and the writing of a critical essay on another. The difference

that Eliot cannot reconcile—nor will he ever, I think, bridge this gap successfully— is the real difference that exists between the poet, who from his private hell conceived "Prufrock," *The Waste Land*, *Ash-Wednesday*, and that other person who owes his very existence to the poet, a public figure. The second person, beyond the fact that he would be quite unknown but for the poet's genius, is the result of an ironic accident. He grew to full size with a reversal of the critical abuse that made "Prufrock" and *The Waste Land* notorious and he became, like those newsreels of Hemingway fishing in Florida waters, a symbol of the post-war expatriated American. What he wore and how he dressed, his politics and personal religion, became a matter of public interest. It was he who in 1928 announced himself as possessing a point of view so often recited in subsequent essays on Eliot that it is quite unnecessary for me to repeat it here.

In *After Strange Gods*, it is clear that the reception given this "summary declaration of faith" still haunts the uneasy composite of poet and public figure that Eliot has become. He now believes that the statement was "injudicious" and sees the danger of suggesting to outsiders that the Faith is a political principle or a literary fashion, and the sum of all a dramatic posture. But having once started on the road toward making his private convictions public, he finds it difficult to stop. He veers, as any Man of Feeling might, from too great reticence into intimate confidence, from the extremes of caution into serious tactlessness, until at last we hear him saying to a Southern audience: "What is still more important is unity of religious background; and reasons of race and religion combine to make any large number of free-thinking Jews undesirable."

The public figure is then revealed as an unhappy, persecuted, lonely man, an

American born in St. Louis, of New England education and heritage, who has lived as an expatriate in London for a number of post-war years and has now fallen naively into the same trap that is set for any visitor who steps upon an American lecture platform. I know of nothing so disastrous since the arrival and unregretted departure from these shores of Count Hermann von Keyserling. There seems to be something fatal in the calm worship that an American audience bestows upon its idols—a truth, an "actuality" which the poet Eliot should have perceived at once and noted with the irony that had served him so well in "Prufrock." There can be no doubt of the sincerity that prompted his remarks on heresy and orthodoxy, of his belief in the hellfires waiting for D. H. Lawrence and Ezra Pound and even strong-willed Irving Babbitt. And to this company (not without regret) he adds Confucius, John Dewey, and I. A. Richards. All, all, go down with Shelley and the rest, until the public remains of Eliot are left talking to the little band of contributors to a symposium called *I'll Take My Stand*.

All this, of course, is scarcely the result of "intellectualizing" his position, or even exerting to the best advantage his sensitive critical instrument to the times. By this I mean that the larger problems of "faith" are ignored in favor of justifying a personal situation. His private hell, his fear of being misunderstood, is all too evident. His sense of personal salvation cannot, naturally enough, gratify a demand for public action. Nor does his sense of public "right" and "wrong" condone a course of conduct that allows him the freedom to walk alone. Loneliness is therefore stripped of all its pretensions to glory and horror and martyrdom (this last was the role of Baudelaire) that he might claim as poet.

There is nothing, I think, in modern literature that exposes at such length the emotional temper of an individual dilemma as these two documents of a year's visit in America. "Feeling" and the precision of emotional expression that Eliot so frankly admires in Shakespeare is here produced in liberal measure, yet it refuses to extend toward the necessary intellectual formulation that he observes in Machiavelli and in Dante. The public figure of the poet looms too large; the *Paradiso* is all too distant and the hell too near. Will the fact that the Virginia lectures were first published in Seward Collins's *American Review* align Eliot irrevocably with our Southern Agrarians? I think not. He will again split off into a singular position where he will be heard with greater authority, but will command less influence. It will be a loneliness comparable to that which is now facing F. Scott Fitzgerald, Ernest Hemingway, and Glenway Wescott.

***

S. Ichiye Hayakawa. "Mr. Eliot's Auto da Fé." *Sewanee Review* 42 (July–September 1934), 365–71.

***

The follower of T. S. Eliot's reputation remembers the alarm and scorn with which numbers of his young disciples repudiated his leadership upon the publication of *For Lancelot Andrewes*. Mr. Eliot became overnight, as he himself pointed out with dry amusement, a lost leader, or perhaps a lost lamb. Those who had read, with excitement and enthusiasm *The Waste Land*, suddenly dug their heels into the ground, and refused to be led into the land beyond where, in the rich spiritual significance of the Christian tradition, Mr. Eliot found the fructifying principle, the abundance of "water" that our waste land lacked. Some of us, however, slower to reject a leader from whom we had learned so much, have followed patiently and loyally, and have discovered much that we needed to know by reading, more sympathetically than we could have done without his stimulation, the religious writers whom he recommended. All thoughtful Americans, nourished (or undernourished) in the dry Protestant tradition of liberals like Channing and Puritans like Edwards, owe to Mr. Eliot an enormous debt. He restored theology to us as a living subject so that, perhaps for the first time in almost a hundred years, it has become no uncommon thing for young literati here and there throughout America to discuss in perfect seriousness such subjects as Grace, Redemption, Original Sin, and Sacramentalism. Mr. Eliot lost many followers when he announced himself as anglo-catholic, but what his influence has lost in extent, it has at least partially gained in intensity.

To one who has sat unashamed at Mr. Eliot's feet for years, his latest volume is perplexing and distressing. The result of the discovery of a set of positive religious beliefs, one has always been led to imagine (even from *The Waste Land*), is a heightening of experience: the pleasurable or the admirable becomes Good, the disagreeable or the misdirected becomes Evil. [. . .] Religious belief is an intensification of life, so one had gathered from great religious writers, which replaces regret with remorse, complacency with joy, and stoicism with serenity.

It is therefore disconcerting for the ardent student of Eliot to find in this most recent book no indication of a richer spiritual life as the result of his conversion. [. . .] *After Strange Gods* [. . .], far from showing any enrichment of Mr. Eliot's life, indicates on the contrary an increasingly fastidious [. . .] disapproval of men, manners, and ideas. I would not for a moment suggest that there are not things in the modern world that ought rightly to be disapproved of; however, it is profoundly indicative of the peculiarities of Mr. Eliot's temper that he has found in Christianity a convenient platform from which to indulge his favorite pastime of deploring (to use a favorite word of his), instead of a river of life from which to irrigate and fructify his waste land. Distasteful as such an obvious line of explanation is to an admirer of Eliot, one finds difficulty in escaping the conclusion that he has inherited from his New England [. . .] background so strong a habit of disapproving that he can make no greater progress in Christianity than to advance from witch-hunting to heresy-hunting.

There is little to quarrel with in Mr. Eliot's judgments of individual authors. Of Katherine Mansfield's story "Bliss," he writes,

> We are given neither comment nor suggestion of any moral issue of good and evil, and within the setting this is quite right . . . the moral and social ramifications are outside the terms of reference. [. . .] [I]ndeed our satisfaction recognises the skill with which the author has handled perfectly the *minimum* material [. . .].

This is an excellent explanation of the peculiarly expert smallness of Katherine Mansfield's work. Professor Irving Babbitt indeed "seemed to be trying to compensate for the lack of living tradition by a herculean, but purely intellectual and individual effort," although to quarrel with his "addiction to the philosophy of

Confucius" seems unfair [. . .]. Again, Mr. Eliot is right in pointing out the "powerful and narrow post-Protestant prejudice" that "peeps out from the most unexpected places" in the work of Ezra Pound. Mr. Eliot's summary of the progress William Butler Yeats has made towards greatness, overcoming "the greatest odds," will find few dissenters. Especially brilliant is Mr. Eliot's analysis of the weakness of Hardy:

> It is only, indeed, in their emotional paroxysms that most of Hardy's characters come alive. [. . .] [I]t is a cardinal point of faith in a romantic age to believe that there is something admirable in violent emotion for its own sake, whatever the emotion or whatever its object. But it is by no means self-evident that human beings are most real when most violently excited [. . .].

"What again and again introduces a note of falsity into Hardy's novels is that he will leave nothing to nature, but will always be giving one last turn of the screw himself [. . .]." Mr. Eliot is not alone in entertaining these suspicions; and if Hardy has ever failed to arouse suspicions as to the purity of his motives himself, his admirers have done so for him. In opposing to these writers who face imperfectly the problems of life, James Joyce, as the one contemporary artist who approaches the central problem of good and evil in a "traditional" and "Christian" manner, Mr. Eliot has triumphantly demonstrated that Joyce, whatever his virtues or shortcomings, has been both acclaimed and reviled for the wrong reasons. In a real sense Joyce is central while Lawrence and Hardy are peripheral.

Mr. Eliot's literary perceptions [. . .] are extraordinarily acute, and their acuteness is sharpened by his ethical sensitivity. Tradition is, according to him, "a way of feeling or acting which characterises a group throughout generations; and . . . it must largely be, or . . . many of the elements in it must be, unconscious." Mr. Eliot, who is as richly cosmopolitan in his learning as Babbitt or Pound, has a genuinely traditional way of feeling about literature: his erudition and sensitive reading have given him [. . .] a European tradition, the lack of which has made possible the many and various heresies of the modern world which he rightly deplores. The heresies which are uttered in the name of self-expression, nationalism, romanticism, science, and society, would be impossible, if a unified "way of feeling" based upon the past experience of the race had a more lively existence. We are sadly in need of traditional men, in Mr. Eliot's sense. [. . .] Our society is, in Mr. Eliot's words, "worm-eaten with Liberalism." Mr. Eliot demonstrates, in his own literary criticism, the advantages of a traditional literary culture as a safeguard against erratic and half-formed ideas.

Unfortunately, Mr. Eliot does not come to us in these lectures as a literary critic; he writes, "I ascended the platform of these lectures only in the role of moralist." Therefore the social implications of his definition of tradition become matters of great importance in his book. It is here that Eliot reveals prejudices that distinctly mark his thought as, in some respects, "trifling and eccentric," [. . .] to use his own terms of derogation.

In order to develop tradition, Eliot maintains [. . .],

> The population should be homogenous; where two or more cultures exist in the same place they are likely either to be fiercely self-conscious or both to become adulterate. [. . .] What is still more important is unity of religious back-ground; and reasons of race

289

and religion combine to make any number of free-thinking Jews undesirable. There must be a proper balance between urban and rural, industrial and agricultural development. [. . .] [T]he concept of the nation is by no means fixed and invariable. [. . .] [L]ocal patriotism, when it represents a distinct tradition and culture, takes precedence over a more abstract national patriotism.

Mr. Eliot is here obviously talking about a very different thing from the tradition the absence of which induces the many heresies he attacks. In a passage such as the above, he is talking about local tradition [. . .]; he addresses his Southern audience and tells them they are in a good position to develop tradition. A comparatively homogeneous population, a homogeneous culture, a smaller degree of industrialization, a comparative freedom from adulterant immigration, are Southern advantages. [. . .] But is this the tradition that has enriched Mr. Eliot's own background? [. . .] Obviously not. One need not belittle the value of local tradition to point out the fact that Mr. Eliot is what he is at his best because of the enriching power, not of local, but of general European tradition. Mr. Eliot is a civilized Occidental, whose traditions derive [. . .] in important essentials, from all the cultivated Western world, from Judaism, from Greece, from Rome, from France, Italy, Germany, England, and America at their best, in all the writers, great and small that he absorbed in his extensive reading. This greater tradition Mr. Eliot shares with all the best cosmopolitan minds of Europe.

Mr. Eliot confuses, it is to be feared, the tradition he desires as a moralist with that which he represents as a literary critic. The latter form of tradition most of us assent to willingly, but the former, especially in America, is not only futile, but

distinctly hostile to "right living" and "right thinking." [. . .]

Perhaps this gives us a clue to some of the things that have disturbed us about Mr. Eliot's work even at times when we have admired him most [. . .]. Enthusiastic as we have been about his work, there are few of us who have not ground our teeth at one time or another at some of his mannerisms. He has the irritating habit of explaining at great length things that are obvious to the reasonably cultivated reader, and the accompanying habit of saying in a subordinate clause (or in a parenthesis) things that really need no further elaboration or explanation. [. . .] In *After Strange Gods*, his mannerisms have become accentuated (partly, perhaps, because the essays were lectures), and there is an amazing increase in the number of cautionary phrases such as "I do not mean that . . ." "What I really mean is that . . ." [. . .] "I am very far from asserting that . . ." [. . .] etc., etc. There is, in the sum-total of these mannerisms which always mark Mr. Eliot's prose, an unmistakable condescension, a superciliousness toward his readers.

These stylistic eccentricities, like the eccentricities of his social and moral views just examined, are trifling and personal. If they merely trespassed momentarily upon our enjoyment of his splendid literary criticism, they would cause little concern. But they go more deeply than that. The snobbery that these eccentricities reveal explains why the negative aspects of belief [. . .] are more congenial to him than the positive aspects of belief—joy and serenity and cheerful labor in the vineyards of the Lord. It is surely not without significance that "deplore" and "deprecate" are his favorite verbs. [. . .] Mr. Eliot is a great writer; for all his eccentricities, it is not without reason that everything he says and writes commands the immediate and respectful attention of the entire English-speaking world. One looks forward, therefore, to his next book with keenest interest; the general expectation is, of course, that he will grow narrower and more disapproving in tone as he grows older. But Christ has worked miracles before.

---

*F. R. Leavis.
"Mr. Eliot, Mr. Wyndham Lewis, and Lawrence."
Scrutiny 3 (September 1934), 184–91.

After Strange Gods, like the last set of printed lectures, is clearly not a book the author would choose to have written, and one is tempted to pass it by with a glance at the circumstances of production. Yet the weaknesses, the embarrassing obviousness of which is partly to be explained by those circumstances, cannot, after all, be dismissed as having no significance. Mr. Eliot is too distinguished, his preoccupations have too representative an importance, and the subtitle of the book, recalling as it does an old and notorious promise, invites us to consider their presentment here as embodying a certain maturity of reflection.

His themes are orthodoxy and tradition, and, as one would expect, he says some memorable things. Tradition, for example, he describes admirably as "the means by which the vitality of the past enriches the life of the present." And when he describes "the struggle of our time" as being "to concentrate, not to dissipate; to renew our association with traditional wisdom; to re-establish a vital connexion between the individual and the race," one again assents with pleasure. But when he goes on, "the struggle, in a word, against Liberalism," it seems an odd summary.

Mr. Eliot's stress in this book, of course, falls explicitly upon the religious needs of the age. And, with conscious inadequacy, holding on to what one is sure of, one agrees that "to re-establish a vital connexion between the individual and the race" means [. . .] reviving what it may be crude to call the religious sense—the sense that spoke in Lawrence when he said, "Thank God I am not free, any more than a rooted tree is free."

[. . .]

The relevance of this [. . .] is plain: "when morals cease to be a matter of tradition and orthodoxy—that is, of the habits of the community formulated, corrected, and elevated by the continuous thought and direction of the Church—and when each man is to elaborate his own, then *personality* becomes a thing of alarming importance." Mr. Eliot has no need to talk hesitantly about the "need for a religious sense"; he adheres to a religion, and can point to his Church and recite its dogmas.

Nevertheless, those of us who find no such approach to tradition and orthodoxy possible can only cultivate the sense of health they have. "The number of people in possession of any criteria for distinguishing between good and evil," writes Mr. Eliot, "is very small." As we watch his in use, we can only test them by reference to our own surest perceptions, our own modest stable grounds of discrimination. When, for instance, he says that he is "applying moral principles" to literature, we cannot accept those principles as *alternatives* to the criteria we know. "What we can try to do," he says, "is to develop a more critical spirit, or rather to apply to authors critical standards that are almost in desuetude." [. . .] To put it another way: moral or religious criticism cannot be a substitute for literary criticism, it is only by being a literary critic that Mr. Eliot can apply his recovered standards to literature.

It is only by demonstrating convincingly that his application of moral principles leads to a more adequate criticism that he can effect the kind of persuasion that is his aim. In these lectures, if he demonstrates anything, it is the opposite: one can only report that the criticism seems painfully bad—disablingly inadequate, often irrelevant and sometimes disingenuous.

And it has, more generally, to be said that since the religious preoccupation has become insistent in them, Mr. Eliot's critical writings have been notable for showing less discipline of thought and emotion, less purity of interest, less power of sustained devotion, and less courage than before. All this must be so obvious to those who read him (except to the conventional and academic who, having reviled him, now acclaim him) that there is no need to illustrate—the only difficulties in doing so would be to select and to stop. [. . .]

These comments one makes, in all humility, as essential to the issue: they are to enforce the point of saying that it is not as a substitute or an alternative that what Mr. Eliot nowadays offers us could recommend itself, but only as a completion [. . .]. One may at any rate venture that health—even religious health—demands a more active concern for other things than formal religion than Mr. Eliot now shows or encourages. Indeed, it seems reasonable to restate in terms of Mr. Eliot's situation his expressions of fear regarding Lawrence, fear that Lawrence's work "will appeal not to what remains of health in them ['the sick and debile and confused'], but to their sickness."

There is hardly any need to be more explicit: it must be plain why for those preoccupied with orthodoxy, order, and traditional forms, Lawrence should be especially a test. [. . .] What one demands is a truly critical attitude—a serious attempt to discriminate and evaluate after an honest and complete exposure to Lawrence. Mr. Eliot has in the past made me indignant by endorsing, of all things, Mr. Middleton Murry's *Son of Woman* while at the same time admitting to a very imperfect acquaintance with Lawrence's work. *After Strange Gods* exhibits something much more like a critical attitude: there has obviously been a serious attempt to understand in spite of antipathy.

> It is characteristic of the more interesting heretics, in the context in which I use the term, that they have an exceptionally acute perception, or profound insight, of some part of the truth: an insight more important often than the inferences of those who are aware of more but less acutely aware of anything. So far as we are able to redress the balance, effect the compensation, ourselves, we may find such authors of the greatest value.

This is not explicitly said of Lawrence; but it suggests fairly Mr. Eliot's implied estimate of him: he is spoken of with respect, as (what he obviously is) "a very much greater genius" than Hardy, and there is "a very great deal to be learned" from him. We are decidedly far away from the imagined "frightful consequences" of Lawrence the don at Cambridge, "rotten and rotting others." It would, indeed, have been ungracious to recall this unhappy past if Mr. Eliot's attitude now had been consistently or in general effect critical, to be agreed or disagreed with. But it is not; its main significance still lies in its being so largely and revealingly uncritical—and so equivocally so.

> The first [aspect of Lawrence] is the ridiculous: his lack of sense of humour, a certain snobbery, a lack not so much of information as of the critical faculties which education should give, and an incapacity for what we ordinarily

call thinking. Of this side of Lawrence, the brilliant exposure by Mr. Wyndham Lewis in *Paleface* is by far the most conclusive criticism that has been made.

The charge of snobbery [. . .] may be passed by; what damage it does is so obviously not to the object. But why, one asks, this invocation of Mr. Wyndham Lewis? With all his undeniable talent, is he qualified to "expose" any side of Lawrence? No one who can read will acclaim Lawrence as a philosopher, but "incapacity for what we ordinarily call thinking"—does not this apply far more to Mr. Wyndham Lewis than to Lawrence? Mr. Lewis stands, in a paradoxically high-pitched and excited way, for common sense; he offers us, at the common sense level, perceptions of an uncommon intensity, and he is capable of making "brilliant" connections. But "what we ordinarily call thinking" is just what he is incapable of [. . .].

When we look up Mr. Wyndham Lewis's "brilliant exposure" of Lawrence in *Paleface*, we discover that it is an "exposure" of Lawrence and Mr. Sherwood Anderson together. Now the primitivistic illusion that Mr. Wyndham Lewis rightly attacks was indeed something that Lawrence was liable to (and could diagnose). Just how far, in any critical estimate, the stress may be fairly laid there is a matter for critical difference. But that Lawrence's importance is not anything that can be illuminated by assimilating him, or any side of him, to Mr. Sherwood Anderson is plain on Mr. Eliot's own showing: "Lawrence lived all his life, I should imagine, on the spiritual level: no man was less a sensualist. Against the living death of modern material civilisation he spoke again and again, and even if these dead could speak, what he said is unanswerable." If Lawrence was this, how comes Mr. Eliot to be using Mr. Wyndham Lewis against him?—Mr. Wyndham

Lewis, who, though he may stand for Intelligence, is as completely without any religious sense, as unqualified to discriminate between the profound insight and the superficial romantic illusion, as anyone who could have been hit on. His remarkable satiric gift is frustrated by an unrestrained egotism, and Mr. Eliot might have placed him along with Mr. Pound among those whose Hells are for other people: no one could with less injustice be said to be destitute of humility.

[. . .]

[The] curious sleight by which Mr. Eliot surreptitiously takes away while giving, is what I mean by the revealingly uncritical in his attitude towards Lawrence. It is as if there were something he cannot bring himself to contemplate fairly. And the index obtruded in that over-insistence on Lawrence's "sexual morbidity" refuses to be ignored. It is an odd insistence in one whose own attitudes with reference to sex have been, in prose and poetry, almost uniformly negative—attitudes of distaste, disgust, and rejection. (Mr. Wyndham Lewis's treatment of sex, it is worth noting, is hard-boiled, cynical, and external.) The preoccupation with sex in Lawrence's work is, no doubt, excessive by any standard of health, and no doubt psychologists [. . .] can elicit abnormalities. But who can question his own account of the preoccupation?—"I always labour at the same thing, to make the sex relation valid and precious, not shameful." And who can question that something as different as this from Mr. Eliot's bent in the matter is necessary if the struggle "to re-establish a vital connexion between the individual and the race" is to mean anything?

[. . .]

Mr. Eliot complains of a lack of moral struggle in Lawrence's novels [. . .]. No one will suggest that in Lawrence we have all we need of moral concern, but, as *After Strange Gods* reminds us, a preoccupation with discipline—the effort towards orthodoxy—also has its disabilities and dangers. These are manifest in the obvious and significant failures in touch and tone. It may be prejudice that makes one find something distasteful in the habitual manner of Mr. Eliot's references during the past half-dozen years to Baudelaire and Original Sin. [. . .]

No one who sees in what way Lawrence is "serious and improving" will attribute the sum of wisdom, or anything like it, to him. And for attributing to him "spiritual sickness" Mr. Eliot can make out a strong case. But it is characteristic of the world as it is that health cannot anywhere be found whole; and the sense in which Lawrence stands for health is an important one. He stands at any rate for something without which the preoccupation (necessary as it is) with order, forms, and deliberate construction cannot produce health.

Checklist of Additional Reviews

*Arthur T. Quiller-Couch. "Tradition and Orthodoxy." *The Poet as Citizen and Other Papers* (Cambridge University Press, 1934), 44–61.

*J. G. *Isis* 890 (22 February 1934), 8.

*K. John. "The Grand Inquisitor." *New Statesman* 7 (24 February 1934), 274.

*Hugh Ross Williamson. "T. S. Eliot's 'Primer of Modern Heresy.'" *Bookman* 85 (March 1934), 468–71.

*Basil de Sélincourt. "A New Cure for the Times." *Observer*, 4 March 1934, p. 5.

*Edwin Muir. "Mr. Eliot on Evil." *Spectator* 152, no. 5515 (9 March 1934), 378–79.

*K. S. T. *Cherwell* 40 (10 March 1934), 190.

*Lyn Irvine. "Mr. T. S. Eliot Annoys the Critics." *Monologue*, 15 March 1934, pp. 1–8.

*John Beevers. "Mr. Eliot, Moralist." *Time and Tide* 15 (17 March 1934), 350–51.

*George Catlin. "A Daniel Come to Judgment?" *Sun Times* [London], 18 March 1934, p. 12.

*J. E. "Books to Interest the Workers." *New Leader*, 23 March 1934.

*Ezra Pound. "Mr. Eliot's Quandries." *New English Weekly* 4 (29 March 1934), 558–59.

*C. H. W. "Mr. Eliot Shuts the Door." *Everyman* 27 (29 March 1934), 167.

*Osbert Burdett. "Literary History and Criticism." *London Mercury* 29 (April 1934), 567.

*"Mr. Eliot's Criticism." *Manchester Guardian*, 3 April 1934, p. 5.

*"After Strange Gods." *Times Literary Supplement* 1681 (19 April 1934), 278.

*Ezra Pound. "Mr. T. S. Eliot's Quandaries." [Letter to the editor] *New English Weekly* 5 (26 April 1934), 48.

*A. M. *Blackfriars* 15, no. 170 (May 1934), 359–60.

*William Rose Benét. "T. S. Eliot and Original Sin." *Saturday Review of Literature* 10 (5 May 1934), 673, 678.

*Ezra Pound. "Mr. Eliot's Looseness." [Letter to the editor] *New English Weekly* 5 (10 May 1934), 95–96.

*G. Martin Turnell. "Tradition and T. S. Eliot." *Colosseum: A Quarterly Review* 1 (June 1934), 44–54.

Robert Peel. "T. S. Eliot and the Classic-Romantic Yardstick." *Christian Science Monitor, Weekly Magazine Section*, 6 June 1934, p. 11.

V. F. Calverton. "T. S. Eliot: An Inverted Marxian." *Modern Monthly* 8 (July 1934), 372–73.

*Brother George Every. *Theology* 29 (July 1934), 56–57.

*John Short. "A Provocative Critic." *Friend*, 7 September 1934.

Conrad Aiken. "After Ash-Wednesday." *Poetry: A Magazine of Verse* 45 (December 1934), 161–65. [Included in reviews of *The Rock* in this volume, pp. 312–14]

*F. C. "Gods True and False." *Granta* 43 (28 February 1936), 292.

THE ROCK
1934

THE ROCK

A PAGEANT PLAY
WRITTEN FOR PERFORMANCE
AT SADLER'S WELLS THEATRE
28 MAY — 9 JUNE 1934
ON BEHALF OF THE
FORTY-FIVE CHURCHES FUND
OF THE DIOCESE OF
LONDON

BOOK OF WORDS BY

T. S. ELIOT

LONDON
FABER & FABER LIMITED
24 RUSSELL SQUARE

*Derek Verschoyle. "The Theatre." *Spectator* 152, no. 5527 (1 June 1934), 851.

The production of Mr. Eliot's pageant play is organized by the Diocese of London, in aid of the Forty-Five Churches Fund, the president of which is the Lord Bishop of London. Apart, therefore, from its place as a contribution to English dramatic literature, *The Rock* is to be considered as an official *apologia* for the campaign of church-building which the fund was started to finance. In both respects it is an extremely interesting work, and in both it is at least partially a failure.

The direct action of the play turns upon the efforts of a group of bricklayers engaged in building a church, and the difficulties (from bad foundations, lack of money, agitators, hostile criticism) against which they have to struggle: their difficulties symbolize as well the general attitude to religion of the secular world. The process of construction is shown in every stage. In the first scene the workmen appear starting on the foundations; later the church is seen half built; finally, it is shown completed and ready for dedication. The Church's requirements of today are illustrated by a complementary series of pageant scenes, presenting episodes in the history of the Church, for the most part the Church in London: the conversion of King Sabert by Mellitus, Rahere's building of St. Bartholomew's, the dedication of Westminster Abbey, outbursts of Puritan iconoclasm. The episodes are linked together by a chorus, which comments both upon the action of the play and upon the present problems of the Church. The hooded figure of the Rock, who lends the play its title, represents the Church's continuity and resistance to dissolution; he takes little part in the action, and exists mainly as a consultant for the chorus. The main theme of the whole production is, in Mr. Eliot's words, the conflict between the Church and the World.

It is a defect in the play, considered as an *apologia*, that the case for neither of these opposed causes is conclusively stated. Mr. Eliot's defense of the Church is based rather on invocations than on definition, and he seems reluctant to commit himself to logical justification. For the most part the Church's cause is assumed and not stated, and at times Mr. Eliot's unwillingness to substantiate his beliefs makes him appear to be doing little more than strike an attitude. His picture of the society in which the Church must work is simplified and thereby distorted. He satirizes Fascists and Communists, plutocrats and social parasites, but admirable as much of his satire is, it is not conclusive. The elements in society which he satirizes do not represent the only, nor even the main, reasons for indifference to the Church today. Acceptance of Fascism or Communism is for many of their followers the result, not the cause, of dissatisfaction with the Church. The causes in many instances lie elsewhere; in, for example, despair of the Church's attitude towards such questions as Housing and Population. Mr. Eliot does not touch upon the latter problem, and only deals fragmentarily with the former. And he neglects altogether opposition to the Church which has other than a materialistic basis.

Nor, apart from its theme, is *The Rock* entirely successful as a dramatic experiment. In the choruses Mr. Eliot uses only verse, and in the choruses alone is a continuous dramatic effect achieved. Mr. Eliot's admirable dramatic verse was spoken in unison by a chorus dressed like carved stone figures, whose beautifully clear delivery and rhythmic skill produced an effect that was both austere and inspiriting. The producer's only error was in their final appearance where, crowded together in a narrow opening between the curtains in the center of the stage, they looked incredibly like a flock of lost and anxious sheep.

In the rest of the play Mr. Eliot uses for the most part prose, and dramatic modes which derive from the ballet, the music-hall, and the pantomime. Many of his points would be better made if they could be made more concisely, and a lack of economy in expression sometimes distorted the balance between the scenes. Some of the pageant scenes made their effect, some had merely the rather tedious plausibility of a carefully dressed charade. It is, perhaps, unwise to insist too much on the superiority of the choruses to the rest of the play, because they had the advantage of being spoken by Miss Elsie Fogerty's admirably trained and disciplined pupils, while the players in other scenes were largely recruited from amateurs from different parishes, in whom the effects of lack of experience and rehearsal were evident. But a hurried reading of the printed version of the play confirms the impression that was made by its presentation on the stage. It remains to add that Mr. Martin Browne's production was ambitious and in many ways impressive, and that much of the music composed by Dr. Martin Shaw had a great deal more than charm.

*Michael Sayers.
"The Drama: Mr. T. S.
Eliot's *The Rock.*"
New English Weekly 5
(2 June 1934), 230–31.

[. . .]

French influence has rarely improved our English drama. Concerning literature of the stage, at least, it is true to say that the Entente exemplifies little more than a reciprocal exchange of misunderstandings. Modern or fairly modern French criticism and poetry [. . .] have impressed Mr. Eliot to the extent of reproduction; and certainly they have led him to dispense as far as possible with the essentially English poetic device which, by a combination of precise communications and evocative suggestions, yields a language continuously creative. Mr. Eliot has struggled nobly and brilliantly against the deterioration, imprecision, and misuse of our language in our time; but, not satisfied by this excellent work, he went on to elevate his negative critical principles into a theory of poetry, and to practice his own teaching. He commenced by deliberately smothering those magnificent sonorities (even when our poetry snored it was magnificent!) which had become the test of good poetry; and substituted in their place the witty café-table rattle, the morbid whine, and the mere boudoir coo characteristic of his favorite French verses. Consequently, even when most earnest, much of Mr. Eliot's poetic writing still strikes the eye more forcibly than the ear. [. . .]

Nevertheless this poet is capable of producing at times extremely lovely-sounding lines, as those beginning: "O greater light we praise thee for the less." And that he is well aware of what might be a deficiency in his work may account for his frequent use of liturgical movements, with rather monotonous results.

For my purposes, then, Mr. Eliot's verse lacks that precipitation of the spirit without which stage dialogue is tedious and flat. His verse "stays on the ground"; it walks, with irregular steps, in a circle. It does not stir us by a bold advance, though it may disappoint us by a feeble recession [. . .]; at best it keeps steadily to an improgressive circumambulation. Its emotional gamut is restricted, dropping from satiric levity down to hopeless despondency, but reaching neither really comic impetuosity on the one hand, nor tragic contemplativeness on the other hand. And in this play *The Rock* [. . .], the content is equally as uninspiring as the form.

Mr. Eliot allows certain limits to be set to his thought and feelings by his beliefs. He does not seek to justify the ways of his God to us; this, it appears, he would consider a piece of impertinence to attempt. He does not concern himself very deeply with the mystery of our existence; this, it appears, would be contrary to orthodoxy. Not to phrase it irreverently, Mr. Eliot's dramatic verse, in its most moving expressions, is the incantation of a Dean *manqué*, who would call strayed Christians into the Catholic Church of England.

Again, these beliefs of Mr. Eliot cause him to voice in most melodramatic utterances (which too often, in this book, take the place of intense feeling), a series of mediaeval platitudes decked out in canonicals; as, for instance, when he expresses his horror at the hygienic practice of brushing the teeth; and also when he declares that our culture is decadent because it ignores the Church, though it is more probable that the Church is degenerate because it has lost touch with our culture. One can only share the lament of the other critics upon the passage of this great literary gentleman into "the Wasteland of Futile Superstition"; and murmur, in the words of the Talmudic funeral oration pronounced upon Rabbi Hillel: "Alas, the humble and pious man, the disciple of Ezra!"

I know that there is a tendency among modern critics to desire to confine the subject-matter of art to an accepted number of abstractions from common experience. Just as we speak in our debates of Communism, instead of the different disciples of Karl Marx; and of Social Credit, instead of individual exponents of Major Douglas's Theory; so, if we wish to make a play or novel about "love," [. . .] we shall no longer create a Romeo and Juliet, [. . .] a Lady Chatterley and the Gamekeeper, embodying our particular experiences and observations of the sexual impulse; but rather choose to deal with universal affections; and write, as it might be, the tragedy of Lingham and Yoni, where only whatever is common to collective experience of sex is allowed. It seems to me that this modern inclination to restrict the field of artistic enquiry would reduce our Western art to the static condition of Chinese aesthetics, which we might call the science of trifling; and we should come to agree with Voltaire that Shakespeare was altogether a barbarian. If, however, some of our dramatists welcome this limitation of material, then in that case they may find Mr. Eliot's forms of verse to be indicative of the sort of vehicle necessary for the conveyance of mass emotions. I think that these verse-forms might be suitable for Comedy, but a very specialized kind of comedy: a Collective Comedy of Manners—e.g., the Calf of Gold episode in the play under review. The tragic experience, like that of the mystic, the poet, and the lover, will remain an individual revelation [. . .].

As a special kind of comedic poet, then, Mr. Eliot indicates in a few passages in *The Rock* how talent, insight, wit, information, chastened sentiment, and proper dignity may be put to use in the modern drama, although it still remains to be done.

[. . .]

Listener 11 (6 June 1934), 945.

The immediate object of *The Rock*, the pageant play now being performed at Sadler's Wells, for which Mr. T. S. Eliot has written the words, is to raise money for the Forty Five Churches fund of the Diocese of London—a purpose which dictates the main theme of the play, the building of a church, against which are shown certain "experiments in time" which illustrate the growth of the churches in London from the time of the conversion of the Anglo-Saxons. But beyond this main object, which deserves all support, the play raises the whole issue of dramatic poetry today, an issue which the author himself has discussed as thoroughly as any contemporary critic. In the course of a dialogue on this subject, written a few years ago, Mr. Eliot put forward certain general propositions with which his dramatic poetry in this *Rock* can now be compared. One was the necessity for something more than pure entertainment. *The Rock* most certainly does entertain; as well as its choruses and historical pictures, it has Cockney backchat, topical references to Redshirts and Blackshirts and the Douglas Credit Scheme, a music-hall song and dance, and even a ballet (of Whittington

and his Cat). But the energy which carries through its diverse scenes and gives the whole performance shape is (as it was in Mr. Auden's *Dance of Death*) the writer's conviction of the importance of his theme. [. . .] Mr. Eliot obviously does have very strong feelings about those who "stray, in high-powered cars, on a by-pass way," and does not care very much about "A Church for us all and work for us all and God's world for us all even unto this last." A second observation, that "Drama springs from religious liturgy and cannot afford to depart far from religious liturgy," is amply illustrated, not only by the actual introduction of parts of the Church service (in the scene showing the blessing of the Crusaders, and in the climax where the Bishop of London blesses the audience) as by the use of the rhythms of the liturgy in certain of the choruses. And this links up with the third proposition, the necessity of providing a verse that will be as satisfactory for us as blank verse was for the Elizabethans. There is no one form of verse in *The Rock*; it comprehends a variety, from the measures of the Psalms to those of music hall; but the point is that they are familiar rhythms, to which the audience's ear is attuned. And so, either sung, or spoken with beautiful clearness by the Chorus which links up the scenes, they present no difficulty in acceptance. Those to whom Mr. Eliot's name is synonymous with "modernist" and "difficult" poetry may be surprised that audiences of bishops, aldermen, church workers, school children and "general public," most of whom are probably unfamiliar with his other works, should be able to join in anything written by him as they do in the last chorus of all. Those, however, who remember the smart rhythms of *Sweeney Agonistes*, or the clear lines of the *Journey of the Magi*, will not be in the least surprised; but simply pleased that a great contemporary poet should have been given

302

the opportunity of writing directly for a popular audience.

*"Mr. Eliot's Pageant Play."
Times Literary Supplement 1688 (7 June 1934), 404.

Evidently Mr. Eliot has prepared, step by step, to enter the theatre. *The Rock* is not actually a drama, being first a pageant; but it is a work for the stage, and may be regarded—Mr. Eliot having advanced so far—as a notable demonstration of possibilities. That his approach has been deliberate, preceded by much critical examination, is apparent from previous writings.

The contemporary theatre presented him with two obstacles: first, the dislike or fear of poetry on the stage; second, the lack of a recognized morality either on the stage or in the audience. [. . .] Perhaps, in order to seek guidance for his advance, he made his study of former dramatists, especially the Elizabethans; and within recent years enunciated his discovery that poetry and drama are not contradictory, as this century assumes: the best drama is in fact that which comes nearest to poetry, and *vice versa*. This declaration gave confidence for experiment, and he wrote several fragments. But now the request to write for a church audience, in support of a church extension campaign, solved for him the second problem—at least for the occasion: Christianity was present on both sides of the curtain.

Mr. Eliot is not alone among modern writers in desiring a poetic drama. And internal evidence shows him sensitive to what others are doing, to the ground won, the methods employed. His genius, indeed, might be said to rest on a careful regard of other artists, predecessors and contemporaries. He balances two forms of awareness, which might be described as horizontal and vertical, more nicely than anyone today. In this play the vertical (or past) influences are obvious and glorified in. Liturgy, which gave birth to English drama, is a model; there is antiphonal use of choric speaking; and many scenes, which are all linked on the theme of church-building, contain portions of actual liturgy. The Latin ritual for taking the Cross for the Crusades is bodily inserted. There are also bits of sermons. Early moralities authorize comic relief to the most serious intentions; and that relief, naturally enough, is expressed in terms of the music-hall and pantomime we know. The cockney builders of a church, which is gradually erected as the pageant proceeds, are ready to indulge in jokes, arguments, songs, and humble reverence, as required. Each difficulty in church-building is illustrated by a scene showing a similar (or worse) difficulty overcome in the past. Liturgical chanting and mime are used in these scenes, which include such occasions as Mellitus's conversion of London, Rahere's building of St. Bartholomew's, the rebuilding of Jerusalem, and the Danish invasion of England.

As already suggested, awareness of present writers is shown. With them, what might be called the modest or non-sublime approach to poetic drama has become almost a convention. They take the popular stage forms today (the modern "folk" forms), such as musical comedy or *revue*, and use them as a basis. There was recently Mr. O'Casey's *Within the Gates*; and echoes of its sing-song choruses, its pervasive harping on modern down-and-outs find their way into *The Rock*: [quotation of lines 102–05 of *The Rock*, Chorus I]. Mr. W. H. Auden is another experimenter;

he is marked by strangeness and an arrogant threatening of a doomed society, as he sees it. Him, too, Mr. Eliot recalls on occasion: "Though you forget the way to the Temple / There is one who remembers the way to your door." His gift of parody may unconsciously lead him to this. But conscious parody appears elsewhere, as in the Communists' verses—typographically parodied also.

The scene where this occurs, set in 1934, is most characteristic of the Eliot known through his poems. (It should be made clear that the scenario is by another hand, Mr. E. Martin Browne; Mr. Eliot is author "only of the words." As he explains, "Of only one scene am I literally the author," and this modern scene is presumably the one.) The chorus, despondent, wonders if the young offer hope of better things. Bands of Redshirts and Blackshirts are questioned. Their replies are, with exaggeration, unsatisfactory. The chorus says: "There seems no hope from those who march in step." A Plutocrat enters, criticizes the Church and, instead, offers to the crowd a golden calf, for which they fight. As a comment on our modern situation, it cannot be said that in this the pessimism of *The Waste Land* has been abandoned.

Mr. Eliot takes a hard view of the Christian struggle. The emphasis of his chorus counters the optimistic scenario, an emphasis such as is expressed in:

> The desert is not remote in southern
> tropics,
> The desert is not only around the
> corner,
> The desert is squeezed in the
> tube-train next to you.

These choruses [. . .] exceed in length any of his previous poetry; and on the stage at Sadler's Wells they prove the most vital part of the performance, being excellently spoken. They combine the sweep of psalmody with the exact employment of colloquial words. They are lightly written, as though whispered to the paper, yet are forcible to enunciate.

[Quotation of lines 30–36 of *The Rock*, Chorus III]

In *The Rock* Mr. Eliot's success is certainly lyrical; the action scenes have immaturities and faults, for which, on account of collaborators, he may not be entirely blameworthy. The cockney humor is often curiously feeble; sometimes alien points of view, such as the Agitators', are thinly projected. But with his use of the chorus he has regained a lost territory for the drama. Nor is it only satiric, as the tender music of the closing scene may exemplify: "In our rhythm of earthly life we tire of light. We are glad when the day ends, when the play ends; and ecstasy is too much pain [. . .]." Mr. Eliot, having at last entered the theatre, may well continue towards a proper play in verse. There is exhibited here a command of novel and musical dramatic speech which, considered alone, is an exceptional achievement.

---

*Richard Sunne. "Men and Books." *Time and Tide* 15 (16 June 1934), 774.

The relation of the poet to his times raises problems which can never, perhaps, be satisfactorily determined. Does the poet make the thought of his time? Or represent it? Is he himself remarkable only because of a responsive quickness of intellectual and spiritual hearing which enables him to catch sounds while they are still unheard by most of us? Or does he actually originate the rumors which, as he gives them force and form, become bruited over the world in which he lives and the very voice of the time? [. . .] I suppose the truth is, as usual, with both views. The poet does hear quicker and more surely; but to what he hears he will, if he be true poet, give a new overtone; the murmurs of the new thought which is coming will be transmuted by him into something which will always be inalienably his own, held with a precision and a purity which are beyond the capacity of those who can only hear, not what he hears, but a distortion of it, a sound confused by prejudices and ambitions and self-seeking aspirations. The poet, as poet, will never wish to lead men; even the fact that he inspires them is to him only incidental. It is his business not to improve this world, but to reveal a new world by his interpretation and criticism of this.

Mr. T. S. Eliot's position among modern poets is largely due to his sensitive awareness of this characteristic of the true poet. He is remote, not because he is unconcerned in modern perplexities and problems (few men are more concerned), but because he can relate and control his concern by reference to his own vision. He is remote, I feel, even from himself, knowing well the difference between the poet in him and the propagandist, and never allowing the propagandist to get the better of the poet in his poetry. Much of his work has seemed to be representative of the particular dis-ease of his time; he has been accused of leading his generation into a waste land which otherwise it would not have occupied. I believe, however, that in that early work Mr. Eliot did something different. He disclosed the waste land to people who were living there, and still cozened themselves that they were in the happy valley, or, at worst, daring some dangerous mountain; and he himself, as poet, always knew that he and his generation must go through

the waste land, and never could do that until they confessed to themselves the true nature of the country they were inhabiting. It is not his fault if some of those to whom he disclosed the true nature of their lives elected to remain in the waste land, and have refused either to join him on his way out from it, or to discover any way of their own. No poet, especially no dramatic poet, can be blamed because some of his readers will stay obstinately faithful to a vision which the poet has proclaimed, but not praised. If a man thinks the world of *Troilus and Cressida* or of *Timon of Athens* is nearer to truth and beauty than the world of *The Tempest*, it is his own fault, not Shakespeare's. What is exciting to the critic who refuses to separate literature from life is the problem whether Mr. Eliot in his later poetry is once again, as in *The Waste Land*, overhearing the first faint murmurs of a thought which will become as general as the thought expressed in his earlier work.

It would be a mistake to stress too much the fact that at the performances of *The Rock* at Sadler's Wells Theatre the house was packed—on the night I went there was hardly standing-room—for the whole fortnight of the production. There were other than artistic reasons for this popularity. It would be a graver mistake to suppose that the audience consisted mainly of earnest Church-people, and of friends of the actors and actresses who had given their services for the performance of this impressive pageant-play. The value of *The Rock* can be estimated from the printed "book of words." It is a religious play; and at moments, as I listened to the words, and even more now I read them, I discerned in Mr. Eliot an allegiance which I had not previously found in his work. There were plenty of echoes, parodies, and side-glances at modern poets and modern heresies; here a touch of Mr. Auden, occasionally a note of his old friend

Mr. Ezra Pound—in the comic scenes, dialogue and a song of which Albert Chevalier would not have been ashamed. The name that kept on recurring to my mind, however, was one an older than these. It was the name of Wordsworth. It is likely that Mr. Eliot will suffer from the same injustice as was for so long Wordsworth's fate [. . .]. A rebel who changes from rebellion to acceptance of habit often retains his popularity, and is not suspected as a traitor; a rebel who, retaining the spirit of rebellion, enlarges the scope of his rebellion, is too often abandoned by old associates and remains misunderstood by possible friends. Mr. Eliot is, as Wordsworth always was, a free thinker; but his freedom has taken a direction at present so unfashionable in the ranks of the intelligentsia, that it is hardly understood. Mr. Eliot not only believes in liberty, in the rights of men, in the duties of the brotherhood; he actually believes that this liberty, these rights, and these duties must somehow be conserved for men's happiness, and that the surest, the only certain safeguard for them is the Christian religion. There is much else in *The Rock* besides this simple statement: but that is the play's key. Against the servile state, against the bondage of pleasure, against the worship of success, against the vulgarity of civilization *The Rock* stands.

[Quotation of lines 28–36 of *The Rock*, Chorus III].

The Rock is at once an assertion and a denial of individualism. Mr. Eliot believes, as firmly as any Communist on Fascist, in a whole of which individuals are part; but the needs of that whole can only be gained by the voluntary transcendence, not the compulsory suppression, of the individual. And when the whole is duly served, there will result a richer individualism, a truer freedom than are possible otherwise. Only

so can man overcome that other spirit which dominates a world where "men have forgotten All gods but Usury, Lust and Power."

Theology 29 (July 1934), 4–5.

The text of the Sadler's Wells London Church Pageant, *The Rock*, by T. S. Eliot, is now available, and very good reading it is. Our only criticisms are that it is difficult to grasp at a single hearing, and that the modern London workingman does not speak as he is here made to do. Ethelbert, Alfred, and young Edwin are at once too intelligent and too illiterate. But what a blessed relief, after the Wardour Street lamb-doodle sometimes put forward as the language of Church-plays, to have words with a bite in them, full of wit, satire, and poetry. It is a genuine modern exposition of belief in the Church, as an ancient, unpopular, hard-pressed, conquering, divine society. It is modern in that it is aware of the modern situation (we even have the Douglas scheme of Social Credit—"that bein' the case, I say: to 'ell with money"), and of Redshirts, Blackshirts, and so forth, but in a deeper sense it is modern in that we have in it the *confessio fidei* of a modern Churchman, a real faith expressed in the language of today. Above all it is a pageant, with Mellitus, Rahere, and even Nehemiah to reassure the builders of today. The time-series is used with freedom. Bishop Blomfield comforts the leader of the Chorus with a reminder of the Crusades, and we at once see a mediaeval Bishop giving the Cross, with Latin prayers and benediction, to two young Crusaders, and the next moment the twentieth-century builders are patting one another on the back because the difficulties have miraculously vanished. We congratulate the Diocese of London on having secured Mr. Eliot to write their book.

---

*D. W. Harding.
"The Rock."
Scrutiny 3 (September 1934), 180–83.

"The view that what we need in this tempestuous turmoil of change is a Rock to shelter under or to cling to, rather than an efficient aeroplane in which to ride it, is comprehensible but mistaken." The attitude expressed by Dr. Richards here is one that many people now find less alluring than once they did, and to them the general theme of *The Rock* will be welcome. The whole book bears witness to the conviction that the only possible advance at the present time is a "spiritual" one and has little to do with anything specifically modern, nor any appeal for those who

> . . . constantly try to escape
> From the darkness outside and within
> By dreaming of systems so perfect that
>   no one will need to be good.

Mr. Eliot's subtle tone of humble and yet militant contempt could hardly be improved upon. What is not convincing, however, is his suggestion that the Church is the only alternative, for his pleading relies upon false antitheses. It puts the plight of the uncultured vividly but it does not show what the Church would do for them. A description of the breakdown of social and particularly of family life ends "But every son would have his motor cycle, / And daughters ride away on casual pillions." But the alternative to the pillion is not suggested. As far as we can judge from the time when such families were more stable, it would be the horsehair sofa, in a front parlor left vacant by the rest of the family with appropriate pleasantries. The only alternatives to godless restlessness that this book gives are the rough diamond piety of the builders' foreman, and more impressive, the satisfactions of the highly cultured who happen to be within the Church.

[Quotation of lines 26–28 of *The Rock*, Chorus IX]

But the plight of people capable of appreciating such culture and still outside the Church is not put. In so far as *The Rock* is pleading for certain attitudes which the Church at its best supports it is undoubtedly effective, but as an assertion of the necessity of the Church to the establishing or maintenance of those attitudes, it is invalidated by its false antitheses. Undoubtedly it is more effective in its denunciatory description of things as they are, of the misery of the poor and the spiritual vacuity of the well-to-do, than in the remedy it proffers. And it is in the choruses where these descriptions occur that the greatest intrinsic value of the work is to be found.

The prose dialogue which maintains the action of the pageant is distressing. It is difficult to believe that the spinsterish Cockney of the builders was written by the author of the public house scene in *The Waste Land*, and the speeches of the Agitator and the fashionable visitors to the Church are just the usual middle-class caricatures of a reality that has never been accurately observed. They are the caricatures of a class by a class, and well-worn and blurred they are, inevitably. The reach-me-down character of the dialogue is partly responsible for and partly derived from—in fact is one with—the banal and sentimental treatment of a scene like "The Crusaders' Farewell," which offers so painful a contrast to the dignity of the liturgical Latin that comes next. Only in some of the ingenious pastiches of archaic styles which Mr. Eliot introduces from time to time is the prose readable with even mild pleasure.

The verse is altogether more interesting. Naturally in a work written to order and presumably in a limited time there is included some which is not as fine as most of what Mr. Eliot has published. Necessarily, too, this verse cannot have the concentration and subtlety of a short poem intended for many attentive readings. Its interest lies rather in its experimentation with a tone of address. Innovations of "tone" (in Richards's sense) are at least as significant as innovations of "technique" in the restricted sense, and in the addresses of the Chorus and the Rock to the decent heathen and the ineffectual devout, who are taken as forming the audience, Mr. Eliot achieves a tone that is new to contemporary verse. Its peculiar kind of sermonizing is especially welcome in contrast to the kind the young communist poets offer us: in particular it succeeds in upbraiding those it addresses while still remaining humble and *impersonally* superior to them:

> The Word of the LORD came unto
>   me, saying:
> O miserable cities of designing men,
> O wretched generation of enlightened
>   men,
> [. . . . .]
> Will you build me a house of plaster,
>   with corrugated roofing,

To be filled with a litter of Sunday
  newspapers?

[Quotation of lines 11–13 of *The Rock*, Chorus VI and of lines 46–47 of *The Rock*, Chorus I]

Closely bound up with the tone of address is the texture of the language. The idiom Mr. Eliot developed here is admirably suited to, and has evidently emerged from pressure of, the practical circumstances of the work: its dramatic presentation before an audience whose muzzy respect for the devotional had to be welded to a concern for contemporary realities. A particularly successful and characteristic trick of idiom is the quick transition from vaguely Biblical language to the contemporary colloquial. It can be seen in this: "I have trodden the winepress alone, and I know / That it is hard to be really useful . . ." [. . .] This passage also illustrates the dominant feeling of the denunciatory choruses, a dry contempt which has passed beyond the stage of tiredness and now has a tough springiness.

[Quotation of lines 59–60 and 66–71 of *The Rock*, Chorus III]

The Rock is in many ways typical of Mr. Eliot's later work. Far less concentrated, far less perfect, far more easy-going than the earlier work, it has an increased breadth of contact with the world which takes the place of intensity of contact at a few typical points. The change is not one that can be described briefly. It can be roughly indicated by saying that the earlier work seemed to be produced by the ideal type of a generation, and asked for Mr. Eliot to be looked upon almost as an institution, whereas this later work, though not more individual, is far more personal. What seems certain is that it forms a transition to a stage of Mr. Eliot's work which has not yet fully defined itself.

*A. M.
Blackfriars 15, no. 174
(September 1934),
642–43.

Mr. Eliot has come out of the waste land. His sojourn in the desert was not, as his less intelligent disciples seem to have thought, an intellectual antic: it was a necessary asceticism, and an asceticism for poetry. Analogous renunciations are observable in other arts. All are stripping to structure in order to regain tradition. But the desert is a dangerous place: there are devils in it as well as God. Surrealist paintings suggest that it is the devil whom the painters have met in the desert.

Mr. Eliot has come out of the waste land a Christian. This play, which ran for a fortnight at Sadler's Wells, with crammed audiences [. . .], is an explicitly Christian play, it is vulgar propaganda, it is to collect cash for Church extension. It is a phenomenon to be noted when the greatest living English poet finds it an honor for poetry to be an *ancilla Fidei*.

The play is built on several planes. In the foreground two Cockney bricklayers are trying to build a church in a swamp. On another plane are the appearances of great church-builders of the past who come to encourage the workmen—Rahere, Nehemiah, Blomfield. Then there is the contemporary "world," with its aimlessness and lucre lust, and its panaceas of Fascism and Communism. And behind all is the mysterious figure of the Rock. The Rock is Peter.

Mr. Eliot has always claimed that the poet should be in organic relation with the community: in this play he has achieved that relation, and without any loss to his poetry, for the great choruses which weld the play together contain some of the noblest poetry he has written. Only the language of the Cockneys is a little uninteresting: Cockney is more than misplaced h's, and Mr. Eliot would do well to rely on his own judgment in this matter, since the advice he says he has taken seems not to have been very helpful. But this is to carp at a work which as a whole is a magnificent and thrilling success. The temptation to quote is furious, but we must be content to conclude with the refrain which is the "motive" of the entire play: "A Church for us all and work for us all and God's world for us all even unto this last."

Robert Peel.
"A Classical
Contemporary Pageant
from Mr. T. S. Eliot."
*Christian Science Monitor,
Weekly Magazine Section*,
14 November 1934, p. 12.

For many people Mr. Eliot is the poet of chaos, and that is all. They think of him as dwelling perpetually among the splintered, splendid agonies of *The Waste Land*, grasping at such fragments of meaning as are momentarily visible in the nightmare light of that region of the imagination. Readers of his prose know a very different sort of man, a cool, self-possessed reasoner, a lover of precision, proportion, and established values, a believer in the sublime destiny of man. Those who have followed his recent development closely know that Mr. Eliot, like a modern Canute, has been quietly undertaking to turn back the sea of sensibility which so long threatened to engulf him, that he has been gradually extending the empire of law over the profoundly disturbed depths of his own submarine nature. The present work marks the extent to which he has succeeded.

If the sea has refused to turn back, it at least moves in with a beautiful regularity, an ordered grandeur, in which not more than every seventh wave lands on the shore with a perceptible shock. So far as his form and method and even his aims are concerned, Mr. Eliot has obviously passed from the tempest-tossed age of Donne to the stately age of Dryden. *The Rock* is a pageant play for which the poet has written the words alone, the scenario having been furnished by Mr. E. Martin Browne. Nothing could better illustrate the extent to which Mr. Eliot's nervous, prehensile imagination has come under the sway of law than his willingness— his positive eagerness, in fact—to adapt his imagination to the structural framework of another's dramatic conception. This is a classicism in its purest essence: the transmuting of an idea common to percipient minds into the form determined by the artist's individual genius working in an accepted medium of expression. Judged as a drama, or even as a pageant, the play is very uneven in its merits. It concerns a group of Cockney bricklayers engaged in building a church in contemporary London. To them, in rather muddled fashion, come glimpses of the past, near and remote, intended to show that the church is always being built, always being destroyed, but is perpetually alive in the consecrated efforts of good men to make it a permanent and visible reality on earth. Prose scenes of Cockney realism and humor alternate with rather high-falutin poetic scenes, and a good measure of satirical symbolism is introduced by way of getting in a dig at the many shallow-pated, conventional opponents (and supporters) of the church today. There is much that is excellent, considerable that is specious, and a little that is painful in all this; but overwhelming the consideration of all else are the magnificent choruses which sweep the play into the realm of major art.

In the best of them Mr. Eliot overtops Dryden in majesty, while preserving faultlessly the simplicity and directness of common speech. He has never written anything better than the lines that occur at the beginning of the play:

> The Eagle soars in the summit of
>   Heaven,
> [.............................]
> Where is the Life we have lost in
>   living?
> Where is the wisdom we have lost in
>   knowledge?
> Where is the knowledge we have lost
>   in information?

The answer to these questions is all too explicit in many of the scenes that follow, but again and again the choruses lift the reader above the clutter of well-meaning arguments and heroics to lonely, solemn heights of impassioned thought. The present reviewer tried the experiment of reading the choral paean to light at the end of the play immediately after reading the great hymn to light at the beginning of Book 3 of *Paradise Lost*. Granted the greater *weight* of Milton's verse, he found that Mr. Eliot's lines did not suffer diminution of beauty, sincerity, or passion by association with so superlative a passage of poetry. Technically these choruses can bear comparison with the best of English poetry, though their simplicity may delude some people into thinking them easy of achievement.

Mr. Eliot has pointed the way to a generation of poets. They could do worse than to follow him (as poet, *not* as dogmatic theorist) in the new direction that he has chosen. It is time for the light to move on the face of the waters. It is time for poets, as well as other men to *build*; to construct, however fumblingly, temples in which the spirit of Truth may dwell. One may disagree with much of the reasoning of Mr. Eliot's play, but one can hardly fail to respond to its ideas, gracefully epitomized in the "Builders' Song" with which the play ends [. . .].

"*The Rock*: Ecclesiastical Revue."
Theatre Arts Monthly 18 (December 1934), 926–29.

The London Diocese, faced with the necessity of building and endowing forty-five churches for a half-million inhabitants of the new suburbs, realized the value of the theatre in clarifying such a problem, and asked E. Martin Browne, who had been director of religious drama for the Chichester Diocesan Players, to evolve a play that would set forth the difficulties of the campaign and initiate the drive for funds. Mr. Browne invited T. S. Eliot to do the writing, and engaged Martin Shaw as composer and Stella Mary Pearce as designer. His scenario took the form of what the papers later called an ecclesiastical revue, a device unusual enough to pack the house for every performance but one whose success can be judged at this distance only by the accompanying pictures of the production and the recently published version of Eliot's script, called *The Rock*.

Superficially, the choice of Eliot as author is as unusual as the form of the play itself, for the poet's contact with the theatre has been slight. But, perhaps, for that very reason, Eliot has been able to bring to the writing of *The Rock* an unconventionality and a freshness that set it apart from the ordinary run of dramatic production. Mr. Browne's story-framework for Eliot's verse is built around "The Rock, The Watcher, The Stranger," who is to show

> . . . the things that are now being done,
> And some of the things that were long
>   ago done,
> That you may take heart. Make
>   perfect your will.
> Let me show you the work of the
>   humble. Listen.

What he shows is a group of Cockney workmen who have been hired to build a church in London, and how the difficulties that beset them are remedied by momentary appearances of Church figures of the past, who describe or reenact their own troubles when they were doing God's work in a younger world. Eliot's previous work offers no prophecy of the fertile theatric invention used in his presentation of these episodes: poetry and prose, mime and ballet. As accompaniments and alternatives to these diversified scenes are choral comments, by groups of unemployed and of builders, and, most important, by a formal chorus that symbolizes the foundations of the Church. Eliot has written some fine poetry for these passages, such lines, for example, as these:

> O Greater Light, we praise Thee for
>   the less;
> The eastern light our spires touch at
>   morning,
> The light that slants upon our western
>   doors at evening,
> The twilight over stagnant pools at
>   batflight,
> Moon light and star light, owl and
>   moth light,
> Glow-worm glowlight on a
>   grassblade.
>
>   [. . .]

But there is much mediocre poetry, as in the recurring "Builders' Song," and in general the prose is more felicitous, since Eliot seems to attain humor and truth more often and more easily in that form:

> You needn't believe in God but you've got to believe in a buildin'. It goes up and up in the sky, and on and on through the years, and it speaks with its lights and its bells in the night and in the sunshine—and it stands when you and I are dust, what built it for the glory of God—and that church 'as been put up with 'ands, buildin', buildin', buildin'—all through the years—in the ruddy rain and 'eat and 'ail and snow—workin' in bricks and mortar, goin' on forever and ever and ever, buildin' the Church of God.

As it appears on the printed page, *The Rock* lacks the dramatic power, the sweep and profundity, that it must have had on the stage, a truism in any comparison of published and acted versions of plays. Such divertissements as a children's ballet of Dick Whittington and an old music-hall song-and-dance come out better in performance; and mimes have little color and movement when they are confined within three or four lines of prosy description. And although it is Eliot's virtue, perhaps, that he can generally set beauty beside the homely and rob neither of its distinctive values, cold print cannot hide the crudity of colloquialism when it is placed next to ardent verse in such an allegory. *The Rock*, when it is read, is too often a mixture of contradictory impulses.

The stage version is another story. The reported success of the Martin Browne production is an indication that the play is scaled for the theatre and had a color and rhythm, an impassioned virility, at which the book only hints. In any medium, however, *The Rock* composes one of Eliot's most thoroughgoing tributes to the faith.

Conrad Aiken. "After *Ash-Wednesday*." Poetry: A Magazine of Verse 45 (December 1934), 161–65.

[Review of *After Strange Gods* and *The Rock*]

To read these two new books of Mr. Eliot's together is to be made more than ever uncomfortable about his present predicament, his present position and direction. It is unfair to examine a lecture as closely as one would an essay in criticism, and *After Strange Gods* consists, of course, of three lectures delivered at the University of Virginia. It is equally unfair to judge the printed text of a pageant, a pageant written in cooperation with others and for performance on a special occasion, as one would judge a new book of poems presented in the ordinary way. In other words, one must begin by discounting both books as not quite "pure" Eliot. Nevertheless, there they are, they must be fitted into the Eliot tradition, they fall into line, and Mr. Eliot himself invites the comparison by publishing them; and it must be confessed that they leave one with a feeling of dissatisfaction and uncertainty.

The lectures consist chiefly of an extension and elaboration of the now famous essay in *The Sacred Wood*—"Tradition and the Individual Talent." It is difficult to see that they add much of importance, whether in refinement or perception, or in division or addition; if anything, they are a dilution of the earlier work, they seem a little thin. Of course, as we all know, Mr. Eliot has turned to religion in the interval of thirteen years between *The Sacred*

Wood and *After Strange Gods*, and it is not without a melancholy interest to consider the later book in this special light. From "tradition" to "orthodoxy" was, in the circumstances, a natural semantic and mantic step to take; Mr. Eliot takes it, and is not at pains to conceal it. Everywhere here is the implication that not only is it of vital importance for the artist (as individual) to remain in a sort of conscious connection with the tradition from which he springs, but also that if this contact can be further or more deeply extended to include a connection with the Church he will be safer still. Leaving aside, as one must, the whole question of religious belief, or of orthodox religion, nevertheless one is at once aware that the change in Mr. Eliot's critical attitude is decidedly in the direction of limitation. Already, in "Tradition and the Individual Talent," his emphasis was not so much on the *freedom* offered the artist by tradition as on the *restrictions*; the use of tradition was rather to hold one back than to release one for a forward step of exploration; in short, the position was a cautious one. The effect of orthodoxy is not unnaturally to deepen this timidity. If little room was then left for the individual's "free play," there is now very much less. As a mother of the arts, Mr. Eliot's "tradition" would be a very anxious and possessive one indeed; and (one is afraid) very crippling. Individualism must go by the board—if such a program should become universal—and the creative renewal of the arts fall to so low a level as to lead inevitably to stagnation. With the death of the individual would come the death of tradition; and art would be simply a history.

A curious state of things, a curious attitude in one who has himself been one of the most pronouncedly and creatively "individual" of contemporary writers, and himself therefore a pretty violent *creator* of tradition; and one immediately begins to wonder what effect his doctrines will have on his own poetry. *The Rock* alone cannot give us much of an answer, for as observed above, it is not a "pure" offering, but an amalgam. In conjecture, however, with the handful of poems which Mr. Eliot has given us in the twelve years since he published *The Waste Land*, it is enough to make one uneasy. Without in any way detracting from the extraordinary beauty of *Ash-Wednesday* or *Marina*, or from the occasional brilliance of other of the later poems, one cannot fail to notice a contraction both of interest and power in the recent work. *Ash-Wednesday*, let it be said at once, is perhaps the most beautiful of all of Mr. Eliot's poems: it seems not unlikely that its "value" will outlast that of *The Waste Land*. It is purer and less violent; it depends less on shock, though elements of shock are still there, enough of them to give energy; in Mr. Eliot's own sense, it is more absolutely a poem, has a new being and constitutes a new experience, and is so much more without "reference," or conscious reference, and so much more heavily weighted with *un*conscious reference (or *affect*) as to approach the kind of heavenly meaninglessness which we call pure poetry. But, though we can like it better than *The Waste Land*, or feel it to be finer, we also feel it to mark the beginning of a diminution of vigor and variousness: the circle has narrowed, and it has gone on narrowing.

We cannot, of course, argue that this charge is due to the change in Mr. Eliot's views, any more than we can argue that some deeper diminution of energy led to the change of view; all we can do is observe that the two things have gone together. In *The Rock*, the choruses are not the very best Eliot, though they are skillful and beautiful; they are admirably calculated for declamation; they have an excellent hardness and plainness; but at times one feels the cunning of the rhetoric and

313

the rhythm to be almost too glib and easy, and as if usurping the place of what would formerly have been a richer and more natural inventiveness.

Mr. Eliot remarks, in *After Strange Gods*, that to write religious poetry is one of the most difficult of all things. *Orthodox* religious poetry, yes: for that is merely to state, or to state by referring, or to argue: which is propaganda, or something very like it, as long as it remains within that given frame of traditional or taught conviction, as it must. It is this that makes one uneasy about Mr. Eliot's future: this and his converse belief that poetry, or the poetic genius, cannot be a substitute for religion. To many of us it must appear that "orthodox religion," on the one hand, and "tradition," on the other, are simply nothing but a temporary conservatism, or freezing in formula, of the initial poetic impulse. Beyond a certain point, or for more than a given time, it *cannot* be formalized: along comes a poet who reaches through it to the thing itself. Perhaps Mr. Eliot's experiment with dramatic form in *The Rock*, which must have been as highly suggestive to himself as to his auditors and readers, will release him once more in ways which neither he nor ourselves can foresee.

M[orton] D. Z[abel].
"Poetry for the Theatre."
Poetry: A Magazine of Verse 45 (December 1934), 152–58.

Sean O'Casey's play, *Within the Gates*, has now been produced in New York, and Mr. Eliot's *The Rock* was staged last June in London; accordingly, the question of a modern poetic drama is again in the air. O'Casey's play is an appropriate stimulus to argument, since it comes from the country which has yielded the finest verse plays in English in our time. Mr. Eliot's "book of words" for the pageant of the Diocese of London is also of special moment; it follows on his "Aristophanic fragments" in *Sweeney Agonistes* as an apparent effort to put into practice the ideas on poetry for the modern theatre which he outlined in two of the best essays in *The Sacred Wood*. O'Casey's avowed aim is to liberate the creative spirit of the dramatist from the shackles and tedium of naturalism; he wants to arouse the *élan* of a ranging imagination, the vital force of an ideal symbolism. "All fresh and imaginatively minded dramatists are out to release drama from the pillory of naturalism and send her dancing through the streets," he says, and his latest play carries him even farther than *The Silver Tassie* from his brilliant achievements in natural humor or pathos in *Juno and the Paycock* and *The Plough and the Stars*. Mr. Eliot has taken the cause of the Forty-Five Churches Fund as an opportunity to test "the temper of the age" on its direct capacity for poetic speech—"a preparedness, a habit on the part of the public, to respond to particular stimuli" which has been dwindling since the days of Marlowe and Shakespeare. In doing so he has put his talent to its longest test since *The Waste Land* and indicated what may again become a serious ambition among poets.

[. . .] [T]here is a fund of the best poetic energy in our time tending toward the dramatic form, to claim for spoken poetry its natural setting in the theatre, and to bring verse back to one of its time-sanctioned and impressive uses. But with this realization comes another. The fund of poetic ambition today is exceeded only by its diversity; this diversity corresponds to an equal instability in interest and sympathy in the modern audience; and this instability (which only the commonest denominators of humor, farce, sex appeal, and sensation seem able to localize or resolve) is the factor that can usually be counted on to make poetry in the modern theatre seem trivial, and its speech and appeal ridiculous.

It is one thing for an audience to attend an Elizabethan play, with its sanctions of tradition and reverence, and quite another to find the same literary processes applied to the events and speech of contemporary life, from which newspapers, films, and similar liberties have done their best to extract the elements that make poetry possible. [. . .] The triumph of realism is photography, and photography has apparently triumphed over any powers that language now ordinarily has to impress the masses. The minority of students and poetry-readers who welcome poetic drama are an insignificant proportion of the public that has exhausted, usually before the end of adolescence, most of the impulses and mysteries of life which a poet takes seriously. Accordingly, even serious poets, turning to drama, do so by "stepping up" the material of common realism to a poetic level. This was Mr. Eliot's idea when he advocated the music-hall comedian as a fit medium for poetic transformation; and he followed his own advice by taking the banalities of musical comedy for his material in *Sweeney Agonistes*. That work, however, left one with the conviction that the use of "jazz as a medium for tragedy" (one critic's interpretation) is a project more high-sounding and exciting than practicable. *The Rock*, without descending to jazz or rising to tragedy, again uses music-hall methods, this time for the purposes of a morality, but the effective parts of this play are hardly due to them. In O'Casey's play the vulgarity is not so much a matter of deliberate

intention as of the poetic limitations of the author.

[. . .]

No one can question the serious value of both O'Casey's and Eliot's plays. The life in them is vastly superior to the rhetoric of dramatists like Philips and Rostand [. . .]. The defect appears to lie, rather, in a conscious externalizing of poetic values, of applying the poetry to an admittedly barren or non-poetic subject-matter. A fault that springs from a recognition of obstacles is often more emphatic than one which grows out of a mere ignorance of them. The Elizabethans are ideally the poets who possessed no separate consciousness of their environment, their theatre, and their art: the three met at a single focus of vision and acceptance. [. . .]

Yeats's concern for poetic drama has been life-long, and early in his career he referred to the unity of interest in an audience on which the subject-matter of a play depends. That popular agreement he identified as "religion," and indicated thereby the fixity of purpose and assent on which a dramatic language, free of either rhetorical pretension or mere catchpenny novelty, relies.

> [. . .] The more religious the subject-matter of an art, the more will it be as it were stationary, and the more ancient will be emotion that it arouses and the circumstances that it calls up before our eyes.

The assent to which [Yeats] refers—whether social or political, moral or religious—is particularly necessary to the audience of poetic drama. The present moment may be the worst in which to look for it; there is little in current literature to indicate that it exists. Possibly drama will have to revive or develop it before it can rely on it. But it is almost certain that without such reliance the ephemeral novelty of speech, the apologetic artifice of method, or the easy return to convention will not disappear from attempts in this line. Genuine poetry allows none of these; it is, more than drama, a "means of expression" that becomes authentic only when it has something to express, and that subject-matter must be grounded in the deepest nature and intelligence of the poet. A new poetic drama that realizes this may ultimately count itself not only the reviver of a particular literary form, but of something more essential—a purpose, implicit in age and people, of which true literature is the expression. Whether a play is written to reprove religion, like *Within the Gates*, or to defend it, like *The Rock*; whether it is written for social propaganda or political; its greatness will exist in direct proportion to the dramatist's respect for this law. The conditions hostile to poetic drama may possibly be auspicious. They may drive poets not only to revive a form, but to create the audience that will make a poetic theatre imperative.

Checklist of Additional Reviews

*Francis Birrell. "Mr. Eliot's Revue." *New Statesman* 7 (2 June 1934), 847.

*D. G. Bridson. "Mr. Eliot Again." *New English Weekly* 5 (5 July 1934), 285–86.

*L. A. G. Strong. *Observer*, 22 July 1934, p. 8.

Edward Shillito. "The Faith of T. S. Eliot." *Christian Century* 51 (1 August 1934), 994–95.

Tablet 164 (4 August 1934), 138.

Everyman 47 (17 August 1934), 189.

William Rose Benét. "*The Rock*." *Saturday Review of Literature* 11 (22 September 1934), 129.

Sunday Times, 30 September 1934, p. 12.

*Harry Thornton Moore. *Adelphi* 9 (December 1934), 188–89.

**Poetry Review* 26 (January–February 1935), 78–79.

Percy Hutchison. "T. S. Eliot's Pageant-Play of Faith." *New York Times Book Review*, 14 July 1935, p. 8.

Frederick A. Pottle. "Drama of Action." *Yale Review* 25 (December 1935), 426–29. [Included in reviews of *Murder in the Cathedral* in this volume, pp. 333–35]

Harris Downey. "T. S. Eliot—Poet as Playwright." *Virginia Quarterly Review* 12 (January 1936), 142–45. [Included in reviews of *Murder in the Cathedral* in this volume, pp. 337–38]

MURDER IN THE CATHEDRAL
1935

MURDER
IN THE CATHEDRAL

by

T. S. Eliot

London
Faber and Faber Limited
24 Russell Square

*"Mr. Eliot's New Play." Times Literary Supplement 1741 (13 June 1935), 376.

Mr. Eliot's new work of poetic drama has moved farther from the theatre than his previous attempts and come nearer to the Church. It is written for production in Canterbury Cathedral this week. Its conventions have more in common with ritual than with the stage, as in the earliest English drama; and these conventions which he has adopted, including strong use of a chorus, are well assimilated to the whole texture. In *The Rock* they were often self-conscious, but here they have become subordinate, natural, appropriate. The play might be described as a poem for several voices used liturgically.

The subject covered by a title that echoes detective fiction is Thomas Becket's assassination. It is told without an obvious propagandist intention, which was not the case with *The Rock*. We open with Becket returning after seven years abroad, to a scene which has been prepared by a chorus of Canterbury women, who speak in strikingly simple language:

> Here is no continuing city, here is no
>   abiding stay.
> Ill the wind, ill the time, uncertain the
>   profit, certain the danger.
> O late late late, late is the time, late
>   too late, and rotten the year;
> Evil the wind, and bitter the sea, and
>   grey the sky, grey grey grey.
> O Thomas, return, Archbishop;
>   return, return to France.

But Becket, who is shown throughout as one ready for death, will not accept any warning. Tempters appear. One tempter would have him revive the worldly pleasures of his youth, and when rejected remarks: "I leave you to the pleasures of your higher vices." Another tempter would have him re-seek the power he once held as Chancellor. To whom Becket replies:

> Those who put their faith in worldly
>   order
> Not controlled by the order of God,
> [. . . . .]
> Degrade what they exalt.

A third tempter would have him lead rebellion against the king; a fourth makes a subtler appeal—to triumph over his enemies by martyrdom:

> Think, Thomas, think of enemies
>   dismayed,
> Creeping in penance, frightened of a
>   shade;
> [. . . . .]
> Think of the miracles, by God's grace,
> And think of your enemies, in another
>   place.

But Becket is aware of the danger of this last temptation: "To do the right deed for the wrong reason."

As an interlude we see him preaching in the cathedral on Christmas morning, 1170, when he pronounces his view that a Christian martyrdom is not the effect of man's will to become a saint. He says: "[. . .] [t]he true martyr is he who has become the instrument of God, who has lost his will in the will of God [. . .]." He concludes his sermon by saying he does not think he will ever preach to them again.

In Part II, the murder takes place. First, the four knights accuse Becket. The priests try to persuade him to take sanctuary, but he is more than ready for death: "I have had a tremor of bliss, a wink of heaven, a whisper, / And I would no longer be denied." When the priests carry him by force into the cathedral, he makes them unbar the doors. The knights enter, slightly

319

tipsy, and kill him. They then, in mock-elaborate prose, justify themselves, urging that their act is disinterested, that Becket's crime was his failure to unite temporal and spiritual office (Chancellor and Archbishop), "an almost ideal State," and that by his attitude he more or less killed himself.

All through the play the two main notes are of Becket with his *idée fixe* of fulfillment in death and of the chorus exhibiting a sense of approaching death. Mr. Eliot's talent seems to be most effective in this second note, of imminent desolation:

> The forms take shape in the dark air:
> Puss-purr of leopard, footfall of the
>   padding bear,
> Palm-pat of the nodding ape, square
>   hyena waiting
> For laughter, laughter, laughter.

Or, again, a recurrence of the undersea imagery of his early work: "I have lain on the floor of the sea and breathed with the breathing of the sea-anemone, swallowed with ingurgitation of the sponge. I have lain in the soil and criticised the worm." But those former contradictions which were the special surprise of Mr. Eliot's verse are here fused. This is his most unified writing. He has admirably brought to maturity his long experimenting for a dramatic style, the chief merit of which lies in his writing for a chorus.

---

*I. M. Parsons.
"Poetry, Drama, and Satire."
Spectator 154, no. 5583 (28 June 1935), 1112–14.

Artists, it has been said, usually know what is best for themselves. And certainly Mr. Eliot's preoccupation with religion, in which many critics saw the end of his poetry and the stultification of his criticism, wears a different aspect in the light of his latest work. *Murder in the Cathedral* is a historical episode, or series of episodes, dealing with the life and death of Thomas Becket. The action takes place alternately in the Archbishop's Hall and in the Cathedral at Canterbury, and covers the last few weeks of Becket's life. The episodes are linked by a Chorus of Women of Canterbury, and divided into two parts by a prose interlude in which Becket preaches in the Cathedral on Christmas Day, 1170. So much for the frame of the piece. To suggest its essential quality is not so simple. One might begin by referring to the choruses, used in the Greek manner to create an atmosphere of impending evil, among an audience expectantly acquainted with the outcome of the plot.

> Some presage of an act
> Which our eyes are compelled to
>   witness, has forced our feet
> Towards the cathedral. We are forced
>   to bear witness.

Or to Becket's tempters, advocates in turn of luxury, temporal power, and spiritual glory through martyrdom, whose arguments are used both to reveal Thomas's character and to introduce relevant details of his past life: "If you will remember me, my Lord, at your prayers, / I'll remember you at kissing-time below the stairs." Or to the Christmas sermon, Becket's final affirmation of his position, which acts as a bridge between the psychological action of Part I and the physical action of Part II. All these are important to the play's effectiveness, contribute to its atmosphere, construction, and presentation of character. But equally one might mention those passages of the chorus in which the stress is not on the fate that is foreboded, but on the fate that is the portion of the common man: "Of the men and women who shut the door and sit by the fire," passages in which Mr. Eliot's particular touch is most revealing and most assured. Or to the skillful variety of tone and modulations of rhythm in the Tempters' speeches; or to the scene immediately following the murder when the four knights advance and address the audience in justification of their act: a scene whose satire gives point to the main theme of the play, while relieving the tension created by the climax and providing a smooth elision to the exaltation of the final chorus. All these again are part of the play's quality, though still only part. Its main quality is bound up inextricably with the written word, which cannot be paraphrased. And if one were to start quoting it would be hard to know where to begin or where to stop. For the play is a dramatic poem, and has an imaginative unity which does not lend itself to brief quotation. An imaginative unity ... there perhaps is the essence of the matter. Many people could have made a play out of Becket's murder—an instructive play, a witty play, a good thriller or a moral tale. Mr. Eliot has done more: he has reanimated a literary form which in England has been dead or dormant for nearly three hundred years, and in doing so he has found himself anew as a poet, only with an added ease, lucidity, and objectiveness.

*Edwin Muir.
"New Literature."
London Mercury 32 (July 1935), 281–83.

Mr. Eliot's latest play is an interesting and moving piece of work and, unlike *The Rock*, a unified one. The drama is simple, direct and closely knit, and it proceeds within an intellectual scheme which is stated quite early in the play and is never forgotten during the rest of the action, which in turn is circumscribed by it and takes its governing significance from it. The scheme of the action, that is to say, is related to or rather becomes part of a scheme of human action in general, seen timelessly. This scheme of human action is tentatively stated in the first chorus by the poor women of Canterbury with which the play opens:

> We wait, we wait,
> And the saints and martyrs wait, for
> those who shall be martyrs and
> saints.
> Destiny waits in the hand of God,
> shaping the still unshapen:
> I have seen these things in a shaft of
> sunlight.
> [....................................]

It is stated more definitely by Thomas at his first entrance, in a reply to one of the priests who had reproved the women for "croaking like frogs in the treetops":

> Peace. And let them be, in their
> exaltation.
> They speak better than they know,
> and beyond your understanding.
> They know and do not know, what it
> is to act or suffer.
> They know and do not know, that
> action is suffering
> And suffering is action. Neither does
> the agent suffer
> Nor the patient act. But both are fixed
> In an eternal action, an eternal
> patience
> To which all must consent that it may
> be willed
> And which all must suffer that they
> may will it,

321

That the pattern may subsist, for the
    pattern is the action
And the suffering, that the wheel may
    turn and still
Be forever still.

[. . .]

This is Mr. Eliot's image of earthly life: the wheel that turns and is forever still. But as man is a spirit he is not completely bound to this wheel with every power; and this is the other aspect of the intellectual scheme of the play. The first clear statement of it comes at the end of the first act, when Thomas deliberately embraces his martyrdom, which he sees is bound to follow:

                       I know
What yet remains to show you of my
    history
Will seem to most of you at best
    futility,
Senseless self-slaughter of a lunatic,
Arrogant passion of a fanatic.
[. . . . .]
I shall no longer act or suffer, to the
    sword's end.

The last line is the crucial one, for it declares that Thomas, by purification of the will, has set himself free from the wheel. This mystery is dealt with more fully in the sermon which follows, forming an interlude between the first and the second (and last) act, and dealing with martyrdom.

Saints are not made by accident. Still less is a Christian martyrdom the effect of a man's will to become a Saint, as a man by willing and contriving may become a ruler of men . . . A martyrdom . . . is never the design of man; for the true martyr is he who has become

the instrument of God, who has lost his will in the will of God [. . .].

These quotations should make clear the main lines of the action, which is both earthly and transcendental, a matter therefore both of grief and rejoicing (part of the sermon deals with this question, how believers can sorrow and rejoice at the same action). The meaning of the whole play is summed up in a few lines spoken by Thomas before his death: "I give my life / To the Law of God above the Law of Man [. . .]." That expresses both the nature of Thomas's action and the mystery implied in it. And this is what Mr. Eliot is mainly concerned with, and without bearing it in mind the drama loses most of its meaning.

It is not for a reviewer to agree or disagree with the intellectual scheme of a work of imagination; all that he need be concerned with is its consistency, and its imaginative and dramatic force. From the outline I have given I think it will be clear that the intellectual fabric of this play is quite unusually consistent and closely knit, and also imaginatively impressive. But it is the dramatic force that it conveys to the action that is perhaps most striking of all; for one might almost say that the action owes its ultimate force to the consistency with which Mr. Eliot's imagination has moved within the bounds of his general conception of human action, stated abstractly in the passages which I have quoted. It may be said, of course, that every work of imagination moves within the limits of its author's general conception of human action; but here the conception is held far more clearly and consistently than in most dramatic works, and the result is not only a greater intellectual, but a greater dramatic intensity, for every utterance of the actors being given its exact place in the scheme, is given also

322

a more packed and full meaning. Sometimes, it seems to me, Mr. Eliot secures this precision at the expense of imaginative freedom, particularly in the figures of the four knights, who represent the ordinary man of action. But the action itself as he conceives it is truly dramatic; the figure of Thomas in particular is beautifully imagined: the scene between him and the Tempters being probably the finest in the play.

Obviously a play conceived on such terms as these must have a number of meanings apart from or flowing from the main one. "I give my life / To the Law of God above the Law of Man" clearly expresses one of them, and one which at present is of the utmost urgency: the rival claims of religion and politics. In this question one feels that Mr. Eliot is on the same side as Thomas Becket; but what he has written is a play, and so he has to state both sides. In the first act both sides are finely balanced, and that is what makes it so strong dramatically; in the second the murderers of Becket are somewhat burlesqued and belittled, and even though they may have been in themselves quite commonplace or even ridiculous characters, Mr. Eliot by making them actually so loses the feeling, which he catches so finely in the scene of the Tempters, of the deep and permanent worldly power which they represent: they have not enough behind them. He holds the balance between the two powers in the first act, but in the second he actually gives the impression of making Becket's triumph too easy, perhaps a strange complaint to make about a dramatic representation of martyrdom. The Chorus immediately preceding the murder, on the other hand, is one of the finest in the whole play. But this poetic drama, unlike *The Rock*, does not depend on the choruses. It is a unified work, and a work of great beauty.

*James Laughlin. "Mr. Eliot on Holy Ground." *New English Weekly* 7 (11 July 1935), 250–51.

... wherever a martyr has given his
    blood for the blood of Christ,
There is holy ground, and the sanctity
    shall not depart from it
Though armies trample over it,
    though sightseers come with
    guide-books looking over it ...

However you want to feel about Mr. Eliot's "position," *Murder in the Cathedral* proves that he is still a great master of metric and that he knows how to put together a play. These new lines do not sparkle as do those of *The Waste Land*, but in their quiet way they are perfect.

The mind jumps at once to the problem of poetry and belief, but I don't want to get myself entangled in that. Mr. Eliot himself has treated it quite adequately in his essay on Dante. It is enough to say that although an Anglican vicar will naturally feel more excited about this play than others would, agnostics and heretics need not abstain, as it contains enough intellectual pabulum to hold all their attention. For example, you can do a lot of thinking about Mr. Eliot's blending of the Aristotelean tragedy with Christian dogma.

The play begins in the best Greek manner with a Chorus (of the women of Canterbury) chanting of bad things to come and a Herald ushering in the Protagonist. But with Becket's first speech you realize that here is no Oedipus about to be battered from all sides by bland fate, but a Christian martyr forging his own destiny with eyes open to the forces moving against him, [who knows]

> [. . .] that action is suffering
> And suffering is action. Neither does
> the agent suffer
> Nor the patient act. But both are fixed
> In an eternal action, an eternal
> patience
> To which all must consent that it may
> be willed
> And which all must suffer that they
> may will it,
> That the pattern may subsist, for the
> pattern is the action
> And the suffering that the wheel may
> turn and still
> Be forever still.

These lines deserve your careful analysis, for they are not only the principle motif of the play, but as well, I think, a deliberate expression of the poet's philosophy. Roughly I interpret them as orthodox Thomism; in any case they indicate the intellectual nature of Eliot's faith.

Reading Sophocles I always get the impression of fly-swatting—of a superhuman hand suddenly reaching down from nowhere to crush a bewildered little animal. Thus in the Greek frame such a line as "And which all must suffer that they may will it," is all out of drawing. What is Eliot's purpose in this distortion?

An examination of the psychological angle provides the clue. Aristotle's criteria call for pity and terror to induce the catharsis. But the fall of Becket produces neither; he foresees his doom and declines escape though it is offered—hence not terror; he is obviously ready for death and glad to fulfill his faith—and so no pity. And yet the play's action does release emotion within the observer. Of what kind? The same, I think, as is aroused by a Mediaeval Mystery or Miracle, one of religious exaltation, of completion of faith. It is clear then that Eliot has attempted a fusion of the Classic and Mediaeval dramatic formulae. Perhaps this will offend the purist, but for me it is curious and thought-provoking.

Is this fusion purely a technical matter, or does Eliot intend a deeper meaning? Does he wish to indicate a fundamental affinity between the Classic and Christian tempers? Does his duality reflect a similar tendency in his own thought? Or is he, in blending an act of faith with tragedy, merely recalling that Greek drama had its origin in the religious ritual of the Goat Song, in which masked priests induced a mystic ecstacy in the celebrants by their chant and pantomime? I guess you would have to ask him.

To make his work completely solid Eliot presents through the assassins' after-murder speeches a clear analysis of the historical forces conditioning the event. Becket would not compromise between Church and State and was put on the spot. The knights speak in prose.

Throughout *Murder in the Cathedral* the versification is of a high and even quality. There are few lines which will catch in your memory and stick there, as do so many of those of *The Waste Land*, and the poems in *Prufrock*, but neither is there a faulty line. There is no fixed meter, but there is, in the best sense, a fine free metric. Mr. Eliot has been to school and knows his language-tones and sound-lengths as few others do. He can cut a line of sound in time so that it comes off the page to you as a tangible design. His cadences are soft and cool and flowing, but there is never an unnecessary word. The language is highly charged with meaning, but there is no looseness of rhetoric. The craftsmanship of the verse is so unostentatious that you must look closely to see all the richness of detail.

> We are not ignorant women, we know
>   what we must expect and not
>   expect.
> [. . . . .]
> We have seen the young man
>   mutilated,
> The torn girl trembling by the
>   mill-stream.
> And meanwhile we have gone on
>   living,
> Living and partly living
> [. . . . .]

Yes, it's a long, long way to *Prufrock*, it's a long, long way from here. There has been much change, but I think it is in the nature of a fertile evolution and not a sterile decline.

And yet is the change so great? *Murder in the Cathedral* . . . is hardly a title chosen by a religious recluse! And even back in 1917 (with apologies to "The Hippopotamus") we find that "the True Church can never fail / For it is based upon a rock."

Conrad Aiken [pseudonym, Samuel Jeake, Jr.]. "London Letter." *New Yorker* 11 (13 July 1935), 53–55.

We ought, of course, to have gone to Ascot to see the gray top hats and lovely dresses (not to mention the umbrellas) and perhaps a horse or two; instead we joined a very different pilgrimage, and one with an even statelier history than Queen Anne's Royal Ascot. In short, we went to Canterbury. It was the week of Canterbury's annual Festival of Music and Drama, an affair organized by the Friends of Canterbury Cathedral, its admirable object being to raise funds for the upkeep and repair of the church. The program of entertainment was unusually good this year—first-class concerts in the Cloisters by the B.B.C. Orchestra, and also in the Cathedral itself (the only regrettable feature of this being that for the moment one was unable to see the newly restored tomb of the Black Prince, now bright gold), with music by Bach, Ravel, Holst, Vaughan Williams, Scarlatti, and so forth. No wonder the little town was crowded, swarms of uniformed schoolgirls being especially conspicuous, but the strangest thing of all was the fact that this year the chief attraction was actually the work of an American. To be exact, an ex-American. T. S. Eliot had been invited by the Friends of the Cathedral to write a play for the occasion—no doubt because of his production of *The Rock* last year at Sadler's Wells, in aid of the City churches—and he complied, giving them *Murder in the Cathedral*. Thus, without any preliminary fuss or fanfare, without advertisements in the newspapers, or any advance announcements except through Church channels, a poetic play was staged in the Chapter House which may well mark a turning point in English drama.

Making every allowance for the extreme impressiveness of the surroundings—the hall of the Chapter House is, of course, magnificent—and for the extraordinary associational aid in the fact that a play about Thomas Becket's martyrdom was being performed on the very spot where the martyrdom itself had been enacted—a combination of circumstances which must remain unique—nevertheless, one hadn't listened five minutes before one felt that one was witnessing a play which had the quality of greatness. If one had become uneasy about the effect of Eliot's churchward leanings on his poetry, one forgot that at once. Performed in a barn, and before an audience of skeptics, *Murder in the Cathedral* would still be a profound and beautiful thing. It transcends the particular beliefs on which it has been built—or, rather, it creates its own beliefs out of its own sheer livingness—exactly as *Everyman* does, or *Oedipus Rex*, and, incidentally, with striking technical resemblances to both. The use of the chorus of ten women, and the choruses themselves, were superb. One's feeling was that here at last was the English language literally being *used*, itself becoming the stuff of drama, turning alive with its own natural poetry. And Eliot's formalization wasn't at all the sort of thing one has grown accustomed to expect of poetic drama—no trace of sham antique or artiness about it; nothing, in the "dead" sense, "poetic." No, the thing was directly and terribly real, the poetry of the choruses was as simple and immediate in its meaning as our own daily lives, and the transition into satirical modern prose at the end, when the four knights turned and addressed the audience, came without shock. It is a triumph of poetic genius that out of such actionless material—the mere conflict of a mind with itself—a play so deeply moving, and so exciting, should have been written; and so rich, moreover, in the various language of *humanity*. That is perhaps the greatest surprise about it—in the play Eliot has become human, and tender, with a tenderness and a humanity which have nowhere else in our time found such beauty of form.

The production by Martin Browne was perfect. The stage was of the simplest, the actors approaching it from the center aisle of the hall, through the audience; the chorus, when not speaking, sitting at the right and left in the niches between little columns, as if merely a part of the design. Robert Speaight, as Becket, was superb. The other parts were taken by amateurs, the Cathedral Players, who give a performance that professionals might envy. And the speaking of the choruses was so beautiful that one actually resented at moments the singing which served as a counterpoint for it, from the gallery at the other end of the hall; for once, the spoken word was all one wanted. Altogether, an event; and we shall be surprised if later this lovely thing isn't given a run in the West End of London, or even put on by the Theatre Guild in New York.

[. . .]

Mark Van Doren. "The Holy Blisful Martir." *Nation* 141 (9 October 1935), 417.

It is only in a minor sense that the action of Mr. Eliot's play can be understood as taking place at Canterbury. The stage directions put it there; the Chorus is composed of women from the town; the Archbishop stands and talks in his own hall, and at the end is murdered by four English knights while he prays before the cathedral altar; and the date, 1170, is displayed with sufficient prominence. But the peculiar merit of the poet has little to do with all this. It has rather to do with the fact that Mr. Eliot has confined himself with a strict and icy purity to the one aspect of the story which he was equipped to treat. This aspect is such as not even to suggest a comparison with Shakespeare, whose kind of humanity Mr. Eliot nowhere attempts. It suggests only Mr. Eliot, who achieves perfection here to the degree that he explores his own mind and employs his own art.

He is concerned first and last with the morality, or perhaps it is the theology, of martyrdom. Chaucer's "holy blisful martir" is so far from blissful in these pages as to strike a kind of silent terror in the spectator's heart through the spectacle of his bleak and puzzled loneliness. And as for his holiness—ah, that is a question which Mr. Eliot is unable to answer. Indeed the impossibility of answering it is the theme of the play. For who can say that Thomas Becket was without spiritual pride when he determined to obey his instinct of martyrdom? Who can say that he exposed himself to swords for any better reason than a certain tempter gave him—this tempter being the last of four, and the most deadly of them because he urges "the right deed," namely martyrdom, for "the wrong reason," namely glory? The point is plainly made that if Thomas suffered death for the sake of power and glory he was not holy; and there is abundant evidence, both before and after the catastrophe at the altar, that most of England felt a fanaticism in his final act. But the point is as plainly made that this particular martyrdom may have been designed in heaven, where "the Saints are most high, having made themselves most low." As for an earthly solution to the problem, there is and can be none; nor can Thomas's own words to himself be taken as testimony, since he dies a man and not a saint, and speaks accordingly—as one, that is to say, who desires to know rather than knows.

Murder in the Cathedral has been compared with *Saint Joan*, but it is both higher and thinner than that; higher because it rises above the merely political problem of obedience to authority, and thinner because theology must always be thin on any stage, even the stage to which Mr. Eliot adapts himself with such dignity, simplicity, and skill. Within its limits the play is a masterpiece, a thing of crystal whose appearance of flawlessness is not altered by the weird reality of the four speeches in prose delivered by the murderers after their job is done. For the irony which tinkles through those speeches is merely the accompaniment of an irony pervading the whole, and reaching its deepest tones in the last words of Becket. Mr. Eliot has written no better poem than this, and none which seems simpler. It is of course not simple; but that is another of its ironies.

F. O. Matthiessen. "T. S. Eliot's Drama of Becket." Saturday Review 12 (12 October 1935), 10–11.

That *Murder in the Cathedral* was produced at this summer's Canterbury Festival with apparently considerable success should not surprise anyone who has tried reading it aloud. For not only do its lines fall naturally into spoken patterns, but, even more importantly, its structure is dramatically conceived *as a whole*, each of its two parts building strongly up to a climax. In this respect it is in marked contrast with Eliot's two previous experiments with drama. *Sweeney Agonistes*, 1927, which broke away from the packed intricacy of his former poetry by attempting to utilize music-hall rhythms, was left as a fragment. *The Rock*, which was written for production at Sadler's Wells last year, was more in the nature of a ritualistic pageant than a play.

But in this play presenting the martyrdom of Becket, the poet has worked out an original and effective form. Its general construction and its choruses bear a kinship to the kind of classical drama represented by Milton's *Samson*; in its characterization by types, especially in the four tempters in the first part and the four knights in the second, it shows a relationship also to the mediaeval morality plays. But it is naturally far more supple than these latter. The varied movement of its long lines seems often to have sprung from the response of the poet's ear to the cadences of the Bible and the Catholic Mass. As a result it demonstrates at last the fruitfulness of the belief that Eliot voiced in his "Dialogue on Dramatic Poetry" in 1928, that the essentially dramatic quality of church ritual might again furnish a stimulation and release for poetic drama.

Recent criticism has tended to insist that a poet should find his material in his immediate surroundings, claiming that otherwise he takes refuge in a world of his own fancy and fails to portray an authentic relation with the urgent problems of society. And it is probably a matter of considerable skepticism to many readers as to wherein the career of a twelfth-century archbishop can have much relevancy to existence as they know it. What Eliot argued, in pointing that Pound's translations from the early Italian poets are often much more "modern" than the contemporary sketches, seems to me far more searching: that "it is irrelevant whether what you see, really see, as a human being is Arnaut Daniel or your greengrocer"; the important consideration is to grasp the permanent elements in human nature. To what degree Eliot has grasped and portrayed such elements in this poem can be briefly suggested by a speech in which Thomas, addressing one of his priests, meditates on the lot of the Chorus, the working women of Canterbury.

[Quotation of lines from "They speak better than they know, and beyond your understanding. / They know and do not know, what it is to act or suffer" to "That the pattern may subsist, for the pattern is the action / And the suffering, that the wheel may turn and still / Be forever still," *Murder in the Cathedral*]

The full weight and meaning of such a passage can be appreciated only in its context; but it is at once apparent how closely its assumptions relate to Eliot's long absorption in the view of life that has been best expressed in poetry by Dante. Here, in this speech of Becket's, Eliot reveals an increased share of the depth of understanding which also characterizes Dante, not merely of an acute part of life but of its total pattern, a pattern that embraces not only "the eternal burden" but "the perpetual glory" as well. Here is a voicing of the subtle interweaving of suffering, striving, and acceptance that unite to form the attitude that finds expression in such a line in the *Paradiso* as "la sua voluntate è nostra pace." Here, in this mature reflection on the incalculably intricate relation between feeling and action, is the poetic statement of what Eliot has in mind when, discussing the relation of the individual to society, he refers to "the Catholic paradox": society is for the salvation of the individual and the individual must be sacrificed to society. Communism is merely a heresy, but a heresy is better than nothing.

The dramatic conflict in the first part of the work is an inner one, of a sort that shows Eliot even more clearly than ever in the tradition of Henry James, and, more especially here, of Hawthorne. For the conflict is Becket's struggle against pride and his final transcendence over it. The last tempter speaks to him insidiously in words that had often been Becket's thoughts, luring him on to martyrdom not as a result of losing his will in God's, but as an act of self-aggrandizement, as a final overweening of his pride. Tortured by a dilemma in which

328

it seems to him that he can "neither act nor suffer without perdition," and where all existence consequently seems unreal, he fights his way through to his final resolve:

> Now is my way clear, now is the
> meaning plain:
> Temptation shall not come in this kind
> again.
> The last temptation is the greatest
> treason:
> To do the right deed for the wrong
> reason.

Thus fortified, his will at last made perfect in acceptance of God's will, he continues to maintain the supremacy of the law of God above the law of man, and goes forward, in the second part, to his death at the hands of the knights.

It is upon his consecration to perseverance in his career and the world's denial of its value that the dramatic conflict of the second part hinges. Immediately after the murder, in the most effectively unexpected passage of the play, the knights themselves turn to the audience, and, speaking in prose, conduct a systematic defense of their act. The writing of their speeches is masterly in its wit and irony: the knights fall naturally into all the clichés of an actual present day parliamentary debate.

The contrast between them and Becket is thoroughly presented. Becket argues throughout—in passages which illuminate Eliot's apprehension of human history— that the knights, by judging only from results, by deferring always to the appearance of social circumstance, have blurred all distinction between good and evil. In consequence of their conception of deterministic process, no individual can be blamed for oppression, exploitation, or crime that he undertakes in the cause of the State. There are only social forces and expediency, the responsibility of a human will for its own actions has been utterly lost. But in opposing this doctrine with his

life, in reasserting the value of the idea as rising above that of fact, Becket's is never a plea for the individual without the deepest obligations to society. His most characteristic tones sound in his experienced thoughts, again concluding in the image of the turning wheel, on the inexorability of man's fate as part of a force greater than himself:

> We do not know very much of the
> future
> Except that from generation to
> generation
> The same things happen again and
> again.
> [. . . . .]
>
>   Only
> The fool, fixed in his folly, may think
> He can turn the wheel on which he
> turns.

The samples of the verse that I have been able to include here by no means suggest its freedom and variety. Never departing in any of his variations far enough from the norm of blank verse to break down his formal pattern, Eliot reveals throughout the controlled mastery of technique that, among other living poets writing in English, only Yeats can rival.

The lines quoted are sufficient, however, to show this play's principal defect. Though the language is both sharp and precise, it is extremely bare. It avails itself very little of new life that comes from sensuous imagery; and compared with Eliot's early work, many passages, particularly those spoken by the priests, seem attenuated. A relative lack of density also emerges in comparing the play as a whole with *The Waste Land*. This is partly owing to the fact that in *The Waste Land* the poet employed symbols which maintained the action continually in the present at the same time that he was exploring analogies with the past. In the play, though centering throughout on problems that reveal the "permanent in human nature," he has not made that complete fusion. His imagination has not created the illusion of a four-dimensional world; the characters remain partly abstractions. Putting it in terms of the usual objection to historical fiction, one could say that the life represented is lacking something in immediacy and urgency, an objection that is forgotten only in the face of a *Coriolanus* or a *Phèdre*. Nevertheless, this play—the title of which, with its unfortunately smart suggestion of a detective story I have done my best to avoid—even though it does not reach the rank of Eliot's most nearly perfect work of art, *Ash-Wednesday*, demonstrates how Eliot has survived both popularity and unpopularity, both generously bestowed frequently for the wrong reasons. He has gone on undistracted, cultivating and perfecting his craft, and bringing to bear upon it his accruing experience.

Peter Monro Jack.
"T. S. Eliot's Drama of
Beauty and Momentous
Decision."
*New York Times Book
Review*, 27 October 1935,
p. 11.

Mr. Eliot's play was written expressly to fit into the annual week of music and drama at Canterbury; it opened there in the Chapter House last June under the supervision of Martin Browne, the scenarist of *The Rock*. It is a dramatization about the killing of Thomas Becket, murdered, as one remembers from the schoolbooks, on the word of the king, Henry: "Will no one rid me of this saucy knave?"—murdered and martyred in the cathedral by four knights of the king as the first symbolic act (1170) of the rivalry between crown and church.

The historical matter is taken for granted and the chronicle material comes in by the way. This is strictly a characterization of Thomas about to meet his death, and, by extension, of the Christian martyr. The possibilities of dramatic conflict are crowded into the introspection of Thomas. He has to face and answer four tempters. One of these reverts to his chancellorship days when he enjoyed the king's favor and had good times and easy dinners. Another suggests the desirability of temporal power: the patronage, the intrigues of a master politician. A third cautiously intimates the possible power of the people: Thomas might become a demagogue, on the side of the plain people against the usurpations of king and baron. A fourth, the most insidious and treasonable of all, whispers of the glories of martyrdom, the name, the fame, the reclaim of personal sacrifice, accruing with the centuries.

All of these are in Thomas's reach, and his response is a measure of his faith or failure. There is no other drama. But outside this, and preceding it, is the Chorus of poor women of Canterbury, desiring only peace and the ordinary means of living; disturbed by the doom felt in the air, not understanding it, and wishing only that Thomas would return to France and keep his metaphysical problems from interfering with the ordinary business of crops and rent. The priests who appear next on the stage are more nearly implicated: they welcome the return of authority.

And indeed, when Thomas enters Eliot's imagined scene of twelfth-century theocracy, he brings the authority of a great spiritual protagonist, "fixed in an eternal action, an eternal patience." He comforts the women, quiets the priests,

330

and turns to the tempters who appear on the stage singly, confronting them with power and dignity, until he is visibly taken aback by this fourth tempter, whom he had not expected, this Frankenstein of his secret *personal* ambition of martyrdom—it is this he has chiefly to conquer.

An interlude is given him in the form of a magnificent sermon as a prelude to his martyrdom and an apology for his death: "A martyrdom . . . is never the design of man; for the true martyr is he who has become the instrument of God, who has lost his will in the will of God [. . .], [the martyr] no longer desires anything for himself, not even the glory of being a martyr . . . I do not think I shall ever preach to you again."

The verse throughout is plain and direct, so diversified in rhythm that it appears to be constantly changing with the dramatic mood: there is a remarkable passage in alliterative stress, others are in odic style, others in set stanzas. Such resources as Mr. Eliot's have probably never before been brought to liturgical drama. But it seems to us that the theatre as well as the church is enriched by this poetic play of grave beauty and momentous decision, and that if our stage were capable of presenting and speaking it, it would be a memorable thing to hear.

Geoffrey Stone. "Plays by Eliot and Auden." *American Review* 6 (November 1935), 121–28.

The poetry of T. S. Eliot, Wyndham Lewis has somewhere said, has been like a small particle of musk which scents an entire room; small in bulk, it has given its tone to the verse of a whole generation. Mr. Eliot's criticism has elucidated his poetry and made for its acceptance; it has laid down principles or pointed out characteristics in works of the past which might be discerned in his own work, and while there are those who applaud Mr. Eliot's verse and condemn his criticism, and a small number who do the converse, in general it can be said that once Mr. Eliot's critical theories are subscribed to, his verse is found to be rich in the elements that have marked the great poetry of every age. For not only is there homogeneity in Mr. Eliot's writing, but he is also conscious of the impulses and needs that underlie his work—a consciousness that is not manifest in a great deal of modern writing, which is often the product of superficially conflicting tendencies resulting from unexamined and invalid assumptions. Much that his contemporaries and juniors have taken over from Mr. Eliot's work is not his most profound. In his recent book on Paul Elmer More, Robert Shafer has called Mr. Eliot a purely aesthetic critic. This statement denies the best that is in the man's writing, but it does serve to underscore a significance that he holds for a large portion of his public. It is a significance, one might say, imposed on him rather than implicit in his work: the age has taken from his books what it has brought to them, or, more exactly, it has taken from them a technique for expressing the mood in which it has gone to them.

[. . .]

Hitherto Mr. Eliot has used his technical resources in the service of tension and compactness; *The Waste Land*, which is ranked as a "long poem," is about the length of "Lycidas." A loosening of technique was discernible in his pageant play of last year, *The Rock*, and has been carried to further length in this year's play, *Murder in the Cathedral.* Loosening of technique is not meant in any individual sense; it is not discipline and care that have been relaxed but lyric intensity. Mr. Eliot has, so to speak, limited his poetic vision to the immediate materials of his drama, and this allows him to support it with less strain. Such a move seems to be in the right direction, for a play, even a poetic drama, if it is meant for production, cannot be accorded the same attention and study as a poem, designed to be read, and the ear must be enabled to take in a great deal of it at a single hearing. Style and substance, Charles Maurras has said, are one; but the surface simplicity of *Murder in the Cathedral* does not mean that its subject is a shallow one, for true simplicity is only attained when many complexities have been considered and what is non-essential and what is abiding in them have been decided.

The murder of the play's title is the murder of Thomas Becket. The actual character of the historical Becket and the political forces that brought about his assassination are not Mr. Eliot's primary subject-matter. He is concerned with an issue of more fundamental character, and it is an issue intrinsically dramatic. Despite Mr. Day-Lewis's assertion that literature must become more concerned with the relations between classes and less with the relations between individuals, the greatest drama always has been, and always will be, concerned with the individual, for the individual is the unit from which life takes meaning: he is the center to which relates the intelligibility of the universe. For the purposes of action, the dramatic conflict in the individual must be with other individuals, but in so far as that conflict has meaning it is less a matter of the relation of man to man and more a matter of man's relation to things beyond him. Thus what moves us most in the drama of Oedipus is not his relations with Jocasta or the people of Thebes but with something less easily named; Hamlet's questions are not to be answered by Gertrude or Ophelia, since in the end they reduce to the question of "to be or not to be" and the manner of that being. And Thomas's concern is as to what his aspiration to goodness will actually be in God's sight; he finds the way to holiness no more easy in being chosen than in being traversed:

> The last temptation is the greatest treason:
> To do the right deed for the wrong reason
> [. . . . .]
> Ambition comes when early force is spent
> [. . . . .]

This is fundamental because it asks: Do we do good for good's sake? It is dramatic because it uncovers a conflict within the individual himself and an outcome of his nature.

Whether or not Thomas's choice of martyrdom is noble Mr. Eliot does not say. But such a judgment is perhaps one that we cannot ask any dramatist to make; he cannot speak with the finality of the casuist or he will seem to have stacked the cards against his character, whatever his decision. However, a dramatist cannot write at his most effective if he assumes that the moral worth of the actions he depicts is a small matter; for the moral worth of action is its human worth, and without recognition of this a drama is merely a spectacle of variously amusing puppets. Mr. Eliot's religious sense has greatly aided him here. Religion teaches a distinction between right and wrong, between good and evil, and makes the knowledge of this distinction essential to salvation, so that the concern with right and wrong goes beyond a mere interest in personal happiness. The awareness of this distinction, and the fact that it is a real one, illuminates *Murder in the Cathedral* and gives a sweep and grandeur to Thomas's struggles which show them to be as central in our day as they were in his own. For Thomas, as a person, confronts something more than personal and proves that men do not dwell forever "each in his prison." This is made possible through the reality which evil is given in these pages; the struggle is not with an illusion engendered in the self but with an actual exterior force:

> I have seen
> Rings of light coiling downwards, descending
> To the horror of the ape. Have I not known, not known
> What was coming to be? It was here, in the kitchen, in the passage,
> In the mews in the barn in the byre in the market-place
> [.................................]

Sometimes, it must be said, Thomas's problem seems more real than Thomas himself and the people who surround him—the characters become convenient abstractions and the play loses in dramatic quality, its story told more through the ruminations of its author than through the actions of its characters. This is surprising in Mr. Eliot, who has showed a high talent for dramatic presentation even in his lyric pieces. One might also complain of the low key of the verse and its eschewal of rich metaphor. Here Mr. Eliot may be striving for an exclusive concentration on what he sees as the main imports of his drama, but the result now and again has the appearance of thinness rather than austerity. Remembering that Mr. Eliot has

said that Shakespeare reached his most poetic in his most dramatic, it does not seem consistent of him to have come so close to using a prose tempo. But these are not judgments on the play as a whole.

[. . .]

Frederick A. Pottle. "Drama of Action." *Yale Review* 25 (December 1935), 426–29.

[Review of *The Rock* and *Murder in the Cathedral*]

Drama in our days is struggling towards a new birth; the change can best be described by saying that our most gifted authors are deeply dissatisfied with drama of character and are turning to drama of plot. Their lively interest in Greek tragedy is symptomatic. Mr. MacLeish studies Sophocles and Mr. O'Neill refers to Aeschylus. But to write genuine drama of plot, of action, in our days is not altogether a matter of choice. The essence of Greek drama is religious certainty; an unshaken conviction that there is an order of things in the universe more real and more important than the individual hero. The difficulty which most modern playwrights face is that, lacking religious certainty, they have to invent an equivalent—to set up deliberately the external sanctions by which alone drama or plot can be organized. They start with a considerable—perhaps an insuperable—handicap. An artist who really feels dogmatic Christianity will have the advantage; and so also, it appears, will a convert to that most striking of modern religions—communism.

In June, 1934, Mr. T. S. Eliot published his first completed drama, *The Rock*, a pageant-play written and produced in the interest of a London church fund. *The Rock* was admitted Anglican propaganda. A clergyman furnished Mr. Eliot with a scenario for which he wrote words. The internal evidence of collaboration is abundant. No one, familiar with Eliot's earlier works, would expect him to have chosen just that subject matter, nor to have put it together in just that way. Yet the foreign matter is, to a remarkable extent, dominated by his astringent personality, and the overtones of the piece are so characteristic that one wonders whether they may not have caused his clerical sponsors some misgivings. He introduced a chorus, and within the speeches of the chorus (which probably contain the best Christian poetry of our time) he moved freely, reiterating that arid and austere Christian faith which he had announced in *Ash-Wednesday*. His scenario, one fancies, must have tended towards a facile optimism, but for him the air was still thoroughly small and dry. He repudiated the notion of progress in the Church Militant. Churches must be always building, not as part of a slow but ultimately triumphant penetration of the powers of darkness, but because churches are always decaying and we must bear witness.

[Quotation of lines 31–34 of *The Rock*, Chorus VI]

Man's duty is simple and single: it is to "make perfect his will."

In *Murder in the Cathedral* Eliot resumes that text and founds an entire action upon it. The murder of Thomas Becket is only a terminus, clearly announced from the very beginning of the piece. Far from striving to escape martyrdom, Thomas welcomes it. His struggle is to make perfect his will before the event; to purge himself of the last and most deadly manifestation of pride, which is "to do the right thing for the wrong reason." Parallel with his struggle runs another, expressed in the speeches of the Chorus of poor Canterbury women: the struggle of the ordinary unsaintly mortal to nerve himself for the bloody working out of Destiny. The Archbishop is only too eager for the consummation; the women in sick and shuddering suspense beseech him to depart out of their coasts and spare them the awful intrusion of the Divine Will into the tolerable pattern of their lives. With this starkly simple plot, Eliot achieves a drama perhaps more nearly Greek in its method than anything hitherto written in English.

In dramatic writing Eliot deliberately avoids that obscurity, both of style and sequence, which makes *The Waste Land* and *Ash-Wednesday* such slow reading. *Murder in the Cathedral* can be read rapidly, but like other good verse tragedies it contains some lines which give up their full content only after patient study and some others concerning the meaning of which there will always be difference of opinion. The method is completely unhistorical and unrealistic: Thomas's four tempters instance "The Catherine wheel, the pantomime cat, / The prizes given at the children's party, / The prize awarded for the English Essay" as examples of life's disappointments; and the Third Knight, justifying himself to the audience for the murder, shows that he has heard of the execution of Archbishop Laud and the humiliation of Archbishop Davidson in the rejection of the Revised Prayer-Book. Some of the lines assigned to the chorus have no dramatic propriety—as, for example, that extremely powerful and metaphysical passage in which the women proclaim the identity of their flesh with the worms of the soil and the living creatures of the deep. In this it may be thought that Mr. Eliot has been too clever. The chorus which follows immediately after the murder is peculiarly in character for the "scrubbers and sweepers of Canterbury," and seems to gain tremendously thereby:

> Clear the air! clean the sky! wash the wind! take stone from stone and wash them.
> The land is foul, the water is foul, our beasts and ourselves defiled with blood.

The verse shows Eliot's curious and inexhaustible resourcefulness in both rhymed and unrhymed measures, and he reveals in addition a fertility of dramatic invention which will surprise those who have not read *Sweeney Agonistes* and *The Rock* with attention. To devote an entire scene to a Christmas sermon preached by Thomas in the cathedral four days before his death was daring, but the device succeeds. Even more audacious is that of having the four knights, after the murder, step forward in turn and justify their deed in Shavian prose—a device for bringing various modern historical judgments of Thomas into the framework of the play. But to my mind the most impressive of all Eliot's feats are his liturgical adaptations in the second part of the play: the three introits at the beginning; the parody of the *Dies Irae* spoken by the Chorus outside the cathedral against the singing of the hymn inside; the concentration of blasphemy achieved just before the murder by having the four knights, slightly tipsy, speak in turn lines from a revivalist hymn and a Negro spiritual.

[. . .]

Edward Shillito. "*Murder in the Cathedral.*" *Christian Century* 52 (18 December 1935), 1636.

At the Canterbury Festival in June, Mr. T. S. Eliot's play, *Murder in the Cathedral*, was produced. It marks an advance in the work of this poet. Last year he wrote *The Rock*, but in his new play he has done what he could not do in that; he has shaped a drama which has a unity throughout, such as a Greek drama had. In his earlier work it was chiefly in the choruses that the reader looked for the mind of Mr. Eliot. The new drama, which deals with the death of Archbishop Thomas Becket, is of one piece and everywhere shows the same creative imagination. Mr. T. S. Eliot in his new work has won for religious drama a fresh hearing. Whether we admire it or not, we cannot ignore it. In my judgment it is a noble drama of enduring worth.

Like other supposed revolutionaries in literature, Mr. Eliot is in reality a reverent student of the great traditions. His method is in many ways like that of the Greek tragedians and yet it is new, since it is handled by a new thinker living in new spiritual realms.

It is strictly historical and yet while all the time the reader is in the Canterbury of 1170, he is haunted by the thought that the conflict is still taking place. All the great spiritual conflicts are never finally answered. It belongs to the greatness of a play that, even when the modern scene is not mentioned, it should be before the reader's inner eye. While he thinks of Canterbury 1170, he may be in Moscow or

Munich 1935. There is still the question before us how the two kingdoms are to be related, the kingdom of nature and the kingdom of grace; the state and the church; the prince and the spiritual ruler; the law of man and the law of God.

The one supreme difficulty for the writer of religious drama is to find a scene of action in which the spiritual world shall find true and indeed inevitable expression. The murder of Becket in the cathedral provides such an action. It was no accident; the deed was not done by some madmen with no intelligible purpose. As the poet tells the story, it was a significant deed, taking its place as a crisis in a drama, which deals with one of the great issues for man, not in that age but in all ages. St. Thomas himself sees clearly what his death means:

> [. . . . .]
> I give my life
> To the Law of God above the Law of
>   Man.

> [. . .]

There had been times in the life of Becket, in which the loyalties of his life had been disordered. He had submitted himself to the temporal power to secure his ends as a servant of God. Now he resists one by one the tempters who call him back to this and other passages of his life. He stands before us in the play not as a man who has kept one way from youth. Thomas says of himself:

> Thirty years ago, I searched all the
>   ways
> That lead to pleasure, advancement
>   and praise.
> Delight in sense, in learning and in
>   thought
> [. . . . .]

And afterwards ambition had come to him to win power as the servant of a king. But then the call had come to him to serve God above all other services. It is with this Thomas Becket that we have to do. Tempters in the play call him back to the easier ways of his past. But he scorns them. One tempter alone makes an appeal to him and this because he interprets to him the secret thoughts and desires against which he has always to fight.

Why is he ready to die? What motive is moving him? Why do martyrs die? The Fourth Tempter reveals the temptation which may come to the servant of God who is set in a place where he may retreat or be faithful even unto death. Thomas may win a kingly rule from his tomb; at his glittering shrine men would bend the knee. The time would come when that sanctuary would be pillaged; yet he would be in a glory surpassing all that earth would give. Who would not suffer the brief pain of death for this glory? [. . .]

Thomas knows [. . .] that the man who is faced by death for the sake of God may be tempted to do the right thing for the wrong motive. But in the sermon which he preaches on Christmas morning he tells what Christian martyrdom is and in the spirit of his own words he makes perfect his will: "[. . .] A martyrdom is always the design of God, for His love of men, to warn them and to lead them, to bring them back to His ways. It is never the design of man; for the true martyr is he who has become the instrument of God [. . .]." In this faith the archbishop offers himself to God, ready to suffer with his blood.

> [Quotation of lines from "This is the sign of the Church always," to "My death for His death," *Murder in the Cathedral*]

It is not hard, even for those who have not seen the drama, to imagine how impressive it must have been. Not since *Saint Joan* has there been any play on the

English stage in which such tremendous issues as this have been treated with such mastery of thought, as well as dramatic power.

[. . .]

Harris Downey. "T. S. Eliot—Poet as Playwright." *Virginia Quarterly Review* 12 (January 1936), 142–45.

[Review of *The Rock* and *Murder in the Cathedral*]

If Mr. Eliot's last two volumes, *The Rock* and *Murder in the Cathedral*, be considered good poetry, then they stand as further contradictions to the old idea that the poet is good to the degree that he deviates from his theory. For even though the scenario of the first was not original with Eliot but was provided for him by Mr. Martin Browne, and even though both the works show the author's determination to turn toward other forms rather than to rest the development of one manner, the pageant and the play incorporate predilections of the earlier poetry and tenets of the criticism. The verse of these two volumes differs from the earlier verse only in degree, but they provoke a more specific consideration of the choice of the dramatic rather than the reflective quality, of the importance of form and condensation, and of religion as subject matter.

In his essay on *Hamlet*, Eliot says that the only way of expressing emotion in the form of art is by finding an "objective correlative." [. . .] For the Elizabethan playwright, the objective correlative was the plot, and the action and thought of the characters who moved through the plot were identical. Eliot, who has said that poetry is the emotional equivalent of thought, has reached the same end even in his early poems by the selection of a similar externality, an object or a situation which constituted the formula of a particular emotion. Just as the Elizabethan play is more than the usually borrowed plot, the images of poetry stand for something much larger than themselves; that is, the "consciously concrete" suggests the "unconsciously general." The early poems are really soliloquies objected by the poet's selection of a correlative—a girl standing at the top of a stairway, an old man being read to by a boy, and so on. But the poems through "Gerontion" have secured their dramatic quality by the objectifying of thought through detail, the method of the metaphysicals; and that poetry's characteristic is complexity. Eliot has felt that the ideal medium for poetry is the theatre, where

> For the simplest auditors there is the plot, for the more thoughtful the character and conflict of character, for the more literary the words and phrasing, for the more musically sensitive the rhythm, and for auditors of greater sensitiveness and understanding a meaning which reveals itself gradually.

The pageant and the drama show the poet to be moving in the direction of these several levels of significance.

The correlative has become a grander and more obvious externality; the medium is story rather than conceit; and, were it not that the poet has been careful to deal with actuality and to preserve a degree of the metaphysical mosaic or were it not that we think of allegory in the tradition of Spenser rather than of Dante, the method of *The Rock* and *Murder in the Cathedral* would be called "allegorical." If there has been some sacrifice of the wealth of allusion and image for the sake of simplicity and dramatic action, there remains, in the "allegory," a compensation for the audience of greater sensitiveness and understanding. [. . .]

Saying that poetry is the emotional equivalent of thought, Eliot expresses Mallarmé's contention that poetry is written with words rather than with ideas; and, creating in accord with his theory, he presents a form characterized by a "contrast between fixity and flux . . . which is the very life of verse." In *The Waste Land* this contrast arises principally from the surprise of the sudden turns of words and figures, of the mutilation of a familiar quotation, or of the appearance of an "anthropological ghost"; in the later poetry, it rises mainly from the irregular rhythms of the dialogue and the song and from the interchange of verse and prose. To compensate the loss of many phrasal contrasts, the dramatist has used the action of the play to offer a grander contrast, the most striking instance being in the last work, where after the murder of Becket and the recitation of one of the most exalted choruses of the play, the First Knight advances to the front of the stage and, addressing the audience with "We beg you to give us your attention for a few moments," proceeds in prose to analyze the English audience and to present each of his accomplices that they may explain the rash deed. In this respect, Eliot shows that he has appreciated the consciousness of such creators as Webster, who found that prose was not only the prince of comedy but also one of the most effective means of contrast and certainly the only medium for the character who lets the audience probe his intellect rather than the depth of his spirit.

This play is probably the best example of Eliot's practicing his theory. From the reading of it, one may conclude what the critic said before the poet wrote: "if we are to express ourselves, our variety of thoughts and feelings, on a variety of subjects with inevitable rightness, we must adapt our manner to the moments with infinite variations. [. . .]" This precept, Eliot has successfully followed; and though in this drama there are few lines that will linger in the memory of the listener, though there is hardly enough action for the simplest level, and though there awaits disappointment for him who prefers such passages as those of *The Waste Land*, there is poetry of lucid words, of clear visual image, and of immediate intelligibility. In short, here is poetry "standing naked in its bare bones."

A third significance of these two volumes is the belief [. . .]. The present is said to be a time in which everyone asks questions to which none can find answers. Eliot has chosen to answer, and whether or not Anglo-Catholicism makes provision for Communism or Methodism or any other dogma is of little consequence; for what a poet believes is not necessarily a hindrance to his expression of "the greatest emotional intensity of his time." He who would condemn belief would have little poetry; his principle, in extension, would eliminate even metaphor. [. . .]

Ashley Dukes. "The English Scene: Listener's Theatre." *Theatre Arts Monthly* 20 (January 1936), 25–26.

[. . .]

T. S. Eliot's *Murder in the Cathedral* [. . .] was first done in the Chapter House of Canterbury last June. Any experienced theatre observer visiting Canterbury and seeing Martin Browne's sensitive production of this work could have foreseen that it would fill London theatre for a run. Its qualities of universal appeal positively could not be overlooked: although the Chapter House made a lovely setting for it, scene after scene cried out for production in theatre lighting and under theatre conditions. It was also the one play of the year that could be relied upon to draw the occasional dramatic audience—in other words the absentee audience from the contemporary playhouse. I therefore claim no credit whatever for having (with Eliot's permission) reproduced the Canterbury production on a small stage, in a small theatre which is to be specially devoted to plays for listeners. Martin Browne's original rendering had been necessarily intended for a long Gothic auditorium where poetry ran the risk of being lost in echoes; but I think he adapted it very subtly to the new surroundings.

The play is not easy. I had read it before seeing it in Canterbury—and there can hardly be a work that is less suited to being read without being seen. Any hard-headed person who cares to do so can prove logically that whole passages are moonshine—chiefly passages in which the Chorus of Women of Canterbury interpret the drama that passes before their eyes. But in the actual test of performance everything carries, and the most prejudiced spectator has to admit that he is dealing with a natural dramatist. Looking at the play from a technical standpoint, I would stress the simplicity of approach that makes it possible to create four mystical figures as tempters of Becket, perfectly defined in character and distinguished in utterance, who materialize later in the four assassin–knights and still retain their individual salt of mind and humor. It is the dream of every actor to stand before a hushed audience as these

actors stand, creating a drama of their own within the drama. As for the figure of Becket, it is the creation of a mind that stands above every device of dramatic convention and every special pleading of intellectualism, and employs the art of poetry consciously to achieve a spiritual fusion. The dramatist requires assent and not dissent from his audience. And not assent to this or that intellectual proposition, least of all to the theological dogma that seems paramount; but assent to standards of action and thought and will. Robert Speaight, who plays Becket, understands these things and does not allow his unique gift for verse-speaking to lull the true sensibilities of the listener gently and lyrically to sleep. The thread of argument (which is not argumentative) is held taut and firm. And actors of more and less experience than his own, playing the priests and tempters, maintain the same firmness of attack. So in their own fashion do the Chorus, whose training has given them the quintessentials of dramatic speech.

[. . .]

Horace Gregory. "The Mixed Role of T. S. Eliot." *New York Herald Tribune Book Review*, 12 January 1936, p. 4.

[. . .]

This dramatization of Archbishop Becket's martyrdom is Eliot's poetry in a new proportion, or, rather, it is one step forward toward gratifying Eliot's old ambition. Eliot was among the first of modern poets to express a hope that the new poetry be converted into a medium for the stage. The lyrical structure of "Prufrock" and *The Waste Land* contained dramatic implications; the monologue of "Prufrock" and certain sections of *The Waste Land* were written as though they were possible fragments of a play. Then came *Sweeney Agonistes*, an attempt which failed, then *The Rock*, a more conclusive failure than the first, with its Christian propaganda showing through threadbare, ill-devised Cockney speeches, a fake and patronizing Cockney, such as might well be written by an American—and the choruses, worst of all, a feeble parody of Eliot's own music, as though it were heard at a great distance. But with *Murder in the Cathedral* he takes a fresh start; a new or, rather, regained control over his medium is now in evidence; and the play itself is not so much the re-enactment of an old melodrama as an analysis of martyrdom.

[. . .]

Eliot's grasp of characterization has never been of great variety: Gerontion shades into Prufrock, Prufrock into Tiresias, Tiresias into the speaker of *Ash-Wednesday* and from this voice into the voice of Becket answering four tempters in the play. I agree with Mr. [F. O.] Matthiessen that we must not identify this character too closely with Eliot himself—he represents, I would say, merely the symbol of the poet's indecision, moving toward and away from its objects of desire. It is significant, I think, that the fourth and last tempter in *Murder in the Cathedral* offers martyrdom and everlasting fame; that is, the actual martyrdom is the decision to become a martyr—the difficulty of deciding *anything* is more important than the final action.

The introduction of four tempters is a hint toward the real foundation of the play or poem; it is to be seen or read as a miracle play; we are not to ask for characters or for the detail of historical incident. [. . .] [W]e have bitter commentary upon the power of the state, an interlude which is a sermon, and at the play's end, passages in prose which may be read as an ironic parody of legalized justice, an apology for murder. There are at least five passages in the play which contain some of the best of Eliot's poetry and never before has he sustained himself at such great length. The action of the play is clearly visible and is effective upon first reading which means that there is little room for confusion in the actual production.

Granting that this play comes closer to perfection than anything that Eliot has written, there remains some doubt, I think, as to whether it is actually better than the less clearly written "Prufrock" and *The Waste Land*. Though it may be difficult to revive an old myth or a legend into a convincing symbol for our time, there is a much more intense (and larger) aesthetic problem involved when a poet attempts the direct transfiguration of contemporary material. The risks are greater; he is making a myth—and chances are that much of his work will be outmoded. From first to last, he is converting living subject matter into verse and any biologist will tell us how perishable life is and how much waste attends its continuity. This is a truism that Browning knew well: there is considerably less poetic imagination at work where legend and myth have become crystallized. And that is why I think *The Waste Land* and perhaps Auden's charade *Paid on Both Sides* contain a vitality beyond the reaches of this excellent revival of Becket in *Murder in the Cathedral*.

Marianne Moore.
"If I Am Worthy, There Is No Danger."
Poetry: A Magazine of Verse 47 (February 1936), 279–81.

In this drama of the death of Becket, Archbishop of Canterbury, we have in Part I, powers invisibly moving that in Part II culminate in the murder of the Archbishop; his sermon on Christmas Day standing as interlude between the two parts. The women's chorus of Canterbury's poor bespeaks the apprehensiveness of the people, tremulous at the thought of business and private peace interfered with. And the priests, concerned for the Church, the Archbishop and themselves, aware that "Had the King been greater, or had he been weaker / Things had perhaps been different for Thomas," ask "What peace can be found / To grow between the hammer and the anvil?" It is difficult even today for conscience to know how justifiably inexorable the King might have been, or how morally compelled to inflexibility the Archbishop was.

Four tempters appear to Thomas; the first advocating easy compliance; the second, churchly authority: "Disarm the ruffian, strengthen the laws, / Rule for the good of the better cause." The third advises that he be one with the people, ignoring the King; and the fourth, "the right deed for the wrong reason," martyrdom and fame through sanctity—the apex of seduction, "Dreams to damnation."

The historical re-realizing of the character of Becket is a literary *tour de force*. Wickedness is less troubling to those who are immersed in it than it is to a man like Job whose one thought is to serve and obey. It is easier to be faithful than it is to have faith; and to act with courage than to suffer with patience; but the mere martyr becomes the saint when he is able to say, as Becket does to the dismayed priest, "I am not in danger; only near to death." The profiteer is reluctant to think of duty, or evil, or of the law of God. It is only a Samson of incorruptibility who is driven to exclaim, "Can I neither act not suffer without perdition?" [. . .]

One may merely mention the appropriateness of verse to subject matter and the consequent varying rhythms; the unforced suitability and modesty of presentation; the evidence that originality is not a thing sealed and incapable of enlargement, but that an author may write newly while continuing the decorums and abilities of the past; touches reminiscent of early idiosyncrasy, as "Sometimes at your prayers, / Sometimes hesitating at the angles of stairs," or "the dark green light from a cloud on a withered tree"; accuracies such as "the evasive flank of the fish," "the western seas gnaw at the coast of Iona"; and the self-condemnation of the four tempters as they declare life to be "a cheat and a disappointment,"

> The Catherine wheel, the pantomime
>   cat,
> The prizes given at the children's party,
> The prize awarded for the English
>   Essay,
> The scholar's degree, the statement's
>   decoration.

Mr. Eliot is sarcastic but not sardonic; we are made to realize the egregiousness is not primitive more than it is modern, and that we are ourselves satirized in the murderers' attitude to their deed; the Second Knight being "awfully sorry" and at pains to assure the public that "*we* are not getting a penny out of this"; another alluding to the balderdash of his companion as "his very subtle reasoning," and hazarding the further subtlety that the Archbishop had used every means of provocation, had determined upon death by martyrdom, and could not but receive the verdict, "Suicide while of Unsound Mind."

Mr. Eliot steps so reverently on the solemn ground he has essayed that austerity assumes the dignity of philosophy and the didacticism of the verities incorporated in the play becomes impersonal and pervasive.

Brooks Atkinson. "Strange Images of Death." *New York Times* 20 (29 March 1936), sec. 9, p. 1.

Fortunate is the poet who has a resourceful director to stage his play. [. . .] Halsted Welles has performed a service that is [. . .] creative on the withering text of T. S. Eliot's *Murder in the Cathedral*, which is now visible and audible at the Manhattan Theatre under WPA[1] auspices. Mr. Eliot is not a theatre man. Like Archibald MacLeish, whose *Panic* was experimentally acted last Spring, he writes a taut and stringent form of verse that puts a considerable strain upon the nerves of the theatre. He pulls the lines tight. His imagery is like the small strokes in an etching. For the sweep of the theatre he substitutes many "brown sharp points of death" which are virtually invisible in a large auditorium. The Victorian poets failed in the theatre because their verse was too wordy and flat-ulent. Excepting Mr. Anderson, who is a trained theatre man, the modern poets are likely to fail because their workmanship is too fine, their emotion is too acid, and their scope is too narrow. They are still writing closet drama.

And yet the fact remains that *Murder in the Cathedral* is one of the most profoundly moving dramas the season has given us. Where Mr. Eliot left off in his masque of Thomas Becket's martyrdom Mr. Welles has come in with his panoply of theatre dynamics and without violating the dark and baleful mood of the text he has given it theatre compass. The vast expanse of sky in Tom Cracraft's formalized setting brings the drama out of the monk's cell into the world where people are accustomed to move easily. In directing the text Mr. Welles has avoided the audible monotony of the choral chants by breaking up the long passages into separate lines for individual performers, and the variegated color of their voices heightens the excitement of the frightened comments they make. In directing the movements of the performers Mr. Welles has also released the tension of the text by violent groupings and the unobtrusive rhythm of choral masses. The murder of Thomas in the text is so barely chronicled that it might pass almost unnoticed in a large theatre like the Manhattan. But this bloody climax to a long and poignant martyr's meditation Mr. Welles has powerfully expressed by bringing in, on a strange incline, an impersonal line of lancers which slowly encircles Thomas like the shrouding wings of death, and although the murder is not painful, it is terrifying—a cardinal sin, deliberately performed.

To the formal church music which Mr. Eliot's text provides for, and which is glorious, A. Lehman Engel has added a sternly prescient score that cries a swiftly phrased warning and gives *Murder in the Cathedral* audible architecture. [. . .] [W]ithout creative direction Mr. Eliot's play would be only a literary rite. Resourcefully directed, it becomes a liturgical drama of exalted beauty.

Mr. Eliot is telling in vitally classic form the story of Thomas Becket's return to England on Dec. 2, 1170, and his murder in the Canterbury Cathedral on Dec. 29. In his youth Thomas was an active and versatile servant of the King, well informed on matters of canonical law, courageous on the battlefield, influential in the court. As soon as he was made Archbishop, however, he transferred his allegiance to the church and was soon at loggerheads with the King and the barons. As a fighter, he was always a formidable opponent. Although no one doubts the validity of Thomas's passion for justice, students suggest that the restlessness of his personality stirred up trouble that a more tranquil spirit might have avoided. Mr. Eliot's play begins after Thomas's active career was finished and dramatizes the contemplation of his spirit when he is wrestling with the temptations of policy and preparing his soul for martyrdom. From the lay point of view the points are often minute. But to a man of spiritual eminence purity of motive is the first essential: "To do the right deed for the wrong reason" is unpardonable—"the greatest treason." Mr. Eliot's play shows how devoutly Thomas prepares himself for martyrdom, how selflessly he faces his murderers, and it concludes with what turns out to be in the theatre a highly amusing satire on the pompousness and superciliousness of men of the world when they are confronted with a strong man of spiritual superiority.

It is no secret that Mr. Eliot is an exacting poet. Even in this play, which has had a remarkable popular success, he writes many lines of what is known nowadays as "private poetry." He is a scholar as well as a bard and he tortures his scholarship with oblique phraseology. Now, a poet may be difficult to comprehend for two reasons: One, he is writing in an original style about recondite matters and the dance of his thought may be difficult to follow; or, two, his readers may be stupid, which is perhaps the same thing. But there is a very apparent difference between obscure attitudinizing and genuine poetry, and you can recognize a genuine poet on his first page.

Since golden October declined into
  sombre November
And the apples were gathered and
  stored, and the land became brown
  sharp points of death in a waste of
  water and mud,
The New Year waits, breathes, waits,
  whispers in darkness.

That comes from the first page of *Murder in the Cathedral*. Although some of the rest of it is as abstract as *The Critique of Pure Reason* the total impression is strangely unearthly and devoutly sincere. The verse has the bite and fearlessness of the agony of a spirit. Without being a man of the theatre Mr. Eliot has given the theatre a remarkably stirring play.

Notes

1. Works Projects Administration. See another reviewer's full note at p. 535.

Joseph Wood Krutch. "The Holy Blissful Martyr." *Nation* 142 (8 April 1936), 459–60.

The Federal Theater Project has undertaken plays of various sorts, from the simple entertainment to the revolutionary drama heavy with the problems of today. [. . .] Who [. . .] would have supposed that its one real "hit" to date would be a drama in verse dealing with certain complicated events in twelfth-century England? T. S. Eliot, the author, is not an easy writer, and the question of the extent to which the character of Thomas Becket was truly saintly is hardly a burning one today. The relevance to contemporary problems is indirect, to say the least, and it would be easy to prove that no one with a head on his shoulders or a heart in his breast could possibly concern himself with it just now. Yet *Murder in the Cathedral* (Manhattan Theater) is a hit. [. . .]

When the play was published here last fall, it was reviewed by Mark Van Doren in our issue for October 9. [See "The Holy Blisful Martir" in this volume, pp. 326–27.] What chiefly remains to be said is that it acts extremely well and that Mr. Eliot, whom we thought of as a lyric and reflective poet of intense if constricted force, can write lines which are speakable and chantable with striking effect. To say this is not—as any prospective spectator unfamiliar with the text should be warned—to say that he writes in what we are accustomed to think of as the natural style of poetic drama. He does not attempt to adapt the manner and moods of poetry to contemporary theatrical practice [. . .]. Neither does he make any effort to achieve the Shakespearean effect, produced through the fact that the language and versification are so flexible, so varied in accordance with the situation and the character, that dramatic verse becomes something entirely different from lyrical or reflective poetry, and that in consequence one comes to be more aware of its richness and adaptability than of the fact that it is verse. Mr. Eliot has neither the vitality, the exuberance, nor the broad sympathetic understanding of men and tempers for anything of the sort. He is intense rather than [. . .] in this sense catholic. For all his critical studies in the field he is [. . .] by no means Elizabethan. He is mediaeval instead, and what one thinks of is not *Hamlet* but *Everyman*, the liturgical drama of the church, not the popular if exalted entertainment of the sixteenth-century inn yard.

To some extent, of course, this effect is due to the fact that some of his characters are pure abstractions—the four tempters for example; that other characters, like the women of Canterbury, are symbols not persons; and that the action is conducted in a manner closer to that of the pageant and processional than to that of the more complexly evolved drama. But its mediaeval character goes deeper, pervading as it does the whole conception both of what is suitable expression and what is the nature of essential reality. The tone is uniform not varied, because the sense of the importance of personality as expressed in individual variations is foreign to the spirit of a drama dealing with conceptions not persons, and because, therefore, it is through formalization rather than through representational variety that the intended effect can be achieved. And unless I am very much mistaken, the point of view of the dramatist, the judgment which he finally makes upon the events with which he has been dealing, can also be grasped only in these essentially mediaeval terms.

Eliot begins when the people of Canterbury, cleric and lay alike, are awaiting the return of Thomas from his seven years of exile. He shows the Archbishop beset by four tempters, the last and most dangerous of whom whispers that the crown of martyrdom is the only crown really worth a great man's ambition. And he ends with the lamentations of the people, who, as he had told them in a sermon true Christians must often do, find themselves mourning and rejoicing at the same time over a Christian mystery, this time the mystery of martyrdom. At no time is there any attempt to hide the human and often unworthy forces at work. Just as Thomas is not only a saint but an ambitious man as well, so the conflict between Henry and the Pope is a struggle for power as well as a struggle between the idea of earthly sovereignty and the idea of the Divine Will, to which even kings should be subject. Yet the whole emotion of the play would be meaningless if these facts were interpreted in accord with the habit of post-Renaissance rationalism. Mr. Eliot is certainly not saying that Becket was a fraud and his martyrdom no more than an incident in a political struggle. After all, the Middle Ages knew as well as we know that men were fallible and their motives mixed. Mr. Eliot is saying, or rather putting us in the mood to feel, that it was, nevertheless, rather they than we who knew how to interpret that fact. The human and the unworthy are incidental, not central, and the mystery of martyrdom is more real than the circumstances amid which it occurs. It is we not they who mistake what seems to be for what really is.

Halsted Welles, who staged the present production, [. . .] has pulled things together in surprisingly effective fashion. The little comic interlude toward the end in which the four assassins address the audience is a superb piece of parody. The following note—doubtless not formulated with this production in mind—appears on the program: "The Federal Theater Project is part of the WPA[1] program. However, the viewpoint expressed in this play is not necessarily that of the WPA or any other agency of the government."

Notes

1. Works Project Administration. See another reviewer's full note at p. 535.

Philip Rahv.
"A Season in Heaven."
Partisan Review 3, no. 5 (June 1936), 11–14.

It is only natural that T. S. Eliot, who has been sufficiently publicized as the fugleman of literary reaction, should have written a verse drama asserting his belief in death and man's utter wretchedness. Eliot has long held the view that this is what any "really serious belief in life" must come to. Where the surprise came in— most unpleasantly for the left critics—was in the fact that Eliot spoke his message of darkness in the unmistakable accents of a major poem. The critics had decided that Eliot's godliness had done for him, and here he was flying in the face of their stigmas.

To say that great art has a way of making even the death-rattle sound like the rattle of tambourines is all too easy [. . .]. Caught short by the contradiction between their habitual simplicities and Eliot's performance, several of the left critics declared the play to be fascist, and hence, by implication, beyond the pale of analysis and interpretation. By itself such a procedure is ludicrous enough, but here it is doubly so. The conflict the play portrays is between Church and State, the spiritual and temporal orders, the spirit and the flesh; and this conflict is so pointed as to pillory all profane aspiration and power. If classic Christianity be fascism, then Christ becomes the prototype of Hitler and every priest a storm-trooper. By the same token, in stressing another aspect of Christian doctrine, one can make out a case for Christ as the prototype of Marx. And, indeed, a horde of humanitarian gents are quite adept at this game.

[. . .]

In criticism, as in science, exactness of observation and statement is indispensable. Without it, even if our general principles are right, we somehow manage to be specifically wrong. Thus it is one thing to say that the religious denial of the world is purely theoretical, and that in the main religion accommodates itself to fascism as it has accommodated itself to capitalism. But to claim that Eliot's play is fascist is something else again. All we can say is that though its internal drive is really against all politics, in a sense its social use is nevertheless political. In essence the spiritual slavery promulgated by the Church is but the ideological reflex of real social slavery, in the flesh. But historic facts of this order cannot excuse the frivolity of some Marxist critics, who make a practice of skipping intrinsic stages and distinctions in order the more easily to blur the difference between the specific content of a work of art and its possible objective effects, which more often than not are rather vague and remote. Moreover, criticism that discards such basic distinctions must end in equating literature with life. And the failure to distinguish between literature and life is almost as bad as the failure to see their close and necessary relationship.

To my mind, in *Murder in the Cathedral* Eliot has written his best poetry since *The Waste Land*. Its magnificent lucidity, so much in contrast to the symbolic mazes of his previous devotional verse, mirrors itself in a trembling and dolorous music. The diction is lyrical, yet dry and firm, its slight biblical cast and rare ecclesiastical phrase tempered by the neutral words of current speech. The obligations of a definite historical theme as well as the clear pattern imposed by the dramatic medium seem to have prevented the poet from

clawing his way through caverns of history and mythology, as is his wont. If *The Waste Land* was written in water, this new poetry is cut into stone.

The structure, too, is simple and ingenuous. Thomas Becket returns to Canterbury after a long exile abroad. The first conflict represented is self-conflict, with Becket's soul in the arena, when he casts out the devils within himself—the four tempters arguing earthly pleasure, ambition, treason, and pride. After the *entr'acte* of the Christmas morning sermon, in which Becket heeds the summons of martyrdom and resigns himself to die, the main conflict comes to a head. The four knights appear—messengers of the king, figures out of earth, cruel and lustful—who kill Becket as they blaspheme. At once a metaphorical curtain is dropped on the historic scene as the knights step out of their parts and address the audience in the corrupt and ingratiating speech of modern politics. This is the continuation of blasphemy, ironically transposed into the typical clichés of British respectability and parliamentary eyewash. [. . .] Here the poetry of exaltation takes the cure in the prose of private convenience and genial demagogy. The result is comic relief, a vertiginous reversal of tone and tempo. In an instant the reader or spectator, laughing cynically, turns hard-headed and a bit rowdy. The final chorus, intoning a beatific vision, sounds uninspired, as dull as a hymn or a patriotic ode. The spell has been broken. The poet wanted to show us the sameness of history, that nothing changes, but history threw him aside to repeat itself as farce. [. . .] Can it be that Eliot's religion is really a form of willful aesthetics? If so he is man enough to be damned, and we shall not be prevented "from praying for his repose."

It has been said that every work of art is an act of collaboration between reader and creator. Let us measure, then, the truth of that statement against Eliot's play. Did our sensibility really respond to the desiccated pattern of theological salvation? It cannot be that we were pleased by the stale art of the old-time vamps! No, it is not Becket and the women of Canterbury, the knights and the tempters, but we ourselves who are here represented. The pattern has been rent asunder by a tragedy altogether temporal—and to the poet perhaps both absurd and terrifying—giving the play overtones and meanings in another sphere, one close to our interests and desires.

[. . .]

Moreover, what has become of the Christian man, man in the singular, that *identical* creature of dogma? Why does the chorus harp upon the image of the "common man," the "small folk"? Throughout the action Eliot–Becket, the clerical philosopher, answers the complaints of those "who acknowledge themselves the type of the common man" in contrast to those who walk "secure and assured" in their fate. Who hatched this heresy of a plural man, veritably a class conception in disguise? Has Eliot heard of the role of the masses in history, of their refusal to become the fodder of eternity? Is the image of the small folk the poet's bad conscience?

> Archbishop, secure and assured of your fate, unaffrayed among the shades, do you realise what you ask, do you realise what it means to the small folk drawn into the pattern of fate, the small folk who live among small things . . .

The protest of the commoners, however, always meets the stopgap reply: The sin of the world is upon your heads. Yet it is in the self-portrayal of these plebeians that concrete life emerges. Sometimes the corn fails them, one year is a year of dryness, another of rain, there have been oppression and taxes, girls have

unaccountably disappeared, still they have gone on living, "living and partly living." (This word *partly*, denatured, unpoetic, recurs throughout and throughout turns into its opposite. Loaded with the burden of the real, it violates its many "poetic" contexts, thus animating with a superior poetry, the genuine poetry of surprise and humility.)

The dislocation of the poet's intention continues. We do not feel the "joyful consummation" heralded as the play ends. The formal cause of the horror expressed by the chorus—the crime of murder absolutized in "an instant eternity of evil and wrong"—remains an abstraction. The Horror is not realized as such, its language is nowise equivalent to the peculiar logic of its indicated motivation. History, ever determinate, will not be cheated of its offspring; though the poem recoils from history, only history can give it life. [. . .]

I have suggested a creative contradiction in Eliot that makes him our contemporary in more than a chronological sense. Yet there are many whose distorted critical ideas allow them to see only explicit ideology in a work of art, and unable to share the poet's beliefs, they find themselves unable to enjoy his poetry. This is the real reason for the crude treatment the play received from some of the left critics. What these critics don't see is that their approach isolates them from literature as a historical entity, particularly from the literature of the past. We can understand the immediate pleasure a critic gets from an ideological correspondence between himself and the work he criticizes, but let him beware lest this immediate pleasure become a vice blinding him to other and related values.

[. . .]

I have praised Eliot's poetry; and I believe that its example cannot be ignored by the young revolutionary poets. Precisely as an example of achievement we should see it, rather than as an influence on the actual texture of revolutionary verse. It is a poetry various and complex. It has a historic sense, both of language and of events; it summarizes centuries of experiment and discovery; above all, it is precise, contemporary, sustained by a sensibility able to transform thought and feeling into each other and combine them in simultaneous expression. [. . .]

Checklist of Additional Reviews:

* R. Ellis Roberts. "T. S. Eliot's Drama of Faith." *Church Times*, 14 June 1935, p. 729.

John Hayward. "London Letter." *New York Sun*, 15 June 1935, p. 21.

* Bernard Wall. "*Murder in the Cathedral*." *Catholic Herald*, 29 June 1935, p. 15.

"Book Notes." *New York Herald Tribune*, 2 July 1935, p. 15.

* F. L. Lucas. "The Guilty Knights." *Sunday Observer*, 27 July 1935, [page no. unknown].

* T. R. Barnes. "Poets and the Drama." *Scrutiny* 4, no. 2 (September 1935), 189–91.

H. S. "T. S. Eliot's Confidence in the Superiority of the Past Colors His Latest Work." *Dallas News*, 22 September 1935, [page no. unknown].

I. F. "Literary Fascism." *Christian Science Monitor*, 25 September 1935, p. 18.

* Richard Rees. "*Murder in the Cathedral*." *Adelphi* 11 (October 1935), 60–61.

H. M. "Book Parade." *Stage* 13 (November 1935), 97.

*[*Murder in the Cathedral*]. *Times*, 2 November 1935, p. 10.

Allardyce Nicoll. "Eliot Play Opens in London Theatre." *New York Times*, 2 November 1935, p. 12.

Louise Bogan. "The Season's Verse." *New Yorker* 11 (9 November 1935), 85.

Tench Tilghman. "Realm of Poesy." *Baltimore Evening Sun*, 9 November 1935, p. 6.

Humphrey Jennings. "Eliot and Auden and Shakespeare." *New Verse* 18 (December 1935), 4–7.

"Play for a Cathedral." *Christian Science Monitor* 28 (3 December 1935), 30.

* Rolfe Humphries. "Eliot, Auden, Isherwood, and Cummings." *New Masses* 18 (31 December 1935), 23–24.

Hugh Ross Williamson. "Medieval Drama *Redivivus*." *American Scholar* 5 (1936), 49–63.

Newton Arvin. "About T. S. Eliot: *Murder in the Cathedral*." *New Republic* 85 (15 January 1936), 290.

Euphemia V. Wyatt. *Catholic Weekly* 142 (March 1936), 760–61.

"Temptation." *Commonweal* 23 (13 March 1936), 560.

"Federal Theatre Presents a Play." *Brooklyn Eagle*, 21 March 1936, p. 15.

Brooks Atkinson. "The Play. Meditation of a Martyr in T. S. Eliot's *Murder in the Cathedral*." *New York Times*, 21 March 1936, p. 13.

Howard Barnes. "T. S. Eliot's Poetic Melodrama Opens at the Manhattan." *New York Herald Tribune*, 21 March 1936, p. 12.

J. C. "WPA Stages T. S. Eliot's Poetic Drama." *New York Daily News*, 21 March 1936, p. 27.

Gilbert W. Gabriel. "*Murder in the Cathedral*." *New York American*, 21 March 1936, p. 11.

Robert Garland. "WPA Presents Drama of Thomas à Becket." *New York World-Telegram*, 21 March 1936, p. 6c.

Richard Lockridge. "The Stage in Review: Poetic Martyrdom." *New York Sun*, 21 March 1936, p. 9.

Carolyn Marx. "Bookmarks for Today." *New York World-Telegram*, 21 March 1936, sec. 3, p. 3.

Wilella Waldorf. "*Murder in the Cathedral* Given by Federal Actors." *New York Evening Post*, 21 March 1936, p. 8.

John Anderson. "Federal Project Actors Present Drama of Thomas à Becket." *New York Evening Journal*, 23 March 1936, p. 16.

"Ibee." "*Murder in the Cathedral*." *Variety*, 25 March 1936.

"Thoughtful and Moving Drama of a Martyr's Murder." *Newsweek* 7 (28 March 1936), 26.

Robert Benchley. "The Government Takes a Hand." *New Yorker* 12 (28 March 1936), 32.

Ann Hawkins. "An Enduring Poem." *Pacific Weekly* 5 (28 March 1936), 174–75.

"Playbill." *New York Herald Tribune*, 29 March 1936, sec. 5, p. 1.

Richard Watts Jr. "Bringing the Middle Ages to Broadway." *New York Herald Tribune*, 29 March 1936, sec. 5, pp. 1, 5.

John Mason Brown. "The High Excitements of *Murder in the Cathedral*." *New York Evening Post*, 30 March 1936, p. 18. [Reprinted in *Two on the Aisle* (New York: Norton, 1938), 124–26]

S. Gorley Putt. "This Modern Poetry." *Voices* 85 (Spring 1936), 58–61.

Grenville Vernon. "The Play and Screen: *Murder in the Cathedral*." *Commonweal* 23 (3 April 1936), 636.

Stark Young. "Government and Guild." *New Republic* 86 (8 April 1936), 253.

Edith J. R. Isaacs. "Saints and Lawmakers: Broadway in Review." *Theatre Arts Monthly* 20 (May 1936), 341–43.

Mary Colum. "Spiritual and Temporal Order: *Murder in the Cathedral*." *Forum and Century* 95 (June 1936), 346–47.

Horace Gregory. "Poets in the Theatre." *Poetry: A Magazine of Verse* 48 (July 1936), 227–28.

*Michael Sayers. "A Year in the Theatre." *Criterion* 15 (July 1936), 653–55, 657.

Roy Daniells. "The Christian Drama of T. S. Eliot." *Canadian Forum* 16 (August 1936), 20–21.

John Haynes Holmes. "Murder in the Cathedral." *Unity* 117 (3 August 1936), 218.

John Crowe Ransom. "Autumn of Poetry." *Southern Review* 1 (Winter 1936), 619–23.

Ashley Dukes. "The English Scene." *Theatre Arts Monthly* 21 (February 1937), 103–04.

*John F. Butler. "Tragedy, Salvation, and the Ordinary Man." *London Quarterly and Holborn Review* 162 (October 1937), 489–97.

COLLECTED POEMS 1909–1935
1936

Collected Poems
1909-1935

by

T. S. Eliot

London

Faber & Faber Limited

24 Russell Square

*Edwin Muir.
"Mr. Eliot's Poetry."
Spectator 156, no. 5623 (3 April 1936), 603–04.

The first eighty pages in this volume are taken up by the poems which have already appeared in *Poems 1909–1925*; the remaining hundred pages contain Mr. Eliot's poetic production for the last ten years, except for *Murder in the Cathedral*, which is not included. The second part begins with "Ash-Wednesday," embraces two unfinished poems, *Sweeney Agonistes* and *Coriolan*, ten choruses from *The Rock*, four Ariel poems, thirteen minor poems, and ends with "Burnt Norton," which is in some ways different from any of Mr. Eliot's other poems, and is one of the most remarkable, I think, that he has yet written.

It will be seen from this that Mr. Eliot has been considerably more productive during the last ten years than during the sixteen years before; but it is very difficult to judge whether he has been productive on the same level, firstly because a writer of such individuality as his changes the taste of his readers, and they come to his later work with a different mind, and secondly because his style has altered. The alteration has been towards a greater explicitness of statement; "Ash-Wednesday" is far more explicit than any poetry that Mr. Eliot wrote before it, and it represents, I think, a turning point in his development. *The Waste Land* is no doubt his greatest work, but there is in it, compared with his later work, a certain blindness both in the despair it expresses and in turning away from despair at the end. Since "The Hollow Men," where that despair reached its lowest depths, Mr. Eliot has

never expressed it again; he has taken it as a theme, certainly, in *Sweeney Agonistes* and other poems; but though he is still in the midst of it, he is no longer within it. That is to say that he is not so firmly under the influence of his time and is more deliberately concerned with permanent things. The difference may be seen by setting side by side: "These fragments I have shored against my ruins" from *The Waste Land*, and "Redeem the time, redeem the dream / The token of the word unheard, unspoken" from "Ash-Wednesday." This difference, the difference between despair and faith, is so great that it is very hard to compare the two kinds of poetry that derive from it. A good deal of the second kind is obscure, like the first, but with a different obscurity: not the obscurity of deep darkness, but rather that of darkness against light. It is consequently less heavily charged and more easy to understand, more finally comprehensible. This must be admitted to be in its favor, unless we are to regard obscurity in itself, deep and total obscurity, as poetic virtue.

The second half of the volume is nevertheless more unequal than the first. *Sweeney Agonistes,* brilliant as it is, is definitely in a lower class of poetry than the rest, and doubtless is intended to be. The choruses from *The Rock* are first of all choruses, that is compositions intended to be spoken and to be comprehensible as soon as spoken. They contain some beautiful poetry, they are original in form, but they naturally lack the condensation which Mr. Eliot's poetry has at its best. On the other hand, almost all the shorter poems have intense concentration and perfect clarity at the same time; "Ash-Wednesday" and the four Ariel poems are works of great beauty; and "Burnt Norton" is surely one of the best poems that Mr. Eliot has ever written. Its subject is Time and its main text a quotation from Herakleitos to the effect that the road upwards and downwards is one and the same road. This poem is different from the others inasmuch as it is not at all dramatic, being a pure intellectual enquiry into the nature and forms of Time. It alternates between the most close argument and the most vivid imagery expressing the contradiction of Time, a contradiction implicit in the recurring phrase, "At the still point of the turning world." It contains lines of great beauty:

We move above the moving tree
In light upon the figured leaf
And hear upon the sodden floor
Below, the boarhound and the boar
Pursue their pattern as before.

That is a far more rarefied poetry than

In the juvescence of the year
Came Christ the tiger
In depraved May, dogwood and
    chestnut, flowering judas

but is has something in common with it, a sense of the fabulous; the difference is that the second kind is very much more figured and patterned (to use the words that recur frequently in it), which means that it is more thoroughly worked out. Imagery which is thoroughly worked out often becomes mechanical and lifeless; but in this poem both the thought and the imagery are intensely concentrated, and gain immensely from the development. Whether this poem owes anything to Dante I do not know, but one might chance the guess that Mr. Eliot's later development as a poet has been away from the Elizabethans, by whom he was so much influenced at the beginning, towards Dante.

Mr. Eliot's position as a poet is established, and his work has been more thoroughly discussed than that of any of his contemporaries. His influence on poetry has been decisive. The influence was due chiefly to his genius for poetry, but it was due also to certain qualities which he held in common with some other men in his age. He has had an influence on the form and on the attitude of poetry. By this I do not mean that he has encouraged a kind of poetry in which all sorts of poetical quotations and reminiscences alternate with the realistic descriptions of contemporary life. This method was employed very effectively in *The Waste Land* because it was a natural part of the scheme; it has not been employed successfully by any of Mr. Eliot's imitators, and as a set of poetic method it is obviously ridiculous. Mr. Eliot's dramatic approach has influenced the form of poetry away from the purely lyrical, and his exercise of the historical sense has influenced the attitude of poetry. The first influence has been entirely salutary; it has led to a necessary reform of poetic language and a spirit of objectivity which had been buried in the degeneration of Romanticism. The reliance on the historical sense Mr. Eliot himself seems to have lost in his later work; it does not go with religious poetry; it cannot survive the vision of "the still point of the turning world." But even in *The Waste Land* he used it conditionally, for there too, if less explicitly, he was concerned with permanent things, which are not affected by history. When the historical sense is employed without reference to these permanent things it leads to a shallowness of the imaginative faculty, for it robs the individual existence of meaning and can in itself give no meaning to society, since society is still in becoming, and by the laws of history will always be. Where the historical sense has been used in this way, the responsibility is not Mr. Eliot's; but it partly explains why his influence should be so great with poets who do not hold his beliefs.

*Peter Quennell. "Mr. T. S. Eliot." New Statesman 11 (18 April 1936), 603–04.

[Review of *Essays Ancient and Modern* and *Collected Poems*]

Were a bibliography to be composed of the various critical studies that have been devoted to Mr. T. S. Eliot during the last ten or fifteen years, it would make up a fairly considerable volume. For almost every modern critic has had his say. There are, indeed, very few literary undergraduates who have not, at one time or another, voiced their appreciation of his poems; and, even in the Far East, solemn spectacled faces are earnestly bent, and round shaven skulls dolorously scratched, over *The Waste Land*, "Prufrock," or "Ash-Wednesday." At Oxford, ten years ago, admiration of *The Waste Land* had given rise to a new and, now and then, extremely tiresome form of intellectual snobbism. The intelligentsia were as knowledgeable and talkative about the relationship and precise significance of Mr. [Eugenides] and Phlebas the Phoenician as their Bullingdon equivalent about the genealogical complications of the Stud Book; "La Figlia che Piange" provided the *leit-motif* of a dozen adolescent love-affairs. And yet, although the mass of writing around Mr. T. S. Eliot is by now probably much more voluminous than the whole corpus of his published verse and prose, it is still possible to retrace one's steps through his poems, experiencing as one reads a continuous movement of pleasure, interest and surprise. Perhaps surprise is the final criterion of poetic excellence. However hackneyed

it may have become, no poem of real quality can quite lose the power of administering that kind of salutary emotional shock which, if only for a few minutes, possesses the brain and shows us the familiar universe in a refreshing light. *Collected Poems* embraces Mr. T. S. Eliot's entire poetic output between 1909 and 1935. It covers the same ground as *Poems*, published several years back, but includes "Ash-Wednesday," four poems published in the Ariel series, a quantity of minor and unfinished work, as well as a new and remarkably accomplished poem, "Burnt Norton."

Here is a panorama of Mr. Eliot's poetic achievement. Beginning with the section headed *Prufrock, 1917*, one is at first startled by the brilliance and liveliness of those early poems—we know them so well; yet, even today, how well they stand rereading!—then a little puzzled and disconcerted because, although certain elements in *Prufrock* have continued to develop until we reach the uncommon rhythmic virtuosity of "Burnt Norton" (written nearly twenty years later) they contain another element that has very largely disappeared. In "The Love Song of J. Alfred Prufrock," Mr. Eliot displays a gaiety, energy and satirical versatility that he has long since discarded. The influence of Jules Laforgue is extremely strong; but this is a Laforgue with additions and, I think, at least from the Anglo-Saxon point of view, very definite improvements. He has Laforgue's wit and dexterity without his fragility—Laforgue's skill without the touch of flatness and thinness that gives so many of Laforgue's *vers libre* essays a slightly consumptive and debilitated air. For there is a background of something we can best describe as *gusto*—a sense of enjoyment that may coexist with a knowledge of human suffering, a love of life not incompatible with the horror of humanity;

and from more recent works that element of gusto proved strangely lacking. The *peur de vivre* had broken down his poetic defenses; the poet was in full retreat through *The Waste Land*.

Having entered it, he was obliged to find an issue. If the influences of Laforgue had done much to shape *Prufrock* (1917) and *Poems (1920)*, even to the extent of suggesting images, lines and whole passages, Baudelaire (with Tristan Corbière as a secondary influence) was the presiding spirit of that extraordinary poem which burst, like an organ cactus dominating a herbaceous border, from among the pleasant flower-beds and meandering grass-walks of Georgian poetry. But now compare the methods of master and disciple. When I ventured to observe that Eliot lacked gusto, I did not, of course, mean to complain that he lacked optimism, that he was a perverse and atrabilious highbrow malcontent. No poet has ever expressed a deeper or more unrelieved despair, a more uncompromising and embittered attitude towards contemporary society, than the author of *Les Fleurs du Mal*. And yet how solid, sensuous and—in spite of condemnation, disgust and disenchantment—how almost *appreciative* is his rendering of the real world! [. . .] Nineteenth-century Paris, with the old struggling against the new, [. . .] was a city full of phantoms and stalking memories: "Fourmillante cité, cité pleine de rêves, / Où le spectre en plein jour raccroche le passant." There was no end to the emotions of wonder and horror that it aroused; it was intensely real to the poet, even though its reality may have been intensely unpleasing; whereas the landscape of twentieth-century London, glimpsed in *The Waste Land*, seems, by comparison, as drab, low-toned and shadowily inconsequent as the stream of spiritless human automata trudging to their work over London Bridge:

Unreal City,
Under the brown fog of a winter
  dawn,
A crowd flowed over London Bridge,
  so many,
I had not thought death had undone
  so many.
[. . . . .]

For Mr. Eliot shares the malady of his epoch; and that malady—at any rate, among intellectuals—comes not so much from a positive misdirection of energy as from a mere lack of vitality, not so much from any failure of sensitiveness as from a general lowering of temperature that leaves us face to face with a world where the good is flavorless, the bad insignificant, where our values, slowly and quietly, seem to be crumbling away to form part of a general desert-level of indifference and ill-will. Such is the predominant mood of *The Waste Land*. And a historian of the future may find that the poem affords him interesting material for a study of the period, noting, moreover, that when Mr. Eliot escaped from the wilderness he did so by taking refuge in a narrow and sectarian, but evidently absorbing and satisfying, faith, and that, under the influence of this new faith, he was to achieve some of his most exquisite and finely balanced later poems. We may regret that the gaiety and gusto of "Prufrock" should already have begun to disappear in *The Waste Land*; and we may regret that, on emerging from *The Waste Land*, he should have limited himself to a smaller poetic field; but a poet, after all, can only progress along the lines that his individual temperament lays down; and, by remaining faithful to his temperament—one of Protestant and transatlantic puritanism, exasperated by contact with an alien culture—Mr. Eliot has continued to perfect his gift. *Collected Poems*, then, is a valuable and fascinating book because it gives a bird's-eye view of his poetic progress, from his early, brilliant but derivative excursions, right up to the present day. It is particularly interesting, for example, to see the admirable choruses of *The Rock* divorced from their somewhat less stimulating context, and be able to trace Mr. Eliot's link with the main tradition of English devotional verse. About the poems in "Ash-Wednesday" there was an occasional touch of almost pre-Raphaelite prettiness; and, personally, I prefer the choruses; since Mr. Eliot must be numbered among the very few modern poets who have learned to combine eloquence and simplicity of statement with a feeling for poetic expression in its more allusive form.

[Quotation of lines 28–36 of *The Rock*, Chorus III]

Nor is "Burnt Norton" disappointing. In harmony and flexibility it is the equal of Mr. Eliot's earlier poems; and, though the first section opens in a style rather too reminiscent of the text-book, [quotation of lines 1–5 of "Burnt Norton," Part I] it closes with a long passage of remarkable felicity, to which quotation and abbreviation do less than justice.

[Quotation of lines 9–15 and 19–48 of "Burnt Norton," Part I]

But, if the acquisition of faith has added to the delicacy—while detracting, I believe, from the breadth and variety—of Mr. Eliot's poetic method, it has had another effect on his discursive and critical work. *The Sacred Wood* and *Homage to John Dryden*, though often abused by academic journalists, were among the most exciting and illuminating critical products of their time. *For Lancelot Andrewes*, which contains a suggestion that Andrewes was a finer stylist than John Donne [. . .] struck a sad shock through the heart of many a hopeful reader, who expected something as good as Mr. Eliot's essays on the Elizabethan dramatists and seventeenth-century poets. *Essays Ancient and Modern* is [*For*] *Lancelot Andrewes* revised, corrected and brought up to date. The all-too-famous foreword—plumping for classicism in literature, royalism in politics and anglo-catholicism in religion—is now judged to have served its purpose and has been removed. Studies of Machiavelli and Crashaw, which their author considers unsatisfactory, have also been deleted; while a paper on Middleton does not appear since it has found a place in Elizabethan Essays. To fill the gap, we have two articles written round religious or semi-religious themes, "Religion and Literature" and "Catholicism and International Order," an essay—sound, but not particularly exciting—entitled "Modern Education and the Classics," an introduction to the *Pensées* of Pascal (in which Mr. Eliot explains the dangerous fascination of Montaigne by comparing that unfortunate sage to "a fog, a gas, a fluid, insidious element") and a note, in his best manner, on the poetry of Tennyson. Here the critic uses only aesthetic arguments; and the result is wise, sensitive and brilliantly expounded.

*Cyril Connolly. "Major Poet: The Influence of Mr. Eliot." *Sunday Times*, 3 May 1936, p. 8.

A good way to gauge the importance of a writer is to try to imagine what his subject would have been like without him. Let us suppose Mr. Eliot had never existed, what would English poetry be like today? I think it would have advanced no further from the Georgian poets than they had progressed from the 'nineties. There would be Yeats, of course, but otherwise we would still be reading Flecker and Housman and Ralph Hodgson, and writing like them. They would have been the intellectual poets, themselves in advance of other Georgians, with Sassoon and the Sitwells as the last word in youthful and ferocious opposition. Pound, without Eliot's appreciation and adaptation of him, would not be important. Auden would have been no more than a young Kipling of the Left (which he may yet become), Spender a deflated Rupert Brooke, Day-Lewis a baby W. J. Turner, while MacNeice and Barker could not have existed at all. [. . .]

The theme of poetry would still be the lyrical expression of simple nostalgia; Babylon, Popacatapetl, Innisfree, Grantchester, Sussex—"The meadows of England shining in the rain"—we would not have got beyond them, and the best poetry would still consist of exercises in homesickness and be written by old laureates or young medalists, or by imitative and large-hearted women. Eliot, in fact, has brought to English poetry dignity and intellectual distinction, without which it might well have gone the way of most modern English music, novel-writing, and architecture. But he has brought to it as well an exquisite lyrical gift: that real beauty of diction which provides the aesthetic reader with a unique emotion, and to which hardly any other modern poet, except Yeats, can lay claim.

How many single lines, for instance, can you remember from Auden, Spender, and Day-Lewis, or, for that matter, from more conservative poets? Yet Eliot is packed with them. "There will be time to murder and create," "The troubled midnight and the noon's repose," "Supine on the floor of a narrow canoe," "The infirm glory of the positive hour," "The awful daring of a moment's surrender."

I often think what an experience it must have been, during the second year of the war, to have come upon that small paper-covered, biscuit-colored volume with the odd title, *Prufrock*, and to have opened it at the first poem:

> Let us go then, you and I,
> When the evening is spread out
> against the sky
> Like a patient etherised upon a table.

It must have provided one or two people with the fine shock of discovering a new talent [. . .].

Unfortunately, the extraordinary freshness, the special gaiety of *Prufrock*, a gaiety partly due to the influence of Laforgue, from which much is imitated, and partly to the dandyism of those young men of 1913 (we find it also in *Crome Yellow* and in Ronald Firbank), disappears from the later Eliot. This is largely due to the influence of Pound, who brings, after the "clever" period of the "Sweeney" poems, in which his dandyism is finally stifled by his horror for life, two new features into Eliot. They are the introduction of unassimilated quotations into the body of his work, and the more serious introduction of a mystical, but also rather muddy and disingenuous bardic quality into his thought. He is no longer the pleasant young man who confides in the reader, but the prophet, the maker of mysteries, descending only to tell us, as of "Shantih," for instance, that "The Peace which passeth understanding is a feeble translation of this word." Through the despair of the "cactus" poems, the hopefulness of "Ash-Wednesday," and the severity of the choruses from *The Rock*, the same lyrical power persists however, and it is found in equal purity in the long new poem, "Burnt Norton," a philosophical meditation on Time, with which this book closes.

[. . .]

The work of any great writer is like a train running through various stations. At each station some admirers get out and begin to say, "Such a pity the train ever went on to the next station." Sometimes if they say this loud enough they do actually stop the train from going any further, and then all is over with it. This is particularly true of Eliot, who has one lot of passengers still waiting at the terminus of *The Waste Land*, and another which is not willing to follow him into the Drama, with his two Church of England plays, *Murder in the Cathedral* and *The Rock*.

It is obvious, however, that the art of Mr. Eliot is still a living spiritual force, anything may happen to it, and whatever happens will be vastly interesting. There is no reason even, now that he has found peace of mind in religion, why his early lyrical and ironical high spirits, driven out by post-war depression, should not return, or else why his mastery of language, and his incessant and conscientious experiment and adaptation (for Mr. Eliot is one of the few writers who deliberately imitate, yet are able to absorb and give, unlike Pound, an added power and meaning to the thing imitated) should not lead him into unpredictable discoveries. For he is gifted with that great rarity these days: an imaginative and emotional staying power, poetical long-life.

Marianne Moore. "It Is Not Forbidden to Think." *Nation* 142 (27 May 1936), 680–81.

The grouping of these poems—chronological through 1930, and inclusive except for *Murder in the Cathedral*—seems to point to a mental chronology of evolvement and deepening technique. But two tendencies mark them all: the instinct for order and certitude, and "contempt for sham." "I am not sure," Mr. Eliot says in *The Use of Poetry*, "that we can judge and enjoy a man's poetry while leaving wholly out of account all the things for which he cared deeply, and on behalf of which he turned his poetry to account." He detests a conscience, a politics, a rhetoric, which is neither one thing nor the other. For him hell is hell in its awareness of heaven; good is good in its distinctness from evil; precision is precision as triumphing over vagueness. In *The Rock* he says, "Our age is an age of moderate virtue / And of moderate vice." Among Peter the Hermit's hearers were "a few good men, / Many who were evil, / And most who were neither." Although as a critic, confronted by apparent misapprehension, he manifests what seems at times an almost pugnacious sincerity, by doing his fighting in prose he is perhaps the more free to do his feeling in verse. But in his verse, also, judgment remains awake. His inability to be untormented by "the Demon of Thought" as action, in "Prufrock," posits an overwhelming question: "Oh, do not ask, 'What is it?' / Let us go and make our visit"; and as writing, is satirized in "Lines for Cuscuscaraway and Mirza Murad Ali Beg":

How unpleasant to meet Mr. Eliot!
With his features of clerical cut,
[. . . . .]
And his conversation, so nicely
Restricted to What Precisely
And If and Perhaps and But.

One sees in this collected work conscience—directed toward "things that other people have desired," asking "are these things right or wrong?"—and an art which from the beginning has tended toward drama. *The Waste Land* (1922) characterizes a first period. In "Ash-Wednesday" and later Mr. Eliot is not warily considering "matters that with myself I too much discuss / Too much explain"; he is *in* them; and "Ash-Wednesday" is perhaps the poem of the book, as submitting in theme and technique to something greater than itself.

> A spirit of the river, spirit of the sea,
> Suffer me not to be separated
>
> And let my cry come unto Thee.

This is a summit; an instance, as well, of increased pliancy in rhythm, the lengthened phrase, gathered force of rhymes suddenly collided being characteristic of the later poems.

Mr. Eliot's aptitude for mythology and theology sometimes pays us the compliment of expecting our reading to be more thorough than it is; but correspondences of allusion provide an unmistakable logic: stillness, intellectual beauty, spiritual exaltation, the white dress, "the glory of the humming bird," childhood, concentration and wholeness of personality—in contrast with noise, darkness, drugs, dreams, drowning, dust on the rosebowl, Dusty the makeshift enchantress, cards, clairvoyants, serpents, evasiveness, aimlessness, fog, intrusiveness, temptation, unlogic, scattered bones, broken pride, rats, drafts under the door, distortion, "the sty of contentment." Horror, which is unbelief, is the opposite of ecstasy; and wholeness, which is the condition of ecstasy, is to be "accepted and accepting." That is to say, we are of a world in which light and darkness, "appearance and reality," "is and seem," are ineludable alternatives.

And there are words of special meaning which recur with the force of a theme: "hidden," referring to poetry as the revelation of a hidden life; "the pattern" contin-uing the Aristotelian concept of "form" as the soul, the invisible actuality of which the body is the outward manifestation. Fire, the devourer, can be a purifier; water has in it the thought of drowning or of drought ended by inundation; as God's light is for man, the sun is life for the natural world. Concepts and images are toothed together and the poems are so consistently intricated that one rests on another and is involved with what was earlier; the musical theme at times being separated by a stanza, as the argument sometimes is continued from the preceding poem—"O hidden" in "Difficulties of a Statesman" completing the "O hidden" in "Triumphal March." The period containing "Ash-Wednesday," concerned with "the infirm glory of the positive hour," is succeeded by the affirmative one to which *Murder in the Cathedral* belongs; also "Burnt Norton," a new poem which is concerned with the thought of control ("The high road and the low are one and the same") embodied in Deity and in human equipoise, its temporal counterpart.

[Quotation of lines 10–15 of "Burnt Norton," Part II]

In "Usk," also, Mr. Eliot expresses the conviction that the *via media* of discipline and self-control is the valuable one:

> Where the roads dip and where the
>   roads rise
> Seek only there
> Where the grey light meets the green
>   air
> The hermit's chapel, the pilgrim's
>   prayer.

One notices here the compactness, four thoughts in one—the visible, the invisible, the indoors, the outdoors; and that in the later poems, although statement is simpler, the rhythm is more complex.

Mr. Eliot has tried "to write poetry which should be essentially poetry, with nothing poetic about it, poetry standing naked in its bare bones, or . . . so transparent that in reading it we are intent on what the poem *points at* and not on the poetry." He has not dishonored "the deepest terrors and desires," depths of "degradation" and heights of "exaltation," or the fact that it is possible to have "walked in hell" and "been rapt to heaven."

Those who have power to renounce life are those whose lives are valuable to a community; one who attains equilibrium in spite of opposition to himself from within is in a stronger position than if there had been no opposition to overcome; and in art, freedom evolving from a liberated constraint is stronger than if it had not by nature been cramped. Indigenous skepticism, also constraint, are part of Mr. Eliot's temperament; but at its apex art is able to conceal the artist while it exhibits his "angel"; like the unanticipatedly limber fluorescence of fireworks as they expand into trees or bouquets with the abandon of "unbroke horses"; and this effect we have in "Cape Ann"—denominated a minor poem, perhaps as being a mood or aspect rather than part of a thought-related sequence.

[Quotation in full of "Cape Ann"]

Babette Deutsch.
"The Most Influential Poet of Our Time."
New York Herald Tribune, 31 May 1936, p. 7.

Having been told by the poet that it is impossible to understand his poetry unless one accepts the doctrine of Original Sin, the dissident might hesitate to accept this volume. But Eliot has also said that it is possible to enjoy poetry one does not understand, so that the reader may take heart of grace. Certainly those who do not share Eliot's beliefs, from members of his own unhappy generation down to the young revolutionaries who see "the Church blocking the sun," can find in this volume much more than food for enjoyment. For Eliot, though not the most distinguished, is easily the most influential poet of our time, important not merely because of what he has contributed to the body of poetry produced by his predecessors, but also because he has impressed himself so deeply upon his juniors. He is significant further as a representative of an attitude which, if valid only for the few, is grounded in a disgust with current evils that may be symptomatic with the rebellion of the many.

It is some ten years since the publication of his *Poems 1909–1925,* including *The Waste Land.* It is nearly twenty since the appearance of *Prufrock* startled the discerning into recognition of a new voice. The interval allows us to discover the course of the poet's development, a development that has curiously reversed the usual order. Of the many astonishing facts about "Prufrock," not the least is that it was the product of a boy of twenty-two. [. . .] At the very outset the poet objectified feelings, put on a mask. "Prufrock," like "Portrait of a Lady," which was written even earlier, might be described as a dramatic lyric, though scarcely reminiscent of Browning. Eliot had been reading not merely the Elizabethan playwrights, but the French symbolists, to advantage. He introduced an exciting juxtaposition of the poetic and the anti-poetic, the talk of the man in the street and the learned in a library.

The most startling aspect of these pieces, however, was not the novel technique exhibited, but the fact that this very young man was writing depersonalized poetry. And, curiously enough, he was not dramatizing himself, with a desire to exhibit himself in the role of some hero out of the antique world or some personage of the Middle Ages, but dramatizing his response to the world about him. It is an index both to the success of his method and the actuality of the sordid empty scenes he was evoking, that a young poet born in Whitechapel, two years after "Portrait of a Lady" was written, should grow up to use the same rhythms, almost the same phrases, in a bitter poem on the unemployed. What was evident in the *Prufrock* poems was an extraordinary gift for cadence, a matchless ability to assimilate and convert to his own uses the discoveries of earlier men, and in an irony bred of a distaste for the vulgar that was linked with fear.

> I have seen the moment of my
> greatness flicker,
> And I have seen the eternal Footman
> hold my coat, and snicker,
> And in short, I was afraid.

With the exception of "Gerontion," the second group of poems shows the influence of Gautier almost equally with that of Laforgue. There is the strict quatrain, with its regularly recurrent rhymes; there is the Parnassian precision of objective detail; and as usual Eliot allows himself the unscrupulous theft of entire phrases scrupulously placed in a new setting. But the insistence of the grotesque, the ironic implications of the symbolist, remain, pointing, in a yet more private fashion than before, to a wincing hatred of the mob. Eliot's mob is not quite the "rank-scented many" abhorred by Coriolanus.

In it one finds Bleistein, the parvenu. One finds Sweeney, the lowest common denominator of the average sensual man. Bleistein and Sweeney want neither food nor bread for circuses. They are not even pitiable, like the timorous Prufrock or the poor women of Canterbury. They are the Laodiceans of Eliot's modern Agon, bored with the meaningless cycle of "birth, and copulation, and death," more terrifying than terrified.

Seen in perspective, against the background of Eliot's earlier work and as a background to what came later, *The Waste Land* appears as the poem toward which all the previous poems tend, and as the germ of those that are to follow it. It is "such a vision of the street / As the street hardly understands." And, as in that almost forgotten trifle called "The *Boston Evening Transcript*," it is as "if the street were time," and the poet nodding goodbye to one at the end of the street. Prufrock merged into Gerontion, here Gerontion merges into Tiresias. The Lady, whom we remember slowly twisting the lilac stalks and asking unanswerable questions, has undergone a similar transmutation. Bleistein and Sweeney may be inferred; the mob presses closer than before. The sense of waste, dispersion, frustration, the horror of rootlessness which to Eliot, as to Dostoevsky, is the source of evil, are omnipresent. Technically, we revert from Gautier to Webster and Laforgue. The familiar images recur, more meaningfully. The method of symbolism is preferred; the past impinges on the present, sordid ugliness is ironically contrasted with lost grandeur; the crowding illusions, the rapid associations enhance the effect of disorder, throng the street with shapes of death. It is only at the very close, with the injunctions from the Buddhist fire-sermon, that hope stirs, faintly. Order will come out of chaos, peace will descend upon the spendthrift and the impotent, when men learn how to give, angels to sympathize, gods to control.

The Waste Land is the definite example of a phase of Eliot's work, but it did not mark the end of that phase. The horror of vulgarity is no less patent in "The Hollow Men." In "Journey of the Magi," for all its debt to Pound, may be found echoes of the desperation of Gerontion, and "A Song for Simeon" reads like Gerontion transposed into a religious key. There are passages in the choruses from *The Rock* that suggest *The Waste Land*. But if the sense of evil persists, the emphasis changes. Under all the poems that follow is the voiceless cry: What must we do to be saved? And already in "The Hollow Men" there begins a new music. The religious craving, growing more insistent, introduces a purer lyricism. The emotion is decreasingly depersonalized. And though Eliot is now actually writing poetic dramas, he seems to be speaking for himself more clearly and openly than he dared to do in such a poem as "Prufrock."

"Ash-Wednesday" is generally regarded as exhibiting a new aspect of Eliot's work. This is suggested by the very opening line: "Because I do not hope to turn again"—an odd version of the first line of the ballata written by Cavalcanti upon his exile to Sarazan. Yet there are melodies in "The Hollow Men," unlike those in "Ash-Wednesday," and the persistence of images of drought, the allusion to Phlebas, the drowned sailor, in such a line as "Wavering between the profit and the loss," to "death's dream kingdom," to "La Figlia che Piange," in "Blown hair is sweet, brown hair over the mouth blown, / Lilac and brown hair," all help to remind us of the continuity of Eliot's performance. In all his transitions he preserves his identity, retains that personality which, he has told us, without tradition and orthodoxy, is apt to become "a thing of alarming importance."

The interest attaching to "Ash-Wednesday" lies partly in its retention of familiar symbols, partly in its novel and exquisite music, and largely in its shift of emphasis from flinching contempt of the world to penitent seeking for God. In the light of this poem one may conceive *The Waste Land* as a horrified expression of a sense of sin, and the later poems as a seeking for salvation. For Eliot, as he has not tired of making explicit, salvation is to be found only in the lap of the Anglo-Catholic Church. Yet those of us who would never think of looking for it there can yet delight in "Ash-Wednesday" both for its music and its meaning. The concluding lines, and more especially the repeated supplication "Teach us to care and not to care / Teach us to sit still" could be uttered by the veriest agnostic in those hours when man's endurance is taxed to its limits.

The lyricism of "Ash-Wednesday" informs the poems that follow, which include more personal verse than other groups, notably "Animula." Here, too, is the famous "Marina," a lyric which wonderfully answers Coleridge's demand for poetry that should be untranslatable into words of the same language without injury to the meaning. The hopefulness expressed in this poem is nowhere else apparent, and its tenderness is emphatically denied in *Sweeney Agonistes* [. . .].

Eliot has never been noted for his love of created beings. The scorn implicit in "Prufrock," explicit in the Sweeney cycle, is absent from "Ash-Wednesday" and from "Marina" because there the poet's eye is turned inward and he has the humility of the soul in search of salvation.

[. . .]

363

Morton Dauwen Zabel. "Poets of Five Decades." *Southern Review* 2 (Summer 1936), 168–71.

The unity for which one gropes in combining seventeen new books of verse comes, unexpectedly, less from what they show of the habits of poets during the past five months than from the changes they reveal in fifty years of modern poetic history.

[. . .]

When this cycle of half a century began, poets were still writing *Man* with the monumental initial of moral supremacy. The word soon dwindled to the water-written characters of spiritual illusion; it diminished to the pale letters of self-excoriation and humility; it shrank into the shadow.

[. . .]

When Eliot began to write, the moment for this kind of spiritual illusion had passed from the serious poets of the English scene. He subtitles his *Collected Poems* with the dates *1909–1935*, and by 1909 whatever heroic assumptions remained among the older poets (Swinburne, Meredith, or Moody) passed with the deaths of those men. It had in any case been long reproved by the tragic sarcasm of Hardy, Housman, and Robinson, or—for Eliot more forcibly—by the withering irony of the later Symbolists. There was no further opportunity to lean toward dreams and visions, or upon the ennobling humility of public confession and absolution. If the heroic emerged from the past it did not console the poet either when he borrowed its language or adapted its legends. It diminished to further frailty his dispossession and mediocrity. But

curiously, where the promise of oblivion and oneness in "the Dream" deceived Æ into making ineffectual splendor of his own destiny, the extreme contempt of human meanness in a poet like Eliot led to a tangible grasp of what there was in him to be exalted. This produced in the end an illumination of selfhood which achieved the hard and concrete permanence of a legend. It is to legend that Prufrock and Sweeney belong. They cleanse the conscience of modern man by a species of critical purgation. Long as we have read and pondered them, they still give the pleasure of severe epitomes of the meaning of experience.

But as everyone knows, Eliot has moved far from the style and spirit of those poems. *The Waste Land* showed his transition toward a less personal idiom, and a less sympathetic participation in the modern problem. "The Hollow Men" marked a release from, and a disintegration of, the critical intelligence of the earlier verse, showing this not only by its greater flexibility of structure and cadence, but by the words employed. These words begin to modify the sharp epithet and accent of the satires, and to weave around the sensibility within the poems a subtle web of logical complexity and the casuistries of dialectic argument. It is not too much to claim that this development in Eliot's style reveals the exchange of his powers of introspection for something superior to and beyond personality. His themes change from the dramatic situation of "The Love Song," and "Portrait of a Lady," where self-scrutiny is remorseless and laconic, to the delirium of "The Hollow Men," the self-effacing abnegation of "Ash-Wednesday," and finally to the abstract considerations on the nature and meaning of Time in his latest poem, "Burnt Norton." Here also is a growth away from the meagerness of personal agony toward the freedom of impersonal speculation. But the best quality of

"Burnt Norton" resides in its reminders of how severe, strenuous, and practical was the poet's approach toward the present enlargement of his philosophic vision.

Eliot's poems show remarkable changes in these two hundred pages. While they have become more abstract and intricate in their ideas, they have grown simpler and more expository in method. They have exchanged the pithy terseness of the early allegories for the sinuous devices of metaphysical search. Their language has almost entirely lost the colloquial formality of the *Prufrock* volume. Where this persists, and where he still employs the contrasts of cheap modernity with past greatness (as in the two "fragments of an Aristophanic melodrama" of two poems— "Triumphal March" and "Difficulties of a Statesman"—now grouped as parts of an unfinished work called *Coriolan*), the yoking seems to have the obvious violence of a patented device. By contrast this gives a superior effect to later poems that avoid such conjunction, "Ash-Wednesday" and "Marina." Oblique humor has also disappeared from the later work (though not entirely from the volume, for Eliot here prints a number of nonsense pieces, "Five-Finger Exercises," which hardly impress as important). He has become on the whole a more patient and explicit—that is, a more popular—poet. No doubt there are derivations concealed in his later work [. . .]. I have not traced them far; "Burnt Norton" seems to derive its Time-theme as much from speculators like Whitehead and Dunne as from the lines of Heraclitus printed below the title. But these poems, like the choruses from *The Rock* and *Murder in the Cathedral*, impose no such task of identification on the studious reader as was demanded by every line and page of *The Waste Land*. Their subtleties are organic to themselves; the poem's whole problem is contained within the poem and does not fly off at the tangent of each literary echo or historical reference. And at times, as in "Animula" and "Marina," the feeling and utterance of the poet concentrate into passages of superb lyric vision.

When Eliot stood isolated and dispossessed among the ruins of a familiar universe, every nerve and sensation quivered with its own life. The antennae of his intelligence were alive with nervous vitality. This resulted in images and allegories of great focal sharpness. In more recent years, approaching stranger territory, this grip on identity is no longer held, and with its relaxation the nervous sensibility of his diction and cadence has lessened. He writes either a more relaxed and speculative verse, or a sort of argument which attempts to extend his intellectual problems beyond their own limits. He has become a poet of more public qualities, of religious responsibilities, and even (in *The Rock*) of social concerns. These have entailed a change from a style of cryptic historical reference and erudition to one of dialectic lucidity, or even of popular simplification. He also has doubtless felt "a drift in the times." He has been compelled, as churchman and citizen, toward popularizing and clarifying his language, even though he has not descended to simplifying his metaphysical vision. But that his address has broadened is obvious. One has only to recollect his essays on poetic drama in *The Sacred Wood*, or his remarks on poetic popularity in the study of Tennyson in his new book *Essays Ancient and Modern*, to be aware of his long-standing inclination to enlist moral support and affirmation of a wide human public.

There remains the question of which of these two kinds of poetry—the personal and allegorical or the more human and explicit—he shows greater mastery in. "Ash-Wednesday" and *Murder in the Cathedral* are brilliant achievements. They may bear the more lasting signs of poetic authority. They rise above that poetic value which is restricted to the circle of initiates. But Eliot's creative temperament still stands in its original and fundamental quality in the poems before 1925, and is corroborated there by the essays of the same period. Moreover, those earlier poems were in their way primary creations. They embodied a specific poetic method, and the form of the poems exactly conveyed the matter presented and the kind of experience defined. In later works the hortatory or penitential style is often weakened by such pastiche of his own earlier manners as mars the pages of *The Rock*. Humor and skepticism now seem to sprout artificially from the thicker stem of religious faith, and we are left uncertain of just what is essential and what is not.

[. . .]

Peter Monro Jack. "T. S. Eliot, Poet of Our Time." *New York Times Book Review*, 14 June 1936, pp. 1, 14.

Mr. Eliot has become a classic in his own time without having been very well understood or much read. The quality of his poetry had been obvious since 1917, when *Prufrock and Other Observations* was issued from Bloomsbury Street. General recognition, or as one might say, a general offensive, started in 1922, when *The Waste Land* (a *Dial* prize winner) was published. From then on Mr. Eliot's poetry was largely ignored. Instead he became a public issue. Those who could not read him and those who did not try turned him into a sort of stoolpigeon for

almost every contemporary controversy: the bad effects of expatriatism, for instance; the cult of unintelligibility; the traditional "ancient and modern" quarrel; the humanism–fascism–communism, Puritan–Anglo-Catholic, Royalist–democratic, escapist and look-at-the-facts schools; Mr. Eliot was supposed to represent all of them, while he was being used merely as an excuse to talk of them. The name started a fight whenever it was mentioned, or when it appeared in a magazine or review. Every one seemed to feel that he was important and to find him unintelligible, and the result was a series of critical errors that no one can be very proud of today. The misapprehensions persist. Only last month a Pulitzer prize winner (in poetry) complained that Eliot belonged to the Art for Art's Sake school.

Looking over the variety and versatility of *Collected Poems* one can see that its obvious distinction is to be "useful" poetry. It has expressed, as no one else has done, the critical and creative intelligence of our day, in its utmost seriousness as well as its potential farce. Consider the serious comedy of J. Alfred Prufrock in his "Love Song," written by Mr. Eliot before he graduated from Harvard at the age of 22. Here already is an astonishingly effective technique in poetry, so admirable that it at once became a formula. (Needless to say Mr. Eliot did not himself repeat it. The "Portrait of a Lady" which follows in all the editions was written a year earlier, and is obviously an approach to the perfected form of "Prufrock.") This "Love Song" set the tone of contemporary verse. It restated the dramatic monologue with a new accent, free from the tricks of Browning and Tennyson's sententiousness, and (we may add) was much more integrated than the examples that Ezra Pound was then producing. It used free verse with stylistic assurance, took over a Dostoevski confessional attitude with its later psychoanalytic implications, explained itself through allusive imagery, and set the whole to a discordant music, mostly recitative, with occasionally, a half-formed melody—to make a poem so exactly expressive, so intelligently aware of its effect, that one felt a new certainty in poetry. That it dealt with the difficulties and uncertainties of life made the precision of its form even more remarkable.

The shorter poems that follow show that he had been reading the French Symbolists and that he had learned from them that a poem is more valuable when it stands alone, not subsisting on the author's personality. In Eliot's hands this was to move from romanticism toward classicism, to think of a poem in terms of a finished effect, a final symbol, rather than (as with romantic poets) the beginning of an acquaintance with a personality. There are a few doubtful phrases in these poems. The second couplet here is more smart than witty ("Morning at the Window"):

> They are rattling breakfast plates in
>   basement kitchens,
> And along the trampled edges of the
>   street
> I am aware of the damp souls of
>   housemaids
> Sprouting despondently at area gates.

But the poems have been so carefully formulated from the first that lapses such as this (if this is one) are rare, and only one poem ("Ode" from *Ara Vos Prec*, a mannered and distasteful poem), has been dropped from the collection. The section ends with the lovely "La Figlia che Piange," designed for an anthology.

"Gerontion," a curiously prophetic poem (dated before 1920), seems to have all the elements of both *The Waste Land* (1922) and "Ash-Wednesday" (1930) without a clear articulation. Here is the loss of desire in the symbol of old age, the memories and the questioning that have

replaced passion and faith, and the despair at the little that is left. But still there is Christ, the tiger, the conscience that still devours us, the eternal symbol from which there is no escape: "Think at last / We have not reached conclusion, when I / Stiffen in a rented house." It is a difficult poem (perhaps the only difficult poem Mr. Eliot has written), not only because it is unresolved, but because it is too complex for its form and too pregnant with its possibilities.

The astonishing poems that follow in formal quatrains, the Burbank–Bleistein–Sweeney poems, with "The Cooking Egg" (an egg not quite fresh, like Mr. Eliot's symbolic world) are acknowledged masterpieces of style. Like "Prufrock" and "Gerontion," their theme is the weakness or the absurdity or the futility of worldly desire, in this person or that; mocked by the heroic tradition of the past and made uneasy by the ever-living conscience of the future. Here Mr. Eliot is at his most savage, pitilessly exposing the poorest pretensions of our day. But again there is the counterpoint that was to be heard more clearly in "Ash-Wednesday." The sensual Sweeney stirs in his bath, the subtle professors discuss theology, but

> A painter of the Umbrian school
> Designed upon a gesso ground
> The nimbus of the Baptized God.
> The wilderness is cracked and
>   browned
>
> But through the water pale and thin
> Still shine the unoffending feet
> And there above the painter set
> The Father and the Paraclete.

It repeats the tone of Shakespeare

> (those holy fields
> Over whose acres walk'd those blessed
>   feet
> Which fourteen hundred years ago
>   were nail'd
> For our advantage on the bitter cross.)

and repeats it to our disadvantage, for the easy style of Shakespeare can be sustained only dryly and wryly.

After this *The Waste Land* should have been no surprise, though it must be said that one was not prepared for its brilliance. It put an epic into a short poem, a music into our distraught and demoralized ideas, an ultimatum for our faith, a final immersion in our destructive element, and all of it ringing with memories of Shakespeare and Webster and Donne, Marvell and Day and Baudelaire and Verlaine, Dante, Lucretius, and St. Augustine, Spenser, Milton, Wagner, Tiresias (Ovid), Sappho, Froude, Frazer, Bradley, and the Vedic books: as if to say, "Look here, upon this picture, and on this." No such documentary prosecution of a contemporary age had appeared before, no such challenge; but it was clear that Mr. Eliot could not continue his catalogue of broken images. "The Hollow Men" (1925) is the last and perhaps the most masterful descant on the deadness of an unspiritual life, though following it Mr. Eliot should have printed his incomparable farces of *Sweeney Agonistes* (1926), the last twist of the knife for our vulgar civilization, as if administered by Aristophanes. The dates here are deceptive. The *Ariel* poems here precede "Ash-Wednesday" but "Journey of the Magi" (1927) and "A Song for Simeon" really are precursors, though they are printed as aftermaths. Still one has to be cautious. "Ash-Wednesday" was published in 1930, but at least one of its sections (No. II) was published in Mr. Eliot's *Criterion* in January 1928, and entitled "Salutation." "Doris's Dream Songs" are incorporated here for the first time, looking like late poems, though they had been printed in Harold Monro's *Chapbook* in 1926, and the third section had become a piece of "The Hollow Men." It is too easy to be dogmatic about Eliot's progress and his so-called conversion: both were implicit from the first, and the only comment is that his later style is as surprisingly novel and proper as his earlier.

"Ash-Wednesday," a simple and lovely exercise in devotion coming after the tortuous patterns of his early poems, has by no means exhausted Mr. Eliot's versatility. The choruses from *The Rock* are here, dramatic and exhortatory; the argumentative rhetoric of "Burnt Norton," the pieces (for children?) that are evidently to go into "Pollicle Dogs and Jellicle Cats," the little imagistic landscapes from New Hampshire, Virginia, and Scotland, with a peculiar rhyme-echo scheme—a good deal of quiet minor poetry that probably marks the beginning (as has usually been the case) of a new major development. It is most likely to be in the direction of *Coriolan*, the same sort of speech that went into the last act of *Murder in the Cathedral*, startlingly direct, caustic, and dramatic, a speech for the people. Certainly the effective stress, rhythm, and pitch (the "stone" always low, the rest higher) of "Triumphal March," "(Stone, bronze, stone, steel, stone, oakleaves, horses' heels / Over the paving)" are new to him. But whatever he does is readily interesting and bound to be influential. He has been a poet's poet (though not all poets) and now he might very well be a people's poet. His direction seems to be toward that, and we hope it might be so.

*Rolfe Humphries. "Eliot's Poetry." *New Masses* 20 (18 August 1936), 25–26.

Half this book is a reprint of Eliot's *Poems: 1909–1925*. That work formed the basis of the finest Marxist criticism of poetry in this reviewer's experience, D. S. Mirsky's essay "T. S. Eliot and the End of Bourgeois Poetry." Concerning this half of the present collection, it is sufficient here to refer the reader to the version of Mirsky's essay which appeared in the *New Masses* (November 13, 1934), or, if he knows French, to the fuller statement in the files of the Paris magazine *Echanges*.

"What distinguishes Eliot," Mirsky sums it up, "is that with him a rare poetic gift is allied with a social theme of real significance, with indeed the sole historically valid and sincere theme accessible to a bourgeois poet of today. His contemporaries are but manifestations of the death of bourgeois poetry and civilization; he alone has been able to create a poetry of this death."

The risk run by such a poet is that of exposing himself to the infection of his material. Eliot, who has created a poetry of death, may survive to demonstrate, in his personal history, the death of poetry. In the poems from "Ash-Wednesday" on, there is perceptible evidence of the fatal trend. There is repetition, if not self-imitation: the minor poems, "Eyes That Last I Saw in Tears," and "The Wind Sprang up at Four O'Clock," for instance, contain phrases that seem like scraps left over from their use in "The Hollow Men" or *The Waste Land*. There is a doggerel and triviality: items IV and V of "Five-Finger Exercises," for instance, seem a bit unworthy of one who may aspire to saintliness, and the spectacle of an ascetic copying the attitudes of Edward Lear is ghastily incongruous rather than genuinely comic or edifying. The much-admired choruses from *The Rock* seem to me to contain, rather than to be, poetry [. . .].

If we elevate Eliot above his contemporaries and entitle him the ideal classical poet of an age in break-up, we do not thereby intend to accept his own valuation

of himself as classicist—a romantic and pathetic gesture in the teeth of his time. But his genius, unusually sensitive to an atmosphere of disintegration, has contrived to resist its attraction by his art, to make aesthetic use of the phenomena of dissolution. He has a power of dealing with fragments; both in their invention and synthesis, Eliot has elevated the status of the fragmentary from accident to design. "These fragments I have shored against my ruins" runs the last completely intelligible sentence of *The Waste Land*; and in subsequent work he seems to take comfort in their creation as well as in their use. Thus we have before us fragments of an agon, fragments of a prologue, unfinished poems, five-finger exercises as such; "Ash-Wednesday" includes scraps of the litany, the choruses from *The Rock* of the *Te Deum*. "A Song for Simeon" of the *Nunc Dimittis*; and elsewhere can be found, as mentioned, lumps of Edward Lear, or Gertrude Stein.

[Quotation of lines 11–19 of "Ash-Wednesday" V]

[. . .] [T]here are signs of a reduction of temperature from the white-hot fervor of energy which fused and smelted the scrap-metal in *The Waste Land* to a durable poetic amalgam. Or, to vary the metaphor, what we are permitted to see at times now in Eliot is the undigested substance in the crop of the dissected bird rather than its conversion to formal discharge of energy in poetic flight.

There is more light and less heat in Eliot now, more radiance and less candor, but whatever details of weakness appear in his work are in it, rather than of it. They are there as tendencies which will perhaps be magnified and accelerated as Eliot attains to that state of senile blessedness to which he professes to aspire; at present they reside in him only in the same sense that a man in the prime of his life houses, barring accident, his own peculiar dissolution, predictable enough by the expert in prognosis.

> Little by little we see rising against the Laforguian atmosphere that pervades the verse of the young Eliot a poetry altogether different, freed from the vacillating ambiguity of the decadent, a poetry in which irony cedes before the tragic, and the sexual ambivalence of the consumptive is replaced by the renunciation of the aesthete.

Eliot's later work confirms the accuracy of Mirsky's prediction. We are not yet beyond earshot of ambivalence: the *Sweeney* fragments in the present collection, placed after the "Ash-Wednesday" and Ariel sequences, testify to the temptations assailing the soul, which "cannot be possessed of the divine union, until it has divested itself of the love of created beings." [. . .] [A]s the attraction of high austerity and low vulgarity make war on each other, out of their conflict he achieves his finest poetry; his spirit announces "the completion of its partial ecstasy, the resolution of its partial horror" in the beautiful musical despair of the final poem, "Burnt Norton."

"All the arts," Eliot has quoted Pater to us, "aspire to the condition of music and their meaning reaches us through ways not directly traceable by the understanding." More than ever, Eliot seems to feel that words fail him; more than ever, he grows in his capacity to make them assume the functions of music. There is a sense in which the *Collected Poems* are one whole—a symphony, with deliberately introduced dissonances, with studied repetitions of theme and phrase [. . .]. How beautifully, in "Burnt Norton," Eliot winds the theme, from the simple statement that perhaps any dialectical materialist would accept:

Time present and time past
Are both perhaps present in time
    future
And time future contained in time
    past.

to the conclusion that any revolutionist might find difficulty in understanding: [Quotation in full of "Burnt Norton, V]. How beautifully it is done!

We must not let ourselves become insensitive to this means of communication, no matter how thoroughly we are bent on understanding that the apparent motions of Eliot's art and the real motions are by no means identical. It would be too easy to let Eliot's sense of moral resignation conduce to our sense of moral outrage, and declare a boycott on all his works: but if Marxist criticism of poetry is presumed to partake of the nature of economic science, it would be poor economics. To that science, wrote Engels, "moral indignation, however justifiable, cannot serve as an argument, but only as a symptom." Eliot is not a proletarian poet, nor has he urged a classless society even in heaven. Still, he is a prophet of revolution; he has written, with poetic authority too great to be questioned, the elegy of an age that is passing. Let us not be so boisterous shouting our war songs that we fail to hear from the citadel of our enemies the cry of capitulation.

---

*D. W. Harding.
"T. S. Eliot, 1925–1936."
Scrutiny 5 (September 1936), 171–76.

This new volume is an opportunity, not for a review—for "The Poetry of T. S. Eliot" begins to have the intimidating sound of a Tripos question—but for asking whether anything in the development of the poetry accounts for the change in attitude that has made Mr. Eliot's work less *chic* now than it was ten years ago. Perhaps the ten years are a sufficient explanation—obvious changes in fashionable feeling have helped to make the sort-of-communist poets popular. But on the other hand it may be that these poets gratify some taste that Mr. Eliot also gratified in his earlier work but not in his later. If so it is surely a taste for evocations of the sense of protest that our circumstances set up in us; for it seems likely that at the present time it is expressions of protest in some form or other that most readily gain a poet popular sympathy. And up to *The Waste Land* and "The Hollow Men" this protest—whether distressed, disgusted, or ironical—was still the dominant note of Mr. Eliot's work, through all the subtlety and sensitiveness of the forms it took. Yet already in these two poems the suggestion was creeping in that the sufferers were also failures. "We are the hollow men," but there are, besides, "Those who have crossed / With direct eyes, to death's other Kingdom."

And in all the later work the stress tends to fall on the regret or suffering that arises from our own choices or our inherent limitations, or on the resignation that they make necessary. Without at the moment trying to define the change more closely, one can point out certain characteristics of the later work which are likely to displease those who create the fashions of taste in poetry today, and which also contrast with Mr. Eliot's earlier work. First it is true that in some of the poems (most obviously in the choruses from *The Rock*) there are denunciation and preaching, both of which people like just now. But there is a vital difference between the denunciation here and that, say, in "The Dog Beneath the Skin": Mr. Eliot doesn't invite you to

step across a dividing line and join him in guaranteed rightness—he suggests at the most that you and he should both try, in familiar and difficult ways, not to live so badly. Failing to make it sound easy, and not putting much stress on the fellowship of the just, he offers no satisfaction to the craving for a life that is ethically and emotionally *simpler*.

And this characteristic goes with a deeper change of attitude that separates the later work from the earlier. Besides displaying little faith in a revolt against anything outside himself, Mr. Eliot in his recent work never invites you to believe that everything undesirable in you is due to outside influences that can be blamed for tampering with your original rightness. Not even in the perhaps over-simple "Animula" is there any suggestion that the "simple soul" has suffered an avoidable wrong for which someone else can be given the blame. Mr. Eliot declines to sanction an implicit belief, almost universally held, which lies behind an immense amount of rationalization, self-pity and childish protest—the belief that the very fact of being alive ought to ensure you being a satisfactory object in your own sight. He is nearer the more rational view that the process of living is at its best one of progressive dissatisfaction.

Throughout the earlier poems there are traces of what, if it were cruder and without irony and impersonality, would be felt at once as self-pity or futile protest: for example, "Put your shoes at the door, sleep, prepare for life. / The last twist of the knife," or,

Wipe your hand across your mouth,
    and laugh;
The worlds revolve like ancient
    women
Gathering fuel in vacant lots.

Obviously this is only one aspect of the early poetry, and to lay much stress on it without qualification would be grotesquely unfair to "Gerontion" especially and to other poems of that phase. But it is a prominent enough aspect of the work to have made critics, one might have thought, more liable to underrate the earlier poems than, with fashionable taste, the later ones. For there can be no doubt of the greater maturity of feeling in the later work:

> And I pray that I may forget
> These matters that with myself I too
>   much discuss
> Too much explain
> [. . . . .]

This may be called religious submission, but essentially it is submission of maturity.

What is peculiar to Mr. Eliot in the tone of his work, and not inherent in maturity or in religion, is that he does submit to what he knows rather than welcoming it. To say that his is a depressed poetry isn't true, because of the extraordinary toughness and resilience that always underlie it. They show, for instance, in the quality of the scorn he expresses for those who have tried to overlook what he sees: "the strained time-ridden faces / Distracted from distraction by distraction [. . .]." But to insist on the depression yields a half-truth. For though acceptance and understanding have taken the place of protest, the underlying experience remains one of suffering, and the renunciation is much more vividly communicated than the advance for the sake of which it was made. It is summed up in the ending of "Ash-Wednesday": [quotation of lines 25–35 of "Ash-Wednesday" VI]. This is the cry of the weaned child, I suppose the analysts might say; and without acquiescing in the genetic view that they would imply, one can agree that weaning stands as a type-experience of much that Mr. Eliot is interested in as a poet. It seems to be the clearer and more direct realization of this kind of experience that makes the later poems at the same time more personal and more mature. And in the presence of these poems, many who like saying they like the earlier work feel both embarrassed and snubbed.

However, all of this might be said about a volume of collected sermons instead of poems. It ignores Mr. Eliot's amazing genius in the use of words and rhythms and his extraordinary fertility in styles of writing, each "manner" apparently perfected from the first and often used only once (only once, that is, by Mr. Eliot, though most are like comets with a string of poetasters laboriously tailing after them). One aspect of his mastery of language may perhaps be commented on here because it reaches its most remarkable expression in the latest of the poems, "Burnt Norton." Here most obviously the poetry is a linguistic achievement, in this case an achievement in the creation of concepts.

Ordinarily our abstract ideas are over-comprehensive and include too wide a range of feeling to be of much use by themselves. If our words "regret" and "eternity" were exact bits of mosaic with which to build patterns much of "Burnt Norton" would not have had to be written. But

> Words strain,
> Crack and sometimes break, under the
>   burden,
> Under the tension, slip, slide, perish,
> Decay with imprecision, will not stay
>   in place,
> Will not stay still.

One could say, perhaps, that the poem takes the place of the ideas of "regret" and "eternity." Where in ordinary speech we should have to use those words, and hope by conversational trial-and-error to obviate the grosser misunderstandings, this poem is a newly-created concept, equally abstract but vastly more exact and rich in meaning. It makes no statement. It is no

372

more "about" anything than an abstract term like "love" is about anything: it is a linguistic creation. And the creation of a new concept, with all the assimilation and communication of experience that involves, is perhaps the greatest of linguistic achievements.

In this poem the new meaning is approached by two methods. The first is the presentation of concrete images and definite events, each of which is checked and passes over into another before it has developed far enough to stand meaningfully by itself. This is, of course, an extension of a familiar language process. If you try to observe introspectively how the meaning of an abstract term— say "trade"—exists in your mind, you find that after a moment of blankness, in which there seems to be only imageless "meaning," concrete images of objects and events begin to occur to you; but none by itself carries the full meaning of the word "trade," and each is faded out and replaced by another. The abstract concept, in fact, seems like a space surrounded and defined by a more or less rich collection of latent ideas. It is this kind of definition that Mr. Eliot sets about here—in the magnificent first section for instance—with every subtlety of verbal and rhythmical suggestion.

And the complementary method is to make pseudo-statements in highly abstract language, for the purpose, essentially, of putting forward and immediately rejecting ready-made concepts that might have seemed to approximate to the concept he is creating. For instance: "Neither from nor towards; at the still point, there the dance is / But neither arrest nor movement. And do not call it fixity, / Where past and future and are gathered. [. . .]."

In neither of these methods is there any attempt to state the meaning by taking existing abstract ideas and piecing them together in the ordinary way. Where

something approaching this more usual method is attempted, in the passage beginning "The inner freedom from the practical desire," it seems a little less successful; admirable for the plays, where the audience is prominent, it fails to combine quite perfectly with the other methods of this poem. But it is Mr. Eliot himself who, by the closeness of his approach to technical perfection, provides a background against which such faint flaws can be seen.

Louis Untermeyer. *Yale Review* 26 (September 1936), 165–66.

T. S. Eliot has become a symbol of all that is advanced in poetry, and yet he is an anachronism in the sense that he is both futurist and *fin de siècle*. No one, as far as I know, has compared him to the aesthetes of the Nineties; yet his course and theirs are curiously similar. They mixed Anglican intellectuality and Parnassian impressionism; he combined academic erudition and French symbolism. They found their own times ugly, and retreated into the remote and exotic; he, equally horrified by his world, pitted a beautiful past against an evil present, and explored an unreal limbo where even the brutal was bizarre. They— Lionel Johnson, Ernest Dowson, Oscar Wilde, Aubrey Beardsley—could no longer face their own distortions and turned to the Catholic church, which supplied them with new color as well as a new impetus; he, unable to dwell in his Waste Land, with its nightmares of vulgarity, had found an Anglo-Catholic haven, and in return, the church has given him another kind of subsistence as well as fresh subject matter. With their desperate audacities they marked the end of the century; with his confused desperation he marks the end of an epoch.

Eliot's *Collected Poems*, including all the poetic work he wished to print with the exception of *Murder in the Cathedral*, his simplest and most moving creation, presents still a further paradox. The early poems—the poems of contempt, frustration, and horror—are more compelling than the later penitences and salvations. Eliot communicates his aversions through "Sweeney" and "Bleistein" far more successfully than his resignations through "Burnt Norton." "The Love Song of J. Alfred Prufrock," that remarkable study of futility, written when Eliot was an undergraduate, scarcely depended on abstractions. Here, and in the poems that immediately succeeded it, Eliot expressed his hatred of his times in biting, if bewildering, stanzas. *The Waste Land*, with its sequential "The Hollow Men," was the impasse; the poet could descend no further into boredom, emptiness, drought. "Ash-Wednesday" points the way out; "A Song for Simeon" and the choruses from *The Rock* define it.

And what is the sum of the contrasts and shifting now they are collected in one volume? Is the final effect a growth of incongruity? It is an uncertain mixture of all. Eliot can be the most solemn of poets; there are times when his solemnities are sillier than his purposeful nonsense. The burlesque of third-rate comic opera in *Sweeney Agonistes* is mildly amusing, but prefixing his absurdities with a quotation from St. John of the Cross is both pretentious and funny. There is no fusion, not even a "lunar synthesis." There are remarkable images, strange and exciting juxtapositions, sweet and acidulous discords, bleak hope matched with no final faith, the words of other men shaped into new cadences. Eliot's very idiom—and there can be no doubt of its individuality—is a paradox, being largely composed of idioms not originally his own. His lines are a mosaic of fragments from poets as incongruously joined as Browning and Paul Dreiser (Theodore Dreiser's brother and composer of "On the Banks of the Wabash"), Shakespeare and the *Upanishads*, Ovid and Verlaine, Dante and Edward Lear. Certain borrowed lines, often without benefit of quotation, appear again and again; for example Dante's "At the still point of the turning world" occurs in "Triumphal March" and the still more recent and seemingly autobiographical "Burnt Norton."

Yet there is no questioning Eliot's influence or his authority. The authority, however, lies not so much in what Eliot says as in his manner of saying it, even in his manner of making others say it. It lies in the very amalgam of accents, in his timely sense of confusion, and his peculiarly persuasive techniques of escape. In spite of major sonorities and an often exalted pitch, Eliot is not a major poet, but a new kind of minor poet—a minor poet in the grand manner.

Checklist of Additional Reviews

John Hayward. "London Letter." *New York Sun*, 28 March 1936, p. 19.

Malcolm Cowley. "Afterthoughts on T. S. Eliot." *New Republic* 87 (20 May 1936), 49.

William Gilmore. "The Poetry of Eliot: An Oasis in the Waste Land." *Brooklyn Eagle*, 24 May 1936, p. 10.

"Royalist, Classicist, Anglo-Catholic." *Time* 27, pt. 2 (25 May 1936), 90–91.

H. Jeffrey Smith. "Along the Bookshelf." *Person* 17 (Summer 1936), 330–32.

*Ivan Black. "A Note on T. S. Eliot." *Verse*, June 1936.

Joseph Carroll. "The Dry Crackle of *The Waste Land* Haunts His Measures." *Chicago Daily News*, 3 June 1936, p. 19.

Mildred Boie. "Book Reviews." *North American Review* 242 (Autumn 1936), 189–92.

*C. E. B. "Books of the Day." *Illustrated London News* 189 (12 September 1936), 428.

Kerker Quinn. "Out of the Slough of Despond." *Virginia Quarterly Review* 12 (October 1936), 621–22.

*Arthur W. Fox. "Collected Poems of T. S. Eliot." *Papers of the Manchester Literary Club* 63 (1937), 23–40.

**Dallas Kenmare. "Story of a Pilgrimage." *Poetry Review* 28 (January–February 1937), 23–27.

R. P. Blackmur. "The Whole Poet." *Poetry: A Magazine of Verse* 50 (April 1937), 48–51.

B[lanche] K[elly]. *Catholic World* 145 (May 1937), 245–46.

THE FAMILY REUNION
1939

THE
FAMILY REUNION

a play by

T. S. Eliot

Faber and Faber Limited
24 Russell Square
London

*"Mr. Eliot in Search of the Present."
Times Literary Supplement 1938 (25 March 1939), 176.

Mr. Eliot must be admired for his persistence in making experiments for a modern verse drama. The box-office success of *Murder in the Cathedral* may have given him an unexpected and fortunate filip. It is possible, indeed, that he, more than other poets on the scene at the moment, may establish an altered theatre. His work is ritualistic, a thing which will be increasingly appropriate, without doubt, in the coming years. Yet, strangely enough, in his new play, *The Family Reunion* [. . .], he clings in the text to naturalism of surface and the naturalistic time. For all the versification, he may be said to have hardly broken with the main tenets of Shaftesbury Avenue.

Here we have the fixed drawing-room and library of an English country house. The slight ceremonies of such a place may make a preliminary appeal to Mr. Eliot. The verse is so apologetic it might often hardly be noticed: "She's a nice girl; but it's a difficult age for her. / I suppose she must be getting on for thirty?" This is perhaps an experiment in infiltration, of "getting by" with verse before the Philistines suspect it. It has the flat simplicity of Frost, the studied casualness of certain Frenchmen, but it does not seem especially dramatic; nor is it compact. At times it is both clumsy and diffuse, reminding us rather of the novel of analysis, now passing, than of a possible poetic drama. It has less natural music than that of certain dramatists who take conversation and subtilize it and make it dance to its inherent tunes. Too often he imposes rather than educes the music. What the theatre requires is the dance of the text; whether verse or prose does not matter. [. . .]

The Family Reunion, to some extent, reflects the state of the modern theatre, both in its treatment and story. Old appearances are kept up, but always there is a sense of another thing, in this case horrible, ready to explode beneath. At intervals a choric frankness breaks forth, and the Eumenides are sighted for a second in a window embrasure. We realize it is inevitable that the surface will break completely, in the end, and that is all: a negative approach. The general effect is static and descriptive. We had imagined a dynamic and cursive drama, learning from the Greek, but moving away from it too. This is the contrary. Characters are erected like statues [. . .] here and there about the desiccated stage. They are the statues of an intellectual commentary, not bold complete figures in Greek sunshine, but tenebrous with nineteenth-century Gothic guilt.

[. . .]

Mr. Eliot is a poet with a sense of the past in search of an equivalent present. His poems contrasted slick Modernism with ancient greatness, to the former's disadvantage. Here he has tried to insert guilt in the ancient style, into a drawing-room. He spoke in an essay once of Hamlet being

> dominated by an emotion which is inexpressible, because it is in *excess* of the facts as they appear. And the supposed identity of Hamlet with his author is genuine to this point: that Hamlet's bafflement at the absence of objective equivalent to his feelings is a prolongation of the bafflement of his creator in the face of his artistic problem.

His own words describe the impression that *The Family Reunion* makes.

Again, this is the past looking for a present, not the present reabsorbing the past [. . .]. Mr. Eliot is perhaps an illustration of the Orpheus legend. He has visited the world of the dead and is bringing back what he needs to enrich the modern time. But it is ordained that the poet must keep his eyes well on his own brief day lest, ironically, the world of the dead should cease to help him.

---

*Phoebe Fenwick Gaye. "Expiation Becomes Orestes." *Time and Tide* 20 (25 March 1939), 388–89.

There is more connection between this fine play and O'Neill's *Mourning Becomes Electra* than the fact that both have received their first London production at the Westminster. There is a source of inspiration common to both and the same Hellenic skeleton has served both authors on which to build up the muscles and fleshly outline of new characters. The producer, Mr. Martin Browne, sums up the play's argument admirably when he describes it as the tale of Orestes in a contemporary English setting in which "the pursuing forces let loose by an evil tendency in the family . . . lie close beneath the apparently placid surface of life."

The setting is Wishwood, a country house in the north of England, in which the dowager Lady Monchensey, together with her three sisters and two brothers-in-law, is celebrating a birthday and awaiting the arrival of her children, especially of an eldest and beloved son, Harry Lord Monchensey, who has been abroad for eight years. During this time we gather he has contracted an unfortunate marriage, traveled far and widely and eventually, during the course of a sea voyage, lost his wife in suspicious circumstances. Rumor—and the papers—report it as an accident. Harry, arrived home in the gracious and spacious surrounding of Wishwood, declares abruptly before his assembled relations that it was no accident—that in a moment of long repressed but finally released hatred, he had pushed her overboard.

The reactions to this development are expressed in prose (for the surface comments of every day) and in poetry, often chanted in unison when the unspoken fears and hopes of the company, either severally or individually, are intended. This procedure in less adept hands might have turned actors into robots or mouthpieces as uniform and uncharacterized as a set of *papier mâché* masks taken off the same mold. But Mr. Eliot can draw lineaments with a skill fairly uncommon in poets and the simple optimistic Aunt Ivy, the repressed snob Aunt Violet, the wise Aunt Agatha, the fumbling, fuddled Uncle Charles and the retired Colonel who is Uncle Gerald are as distinctly and individually expressed whether they talk poetry or prose. So is the pathetic, embittered figure of self-will which is Harry's mother and the gentle insufficiency of his cousin Mary. Every character in short conforms with a satisfactory precision to its original conception and expresses itself only in terms acceptable (because fundamentally truthful) both to itself and the audience.

The poetry is as clear in outline as the characterization, with a metallic precision about it. That it accords so well with the Greek framework is odd since I have always considered Mr. Eliot to be one of the most twentieth-century of poets—his lines so clean and bright and hard that sometimes they appear a little as if they were sprayed over with chromium plating—guaranteed not to warp, crack or tarnish under the roughest usage. Yet here the chromium-plated effect was in abeyance; instead the severity and accuracy of the descriptive lines, and the meticulous diction of the speakers of them were, like the stony folds in the cloak of the Apollo Belvedere or in the gown of the sleeping Ariadne, a kind of rigid but absolutely right decoration to a piece of Greek origin.

This cuts both ways of course. For just as the Apollo though beautiful never moves, and the sleeping Ariadne never wakes, so this family of Monchensey never puts on living, breathing, human flesh. If they have the pure outline of marble they have also its insensibility. No real family, for instance, would sit quietly at home awaiting the arrival of an eight-years-absent son and heir—somebody or other, one feels, would have taken the trouble to go to the station to meet him or at least to wait on the steps looking out for his car. And no real sister would be able, like Agatha, to relate with such dispassionate detachment the details of a plan to murder her sister—however long ago it all occurred, and however little the bond of sympathy between them. That we, the spectators, feel for the family and are moved by their circumstances is a proof that despite their lack of the smaller humanities they still make admirable dramatic material. After all, we have had more than enough of the man-in-the-street in drama, and this play has been a welcome reminder that gods and devils, ghosts and furies, angels and ministers of grace are also legitimate members of a cast.

The argument was less easily assimilated than the characterization. It would appear to be that Orestes–Harry, having finally returned to his birthplace and home of not too happy childhood: "the sideways looks that bring / Death to the heart of a child" must unburden himself of the sense of guilt which has been pursuing him ever since the accident (was it accident? was it deliberate?) occurred; must learn of his antecedents and that he suffers less as a single sinner than as a scapegoat for the sins of the entire family (his father had had homicidal tendencies); must go out again into the night, led on by a species of Eumenides or avenging furies to an unknown destination but accepting them and not running away from them—and from himself—for the first time:

> It is love and terror
> Of what waits and wants me and will
>   not let me fall.
> [. . . . .]
> I must follow the bright angels.

[. . .]

---

*Desmond MacCarthy. "Some Notes on Mr. Eliot's New Play." *New Statesman* 17 (25 March 1939), 455–56.

[. . .] Mr. T. S. Eliot's new verse play, *The Family Reunion*, [. . .] is a drama of the inner life. The character contrast which runs through it—the test applied to all the characters in the play—is whether he or she attempts to live on the surface and *pretends* (that is all that is possible) to ignore the spiritual destiny of man, or accepts a predicament which is essentially tragic. [. . .]

The theme of this drama is retribution and expiation. It postulates a supernatural conception of sin. The dramatic method employed is (*a*) a blending of symbolism and realism (Ibsen's later method and the most poetic way of dealing with dramas of the inner life) and (*b*) a device which Eugene O'Neill used in that extraordinarily interesting experiment, *Strange Interlude*, namely, that of making the characters on the stage speak their thoughts and feelings aloud, not as in traditional drama in the form of brief conventional asides or set soliloquies, but in order to convey to the audience a running contrast between what they are saying to each other, and those thoughts and feelings they are withholding or even stifling unconsciously in themselves.

This is obviously an extremely difficult device to handle. I cannot say that Mr. Eliot has employed it throughout with that psychological tact towards his audience which is absolutely essential if the effect is not to be more grotesque than impressive. In a sense, too, it is a "get-out." It is a way of circumventing what is the great difficulty in handling on the stage a drama of the inner life; namely, of writing a dialogue which shall be realistically plausible and yet every line of which, however commonplace and natural, shall *suggest* to us what is going on privately at the back of the speakers' minds. Ibsen was the great master of this art. Chekhov hit upon a device which was a sort of half-way compromise, realistically justified by the Russian temperament—that of the soliloquy *à deux*. Recall how often in his plays conversation between two or more characters takes the form of each pursuing aloud their own thoughts instead of answering directly what is said to them. [. . .] In fiction, Virginia Woolf uses this monologistic form of dialogue at points where traditional novelists (claiming the privileges of an omniscient observer) would have simply stated what was going on inside the heads of people, while they were *talking* about something else. The O'Neill

experiment, which Mr. Eliot has followed, is deliberately to make the thoughts or feelings of his characters audible to the audience, without attempting to make soliloquy, as Chekhov did, consonant with the realistic surface of the dialogue. Indeed, Mr. Eliot goes a step further. At certain points in the dialogue where a group of people are presented as embodying the same reactions, they are made to speak the same words in chorus. Thus, suddenly, in the middle of humorously realistic chit-chat, to which in turn each of them has contributed some characteristic trifle, Harry's uncles and aunts (always with the exception of Agatha, who does not cling to the make-believe surface of life) will start speaking the same words in chorus. This device is a failure, and for two reasons. It weakens still further the actuality of the scene before our eyes, and thus the intensity of what we feel about it; and secondly, words muttered in unison have the inevitable effect of ritual responses—as it might be, "Lord, have mercy upon us and incline our hearts to obey this Law." Realism, whether on stage or on the written page, is primarily a means to increasing our fellow-feeling with imaginary characters and strengthening our faith in the situation presented. It is a very powerful means indeed, never to be lightly sacrificed, except in order to gain another intensity, poetic or symbolic, more valuable still. Here the destruction of plausibility is complete. The audience may have adapted their imaginations to the new convention of characters speaking their private thoughts aloud; but when a London clubman, a Bayswater boardinghouse lady, a retired colonel and a well-to-do widow, who the moment before have been making typical remarks, suddenly start murmuring in chorus, then the last refuge of willing make-believe in us is destroyed. It is hard enough for actors to mark by their delivery from the stage the difference between the spoken *thoughts* and the spoken *words* which the author puts in their mouths. It can only be done by uttering the former with a peculiarly personal self-withdrawn intonation, and this is impossible when they are made to speak in unison, when to be audible they have to keep in strict time with each other. It is the difference between walking and marching. A man may express his individuality by his gait, but not in the ranks. Thus in this play at times when the words should seem to be proceeding out of the depths of an individual mind, they reach our ears like a singing-lesson or a liturgy. Mr. Eliot's "chorus" of uncles and aunts implies a violation of auditory psychology.

How did he come to make it? That is an interesting question connected with my fundamental criticism of his play. Evidently his theme—retribution and expiation—occurred to him first in the form of Greek drama. Eugene O'Neill had adapted in *Mourning Becomes Electra* with extraordinary, tragic effect the Greek conception of Destiny and the whole of the Clytemnestra–Agamemnon story. It was a masterpiece, thanks fundamentally to the inspiration which made him perceive in the modern theory of the Unconscious— a power which pushes us into behaving against our will—a close parallel to the Greek conception of Destiny. Mr. Eliot has perceived a relation between the Greek Furies and remorse or maddened conscience. But note this. O'Neill got his effect without using Greek mythology. Had he introduced the Eumenides in the last Act as symbols of Harry's remorse, they would not only have left us cold but made nonsense of an intensely tragic situation. The Eumenides are not for us recognized symbols of remorse and retribution. They are not part of the furniture of our minds as, in a shadowy way, guardian angels and devils still are. They carry no guns, so

to speak; the mention of their name, let alone a glimpse of them through a modern drawing-room window, awakes no sensation of dim disgust and terror in our hearts. They are hopeless symbols for Mr. Eliot's purpose. If he had put his story of remorse and expiation into a Greek setting, Furies would have been in place, but he could not expect us to shiver at the idea of a young lord being pursued on his travels by those monsters (visible also to his chauffeur and a young lady cousin) and of his finding them waiting in his old home.

It is the greatest pity that Mr. Eliot in writing this play about the place of the conscience in life ever took off on a Greek foot. The temper of his mind, too, is entirely Christian, not Greek. I know the Greeks to propitiate evil powers called them by flattering names, and the Eumenides were superstitiously referred to as "the good ones" for fear of being dogged by them. But the whole point of Mr. Eliot's play is that they (these embodiments of remorse and thwarted spiritual aspirations) are really guiding angels which must be welcomed and followed, if man is to find peace. Why in that case introduce Greek mythology at all? It is maddening. This play shows that Mr. Eliot has it in him to write a masterpiece on a theme nearer his thoughts than any other: on the problem of wickedness and the salvation of the soul. But the Greeks are the last people in the world to help him in that. He might have presented this young man, who perhaps—it is even in doubt whether he ever did more than contemplate doing it—pushed his silly wife overboard, as *haunted* on his return to take up his life as a country squire. We can still suspend disbelief in regard to revengeful ghosts, and be interested in them too, if they stand at the same time for spiritual torture. But (*vide* Macbeth) certainly no one else ought to see the specter of his conscience.

[. . .] The play is [. . .] an example of how to write a modern play in verse. Mr. Eliot has used a kind of subtle verse, based on iambic blank verse, which can be delivered as prose, or at moments of high emotion, stressed rhythmically so as to carry us into the region of poetry: a great achievement and one of pioneer importance. The diction, too, is fine, clear and impeccable.

*"The Family Reunion. A Play by T. S. Eliot." *Listener* 21 (6 April 1939), 750.

No one should miss reading this play, if it happens, as may well be, to prove a failure on the stage. As an imaginative work of art, a book to read, it compares with the most sensitive of the short novels by Henry James. It is fashionable to say boldly that there is no place in the library for the dramatic poem; poetic drama is written for the stage, we are told, and if it fails there, it is useless. But just conceivably the poetic drama is developing in two directions; one, in the plays of Auden and Isherwood, certainly towards the theatre; the other, of which this play is a striking example, towards narrative poetry.

The plot of *The Family Reunion* is extremely simple. The scene is a family party to celebrate the birthday of its senior member, Lady Monchensey, the mother of the hero, Harry. A shadow is cast over the proceedings by the fact that Harry's wife, whom the family always disliked, has been drowned by falling overboard during a voyage at sea. Everyone assumes that this is either suicide or an accident. However, when Harry returns, he disconcertingly reveals that he either has, or believes he has, pushed her overboard. The family assures him that this is the working of his fevered imagination. However, he is a modern Orestes, pursued by the Eumenides. Moreover, the crime is not just his, for it has been repeated in the family; his father has also wished to murder his mother. This leads us to think that in all probability neither of these murders exists outside the hearts of the protagonists. But Harry has to suffer: "It is possible / You are the consciousness of your unhappy family, / Its bird sent flying through the purgatorial flame [. . .]." The upshot is that Harry leaves his family to follow the "bright angels" of the Eumenides and to atone for his crime in isolation.

Various features of this plot must surely mar it on the stage. In the first place, the main piece of action, the murder, is an unexplained mystery, which may even not have happened. It has only a symbolic significance. The actual action on the stage is of a quiet, domestic drama, in which one of the characters has a load of guilt on his mind: and yet one feels that there is more than that to it, that something violent ought to *happen*. The Eumenides idea, and the idea of the repeated crime, are surely purely academic; it would be much simpler if one member of the family was faced with the problem of his own sin, and the rest of the family were spectators, entering into his consciousness at various levels. These things do not bother one so much when one reads the play; although the obscurity of the action sometimes makes it a little tiresome to follow. But what is wonderful is the marvelous opening out of consciousness, the flowering of meaning, which makes this play an account of a spiritual experience. There are passages of great poetic beauty, and statements which are the fruits of a lifetime devoted to poetry. To find any parallel to Mr. Eliot's moral sensitivity, to his capacity for feeling life and opening out layer after layer of consciousness, we are brought back again to his great compatriot the New Englander, Henry James.

*P. T. [Pamela Travers]. *"The Family Reunion."* New English Weekly 14 (6 April 1939), 397–98.

[. . .]

The great virtue of [Mr. Eliot], both as dramatist and poet, is that he refuses to live in or to record only the isolated moment, that packed particle of time in which, looking neither backwards nor forwards, the common ruck of men dwell throughout their lives. Rather, he uses the moment as a sieve through which past is poured on its way to become future. Now, for him, is only significant when it is the effect of Then and the cause of Maybe. He performs for us a grateful service when he reveals the present as a mere focal point for the antique and unborn worlds. For thus he reminds us at once of our heritage and our hope. With *Murder in the Cathedral* he brought up an old sequence of events to illustrate the living instant. With *The Family Reunion* [. . .] he goes deeper into time and brings back the stones of Argos to build a house in Yorkshire. Orestes, too, comes with him and moves amid the purple ling, as haunted and hunted as among the Arcadian rocks. Yet so apt is Mr. Eliot at binding together the sections of time that we are aware of no strain, no discrepancy when the Erinnys of the ancient world break through the barrier that separates myth from our moment. For that barrier is imponderable and intangible and consists only in the changed habitation of Fate. Of old, Nemesis was conceived as acting from without, an incarnation separated in substance from, though endlessly bound to, the object of pursuit. But the advent of Christianity changed the locale and Nemesis now acts from within, inseparable and indistinguishable from the personified cause of its existence. It is a truism that all our lives are haunted by imminent pasts and futures. Argos builds itself second by second in every one of us. But till now, for all the drama implicit in such realization, no modern dramatist has dared to hint at it. The wedding ring of Heaven and Hell is difficult enough to forge in poetry. In drama, where the artificer must in addition stamp the immediate moment on the circlet, it is a task for Hephaestos. And, if you stretch the inelastic, unapprehensive modern mind to include immortal intimations the process is as likely to shatter it as enlarge it. The risk is very great.

Mr. Eliot has taken the risk, however, and *The Family Reunion* must be judged in the light of this and other difficulties inherent in its theme. Theatrically, and as a dramatic form wherein characters are hounded backwards and forwards from plane to plane, from mere existence plunged into true being and by deep tides lifted back to the parched sand, it succeeds triumphantly. Its transformation from the prose to the poetry of life is so subtly and fluidly achieved that the play moves, like a river, in one unbroken rhythm. The chorus of Uncles and Aunts, supplying the worldly comment on the event, alternating their inward thoughts with those imposed by tradition and convention, is a gorgeous theatrical device. If we could by law introduce a chorus into every serious play—the frivolities have it already, though in a bastard form that does not know its father—we should have a drama worth matching with the time. For the chorus is the particle of dust, the immortal matter, the atommass of humanity, about which idea and individual cohere and grow to being. On the opposite side from the chorus, where the mass throws up the pyramidal one, stands the figure of Agatha, lover of the father, absolver of the son. In this character resides the whole significance of the play, a significance which thrusts her out of mortal dimensions to those of avenging goddess—Athene with a word-stroke setting free her own. She it is who reveals to Harry—or Orestes—what is, in fact, the play's own revelation; that the Erinnys are only furies when they are fled. Face them and they become Eumenides, the kindly ones; pursue them and you are at the heels of the bright angels. Thus, in a moment, the theatrical purpose of the play is effected and what seems to be an endless circle springs suddenly to the spiral. No action prepares it; the change is wrought by word. But there are moments in drama, as in life, when word becomes action. It is not the static climax, therefore, nor the intellectual revelation, that leave us in doubt. But in its emotional aspect the story appears too cloudy and insufficiently digested. Throughout its unfolding our minds are vividly alive, riding Mr. Eliot's intellectual horse, its bright mane of poetry blowing strongly back upon our faces. Unfortunately, no Pegasus is provided for the emotions. They remain sadly upon the moor, huddling like grouse between the earth and the branched heather. It is not the austere quality of the play that prevents them taking wing, for austerity opens a window upon feeling, but the fact that occasionally the austere descends to the pompous. Even if this were not so it must be remembered that emotion can only function in a human habitation and there is about the great house of Wishwood an extra-human atmosphere. Accepting this, we must also accept the emotional cloudiness as inevitable. Even clarity and perfection must be sacrificed in the cause of truth and if our theme be gods and demons the

human sign that links them must suffer diminution. [. . .]

---

*Maud Bodkin. "The Eumenides and Present-Day Consciousness." *Adelphi* 15 (May 1939), 411–13.

Of T. S. Eliot's play, *The Family Reunion*, at the Westminster Theatre, one critic—in the *Observer*—wrote "Christian and Pagan do not mix. How can a Christian accept the idea of a family curse at all?" Another—Desmond MacCarthy in the *New Statesman*—similarly questions: Why introduce the Furies—"hopeless symbols for Mr. Eliot's purpose"—in a play of Christian temper "about the place of the conscience in life"? A vengeful ghost, visible, as in *Macbeth*, to the haunted sinner alone, would, Mr. MacCarthy suggests, win from us a readier response. [MacCarthy's review is reprinted on pp. 381–84.]

A play by Mr. Eliot is more than an event of the theatre. A critic reviewing the play—in the *Listener*—as "an imaginative work of art," that "no one should miss reading," praising Eliot's "moral sensitivity," his "capacity for feeling life and opening out layer after layer of consciousness," yet repeats the complaint concerning the use of the myth of the Eumenides. He pronounces it "purely academic; it would be much simpler if one member of the family was faced with the problem of his own sin and the rest of the family were spectators."

Does it not seem a little odd that critics, recognizing the poet's moral sensitivity and power to bring new issues to consciousness, should yet so lightly propose change in the play's central imagery, as if they knew better than the author what experience this imagery should illumine?

Is this a play about an individual conscience haunted by an individual sin? Eliot—I think—tries to guard against just such an apprehension of his theme. The play's chief character, Harry, the returning heir, speaking to his assembled family, dismayed to find him, as it seems, conscience-haunted, believing himself guilty of the murder of his wife—insists that they do not understand:

> It goes a good deal deeper
> Than what people call their conscience
> [. . . . .]
> It is not my conscience,
> Not my mind that is diseased, but the
> world I have to live in.

And again:

> You go on trying to think of each
> thing separately,
> [. . . . .]
> I was like that in a way, so long as I
> could think
> Even of my own life as an isolated
> ruin,
> [. . . . .]
> But it begins to seem just part of some
> huge disaster.

Of the haunting to which these words refer we can best gain understanding, it seems to me, if we search our own spirits, and putting aside demands of theatrical convention, use the poet's fable and imaginative speech to objectify our own deeper experience at this moment of our individual and collective destiny. For us, too, horror grows of overshadowing disaster. Our world is diseased, constrained to self-destroying violence; and when we question: "Can devastation of our own homes be averted? Can we, if war comes,

refuse a part in it?" do we not feel that our questions falsely "isolate the single event," "making small things important"?

It is indeed one necessity of life to isolate, concentrating upon our small individual range; yet there is another need: to be aware of a reality more comprehensive. There is a vision of the real pressing on our spirits that only myth and imagery can convey. At a time like the present, in a world where [. . .] the air around us is dark with the wings of curses coming home to roost, surely the myth of the Eumenides—dread pursuers that avenge not private but communal crime—far from being academic, has dreadful relevance.

Of the pursuing forces in Eliot's play, the fugitive says:

> Were they simply outside,
> I might escape somewhere, perhaps.
> Were they simply inside
> I could cheat them perhaps with the
> aid of Dr. Warburton—
> [. . . . .]
> But this is too real for your words to
> alter.

So with us; when the horror of reported events becomes unendurable, we escape to private interests; when the pain of our own spirits overwhelms us, we practice devices of mental hygiene. But our trouble is both within us and without. For such modes of escape it is too real. Is any escape possible?

The play suggests an answer. For such a problem any solution a poet may suggest can be no more than a hint, partial and tentative, to which an individual spirit may respond.

Harry learns that his sin against the wife he hated was foreshadowed in his father's sin of intention against his mother; that his suffering has its counterpart in that of the woman, his aunt, who loved his father, and had known and loved himself as though he had been her son. [. . .]

387

The revelation of the nature of the haunting sin, with fellowship in suffering, is found to liberate. The specters seen again by their victim, released from the "awful privacy of the insane mind," are seen without fear or wonder. "This time, you are real, this time, you are outside me, / And just endurable [. . .]."

So of this horror laid on us; though we do not know, individually or collectively, the path we must tread, we perhaps know this at least: that what horrifies us is real. We cannot escape it; we must not, like the unseeing aunts and uncles of Eliot's chorus refuse to know what lies beyond our narrow circle, blindly insisting "that the world is what we have always taken it to be." We have to seek knowledge of the sin—in ourselves and in our world— that now is fulfilling itself in such monstrous shape. In conscious fellowship with others, enduring sin's consequences that cannot be averted, we also must sustain hope hereafter to achieve expiation of the curse, resolution of the enchantment under which we suffer.

Louis MacNeice. "Original Sin." *New Republic* 98 (3 May 1939), 384–85.

The Family Reunion seems to me a better play than *Murder in the Cathedral*, better integrated, less of a charade. This time the subordinate characters are real persons, fuller, more differentiated, more sympathetic; and the ideas behind the play are fused into the action and the characters; it is difficult (and this is as it should be) to divorce the theme or the moral from the play itself. It would be an easy play to ridicule—hag-ridden hero who appears in a vague mess and disappears toward a vague solution—but such ridicule would be misplaced. Aristotle thought that the soul of a play is action. If we interpret action in the narrow or external sense, then according to Aristotle this play is not dramatic. But Mr. Eliot has always been more interested in action, and the correlative suffering, on the spiritual plane. [. . .] We may regret that he seems to put all his money on the religious conscience as distinct from practical morality, but at the same time we must recognize that he asserts certain truths (even if these are truths of the Unknown God) which are now commonly neglected and whose neglect may in the long run sap the life from our utilitarian ethics [. . .].

Though the subject of his play is Original Sin, Mr. Eliot has embodied it in characters who on the surface plane also are involved in dramatically interesting relationships to each other (this set of characters in the same situation could in fact have been treated by Chekhov). There is a compromise here between naturalism and mysticism. The definite surface facts—the mother's birthday, the family house, the brothers' accidents, the hero's homecoming, the previous death of his wife, the death in the last scene of his mother— may be from Mr. Eliot's point of view merely incidental, but they act as girders to the play. Thus the hero, like Orestes, has apparently committed (or thinks he has committed) a murder; this murder is merely incidental to, or at most symptomatic of, a far more basic and less particularized sin which he has to expiate. The Eumenides who haunt him appear at first sight to be subjective phantoms but are discovered, to the hero's own relief, to be forces outside him. His expiation on the face of it seems to consist in leaving his home forever; this is in fact the outward and visible sign of a profound spiritual change. This change being still obscure, Mr. Eliot was of course right to stress the outward and visible signs. For this reason the play seems to me more suited to the stage than *Murder in the Cathedral*.

The trouble with *Murder in the Cathedral* was that the essential conflict was between Becket and himself as represented by the Tempters; the murderers merely arrived out of a machine. In *The Family Reunion*, the hero is again struggling with himself, but the conflict is made more palpable by the antipathies between various members of his own family—between the hero and his family in general or his mother in particular, between his mother and the aunt who had stolen her husband, between this aunt and the other aunts and uncles, between the dead father and the mother, between the inhibited young cousin Mary and the mother and aunts. These characters are not treated satirically; even the stupidest uncle is allowed a certain human feeling and an inkling of truth outside himself. The old mother, who in a sense has been a vampire to her son, yet compares favorably with the mother in Messrs. Auden and Isherwood's *The Ascent of F-6*, who is almost a Freudian dummy.

Technically the verse of this play is most successful, though some people have accused it of not being verse at all. Mr. Eliot has quite rightly avoided inserting any hunks of obvious prose; no prose-plus-verse play in recent times has as yet managed to be homogenous. He has therefore had to contrive a versification elastic enough to be incantatory at one moment and to represent the banalities of conversation at another. This is a very considerable achievement. He uses his favorite devices—hypnotic repetition, antithesis, paradox, the overrunning of sentences from line to line, the simple and sharp but yet mysterious use of imagery: "the sobbing in the chimney / The evil in the dark

closet?" And there are echoes from his previous poetry—"south in the winter," "You don't see them, but I see them" (the key line from the *Choephoroi* of Aeschylus). It is foolish to cavil at these echoes when they are so well integrated into the present piece. Thus a scene between Harry and his Aunt Agatha is a reminiscence of "Burnt Norton," but is a magnificent presentation of the world of unfulfilled choices: [quotation of lines from "I was not there, you were not there, only our phantasms" to "And I ran to meet you in the rose-garden," *The Family Reunion*].

Most of the characters speak at one time or another as if they were a chorus; this is one of the advantages of a poetic play. Further, Mr. Eliot here has not introduced any external chorus (a disrupting influence on the modern stage) but on occasions (with a certain irony?) he makes the four stupidest characters step out of their proper parts and speak a commentary in unison. I am not sure if this will succeed on the stage, but it is at least a hopeful experiment. It is probable, however, that this could have been dispensed with and that characters like Agatha could have been left to speak the commentary singly and still more or less in character.

Lastly, this is a very moving play both as a whole and in its passing pictures, its ironic comments, its pregnant understatements, its bursts into liturgy. Witness Mary's criticism of Harry: "you attach yourself to loathing / As others do to loving [. . .]." Or Harry's comment on himself as a person that his family has conspired to invent. Or one of his first remarks on re-meeting them after eight years: "You all look so withered and young." Or his mother's dying words: "The clock has stopped in the dark." Or the brilliant reminiscences of a neurotic childhood. [. . .] Mr. Eliot's own poetry may appear to be taking the opposite direction, but the reader of this play cannot, I think, object to it, as he could to *The Waste Land*, that it is essentially defeatist; it embodies a sincere belief and a genuine courage.

Cleanth Brooks.
"Sin and Expiation."
Partisan Review 6
(Summer 1939), 114–16.

The work of few poets shows the intense continuity which we have learned to expect in the work of T. S. Eliot. It was to be predicted that *The Family Reunion* would contain a recapitulation of the symbols which dominate Eliot's earlier poetry. They are here: the purposeless people moving in a ring ("in an overcrowded desert, jostled by ghosts") of *The Waste Land*; the "hellish, sweet smell" that accompanies the apprehension of the supernatural from *Murder in the Cathedral*; the purgatorial flame of "Ash-Wednesday." But most of all, perhaps, the play is illuminated by that rather dry and not sufficiently appreciated poem, "Burnt Norton"; and in one sense, at least, the play may be said to be a restatement of "Burnt Norton" in terms of drama.

The world of the play is the world of *The Waste Land*: a world inhabited by thoroughly respectable upper-class English ladies and gentlemen, "people to whom nothing has ever happened," and who consequently "cannot understand the unimportance of events," people whose "life" is "the keeping up of appearances. The making the best of a bad job."

But to Harry, the young head of the family, something has happened, something which breaks through the death-in-life in which he has lived, and his return to

the family home completes his birth into the real world. At the end of the play, like Arnaut, he is, with joy, committing himself to the purgatorial flame, but he despairs of making the family understand what has happened to him, and why he cannot take up his place as head of the family and master of Wishwood. As he says late in the play:

> when one has just recovered sanity,
> And not yet assured in possession,
> that is when
> One begins to seem the maddest to
> other people.

His is essentially the position of the protagonist at the end of *The Waste Land*— "Hieronymo's mad againe."

But Harry's difficulty is Eliot's difficulty. The audience for whom he writes are quite as secularized as are the characters of the play, and they are far more hard-boiled in their rationalism. They are not more likely to understand the treatment of the relation of time to eternity expressed in "Burnt Norton"; they are even less likely to be sympathetic with it. Eliot has set himself a very difficult task in the play. For many readers, Harry's action will be quite incredible, and the play will consequently be murky and dull—another instance of Eliot's retreat into Anglo-Catholic mysticism.

But precisely because Eliot has faced this basic problem frankly, the play is a triumph. The dramatic fact, kept steadily in focus, is Harry's awareness that, intense and meaningful as the experience is to him, it is quite impossible for his uncles and aunts to understand it. There is even a grim humor in the fact that the revelation has come through Harry's sin. (One remembers Eliot's comment in the essays, "and it is better in a paradoxical way to do evil than to do nothing; at least we exist.") Harry is conscious of the humor, just as he is willing to entertain the belief that he may be mad. The play does not turn into preaching. It remains focused on Harry's exploration of his experience.

It is symptomatic of the play's closeness of texture that one cannot separate out gobbets of poetry and have them retain the intensity which they undoubtedly possess in the context. The poetry is very closely integrated with the other elements of the play. The verse is one which allows Eliot to shift from the casual, fatuous, after-dinner conversation into the passionate language of Harry's colloquies with Agatha. There is a sense of dramatic acceleration, but not of strain; and this, in part, of course, is because the contrast is not superficial and external, but a part of the central dramatic fact. The contrasts occur, therefore, at the proper level, and thus allow Harry's experience to grow out of the family history, as they allow his crisis to grow legitimately out of the rather boring normality of a family reunion.

By the same token, the choruses are natural: the characters do not strike a pose as they begin their choruses. They are merely speaking aloud (by conversation) their unspoken thoughts in the awkward silences which occur as they wait for dinner. I have not seen the play performed, but my feeling is that it would gain from being acted, and this, again, is further testimony to the fact that Eliot has consciently subordinated every detail to the total effect of the play as a play.

A review so brief as this cannot hope to penetrate very far into the more interesting problems of organization which the play raises. Perhaps it is more important to try to say a further word about the reader's problem of belief. The play obviously has something to say to people who cannot accept Eliot's metaphysic. It would be folly to argue that his metaphysic is of no importance in this play in which it finds, perhaps, its most explicit statement. But it is also folly to prejudge the play as representing

an intolerable narrowness of interest by narrowing our own interests in advance. For the reader who is likely to be troubled by this problem, one may suggest some such approach to the play as the following. Eliot has not lost touch with the realities. The desiccation, the fatuousness, the deadening complacency of the British upper classes are revealed in this play quite as mercilessly as Auden reveals them. Harry's vision of a different world is certainly not Auden's vision, but he occupies a position in relation to society basically similar to that occupied by Auden's characters. (Auden's "converted" characters have their problems of communication too, and their problem of expiation.) There will be time enough, and room enough, outside the play, to argue the relative truth of the two visions. Suffice it to say here that Eliot, with a dramatic consistency and integrity which rarely lapses, has exploited the dramatic values inherent in the situation. And it is ultimately by a test which takes this dramatic integrity into account that his play will have to be appraised.

Philip Horton. "Speculations on Sin." *Kenyon Review* 1 (Summer 1939), 330–33.

It is perhaps scarcely legitimate to compare *Murder in the Cathedral*, which is more properly a pageant than a play, with Eliot's latest work, yet at one point such a comparison will serve to illustrate what I feel to be the radical weakness of *The Family Reunion*. Doubtless there are several reasons for the surprising stage success of the earlier piece, including its character as pageant, but not the least of them is the fact that the audience is at once put in possession of the knowledge why the action is necessary. Whatever else may escape them—the further reaches of theology and irony—they know that Thomas is to become a martyr, and understand at least enough of the circumstances and the character of the man to make the action seem plausible, if not, indeed, necessary.

It is precisely here—in point of adequate motivation—that *The Family Reunion* seems to me to fail. To be sure, we know the general subject of the play; it "is not a story of detection, / Of crime and punishment, but of sin and expiation." But this is not enough. In order that the action be convincing, the sin must be sufficiently defined to make clear not only the nature of the relations between characters, but also the terms of the central conflict. Without such elementary definition, it seems to me, there can be no adequate motivation. What Eliot offers in its stead—a complex of possible sins almost Jamesian in its ambiguities—hardly constitutes, however rich its materials, a workable substitute.

These are the essential facts of the play. Harry, the eldest son of Lady Monchensey, returns from abroad after an absence of eight years. During this time he has taken a wife whom he later murdered (or thought he murdered), and since then has been pursued, like Orestes, by the Eumenides. Presently he becomes aware of some "origin of wretchedness" behind his childhood, and upon questioning Agatha, one of his mother's sisters, learns that his father, long since dead, had really been in love with her, Agatha, had lived with his wife for a few years only under duress, and had wished and even planned to marry her. After this revelation Harry comes to a decision to leave home again in pursuit of expiation—a decision that is directly responsible for his mother's death at the end of the play.

Now, however it may be for theology, it is not enough, I think, for the purpose of dramatic motivation simply to name the sin; it is also necessary to ground it in circumstance, to supply its rationale. Admitting that it is immaterial whether Harry actually caused his wife's death, why did he desire it? Had she been unfaithful to him; or was their marriage, like that of his parents, corrupted by a less patent immorality; or have we to deal here with a Freudian situation where the desire for the death of the wife represents the desire for the death of the mother? (There is some support of the last suggestion in the highly effective scene where Harry plays grimly upon the phrase, Her Ladyship, which may refer equally to his dead wife and to his mother.) Nowhere in the play are these questions answered. With the family sin, however, things are a little more clear. Harry's father is also guilty of desiring his wife's death; but in his case the motive is supplied: he was in love with Agatha. In the eyes of a theologian like Eliot—if one wishes to press matters—this might well make him guilty of three sins: murder, adultery (since he lusted after another woman), and fornication (since there was no love between him and his wife). But though the rationale of the family sin is relatively clear, I still do not feel that it serves as adequate motivation, for the reason that Eliot does not indicate on Harry's part any decisive or commensurate reaction to it. Neither in speech nor in behavior does he betray any increment of guilt or horror at Agatha's revelations, nor is one made to feel that this knowledge radically changes or determines his course of action. It contributes to it, to be sure; but neither the family sin nor the "murder" of his wife is clearly defined in terms of the dramatic conflict (i.e., in terms of Harry's consciousness). The burden of motivation seems to fall somewhere between the two. The resulting ambiguity may be seen in Agatha's tentative statement of the central problem in the next to the last scene. Its very tentativeness may serve as a measure of my objections.

> It is possible that you have not known what sin
> You shall expiate, or whose, or why
> [. . . . .]
>   It is possible
> You are the consciousness of your unhappy family,
> Its bird sent flying through the purgatorial flame.

From this passage it would appear that the ambiguity was deliberate on Eliot's part. If this is true, one may perhaps find an explanation for it in the fact that the sin and the expiation are spoken of variously in terms of Christian dogma (defilement, pilgrimage, intercession, redemption), in terms of pagan thought and ritual (the season of sacrifice, the Eumenides, exorcism, consummation of the curse), and possibly in terms of psychoanalysis as well (the creeping back through the little door, the private worlds of make-believe and fear, the wife–mother, the search for the father.)

All this would seem to indicate that Eliot, instead of supplying the play with a *definition* of the specific sin in question, has used the play as a vehicle of *speculation* on the nature of sin. It is important to note that the one does not necessarily exclude the other. The speculation, if indulged through the consciousness of the hero, as in *Hamlet*, might well have become a legitimate and effective agent in the dramatic conflict. But Eliot has carried on his speculation *in his own person as playwright* by his manipulation of the materials and structure of the play: by the incantations assigned variously to Agatha, Mary, and Harry; by his treatment of the Eumenides (he has followed Aeschylus in transforming the spirits from the Erinyes, the "sleepless hunters," who pursue, into

the "bright angels," who guide, without, however, making clear the logic of the transformation); and by the deliberate ambiguity with which he has cloaked the nature both of the sin and of the expiation that is to follow. Now for the "higher levels of significance" in drama such mysteries and ambiguities are often highly desirable, but only provided that the action, far from depending upon them for its motivation, is supported, as in *Hamlet*, by a relatively simple rationale that will be immediately available to the audience. Furthermore, it seems to me that such ambiguities should not be left implicit in the structure of the play, but should be made explicit through the characters. In failing to do this, Eliot has, to my mind, handled his materials as if he were writing, not a poetic drama, but a dramatic or philosophical poem, like *The Waste Land*, with the unfortunate result that the ideas, the speculation, tend to take precedence over the characters both as the principal agents of the action and the center of interest.

The radical weakness of the play is all the more regrettable since in other respects—in the richness and complexity of its subjects, in its flexible adaptation of simple idiomatic speech to blank verse, in the skillful manipulation of dramatic materials in certain scenes—it represents a distinct achievement in the advance of contemporary poetic drama.

Frederick A. Pottle.
"A Modern Verse Play."
Yale Review 28
(June 1939), 836–39.

Mr. Eliot's experiment in domestic drama is an even more decisive technical triumph than *Murder in the Cathedral*, not because it contains actually better verse but because the problem to be solved was more difficult and he does well with it. The martyrdom of Thomas, the subject of his first play, seems naturally "poetic," but it is another thing to make credible an apparition of the Eumenides at Wishwood. We have known the specifications of this kind of play for a long time: it must give us a prevailing surface of dialogue so close to prose in its rhythms and sentiments as to create the illusion of common reality, but it must also manage to invest its matter with the urgency which we associate with verse. To be prosaic: to be literary—these are the poet's Scylla and Charybdis. It seems pretty certain that Mr. Eliot has come through more prosperously than any of his predecessors. His conversational lines have a surface which we recognize as the familiar level of prose, but when we venture on it, we feel it to be precarious; maintained, as it were, not by gravitation but by an unnatural tension. Beneath, and momentarily breaking through, is the real world, a world of poetry in which people see strange sights and say things never heard in any drawing room.

The device of the chorus is masterly. It was perhaps suggested by *Strange Interlude*, but in its effect is quite original. The four characters who compose it express, in their normal roles, no sentiment not strictly in prose character. The "choruses" consist not of what they would ever actually say, but of what they are thinking—or would be thinking if they had the poet's power of expression. I find no verse here so memorable as parts of *The Rock* and *Murder in the Cathedral*, but that was, no doubt, Mr. Eliot's intention. He had to be extremely careful in this piece not to pitch any passages so high as to make them seem verse interludes in a prose context.

A brilliant feat; but if my own feelings can be trusted, the least satisfactory of Mr. Eliot's long poems. I do not feel in it that strong current of excitement which has previously swept me on through dense and rare. One should have seen the piece presented before attempting to diagnose its faults, and I have not had that opportunity. But I venture the following criticisms.

The exposition should be clearer. This is emphatically not closet drama. It deals, as Mr. Eliot's chief character is at pains to point out, with states of mind, not with events; but without knowledge of certain crucial events, a good deal of the language is radically ambiguous. The explanation of the mystery comes very late: the play is more than two-thirds over before Agatha reveals the crucial bit of information that makes sense of what has gone before. Anyone reading and pondering the text will probably convince himself that the central character, Lord Monchensey (Harry), really did push his wife over the steamer-rail, though we are to think of the crime as not his but the sin of his father, mother, and aunt coming to completion through him. No person merely seeing the play presented will be sure that Harry did not imagine the whole thing. It makes a difference. And we do not know what Harry is going to do at the end of the play. His mother, not unnaturally, infers that he plans to be a missionary; he says that is not it. He has "not yet had the precise directions." It is very hard, if not impossible, to feel that any act is expiatory until we know what it is. In neither case does the ambiguity result from clumsiness; ambiguity is Mr. Eliot's deliberate intention. To object to this is not to raise the old cry against his "obscurity," it is merely to insist that a play to be acted is a different thing from a poem to be read. There seems no escape from the conclusion that the people who are to witness a play must be quite clear as to the gross actions which constitute the plot. If these are not part of history or notorious legend, they must be unequivocally set forth by the author. And "unequivocal" is not the word for Mr. Eliot.

In the second place, I do not think Mr. Eliot so successful as usual in his religious framework. Current criticism charges him with having dwindled into a Christian poet, and some will feel that he is showing his versatility by writing a play from which Christian dogma is entirely excluded and in which Christian phraseology is allowed to appear only in the last scene. It is more probable that he has yielded to a dramatic exigency: having chosen to write a play of modern life, he had to reconcile himself to the religious paucity of the skeptical mind. At Wishwood the stark Greek conception of the ripening curse may barely seem in character, but to add the rest—the massive pagan faith of Aeschylus or Sophocles—would be too much. This makes for dramatic difficulties.

"What we have written," says Agatha in lines that are clearly to be taken as an epigraph, "What we have written is not a story of detection, / Of crime and punishment, but of sin and expiation." Crime and detection have meaning without expressed religious values, but sin and expiation have none. It is too late to bring in the Christian reference at the very end by ritual (a parody of the service of *tenebrae*) and by such words as "intercession," "pilgrimage," and "redemption." The result is to make *The Family Reunion* more than superficially like the works of a dramatist whom I cannot think Mr. Eliot wished to resemble: Ibsen. There is the same plot of inexorable destiny, the same visiting of the sins of the fathers on the children, the same bad manners (I do not remember reading any play in which the chief characters were so consistently rude), the same flaying of bourgeois virtues, the same obsessions—almost, one would say, the same ghosts. The intent, no doubt, was to effect a resolution: to show the solemn forms of Christian faith emerging through disbelief,

petulance, and horror to invest the curse with meaning; but the end seems rather a surprise than a resolution.

Delmore Schwartz. "Orestes in England." *Nation* 148 (10 June 1939), 767–77.

In *The Family Reunion*, T. S. Eliot has attempted to use the Orestes story in modern terms and for his own special purpose. The subject of the play is the hero's gradual understanding of the sin and the guilt which have cursed his family and resulted in his own unspeakable awareness of evil. What happens, in the course of a family reunion, is that the hero learns or seems to learn the reason for the evil which afflicts him and what he must do about it. He must depart from his house, reject his position as head of the family, kill his mother (though indirectly), and pursue the specters who have been pursuing him just as the Erinyes hunted down Orestes. Where he is to go is unknown, but the direction is undoubtedly a Christian one without being named so.

[. . .]

The family guilt, which the hero must expiate, is the crime committed by his mother: she has abused and degraded his father, and driven him from the house. It is the crime, perhaps, of the domination, for the sake of domination, of one person by another. The emphasis is on the intention of the will: adultery and murder are hinted at but never confirmed. Orestes, by contrast, was guilty in a more adequate way from a dramatic standpoint: he had killed his mother, and he is hunted by specters with an exact religious meaning, whatever their truth. The crime in *The Family Reunion* is on the contrary left faint and indecisive, though it is meant to justify the whole crisis of the play, the fact that supernatural beings are actually present. The same indefiniteness dims the whole progress of the play.

Probably there is an immense difficulty in the subject, a peculiar and special difficulty of the present time. In trying to dramatize the presence of the supernatural in nature, in trying to display upon the stage a character's progressive awareness that he has to do with supernatural beings, not with the result of too much drinking, Eliot is faced with the problem of the disbelief inherent in any context of modern life. It is not in the least a question of what the modern audience will believe, for any audience will believe anything from Jules Verne to Walt Disney for the pure sake of seeing what happens to the protagonists. A modern audience will even believe in the supernatural if the protagonists are shown as acting and suffering in ways which are a plausible extension of the common denominator of human experience. But Eliot fails to find plausible extensions; he finds few extensions of any kind. The audience would be willing to assume the existence of what the hero sees, namely, the Furies standing in the window embrasure, if the hero's emotions during the play were with sufficient vividness related to and induced from what we all know of emotion, especially the emotion of nameless guilt. But the best Eliot can do to get the experience of the supernatural upon the stage is such a speech as the announcement by the hero's chauffeur that he too has seen the Furies, or the hero's continual explanation that he cannot explain what he feels and no one else can see what he sees. The first-night audience in London which laughed at the wrong time was justified, although wisdom would perhaps have predicted tears; for modern characters, in the scene as given, do not see the supernatural without undergoing more radical changes—of heart, of mind, of interest—than do Eliot's characters.

Probably it was this difficulty of grounding the supernatural in modern life which made Eliot attempt to get in the dialogue so much of the idiom of modern speech. All the dialogue is supposedly versified, but it is very hard to accept much of it as verse at all, shocking as this may seem to one who recalls Eliot's previous poetry. What can one make of such a passage as this, which is a fair sample of all but two or three parts:

> Nevertheless, Amy, there's something
>   in Violet's suggestion.
> Why not ring up Warburton, and ask
>   him to join us?
> He's an old friend of the family, it's
>   perfectly natural
> That he should be asked. He looked
>   after all the boys
> When they were children. I'll have a
>   word with him.

The speech gains nothing by the division into lines and possesses little rhythm which is not that of prose. The emphasis of emotion, the heightening of an attitude or tone, the exact suggestiveness, the double irony which can be attained by the use of a regular rhythm of verse are wholly absent. Modern speech has defeated the poet, just as modern belief or disbelief has defeated the dramatist.

One might suppose, since the locus of guilt is an upper-class English country house, that this play signifies a new period in Eliot's mind, a rejection of the royalism and conservatism which in [1928] were affirmed as the only secular complement of Anglo-Catholicism. And this rejection might seem related to the poet's sense of what the English ruling class has recently done, so that the inadequacy of the play would flow fundamentally from the poet's new and as yet inadequately considered revulsion and perplexity. Actually, however, the poet of "Ash-Wednesday" also seemed to see "the worship in the desert" in the Church of England, and there has always been an obsessed horror of natural life and modern society in Eliot's poetry. We can say for certain, then, only that the failure of this play, in contrast with the success of "Ash-Wednesday," issues from the fact that it is simpler to accomplish a Christian work of art in which the subject is personal emotion than one in which the subject has become family relationships and supernatural beings in a time and place in which neither Christianity nor any other belief or value can be assumed as genuine and unquestioned by the writer who wishes to show the relevance of his vision of life to other human lives.

Katherine Brégy.
"T. S. Eliot: A Study in Transition."
America 61 (15 July 1939), 331–32.

With the possible exception of Aldous Huxley and Eugene O'Neill—many of whose diverse problems he shares "with a difference"—our contemporary literature in English shows no more exciting study of transition than Thomas Stearns Eliot.

The *Prufrock* verses of 1917 were, like a great deal of work at that time, erudite and sexy; the *Poems* of 1920, more erudite and more sexy. Also they were strikingly imagistic—I recall one dismal picture of the "damp souls of housemaids" at area gates in the early London morning—and heavy with post-War introspection and disenchantment. Their undeniable originality was not lessened because one detected the influence of Ezra Pound or James Branch Cabell—just as one detected the influence of James Joyce when Mr. Eliot's *The Waste Land* captured the *Dial*'s $1,000 prize in 1922. Personally, I found, and still find, that melange of painfully realistic free verse, doggerel, sophisticated *vers de societé* and perverse mysticism largely unintelligible—while the intelligible parts I did not, and still do not, like. Yet there were moments where one felt the living, suffering soul of a true poet hiding beneath all this waste. And one felt it again in the bitter battle cry—"*This is the way the world ends / Not with a bang but a whimper*"—which was the keynote of "The Hollow Men," and borrowed by Huxley for his *Brave New World*.

When "Ash-Wednesday" was published in 1930 the reaction had manifestly set in—the dead bones of the desert were, in the poet's own arresting phrase, "chirping to God." There was an increasing interest in Catholic imagery and liturgy: visions of Our Lady in "blue of larkspur" to sweeten the bitter waters, very human pictures of the Magi to link ancient and modern seekers after the light. And there was not only that "sense of entanglement" which Lionel Johnson years ago found in practically all modern literature, but also that tortured and torturing self-analysis—the Hamlet *motif*—which the poet himself recognizes when he cries—"I pray that I may forget / These matters that with myself I too much discuss / Too much explain."

Through these years, and since, Mr. Eliot was providing a series of thoughtful, critical essays arraigning modern literature and the modern world for its alienation from supernatural faith. Indeed, he has all along written such extraordinarily good sermons that one suspects the "clerical cut" to which he somewhere wittily refers may not apply to his "features" alone. From the rather vague Protestantism of his upbringing, the poet turned to "High" or ritualistic Anglicanism, composing in 1934 the text for a pageant of the Anglican Church produced at Sadler's Wells. One fancies this somewhat exotic production must have been a puzzle to any popular audience: but *The Rock*, as it was called, remains one of Mr. Eliot's most significant works and contains some of his finest poetry. With its choruses of Workmen and Unemployed, its sermons by a Narrator or Preacher and cryptic words from the Rock—representing, of course, the Church of Christ—the cumulative message is, like that of the later Saint Thomas, that we must *make perfect our will*.

[. . .]

Obviously—and counting out the symbolic pun—*Murder in the Cathedral* was built upon *The Rock*. The two things Mr. Eliot's art needed most were concentration and personality. Finding these in the dramatic form and the character of Becket, he created what is so far his greatest work. Thomas of Canterbury, the brilliant and luxurious young clerk, ordained priest and consecrated bishop within a single week that he might be eligible for the post of English chancellor—who from the King's companion became the Church's champion and martyr and was canonized three years after his murder—has always been one of the most dramatic of the Saints.

[. . .]

The event rather surprisingly proved *Murder in the Cathedral* a successful acting play as well as a work of art. But

Mr. Eliot may have feared that what Yeats called the "high window of dramatic verse" set him too far away from his audience. In any case his most recent drama, *The Family Reunion*, has a contemporary setting and its free blank verse is often the rhythmic prose so frequently used by Maxwell Anderson. Here again we have a study in temptation—not present but past: a study of the evil which has gathered a modern English family under its curse as the New England Mannons were gathered in *Mourning Becomes Electra*.

[. . .]

Mr. Eliot's preoccupation, not to say obsession, with *sin* was evident in *The Rock*, where a long dramatic meditation ends with the wise conclusion that "the mystery of Iniquity is a pit too deep for mortal eyes." Looking back now one sees how it penetrated the desolation of *The Waste Land* and was the *raison d'être* of *Murder in the Cathedral*. The poetic unity of the former tragedy is not, it seems to me, quite duplicated in *The Family Reunion*, although the latter's blending of colloquial everyday life with superhuman terror and pity is quite astonishing. Would *confession* be too crude and simple a solution, one wonders, to offer all these tortured people conscious or unconscious of their mysterious curse? For surely the brief Sacrament of Penance is infinitely dramatic in its implications. [. . .]

[Eliot] is his own pilgrim, and the end of his journey is not yet reached. He is, in fact, a great many seemingly contradictory things: an aristocrat of letters speaking to a democratic and proletarian age, an aesthete who is persistently both preacher and theologian. And in the main his theology is, as far as it goes, quite orthodoxly Catholic. "The Church exists for the glory of God and the sanctification of souls," declares one of his essays; "Christian morality is part of the means by which these are to be attained"; and he adds that the "perpetual mission of the Church is to affirm, to teach, to apply true theology" to all human problems. But how much longer can so close a thinker as Mr. Eliot be satisfied to make "the Church" include "the whole number of Christians as Christians"? Judging this theology from its reflection in his poetry, one suspects a taint of Jansenism—a certain rigidity producing scrupulosity. He is at the other extreme from the robust and joyous Chesterton. But in a world of transition, extremes often meet!

---

*Desmond Hawkins. "Hamlet and T. S. Eliot." *New English Weekly* 15 (20 July 1939), 221–22.

T. S. Eliot's new play has been so widely reviewed and discussed that I feel myself excused both from providing a descriptive *précis* and for delaying this review until I had had the opportunity to read the book several times at decent intervals. For a somewhat similar reason I propose to deal only cursorily with the play's evident merits. It is—need I say?—the most important play of the year. [. . .] The verse is always dramatic, flexible, extremely moving in certain parts, and sustained at the pitch of authentic tragedy. The play moreover is packed with sudden illuminations and keen-edged paradoxes which root into the mind and will recur in one's thoughts enduringly. Whether the play succeeds or fails in its total pattern, the author is fertile enough as a personality [. . .] to have impregnated it with incidental riches of perception and statement. If we judge *The Family Reunion* within the perspective of

current drama, we must conclude that Mr. Eliot is an extremely civilized man in an extremely cretinous neighborhood.

[. . .]

In reading the play one is struck by its affinities with "Burnt Norton." The major image of the rose garden is reintroduced, and the "still point" which is the fulcrum of past and future is one of the key motifs in Harry's thoughts. [. . .]

But these passages are set within the framework of a play, and it is rather upon the action of the play that I want to concentrate. Dramatic form provides new obstacles as well as new opportunities: in particular, it requires an objectification of emotional sources. Its dumb-show of murders, treachery and the whole bag-full of deeds is useful because it keys us up to the emotional pitch of the participants. We are deeply and unreservedly moved by high feeling when we command a comprehensive view of its occasion, when we perceive the relevance of the response to the situation. Mr. Eliot has dealt with this subject of finding the "objective correlative," in his essay, "Hamlet," where he writes "Hamlet (the man) is dominated by an emotion which is inexpressible, because it is in *excess* of the facts as they appear."

I have not the space to illustrate a parallel between Harry and Hamlet, but I think it is not difficult to see. The central action of the play indeed is a search for "facts" which tally with the emotion dominating Harry. Faced with the technical difficulties of so subjective a drama, Mr. Eliot creates two brilliant devices—the Furies and the curse motif. As an audience we cannot instantly be "at home with" so exotic an apparition as the Furies, and they tended to be nebulous in the production; but they must be counted an inspired gamble in a desperate situation, a solution *faute de mieux* to which we shall gradually habituate ourselves. The curse, closer to our tradition and in the mainstream of Mr. Eliot's talent for supernatural incantation, is completely effective: the speeches with which Agatha, skillfully absorbing the role of chorus, closes each act are electrifying in their oppressive power. The forces bearing upon Harry are thus excellently dramatized. That which in a secular drama [. . .] would be the most difficult element to objectify presents little resistance to Mr. Eliot's theological tools, and on this score the play is an invaluable exploration of new ground. What remains to be examined is Harry's connection with these forces. How does he enter the orbit of these spells and furies?

I think the play stands or falls on Harry's character. The whole action is a tremendous postmortem in which he is both corpse and witness. What we are shown is the epilogue to one life of Harry and the prologue to another: in a sense, the whole of *The Family Reunion* is simultaneously the third act of one play and the first act of another, and it can hold its unity only by a strong conviction at both ends. We have no direct vision of the situation that is being resolved, nor of the durability of the resolution. Becket, in *Murder in the Cathedral*, has concrete alternatives to choose from, and he seals his choice with his blood. Harry, on the other hand, is both obscure and ambiguous. In him "the motive and the cue for passion" are difficult to decipher, and it is even possible to dispute whether or not he did push his wife overboard. [. . .] He [. . .] is on the further side of conventional sanity, but nevertheless he is the only witness and as such he must presumably be believed. If we cut Harry from ourselves with the word "delusions" we shatter the play. He must be accepted, and I believe he is meant so to be accepted, as the heroic protagonist.

Nevertheless one asks for certain assurances from such a character. The suspicion to be allayed is that Harry is a spiritual snob, a man who enjoys his suffering, a willful self-persecutor nourishing his tragedy in a kind of perverse pride for the sake of the attention it gains. I have called him ambiguous because it is possible to document this suspicion: Harry continually insists that he is much too complex and extraordinary to be understood (to the point of making a virtue of it); he feels nothing but contempt for his family when contrasting them with himself; and he makes a significant error when Dr. Warburton opens a conversation with him. Harry at once concludes that the conversation is to be about himself, whereas Warburton later reveals that he wished to discuss the health of Harry's mother; though this is still further ambiguous because Warburton may be lying (he has been called in, a handy Rosencrantz-cum-Guildenstern, to watch Harry).

[. . .]

And yet the suspicion remains—not more than a suspicion but not less either—that in spite of the bright angels one might find Harry a year or two later somewhere in the South of France, a virtuoso in suffering, an armchair saint still rending himself for lack of a better occupation, while the faithful chauffeur packs up and starts the car again. That it is possible to harbor this suspicion is due primarily, I think, to the same fault that Mr. Eliot finds in *Hamlet*. At one point Harry exclaims "It is not my conscience, / Not my mind, that is diseased, but the world I have to live in." [. . .]

Here surely is emotion in excess of the facts, although no brief quotation can convey the all-pervading and universally diffused disgust which goes down to the roots in Harry and overwhelms everything else in the play. The horror that obsesses him is as total, as panoramic and as undirected as Hamlet's. It is a horror before the whole spectacle of the human comedy. At the end of the play Harry has still the world to face; and it is the world of generalized life (not specific persons) which repels him. Like Hamlet he is appalled by the visible world as it enters him in the act of self-knowledge; but without the compassion and the exquisite sensibility of Hamlet. It is perhaps not fanciful to speak of the puritan's tincture of fascinated cruelty in Harry.

It may be objected that Harry's attachment to loathing (as Mary describes it) is a symptom of the condition which Agatha helps eventually to exorcize. It may be so. But the insoluble difficulty is that Harry can find no objective act of dedication—as Becket could—to proclaim and confirm his new allegiance to "the bright angels." He is reduced to calling for his chauffeur and going out into the night. The ambiguity remains. The intensity of his repugnance, the hints of an unapproachable private obscenity, brood after his exit: a terrible irony that recalls the end of *Heart of Darkness*. We have witnessed an attempt "to express the inexpressibly horrible" (I quote again from Mr. Eliot on *Hamlet*). Its nature is foreshadowed in the epigraphs to *Sweeney Agonistes*, which provide the terms of Harry's agony; and if the action breaks it is because the burden of unattached emotion in Harry is too great to be borne by the character and cannot be relieved by anything in the action. To that extent Harry, like Hamlet, is constantly passing over the frontier of sanity, an ambiguous and cryptic figure, a Mona Lisa of literature.

Mr. Eliot, in short, has written his own *Hamlet*, and it will probably fascinate and defeat generations of actors. To my mind it is a bigger work—although less perfect—than *Murder in the Cathedral*. In the character of Harry Mr. Eliot has created, not a viable *dramatis persona*, but a myth-figure, a protagonist of the age, a haunting and ubiquitous voice which will trouble and excite us as the Fausts and Tamburlaines and Hamlets disturbed the Elizabethans.

John Crowe Ransom. "T. S. Eliot as Dramatist." *Poetry: A Magazine of Verse* 54 (August 1939), 264–71.

A new creative work by T. S. Eliot is not going to be simple, even if he has reverted to a simpler literary form, and simple judgments by the critics will misrepresent it. His latest work is the play, *The Family Reunion*. He may be said by this time to have entered upon a new literary career, as playwright. But it would be idle to expect that the new plays will be out of relation with the old poems and critical prose. He keeps a foot in each of two worlds: the new world of naturalistic or realistic psychological drama, and the old world of poetry which, for him, means metaphysics. He will soon make ordinary drama look cheap because of its lack of metaphysical interest, just as he had part in making the ordinary shallow poetry of twenty years ago look the same way, and for the same reason.

As a dramatist working in the contemporary, Mr. Eliot resembles Ibsen much more than Shaw, to call names of comparable stature with his. His satiric touch is devastating, and he turns it onto living English types to show up their social and political silliness, among other things. That sounds like Shaw, and in fact as a satirist he compares unfavorably with Shaw only in that he does not sustain the satire uproariously; but Shaw does that because he has nothing else to do; for Shaw is a social gospeler, except that we must allow something also for his miscellaneous and professional wit. Ibsen could confine himself to social satire, but characteristically he was deeper than that; he quickly got to the point where he could make scornful play with his fighting terms, "Ideal" and "Liberal"; he was really a poet, and had the metaphysical dimension in his thinking.

Shaw inherited a part of Ibsen. It might be quite mistaken to say that Eliot has inherited any of him, since he has come to drama by his own private ways. But there is common property between the two, if we compare *The Family Reunion* with many Ibsen plays, such as *The Wild Duck* and *Rosmersholm*. Each is a poet working in an age which is metaphysically innocent and childlike. Or should I say, working in a medium which rejects the metaphysics? But for a few schools, such as the Greek tragedy and the Japanese Noh drama, the statement would not be, I think, wide. So each tries to import the metaphysical into the dramatic structure, which without it already is formally complete, and to the satisfaction of its customary auditors. [. . .]

On the realistic level Mr. Eliot is superb in his mastery of characterization (both the satiric and the sympathetic), handling of plot-sequence, exposition of background through dialogue, and, I imagine, such other techniques as belong to an oral form like drama. It is comforting to find that an intellectualist, so strict and unconceding that he has been accused of living in a tower, has picked up without any fuss the knack for the close structural effects of drama; it argues that his famous and original capacity as poet was inclusive rather than exclusive, and that our popular stage-drama, with whatever rigor it may claim, is not a very wonderful exercise of genius, and not a thing to which first-rate minds need feel under obligations to become addicted. Success on that level is a hollow triumph for Eliot.

But the success is unquestionable. Such is the cogency of the play as a mere drama that deals with the individual characters and collective fortunes of a family.

[. . .]

I do not know how genuinely Mr. Eliot is under conviction about ancestral curses and their expiation. He may feel that the necessity of the doctrine, given such situations as these, is very deep in the nature of things. It is certain that dramatically the terror of the mysterious curse is very much more emphasized than the beauty of the idea of expiation, which comes in almost as an afterthought. But I think there is a rule of dramatic propriety by which these Eumenides are not sustained as vehicles of the curse. They belong not only to an age of faith, but to an age when faith was different from what it is likely to be again. In other words, the audience, I think, will see them and will not believe in them. The hard-boiled audience, I mean; and as for the sensitive and literary people, who will infallibly constitute much of the audience for this kind of play, even they will think these creatures too "literary" to express the metaphysical realities, and too readily picked up from another context. They belong in a more imaginative order of literature than realistic drama if they are to be vitalized.

I like the air of mystery that thickens steadily throughout the play. We see the "natural" action gathering occult significance. I think there will not be an intelligent auditor who can resist being powerfully impressed; not by the Furies, but by the talk and actions of the characters. As in all metaphysics speculations, a reality deeper than the visible world is indicated.

[. . .] There is nothing particularly Christian in this play. A Christian entity to do the work of the Eumenides probably was not forthcoming; or if it was, it seemed unavailable for this drama, for drama now. Ibsen many times experimented with mysterious symbols in trying to express the occult effects by which he proposed to explode the naturalism of drama. They were not apparitions but words; words which had power with the actors in the main action, therefore with the other actors, and with the audience. It is my impression that when there are no orthodox supernatural beings in the vogue of drama at the time, fresh symbols—which it is as wrong to push to a high visibility as it is not to have them at all—are the best recourse that dramatists have. Unless, at least, they want to leave drama for forms in which imagination need not be so constrained.

The poetic diction probably does well enough—for a play. [. . .] There is just occasional poetic language independent of drama, or in set and undramatic speeches. But it is an atmospheric play. Mary, the cousin who would have married Harry, and who is made sensitive by the slight, says:

> The cold spring now is the time
> For the ache in the moving root
> The agony in the dark
> The slow flow throbbing the trunk
> The pain of the breaking bud.
> [. . . . .]

[. . .]

I like that on the whole, and in a play especially, because it is better than I had bargained for. But it is not the Eliot we knew as a poet. It is that Eliot warmed over, for "theatre."

---

*Horace Gregory. "The Unities and Eliot." *Life and Letters* 23 (October 1939), 53–60.

Whatever else Mr. T. S. Eliot has done or has not done, he has frequently given his critics an excuse to exercise their feelings or opinions, their wit or will, either good or bad, or their ingenuity. In America, book reviewers have been unusually hospitable to his new play [. . .]. I strongly suspect, however, that *The Family Reunion* will finally turn out to be one of the more conspicuous of Mr. Eliot's successful failures. Nor do I believe that its arrival has been spontaneously conceived, for it may be said that Mr. Eliot has had designs on the theatre since 1919 and that his serious intentions toward the general direction of the modern stage have been foreshadowed in his two essays, "Rhetoric and Poetic Drama" and "A Dialogue on Dramatic Poetry." *The Family Reunion* is his first full-length play [excluding *Murder in the Cathedral*], and is, therefore, the first sustained proof of his willingness to test his theories concerning poetic drama before an audience. If mere failure were all that it accomplished, or if Mr. Eliot were another kind of poet than he is, his adverse critics could drop back into the brief security of the moment in 1922 that followed the spectacular publication of *The Waste Land*. It now seems clear that *The Waste Land* was neither a hoax nor the greatest poem of its time, but was the first success that Mr. Eliot had achieved through failure. Both "Prufrock" and "Ash-Wednesday" are better poems, yet *The Waste Land* represents the turning point in Mr. Eliot's career and its very title has become identified with the literary decade preceding 1930.

I can think of no poet of Mr. Eliot's generation who has gained or learned so much from failure as he, or who has become more formidable after his critics have announced him dead and buried. It is for this reason, among others, that I believe *The Family Reunion* should be regarded with particular wariness and, whatever should be said against it, demands some recognition of the serious intentions which lie behind it. For the moment we have no proof that Mr. Eliot will continue to write plays, but if he does, *The Family Reunion* contains promise of being the most important event in the English-speaking theatre since a certain evening in 1893 when non-paying guests were invited to see a performance of Mr. Bernard Shaw's *Mrs. Warren's Profession*. [. . .]

I can well imagine that Mr. Eliot's desire to restore the Greek unities of time and place seem genuinely foreign on the British stage. But here again we must look for an American precedent in viewing Mr. Eliot's intentions. If, as D. H. Lawrence once remarked, early American novelists were haunted by the ghost of the American Indian, it should also be remarked that American poets have been haunted by the perfection, the remoteness, the undying vitality of Greek poetry. One might say that it is almost natural to discover in Whitman an embryonic attempt to reproduce the sound of the Greek hexameter beneath the Biblical rhythms of his unrhymed verse. [. . .] To the American public that reads contemporary verse and goes to see a modern play, the revival of a Greek theme in Mr. Eliot's new play is no more extraordinary than Mr. Robinson Jeffers's adaptation of the Orestes myth in *The Tower Beyond Tragedy*, or H. D.'s translation of the *Ion* of Euripides, or the Homeric undertones of Mr. Ezra Pound's first "Canto" or Mr. Eugene O'Neill's *Mourning Becomes Electra*. The theme of Mr. Eliot's new play takes its place within that tradition, if it may be called so; meanwhile its setting recalls the atmosphere of the bourgeois melodrama as it was once conceived by Sir Arthur Wing Pinero. There is neither a Mrs. Tanqueray nor a notorious Mrs. Ebbsmith [. . .] to enliven its performance and make its setting plausible to a London audience. What we have instead is a mixture of at least two insoluble elements over which a dark blood-stained atmosphere floats, reproducing something that has the obvious intention of arousing discomfort and fear [. . .]. What actually emerges are two things in conflict: the contemporary environment of a country house in the North of England and a vision of the Eumenides.

In theory Mr. Eliot's play appears well disciplined. [. . .] The first act is kept alive by the anticipation of Harry's entrance and the surprise of his early arrival: but in the unfolding of the Orestes story—Harry's conviction of his responsibility of his wife's death, his inheritance of that same sense of guilt from his father, his vision of the Eumenides—the play drags and becomes increasingly unreal and "experimental," quite as though one were witnessing an amateur performance given in a "little theatre." One waits for the fine choruses, one of which is written for the last act, and then and only then does one feel at ease. Part of the discomfort is, of course, the deliberate intention of the author. His characters are stripped of their security with the same critical perception that is conveyed when one reads in *The Waste Land*: "One of the low on whom assurance sits / As a silk hat on a Bradford millionaire."

The same harsh light of irony plays over the people who move behind the footlights of *The Family Reunion*. And realizing this, it would be an easy matter to interpret the play in terms of social irony. Its commentary on the British upper middle class is obvious enough: the characters that Mr. Eliot has called together for a family reunion are terrible and terrifying people and my regret is that they do not terrify us with the absolute conviction we desire. The Eumenides who uncover Harry's guilt and disclose the theme of the play to the spectator's eyes are untranslated elements in the environment where they appear. They are as significant and as false as Mr. Eugene O'Neill's use of masks in *The Great God Brown* and should not be tolerated for a single moment.

If the Eumenides in *The Family Reunion* seem imposed by the will of the author from outside the play, then why do we accept the witches in *Macbeth*, the dead king's ghost in *Hamlet*, or the hovering, invisible presence of the White Horses in *Rosmersholm*? These, too, are the supernatural signs of an internal conflict within the human heart and mind and are the springs of dramatic action within the play. I need not, I hope, go into the detail of why or how they are made to seem inevitable within their separate plays; commentators on Shakespeare and on Ibsen have already done so to the satisfaction of their colleagues as well as to the understanding of the public. The witches, the White Horses, and the king's ghost convey their power through the very conventions of the play that they inhabit; they are in the language of the play's worldly environment, they are of that world and of none other. In *The Family Reunion* we are forced to take specific creatures of a distant time and culture on larger faith than anything within the play implies; nor is there anything in the cast of Harry's imagination, as we hear him speak, that points inevitably to a selec-

tion of the winged sisters, leaping to being from the blood of mutilated Uranus to follow him until he turns upon them at the country seat of his name and household. This is not to argue against his sense of guilt, nor against the fact that his state of mind may be one which is commonly called "possessed by furies." That reality is granted at the moment of his first confession. The unreality is attached to the specific symbol of his guilt; unlike the White Horses of *Rosmersholm*, who signified within the neighborhood of Rosmer's guilt-ridden threshold the grief and madness that possessed his mind, Harry's Eumenides are neither of earth nor air, and though he is careful not to name them, his author has, so that the reader is forced to struggle with them against unbelief.

Whatever flaws Mr. Eugene O'Neill's *Mourning Becomes Electra* contains, and those of inflated language and loose writing are among them, the play solves the very problem in translation that Mr. Eliot leaves undone, and until he does so, his intention to revive poetic drama in full stature on the modern stage will remain a brilliant amateur's performance in the theatre. In contrast to Mr. Eliot's version of the Orestes myth, *Mourning Becomes Electra* is omnibus drama, each situation overdramatized at such length that its great energy loses meaning in protracted violence. But the translation of the Orestes cycle is fully realized in the terms of the New England setting recreated by Mr. O'Neill—and for this reason, I believe, Mr. O'Neill's critics and audiences felt or saw something of a true vision of guilt and horror that Mr. Eliot's audiences do not.

The unities of time and place for which Mr. Eliot pleads so eloquently in his dialogue on dramatic poetry and which appear as though a promise had been fulfilled in *The Family Reunion*, display their usefulness in the writing of poetic drama, and it is good to rediscover their merits on the modern stage. They cannot save a bad play, but they do tend to conserve the energy required in hearing verse spoken on the stage, and above all they concentrate the attention of the audience upon individual lines of poetry. There are other unities, of course, and not the least of them (which Shakespeare's quick intelligence discovered) are unities of human motive, speech, and imagination that exist within the play itself and are not to be destroyed. The dramatic reality of Mr. Eliot's *Murder in the Cathedral* suddenly evaporated when its Four Knights stepped to the footlights and spoke their reasons for killing Becket as though they had walked out of a script conceived and written by Mr. Bernard Shaw. Something of the same violation of the play's integrity—and I am speaking of the play's integrity and not its author's—occurs when Harry sets out to pursue the Eumenides in his car.

"Go face the Furies, turn tables on them and track them down," says Mr. Eliot. This is surely excellent advice to many members of Mr. Eliot's generation who fear to face any reality within themselves. The advice contains the same perception into the world that Mr. Eliot now inhabits as the mere title of *The Waste Land* once conveyed to its immediate contemporaries. The same restless sensibility is alive within it, the same disquiet note of warning is heard above the ruins of a notably imperfect play. It is the quality of Mr. Eliot's failures in verse and on the stage that endows them with unusual distinction. [. . .]

The last impression to be carried away from *The Family Reunion* and its revival of the Orestes story is that Mr. Eliot never seems more American than when he is most European. The divided, sleepless sensibility that creates a play and then destroys it, that is most un-British in its seeking-out of an absolute, a classical serenity, still evokes emotions of significant discomfort on both sides of the Atlantic.

George Anthony. "Myth and Psychosis." *Sewanee Review* 47 (October–December 1939), 599–604.

For many years T. S. Eliot has been concerned with the possibility of a modern poetic drama. *The Family Reunion* is evidence that such a possibility exists. The play is far and away the best dramatic work Eliot has given us. It is definitely theatrical; it treats a contemporary situation and a modern theme. And the verse is a flexible verse for the speaking voice.

As in most of his later work, Eliot has drawn upon classic literature and myth for reinforcement. Here the obvious reference is to the *Oresteia* of Aeschylus. The mistake must not be made of approaching *The Family Reunion* as an *Oresteia* reworked into modern terms. The direction is just the opposite. The Orestes myth is not a source, but a reinforcement for the modern play; and this reinforcement is provided as much by contrast as by similarity.

On the use of myth in modern literature Eliot wrote, in a review of *Ulysses* published in the *Dial* in 1923:

> In using myth, in manipulating a continuous parallel between contemporaneity and antiquity, Mr. Joyce is pursuing a method which others must pursue after him . . . It is simply a way of controlling, of ordering, of giving a shape and a significance to the immense panorama of futility and

anarchy which is contemporary history . . . Psychology [. . .], ethnology, and *The Golden Bough* have concurred to make possible what was impossible even a few years ago. Instead of narrative method, we may now use the mythical method. It is, I seriously believe, a step toward making the modern world possible for art . . .

[. . .] [I]t is, in connection with *The Family Reunion*, most interesting as a statement of intention by Eliot. The myth is a control for, and a key to our modern world. But illumination by our recently acquired knowledge of psychology and ethnology is necessary to permit its effective use.

Although I do not believe that the same kind of equivalences discovered by the exegetists in the *Ulysses* of Joyce and that of Homer are to be sought in the work of Eliot and his mythical parallel, I do believe that a critical approach to Eliot neglects the myth on peril of missing the point.

One recalls that, in the *Choephoroi*, the exiled Orestes returns, and, to avenge his father's death, murders his adulterous mother and her paramour. The third part of the *Oresteia* is concerned with the flight of Orestes from the Furies, his release from their punishment, and their elevation to the rank of Eumenides, "benign goddess."

Mr. Eliot's play is nothing like that. In the first place, it is impossible to so neatly summarize the plot. If a plot is considered to be a sequence of events which control the action of the play, there is none. What happens in this play happens without such foundation. In the first scene, Eliot warns us: "All that I could hope to make you understand / Is only events: not what has happened. [. . .]"

What does occur is roughly as follows: A family reunion is taking place to celebrate the birthday of Amy, Dowager Lady Monchensey. Harry, the eldest son, has been absent eight years. Before his return we are informed by conversations among the relatives, that in his absence he had married a woman of whom they all greatly disapproved, and who had been swept overboard in a storm at sea. The family feels that the meeting with Harry may prove difficult.

The meeting is more difficult than they had imagined. Almost immediately upon his entrance he announces that he "pushed his wife overboard." [. . .]

In the next scene, the Eumenides appear for a brief moment in the window embrasure. We are kept in suspense for some time as to whether these creatures exist only in Harry's mind or are visible to other members of the family present. The resolution of the drama cannot be reached until Harry discovers that both Mary and Agatha have seen them; that they are real and outside himself.

Here, it seems to me, lies a very practical value of the myth. Obviously the supporting myth is necessary if the Eumenides are to exist outside the imagination, and are not to become ridiculous. But to have had them imagined by Harry would have destroyed the whole point of the play. For then their vengeance would have to be directed toward a personal sin, and that is not what Eliot means.

Ancillary to, but encompassing, the struggle in Harry's mind (which includes his mother, his dead wife, his dead father) is the drama between his mother and her sister Agatha. Actually it is around Agatha that the play turns. It is Agatha who persuades Harry to leave his mother; it was Agatha who "stole" his mother's husband many years before. This history carries the sin back one generation. (Harry murdered his wife; Harry's father wished to murder his), and charges the drama with a sense of a family curse parallel to the curse on the House of Atreus.

This "is not a story of detection, / Of crime and punishment, but of sin and expiation." And so sharp a distinction does Eliot make between sin and the events of crime that he will not permit us to be certain that any crime has been committed. At the end of the play we are not sure whether Harry killed his wife or wished to kill her. The actual crime is unimportant.

This conception is Christian, not Greek. But it has been remarked before that from Greek Curse to Christian Original Sin, transition is not too difficult.

Although this is a drama of sin and expiation, the resolution of the conflict in Harry's mind is not effected by orthodox redemption but by a process very similar to the "cure by solution" of psychoanalysis. Eliot nowhere makes the error of permitting a direct reference to psychiatry, but throughout the play there is an awareness of the validity of an interpretation impossible without the results of recent studies is psychology. The problem of split personality is introduced through a purely literary image, and with a reference to Henry James's "The Jolly Corner," where a similar subject is treated. Gradually this problem acquires psychological significance—the fairy tale becomes credible. The murder of the wife, where the myth has the murder of the mother; the confusion between wife and mother in the Sergeant Winchell episode, acquire meaning only by reference to the Freudian theories of substitution. And in the conversation between Harry and Agatha "the little door" is an obvious symbol. This symbol introduces a further element of sin, here equivalent to incest because of the peculiar relationship Agatha feels between herself and Harry.

At the close the curse is described as "a power not subject to reason" and operating not in the "world where we know what we are doing,"

But in the night time
And in the nether world
Where the meshes we have woven
Bind us to each other.

It is Agatha speaking. Agatha who is at once the analyst and the Athene of the modern play. And it is with Agatha that the play ends. The mother has died. Agatha and Mary perform a ritual—walking around the birthday cake, with its lighted candles, and blowing out the candles a few at a time so that the play ends in darkness.

The intention and the accomplishment are very great. Where the intention is not clear, the reader is left with an acute sense of frustration. This seems to me to be due to Eliot's failure to correlate the various planes in which his characters are operating. The ritual is sufficient. The trance-talk, which takes the place of chorus, should be particularly illuminating, but is often merely bewildering. The interpolation of the dialogue on the sorrows of spring can be nothing but an attempt to introduce an anthropological significance which is not needed.

Nor is it wholly undisturbing that one cannot avoid the suspicion that a very slight shift in accent would transpose this so serious drama into broad farce. The wit [. . .] is sometimes preposterously pompous wise-cracking. For example: "A brief vacation from the kind of consciousness / That John enjoys, can't make very much difference" [. . .] or "This is what the Communists make capital out of." [. . .]

Perhaps it is Eliot's intention that this play may also be viewed on the plane of comedy. [. . .]

But on its several serious planes *The Family Reunion* is so fine an achievement that it is doubtful if this kind of humor can add anything to it.

Checklist of Additional Reviews

*"Entertainments: Westminster Theatre." *Times*, 22 March 1939, p. 12.

*"T. S. Eliot's New Play." *Manchester Guardian*, 22 March 1939, p. 13.

*W. A. Darlington. "T. S. Eliot's New Verse Play." *Morning Post*, 22 March 1939, page no. unknown.

*"Wasteland of Words." *News-Chronicle*, 22 March 1939, p. 8.

*R. E. R. KKK "Mr. Eliot's New Play." *Church Times*, 24 March 1939, p. 305.

*Derek Verschoyle. "Stage and Screen: The Theatre." *Spectator* 162, no. 5778 (24 March 1939), 484.

*James Agate. "The Eumenides at Home, Audience at Sea." *Sun Times*, 26 March 1939, p. 4.

*Ivor Brown. "*The Family Reunion*." *Observer*, 26 March 1939, p. 15.

*"Watchman. T. S. Eliot's *The Family Reunion*." *British Weekly* 105 (30 March 1939), 466.

Ralph Thompson. "Books of the Times." *New York Times*, 30 March 1939, p. 21.

*L. G. D. KKK "Theatre: *The Family Reunion*." *Poetry* 1, no. 2 (April 1939), unpaged.

*Michael Roberts. "Mr. Eliot's New Play." *London Mercury* 39, no. 234 (April 1939), 641–42.

*T. F. B. KKK "Mr. T. S. Eliot's New Play." *Tablet* 173 (1 April 1939), 424–25.

*Sherman Conrad. "T. S. Eliot's New Play." *Saturday Review* 19 (1 April 1939), 12.

Donald C. Gallup. "T. S. Eliot Imitates Greeks." *Dallas Morning News*, 2 April 1939, sec. 2, p. 9.

Burton Rascoe. "Shreds and Tatters." *Newsweek* 13 (3 April 1939), 40.

*"A Poet's Play." *Picture Post: Hulton's National Weekly* 3 (8 April 1934), 34.

W. A. Darlington. "Benign Note on T. S. Eliot and the Highbrows." *New York Times*, 9 April 1939, sec. 10, p. 1.

Peter Monro Jack. "T. S. Eliot's Modern Variation on the Eumenides Myth." *New York Times Book Review*, 9 April 1939, pp. 2, 20.

Louise Bogan. "Verse." *New Yorker* 15 (15 April 1939), 103–05.

Julian Symons. "*The Family Reunion*." *Twentieth-Century Verse* 18 (June–July 1939), 44, 46, 48.

*John Garrett. "Drama." *English-Speaking World* 21 (June 1939), 278–79.

*Bernard Kelley. "The Family Reunion." *Blackfriars* 20 (June 1939), 469–71.

*Martin Turnell. "Mr. Eliot's New Play." *Scrutiny* 8 (June 1939), 108–14.

Babette Deutsch. "Ghosts of Mr. Eliot." *New York Herald Tribune*, 4 June 1939, p. 6.

Edgar C. Knowlton. "A Playwright Preoccupied with Sin." *South Atlantic Quarterly* 38 (October 1939), 467–68.

Francis Fergusson. "Notes on the Theatre." *Southern Review* 4, no. 3 (1940), 562–64.

Morton D. Zabel. "Two Years of Poetry: 1937–1939." *Southern Review* 5, no. 3 (1940), 590–92.

C. L. Barber. "Strange Gods at *The Family Reunion*." *Southern Review* 6 (Autumn 1940), 387–416.

Theodore Spencer. "Mr. Eliot's Orestes." *Boston Evening Transcript*, 9 November 1940, sec. 3, p. 6.

*Stephen Spender. "Books and the War–VII." *Penguin New Writing*, no. 18, ed. John Lehmann (New York: Penguin, 1941), 125–32.

THE IDEA OF A CHRISTIAN SOCIETY
1939

The Idea of
a Christian Society

T. S. Eliot

HARCOURT, BRACE AND COMPANY

NEW YORK

*"A Christian Society. Mr. Eliot on Ideals and Methods. Democracy's Spiritual Problem."
Times Literary Supplement 1970 (4 November 1939), 640, 642.

Only those who have done some hard thinking for themselves concerning the nature and destiny of contemporary society will appreciate how much objective analysis and self-scrutiny has gone to the making of this slim book by Mr. T. S. Eliot, *The Idea of a Christian Society*. It was written before the outbreak of war; its origination, Mr. Eliot tells us, was in the moral shock produced upon him by the crisis of September 1938, which caused in him "a feeling of humiliation . . . not a criticism of the governments but a doubt of the validity of a civilization." But it was written with the possibility of war in mind, and it is acutely pertinent to the situation today.

What is the idea—in Coleridge's sense of the word—of the society in which we live? Mr. Eliot begins by asking. We conceive of it under several different phrases the meaning of which we forbear to examine; they are regarded as sacrosanct, as sufficient in themselves to establish the superiority of our form of society over its new and now insistent rivals. We speak of it sometimes as a "liberal" society, less often as a "Christian" society; but the blessed word which is chiefly used to validate it is "democracy."

[. . .]

Mr. Eliot [. . .] declares that he does not understand what is meant by democracy, as the word is used today; and he is on firm ground when he insists that the word "does not contain enough positive content to stand alone against the forces you dislike—it can easily be transformed by them," for what is in fact meant by "democracy" is a system that might well be used to introduce totalitarianism. In so far as the word includes the attitudes known as "liberalism," it is enough to say that they are disappearing; the sphere of private life which "liberalism" nominally defends is being steadily whittled away. The tradition of "liberalism" derives from our achievement and successful practice of religious toleration; but that worked because in fact the members of the various communions were all substantially agreed in their assumptions concerning social morality. The comfortable distinction between public and private morality is no longer valid; now the individual is increasingly implicated in a network of social and economic institutions from which, even when he is aware of their control of his behavior, he cannot extricate himself. The operation of these institutions is no longer neutral, but non-Christian. Mr. Eliot sums up his examination of the present condition of our society: it is in a neutral or negative condition; it has ceased in any effective sense to be a Christian society; and, if the forces now operative are allowed to continue without a deliberate and successful attempt to control them towards specifically Christian ends—an effort of which the magnitude can only be dimly conceived—this neutral condition of society will either proceed to a gradual decline "or (whether as the result of catastrophe or not) reform itself into a positive shape which is likely to be effectively secular."

The Secular Ideal

Unfortunately, the majority of people who think about contemporary society regard the second alternative as the ideal, and even a majority of the professed Christians who think about it are content with it. As Mr. Eliot dryly observes, we need not assume that this secular society will be very like any at present observable: "The Anglo-Saxons display a capacity for *diluting* their religion, probably in excess of that of any other race." But those to whom a diluted religion of the state is as repugnant as the prospect of what D. H. Lawrence called "the greasy slipping into decay" should make up their minds that the only possibility is that of a positive Christian society, the idea of which Mr. Eliot proceeds to outline.

He distinguishes three elements, or aspects, of the Christian society: the Christian state, the Christian community, and the community of Christians. First, the men of state, who need not be ardent Christians, must at least have been educated to think in Christian categories, and be confined both by their own habit of mind and the temper and tradition of the people to a Christian "frame of reference." Second comes the Christian community, whose Christianity will be largely unconscious, and consist mainly in religious observances and traditions of behavior: "The mass of the population in a Christian society should not be exposed to a way of life in which there is too sharp and frequent a conflict between what their circumstances dictate and what is Christian." This condition is very far from being fulfilled in England today; the life of the remoter rural parish comes nearest to it, but this has not been typical of English life for a century, and is, even now, still in rapid decline.

[. . .]

Christian Guidance

To prevent the tendency of the State towards expedience and cynicism, and of the mass of the people towards lethargy and superstition is the function of the third element—the "community of Christians," composed of both clergy and laity of superior intellectual or spiritual gifts, which would give the tone to the educational system, consolidate a religious basis for the culture of society, and "collectively form the conscious mind and conscience of the nation."

The Christian society, thus outlined, is one to which the Church could be in vital relation: by its hierarchy in direct and official relation to the State, by its parochial system in contact with the smallest units and individual members of the community and in the persons of its more eminent "clerks" forming part of the community of Christians. A national Church is therefore necessary—a Church which aims at comprehending the whole nation; but the idea of the national Church must be counterpoised by the idea of the universal Church. Only if it fully recognizes its position as part of the universal Church can the national Church combat the tendency to religious–social integration on the lower level of State or race. The prior loyalty of the member of the national Church is to the universal Church.

[. . .]

It is inherent in the nature of Mr. Eliot's argument that he does not entertain the illusion that it would be easy to bring such a society into being. Not only are the social, economic, and political processes actually in motion today carrying society away from not towards such a goal, but to the majority of the *intelligentsia* the goal itself is undesirable. First, because such an idea of the good society is Christian in a definite sense which is alien to the ordinary vague use of the word and perhaps intolerable to the "liberal" mind; secondly, because such an organization of society (though it is quite reconcilable with our English political system) is, in the true sense of the word, aristocratic. That is enough to scare the "democrat," who is seldom realistic enough to analyze the structure of the democratic society in which we live, or to form a clear conception of the nature of the controlling powers in it.

Abuse of Power

If such a critical attitude towards our society were more prevalent, so would be a realization of the new urgency of the perennial problem of politics: how is power to be made responsible? *Quis custodiet ipsos custodes?* The events of the last twenty years should have compelled us to ponder that problem more anxiously than we are naturally inclined to do: for our instinct, confirmed by a century of relatively privileged and prosperous living, is to trust to the general "sense of decency" in the depositories of power, and to the efficacy of popular protest against abuses of power. A "sense of decency" requires a smiling climate to make it reliable; and under the new strain of totalitarian war, which presses hardest on the professional classes among whom the "sense of decency" is chiefly cherished, it may collapse with surprising rapidity.

[. . .]

As Mr. Eliot recognizes, there is no short way out of the condition in which we are. If we are to avoid, or to even have the power of overcoming, secular totalitarianism, we have to begin at the beginning. The work to hand is primarily a work of education both in the more specific and the more general sense. The latter comes first. Of the elements of the Christian society the first

we can hope to bring partly into being is "the community of Christians," a body of people persuaded that the Christian conception of man is the necessary foundation of a politics that can contend against the demonic forces of a machine age. There, no doubt, is a prime difficulty. Christianity in England, when it is not a social convention, tends to be individualistic, emotional, and eccentric; that it is a system of truth from which flow inexhaustible governing principles in metaphysics, ethics, and politics is too rarely admitted even as a possibility by the intelligent man. To bring the contemporary intelligence to an attitude of respect for Christian thought is an undertaking as arduous as it is urgent. Mr. Eliot's book is a very valuable contribution towards this end.

*Charles Smyth. "Church, Community, and State." Spectator 163, no. 5812 (17 November 1939), 687.

The outstanding qualities of Mr. Eliot's thought, as of his prose, are purity, precision, self-discipline, and a grave sense of intellectual responsibility, particularly in the use of words. In consequence, his statements are characteristically measured, qualified, and guarded; and his argument is at the same time close-knit in its construction and discursive in its range. His thought is therefore as easy to follow as it is difficult to grasp: paradoxically, it is elusive, not in spite of its precision, but because of it.

The Idea of a Christian Society contains the revised text of Mr. Eliot's Boutwood Lectures at Corpus Christi College,

Cambridge, in the academic year 1938–9. As he perceives, the society in which we live is Neutral: that is to say, our culture is largely negative (or "liberalised"), although, so far as it is positive, it is still Christian. But it cannot remain indefinitely Neutral, "because a negative culture has ceased to be efficient in a world where economic as well as spiritual forces are proving the efficiency of cultures which, even when pagan, are positive." Our society must therefore reform itself into a positive shape: and here there are only two alternatives—it must become either Pagan or Christian; and if it desires to thrive and to continue its creative activity in the arts of civilization, it would be well advised to choose the latter of these two alternatives, even if this involves, at least, discipline, inconvenience, and discomfort.

The capital necessity is for a system of Christian education, which would be controlled and unified by the Christian philosophy of life, and which "would primarily train people to be able to think in Christian categories." Thus there would come to be established in the political sphere a Christian framework to which the rulers of this society, whatever their private beliefs or disbeliefs, would be obliged to make their policies conform. "They may frequently perform un-Christian acts; they must never attempt to defend their actions on un-Christian principles." The particular form of government is immaterial: the essential point is that it must be founded upon a Christian political philosophy. For the mark of the Christian society is not that it is composed exclusively or even preponderantly of devout and practicing Christians, but that its rulers "accept Christianity . . . as the system under which they are to govern"; that it is a society "in which the natural end of man—virtue and well-being in community—is acknowledged for all, and the supernatural end—beatitude—for those who have the eyes to see it";

and that it possesses "a unified religious–social code of behaviour" and an Established National Church. [. . .]

All this is, clearly, a contribution to the discussion and analysis of a problem rather than a program for immediate action or a blueprint of an abstract and impracticable future. It is not doctrinaire. But it is academic, particularly in its disregard of "feeling," and in its concentration upon the academic categories of "thought" and "behavior." Thus, "it is not enthusiasm, but dogma that differentiates a Christian from a pagan society." "If we are to accept the idea of a Christian society, we must treat Christianity with a great deal more *intellectual* respect than is our wont; we must treat it as being for the individual a matter primarily of thought and not of feeling." But for the great mass of humanity who compose the Christian community (as distinct from "the consciously and thoughtfully practising Christians, especially those of intellectual and spiritual superiority," who compose the Community of Christians), the "capacity for *thinking* about the objects of faith is small": and therefore the Christian Society, at least in its earlier stages, is a society of "men whose Christianity is communal before being individual." Here *The Idea of a Christian Society* carries one stage further the connection between "orthodoxy" and "tradition" which was previously adumbrated in *After Strange Gods*. "It is only from the much smaller number of conscious human beings, the Community of Christians, that one would expect conscious Christian life on its highest social level": from the rest we must be content with conformity to "a unified religious–social code of behaviour," both as regards their customary and periodic religious observances and as regards their dealings with their neighbors: "for behaviour is as potent to affect belief, as belief to affect behaviour." Is not this essentially

416

an application in a wider, more sociological context, of Pascal's counsel: act as if you believed, taking holy water, having masses said, &c.? But Pascal's argument presupposes the will to believe: whereas Mr. Eliot's system is prepared to wait for it. Rather, we find ourselves back again at the classic paradox with which he startled us, in *For Lancelot Andrewes*, in 1928: "The spirit killeth, but the letter giveth life."

Yet this is dangerous doctrine, in so far as it may seem to leave out of sight the primary necessity of conversion. "There are three sources of belief," wrote Pascal: "reason, custom, inspiration. The Christian religion, which alone has reason, does not acknowledge as her true children those who believe without inspiration. It is not that she excludes reason and custom . . ." But reason and custom are the foundations upon which Mr. Eliot builds his Christian society: and a society which functions within the framework of a Christian system of education and a Christian political philosophy may still be a society unregenerate and unredeemed. This criticism might be irrelevant if he were content to argue that a Christian reorganization of society is desirable on grounds of common sense and common prudence; but, because he is himself a practicing Christian, it is impossible for him to do this: "What is worst of all is to advocate Christianity, not because it is true, but because it might be beneficial."

Taken together, *After Strange Gods* and *The Idea of a Christian Society* mark the resumption of the Tractarian counter-offensive against "Liberalism." It is indeed important that that attack should be renewed. The disintegrated culture, the slovenly subjectivism, the spiritual and the intellectual indiscipline, the irresponsible individualism of our time, which are the fruits of "Liberalism," are real evils. Consequently it is not altogether surprising that Mr. Eliot flinches from the term "religious revival": it "seems to me to imply a possible separation of religious feeling from religious thinking which I do not accept." Yet is not his own *Idea of a Christian Society* open to precisely the same accusation from a diametrically opposite direction? He leaves us with the picture of "a community of men and women, not individually better than they are now, except for the capital difference of holding the Christian faith." It is these words—"*not individually better than they are now*"—that seem to carry within them the stultification of the whole experiment.

To say this is by no means to deny the urgency of attempting to work out a Christian doctrine of modern society and to order our national life in accordance with it: still less is it to disparage the importance of Mr. Eliot's contribution to that endeavor. He has said with great courage and with conspicuous clarity something which, whether right or wrong, and whether practicable or impracticable, unquestionably needed to be said, and as unquestionably needs to be considered, discussed, and criticized. *The Idea of a Christian Society* is a thesis distinguished not less, though less obtrusively, by its moral earnestness than by its intellectual cogency: and it is bound to exercise a lasting influence upon all future investigations regarding the nature, end, and function of social order.

---

*D. W. Harding. "Christian or Liberal?" *Scrutiny* 8 (December 1939), 309–13.

Addressed to Christians, this book is largely about—and obviously meant to influence—those neutral others who support "a culture which is mainly negative, but which, so far as it is positive, is still Christian." Mr. Eliot believes that we must now choose between working for a new Christian culture and accepting a pagan one, whether fascist or communist; unless we aim at a positively Christian society, we are committed "to a progressive and insidious adaptation to the totalitarian worldliness for which the pace is already set." Democracy is not an alternative to totalitarian government; it is fundamentally, though perhaps less forthrightly, just as materialistic and pagan. In intention it merely neglects its Christians and has no coherent system of allegiances to a pagan ideal, but it is none the less developing an increasingly complete network of institutions which invite un-Christian conduct from the Christians who find their everyday life set amongst them.

In pointing out the unsatisfactory features of our society, Mr. Eliot can count on wide respect and agreement. In his attack on flabbiness of mind, on the lowering of standards in literature and "culture" in the narrower sense, on the substitution of a mob led by propaganda in place of a community, and in the sort of concern he shows for education, Mr. Eliot implicitly agrees with much that has been expressed in *Scrutiny* for the last seven years; in his disgust at the financial control of politics and his dismay at the plight of agriculture, he is on ground familiarized by social credit reformers and their allies.

In common with many other thinkers, Mr. Eliot believes that any remedy for these disorders must involve the establishment of a true community, one in which non-materialist values will find an important place and not just survive in chinks and crannies. Again, like many other thinkers, he describes these values as "religious." The society he wants, therefore, is a "religious–social community" [. . .].

His emphasis is markedly on the communal: "I have tried," he writes, "to restrict my ambition of a Christian society to a social minimum: to picture, not a society of saints, but of ordinary men, of men whose Christianity is communal before being individual." And his ideal is a community in which social custom is maintained by religious sanction: "a Christian community is one in which there is a unified religious–social code of behaviour."

It is at this point that the non-Christian's doubts begin to focus. Such societies have been known; and stagnation, oppression, and intolerant regimentation have characterized them. Mr. Eliot, it is true, acknowledges from time to time the need for toleration of the non-Christian and, presumably, toleration within limits of those who question the accepted religious–social code of behavior and its supporting beliefs. But such toleration has not usually marked the effectively Christian societies of the past. Crude and unfashionable as it is—and bad taste though it may seem to the associates of Christian intellectuals—I decline to forget Galileo and his humbler fellow-victims throughout the Christian centuries, or even the attitude of the contemporary Roman Catholic Church to contraceptives. Religious sanction for social custom and customary belief has always produced such things, and there is no good reason to expect a change. "To the unreasoning mind," says Mr. Eliot with sedate surprise, "the Church can often be made to appear to be the enemy of progress and enlightenment." It may indeed; and count me among the unreasoning.

I cannot doubt that such a society as Mr. Eliot wants would be heavily overbalanced towards conservation and stability, at the cost of plasticity and exploration. I believe that greater plasticity and bolder exploration of human possibilities are more urgently needed. Talk, with which we half frighten and half flatter ourselves, about the hectic speed of the changes which humanity is undergoing in our century is excited blah. Human nature is, as it always was, remarkably stodgy and in crying need of greater plasticity.

People cannot be plastic, however, unless they are relatively free from anxiety and from guilty fear of the possibilities of their own nature; and freedom from anxiety and guilt is not a thing whose possibility Mr. Eliot convincingly believes in. It is true that he says "We need to recover the sense of religious fear, so that it may be overcome by religious hope," but the fear very evidently takes first place and goes along with "the evil which is present in human nature at all times and in all circumstances."

All alternatives to this spirit seem to be brought under the heading of what Mr. Eliot calls Liberalism, and hates. His attack is made rather chaotic by sketchy suggestions of the relation between this spirit and political and religious liberalism, and by the unargued conviction that this general spirit is responsible for all the particular social disorders which disturb him.

But the tags are of little account, and what matters is recognizing the distinction between the "liberal" spirit and the "Christian" spirit as Mr. Eliot understands them. As so often happens it can best be expressed in the paradigm which childhood offers. The "liberal" spirit is the child who explores his world without prejudice and sees no reason to stop exploring; he finds neither the world fundamentally hostile nor himself fundamentally inadequate. The "Christian" spirit is the child with an intuitive conviction of the world's hostility and his own unworthiness, who (at his best, which Mr. Eliot stands for) concentrates on fortifying himself to overcome— to overcome the world and himself simultaneously. Mr. Eliot's tense and guarded insecurity, beleaguered by the world, is well expressed in his condemnation of "Liberalism" as "something which tends to release energy rather than accumulate it, to relax, rather than to fortify."

The only alternative he sees to Christianity or paganism is a constant departure from, in the sense of a mere rejection of, all positive convictions. This may have been the character of some movements which have been called Liberal. But it is not the only alternative to the religious spirit. What Mr. Eliot ignores or implicitly denies is the possibility of being content with moving on, in a direction given you by the past, to something which has now for the first time become possible and is even more satisfying that your past activities were. This, which is exploration, seems so unsafe to the Christian that he denies its very possibility. His peace of mind depends on the conviction that he knows what he is ultimately aiming at; all his activity must be directed towards a goal which he has already postulated. By this means he escapes the insecurity of being in the strict sense an explorer and becomes instead a pilgrim.

In some temperaments, including apparently Mr. Eliot's, this conviction of an ultimate goal serves paradoxically to reinforce a peculiar gloom. The goal they postulate must be described as unattainable on this earth, since, of course, it is in the nature of human activity that each new development reveals a new and unattained possibility. Simultaneously with becoming better than we were, we realize that we could be better than we are. To the explorer this seems an unsurprising and undisturbing fact. But by concentrating on their postulated goal, those of Mr. Eliot's spirit can see our every advance almost exclusively in the guise of a relative failure. Observe where the emphasis falls in the following passage:

But we have to remember that the Kingdom of Christ on earth will never be realized, and also that it is always being realized; we must remember that whatever reform or revolution we carry out, the result will always be a sordid travesty of what human society should be—though the world is never left wholly without glory.

The satisfaction of advancing at all is recognized dimly; the satisfaction of seeing that further advance is possible is converted into a disappointment. What is vividly felt is "the evil which is present in human nature at all times and in all circumstances." It is this which turns the explorer into an anxious pilgrim.

---

*Maurice B. Reckitt. "Views and Reviews: A Sub-Christian Society." *New English Weekly* 16 (7 December 1939), 115–16.

[See Eliot's reply: 14 December, "A Sub-Pagan Society." See also letters 21 December 1939 (by Every), 4 January 1940 (by Peck), 11 January (by Demant), 18 January (by Reckitt), and 1 February (by Eliot).]

I cannot resist the feeling of a certain unreality attaching to the attempt to review this book. [. . .] Mr. Eliot's book is so short, so succinct, and written with such a crystalline brilliance [. . .] that no one who is even remotely interested either in Mr. Eliot or in his subject will fail to read

it for themselves, and no one is likely to be particularly interested to know what may be anyone else's opinion about it. [. . .] In any case, the book has been widely reviewed and thoroughly summarized in the press already [. .]. I particularly commend Canon Charles Smyth's notice in *The Spectator*, which also, however, embarrasses me somewhat by saying exactly what I should have wished to say a good deal better than I could say it.

[See "Church, Community, and State" in this volume, pp. 415–17.]

What I have not seen generally pointed out is that this book is not the product of any purely theoretical interest in the subject; it is the response to a shock. Mr. Eliot confesses himself to have been "deeply shaken by the events of September, 1938, in a way from which one does not recover," and to be one (as he suspects) of many who experienced a "new and unexpected feeling of humiliation, which seemed to demand an act of personal contrition, of humility, repentance and amendment; what had happened was something in which one was deeply implicated and responsible"; something which suggested "doubt of the validity of a civilisation. We could not match conviction with conviction." This strongly personal and even emotional statement, the mood of which is reproduced in the admirable letter of Dr. J. H. Oldham written to *The Times* on the occasion itself, reprinted at the end of Mr. Eliot's notes, and which provided, as he says, the "immediate stimulus" for these lectures, is interesting for two reasons. First, because it provides an excellent expression of ideas (or more precisely, facts) to which many people find it hard to attach any meaning—corporate sin and corporate penitence. And secondly, because Mr. Eliot reacted to this experience not, as do most of us if we ever attain to such experiences, by feeling and lamenting, but by thinking. This book is that rare phenomenon in English life—the response to a moral challenge of a Christian mind.

I shall not attempt to praise Mr. Eliot's book, for that would be impertinent, nor to summarize it, for [. . .] that would be superfluous. Mr. Eliot himself describes it as "a discussion which must occupy many minds for a long time," and no review could possibly follow up all the clues which are here suggested. Have we got a Christian society—whatever that may be? No, says Mr. Eliot, we have a neutral one, and its difference in idea from a Pagan one "is, in the long run, of minor importance," but, he goes on to insist, "a society has not ceased to be Christian until it has become positively something else," and though our culture is mainly negative, "so far as it is positive, it is still Christian." But the situation is much more serious than the average Christian realizes, "as the problem is constituted by our implication in a network of institutions from which we cannot dissociate ourselves: institutions the operation of which appears no longer neutral, but non-Christian." The ordinary man who believes himself in some real sense a Christian is in fact

> becoming more and more de-Christianised by all sorts of unconscious pressure; paganism holds all the most valuable advertising space. Anything like Christian traditions transmitted from generation to generation within the family must disappear, and the small body of Christians will consist entirely of adult recruits

who have rediscovered the Faith for themselves. Even if quality thus compensates for quantity (an undoubted tendency, which nevertheless Mr. Eliot seems to me to exaggerate), obviously the prospects are far from bright for the transition from a Neutral to a Christian society—whatever that may be.

[. . .]

So many summaries of this book have appeared that probably all my readers will know that Mr. Eliot distinguishes "the Christian State, the Christian Community and the Community of Christians," as elements of the Christian Society. I do not think these titles altogether happily chosen, but there is no difficulty in understanding what Mr. Eliot is seeking to distinguish, and the distinction is very suggestive of the elements of medieval Christendom, if we take as parallels the ruling caste, the mass of the population, and the religious orders. A hundred years ago Coleridge had an analogous category to the last-named in mind when he coined the term "clerisy," but Mr. Eliot gives good reasons for thinking that this term—at any rate in Coleridge's sense, and it is not much good using it in any other—should be discarded. Mr. Eliot admits he has in mind "a body of nebulous outline"—those of "superior intellectual and/or spiritual gifts" who accept a cultural responsibility on an explicitly Christian basis, and from whom "one could expect a conscious Christian life on its highest social level." From the rulers of the Christian State Mr. Eliot would exact only a "conscious conformity" and such a degree of Christian education (the content of which he does not discuss) as would enable them "to think in Christian categories," for as he very sensibly points out, "it is the general ethics of the people they have to govern, not their own piety, that determines the behaviour of politicians."

But it is when we come to the great mass of the "Christian community" that the question which troubles me arises. When Mr. Eliot says that "their religious and social life should form for them a natural whole so that the difficulty of behaving

421

as Christians should not impose on them an intolerable strain," he is only reaffirming the very important truth stated by M. Maritain more than ten years ago, that it is the business of a social order to make the world not holy (which no social order can be) but "habitable," so that a man is not "obliged to heroism," to live a Christian life in it. And it is relevant to this point to add, as Mr. Eliot does, that "behaviour is as potent to affect belief, as belief to affect behaviour"; hence an order in which the majority can lead a life congruous with Christian values is of importance not only for its inherent validity, but on account of the support it gives to the Faith on which ultimately those values depend.

But Mr. Eliot goes further than this. He says (my italics) "the *religious* life of the people would be *largely* a matter of behaviour and conformity"; and again, he envisages "a community of men and women, *not individually better* than they are now, *except* for the capital difference of holding the Christian faith." One is forced to the question what relation a "religious life" of this quality bears to the religion of the New Testament. No doubt the language of the Epistles—"called to be saints," "the measure of the stature of the fullness of Christ,"—was addressed to "Christian communities" in a situation vastly different from the Christian community Mr. Eliot envisages. But a religion which expects no more than this, nothing more elevated, nothing more heroic, from the mass of its devotees can surely be little more than an official cult and a code of morals. "Social customs," says Mr. Eliot, "would take on religious sanctions." But if this is all that happens, the new Christendom will be likely to repeat those errors of the old which led to so much evil and contributed to the apostasy of Europe by the nourishing of superstition within the ecclesiastical integument, and by a readiness to treat religion as instrumental to social ends. The "moral revivalism" which Mr. Eliot sees as our national weakness, and the inadequacy of which he so effectively exposes, is merely the recurrent reaction which inevitably waits upon any religion which is content to be regarded as "largely a matter of behaviour and conformity"; and there are some among the warmest of Mr. Eliot's admirers for whom this represents no true idea of a Christian society.

Malcolm Cowley. "Tract for the Times." *New Republic* 102 (17 June 1940), 829–30.

T. S. Eliot also has written a tract for the times, and one intended to have a permanent value. Like Waldo Frank, whose *Chart for Rough Water* I reviewed last week, he believes that the world can be saved only by religion. At this point the resemblance between them begins and ends. The religion proclaimed by Waldo Frank is deeply felt but intellectually vague and never completely defined; it is apparently to be achieved by individual acts of conversion. T. S. Eliot's religion, though also deeply felt, is primarily intellectual and institutional; it is orthodox Anglicanism as set forth in the Thirty-Nine Articles.

His book begins by saying that our present society—in the democratic countries—is neither Christian nor pagan; it is negative and therefore essentially unstable. Mr. Eliot believes that it must follow one of two courses. It must either proceed, he says, "into a gradual decline of which we can see no end, or (whether as a result of catastrophe or not) reform itself into a positive shape." If that positive shape turns out to be pagan, we shall have inflicted on us "the puritanism of a hygienic morality in the interest of efficiency; uniformity of opinion through propaganda, and art encouraged only when it flatters the official doctrines of the time." The one way of avoiding totalitarianism—the one hope for control, balance and creative activity—is to build for the first time a positive Christian society.

Such a society, Mr. Eliot says, would be completely different from present-day capitalism, under which people have been finding it harder and harder to lead Christian lives. Yet the change would not necessarily be one of government; a Christian society might be a democracy, a monarchy or even a corporative state of the type recommended by the late Pius XI. The rulers of a Christian society might be infidels in their private lives—that would be their own concern—but they would have to accept Christianity as the system under which they governed. The ordinary citizens would accept it as a matter of behavior and habit. But there would have to be a third group, to compensate for the inertia and self-seeking of the others. That group, which Mr. Eliot calls the Community of Christians, would be composed of people distinguished by their intelligence and spiritual devotion. The church itself would include all three groups. It would be established by law but would remain independent of secular politics and would be united to the Christian churches in other countries. Thus, every citizen would have a double allegiance, "to the State and to the Church, to one's countrymen and to one's fellow Christians everywhere. . . . There would always be tension, and this tension . . . is a distinguishing mark between a Christian and a pagan society." As the alternative to totalitarianism, Mr. Eliot offers us the dualism of church and state. He insists that his readers should make their choice: "If you will not have God

(and He is a jealous God) you should pay your respects to Hitler or Stalin."

To a reader trained in the liberal tradition, the weakness of Mr. Eliot's argument seems to be that he is confusing religion in general with Christianity (and sometimes with the Church of England). The advantages he claims for a Christian state might also be claimed for a Buddhist or Brahman or Mohammedan state; indeed, I suspect that there is a good deal of Buddhist resignation mixed in with Mr. Eliot's orthodoxy. Even liberalism, the frame of mind that he says is leading us to chaos, has of late years developed its own faith, the religion of humanity, which is not a wholly ineffective shield against fascist doctrines. Among Christian sects—with due apologies to Mr. Eliot and the devout Anglicans I knew at college—the Church of England seems one of the most perfunctory and almost the least qualified to create a new world order.

All these are reasons why I did not expect to like *The Idea of a Christian Society*, and yet in the end I was greatly impressed by it. Once you have granted Mr. Eliot his doubtful premises, the rest of his argument moves toward wholly logical conclusions. And you find, even when you are hostile to the main trend of it, that it is full of moderation and worldly wisdom. He does not make Waldo Frank's mistake of expecting too much faith from too many people; nor does he believe that society as a whole can be saved by the conversion of individuals. Although he makes no effort to be original, his statements of more or less familiar ideas often have the force of axioms, like Poor Richard's. "Behaviour," he says, "is as potent to affect belief as belief to affect behaviour."—"Out of liberalism itself come the philosophies which deny it,"—"Good prose cannot be written by a people without convictions."— "If anybody ever attacked democracy, I might discover what the word meant."

Sometimes, by approaching a problem from the standpoint of Christian doctrine, he casts an unexpected light on it. "I have never seen any evidence," he says, "that to be a Buchmanite it was necessary to hold the Christian faith according to the Creeds, and until I have seen a statement to that effect I shall continue to doubt whether there is any reason to call Buchmanism a Christian movement."

Mr. Eliot uses the first-person singular pronoun almost as frequently as Waldo Frank, but with a curiously different effect. His is not the prophetic pronoun of "I say unto you," but rather the self-defining and self-deprecating pronoun of expressions like "I am not here concerned," and "I am not qualified to," and "I do not mean primarily." Mr. Eliot's "I" is the least personal pronoun in English literature; it tells us almost nothing about the author except his limitations. Yet one feels from page to page that he would like to express not only his public ideas but also his heart; one feels that strong emotions are being held in check by equally strong convictions. It is this tension between the personal and the impersonal that gives a special quality to all his work, including his poems. Often it lends emotional force to simple statements of fact; and when Mr. Eliot drops his reserve, even for a moment, he impresses us more than another writer might do by screaming and beating his breast. Such a moment of personal confession occurs at the very end of *The Idea of a Christian Society*. There, speaking in his own voice, the author speaks for a whole generation that was betrayed by its statesmen—and by itself—before it heard the German bombers in the skies:

> I believe that there must be many persons who, like myself, were deeply shaken by the events of September, 1938, in a way from which one does not recover; persons to whom that month

brought a profounder realisation of a general plight . . . The feeling which was new and unexpected was a feeling of humiliation, which seemed to demand an act of personal contrition, of humility, repentance and amendment; what had happened was something in which one was deeply implicated and responsible. It was not, I repeat, a criticism of the government, but a doubt of the validity of a civilisation. We could not match conviction with conviction, we had no ideas with which we could either meet or oppose the ideas opposed to us . . . Such thoughts as these formed the starting point, and must remain the excuse, for saying what I have to say.

Checklist of Additional Reviews

*"The Spirit and the Crisis." *Times Literary Supplement* 1970 (4 November 1939), 641.

*"*The Idea of a Christian Society*." *Tablet* 174 (18 November 1939), 576–77.

Listener 22 (30 November 1939), 1086.

"For 'Christian Society.' T. S. Eliot Outlines a Religious System." *Springfield Republican* [Massachusetts], 7 January 1940, p. 7e.

*Brother George Every. "Christian Polity." *Purpose* 12 (January–March 1940), 31–37.

*Stephen Spender. "How Shall We Be Saved?" *Horizon* 1 (January 1940), 51–56.

*Joseph Ratner. "T. S. Eliot and Totalitarianism." *Saturday Review* 21 (6 January 1940), 7. [See Bishop's letter to the editor 2 March and Ratner's "Letters to the Editor: Mr. Ratner Replies." *Saturday Review* 21 (2 March), 9, 18]

Bernard Iddings Bell. "T. S. Eliot Examines the Spiritual State of Society Today." *New York Times Book Review*, 7 January 1940, pp. 3, 19.

Ralph Thompson. "Books of the Times." *New York Times*, 8 January 1940, p. 13.

Donald C. Gallup. "Our Society Is a Negative One, T. S. Eliot Declares in Essay." *Dallas Morning News*, 14 January 1940, sec. 5, p. 4.

"Recent and Readable." *Time* 25, pt. 1 (15 January 1940), 67.

Harry Lorin Binsse. "About a Possible Future." *Commonweal* 31 (19 January 1940), 288.

Howard Mumford Jones. "Shadow Boxing." *Boston Evening Transcript*, 20 January 1940, sec. 6, p. 1.

Philip Dur. "A Church for All and a Job for Each." *Harvard Progressive* 4 (February 1940), 19.

C. P. H. "*The Idea of a Christian Society.*" *Social Progress* [Crawfordsville, Indiana] 30 (February 1940), 26.

*Reinhold Niebuhr. "Can Church Restrain State?" *Common Sense* 9 (February 1940), 26–27.

*Gerald Vann. "Mr. Eliot's Idea of a Christian Society." *Blackfriars* 21 (February 1940), 119–22.

*Edwin Berry Burgum. "The Road to Rome." *New Masses* 34 (6 February 1940), 27.

John Haynes Holmes. "The World and the Faith." *New York Herald Tribune Books*, 18 February 1940, p. 16.

*J. H. Oldham. *Christian News-Letter* 18, supplement, 28 February 1940. [See Eliot's reply: "Education in a Christian Society." *CNL* 20, supplement, 13 March. See also Oldham's "Professor Clarke and Mr. Eliot." *CNL* 22 (27 March) and "Can Education Survive Organization." *CNL* 23, supplement, 3 April]

Contemporary Jewish Record 3 (March–April 1940), 217.

Jacob J. Weinstein. "Religion and the Wasteland." *Jewish Frontier* 7, no. 3 (March 1940), 25–26.

*Virginia Curry Bishop. "Letters to the Editor. Humble Rebuttle." *Saturday Review* 21 (2 March 1940), 9. [Response to Ratner, 6 January, 2 March]

Robert L. Clayton. "T. S. Eliot's Vision of a Christian Society." *Living Church* 102 (13 March 1940), 10.

"Shorter Notices." *Nation* 150 (16 March 1940), 370–71.

**J. S. Bixler. "The Doubtful Value of Imposed Unity." *Christendom* 5 (Spring 1940), 278–79.

R. P. Blackmur. "It Is Later than He Thinks." *Kenyon Review* 2 (Spring 1940), 235–38. [Reprinted in *The Expanse of Greatness* (New York: Arrow, 1940), 239–44]

Mary M. Colum. "Religion and the Modern Worlds." *Forum* 103 (April 1940), 199.

Edgar Sheffield Brightman. "Christianity Today." *Journal of Bible and Religion* 8 (May 1940), 91.

Brother Leo. "God in Government." *Missionary* [Washington, D.C.] 54 (May 1940), 130.

Charles Edward Shain. "*The Idea of a Christian Society.*" *Milton Bulletin* 3 (May 1940), 8–9.

Brother Leo. "Books and Bookman." *Columbia* 19 (June 1940), 14.

Lionel Trilling. "Elements that Are Wanted." *Partisan Review* 7 (September–October 1940), 367–79.

Francis J. O'Malley. "A Christian Society." *Review of Politics* 2 (October 1940), 488–90.

Moorhouse F. X. Millar. "Society, Law." *Thought* 15 (December 1940), 720–22.

EAST COKER
1940
BURNT NORTON
1941
THE DRY SALVAGES
1941
LITTLE GIDDING
1942
FOUR QUARTETS
1943

EAST COKER

by

T. S. ELIOT

H. W. & Theresa Eliot

from T. S. Eliot

FABER AND FABER
24 Russell Square
London

BURNT NORTON

by

T. S. ELIOT

FABER AND FABER

24 Russell Square

London

THE DRY SALVAGES

by

T. S. ELIOT

FABER AND FABER

24 Russell Square

London

LITTLE GIDDING

by

T. S. ELIOT

FABER AND FABER

24 Russell Square

London

FOUR
QUARTETS

T. S. ELIOT

NEW YORK
HARCOURT, BRACE AND COMPANY

*G. W. Stonier.
"Mr. Eliot's New Poem."
New Statesman 20 (14
September 1940), 267–68.

[Review of "East Coker"]

It is five years since the publication of Mr. Eliot's last poem—a period occupied by criticism, two plays and a volume of light verse—but "East Coker" takes us back to "Burnt Norton," in something more than title, as though scarcely a day had passed. Or rather, since Mr. Eliot is not a writer who repeats himself, it would be better to say that we resume from the earlier point. There is a similar cluster of experience: problems of time and eternity clutched at from the sliding second; the return to country scenes in childhood— a moment is held and then let go with a gesture of resignation; permanence sought in solitude and in art hung like a Chinese vase in time; the desire to escape from a twilit consciousness into bright daylight or darkness; the struggle to fix ever-shifting experiences with words which also break and slip. No need to remark, at this time of day, that the expression, the amalgamation of such attitudes is sharp and poignant, as final as Mr. Eliot can make it; or that the poem carries an authority which marks the work of no other living poet except Claudel. This authority has been compared more than once to that of Arnold, but it seems to me even more powerful and exclusive. We do not approach a new poem by Mr. Eliot as single-mindedly as, for example, we used to open the *London Mercury* to discover a new poem of Yeats. Whether Yeats or Eliot is the "better" poet is beside the point. We expect, and find, a criticism both of literature and life. As we read, the hint of passages in Milton and Spenser carry the mind back to criticism he has written in the past; the nature of writing itself is put to the test: [quotation of lines 1–17 of "East Coker" V]. Here, it seems to me, is an integrity as inflexible and moving as Baudelaire's, involving however a confession of failure which no poet of earlier date has dared venture; the mask of eloquence—the only questionable part of Baudelaire's achievement— has been dropped altogether, with masterly effect. If one says that Mr. Eliot has set an example to modern poets, it is in this sense of self-discipline and sacrifice and not of course with the meaning that anyone should follow or attempt to follow his manner of writing.

There are many threads in Mr. Eliot's poetry. The mingled nostalgia and caricature of the Prufrock period have vanished never perhaps to reappear; the roots of his later poetry, "East Coker" and "Burnt Norton" are to be found in "The Hollow Men." There the lyric, the sardonic jingle, the austere response, were set nakedly side by side; the successes—

Eyes I dare not meet in dreams
In death's dream kingdom
These do not appear
[. . . . .]

—were offset by passages in which fragments from different worlds merely clashed and grated. Since then Mr. Eliot has marshaled his material more harmoniously, and as a whole "East Coker" is a more satisfactory poem than "The Hollow Men," though it contains no passage to equal the lines quoted above. The greater homogeneity is due chiefly of course to religious contemplation which has smoothed many corners.

[. . .]

In [one] section of the poem, [. . .] stoicism leads to one of those catalogues of theological paradox—"what you do not know is the only thing you know, / And what you own is what you do not own"— from which Mr. Eliot derives consolation but which are rather blankly depressing to the reader. His thought seems, at such times, to run into a verbal palindrome from which there is no escape. Having abjured ecstasy, he yet allows himself to fall into a neutral trance; the bare words do not carry all the weight and meaning which they are meant to carry; and here, I think, one can put one's finger on his main weakness. Everyone who has read Mr. Eliot with some enthusiasm and care must have discovered for himself that in almost everything he writes there are dumb notes; notes dumb, I mean, to us, not to Mr. Eliot, for they appear at important junctures and are repeated. Certain passages are inoperative: such, I believe, are many of his statements of faith, the affectation of disjointedness, the use of words like "Shantih" at the end of *The Waste Land*, where obviously more intensity went to putting down the word than comes off the page.

Again his use of quotation, by which he so often imparts a nostalgic flavor to his verse, has curious lapses. In "East Coker," there are examples of both success and failure. The section beginning

O dark dark dark. They all go into the
    dark,
The vacant interstellar spaces, the
    vacant into the vacant;
The captains, merchant bankers,
    eminent men of letters

makes excellent use of a well-known passage in *Samson* ("Dark, dark, dark! The moon . . . hid in her vacant interlunar cave"). But how do the last lines of the following passage, delightful in its scene, strike the reader?

                    In that open field
If you do not come too close, if you do
    not come too close,
On a summer midnight, you can hear
    the music
Of the weak pipe and the little drum
And see them dancing around the
    bonfire
The association of man and woman
In daunsinge, signifying matrimonie—
A dignified and commodious
    sacrament.
[. . . . .]

There the Elizabethan spelling imparts no flavor save perhaps one of pedantry; its only effect is to make us think, "Well, I suppose Eliot, when he wrote that, was thinking of passages in Spenser's 'Epithalamion.'" Yet obviously to Eliot the whiff of the antique has an immediate, an emotional effect, like the reminiscences of Haydn in Prokofiev's Classical Symphony. This is a purely literary failure and the more odd because of all poets Eliot is in certain directions the most precise in his effects. The drawbacks I have mentioned will not come as any surprise to Mr. Eliot's admirers.

Taken as a whole, though, "East Coker" is one of its author's best and most mature poems. Who else now writing in English could have packed into 214 lines so many disparate things? And despite blemishes and minor lapses, the effect is homogenous. Perhaps I am wrong in applying the word stoical to consolations which for Mr. Eliot may have a theological reference, but "East Coker" seems to me the somber and moving utterance of a man looking round him as he grows old. [. . .]

*James Kirkup. "Eliot."
Poetry 1, no. 4 (15 January 1941), 115–16.

[Review of "East Coker"]

Mr. Eliot is the only great English poet living. That is, the only poet who in years to come will be read even when it is fashionable to ignore him. Among the likeable set of brilliant hoaxers and endearing cleversides who have succeeded in charming and bewildering the distracted *entre deux guerres* audience, he alone stands out, with Lawrence, as a genuine poet, one of major importance.

His early satirical verse, even in its most frivolous and disconcerting moments, hints at the qualities and the philosophy which distinguish his latest poem. In "East Coker" we find again the metaphysical anguish of the early poems, the obsession with death and the vision of existence as a state in which death is life and life death:

Earth feet, loam feet, lifted in country
mirth
Mirth of those long since under earth
Nourishing the corn.

The grimness and grinning of Webster are still there, only the lines are longer, the vision mellower and the accent less despairing.

[. . .]

But the implied protest of the early poems and of *The Waste Land* is not to be found in "East Coker." Instead there is, not ennui or lassitude in the face of the inevitable, but a wise humility. The prospect of dying inspires no fear, no raptures, but a calm resignation, comparable to the *Gelassenheit* of the aged Goethe and the visionary humility of Rilke in the *Duineser Elegien*. Mr. Eliot is not the first to have realized that life is not all life, and death not all death, and that existence does not merely consist of one state following on the other, but that both states are one.

And what there is to conquer
By strength and submission, has
  already been discovered
Once or twice, or several times, by
  men whom one cannot hope
To emulate—

This humility which the poet endeavors to attain is an attitude devoid of any conscious nobility, but which is essentially noble. It is a religious or Christian humility, the fruit of patience. We are reminded of the significant lines in "What the Thunder Said":

He who was living is now dead
We who were living are now dying
With a little patience

We begin to see that the stage of humility is an organic development out of an initial despair and an acquired patience. Humility is the keynote of the poem. Only humility can make endurable a vision of unending existence in which "here and now cease to matter." We are reminded again of the lines in "The Burial of the Dead": "I was neither / Living nor dead, and I knew nothing. And the conclusion drawn by the poet, the germ of the poem: "The only wisdom we can hope to acquire / Is the wisdom of humility; humility is endless."

"East Coker" impresses us by that quality which we have come to expect of Mr. Eliot—beauty of language, of which the most dominant characteristic is a hypnotic repetitiveness: "O dark dark dark. They all go into the dark, / The vacant interstellar spaces, the vacant into the vacant." These are Miltonic echoes, recalling the dark of *Samson Agonistes*. [. . .] In parts the intricate weaving and commingling of sounds and the knitting of line into line, expressive of the merged state of life and death, is effective by a frequent use of the present participle:

Keeping time,
Keeping the rhythm in their dancing
As in their living in the living seasons
The time of the seasons and the
    constellations
The time of milking and the time of
    harvest
The time of the coupling of man and
    woman
And that of beasts. Feet rising and
    falling.
Eating and drinking. Dung and death.

The above passage is also a good example of the chasteness of Mr. Eliot's vocabulary. And then we see at the conclusion of the third section of the poem how well the death–life paradox adapts itself again to poetically impressive treatment:

In order to arrive at what you are not
    You must go through the way in
        which you are not.
[. . . . .]

It is this essentially simple nature of thought and language which surprises and satisfies. Here and there, standing our from the serious, almost monotone background of the poem with a lucid sweetness, are controlled lyrical or elegiac passages:

Whisper of running streams, and
    winter lightning.
The wild thyme unseen and the wild
    strawberry,
The laughter in the garden, echoed
    ecstasy.

In "East Coker," Mr. Eliot has written a poem of major importance, moving, serious, sincere, and above all, poetical. It reveals, as "Ash-Wednesday" and "Burnt Norton" revealed to us, the most precious and enduring aspect of his genius. It is the poetry of a mature mind, showing depth of understanding and much humanity, as well as a perfection of the most appealing quality in Mr. Eliot's technique, a reverent and impressive use of words.

He brings us sure proof of the true nature of poetry, for which, at present especially, we are grateful.

*Stephen Spender. "The Year's Poetry." *Horizon* 3 (February 1941), 138–41.

[Review of "East Coker"]

[. . .]

Poetry [. . .] cannot evade the responsibility of interpreting the significance of life at a particular time and relating it to life at other times. The poetry of the past is a very freshly preserved record of the reactions of men who were alive in the same way as we are to sets of circumstances different from ours. How different? They can tell us only if we can also tell them. We have to establish our own value in relations to theirs. We rapidly lose the significance of life in the past if we lose it in the present.

The problem that confronts poets—and, indeed, everyone who is aware and alive—is that external circumstances may arise which destroy the continuity of life sensed by poetry. If it is conceded that this is possible—that the destruction of the values of living, and their supersession by machinery, aims of power, and materialism, might make life meaningless—is the poet justified in stepping out of his poetry, as it were, and taking a hand in altering the world? Is he justified in using poetry as a means of propaganda for traditional values which may, in fact, be revolutionary?

Most contemporary poets seem to have been faced by these questions. Some have replied by abandoning poetry altogether and joining revolutionary movements. Those who have continued to write poetry have often been forced to use their poetry as an affirmation of values rather than as an interpretation of values which they find generally recognized by society.

Eliot is a case in point. [. . .] [H]e has protested in his criticism against the suggestion that the poet is concerned with aims outside poetry. Nevertheless, his recent poetry, especially "Burnt Norton" and "East Coker," shows a tendency to move outside itself and question its own use. After a passage in a dancing measure, he writes, in "East Coker":

> That was a way of putting it—not
>   very satisfactory:
> A periphrastic study in worn-out
>   poetical fashion,
> Leaving one still with the intolerable
>   wrestle
> With words and meanings. The poetry
>   does not matter.
> [. . . . .]

"East Coker" lacks, perhaps, some of the essentially poetic merits of Eliot's earlier poetry. If one can say it is a successful poem without being completely poetic, this is not really a contradiction, for it is a poem whose aim is not entirely poetry. What the poem does is to recreate an experience; and this experience lies outside the poetry, within religion and philosophy; that is to say, it could be created by other than poetic means: in prose, in music, or in a philosophic treatise. For "East Coker" is not merely an experience, it is also a statement. It succeeds in producing the sense of man's isolation in the midst of darkness, and his desire to achieve union with God. These phrases are meaningless, or, rather, are outworn, in themselves; but they are not meaningless in Eliot's poem: he has recreated the experience which they imply.

But what is the effect of poetry which uses poetry as a medium to recreate an experience which is outside the poetry itself? It is, that poetry is stepping out of a world of isolated poetic experiences and insisting on the significance of the kind of truth that poetry can describe in the real world, and, quite literally, in the contemporary situation.

> O dark dark dark. They all go into the
>   dark,
> The vacant interstellar spaces, the
>   vacant into the vacant,
> The captains, merchant bankers,
>   eminent men of letters.

In this passage the poetry seems to say, "This is poetic truth, but also it is literal truth, on which religion is based, existing in the world, which you cannot get away from." Throughout "East Coker" Eliot makes use of religious experience to insist on external and universal truths which have always existed and which exist like shining and rather terrible jewels in the somber contemporary setting which he can convey with greater ease than any other of the moderns.

So, to some extent, Eliot's poetry insists on its presence in the world of actuality. Yet although it invokes religion, and might even invoke politics, it is not a substitute for religion or a loudspeaker of a political party. No. What it insists on is the reality of the kind of truth which poetry can describe: the human situation. It is as though there might be a party of poets bearing not the slogans of politics and psycho-analysis, but the slogans of poetry:

"In His will is our peace"; "Ripeness is all"; and Rilke's "You must change your life." These can be insisted on as statements about reality, and they are also poetic statements. A time is coming when, without being a substitute for anything or propaganda of any cause, they might play their part in giving the world a sense of values.

*H. W. Häusermann. "'East Coker' by T. S. Eliot." English Studies 23, no. 4 (August 1941), 108–10.

[Review of "East Coker"]

"East Coker" is the last, so far, of a series of longer poems, beginning with *The Waste Land* (1922) and "The Hollow Men" (1925), and continuing with "Ash-Wednesday" (1930) and "Burnt Norton" (1935). All of these poems mark important stages in the progress of Eliot's thought and poetic style. Although widely separated in time, they cannot be interpreted individually. They must be considered as a whole which is correlated with what is most immutable and fundamental in the poet's life and character. To illustrate this integrity of Eliot's major poems it may be best to recall his own definition of the unity which underlies all Shakespeare's plays. "What is the whole man," he writes,

> is not simply his greatest or maturest achievement, but the whole pattern formed by the sequence of plays; so that we may say confidently that the full meaning of any one of his plays is not in itself alone, but in that play in the order in which it was written, in its relation to all of Shakespeare's other plays, earlier and later: we must know all of Shakespeare's work in order to know any of it. (*Selected Essays* 193)

In Eliot's view this integrity of a poet's work consists not only in the inevitable and often superficial likeness which may be observed among the various writings of any one author, but it is an essential condition of that work's greatness. For so he declares in his next sentence: "No other dramatist of the time approaches anywhere near to this perfection of pattern superficial and profound; but the measure in which dramatists and poets approximate to this unity in a lifetime's work, is one of the measures of major poetry and drama." I do not doubt that this conception of the unity of an important poet's work is fully relevant to Eliot himself.

If one reads some of the reviews of "East Coker" in the periodical press one cannot fail to notice two things. First, the reviewers' lack of comprehension for "the whole man," for the pattern of the poet's entire work. They recognize, of course, certain threads connecting this poem with earlier poems, but they do not venture to form a definite and clear idea about the meaning of these connections. Secondly, their struggle with obscure passages. One cannot help feeling the interest and the excitement of this struggle, for everyone who has read Eliot carefully and with pleasure will have experienced it. But I make no doubt that a good many of these obscurities are easily cleared up if one has grasped the main issues of the poet's religious and philosophical position. Eliot makes use of a highly personal system of symbols and allegories in order to give objective and universal stature to his deepest emotions and beliefs. Unless you are prepared to recognize and to accept the significance of the symbols and allegories, which, as G. W. Stonier remarks "appear at important junctures and are repeated" (*The New Statesman*, 14 September 1940) [see "Mr. Eliot's New Poem" in this volume, pp. 433–34], they will be "dumb notes" and the passages where they occur will be "inoperative."

Eliot's references were particularly recondite in *The Waste Land* and he had to add seven pages of Notes to elucidate them. Since then, his allusiveness has become more restrained, but there still remains enough of it to puzzle and to vex the common reader. Many of Eliot's literary and theological references are explained in his prose works, especially in his Elizabethan essays and in the papers on Lancelot Andrewes and John Bramhall. But it must be stated again that no amount of explanation of out-of-the-way allusions can give the whole meaning of a poem like "East Coker."

I do not intend, therefore, to comment upon this poem. I merely wish to quote a letter from Mr. Eliot, dated May 24, 1940, in which he explained to me some of the more difficult passages. He writes:

> The title is taken from a village in Somerset where my family lived for some two centuries. The first section contains some phrases in Tudor English taken from "The Governour" of Sir Thomas Elyot who was a grandson of Simon Elyot or Eliot of that village. The third section contains several lines adapted from "The Ascent of Mount Carmel." I think that the imagery of the first section (though taken from the village itself) may have been influenced by recollections of "Germelshausen," which I have not read for many years. I don't think that the poem needs or can give rise to further explanation than that.

Everyone who reads and enjoys "East Coker" will appreciate the interest of these explanations. I am deeply obliged to Mr. Eliot for his kindness in offering them.

The passage from *The Governour* is not difficult to trace, but it may be helpful to complete the other two references. The one is contained in the last twelve lines of the third section of "East Coker," and the reference is to *The Ascent of Mount Carmel* by St. John of the Cross (1542–1591), book 1, chapter xiii. The other refers to the story entitled *Germelshausen* by Friedrich Gerstärker. I am informed that Gerstärker's story is frequently used in American schools as a text book for beginners in German. The compelling beauty of this narrative may account for the lasting impression it made on the poet's mind if he read it, as we suppose he did, when he was a pupil at the Smith Academy in St. Louis.

There are, of course, various other references in "East Coker," but Eliot probably thought they did not require special elucidation, either because they are not so significant for the main import of the poem as those already mentioned, or because they refer to books, such as Dante or Tennyson, whose influence on him had already become apparent in his earlier works.

---

*J. P. Hogan. "Eliot's Later Verse." *Adelphi* 18 (January–March 1942), 54–58.

[Review of "The Dry Salvages"]

In the last war Wilfred Owen prefaced his poems with a disclaimer: "Above all this book is not concerned with Poetry. The subject of it is War, and the Pity of War.

The Poetry is in the Pity." In "East Coker" Eliot makes a similar disclaimer:

> That was a way of putting it—not
>   very satisfactory:
> A periphrastic study in a worn-out
>   poetical fashion,
> Leaving one still with the intolerable
>   wrestle
> With words and meanings. The poetry
>   does not matter.

Later in the poem we hear more of the "intolerable wrestle": [quotation of lines 3–7 of "East Coker" V].

Eliot has something to say; he is desperately anxious to say it clearly and precisely. This is the poetry of an honest man. But "the poetry does not matter." The poetry matters only to the poets who are not poets, who have nothing to say. [. . .]

This poem, like every great poem, tells us clearly what we already know vaguely and diffusely. Above all it demonstrates that genius in word and idiom does not make a poet. What counts first is an inner urgency, the having something to say; and what counts second is the genius to say it in the only words in which it can be said. But the second is dependent on the first; for in the saying is the intolerable wrestle; and you suffer the intolerable wrestle only if you have something to say; and you have something to say only if you are moved by an inner urgency. Eliot's work as a whole is a living testimony to this. With him the intolerable wrestle has been three-fold: with experience, which is the source of poetry; with the meaning of experience; and with the words necessary to utter that meaning.

But even that is too glib [. . .]. The knowledge derived from experience forms a pattern, or a varying series of patterns, which is philosophy. Philosophy falsifies. [. . .] Truth is a shifting sand, and what is true today may not be true tomorrow.

Poetry, being always quick and deriving direct from specific, concrete experience, and not from the knowledge derived from experience, is a prophylactic against hebetude. Poetry compels honesty, cannot lie. To be honest needs an intolerable struggle; and to be honest about your honesty, to make an ever-new beginning, "a raid on the inarticulate / With shabby equipment always deteriorating [. . .]" needs a second struggle.

But this poem is only secondarily (or thirdly or fourthly) a record of the struggle of creation in words. Primarily it is an act of creation. It is about experience; it is about the meaning of experience; about the meaninglessness of giving experience a fixed meaning; and about the struggle with words.

All of which sounds as though the thing were a nightmare of abstractions. On the contrary, it is clear, quick, humble and poignantly beautiful. No word jars, or merely skims precision, or it is redundant. Its wisdom is as concentrated as that of Lao-tzu. [. . .]

There are two planes of experience, two planes of suffering. There is the blind, dumb-ox suffering of the unaware; and the conscious suffering of those to whom the miseries of the unaware are misery and will not let them rest.

> Old stone to new building, old timber
>   to new fires,
> Old fire to ashes, and ashes to earth
> Which is already flesh, fur and faeces,
> Bone of man and beast, cornstalk and
>   leaf.

Eliot, the conscious man, the man moved by an inner urgency, writes not out of a subjective suffering but out of an objective awareness of suffering, of birth and copulation and death, of change and decay, of the ebb and flow of earth's givings and takings.

Then there is Time. You will remember "Prufrock":

Time for you and time for me,
And time yet for a hundred
indecisions,
And for a hundred visions and
revisions,
Before the taking of a toast and tea.

But now the note is deeper:

there is a time for building
And a time for living and for
generation
And a time for the wind to break the
loosened pane
And to shake the wainscot where the
field-mouse trots [. . .].

But the time for living and generation is not our time; ours is a time of waiting: "there is yet faith / But the faith and the love and the hope are all in the waiting."

It is hard to wait, hard not to hope for the wrong thing, hard not to love the wrong thing, hard to do nothing about anything, hard to be humble, and to wait, always to wait—even "without thought, for you are not ready for thought." But there is meaning in this; it is too insistent throughout the poem not to be the very kernel of Eliot's meaning: [quotation of lines 35–46 of "East Coker" III].

Experience, then, does not enable us to eliminate our ignorance, but to realize its extent. The acquiring of wisdom is the process of realizing, in ever-widening circles, the extent of our ignorance and of learning to be humble, of learning to wait. Is this the New Testament? Or the *Tao*? Or both?

The poem closes with a gleam of promise, a moment's pallid sunlight on a stormy day:

We must be still and still moving
Into another intensity

For a further union, a deeper
communion
Through the dark cold and the empty
desolation,
The wave cry, the wind cry, the vast
waters
Of the petrel and the porpoise. In my
end is my beginning.

In "The Dry Salvages," the theme of Time is continued. But first there is a breathing space. "The wave cry, the wind cry" evokes memory of the rocky coast of Massachusetts, the scene probably of Eliot's boyhood.

[. . .]

[P]ure poetry [. . .] describes, reveals, *things*. Adulterated poetry expresses subjective *ideas*. "The Dry Salvages" is full of *things*: a river, a stretch of rocky coast, a whistling buoy. It is so easy to spill ideas, so hard to tell people about things: a tree, [. . .] a whistling buoy. Tremendous humility is needed to do it—the humility of the novelist but more concentrated; for the novelist, with unlimited space and all the perils of prose, is apt to give you his *idea* of the rooms, houses, people, furniture he describes.

You are not the same people who left
that station
Or who will arrive at any terminus,
While *the narrowing rails slide
together behind you*;
And on the deck of the drumming liner
Watching *the furrow that widens
behind you*

The precision of observation in the lines italicized, that objective realization of *things*, is what Shakespeare achieved in songs like "When icicles hang by the wall," &c. We *see* the narrowing rails and the widening furrow as Herrick, for example, makes us feel Julia's silks and hear them swish as she moves.

But where Eliot's especial genius comes in is that he extends the finite, sensible quality of things into what was hitherto the domain of ideas. Time, the protagonist of these poems, becomes as objectively perceived, almost, one might say, as real and finite an entity as his brown river and whistling buoy.

[Quotation of lines 37–46 of "The Dry Salvages" I]

But once again "the poetry does not matter." What matters are the moments of happiness, "the sudden illumination," and the approach of its meaning. "Burnt Norton" opened with:

Time present and time past
Are both perhaps present in time
    future
And time future contained in time
    past.

The difficulties of the earlier poem are now clarified and resolved:

    It seems, as one becomes older,
That the past has another pattern, and
    ceases to be a mere sequence—
Or even development: the latter a
    partial fallacy
Encouraged by superficial notions of
    evolution,
Which becomes, in the popular mind,
    a means of disowning the past.

But the past cannot be disowned: "People change, and smile: but the agony abides. / Time the destroyer is time the preserver. [. . .]"

Nor does the future lie before us; what lies before us is the struggle to give meaning to the past:

We had the experience but missed the
    meaning,

And approach to the meaning restores
    the experience
In a different form, beyond any
    meaning
We can assign to happiness.

[. . .]

This is the poetry of silence and stillness and waiting and endless humility. To hear it read aloud is to feel as though one were listening to a silence, as sometimes one listens to a silence in Beethoven. But the dark cold and the empty desolation are terrifying; one could wish one had been born into a time of living and generation. Indeed, so far as one is able, one hangs on to that world, that other time, that warmth of living and contact and togetherness and humanity.

One hangs on to it, I say, as far as one is able. But we cannot have it both ways. If this poetry speaks to our condition, if Eliot's is the adult voice of our generation, if his words, his meaning, so painfully brought forth, represent the highest we know, then we must accept what he says, we must abide by it and face what it implies.

His may be the saddest poetry ever written, but it is not egoistic or inhuman or didactic. He speaks disinterestedly and objectively. Rarely does the first person singular occur; and when it does it is depersonalized, remote, as though Eliot had given himself a power of attorney to speak on his own behalf. It is remote, not intimate, not autobiographical nor autopsychographical. He speaks as a man who has transcended the limitations of the ego, who has denuded himself of personality.

Personality is the disease of our time. Personality is what Churchill has, what the commercial traveler has, what every comic-cuts of a policeman, parson or postman has. Personality is the condition of the unhumble vacant; one is reminded of

442

Thackeray or one of the Georges: "You take off one waistcoat and find another underneath. You take off that and find a third. And when you have taken off all the waistcoats you find—nothing." We are the hollow men—with a sugary coating of personality. [. . .]

Eliot, by example, gives a final quietus to "self-expression." Of course it will go on, that noisy habit; but it will be a survival, as redundant as Wilde and the Nineties. We learn from Eliot that it is better to be silent than to say nothing.

[. . .]

In Eliot's later work we pass beyond the world of ideas and ideals, of abstractions and absolutes, and enter the green kingdom within where no evil is done as a means to good, where there is no clamor of righteousness in protest against evil. Here one suffers consciously, not blindly, and asks for no insurance policy, no endowment of happiness in return for a premium of anguish.

But the kingdom within is not fenced off, is not proof against the assaults of time and experience, confusion and coincidence, events and interludes and waste. Here is no permanent pattern wrested from disorder; one does not digest only tabloids of spiritual essences; here, just as elsewhere, there is the roughage and the unassimilable. The kingdom within is not a monastic seclusion; for the deeper you penetrate your within-ness the more you are in, though not necessarily of, the outer tumult. [. . .] *Every moment*, mark you. In the kingdom within, where we are liberated from the folly of action and competing and contending, there is no stasis but a new and different and terrible experiencing. This, this above all, is the condition of "a further union, a deeper communion." There is no short cut.

*Muriel Bradbrook. "The Lyric and Dramatic in the Latest Verse of T. S. Eliot." *Theology* 44 (February 1942), 81–90.

[Review of "The Dry Salvages"]

All Eliot's latest verse treats of an antinomy of Time and Eternity. The flash of insight is familiar in many poets—Shakespeare, Wordsworth, Blake, Yeats—perhaps isolated in its own felt intuitive value. With his view that the work of the poet is to "connect," and form new wholes from, disparate experiences, Eliot relates this supreme private moment with the Christian doctrine of Eternity, springing from the fact of the Resurrection and embodied in the Sacrament of the Eucharist. The result is no theory of time, in the philosophical sense, but a series of value judgments. Time theories in modern science and philosophy are no more destructive of the doctrine of Eternity than Copernicus's cosmology was of the Christian interpretation of the universe; for miracles of illumination, if not universal, are yet so general that, if they were delusions, the nature and reason of the delusion would still require explanation.

The personal quality of the experience is preserved by Eliot in that all his later poems are dramatic in form: "Ash-Wednesday" was also written in the first person, but the experience was not projected in so dramatic a fashion. "Coriolan" and "Marina" are typical of his new method, in their vividness—partly dependent, of course, on the Shakespearean reference—and their contrasting varieties

443

of satire and introspection: the one gives a picture of power politics which perhaps seemed exaggerated when it was written but is now generally accepted; the key to the other is given by its motto, "*Quis hic locus, quae regio, quae mundi plaga?*," taken from Seneca's *Hercules Furens*, at that moment when the hero emerges from hell into the light of day. The setting of the granite foggy shore with its islands is taken from Eliot's own childhood; it appears also at the end of "Ash-Wednesday" and in "The Dry Salvages." If "Ash-Wednesday" is Eliot's *Purgatorio*, "Marina" is his *Paradiso*, a glimpse of beatitude in which the moral world of sensuous beauty falls away. "By this grace dissolved in place," and in its place comes a vision:

> What is this face, less clear and
>   clearer
> The pulse in the arm, less strong and
>   stronger—
> Given or lent? more distant than stars
>   and nearer than the eye.

Marina, she who was lost and is found again, is here identified with a very personal recollection, which is also to reappear later. "Whispers and small laughter between leaves and hurrying feet / Under sleep, where all the waters meet."

The power of the poem lies in its rhythm, which combines a choric repetition, bolder than the chiming echoes of "Ash-Wednesday" and looking forward to that of the plays, with a delicate, hesitant movement, depicting the wonder of the recognition, at the moment when the beatific vision reveals itself as something also known and familiar.

[. . .]

In *Murder in the Cathedral* and the new sequence, Eliot is attempting to picture the vision of Eternity with its results in Time; miracles of Incarnation. In the play he uses the mediaeval setting because it helps his purpose, since the mediaeval categories of thought and organization are those he finds most suitable; yet the Tempters, and the Knights, who are the Tempters' embodiments, are rightly played as modern figures. The play demonstrates "The critical moment / That is always now and here. Even now, in sordid particulars / The eternal design may appear." In "East Coker," the Elizabethan forebears of Mr. Eliot are "faded out" into the Second World War. In "Burnt Norton," the "moment in the rose garden," in "The Dry Salvages," the "fog in the fir tree," stand for "the point of the intersection of the timeless with time," the study of which is "an occupation for the saint" and the saint alone; in Thomas such a saint is depicted. The words of the Women of Canterbury were not only the comment on the foreordained assassination, they were the most adequate poetic statement of the feeling of foreboding that culminated in Munich, and its conscious shame:

> We do not wish anything to happen.
> Seven years we have lived quietly,
> Succeeded in avoiding notice,
> Living and partly living.
> [. . . . .]
> But now a great fear is upon us, a fear
>   not of one but of many.

[. . .]

In "The Dry Salvages," the Massachusetts coast of Eliot's childhood fuses with his present sense of the Battle of the Atlantic, and both with their religious context. The abrupt colloquialisms in a poetic setting, the sudden switches of rhythm are the "objective correlatives," the vehicle of this fusion:

> Pray for all those who are in ships,
>   those
> Whose business has to do with fish,
>   and

Those concerned in every lawful traffic
And those who conduct them.

[. . .]

The prayer to the Virgin, the penultimate section of "The Dry Salvages," is, like the lament for the drowned Phoenician sailor in *The Waste Land*, the symbolic center of the poem. It is immediately followed by a loose-flowing satiric section denouncing that old enemy of Eliot, the Fortune Teller, dealer in past and future. The conclusion introduces a new rhythm, heavy yet unemphatic, with a triple-stressed line, a prosaic but not colloquial vocabulary, considerable repetition and reiteration. The whole gives an effect of steady, even power, of a massively representative utterance:

For most of us, this is the aim
Never here to be realised;
Who are only undefeated
Because we have gone on trying [. . .].

Compared with "Ash-Wednesday," *Murder in the Cathedral* and the new sequence have both a new variety and a new monotony. Phrases are repeated from poem to poem; experiences which are recognizably related if not the same reappear in different contexts.

[. . .]

Monotony is inevitable in the attempt constantly to evaluate the experiences of time by the experience of eternity. Herein Eliot's preoccupation with time differs from that of [Wyndham] Lewis, and also of Proust and Joyce—though not from Yeats; moreover, the experience of eternity is acknowledged ineffable in terms of time: "I can only say, *there* we have been: but I cannot say where. / And I cannot say, how long, for that is to place it in time." The *via negativa* of purgation, detachment, and illumination is either understood or not understood. The reader at this point either grasps what Eliot is saying or does not; no half-understanding is possible.

[. . .]

Yet with this uncompromising renunciation Eliot achieves a new flexibility and freedom. *Cantat vacuus*. The image of what things felt like at the beginning of the war ("As in a theatre the lights are extinguished for the scene to be changed . . ."), the personal reflections on poetry in "East Coker" II and V, the satiric yet agonized pictures of the general situation ("O dark dark dark . . .," "The wounded surgeon plies the steel"), establish a connection between past and future, between different modes of being in an evaluative sense, which is the main purpose of this later verse. The poems are a whole, yet they combine epigrammatic lines (e.g., "the general mess of imprecision of feeling") with a readiness in the two satiric sections mentioned to draw equally upon *Samson Agonistes* and Mr. Auden. Eliot has regained his old coordinating power, ordered from a new point of view.

The whole development shows itself in changes in the nature of the poetic "I." Dramatic monologue is an early form with Eliot—e.g., "Prufrock," "Portrait of a Lady," "Gerontion." All of these are impressionistic, dependent on the "coloring" of a particular and limited point of view, which is at the same time subjected to self-satire and self-criticism. The degree of projection for the writer and the reader is a ticklish question [. . .] and the satire does not check but reinforce it, being the most "sympathetic" part. [. . .] The main emotional effect is in the nature of a byproduct ("not a turning loose of emotion but an escape from emotion").

In *The Waste Land* the "negative emotions" are stronger: tedium, accidia, and the frozen pity born of foreknowledge and impotence to avert calamity ("And I, Tiresias, have foresuffered all"). Often the "I" seems indeterminate, but nearer to a personal "I" than to Tiresias [. . .].

445

In "The Hollow Men" the "I" becomes "we," for in the sheer pain of that experience any sense of personality has lapsed; the opening section announces it. The "we" is an indeterminate suffering consciousness, not people. "Ash-Wednesday" is written from a collective personality; the "I" is clear, not as a person, but as a will, and parts of the poem are addresses or prayers. The rhythm, a sure index, is less nerveless, and has a taut power. In the later dramatic monologues the "I" is almost neutral: the old man, the spectator, the stony public figure, no longer tormented by self-satire or insecurity, but by exhaustion and weariness of the flesh. No longer is the tempter the satiric Mephistopheles, debunking all impulses in terms of their origins, but the vehicle of a *Weltschmertz*.

[. . .]

Murder in the Cathedral has only two voices—that of Thomas and that of the Women of Canterbury. The Knights, Tempters, and Priests are significant only in relation to the others. And the Chorus and Thomas perhaps only represent the two voices of Everyman: human frailty conscious of its failure, and human frailty conscious of its power. The theme is the old one: renunciation, purgation, perfection of the will, the *via negativa*. This is the whole duty of man. Thomas must not even crave the glory of being a martyr: "The last temptation is the greatest treason: / To do the right deed for the wrong reason." Illumination, grace, the "wink of bliss," can only so be obtained; to hope to obtain it is to be defeated at the outset.

[. . .]

In the new sequence, the satire which was still perceptible in *Murder in the Cathedral* has almost completely faded; the world, in so far as it enters, is mortal, temporal and therefore incomplete, but neither hostile nor malignant. There is more stability and a new refreshment not only in "the moment in the rose garden," but in the ordinary beauty of the Somerset village, the Massachusetts coast. The "I" is occasionally discursive, commentary, annotative ("East Coker," II, V; "The Dry Salvages," II); sometimes altogether absent, as in the beautiful sestinas of "The Dry Salvages": "Where is there an end of it, the soundless wailing, / The silent withering of autumn flowers . . .?" Now Eliot has written for himself a body of work upon which he can draw, and if there is danger in the repetition of his own themes, the present difficulties of any writer justify the risk, even were it not inevitable in his material.

[. . .]

In an age when traditions are so broken, the poet quickly makes his own tradition, which, if he is only a minor poet, amounts to a few tricks and mannerisms upon which he ever after plays variations; men of thirty today are as helplessly living on their own past work as Wordsworth was at eighty. Eliot's work shows that power to change, and yet to incorporate the work which has been done, which marks a true writer; each separate work fits into the pattern of the whole *œuvre*. The whole is greater than the parts. Eliot, like Herbert, demands to be read extensively.

F. R. Leavis. "Eliot's Later Poetry." Scrutiny 11 (Summer 1942), 60–71.

[Review of "The Dry Salvages"]

"The Dry Salvages" ("pronounced to rhyme with *assuages*") is the third member to appear of a sequence that began with "Burnt Norton," continued with "East Coker," and, one gathers, is to be completed in a fourth poem. Each member is a poem in itself, as the separate publication intimates, but it is plain now, with three of the four to hand, that the sequence is to be a real whole; a total context which each constituent poem needs for its full significance. Now too, with this new poem before him, the literary critic finds himself once more turning over the principle that poetry is to be judged as poetry—turning it over and wondering what it is worth and how far it will take him. May there perhaps be a point at which literary criticism [. . .] finds itself confronting the challenge to leave itself behind and become another thing? Is, in any case, the field of literary criticism so delimitable as to exempt him from the theological equipment he can lay no claim to?

In overcoming this last uneasiness he will have found encouragement in the performances of commentators who have not needed to share it: it will have been so clear that their advantage has not been altogether an advantage, but has tended to disqualify them for appreciating the nature of the poet's genius. They are apt to show too great an alacrity in response; to defeat his essential method by jumping in too easily and too happily with familiar terms and concepts. [. . .] In the poetry [. . .] there is no pretense that the sensibility is not Christian; but it is not for nothing that D. W. Harding described "Burnt Norton," which doesn't stand apart from the body of Eliot's religious verse, as being concerned with the "creation of concepts." [See Harding's review of *Collected Poems 1909–1935*, reprinted in this volume pp. 370–73.] The poet's magnificent intelligence is devoted to keeping as close as possible to the concrete of sensation, emotion and perception. Though this poetry is plainly metaphysical in preoccupation, it is as much poetry, it belongs as purely to the realm of sensibility, and has in it as little of the abstract and general of discursive prose, as any poetry that was ever written. Familiar terms and concepts are inevitably in sight, but what is distinctive about the poet's method is the subtle and resourceful discipline of continence with which, in its exploration of experience, it approaches them. [. . .]

The poetry from "Ash-Wednesday" onwards doesn't say, "I believe," or "I know," or "Here is the truth"; it is positive in direction but not positive in that way [. . .]. It is a searching of experience, a spiritual discipline, a technique for sincerity—for giving "sincerity" a meaning. The preoccupation is with establishing from among the illusions, evanescences and unrealities of life in time an apprehension of an assured reality—a reality that, though necessarily apprehended in time, is not of it. There is a sustained positive effort—the constructive effort to be "conscious":

> Time past and time future
> Allow but a little consciousness.
> To be conscious is not to be in time
> But only in time can the moment in
> the rose-garden,
> The moment in the arbour where the
> rain beat,
> The moment in the draughty church at
> smokefall
> Be remembered; involved with past
> and future.
> Only through time time is conquered.

With these "moments" is associated "the sudden illumination":

> The moments of happiness—not the
> sense of well-being,
> Fruition, fulfilment, security or
> affection,
> Or even a very good dinner, but the
> sudden illumination—
> [. . .]

"Illumination," it will be seen, is no simple matter, and "Ash-Wednesday," where the religious bent has so pronounced a liturgical expression, is remarkable for the insistent and subtle scrupulousness of the concern manifested to guard against the possibilities of temptation, self-deception and confusion that attend on the aim and the method.

[. . .]

"Burnt Norton," the first poem of the sequence to which "The Dry Salvages" belongs, has the effect of being in a special sense a "new start." It is as if the poet were conducting a radical inquiry into the nature and methods of his exploration. The poem is as purely and essentially a poem as anything else of Mr. Eliot's; but it seems to me to be the equivalent in poetry of a philosophical work—to do by strictly poetical means the business of an epistemological and metaphysical inquiry. Of course, in this given case examination of the instruments is necessarily at the same time a use of them in the poet's characteristic kind of exploration. Yet to convey the distinctive character of this poem the stress must fall as I have suggested. Harding, in the illuminating commentary referred to above, registers this character in his own way when he speaks of the poem as being concerned with the "creation of concepts."

The kind of expository generality that distinguished "Burnt Norton" is well illustrated by the opening:

Time present and time past
Are both perhaps present in time
    future
And time future contained in time
    past.
If all time is eternally present
All time is unredeemable.
What might have been is an
    abstraction

Remaining a perpetual possibility
Only in a world of speculation.
What might have been and what has
    been
Point to one end, which is always
    present.
Footfalls echo in the memory
Down the passage which we did not
    take
Towards the door we never opened
Into the rose-garden. My words echo
Thus, in your mind.

The general propositions of the first ten lines have, by the time we have read the rest of the passage, become clearly part of a *procédé* and a total effect that belong to poetry, and not to the order of abstraction of discursive prose. The particular memory evoked is not an illustration of the general propositions; these, rather, represent a pondering, with results in generalized significance, of the memory, the "illuminative" quality of which, along with the unseizableness—

            the sudden illumination—
We had the experience but missed the
    meaning,
And approach to the meaning restores
    the experience
In a different form

—is marvelously conveyed. The unseizableness—the specific indeterminate status of the experience and the elusiveness of the meaning—we can see being defined, or created, in the paradoxical

Footfalls echo in the memory
Down the passage which we did not
    take
Towards the door we never opened
Into the rose-garden.

"Footfalls echo" is a fact, and "memory" becomes the "passage" which, though we did not take it, is thus itself a present fact.

448

The complex effect of a de-realizing of the routine commonsense world together with the evoking of a reality that lies hidden among the unrealities into which life in time, closely questioned, paradoxes itself is clinched by the sudden shift: "My words echo / Thus, in your mind." The "not" and "never" of the preceding sentence are "thus" (finely placed word) in a way countered. To convey the status of what is apprehended, what stands, in this searching of experience, takes both "is" and "is not." The effect is completed by the disjoined next sentence—

But to what purpose
Disturbing the dust on a bowl of
    rose-leaves
I do not know

—which, in its sudden drop to another plane, to a distancing comment, brings out by contrast the immediacy of what goes before, while at the same time contributing directly to the sensuous presentness of the whole—the words that echo "thus" disturb, in front of us, "the dust on a bowl of rose-leaves" ("dust" and "rose-leaves" together evoke one of those co-presences of opposing associations which seem to replace words by immediate sensation, and the whole sentence, of course, relates back with various subtleties of significance to the "rose-garden" and "time" of the opening paragraph).

The re-creation of, or by, "echoes"— "Other echoes / Inhabit the garden"— [. . .] the restoring "approach to the meaning," continues in a sustained way in the remainder of the section, concluding with [. . .] "Go, go, go, said the bird: human kind / Cannot bear very much reality." Regarding this reality we read in the next section:

Yet the enchainment of past and future
Woven in the weakness of the
    changing body,

Protects mankind from heaven and
    damnation
Which flesh cannot endure.

The reality is sought because, by providing an absolute reference, it is to confront the spirit with the necessity of supreme decisions, ultimate choices, and so give a meaning to life [. . .].

"Burnt Norton" develops the specifically religious note no further than the passages quoted above suggest. What is characteristic of the poem is the sustained and marvelously resourceful preoccupation that Harding examines; the preoccupation with re-creating the concept of "eternity."

"East Coker" is at the other extreme from "Burnt Norton": it is personal, running even to autobiography (it is the most directly personal poem of Eliot's we have), and historical. We find ourselves (rightly or wrongly) relating its prevailing mood to Munich and the valedictory editorial of *The Criterion*. With a passing resurgence of the "echoes," those reminders of the possibility of "consciousness"—

Whisper of running streams, and
    winter lightning.
The wild thyme unseen and the wild
    strawberry,
The laughter in the garden, echoed
    ecstasy
Not lost, but requiring, pointing to the
    agony
Of death and birth.

—it is written from "the waste sad time" of the concluding two lines of "Burnt Norton": "Ridiculous the waste sad time / Stretching before and after." It is a discipline of meditation the note of which is

I said to my soul, be still, and wait
    without hope

For hope would be hope for the wrong
        thing; wait without love
For love would be love of the wrong
        thing; there is yet faith
But the faith and the love and the
        hope are all in the waiting.

One section (IV) is a formal and traditional religious poem. The opening section, developing a note of family history,
evokes historical time and change and the
decay of the old organic culture. The last,
starting with a passage of direct autobiography, develops the accompanying reflections and concludes with an inversion, "In
my end is my beginning," of the opening
phrase of the whole poem.

"The Dry Salvages" hasn't the personal and historical qualities of "East
Coker"; nor has it the abstract generality (for, in spite of the easy way in
which we commonly oppose it to "concrete," "abstract" seems the right word)
of "Burnt Norton." In its prevailing mode
it lies between the other two poems. It
is concerned mainly, not with the "creation of concepts," but with dissolving the
habit-created "reality" of routine experience and common sense, with their protective (and constructive) anesthesias. The
genius of the poet strikes us afresh in the
opening section as, subtly and inevitably,
the symbolic significance of the "river"—
"reminder / Of what men choose to forget," and of the sea—"The river is within
us, the sea is all about us," emerge and
are developed. The mind is made to feel
how precariously it resists a lapsing away
into the flux of the unknown and alien
within; our environment of familiarities
and certainties dissolves into a daunting
indeterminateness of shifting perspectives
and recessions. Human experience seems
meaningless and vain in its relativity. Our
sense and notion of time are unsettled into
convicted arbitrariness and vanity by the

evocation of times other than human and
historical:

        time not our time, rung by the
                unhurried
Ground swell, a time
Older than the time of chronometers,
        older
Than time counted by anxious
        worried women
Lying awake, calculating the future.

The subtlety of resource with which the
sapping and unsettling are effected is
complementary to the constructive subtlety analyzed by Harding in "Burnt
Norton."

The day-to-day actuality of life in time,
when we are restored to it in the second section, the inertia of human continu-
ance, presents itself in its most desolating
aspect as "Tomorrow and tomorrow and
tomorrow"—"There is no end, but addition: the trailing / Consequence of further
days and hours." It is against this background that we have the reminder of the
"moments of happiness ... the sudden illumination" that promise a release from the
no-meaning of time:

                I have said before
That the past experience revived in the
        meaning
Is not the experience of one life only
But of many generations

There follow, in the close of the section, new subtleties in the symbolic use of
the "river" and the "sea." The third section develops the paradoxes of time and
change, and the fourth is a formally Christian invocation. It is in the last section
that there comes the culminating move to
which the varied process of constructive
exploration with its accompaniments of
negation and rejection, its indirections and
strategic envelopment, has been leading
up. The passage has behind it—is meant

to be read with a full sense of its having behind it—what has gone before in the complex whole that begins with "Burnt Norton" (to take that as the relevant "new start"). It is introduced immediately by a final preparatory negative, an admirably and characteristically dry dismissal of the usual traffic in the "supernormal":

To explore the womb, or tomb, or
    dreams; all these are usual
Pastimes and drugs, and features of
    the press:
And always will be
[. . . . .]
                    But to apprehend
The point of intersection of the
    timeless
With time, is an occupation for the
    saint—
[. . . . .]
For most of us, there is only the
    unattended
Moment, the moment in and out of
    time,
The distraction fit, lost in a shaft of
    sunlight,
The wild thyme unseen, or the winter
    lightning
Or the waterfall, or music heard so
    deeply
That it is not heard at all, but you are
    the music
While the music lasts. These are only
    hints and guesses,
Hints followed by guesses; and the
    rest
Is prayer, observance, discipline,
    thought and action.
The hint half guessed, the gift half
    understood, is Incarnation.
Here the impossible union
Of spheres of existence is actual.

For the reader who comes charged with doctrine and acceptance, the term "Incarnation" thus introduced will tend to have a greater potency than for another. But in that, as I have suggested at the beginning of this review, he will not, for the appreciation of the poetry and of the genius of the poet, be altogether at an advantage. This poetry, in its "recreation of concepts," is at the same time, and inseparably, preoccupied with the nature of acceptance and belief: one might, in fact, say, adapting Harding, that to take the place of the words "acceptance"and "belief" is its essential aim.

The hint half guessed, the gift half
    understood, is Incarnation.
Here the impossible union
Of spheres of existence is actual

—these are, no doubt, statements, to be taken as such; but though they imply a theological context, their actual context is the poem. It would be absurd to contend that the passage is not an invitation to a relating of two contexts, but nothing is gained from the point of view of either poetry or religion by an abandonment of one context for the other, or by any approach that refuses or ignores or relaxes the peculiar discipline that the poetry is. And the critic can hardly insist too much that this affirmation which seems to strain forward out of the poem must, by the reader of the poem, be referred back to what has gone before. [. . .]

That the poetry seems to invite a given intellectual and doctrinal frame may be found to recommend it. But the frame is another thing (and the prose is not the poetry—Eliot himself has made some relevant observations). The genius, that of a great poetry, manifests itself in a profound and acute apprehension of the difficulties of his age. Those difficulties are such that they certainly cannot be met by any simple re-imposition of traditional frames. Eliot is known as professing Anglo-Catholicism and classicism; but his

451

poetry is remarkable for the extraordinary resource, penetration and stamina with which it makes its explorations into the concrete actualities of experience below the conceptual currency; into the life that must be the *raison d'être* of any frame—while there is life at all. With all its positive aspiration and movement, it is at the same time essentially a work of radical analysis and revision, endlessly insistent in its care not to confuse the frame with the living reality, and heroic in its refusal to accept. In any case, to feel an immense indebtedness to Eliot, and to recognize the immense indebtedness of the age, one doesn't need to share his intellectually formulated conclusions, his doctrinal views, or even to be uncritical of the attitudes of his poetry.

To have gone seriously into the poetry is to have had a quickening insight into the nature of thought and language; a discipline of intelligence and sensibility calculated to promote, if any could, real vitality and precision of thought; an education intellectual, emotional and moral. From such a study it would be impossible to come away with a crudely simplifying attitude towards the problems facing the modern world, or without an enhanced consciousness of the need both for continuity and for "new starts." As remarked above, Eliot's work is peculiarly relevant to the stresses of our time; and this remains true, in spite of the change of fashions that set in at the beginning of the last decade. His relative distinction and his title to respect and gratitude are certainly not less than they were a dozen years ago. To him, in fact, might be adapted the tribute that he once paid to that very different genius, D. H. Lawrence; he preeminently has stood for the spirit in these brutal and discouraging years. And it should by now be impossible to doubt that he is among the greatest poets of the English language.

*George Orwell. "Points of View. T. S. Eliot." *Poetry* 2, no. 7 (October–November 1942), 56–59.

[Review of "The Dry Salvages"]

There is very little in Eliot's later work that makes any deep impression on me. That is a confession of something lacking in myself, but it is not, as it may appear at first sight, a reason for simply shutting up and saying no more, since the change in my own reaction probably points to some external change which is worth investigating.

I know a respectable quantity of Eliot's earlier work by heart. I did not sit down and learn it, it simply stuck in my mind as any passage of verse is liable to do when it has really rung the bell. Sometimes after only one reading it is possible to remember the whole of a poem of, say, twenty or thirty lines, the act of memory being partly an act of reconstruction. But as for these three latest poems, I suppose I have read each of them two or three times since they were published, and how much do I verbally remember? "Time and the bell have buried the day," "At the still point of the turning world," "The vast waters of the petrel and the porpoise," and bits of the passage beginning "O dark dark dark. They all go into the dark." [. . .] That is about all that sticks in my head of its own accord. Now one cannot take this as proving that "Burnt Norton" and the rest are worse than the more memorable early poems, and one might even take it as proving the contrary, since it is arguable that that which lodges itself most easily in the mind is the obvious and even the vulgar. But it is clear that something has departed, some kind of current has been switched off, the later verse does not *contain* the earlier, even if it is claimed as an improvement upon it. I think one is justified in explaining this by a deterioration in Mr. Eliot's subject matter.

[. . .]

What are these three poems, "Burnt Norton" and the rest, "about"? It is not so easy to say what they are about, but what they appear on the surface to be about is certain localities in England and America with which Mr. Eliot has ancestral connections. Mixed up with this is a rather gloomy musing upon the nature and purpose of life, with [a] rather indefinite conclusion [. . .]. Life has a "meaning," but it is not a meaning one feels inclined to grow lyrical about; there is faith, but not much hope, and certainly no enthusiasm. Now the subject matter of Mr. Eliot's early poems was very different from this. They were not hopeful, but neither were they depressed or depressing. If one wants to deal in antitheses, one might say that the later poems express a melancholy faith and the earlier ones a glowing despair. They were based on the dilemma of modern man, who despairs of life and does not want to be dead, and on top of this they expressed the horror of an over-civilized intellectual confronted with the ugliness and spiritual emptiness of the machine age. Instead of "not too far from the yew-tree" the keynote was "weeping, weeping multitudes," or perhaps "the broken fingernails of dirty hands." Naturally these poems were denounced as "decadent" when they first appeared, the attacks only being called off when it was perceived that Eliot's political and social tendencies were reactionary. There was, however, a sense in which the charge of "decadence" could be justified. Clearly these poems were an end-product, the last gasp of a cultural tradition, poems which spoke only for the cultivated third-generation *rentier*, for people able to feel and criticize but no longer able to act. E. M. Forster praised *Prufrock* on its first appearance because "it sang of people who were ineffectual and weak" and because it was "innocent of public spirit" (this was during the other war, when public spirit was a good deal more rampant than it is now). The qualities by which any society which is to last longer than a generation actually has to be sustained—industry, courage, patriotism, frugality, philoprogenitiveness—obviously could not find any place in Eliot's early poems. There was only room for *rentier* values, the values of people too civilized to work, fight or even reproduce themselves. But that was the price that had to be paid, at any rate at that time, for writing a poem worth reading. The mood of lassitude, irony, disbelief, disgust, and not the sort of beefy enthusiasm demanded by the Squires and Herberts, was what sensitive people actually felt. It is fashionable to say that in verse only the words count and the "meaning" is irrelevant, but in fact every poem contains a prose-meaning, and when the poem is any good it is a meaning which the poet urgently wishes to express. All art is to some extent propaganda. "Prufrock" is an expression of futility, but it is also a poem of wonderful vitality and power, culminating in a sort of rocket-burst in the closing stanza:

We have lingered in the chambers of
    the sea
By sea-girls wreathed with seaweed
    red and brown

453

Till human voices wake us, and we
drown.

There is nothing like that in the later poems, although the *rentier* despair on which these lines are founded has been consciously dropped.

But the trouble is that conscious futility is something only for the young. One cannot go on "despairing of life" into a ripe old age. One cannot go on and on being "decadent," since decadence means falling and one can only be said to be falling if one is going to reach the bottom reasonably soon. Sooner or later one is obliged to adopt a positive attitude towards life and society. It would be putting it too crudely to say that every poet in our time must either die young, enter the Catholic Church, or join the Communist Party, but in fact the escape from the consciousness of futility is along those general lines. There are other deaths besides physical death, and there are other sects and creeds besides the Catholic Church and the Communist Party, but it remains true that after a certain age one must either stop writing or dedicate oneself to some purpose not wholly aesthetic. [. . .] Eliot's escape from individualism was into the Church, the Anglican Church as it happened. One ought not to assume that the gloomy Pétainism to which he now appears to have given himself over was the unavoidable result of his conversion. The Anglo-Catholic movement does not impose any political "line" on its followers, and a reactionary or austro-fascist tendency has always been apparent in his work, especially his prose writings. In theory it is still possible to be an orthodox religious believer without being intellectually crippled in the process, but it is far from easy, and in practice books by orthodox believers usually show the same cramped, blinkered outlook as books by orthodox Stalinists or others who are mentally unfree. The reason is that the Christian churches still demand assent to doctrines which no one seriously believes in. The most obvious case is the immortality of the soul. The various "proofs" of personal immortality which can be advanced by Christian apologists are psychologically of no importance; what matters, psychologically, is that hardly anyone nowadays *feels* himself to be immortal. The next world may be in some sense "believed in" but it has not anywhere near the same actuality in people's minds as it had a few centuries ago. Compare for instance the gloomy mumblings of these three poems with "Jerusalem My Happy Home": the comparison is not altogether pointless. In the second case you have a man to whom the next world is as real as this one. [. . .] In the other case you have a man who does not really *feel* his faith, but merely assents to it for complex reasons. It does not in itself give him any fresh literary impulse. At a certain stage he feels the need for a "purpose," and he wants a "purpose" which is reactionary and not progressive; the immediately available refuge is the Church, which demands intellectual absurdities of its members; so his work becomes a continuous nibbling round those absurdities, an attempt to make them acceptable to himself. The Church has not now any living imagery, any new vocabulary to offer: "The rest / Is prayer, observance, discipline, thought and action." Perhaps what we need is prayer, observance, etc., but you do not make a line of poetry by stringing those words together. Mr. Eliot speaks also of "the intolerable wrestle / With words and meanings. The poetry does not matter." I do not know, but I should imagine that the struggle with meanings would have loomed smaller, and the poetry would have seemed to matter more, if he could have found his way to some creed which did not start off by forcing one to believe the incredible.

There is no saying whether Mr. Eliot's development could have been much other than it has been. All writers who are any good develop throughout life, and the general direction of their development is determined. It is absurd to attack Eliot, as some left-wing critics have done, for being a "reactionary" and to imagine that he might have used his gifts in the cause of democracy and Socialism. Obviously a skepticism about democracy and a disbelief in "progress" are an integral part of him; without them he could not have written a line of his works. But it is arguable that he would have done better to go much further in the direction implied in his famous "anglo-catholic and royalist" declaration. He could not have developed into a Socialist, but he might have developed into the last apologist of aristocracy.

Neither feudalism nor indeed Fascism is necessarily deadly to poets, though both are to prose writers. The thing that is really deadly to both is Conservatism of the half-hearted modern kind.

It is at least imaginable that if Eliot had followed wholeheartedly the anti-democratic, anti-perfectionist strain in himself he might have struck a new vein comparable to his earlier one. But the negative Pétainism which turns its eyes to the past, accepts defeat, writes off earthly happiness as impossible, mumbles about prayer and repentance and thinks it a spiritual advance to see life as "a pattern of living worms in the guts of the women of Canterbury"—that, surely, is the least hopeful road a poet could take.

*Kathleen Raine. "Points of View: Another Reading." *Poetry* 2, no. 7 (October–November 1942), 59–62.

[Response to George Orwell's long piece on *Four Quartets* in the same issue of *Poetry*. See this volume, pp. 452–55]

I

I have been asked to write on Mr. Eliot's three latest poems, because my point of view at once differs from that of Mr. Orwell, and expresses the point of view of many of my generation. I admire Mr. Orwell's article in certain limited respects. He avoids the more obvious pitfalls, in applying political, rational, non-poetic standards, to poetry. Mr. Orwell does not fall into the error that Communists usually make in such cases, of failing to see that a problem exists that is not stated in terms of dialectical materialism. My point is that Mr. Orwell has fallen into the error of which he accuses Mr. Eliot—that of pursuing a line of thought that has become a dead end; of accepting certain statements about the universe as final that are, like all knowledge, provisional.

Mr. Orwell does not misrepresent Mr. Eliot when he quotes him as saying that "the only people ever likely to reach an understanding of the universe are saints, the rest of us being reduced to 'hints and guesses.'" Nor is he wrong when he says that "so long as man regards himself as an individual, his attitude to death must be one of simple resentment." But one cannot accept Mr. Orwell's conclusions. Who, then, does understand the universe? About the individual resenting death, St. Paul himself could not have stated more concisely the point of the Christian attack on the self-loving ego. But man does not necessarily, as Mr. Orwell implies, think of himself first and foremost as an individual. Freud, in his concept of the *id*, the death-instincts, and indeed, the unconscious mind altogether suggests that many doors open out of that individual entity. James Joyce has drawn a picture of the mind of man, that has little of the individual contour about it. A world inside us presents a landscape as impersonal, vast, and beyond our reach and knowledge, as does that which opens on the other, the outer side of our senses. Picasso, too, has stripped the contours from the object and the individual, and presented us with an image of man liberated from himself, that gives life a scope that explodes like a balloon the individual pigmy, and his squeaking ghost.

Those two artists—and Mr. Eliot is a third—have been quicker in the uptake of the new sciences than those who, like Mr. Orwell, stand firmly by the values that were solid before Einstein; before biochemistry; before modern physics, genetics, psychology; [even before] Joyce, Picasso, and the Cubists tore down the old limits (drawn not by nature, but by habits of thought and language) and put up others that have made the world look very different. We live not only at the end of a decadent materialist age, but at the beginning of a new period—one in which the concern for humanity will be with values more than with facts. For the circumnavigation of the material sciences has been completed. There are no more Eldorados of science. In essence, we know what is in the material universe, as we know the continents and the islands of the earth. Science has long held,

for our imagination, that world of fantastic promise that wishful thinking will always substitute for true values. Some health and wealth science may indeed give, as South America yielded gold and potatoes. But it will not teach us values; and those must come, now as at any other period of civilization, from the human spirit.

Like Mr. Orwell, my point of view is limited. Perhaps I am overlooking more than I know in omitting to consider deeply Mr. Eliot's political importance—the sources and the implications of the Anglo-Catholic Royalist position, without which, Mr. Orwell perhaps rightly says, Mr. Eliot could not have written a line of his work. But whatever point I may be missing, Mr. Orwell misses another—that Mr. Eliot is a poet not a political pamphleteer. If poets are "the unacknowledged legislators of the world" it is by virtue of their poetry, and not of their legislation. Who now cares whether Dante was a Guelf or a Ghibelline? Or even whether Milton was a Royalist or a Cromwellian? Mr. Eliot has been a movement as well as a poet, and Mr. Orwell has seen the movement and missed the poetry—but it is not the movement that remains, but the poetry. Whoever wins the class or any other war will inherit Mr. Eliot's poetry, when his politics concern only the historian. Poetry is an approach to the world, as science and religion are, and a poet is something more than the total of his poems. A poem is not written in a day but in a lifetime. Mr. Orwell has stood still in the Waste Land, and he expects to find that Mr. Eliot is also still there. But the poet is saying something more, "mumbling about prayer and repentance" Mr. Orwell calls it. But what if Mr. Eliot is in advance of his juniors? Never, so far as I know, has the work of a poet been more clearly stated than in "East Coker." Indeed it is one of the main themes of the poem.

[Quotation of lines 18–21 of "East Coker" II]

and again

> So here I am, in the middle way,
> having had twenty years—
> Twenty years largely wasted, the years
> of *l'entre deux guerres*—
> Trying to learn to use words, and
> every attempt
> Is a wholly new start, and a different
> kind of failure
> Because one has only learnt to get the
> better of words
> For the thing one no longer has to say,
> or the way in which
> One is no longer disposed to say it.
> And so each venture
> Is a new beginning, a raid on the
> inarticulate.

Let every poet lay these words to heart. "A raid on the inarticulate" is the work of all poetry, and that work carries poets into strange places.

[Quotation of lines 37–41 of "East Coker" III]

The raid on the inarticulate means, of course, much more than the problem of language. Mr. Eliot's three new poems are concerned with the greatest issue of all—man's place in eternity. His discovery, or re-discovery, will be an influence, during the next poetic generation, as potent as was that of *The Waste Land* on the last.

II

"East Coker" is a stern and dark, but not a tragic poem. Its darkness is the darkness of Dante's hell, or purgatory, that implies the light and the love of paradise. An implicit acceptance of the inherent rightness of the laws that decree also death, darkness, and change, sustains the poem. It is written by a poet who believes that man is a spiritual being. No one who does not see what this means can see that assertions like these are positive: "The only wisdom we can hope to acquire / Is the wisdom of humility: humility is endless." [. . .]

There is Mr. Orwell's pagan hell of squeaking ghosts, too:

> O dark dark dark. They all go into the
> dark,
> The vacant interstellar spaces, the
> vacant into the vacant,
> The captains, merchant bankers,
> eminent men of letters

but for Mr. Eliot, that is a part of the divine plan, not the whole. Mr. Eliot is trying to rediscover that divine plan, "under conditions that seem unpropitious." For those poets who follow him, the conditions are less unpropitious—for they include Mr. Eliot's work.

"Burnt Norton" [. . .] is a less somber poem. Its theme is time. The poem is full of moving and beautiful images of the temporal world—the rose-garden, the pool, the leaves, children, birds, laughter.

[. . .]

[The] ever-present end is love. "Love is itself unmoving, / Only the cause and end of movement [. . .]." Of that love, "Burnt Norton" contains one of the most profound and wonderful descriptions ever written, beginning with [. . .]: "At the still point of the turning world. Neither flesh nor fleshless; / Neither from nor towards; at the still point, there the dance is."

The theme of "The Dry Salvages" is the greater part of life that is not ourselves. For "The river is within us, the sea is all about us." The sea and its rhythm measures "time not our time" and on that sea we are travelers.

[Quotation of lines 16–21 of "The Dry Salvages" V]

Mr. Eliot is not a saint nor a theologian, but a poet. Yet a poet at his best is a saint of his own medium, and performs a miracle in his work. These poems are revolutionary in a sense that transcends the mere use of words. They are a re-assessment of life. Mr. Orwell's evaluation reminds me of the comment that Coleridge made of some critics of Wordsworth who belittled him—I quote, as seems to be the general wartime habit, from memory—that the poet strode so far ahead of his critics, that he was diminished in their eyes by the distance between them.

Perhaps I have given the impression that Mr. Eliot is concerned with spiritual values that refer to another life and not to this one. But he writes of what is most human. I can only speak for myself, but I find that what Mr. Eliot writes about love is nearer the heart's mark than anything that Stephen Spender—to name one of the better poets who speak the language of my generation—has written on that theme. Yet no one, I think, regards Mr. Eliot as a poet of love primarily. [. . .] Mr. Eliot's consistent adherence to the highest values of Christianity, and the inheritance of civilization, shows a deeper respect for the ordinary man than any facile simplification that Mr. Orwell, the BBC, or the *Mass Observer* offer to a public that they at heart despise.

*Robert Speaight. "Little Gidding." *Tablet* 180 (19 December 1942), 302–03.

[Review of "Little Gidding"]

This is the fourth and last of Mr. Eliot's new series of poems, and its publication gives the reviewer an opportunity to assess with rather more certainty than has hitherto been possible the qualities of the poet's later work. There is a type of critic, lofty in brow and very small in sympathy, whose appreciation of Mr. Eliot stops short with *The Waste Land*. I cannot pretend to have much patience with this exclusiveness. Mr. Eliot's verse is not, I agree, of a uniform intensity and merit. No good poet's ever was. But it all proceeds from the same accuracy and integrity of vision which set upon "The Hollow Men," let us say, the unmistakable mark of permanence. Mr. Eliot refuses to falsify his own personality or to borrow the accents of other men. He will hesitate in a periphrasis rather than steal a short cut to the truth. He will perambulate around his subject rather than fail it by an impulsive approach. Above all, he is ever seeking, within the limits imposed by a severe sincerity of purpose, to do something new with words; to fit them in an original pattern to the shape of an original thought.

Judged by this test, the series of which "Little Gidding" is the last appears extraordinarily impressive. There are no other English poems quite like these. They come within the category of Christian verse, and here their mood and emphasis are unique. The intersection of Eternity and time; the necessary asceticism; the drawing onward through the Dark Night to the knowledge of the Divine Love; the certain, sober hope—these themes are all, within a varying framework of imagery and reference, interwoven with each other. Each poem is personal. Each is the utterance of a poet wrestling with the validity of words; doubting sometimes the instruments of his art, as he approaches the Truth that the tongue cannot utter, nor the heart conceive. The poet is not merely singing—he is saving his soul; and he is putting the salvation before the song. It is by these renunciations, when they are necessary, that the highest art is, paradoxically, achieved. For the poet, no less than other men, must lose his soul before he can find it.

"Little Gidding" is like its predecessors in shape. It has the movement and the divisions of a quartet. The free verse, written with a careful ear for assonance, alliteration, repetition, and interior rhyme, is varied by passages in rhymed and in unrhymed *terza rima*. The grand abstractions of Mr. Eliot's thought are clothed in the tissues of time and place. Readers of *John Inglesant* will remember Little Gidding as the home of Nicholas Ferrar and his Anglican community; as a place where "prayer has become valid." And from this *terra firma* of English earth in the seventeenth century, the poet ranges back to Juliana of Norwich with her refrain: "All shall be well and / All manner of thing shall be well," and to *The Cloud of Unknowing* with "the drawing of this Love and the voice of this Calling." The tragic figure of Charles I is the image of every man confronting his doom; the scaffold and the "illegible tombstone" are essentially one destination. The reflections of Mr. Eliot's maturity are perhaps echoed in part by the second figure in the poem. This is the dead master of words with whom the poet "trod the pavement in a dead patrol" during an air-raid, and who "faded on the blowing of the horn." A correspondent suggests Milton to me here, but I think the following lines rather recall the desperate epigrams of the later Yeats, struggling with an invincible vitality.

> the cold friction of expiring sense
> Without enchantment, offering no
>   promise
>   But bitter tastelessness of shadow
>   fruit
>   As body and soul begin to fall
>   asunder.

And then, appropriately enough, the shadow of Yeats is crossed by the shadow of Swift.

> the conscious impotence of rage
> At human folly, and the laceration
> Of laughter at what ceases to amuse.

The reception of Mr. Eliot's central meaning does not, however, depend on picking up this kind of clue. His purpose is clear. "The refining of fire by fire," and "the purification of the motive / In the ground of our beseeching"—this is the teaching of all the mystics; in particular, of St. John of the Cross, whom Mr. Eliot so clearly echoed in "East Coker." It is the burden of all the poet's later verse, expressed with an increasing beauty and precision. Many competent judges will assess this work by literary standards, but only those who are prepared to accept the fundamental doctrines of Christian asceticism at a moment when they have never been more unpopular, will receive the profound thought to which the poetry so rigorously conforms.

---

*L[uke] T[urner].
"Little Gidding."
Blackfriars 24 (February 1943), supplement, xii–xiv.

[Review of "Little Gidding"]

Reviewing the later poetry of T. S. Eliot before the publication of "Little Gidding," a distinguished critic wrote: "It should by now be impossible to doubt that he is among the greatest poets of the English language" [F. R. Leavis, "Eliot's Later Poetry," *Scrutiny* (1942), reprinted in this volume, pp. 446–52]. The new poem decisively supports that judgment. It shows the development of the new poetic phase upon which Mr. Eliot's work entered in the experimental period following "Ash-Wednesday." Shorter poems like "Marina," indeed, are among the loveliest and most satisfying pieces Mr. Eliot has written; but they stand alone, poetically: they do not offer resources capable of technical advance to the length of a major poem. "Burnt Norton" was regarded variously as the beginning of Mr. Eliot's decline and as the greatest poem he had made. In the light of subsequent publications, it seems clear that "Burnt Norton" was, in fact, a transitional piece, and that only now can it be placed; and if the judgment quoted above be accurate, "Burnt Norton" was an important moment in the history of English verse.

A sympathetic understanding of Mr. Eliot's poetry seems to demand an acceptance of two principles which he himself has often enunciated: that the poetry which was adequate for one moment and one set of circumstances can never be valid for any other; and that "for us, anything that can be said as well in prose can be said better in prose. And a great deal, in the way of meaning, belongs to prose rather than to poetry." Once it has been recognized that poetry does not seek to communicate prose meanings, the fact that Mr. Eliot is writing poetry, and striving for the new poetry in the new experience should render unnecessary repetition of the charge of obscurity, which had some relevance in the 'twenties, before the technique of his writing became generally known. Standards of criticism, if true, are objective; but they have to be applied, and applied in relation to the intention of the writer and the particular task he is attempting. And here, as in all his later poetry, Mr. Eliot is attempting something not only more difficult but more important than in his earlier work. *The Waste Land* is a very great poem, in which a range of experience is controlled and organized into poetic language of a pressure which has not often, if at all, been attained in English since the seventeenth century. Yet the problem of communication in "Ash-Wednesday" is a greater one, arising from the utter complexity of the Simplicity with which it is concerned. And since those poems were written, the problems of language have not grown less acute: the work has to be done again, "the intolerable wrestle with words and meanings" has to be undertaken each time a new poem is begun; and the sequence of poems from "Burnt Norton" to "Little Gidding" constitutes a truly noble effort to overcome the supreme difficulties of expressing, in a dying language and at a most unpropitious time, the relations of man with God. The difficulty is the measure of the achievement.

Like all Mr. Eliot's principal poems, "Little Gidding" is not simple, and engages the problem on more than one level. He has never been concerned with the mystery of time, simply; and certainly not in the way in which Proust was concerned with it: that problem is there, but as an aspect of a deeper problem: the relations of God and the world, of the significance of human grasp and endeavor in relation to the still point which is their constant, unifying center, yet also their apparent negation and the denial of their validity. In particular, there is the relation of language to the shifting of experience; and this, for the poet, raises questions which have to be overcome: mastered and not only stated. The whole of this sequence of poems has been concerned with these things; but "Little Gidding," which recalls "Burnt Norton" in technique and fulfills that poem on a higher level, is free from those detailed failures of language, and therefore of sensibility, which could not be overlooked in the two previous pieces.

Indeed, "Little Gidding" is a magnificent completion of a task that might have been thought beyond the powers of a community of poets; and since the death of Yeats (who lived and worked in a wholly different tradition) and the poetic death of Ezra Pound in the *Cantos*, Mr. Eliot has been without the support of any poet of stature comparable with his own. Yet here he adds to his already great achievement with a poem of a strength and generosity beside which all other contemporary verse seems "as straw."

---

*Edwin Muir.
"Little Gidding."
New Statesman 25
(20 February 1943), 128.

[Review of "Little Gidding"]

The theme which Mr. Eliot treats in this poem—as in the three poems preceding it—is very difficult to state except in the form in which he has stated it; the vocabulary we are accustomed to use about time lacks the fitting terms; they have either fallen out of use or not yet come into currency. These poems contain probably the most essential and intimate poetry that Mr. Eliot has written, yet to those who accept the modern conception of time, the conception of development or evolution, it may easily appear remote and tenuous. For it goes beyond the idea of development and concentrates its main attention neither on the past nor on the future, finding no ultimate meaning in the one or ultimate hope in the other. It is concerned with [. . .] that state of human experience which is existence, not change, a state without which our life would be meaningless to us, yet which is embodied in the texture of change, so that it appears as a contradiction only to be described by posing a sequence of contradictions. To ring changes on these, to speak of "the still point of the turning world," [. . .] may appear to some people merely a remote and abstruse game. But it is not only remote and abstruse; it is also intimate. Whether Mr. Eliot has been influenced in the form he has chosen for these poems by Beethoven's last quartets, as has often been said, I do not know, but they certainly resemble the quartets in this combination of remoteness and intimacy, a strange but harmonious combination. They are remote because they pass beyond time as we ordinarily conceive it, and intimate because they go to the hidden heart of human experience and touch "the still point where the dance is."

Their curious quality may be described in another way by saying that they are both very intimate and impersonal. The man who has experienced, questioned, inquired does not appear at all except as a deliberately dramatized figure seen like any other figure, a part of the machinery of the poem, as in the second section of "Little Gidding." [. . .]

Those who accept Mr. Eliot's conception of time and of life will be more profoundly moved by this poem than those who do not, though such assent is not required for an understanding and enjoyment of it. "Little Gidding" is in five movements. The first is introductory and sets the theme. The second is a sort of leavetaking, with a remote echo of *The Waste Land*; the versification in this section is superb. In the next movement Mr. Eliot reaches the resolution of the poem (and of all four poems). Beginning with a passage on the use of memory, which is

For liberation—not less of love but
expanding
Of love beyond desire, and so
liberation
From the future as well as the past

he goes on to assert that "All shall be
well, and / All manner of thing shall be
well," an affirmation caught up in the song
in the next section, which has much the
same resemblance to a simple lyric as the
alla danza tedesca movement in the B flat
major quartet has to a simple dance. The
fifth movement, like the third, is reflective,
playing for the last time with the paradox
of the timeless moment:

[Quotation of lines 11–12 and 19–20
of "Little Gidding" V]

And the end of all our exploring
Will be to arrive where we started
And know the place for the first time.

The mood of still intensity which runs
through the poem deepens towards the
end:

All manner of thing shall be well
When the tongues of flame are
in-folded
Into the crowned knot of fire
And the fire and the rose are one.

This poem, like its three predecessors,
is filled with statements which are both
statements of a paradox and statements
of the things in which Mr. Eliot believes.
Readers who go to the poems for their
poetry cannot be expected to accept all
that Mr. Eliot believes; but it will be hard
for them to question the accuracy and
force with which the paradox is stated, in
a sustained concentration of thought, feeling and imagination, or to doubt that these
four poems are the most original contribution to poetry that has been made in our
time.

*M[uriel] C[lara] Bradbrook. "Little Gidding." Theology 46 (March 1943), 58–62.

[Review of "Little Gidding"]

Whatever we inherit from the
fortunate
We have taken from the defeated
What they had to leave us—a symbol:
A symbol perfected in death.

[. . .]

"Little Gidding" is symbolic in this fundamental sense: not through complication
of overlaid meanings, but through a refinement of discipline issuing in consummation: "A condition of complete simplicity / (Costing not less than everything)."
Much of the material is familiar from earlier poems, but it is used in a new way.
Though this poem completes the series
beginning with "Burnt Norton," there is a
distinctive tone and accent, and a distinctive quality in the vocabulary. The note of
striving and seeking is replaced by certitude. At first, the verse strikes toneless and
cold compared with, e.g., the "wounded
surgeon" passage in "East Coker"; but on
re-reading the peculiar precision defining
with the particularity of a frost, the colorless clarity which is the last reward of
disciplined integrity, penetrates at a deeper
level—the level of "the terrible crystal," of
the final chorus of Milton's *Samson*.

The poem is in five sections: two contrasted visions, a meditative passage, an
apocalyptic lyric, and a conclusion.

The first twenty lines are prelude and
epitome: the dazzle of frosty mid-winter

noon is the paradox of the nadir, "suspended in time between pole and tropic," a midwinter spring, "but not in time's covenant." That strange consolation found only at the center of loss is here marvelously rendered in terms of the frosty blossoming of the hedges. And this experience is also the central experience of Christian life. Mr. Eliot has never concerned himself in his poetry with dogma, but with experience: not with the Truth, but the Way. He has invoked not the creed but the liturgy, not the theologian but the contemplative. And at Little Gidding, which emerges at the end of the journey, it was a way of life that was practiced. Here are no questions of intellectual concepts, but of a mode of living:

> You are not here to verify,
> Instruct yourself, or inform curiosity
> Or carry report. You are here to kneel
> Where prayer has been valid.

"I believe in the communion of saints" is dramatized, where the dead speak to the living, and there is the "intersection of the timeless moment." (It is an article of the Christian belief which must to the non-Christian appear not so much unacceptable as meaningless.) The poet stands here in the relation to the theologian that the love-poet does to the psychologist: he presents and defines an experience both highly personal—as to everyone there is a personal and unique apprehension given—and also genuinely representative. And whilst the religious apprehension is given directly, as experience, the relating and placing, the very highly organized integration, is a matter of the secular context, whether that be daily living or the language of philosophy.

For Eliot does on occasion use philosophy for poetic ends. Christianity is the main vehicle by which European thought has harnessed philosophy to work directly on the refinement of daily living. And it is in the work of great Christian writers, of Dante, Pascal, the company of seventeenth-century mystics and divines who are echoed so subtly throughout the poem, that the delicate art of interpretation is achieved—as Eliot says, not by indifference, not theoretically, but with the full incarnation of the Here and Now, the precision of sensitive life.

The second section gives in dead, echoing monotone the vision of London under fire. Death, suffering, the sense of emptiness and shock that follow a vast catastrophe are not directly invoked: they are *suggested* in terms of a rhythm heavy, yet somehow also serene:

> Ash on an old man's sleeve
> Is all the ash the burnt roses leave.
> Dust in the air suspended
> Marks the place where a story ended.

The strange stillness of bereavement hangs over these stanzas and over the suspended cadences of the dawn scene, where in the blitzed street the form of the "familiar compound ghost" drifts with the dawn wind, a poet came from purgatory to revisit a world not dissimilar: "After the dark dove with the flickering tongue / Had passed below the horizon of his homing." (These lines do not seem to me very happy. The conceit has too fabricated an air and its purpose in pointing forward to the fourth section is too obtrusive.)

The ghost states in words quite glacial in their precision the special sufferings reserved for poets in their age:

> First, the cold friction of expiring sense
> [. . . . .]
> And last, the rending pain of
>   re-enactment
> Of all that you have done, and been.

With a final word, recalling the particular dead master, Arnaut Daniel, whose phrases Eliot has used so often, he speaks of the suffering spirit as being restored by

463

"refining fire"; and so, like Hamlet's father, "faded on the blowing of the horn."

The third section relates these visions of the past and the present, Little Gidding and the blitz, prayer and the craft of verse. They are related through that detachment which alone perceives the pattern binding them. Eliot begins by defining detachment, as distinct from attachment and indifference. Memory is the servant of detachment, liberating the spirit through coordinating its experiences:

> not less of love but expanding
> Of love beyond desire, and so
> liberation
> From the future as well as the past.

(A significant variation upon the praise of detachment in "East Coker": "I said to my soul, be still, and wait without hope.")

So if history is seen detachedly, "history may be freedom." And though the past as it was embodied at Little Gidding cannot be revived, we inherit from both victors and vanquished in those wars. So, too, in turn, if we achieve detachment by the purification of the motive behind our petitions and prayers, we may transmit our best to others: [quotation of lines 47–50 of "Little Gidding" III]. The fourth section—two short rhyming verses—is the poem's focus. It is an apocalyptic vision in which the descent of the Spirit in tongues of flame is blazoned upon a field of fire which is at once burning London, the shirt of flame and deifying funeral pyre of a dying Herakles, and the purgatorial fire of Arnaut Daniel. The fire of agony is seen, as all see it in moments of insight, as Hopkins's nun saw it in "The Wreck of the Deutschland," as the flame of that Person to whom Love is appropriated as His title.

> Who then devised the torment? Love.
> Love is the unfamiliar Name
> Behind the hands that wove
> The intolerable shirt of flame

> Which human power cannot remove.
> We only live, only suspire
> Consumed by either fire or fire.

The ringing vowels, *a*'s and *i*'s, clang over the tolling *o*'s, both excite and bind the feeling which flows up from the complex images resolved in the symbol of fire. As a technical performance it is astonishing. But there is no sense of its being merely a technical performance: nor is "the incandescent terror" merely emotional. It is a triumph of a more elemental kind: all that is not sensuous is spiritual, and the sensuous is completely informed as the vehicle of the spiritual: "A condition of complete simplicity / (Costing not less than everything)."

The conclusion recalls old themes: it is a conclusion to the whole series. The seamless web, only perceived when it is completed; the pattern of words, of lives, of events in history—these have all been illustrated in the preceding sections and in the preceding poems. "History," says Eliot, "is a pattern of timeless moments"—the significant moments which redeem it from being a succession of events, and give life to a nation or a civilization. In the life of a person, his self-discipline may lead him back to his earliest intimations, and Man himself return to the primal garden, when the fire becomes a crown, the thorn a rose, and purgation blends into beatitude.

It will be seen that the theme of this poem is related to the earlier verse and yet that the certainty, the finality of precision is new. The measure of the suffering, which is given in spiritual terms—there are no atrocity close-ups, there is not even a suggestion of any delimited events—is the measure of the integrity and the power needed to present it. "Little Gidding" provides both a standard and a tool for inner reflection on the times. It was a great opportunity worthily met.

*D. W. Harding. "We Have Not Reached Conclusion." *Scrutiny* 11 (Spring 1943), 216–19.

[Review of "Little Gidding"]

The opening of ["Little Gidding"] speaks of renewed life of unimaginable splendor, seen in promise amidst the cold decline of age. It offers no revival of life-processes; it is a spring time, "But not in time's covenant." If this "midwinter spring" has such blooms as the snow on hedges, "Where is the summer, the unimaginable / Zero summer?" With the sun blazing on the ice, the idea of pentecostal fire, of central importance in the poem, comes in for the first time, an intense, blinding promise of life and (as later passages show) almost unbearable.

The church of Little Gidding introduces another theme of the poem. Anchored in time and space, but for some people serving as the world's end where they can fulfill a purpose outside time and space, it gives contact with spiritual concerns through earthly and human things.

A third theme, important for the whole poem, is also stated in the first section: that the present is able to take up, and even give added meaning to, the values of the past. Here too the Pentecostal idea comes in:

> And what the dead had no speech for, when living,
> They can tell you, being dead: the communication
> Of the dead is tongued with fire beyond the language of the living.

Section II can be regarded as the *logical* starting point of the whole poem. It deals with the desolation of death and the futility of life for those who have had no conviction of spiritual values in their life's work. First come three sharply organized rhyming stanzas to evoke, by image and idea but without literal statement, our sense of the hopeless death of air, earth, fire, and water, seen not only as the elements of man's existence but as the means of his destruction and dismissal. The tone having been set by these stanzas, there opens a narrative passage describing the dreary bitterness in which a life of literary culture can end if it has brought no sense of spiritual values. The life presented is one, such as Mr. Eliot's own, of effort after clear speech and exact thought, and the passage amounts to a shuddering "There but for the grace of God go I." It reveals more clearly than ever the articles in the *Criterion* did, years ago, what it was in "humanism" that Mr. Eliot recoiled from so violently. What the humanist's ghost sees in his life are futility, isolation, and guilt on account of his self-assertive prowess—"Which once you took for exercise of virtue"—and the measure of aggression against others which that must bring.

The verse in this narrative passage, with its regular measure and insistent alliteration, so effective for combining the macabre with the urbane and dreary, is a way to indicate and a way to control the pressure of urgent misery and self-disgust. The motive power of this passage, as of so much of Mr. Eliot's earlier poetry, is repulsion. But in the poem as a whole the other motive force is dominant: there is a movement of feeling and conviction outwards, reaching towards what attracts. The other parts of the poem can be viewed as working out an alternative to the prospect of life presented in this narrative.

Section III sees the foundation for such an alternative in the contact with spiritual values, especially as they appear in the tradition of the past. Detachment

465

(distinguished from indifference) allows us to use both our own past and the historical past in such a way as to draw on their present spiritual significance for us without entangling us in regressive yearning for a pattern which no longer is:

> History may be servitude,
> History may be freedom. See, now
> they vanish,
> The faces and places, with the self
> which, as it could, loved them,
> To become renewed, transfigured, in
> another pattern.

Once we accept the significance of the spiritual motives and intentions of the past, even the factions connected with the church and community of Little Gidding leave us an inheritance; we can be at one with the whole past, including the sinning and defeated past, for its people were spiritually alive, "All touched by a common genius, / United in the strife which divided them."

But the humanist's fate cannot be escaped in so gentle and placid a way; a more formidable ordeal is waiting. In contrast to the leisurely meditation of section III, the fourth section is a forceful passage, close-knit with rhyme, and incisive. Its theme is the terrifying fierceness of the pentecostal experience, the dove bringing fire. This is not the fire of expiation, such as the humanist had to suffer. It is the consuming experience of love, the surrender to a spiritual principle beyond us, and the only alternative to consuming ourselves with the miserable fires of sin and error. This pentecostal ordeal must be met before the blinding promise seen in "midwinter spring" can be accepted.

The final section develops the idea that every experience is integrated with all the others, so that the fullness of exploration means a return, with better understanding, to the point where you started. The theme has already been foreshadowed in section III where detachment is seen to give liberation from the future as well as the past, so that neither past nor future has any fascination of a kind that could breed in us a reluctance to accept the present fully.

The tyranny of sequence and duration in life is thus reduced. Time-processes are viewed as aspects of a pattern which can be grasped in its entirety at any one of its moments: "The moment of the rose and the moment of the yew-tree / Are of equal duration." One effect of this view of time and experience is to rob the moment of death of any over-significance we may have given it. For the humanist of section II life trails off just because it can't manage to endure. For the man convinced of spiritual values life is a coherent pattern in which the ending has its due place and, because it is part of a pattern, itself leads into the beginning. An over-strong terror of death is often one expression of the fear of living, for death is one of the life-processes that seem too terrifying to be borne. In examining one means of becoming reconciled to death, Mr. Eliot can show us life too made bearable, unfrightening, positively inviting:

> With the drawing of this Love and the
> voice of this Calling

> We shall not cease from exploration
> And the end of all our exploring
> Will be to arrive where we started
> And know the place for the first time.

Here is the clearest expression of a motive force other than repulsion. Its dominance makes this poem—to put it very simply— far happier than most of Mr. Eliot's.

Being reconciled to death and the conditions of life restores the golden age of unfearful natural living and lets you safely, without regression, recapture the wonder and easy rightness of certain moments, especially in early childhood: [quotation of lines 33–41 of "Little Gidding" V].

The whole of [the] last section suggests a serene and revitalized return from meditation to one's part in active living. It includes a reaffirmation of that concern with speech which has made up so much of Mr. Eliot's work and which could have been the bitter futility that it is for the ghostly humanist. The reaffirming passage (introduced as a simile to suggest the integrated patterning of all living experience) is an example of amazing condensation, of most comprehensive thinking given the air of leisured speech—not conversation but the considered speech of a man talking to a small group who are going to listen for a time without replying. It is one example of the intellectual quality of this poem. In most of Mr. Eliot's poems the intellectual materials which abound are used emotionally. In much of this poem they are used intellectually, in literal statement which is to be understood literally (for instance, the opening of section III). How such statements become poetry is a question outside the range of this review. To my mind they do, triumphantly, and for me it ranks among the major good fortunes of our time that so superb a poet is writing.

F. O. Matthiessen. "Eliot's *Quartets*." *Kenyon Review* 5 (Spring 1943), 161–78.

In the course of an artist's development certain phases may detach themselves and challenge comprehension as completed wholes. Eliot has rounded out such a cycle in "Little Gidding," and we are now able to see the full significance of the experiments with structure which he inaugurated in "Burnt Norton" eight years previously.

He speaks of the four poems which form this cycle as "quartets," and has evolved from them all the same kind of sequence of five parts with which he composed "Burnt Norton." *The Waste Land* was also composed in this fashion, but the contrast is instructive. In his earlier desire for intense concentration the poet so eliminated connectives that *The Waste Land* might be called an anthology of the high points of a drama. It was as though its author had determined to make his poem of nothing but Arnold's "touchstones," or had subscribed to Poe's dictum that no longer poem could exist than one to be read at a sitting. In the intervening years Eliot has given further thought to the problem, and he has recently concluded that "in a poem of any length, there must be transitions between passages of greater and less intensity, to give a rhythm of fluctuating emotion essential to the musical structure of the whole." He has also enunciated "a complementary doctrine" to that of Arnold's "touchstones": the test of a poet's greatness by "the way he writes his less intense but structurally vital matter."

None of the four quartets is much more than half as long as *The Waste Land*, but he has included in them all transitional passages that he would previously have dismissed as "prosaic." His fundamentally altered intention is at the root of the matter. The dramatic monologues of Prufrock or Gerontion or of the various *personae* of *The Waste Land* have yielded to gravely modulated meditations of the poet's own. The vivid situations of his *Inferno* have been followed by the philosophic debates of his *Purgatorio*. He has made quite explicit the factors conditioning his new structures in the essay from which I have just quoted, "The Music of Poetry." As is always the case with Eliot, this essay throws the most relevant light upon his poetic intentions, and is thus a further piece of refutation to those who persist in the fallacy that there is no harmony between his "revolutionary" creative work and his "traditionalist" criticism.

Looking back now over the past generation, he finds the poetry of our period to be best characterized by its "search for a proper modern colloquial idiom." He develops the same theme near the close of "Little Gidding" where he envisages the right equilibrium between "the common word" and "the formal word." Only through their union of opposites do we get "The complete consort dancing together." Eliot, no less than the later Yeats, has helped to restore to poetry the conversational tones which have been muffled by the ornamental forms and diction of the end of the century. But now Eliot is thinking of the other partner to the union, and remarks that "when we reach a point at which the poetic idiom can be stabilized, then a period of musical elaboration can follow." Just as Donne, in his later work, returned to the formal pattern of the sonnet which he had mocked in the broken rhythms of his early lyrics, so Eliot now believes that there is such a "tendency to return to set, and even elaborate patterns" after any period when they have been laid aside.

The present phase of his own return seems to have started with "New Hampshire" and "Virginia," the short musical evocations which grew out of his renewed impressions of America in the early nineteen thirties. The impulse to write a series of such place-name poems led on in turn to the more ambitious "Burnt Norton," which borrows its title from a Gloucestershire manor near which Eliot has stayed. The titles of the other three quartets indicate more intimate relationships: East Coker, in Somerset, is where the Eliot family lived until its immigration in the mid-seventeenth century to the New England coast; the Dry Salvages, a group of rocks off Cape Ann, mark the part of that coast which the poet knew best as a boy; Little Gidding, the seat of the religious community which Nicholas Ferrar established and with which the names of George Herbert and Crashaw are associated, is a shrine for the devout Anglican, but can remind the poet also that "History is now and England."

The rhythmical pattern of "Burnt Norton" is elaborated far beyond the delicate melodies of the brief "Landscapes." Eliot seems to have found in the interrelation of its five parts a type of structure which satisfied him beyond his previous experiments. For he has adhered to it with such remarkably close parallels in the three succeeding quartets that a description of the structure of one of them involves that of all, and can reveal the deliberateness of his intentions. In each case the first part or movement might be thought of as a series of statements and counterstatements of a theme in lines of an even greater irregularity than those of the late Jacobean dramatists. In each of these first movements a "landscape" or presented scene gives a concrete base around which the poet's thoughts gather.

The second movement opens with a highly formal lyric: in "The Dry Salvages" this is a variant of a sestina, rising from the clang of the bell buoy; in "Little Gidding" each of the three eight-line stanzas ends with a refrain—and thus does Eliot signalize his own renewal of forms that would have seemed played out to the author of "Prufrock." In the other two poems, he has also illustrated a remark which he has been repeating in his recent essays, that "a poem, or a passage of a poem, may tend to realize itself first as a particular rhythm before it reaches expression in words." The lyric in "Burnt Norton"— which is echoed perhaps too closely in "East Coker"—is as pure musical incantation as any Eliot has written. Not only does its opening image, "Garlic and sapphires in the mud," take its inception from Mallarmé's line *Tonnerre et rubis aux moyeux*; but the rhythm of the poem in which that line occurs, "M'introduire dans ton histoire," seems also to have haunted Eliot's ear until it gave rise to a content which, with the exception of its opening lines, is wholly different from Mallarmé's.

Following the lyric in the second movement, Eliot has relaxed his rhythms for a sudden contrast; and in "The Dry Salvages," and especially in "East Coker," has carried his experiments with the prosaic virtually over the border into prose:

> That was a way of putting it—not
>   very satisfactory:
> A periphrastic study in a worn-out
>   poetical fashion,
> Leaving one still with the intolerable
>   wrestle
> With words and meanings. The poetry
>   does not matter.
> It was not (to start again) what one
>   had expected.

The sharp drop of incantation is designed to have the virtue of surprise; but it would seem here to have gone much too far, and to have risked the temporary collapse of his form into the flatness of a too personal statement. The variant in "Little Gidding" substitutes for such a sequence a modified *terza rima*, where the poet uses instead of rhyme a sustained alteration of masculine and feminine endings, in a passage that makes the strongest testimony for the value of formal congruence.

What the third parts have in common is that each is an account of movement. In "Burnt Norton" it is a descent into the London underground, which becomes also a descent into the dark night of the soul. In "East Coker" the allusion to Saint John of the Cross is even more explicit. The poet's command to his soul to "be still,

and wait without hope / For hope would be hope of the wrong thing," borrows its sequence of paradoxes directly from the text of the sixteenth-century Spanish mystic. In "The Dry Salvages" where the concluding charge is "Not fare well, / But fare forward, voyagers," the doctrine of action beyond thought of self-seeking is, again, explicitly, what Krishna urged to Arjuna on the field of battle; and we recall Eliot's remarking, in his essay on Dante, that "the next greatest philosophical poem" to *The Divine Comedy* within his experience was the *Bhagavad Gita*. In "Little Gidding" the passage of movement is the *terza rima* at the close of the second part, and the deliberately prosaic lines open the third section. The movement described is the "dead patrol" of two air raid wardens.

The versification in these third parts is the staple of the poems as a whole, a very irregular iambic line with many substitutions, of predominantly four or five beats, but with syllables ranging from six to eighteen. The fourth movement, in every case, is a short lyric, as it was in *The Waste Land*. The fifth movement is a resumption and resolution of themes, and becomes progressively more intricate in the last poems, since the themes are cumulative and are all brought together at the close of "Little Gidding."

It seems doubtful whether at the time of writing "Burnt Norton," just after *Murder in the Cathedral*, Eliot had already projected the series. His creative energies for the next three years were to be largely taken up with *The Family Reunion*, which, to judge from the endless revisions in the manuscript, caused him about as much trouble as anything he has done. With "East Coker" in the spring of 1940 he made his first experiment in a part-for-part parallel with an earlier work of his own. Again Donne's practice is suggestive: when he had evolved a particularly intricate and irregular stanza, he invariably set himself the challenge of following it unchanged to the end of his poem. But in assigning himself a similar problem for a poem two hundred lines long, Eliot has tried something far more exacting, where failure could be caused by the parallels becoming merely mechanical, and by the themes and rhythms becoming not subtle variations but flat repetitions. "East Coker" does indeed have something of the effect of a set piece. Just as its high proportion of prosaic lines seems to spring from partial exhaustion, so its resumption of themes from "Burnt Norton" can occasionally sound as though the poet was merely imitating himself. But on the whole he had solved his problem. He had made a renewal of form that was to carry him successively in the next two years through "The Dry Salvages" and "Little Gidding." The discrimination between repetition and variation lies primarily in the rhythm; and these last two poems reverberate with an increasing musical richness.

A double question that keeps insisting itself through any discussion of these structures is the poet's consciousness of analogies with music, and whether such analogies are a confusion of arts. One remembers Eliot's comment on Lawrence's definition of "the essence of poetry" for our age "of stark and unlovely actualities" as a "stark, bare, rocky directness of statement." "This speaks to me," Eliot remarked a decade ago, "of that at which I have long aimed in writing poetry"; and he drew an analogy with the later quartets of Beethoven. This does not mean that he has ever tried to copy literally the effects of a different medium. But he knows that poetry is like music in being a temporal rather than a spatial art; and he has by now thought much about the subject, as the concluding paragraph of "The Music of Poetry" shows:

I think that a poet may gain much from the study of music: how much technical knowledge of musical form is desirable I do not know, for I have not that technical knowledge myself. But I believe that the properties in which music concerns the poet most nearly, are the sense of rhythm and the sense of structure. I think that it might be possible for a poet to work too closely to musical analogies: the result might be an effect of artificiality.

But he insists—and this has immediate bearing on his own intentions—that "the use of recurrent themes is as natural to poetry as to music." He has worked on that assumption throughout his quartets, and whether he has proved that "there are possibilities of transition in a poem comparable to the different movements of a symphony or a quartet," or that "there are possibilities of contrapuntal arrangements of subject-matter," can be known only through repeated experience of the whole series.

[. . .]

It has been charged against Eliot ever since his conversion that his content has been tenuous; but the range of reflection and feeling in the quartets alone should serve to give a persuasive refutation. The trouble has been that whereas Eliot's earlier poetry was difficult in form, his later work is difficult in thought. The reader of "Gerontion" had to learn how to supply the missing connectives. The reader of the quartets finds a sufficiently straightforward logic, but is confronted with realms of discourse largely unfamiliar to a secular age. Sustained knowledge of the dark night of the soul is a rare phase of mystical experience in any age; and it is at that point that agnostic and atheist readers have been most severe in demanding whether Eliot's lines express anything more than mere

470

literary allusions. The severity is desirable, but is should not be forgotten that authentic poetry often takes us into experiences equally remote from our ordinary hours, as in Oedipus's vision at Colonus, in Rilke's *Duino Elegies*, or in almost the whole *Paradiso*.

[. . .]

Those who demand that a poet's content should be immediately useful will take no satisfaction in Eliot's belief that the poet in wartime should as a man "be no less devoted to his country than other men," but that "his first duty as a poet is towards his native language, to preserve and to develop that language." To the nationalist critics that will seem to beg the question of content altogether. But the cheapness of Van Wyck Brooks's opinion that Eliot is a poet of little hope, less faith, and no charity, should be substantially refuted by the lyric on the kinds of love alone. But such a lyric does not exist alone; its rises organically as the summation of one of Eliot's profoundest themes. And those who are suspicious of the inertness of the passages which urge the soul to wait in the dark without hope, should remember that the final declaration, even in "East Coker," is that "We must be still and still moving." The reconciliation of opposites is as fundamental to Eliot as it was to Heraclitus. Only thus can he envisage a resolution of man's whole being. The "heart of light" that he glimpsed in the opening movement of "Burnt Norton" is at the opposite pole from the *Heart of Darkness*, from which he took the epigraph for "The Hollow Men." Essential evil still constitutes more of Eliot's subject-matter than essential good, but the magnificent orchestration of his themes has prepared for that paradisal glimpse at the close, and thereby makes it no decorative allusion, but an integrated climax to the content no less than to the form. Such spiritual release

and reconciliation are the chief reality for which he strives in a world that has seemed to him increasingly threatened with new dark ages.

Horace Gregory.
"Fare Forward Voyagers."
New York Times Book Review, 16 May 1943, p. 2.

It has been said in certain quarters, thoughtlessly, I think, that the years of the present World War have failed to produce memorable poetry, and it has been implied that poetry in some mysterious way has failed to live up to great occasions. With Mr. T. S. Eliot's *Four Quartets* before me I wish to modify the gloomy accusations that the better poets of our time have been "irresponsible" or have failed to realize the seriousness of living through a difficult hour. For the past twenty years distinguished writers in England and in the United States have been aware of the potential existence of another world war, and they have warned their readers of its hidden forces long before its actual events took place, and in that sense most of the best poetry written in the present generation continues to be "war poetry."

It has been Mr. Eliot's destiny to anticipate, without seeming overtly prophetic, the mutations of feeling which have taken place within the past twenty years, and his perceptions have given him the right to speak with more than merely personal authority when he writes the following statement into his *Four Quartets*: "So here I am, in the middle way, having twenty years—/ Twenty years largely wasted, the years of *l'entre deux guerres*—"

One recalls his *Difficulties of a Statesman*, written long before the Munich pact; one remembers its notes of warning, its moments of satire, and its devotional spirit, for Mr. Eliot has held to the promise he gave his readers in "Ash-Wednesday"and has continued his progress through the choruses of *The Rock*, through the scenes of *Murder in the Cathedral*, and, most impressive of all, in his present collection of four poems, each bearing a place-name, "Burnt Norton," "East Coker," "The Dry Salvages" and "Little Gidding."

To us who read his *Four Quartets*, what do the place-names mean? They mean as much, let us say, as "Tintern Abbey" meant to readers of Wordsworth's early poetry; it is enough to know that the place-name is rich in emotional associations for the poet and whether or not the emotion conveyed to the reader is genuine in quality. We may recognize East Coker as being on a guidebook route from London to Exeter, with beautiful churches nearby and ancient factory yards, or the Dry Salvages as a small group of rocks off our North Atlantic Coast, or, perhaps more significantly, Little Gidding as an Anglican retreat, the scene of Nicholas Ferrar's "Protestant nunnery," which has been so memorably described in J. H. Shorthouse's finely tempered historical romance, *John Inglesant*. But these recognitions may be used as the content of footnotes merely to the four poems; one may photograph each place with anxious care, and yet not feel the emotion that the quartets with the melodic or lyrical interludes convey. The poems must be read for the quality of their emotion and its meaning—and I think I am not wrong when I say that the *Four Quartets* (without being in the least Wordsworthian) represent the best poetry

of their kind since Wordsworth wrote *The Prelude*.

One remembers that *The Prelude* was somewhat portentously subtitled "Or Growth of a Poet's Mind: An Autobiographical Poem," and though it is almost needless to say that Mr. Eliot's *Four Quartets* are not intended to sustain so weighty and so pretentious a claim upon the reader's interest in the philosophy of poetic composition, it is true that Mr. Eliot's new book contains a recapitulation of very nearly everything he has written since *The Waste Land* made its controversial appearance in the *Dial* in 1922. I think it can be said that there is nothing more dangerous than the attempt of a highly respected and gifted poet to imitate himself, to improve upon his original impulses and their expression—yet this is precisely what Mr. Eliot had done in the writing of his *Four Quartets*, and he has succeeded where many another poet has lapsed into mere repetitiousness or dullness. In "Burnt Norton" [. . .], he greatly enriched the devotional premises of "Ash-Wednesday": and with the completion of "Little Gidding" we now know that the earlier poem was the first in a new vehicle of expression for Mr. Eliot's characteristic themes.

[. . .]

More important than these considerations is the beauty of the new statement and its depth of feeling, for I happen to believe that the value of Mr. Eliot's sensibilities has been vastly underrated in favor of paying further tribute to his ingenuity and his acknowledged scholarship. His work is of a character that gives a pedant unholy delight in searching out its sources, and while such labors are not without their rewards, they tend to become irrelevant to the poetic gift which endows the following lyric from "Little

Gidding" with such brilliantly inspired felicity:

> The dove descending breaks the air
> [. . . . .]
> Consumed by either fire or fire.

I submit this quotation as one of the finest lyrics written in our time; and for those who wish to take heart as against others who are convinced that poetry was among the early casualties of the present war, I strongly recommend a reading of Mr. T. S. Eliot's *Four Quartets*.

Malcolm Cowley. "Beyond Poetry." *New Republic* 108 (7 June 1943), 767–68.

T. S. Eliot's *Four Quartets* is one of those rare books that can be enjoyed without being understood. I have heard people of good judgment praising it and, in the same breath, confessing that they didn't know what the poet intended to say. Apparently he gave them a few noble visions and a general impression of austerity, learning, goodness and even saintliness. Reading the book for the first time, I remembered the Swedenborgian sermons to which I half-listened every Sunday morning during my boyhood; I didn't grasp their meaning, but I knew that Bishop Pendleton was a good man and a scholar, and I went home to dinner with a pleasurable feeling of elevation.

Perhaps that is the best way of approaching *Four Quartets*. But if the reader insists on understanding as well as admiring the book, he might begin with the article on mysticism in the *Encyclopedia Britannica*; or better still by turning to the third chapter of Aldous Huxley's *Gray Eminence*, which is perhaps the simplest statement of the mystical way. If the nearest library has the Spring 1941 issue of the *Southern Review*, he might also read the essay on "East Coker" by James Johnson Sweeney, who is a profound student and Scotland Yard inspector of Eliot's later work.

Even after this preparation, there are points that may still escape the reader. My own difficulties began with the second word of the title: why are these poems called quartets? They seem to be spoken in a single voice, that of the author, and each of them is divided into five parts instead of four. The title of the first poem is equally mysterious, considering that the three others have now been explained by the author or his critics. East Coker is supposed to be the birthplace of Sir Thomas Elyot, author of *The Boke Named the Governour*, as well as being the original home of the Eliot family as a whole. It is therefore an appropriate title for a poem that is a mixture of history and autobiography. The Dry Salvages—pronounced to rhyme with "assuages"—is a small group of rocks, with a beacon, off the Massachusetts coast; and the name is set above a poem that deals with the river of time and the sea of timelessness. Little Gidding was the site of an Anglican monastic community that Eliot might have joined, if he had lived in the seventeenth century. But what about Burnt Norton, which F. O. Matthiessen says is a manor in Gloucestershire [*Kenyon Review*, Spring 1943, reprinted in this volume, pp. 467–71]. What is its connection with a poem describing an ecstatic vision? No matter how much he explains, and how many points his critics elucidate, Eliot always leaves us with unanswered questions. Reading his poems is a little like working over a crossword puzzle that will never be completely solved.

But there can be no doubt concerning his general purpose in *Four Quartets*. The book deals with mysticism in its dictionary definition—that is, with the belief in the possibility of union with the divine nature, and the description of methods by which that moment of union may be achieved. It belongs to the mystical tradition that goes back to Vedic days, that was carried to the West by the Neo-Platonists, that was introduced to Christianity by the pseudo-Dionysius in the fifth century, that was Latinized by Scotus Erigena four centuries later, that was continued during the Middle Ages by a whole band of saints and heretics—French, German, Spanish and English—that declined in the days of the Enlightenment, and that is now being revived in our own time of troubles. Eliot's principal source is St. John of the Cross, the Spanish mystic who died in 1591, but he also borrowed largely from the *Bhagavadgita* and, I am told, from the anchoret Dame Julian of Norwich, who wrote *XVI Revelations of Divine Love* and died in 1443 at the age of a hundred. He might have borrowed from many other sources without destroying the unity of his work, for the mystical tradition has changed very little from age to age or from nation to nation. Eliot is not trying to remake that tradition, but simply to recapture it. Even his obscurity is a convention often followed by mystical writers. He says at one point:

> There is only the fight to recover what
>   has been lost
> And found and lost again and again:
>   and now, under conditions
> That seem unpropitious.

What has been found and lost again is the intuition of pure being, the timeless moment of union with the divine. In order to recover it, two difficult steps must be taken. The first is to achieve the good life by means of what Eliot describes as "prayer, observance, discipline, thought and action"—in other words, the practices that used to be demanded of every pious Christian. The second step should be taken only by those who intend to follow the mystic or contemplative life. It consists in a rigorous attempt to empty the mind of all passions, fancies, analytical ideas and mere distractions, while directing one's thoughts solely toward union with God. The process is described at length in the third section of "East Coker," and more briefly in "Burnt Norton": [quotation of lines 25–32 of "Burnt Norton" III].

The reward that the mystic receives for leading the good life and for divesting himself of selfhood is the ecstatic sense of oneness with the divine nature. Eliot describes this ecstasy in many different fashions. Sometimes it is the moment when "the light is still at the still point of the turning world," and sometimes "the point of intersection of the timeless with time." Again it may be "the release from action and suffering," or "a condition of complete simplicity / (Costing not less than everything)," or else a "music heard so deeply / That it is not heard at all, but you are the music / While the music lasts." However described, it is for Eliot the central experience of a lifetime; and he even suggests that history itself is a pattern composed of these timeless moments—

> When the tongues of flame are
>   in-folded
> Into the crowned knot of fire
> And the fire and the rose are one.

I am not qualified to pass on the truth or value of the moral system that Eliot is expounding. Theologians might say that, like all mystics, he is running a grave danger of heresy. Even a layman feels that Eliot's new faith, instead of being Catholic or Anglo-Catholic, has a moral atmosphere that is a curious mixture of Calvinism and Buddhism: it is Calvinist and even New England Congregational in its finely drawn scruples; it is Buddhist in its utter rejection of the world. More interesting to most readers is the fact that Eliot's preoccupation with the contemplative life seems to be carrying him into an abstract sphere beyond the limits of poetry.

It is true that he is still extremely interested in the use of language—in finding "the common word exact without vulgarity, the formal word precise but not pedantic." He is interested in putting words together into a pattern which, like a Chinese jar, "still moves perpetually in its stillness." The pattern of Eliot's verse has never been more skillful and intricate than it is in *Four Quartets*. But the music of poetry, its sense of everyday life and the images with which it recaptures the floating world—all of these are matters beneath the notice of a man bent on union with the ineffable. He is even trying to put them out of his mind, by the contemplative process that leads to "desiccation of the world of sense, evacuation of the world of fancy"— in short, to the total destruction of all the world where poetry is accustomed to dwell.

[. . .]

Indeed, much of *Four Quartets* is on this [. . .] level of bare, abstract and sometimes hermetic expression; it seems to belong in some handbook of mystical philosophy. Much of it, on the other hand, is the sort of poetry that Eliot writes at his best, and the book includes some of his finest lyrics. But one feels that he now writes good poetry by habit or by a talent he is unable to suppress, rather than by intention. He is almost like a skillful bridge player who has abandoned cards as a frivolous occupation, but who sometimes forgets himself and plays a perfect hand.

James Johnson Sweeney. "'Little Gidding': Introductory to a Reading." *Poetry: A Magazine of Verse* 62 (July 1943), 214–23.

"*Qua* work of art," Eliot wrote in an early paper on *Hamlet*, "the work of art cannot be interpreted; there is nothing to interpret; we can only criticize it according to standards, in comparison to other works of art; and for 'interpretation' the chief task is the presentation of relevant historical facts which the reader is not assumed to know." There is no definitive "interpretation" possible for any poem worthy of the name. A poet should aim, as Eliot says in his essay introductory to *A Choice of Kipling's Verse*, "at making something which shall first of all *be*, something which in consequence will have the capability of exciting, within a limited range, a considerable variety of responses from different readers."

To *be*, in Eliot's sense, a poem must have form, or better, structure. As he says, "the poem may begin to shape itself in fragments of musical rhythm, and its structure will first appear in terms of something analogous to musical form." This is the first feature of a poem to win the reader's or listener's interest. It is in part "a language of enticement"—a way of expressing what one has to say in a manner that will hold the reader and persuade him to examine the statement. In fact, according to Eliot, certain poets even find it expedient to occupy their conscious minds primarily "with the craftsman's problems, leaving the deeper meaning to emerge, if there, from a lower level"—either direct to the intelligence or indirectly by suggestion. But we must never lose sight of the fact that "music of verse is inseparable from the meanings and associations of words."

It is not the poet's part to offer recommendations toward a reading of his work. By so doing he would limit its suggestive power. But for a critical approach to an unfamiliar poem, after our first, immediate response, a consideration of its meaning is essential—that is to say, an examination of its fundamental reference points and its allusive materials. This is one sound way to reach the structural skeleton of a poem. The skeleton by itself has no life—no value "*qua* work of art"; nor can such a skeleton ever be outlined clearly. With the true poet, the interplay of thought and the words that express it attain the condition of a dance, valuable to watch in itself. A dancer in his movements does not *do* anything or *go* anywhere. [. . .] "If the sense and the sound, or if content and form, can be easily separated, the poem disintegrates. Chief consequence: the 'ideas' which figure in a poetic expression do not play the same role there, are not at all values of the same sort, as ideas in prose."

For poets such as Eliot, however, there must be some basic schema of "meaning"—a scaffolding to support their structures as they build them, an armature around which their materials may take form. Intentional associations give definition and stability to their expressions through which unintentional suggestions and associations proliferate to give them their textures of detail. And only by a chart of "meaning" can the reader find his bearings among the incidental details of a poem so as to be able to judge the author's organization of them. The working out of such a chart will, and should, differ with every reader. But its delineation is a necessary step in any intelligent reading after our

initial sensory response to a poem. And with a true poem such a schema need not in any way limit the freedom or variety of response to the details which in their individual ambiguities and in the multiple interactions constitute the essence of poetic expression.

The publication of "Little Gidding," the fourth and concluding section of T. S. Eliot's sequence initiated by "Burnt Norton" in 1935, puts us finally in a position to approach the poem as a whole. While each part, as it appeared, seemed quite able to stand by itself, the publication of an additional section threw a fresh light on certain points of significance, or qualities undiscerned in the previous ones. At the same time certain themes and ideas of the first three sections continued to run parallel without achieving any finality or resolution. The contrast of time and eternity; the anomaly of esteeming temporal values in the face of eternal values—appearances in the face of reality; the need for a renunciation of worldly desire for supernatural—the renunciation of "the rose" for "the Rose"; and the constant stress on the omnipresence of pain, change, and disillusionment. Sin and suffering were evidently natural to our world. The situation was persistently restated in each new section. Finally in "Little Gidding" we find the philosophical key to the whole sequence in the famous words of Dame Julian of Norwich "the devout ankress" of the fourteenth century: "Synne is behovabil, but al shal be wel & al shal be wel and al manner of thyng shal be wele." Or as Eliot, in accordance with various modernizations, adapts it, in "Little Gidding":

Sin is Behovely, but
All shall be well, and
All manner of thing shall be well.

Sin is inevitable, unescapable—"behovely" in the fourteenth-century use. But

"Adam's sin was the most harm that was ever done." For this Christ made the "glorious Satisfaction." And in Dame Julian's words: "this Amends-making is more pleasing to God and more worshipful, without comparison, than ever was the sin of Adam harmful." As E. I. Watkin says in *The English Way*:

> She sees sin as God's scourge for our discipline. It humbles us and increases our knowledge of His Love. For redeemed humanity sin is also an occasion of greater good. "Sin is behovely," that is, it has its part in the Divine economy of good . . . God will bestow on redeemed mankind a better gift than we should have enjoyed had man never fallen.

Christ, the second Adam, won redemption for man through His Incarnation, "that central paradox of Christian theology"—in the union of the Divine and the human, of Eternity and time. By this the User imparted virtue to the instrument; the Final Cause operating through subsidiary causes bestowed value on them, with the result that if a man follows a route such as that indicated by St. John of the Cross in *The Ascent of Mount Carmel*, through *The Dark Night of the Soul*, in spite of sin and evil he may yet know "The Living Flame of Love."

> And all shall be well and
> All manner of thing shall be well
> When the tongues of flame . . .

—that is, the love of God—the Pentecostal tongues which are universally comprehensible by the spirit—"are in-folded," with an echo of St. John of the Cross's *The Spiritual Canticle*, "Into the crowned knot of fire," "And the fire" (love) "and the rose" (desire) "are one," as in the last canto of the *Paradiso*, when St. Bernard discloses to Dante the Mystical Rose of divine union.

Renunciation, humility—a recognition of the true Reality behind appearance, of the Timeless beyond the temporal—is the only way. And this by God's grace will, in the words of the anonymous author of *The Cloud of Unknowing*, "at the last help thee to knit the ghostly knot of burning love betwixt thee and thy God, in ghostly one-head and accordance of will."

The theme of "Little Gidding" is love—the renunciation of temporal interests for a loving contemplation of God. The title gives the lead at once. Little Gidding is a small village in Huntingdonshire in England. There, in the early part of the seventeenth century existed the only house dedicated to the contemplative life within the Anglican Church. Nicholas Ferrar, its founder, was a man of conspicuous talents. After an education at Clare Hall, Cambridge, and several years of travel on the Continent, he became actively connected with the Virginia Company. When this Company was deprived of its patent in 1623 Ferrar turned his attention to politics and was elected to Parliament. He was well on his way to a brilliant career when suddenly, awakened by a miraculous preservation from death in the Alps, he renounced the world and adopted a life of obscurity and poverty in which he and his family dedicated themselves wholly to God.

In the opening lines of this last Quartet we have an echo of the figurative associations of physical and spiritual seasons which introduced *The Waste Land*: "April is the cruellest month, breeding / Lilacs out of the dead land [. . .]." But here the image has primarily to do with light, spiritual and physical: "A Vision of Spring in Winter"—Swinburne's "ghost arisen of May before the May." And in view of the seventeenth-century associations of the poem's title, this introductory emphasis on light at once recalls the contrast of natural and supernatural light in Crashaw's "Ode on the

Epiphany" and its exploration of the mysticism of the *via negativa* of "the right ey'd Areopagite." For Richard Crashaw was one of Ferrar's close friends. And the pseudo-Dionysius may be said to be a fundamental inspiration of both Dame Julian and the anonymous author of *The Cloud* as well as the whole Victorine tradition of contemplation.

The experience of a bright day in a dark season for Eliot is the particular through which he sets about to suggest the universal. Like "Midwinter spring," the "eternal brightness of God" "is its own season," sempiternal—"Suspended in time," eternally present. It is a promise "of the new season." In *Murder in the Cathedral* the Tempter offered Thomas Becket a promise of temporal pleasures to come in almost the same words.

> Spring has come in winter. Snow in the
> branches
> Shall float as sweet as blossoms. Ice
> along the ditches
> Mirror the sunlight. Love in the
> orchard
> Send the sap shooting.

But here we have it as an analogue to an intimation of Divine Love, the ultimate reality of the universe. Just as the brief winter sun flames the ice with "A glare that is blindness in the early afternoon," so God may "send out a beam of ghostly light, piercing this cloud of unknowing that is between thee and Him" (*The Cloud of Unknowing*). And such a sudden beam of enlightenment or intuition may leave us dazzled like the three kings in Crashaw's "Ode on the Epiphany"—by "A Darkness made of too much day."

In such a foretaste of Eternity, a promise of the Divine summer, sense is put aside: "there is no earth smell"—no interest in living things: this is the spring promise of a season outside Time. Similarly on a spring day in winter we may see the hedgerow "blanched for an hour with transitory blossom / Of snow . . . / . . . neither budding nor fading / Not in the scheme of generation." Through the grace of God, a "glow more intense than blaze of branch, or brazier, / Stirs the dumb spirit." This is God's love. And as we read in *The Cloud of Unknowing*, there is "a devout stirring of love that is continually wrought in his (man's) will, not by himself, but by the hand of Almighty God."

> There occurs that most delicate touch of the Beloved, which the soul feels at times, even when least expecting it and which sets the heart on fire with love, as if a spark had fallen upon it and made it burn. Then the will in an instant, like one aroused from sleep, burns with the fire of love, longs for God, praises Him and the sweetness of love. (St. John of the Cross, *The Spiritual Canticle*, XXV, 5)

These stirrings are movements of grace. Still it is the constant burden of *The Cloud* and its companion *Epistle of Privy Counsel* that they are a work in which the will, or the soul, is industriously operating: "a naked intent stretching unto God," "a longing desire evermore working." Or as Eliot says in quoting directly from *The Cloud* (Chapter II) in the concluding section of "Little Gidding," "With the drawing of this Love and the voice of this Calling / We shall not cease from exploration."

> Contemplation is a great and a "perfect" state of prayer. To arrive at it, sanctifying or habitual grace is not enough; faith, hope and charity are not enough; there is also required that touch of the finger of God's right hand, and that quick response of the soul thereto, which imply the active operation of the seven great gifts of the Holy Ghost.

When the Holy Ghost descended on the apostles after Christ's resurrection, "suddenly there came a sound from heaven as of a mighty wind coming" (*Acts of the Apostles* II, 1–2.). But the gifts of the Holy Ghost come to the simple Christian informally: "no wind, but pentecostal fire." And "it is the gifts of the Holy Spirit which pour on the soul that exquisite and subtle light, that rapture of attention, that spiritual sensibility, as if new senses had been given us, which combine to elevate ordinary meditation and affection into contemplation" (Bishop Hedley, *Prayer and Contemplation*, quoted by Abbot Butler, *Western Mysticism*).

According to the Neoplatonic school of Christian writers, which included among others St. Augustine, the pseudo-Dionysius, Meister Eckhardt, Dame Julian, the author of *The Cloud of Unknowing*, and St. John of the Cross, "God so transcends as really to be unlike any created thing" (Philip H. Wicksteed, *Dante and Aquinas*). Any assertion as to God cannot possibly have more than a partial or relative truth. To assert that God is this or that would imply some limitation or exclusion and so qualify His all-embracing Being or Super-Being.

> We may indeed say with actual, not only relative, truth that God is in-visible, that He is in-finite, incomprehensible, un-moved, for these are negatives and say not what He is, but what He is not. Since you cannot assert God to be this or that thing, or indeed any *quid* whatever, it follows that He is nothing (*nihil or nihilum*). (Wicksteed, *Dante and Aquinas*)

As a consequence of this belief, Dionysius the Areopagite and his followers in the *via negativa* taught that the return to God (its end and its beginning) is effected by successive denials and abstractions: the initiate must leave behind all things both in the sensible and in the intelligible worlds. Only in this way will he enter that darkness of nescience that is truly mystical—the "Divine darkness" which surrounds God, the absolute Nothing which is above all existence and reason, that unimaginable summer beyond sense, that inapprehensible "Zero summer."

Delmore Schwartz. "Anywhere Out of the World." *Nation* 157 (24 July 1943), 102–03.

Any work by T. S. Eliot is bound to be interesting in a complicated way. But this new work compels, in me at least, a greater complexity of impression than any other of Eliot's works. I speak thus of my own feelings because I know how differently, and with what unmixed admiration, many other readers have greeted these new poems. Yet at the tenth reading I have the same mixed feeling, and this after having tried to force in myself the delight of those who find these poems just what they should be throughout.

Two extended passages, a sestina made more difficult and extraordinary by rhyme and a miraculous exercise in the idiom and method of *The Divine Comedy*, are equal, at least from the standpoint of technique, to any modern poetry. Throughout these poems there is also the invention of new rhythms, of unimagined possibilities in the movement of language, which has always marked Eliot. He is perhaps more original and inventive in rhythm than any other poet in English.

But when this is said, the weakness of other long passages is underscored. These passages are of two kinds. In one, the poet uses conventional forms in an effort to write the kind of lyric which is traditional to English poetry, and here what is to me the inadequacy comes chiefly from the choice of image and phrase: the earth as a hospital "endowed by the ruined millionaire" lacks the permanent surprise, shock, and uniqueness of—to use the used instance, permanently fresh—"April is the cruellest month." Then too the images seem *made*, self-imitative, forced; they have the look of the artificial, and when they are intended as emblematic or established symbols, they look merely decorative.

The other kind of unsuccessful passage is composed of blocks of long lines very close to the rhythm of prose, like much of *The Family Reunion*, and deliberately direct, matter of fact, and prosaic. Nothing is more important to modern poetry than such a use of the prosaic for its poetic quality, for nothing else can give the poet the thickness, the particularity, the full actuality of modern experience, which will justify his avowed emotions and beliefs. The prosaic versification here is so much better than the same kind of thing in *The Family Reunion*, partly because of a greater use of overflow, that it may mark a stage in the mastery of a new style. But in itself, it remains weak and wrong, not only in the triteness of the phrasing—"we have gone on trying," for example—but in the effort, self-consciousness, and falsity of tone. [. . .] It is not enough, in a poem, to say "I am unhappy" or "I have failed"; and especially in the poetry of direct statement the commonplace or colloquial statement must be lifted up to a new light, by one device or another, so that it is not merely itself, but something penetrated and understood as a symbol. The touchstones for this profound usage are Laforgue, Marianne Moore, William Carlos Williams—and Eliot himself, but not in these poems. And then the choice of instances in these passages, "fruit, periodicals, business letters," "even a very good dinner," marks a like relaxation of the poet's sensibility, one which suggests that he is at such times echoing the idiom he himself discovered. Too much is often made of the sheer texture of the language, when modern poetry is examined; but here it is not merely a matter of texture: the crucial instant of insight is betrayed by the language. Thus, at one important moment one gets such a weak play and shift with the meaning of a phrase as "Not fare well, / But fare forward, voyagers," when in "Ash-Wednesday," at a like moment, the poem rose to such a phrase as "Teach us to care and not to care."

However, there can be no doubt about the satisfaction and the success to be found in the modified sestina, the Dantesque interview, and the organized movement of the poems. Especially the encounter with a dead master just before morning in London in wartime strikes one with such astonishment and admiration that some grand rhetorical statement seems proper; so that, as Cocteau declared of the motion pictures, "At last the theatre has an airplane!" one wishes to say, "At last Dante has been translated into English and into modern life." This is literally true in that Eliot has accomplished the effect of *terza rima* in English by alternating masculine and feminine endings without rhyme, thus evading the comparative poverty of rhyme in English and thus instructing future translators and poets. [. . .]

And the organized movement of the four poems makes the title of quartets denote more than the stock analogy of music with poetry. Perhaps later quartets would be still more exact, for as in those of Beethoven, the movement from part to part goes from a passage lyrical, quick, joyous, and exalted; to a passage suddenly slow, turned in upon itself by variation or repetition of the same thought, hovering over divided parts of the same symbol or idea; harsh, flat, discursive, and tortuous; and then once more quickened to certainty, difficult conviction, and the explicit declaration and direct chant of belief.

The belief, made clear by the use of phrases and doctrines in the *Bhagavadgita*, Heraclitus, and St. John of the Cross, is that the only meaningful event in history is the Incarnation, and all else—"the moment in the rose-garden," the place of one's forebears, the practice of poetry, and the whole of one's life—illusory, deceptive, empty, vain, and without meaning except in relation to the Incarnation. Seen in that light, everything still remains false and of little worth, except as a phase to be endured. All that is natural and merely human contradicts itself, love is not love, time is not time, the end of life is the beginning of life, exaltation and despair are the same thing, all desire, effort, and action must be transformed into passages of patient waiting—"waiting without hope"—to be wholly disengaged from everything in this life. Here, as in Eliot's poetry from the start, what declares itself above all is an obsessing desire to be free from "birth, copulation, and death," and to be "divested of the love of created things," to be utterly out of the world. This rejection and renunciation are dominant to such an extent that the affirmation of belief seems only lyrical afterthought. The Incarnation is present for the sake of the rejection of this life, not the renunciation because of the Incarnation. And this suggests once more that Buddhism is perhaps a doctrine just as well suited as Christianity to the poet's mind; perhaps better suited, since the doctrine of reincarnation in some form of natural life becomes true and inexhaustible damnation, given Eliot's vision. To say this is to recognize that the poet's hatred and rejection of this life is something beyond any belief whatever. It must have some personal and private source, but it exists for all readers both as a profound criticism of life and as a necessary phase in the life of the spirit. If there is a phase superior to it, as most Christians, at least, must suppose (how different is the Christianity of St. Francis or Aquinas), the rejection and renunciation which Eliot celebrates is prior and not to be evaded, if one is to be in the full sense a human being. To see that this is true, one has only to remember such very different actualities as the moral disillusionment of our time and the present war; and in literature, such wholly different authors as Céline and Rilke, for *The Duino Elegies* have a cold resemblance to these poems, and these poems, however different in subject matter from Céline's exhaustion of cynicism and despair, are also a journey to the end of the night, inadequate only when the journey is discussed and commended, and not endured.

---

*Paul Goodman.
"T. S. Eliot: The Poet of Purgatory."
New Leader, 14 August 1943, pp. 3, 7.

This poem of personal experience and historical experience, and the experience of eternity, is excellent. So far above the poems that appear these days that one has almost a duty to ally himself with the poet against the average, and write nothing but praise. Easy to do; for on the one hand Eliot has for a long time had no poetic faults, of excess or lapse, of writing beyond what he knows or of merely repeating himself; he writes what he is, for better or worse. And on the other hand, this poem has glorious new perfections. In the diction always a subtle edge of irony and paradox, but an edge even more subtly and beautifully blunted in the interest of the humility that is his theme. And a wonderful conversational use of meters far from the iambic pentameters in which we others have learned to think at our ease. And a thought everywhere so central and self-known that he can go off at liberty yet never divagate, for we are always close to the heart of it. And a symbolism that, more in keeping with his genius, has returned to great overall metaphors and place-names, renouncing the factitious detailed symbolism of his earlier period—"a way of putting it—not very satisfactory: / A periphrastic study in a worn-out poetical fashion." (I do not mean, of course, the high Symbolism that he never attained, and which is precisely sensuous creation itself.)

Yet Eliot is not one of the colossal poets whose truth and attitude we spontaneously advocate, or if we dissent we feel nevertheless that their creating will loom against (and tomorrow overwhelm!) our doubt; thus it is always relevant to ask if what he says is binding. Or to put this another way—for I am not speaking of the compulsion of philosophy, but of spiritual energy and salvation one might say that Eliot is everywhere, but especially in this poem, the poet of Purgatory; and we may ask if there *can* be a great poet of Purgatory; a great poet not *always* attended by some angel of Paradise. But he says, referring to the central theme of this poem,

> But to apprehend
> The point of intersection of the
>   timeless
> With time, is an occupation for the
>   saint—

No occupation either, but something
    given
And taken, in a lifetime's death in
    love,
[. . . . .]
For most of us, there is only the
    unattended
Moment, the moment in and out of
    time,
The distraction fit, lost in a shaft of
    sunlight.

In the nature of the case this is the poet whose voice has a famous "dying fall." But would one not expect that as a poet, not a saint, he could not possibly fail to have an abiding confidence—a confidence not, of course, in his propositions, but in his ability to make something in the medium, the gift ("given and taken") of the Creator Spirit?

Or to put it still another way, looking at what he says we see more clearly here than elsewhere why Eliot is not a Christian poet; how his Christianity is sapped by Indian ideas; and yet he does not have the Indian wisdom either.

What he says—I think it can be synopsized without distortion—is that time, past, present or future, is loss of the soul; that practical desire, action, suffering, inner and outer compulsion, are an endless round; salvation is in the release from these, in abstention from motion, abiding at the still point of the turning world, and this is love; and yet, and this is the capital point, it is only through experience in time, and returning on that experience completed to perceive its pattern, that the timeless may be grasped, for "only through time time is conquered," and

> A people without history
> Is not redeemed from time, for history
>   is a pattern
> Of timeless moments

and therefore, for "a further union, a deeper communion" we must have courage to start on the round again, "we must be still and still moving," "old men ought to be explorers," our destiny is to fare forward, "not fare well but fare forward"—

> We shall not cease from exploration
> And the end of all our exploring
> Will be to arrive where we started
> And know the place for the first time.

The perfection of the earthly paradise of youth is the rose, and the purification of desire is the refining fire; and in the timeless, "the fire and the rose are one." What a relief this noble doctrine is after the wasteland of Anglicanism and new Humanism! It is not ironic to come on precisely the doctrine of Lessing, "fare forward," that used to be singled out for contempt as a cult of experience! And it is even delightful to find T. S. Eliot coming to a kind of antinomianism—"All shall be well, and / All manner of thing shall be well"—for obviously sin also is a venture to fare forward on. And it is moving to hear the poet (in the face of the world-wide catastrophe) speak autobiographically for the first time, and point to his "twenty years largely wasted, the years of l'entre deux guerres." But the doctrine is false. We may theologically take time as a loss and an endless return if we also take it as an illusion; for then there is also prescribed a discipline of ridding ourselves physically of the illusion, an even certain and controllable way of attaining salvation for those who know the science. (This is the Indian way.) But on the contrary, if time is real, as the poem has it, it is impossible for it to be hopeless, for time is the theatre of creation, of creative acts, virtues and miracles, given by grace; not that the sequence of time is a progress, for new evil also abounds, but that God willing it is full of glories, future as well as past.

If faith can move mountains, then the man of faith does move them not only to act out his faith (like Thomas in the *Murder*), but with confidence that their *motion* will do God's work. If pressed, Eliot's despair of material events and his confidence in only the emerging pattern (or in mere meditation on the emerging pattern) would conclude, I think, in denying the Creation itself. (But salvation is in the resources of creative nature, and the hidden God is not an object of experience.) "The faith and the love and the hope are all in the waiting."

Yes, if like Milton, in the sonnet, one knows that "thousands at His bidding speed, and post o'er land and ocean without rest"; or at least that they could do so, given the right inspiration. But *No*, if one imagines that in any case it will make no difference, or will make a difference only in the contemplation of essences, for one essence is as eternal as another and then why consent to fare forward (and do worse).

Even so! the poet is right to torment himself and not to make a commitment where in fact he does not believe. Yet perhaps the divine communities are simple things after all, and all that is easiest is best. I wonder if he did not experience this when he composed the beautiful cadences of these *Quartets*.

John Gould Fletcher. "Poems in Counterpoint." *Poetry: A Magazine of Verse* 63 (October 1943), 44–48.

The great beauty of T. S. Eliot's latest book—and it is a long time since there has been a book of poetry in which the form and the matter seem so appropriate to each other—need not blind anyone to the fact that in each poem of this series, Eliot is dealing with a theme not frequently tackled in modern poetry: the theme of the relation of a supernaturally revealed religion to man, and the question of what man, temporal and accidental as he is, can make of this revelation. The intellectual scheme of each poem in the series represents a further stage in the poet's search for personal adjustment to a set of values already given him by the creed he has embraced; and it is this set of fixed and unalterable values, as given by such Catholic mystics as Saint John of the Cross and Dame Julian of Norwich, that form the framework on which the personal quests of the poet for values that transcend his local and temporal circumstances are set up. The question of the meaning of the whole series has already been ably discussed by James Johnson Sweeney in an article in the July issue of *Poetry* [reprinted in this volume, pp. 475–79], and need not be further dealt with at this point. What I wish to stress is the relation of the content to the form and the degree in which the form combines with the content to produce that "willing suspension of disbelief" which is so characteristic of poetry.

The title *Four Quartets* suggests immediately a musical structure, something on the lines of my own *Symphonies* or *Elegies* or Conrad Aiken's *Preludes*. And it is in this respect that I find Eliot's achievement most impressive. This is the work of a better poet than the Eliot who wrote either *The Waste Land* or "Ash-Wednesday." Where the themes of *The Waste Land* were in brutal juxtaposition, and violently clashed with each other—few poems ever written have been so lacking in transition passages, in progress from detail to detail as this one—and where the main theme of the latter (the abandonment of

temporal love) carried with it details that did not immediately convince one as being appropriate to their purpose, the relation of detail to the main structure here is nothing short of masterly. *The Four Quartets*, in their use of *leit motifs* and variation, in the contrapuntal effect, are the work of a theologically-minded poet determined to explore difficult ground, the ground of the technical analogies between poetry and music. They are by intention and accomplishment musical poems.

But what is a musical poem? Eliot himself has supplied the answer, in [. . .] "The Music of Poetry," [. . .] an essay which I think might have served admirably as an introduction to the *Quartets* themselves, inasmuch as it offers the best possible explanation of them on the technical side. As he points out in this essay, it is quite common among poets for "a poem, or a passage of a poem—to realize itself first as a particular rhythm before it reaches expression in words." In other words, the way a poem should sound as rhythm usually presents itself to a poet before the actual words of the poem are set down. Poets are people who go about with tunes in their heads: and whether the tunes employed be those of Mallarmé or Eliot, or of Kipling and Robert Tristram Coffin, makes all the difference.

The other sense in which the analogy of music holds good for poetry is in the question of structure. The free verse revolution in poetry, coming in English-speaking countries between 1908 and 1914, had as its aim the bringing of poetry back to the rhythm of conversational speech and the renewal of poetic structure in that idiom. As Eliot says in the essay to which I have already referred, "It was a revolt against dead form, and a preparation for new form, or a renewal of the old; it was an insistence upon the inner unity which is unique to every poem, against the outer unity which is typical." Structure, however, must always be a preoccupation of every important poet, whatever the form employed; and the liberation preached by the free versifiers—resulting in much bad prose and some good verse—has seemed most intelligently applied when new devices, bearing a considerable analogy to music, have enforced form on what might have been otherwise formless. These devices are, roughly, the setting of the theme of a poem in several different and contrasting rhythms (for example, sad and humorous); the juxtaposition in the same poem of passages of high lyric intensity with others of conversational comment; the repetition of leading themes with variation; the amplification in sound intensity possible between the open and closed quality of vowel sounds; and finally, the effect of contrapuntal recapitulation possible to sustain by returning to one's leading statements. All these devices have their analogies in music; and it is because Eliot is not only aware of them, but employs them with the utmost skill, that one takes pleasure in his work as a poet.

Is this the only reason why, as a poet, he remains so important today? So far as I am concerned, it is. I do not share his scheme of beliefs, which are familiar to anyone who has read deeply in the Catholic mystics [. . .].

The negative way to salvation, as recommended by the orthodox, seems to me largely valueless in the present crisis. Rather is it important for most men, who have either lost God or never found Him in the existing churches, to build up God again through the operation of the sense of human solidarity. [. . .] The Little Giddings of this world can shed little light on the problem that has come upon this age with renewed force—the problem of creating, while we fight for it, a true democracy. To solve that problem we have to start, not with God as defined by the theologians, but with man, and his relationship towards his fellows. Modern science, though it may help towards a solution, cannot provide one. There is, be it remembered, a mysticism implicit in democracy—a system of beliefs possibly not worked out with the clarity of detail of the medieval schoolmen, but declaring just as surely as Dame Julian of Norwich that "All shall be well, and / All manner of thing shall be well."

Louis Untermeyer. "Eight Poets." *Yale Review* 33 (December 1943), 348–49.

[. . .]

The title of Eliot's later poems, *Four Quartets*, was certain to provoke, and already has provoked, comparisons with Beethoven's later quartets in intention as well as accomplishment. Towards the end, Beethoven fashioned a music to reach beyond music; in his fifties, Eliot employs mind to stretch beyond mind. The result is an intricate paradox: *Four Quartets* is both simpler and subtler than anything Eliot has written since *The Waste Land*. The language is more direct, sometimes even prosaic; the allusions are much less remote and recondite; the connectives are clear. But the meanings are more complex than ever, and the frame which encloses them is deceptively patterned. Structurally *Four Quartets* is magnificent; it unfolds design after design. Some of the patterns are obvious: the series of fours; the mixed symbolism of the four seasons and the four elements, air, earth, water, and fire; the dexterous alternation of unrhymed slow passages and rapidly rhymed lyrics; the turn of the theme with minute variations.

But the best of the four-part poem disguises its effects. Never has a poet used repetition more skillfully and persuasively; never have variations been so insinuating. Here Eliot's chief preoccupations are the sense of time and timelessness, the involution of life, and the difficulty of communication. It is not a narrow interpretation of the poet's art that leads Eliot to complain of the years lost in learning how to use language—"the intolerable wrestle with words and meanings"—the old attempts, the new starts, and the failures "because one has only learnt to get the better of words/For the thing one no longer has to say, or the way in which/One is no longer disposed to say it." [. . .]

The accent of *Four Quartets* is grave, sometimes sadly nostalgic, but it is by no means lugubrious. The music as well as the meaning is solemn, and it will not be to everyone's taste. Eliot's counterpoint of private experience and impersonal mysticism is not easy to follow. But few will question the beauty of the communication; few will doubt the perfection of the poet's art. [. . .]

Peter Monro Jack.
"A Review of Reviews: T. S. Eliot's *Four Quartets*."
American Bookman 1 (Winter 1944), 91–99.

[. . .] [N]o book of poems of this year, or in many years, has been so completely, exhaustively, and earnestly reviewed. One reason is that the poetry warrants this attention. *Four Quartets* is a poetry that has nothing to compare with it today, now that Yeats is no longer writing. It has originated a new style, and almost, one might say, a new thinking, or a way of thought, in poetry. The second reason is that readers of Eliot are perpetually worried about him: what is he up to next? This is an indication of the great impression he has made on his readers. But they are all sorts, and I think their point of view depends pretty largely on what they have first read. Will the new poetry be like "Prufrock," or as good as "Gerontion," or another *Waste Land*, or will it continue "The Hollow Men," or substitute "Ash-Wednesday"?

For Eliot's poetry, being a great poetry, is a controversial poetry, and it reaches every kind of mood and manner and imagination in his readers. Each is concerned with conserving the good that appears to him to be in Eliot's verse. There is no wonder of it. Eliot has reassembled a small and present, and a large and universal, world in our day. Satire, humor, bitterness, pessimism, mysticism, decisions in politics, religion, aesthetics, have taken over his poetry, clearly, obscurely or indirectly; he has especially been the poet of history—the history of legend and ideas—summarizing a civilization in grave, grateful, and sometimes grievous words. This complexity, though it is clearly written, has given Eliot probably the most quarrelsome audience in the world.

There is, however, an almost unanimous decision in favor of the *Quartets*. One might almost think the critics had held a caucus and emerged with their separate opinions clearly coordinated. This again is due to the force of Eliot's poetic personality. He simply drives you to make up your mind about him, or about his subject matter: as Wordsworth, Shelley, Browning, Yeats did; if you begin to read you cannot escape the consequences of reading him. An objective poetry for the most part, in manner, it is really a most intimate poetry in that it makes you feel the importance of knowing and feeling intimately.

[Summary of the following reviews, included in this volume or listed in the checklist: Anonymous, *Time* (June 1943); Horace Gregory, *New York Times Book Review* (16 May 1943); James Johnson Sweeney, *Southern Review* (Spring 1941); G. W. Stonier, *New Statesman* (14 September 1940); Delmore Schwartz, *Nation* (24 July 1943); Edwin Muir, *New Statesman* (20 February 1943); Babette Deutsch, *New York Herald Tribune Books* (18 July 1943); F. O. Matthiessen, *Kenyon Review* (Spring 1943); Raymond Holden, *Saturday Review of Literature* (24 July 1943); Philip Wheelwright, *Chimera* (Autumn 1942)].

These reviews are unlike anything else I have read. They all recognize a book of great distinction. None quite communicates that distinction, conceding that no review can do it justice. They all take refuge, if that is the proper way to put it, in explaining the sources of the poems, the references, allusions, unquoted quotations; and here is an amazing display of scholarship, especially in Sweeney, Wheelwright, and Matthiessen. It makes one take an especial delight in criticism. Eliot has called the act of poetry (and we must include the reaction of criticism) a catalyst; and here is its demonstration. Southerners, New Englanders, English, New Yorkers are all saying practically the same thing in their reviews. One of the two unusual opinions apparent is Miss Deutsch's idea (1) that Eliot ought to write for the majority and (2) that the majority does

not believe in the Church. The other is Mr. Schwartz's scolding Mr. Eliot for his expression of his religion.

Otherwise there is faith in Eliot and unanimity of opinion. I had expected more animosity, since *Time* and Miss Deutsch point out that he is not naturally a sympathetic or popular poet. And yet he has held his readers' attention—it does not matter how many—and his work has produced the best and completest criticism of our time, because it is the best and completest poetry.

E. J. Storman, S. J. "Time and Mr. Eliot." *Meanjin* 3 (Winter 1944), 103–10.

Over the last seven years Mr. T. S. Eliot has been working on a sequence of poems published separately as "Burnt Norton," "East Coker," "The Dry Salvages," and "Little Gidding." These have been recently brought together for the first time in an American edition under the title *Four Quartets*. Thus assembled they make a long meditation, interspersed with lyrics, on the conquest of time and the meaning of history. This is the most considerable thing Eliot has done, and is destined to be of importance in the history of contemporary verse. A much larger claim, however, might be made for it. Our literature is not particularly rich in philosophic poetry of a high order, but here at last is something that can live, as a work of art, in the company of Dante and Lucretius.

It is one of the advantages of Mr. Eliot's work that he has chosen a subject of peculiar significance for modern times. The meaning of the time process has been occupying European thought to an unprecedented degree in this century, as may be conveniently seen, for instance, from Mr. Wyndham Lewis's polemical *Time and Western Man*. Mr. Eliot has the distinction of suggesting at various points the thought of such diverse thinkers and general writers as Whitehead, Bergson, Christopher Dawson, Berdyaev, Spengler, and, behind them, of a mixed company which includes Kierkegaard and Hegel, St. Augustine and Heraclitus. A number of these would, of course, prove inimical to his central position, but he has the virtue of being able to draw on those whom he does not follow for a method of approach or an interesting mental perspective. Thus unexpected windows open out from time to time within the poem, not merely on the subject-matter, but on the history of human thought about it.

The general scheme of *Four Quartets* is suggested by two Greek fragments from Heraclitus which preface "Burnt Norton." One reminds us of the Heraclitean world of flux with its cyclic interchange between the elements of earth, water, air, and fire, between the four seasons, and between life and death. Alternation between these opposites can be considered a "way up" and a "way down," but, since the process is cyclic, these are only two aspects of the same movement. The other fragment concerns the remarkable Heraclitean doctrine of the *logos* or Word. There is a directive principle behind the cosmic flux, and of this human intelligence, and, at a further remove, language, are participations. Symbolism based on this doctrine obviously lends itself to a Christian interpretation. What Mr. Eliot has in fact done is to take the Heraclitean formulas and penetrate them with Christian meaning without quite obliterating their original import. It is possible now to make out the chief structural principles. The poem is in a double sense a "harmony of opposites." Not merely are oppositions in the world of flux and time reconciled, but the cosmic cycles of change and succession are harmonized with the permanence of eternity, repetitions within the world process with the forward movement and ultimate consummation of history. Each of the four poems deals with the Heraclitean alternations, with an emphasis on one particular element and one particular season. In each there is a question either of the conquest of time through contact with eternity in a "timeless moment," or of impregnating time with significance by a prolongation and diffusion of this experience. The synthesis of eternity and time is treated as a consequence of the Incarnation of the Word, and the finalism of history is taken in function of the extension and fulfillment of that unique event.

Such a scheme involves a dialectical movement of thought and feeling which finds issue in a form analogous to that of music, where contrasts can be harmonized and resolved. The musical technique, already suggested by the title, can be seen most obviously in the sudden variations of movement and the complicated interweaving of themes. Each poem is built up of five parts or movements, with statement, counter-statement, and resolution chasing one another throughout. A meditative movement, usually executed in long, loose-fibred lines of *vers libre*, is succeeded by a lyric, which in its turn is followed within the same movement by a further meditation. The third and fifth movements are again meditative (the lines at the end of the fifth being tautened into a shorter measure), while in between them is a short fourth movement consisting entirely of a lyric. The first lyrics deals with some aspect of the Heraclitean rotation of elements, season, etc., viewed either as a resolving harmony, or, more usually, as strife and disintegration. The second treats some form of suffering or self-abnegation.

"Burnt Norton" takes its title, so English reviewers tell us, from a manor house in Gloucestershire, where Mr. Eliot was staying for a time. There is a kind of oscillation between this manor, with its rose-garden, its yew-trees, sunflower, and clematis, and the "gloomy hills of London," region of newspapers and dim trains. The time is autumn, and the Heraclitean element most in prominence is air ("the cold wind that blows before and after time"). The problem of the whole sequence, the "redemption of time," is stated here in such a form as to seem insoluble. In point in fact, however, the initial statement is only a thesis which is to be met with an antithesis, and these are assumed into a synthesis in "East Coker," and, more triumphantly, in "Little Gidding."

The ancient Greek doctrine of the "return of all things," based on a theory of the circular movement of time, would seem to make freedom impossible, and, with it, a significant pattern in history. The cosmic cycles hold on their inexorable way, bringing change which is only repetition. The present and future are contained in the past, the past is repeated in the future. The present is the momentary term of a deterministic process, and could not have been otherwise: "What might have been and what has been / Point to one end, which is always present." Here supervenes the first experience of what Mr. Eliot, possibly borrowing a formula from Kierkegaard, calls the "timeless moment." This seems to be (for Mr. Eliot, though not for the Dane) an imaginative and partly intellectual insight which reproduces on a lower plane some of the conditions of mystical intuition. A sudden hint of eternity is obtained, and the time process seems momentarily suspended.

[. . .]

In "Burnt Norton" the experience is given by way of an excursion from actuality into a world of the "might-have-been" (symbolized by the rose-garden), where childhood is linked with a past that was never realized. Insight comes in the midst of the daydream, but the moment may not last, for "human kind cannot bear very much reality," and the movement ends with a reassertion of the "one end, which is always present." A shift, however, has occurred within the meaning of the word "end," which now indicates primarily the goal or destiny of man, so that the verbal repetition of the initial thesis constitutes in part a real antithesis. Through a moment in time, time itself has been transcended, and the deterministic cosmic forces have been conquered.

A meditation on this experience, in which the contact between eternity and time is represented by "the still point of the turning world," leads to a consideration of the ascetic *via negativa*. Only by the "noughting" of soul and sense can one hope to approach the reality obscurely indicated in moments of insight. By contrast we have a picture of the time-victims ("men and bits of paper") in the London Tube:

> Only a flicker
> Over the strained time-ridden faces
> Distracted from distraction by
>   distraction
> Filled with fancies and empty of
>   meaning

A beautiful "Burnt Norton" lyric on the theme of renunciation leads to an analysis of language as an instrument for the formulation of inarticulate experience and this in turn seems to provoke a repetition of the "timeless moment":

> Sudden in a shaft of sunlight
> Even while the dust moves
> There rises the hidden laughter
> Of children in the foliage [. . .].

The redemption of time has only begun. Escape through the timeless moment is not a final solution. The virtue of that moment must be diffused through the time process, since man must sooner or later return to the changing world. The emphasis in "East Coker" falls on the "exploration" or forward movement in which man is once more caught in the flux, but is already transforming it by contact with eternity:

> We must be still and still moving
> Into another intensity
> For a further union, a deeper
>   communion
> Through the dark cold and the empty
>   desolation.

East Coker is the name of the village in Somersetshire whence Mr. Eliot's ancestors sailed to the New World [. . .]. The poem is of the summer and the return of things to earth. Heraclitus had observed that in a circle beginning and end are the same. This gives rise to two complementary propositions with which Mr. Eliot makes play: "In my beginning is my end," "In my end is my beginning." The application is, as usual, both to human and subhuman forms of existence. Not merely "bone of man and beast, cornstalk and leaf," but the stone and timber of houses go back to earth. In their beginning is their end. "On a summer midnight," the peasants of the past are resurrected in the fields by the village, and dance again round the fire. The rhythm of their dancing is one with the rhythm of the seasons and constellations, of life and death, and so, involved in the cyclic turning, these ghosts go back to earth: "Feet rising and falling./Eating and drinking. Dung and death."

[. . .]

Halfway through the poem the darkness of death is used to suggest the *Dark Night of the Soul* of the Spanish mystic St. John of the Cross, and, since this night is the way to spiritual light, the other aspect of the time process comes into play: "In my end is my beginning." Here we are to think of the doomed Mary Queen of Scots (it may be remembered that the well-known device on her handkerchief read: "*En ma fin est mon commencement*"), and of such dicta as "He that will lose his life shall save it." The solidarity between individual suffering and the redemptive Passion of Christ is then brought out in a curious and felicitous lyric in which stanzas of four-beat measure are ravelled up by final alexandrines. By the end of the poem the various levels of meaning contained within "In my end is my beginning" have been worked out, and hope has arisen out of many kinds of death.

With "The Dry Salvages" we move to the New England coast of America, the home of Mr. Eliot's youth. We are told in a note that the title derives from a "small group of islands" (perhaps once called "*Les Trois Sauvages*") "off the N. E. coast of Cape Anne, Massachusetts." Here, we have to do with winter and the conquering sea. We are back in the world of flux and time with a vengeance. But the bell which tosses on the sea near the islands, "rung by unhurried ground swell," does more than measure time; it sounds an annunciation, which, while being a warning, a herald of pain, is finally also an angelus, and we are reminded of the Virgin's shrine on the promontory. Annunciation and Incarnation, acceptance of the ravages wrought by cosmic change and consequent transformation of time, become indissolubly linked. (At this point, it may be remarked, Mr. Eliot touches on the central thought of Gerard Manley Hopkins' "Wreck of the Deutschland.") With release effected in the soul, we can resign ourselves to the operation of the cosmic cycles on the body:

> We, content at the last
> If our temporal reversion nourish

(Not too far from the yew-tree)
The life of significant soil.

"Little Gidding" is likely to become the most popular portion of Mr. Eliot's work, as the thought content is not as difficult as elsewhere, and the poetic quality can be very readily experienced. Here, for the first time, the poet of *Infernos* and *Purgatorios* (*The Waste Land*, "The Hollow Men"; "Ash-Wednesday," *The Family Reunion*) attempts a *Paradiso*. The torturing history of time turns out after all to be a *Divina Commedia*, a story with a happy ending. The triumph of fire in the periodic general conflagration of the Heraclitean scheme is assumed into the final consummation of history by love through the fulfillment of the Incarnation. But this is to anticipate. The time is the depth of winter, but it is a winter that suggests the spring. Snow in the hedgerows seems like hawthorn blossom, and the "brief sun flames the ice, on ponds and ditches." It is "midwinter spring," however, chiefly in virtue of the heart's heat, and, at the same time, since the bloom is "neither budding nor fading," "not in the scheme of generation," it is an augury of a summer beyond sense. It is characteristic of Mr. Eliot that he refuses to round off his scheme by giving us spring pure and simple: any *Paradiso* he has to offer us will be no easy apocalypse, but "a tremor of bliss, a wink of heaven" out of the midst of travail.

Little Gidding, it may be remembered, was the home of a community established by Nicholas Ferrar in the seventeenth century. The poet Crashaw, among the better known, lived there for a while. It is a place in which the sense of the past is strong: memories of "a broken king" "at nightfall" (Charles I, who once came riding into Little Gidding), and, by association, of "one who died blind and quiet" (presumably Milton), and of the various factions of the seventeenth century, are in the air. One of the chief constitutive elements in this, as in the preceding three poems, is an awareness of the organic continuity of history, of "the past gnawing into the present." Mr. Eliot, in fact, has his own version of that excellent saying "*neminem vere vivere diem praesentem nisi dierum praeteritorum memorem.*" Memory is used to view individual experience, whether of happiness or pain, as of a piece with the past experience of the race: the perspective widens as we look back, so that we come to transcend the limitations of self-interest and live in the general pattern of history. Our lifetime is [. . .] "not the lifetime of one man only / But of old stones that cannot be deciphered" ("East Coker").

History, however, is not only of the past, but very emphatically of the present: it is wartime, and "History is now and England." We move from Little Gidding to London, the London of the air-raids. A "dark dove with the flickering tongue" (a fighter-plane, which, while spitting death like a serpent, is, in a mysterious secondary sense, also an instrument of peace), has "passed below the horizon of his homing," and the shrapnel still falls. In the darkness before the dawn the poet falls in with a "familiar compound ghost" (*cf.* The "affable familiar ghost" of Shakespeare, Sonnet 86), who, when addressed in the language of Dante's *Inferno*, is resolved into Dante himself. A consummate section of *terza rima* (with masculine and feminine endings as the connecting principle instead of rhyme) gives the message of the master of language, a message which is in substance that of the conclusion of *Purgatorio* XXVI (where rehabilitation is effected by *willing* endurance of the "refining fire"). Then, with dawn breaking in the bomb-shattered street, the visitation ceases—"He left me, with a kind of valediction, / And faded on the blowing of the horn."

The last part of "Little Gidding" is dominated by Dame Julian of Norwich, the mystic of an optimism snatched from the fire of pain. Looking over the course of her own suffering, and over the tangle of human history, Julian was able to say: "Love was his meaning." [. . .]

It is the medieval, too, who supplies the refrain, "And all shall be well," with which Mr. Eliot finally brings together the chief themes of his poem in a piece of remarkable symbolism:

> And all shall be well and
> All manner of thing shall be well
> When the tongues of flame are
>   in-folded
> Into the crowned knot of fire
> And the fire and the rose are one.

This is the consummation of history, for the individual, the race, the material universe. Time and change find their issue in redemption.

So much for a general account of *Four Quartets*. The work has, I believe, been sometimes misinterpreted as it appeared in its separate parts, and so there is some point in calling attention to the main movement of its thought. But it is important primarily as a poem, and I am aware that I have hardly begun to speak about that.

---

*Reginald Snell. "T. S. Eliot and the English Poetic Tradition." New English Weekly 26 (14 December 1944), 77–78.

The four poems (three of them, as faithful readers of the *New English Weekly* will be proud to recall, first printed in the pages of this journal) which together constitute one of the most important poetic achievements of our time, have now appeared in a single volume, where they may be—as they always deserved to be—considered as a literary unity. A note speaks of "improvements of phrase and construction," but the only significant alteration from the pamphlet form of the poems, apart from the substitution of "and" for "or" in one place, and a semicolon for a full stop in another, is the appearance of the word "appeasing" instead of "reconciling," in connection with "forgotten wars"—a risky change, considering the emotional overtones to which the newer word now gives rise. The title is a good one: this is the chamber music of poetry, the wholly mature work of a most distinguished craftsman, and the poetic diction is as civilized, as grave and pure as good late Haydn. Each poem consists of five "movements," the fourth being much shorter than the others, and lyrical in form; themes are stated and restated, in the manner of music, inside each separate quartet, and certain phrases are common to them all. Their total length roughly doubles that of *The Waste Land*.

It would be tempting to let the critic in Eliot review the poems himself; the thing could be done, easily enough, from that admirable essay of his, "Tradition and the Individual Talent," which appeared in 1917. For these poems represent precisely the achievement of that true traditionalism which he there describes. Such prose quotations as follow in this article are all taken from that essay. What a remarkable, and what an exciting, development has taken place in Eliot's writing between those early poems of urbane disgust (diffident, private, mannered and in the best sense decadent, they were the final statement of the *kind* of poetry that had preceded them, and were of course immensely competent technically) and these latest poems which are bone and flesh of the English tradition! In one sense, no doubt, nobody but Eliot could have written them, but in another, it does not mater much who did write them—they are part of the whole body of English poetry. *Prufrock* and *Poems (1920)* were first-rate minor poetry, and intensely individual; *The Waste Land* and "The Hollow Men" were already major poetry, but still individual; "Ash-Wednesday" and the Ariel poems were recognizably the poetry of the later Eliot, whose work has reached universality and, in losing individuality, has found it (the same law obtains in artistic creation as in spiritual life). As he himself wrote, if we appreciate a poet without a prejudice in favor of individuality, in the sense of divergence from the main stream of tradition, "we shall often find that not only the best, but the most individual parts of his work may be those in which the dead poets, his ancestors, assert their immortality most vigorously." Much of the significance of the early poems is esoteric—that array of notes to *The Waste Land* (an average of one to every eight lines of the poem) was most of it necessary; but the *Four Quartets*, though parts of them are at least as conventionally "difficult," are in no need of notes. If a reader does not catch every literary allusion as such (and few readers are likely to), it is no great matter. He will certainly enjoy the poetry more if he is familiar with some, at any rate, of the books that the poet has loved and made part of himself (though few people would probably care to challenge him over Elizabethan dramatists, seventeenth-century divines, Seneca's plays, the *Upanishads* and a good many other things), but he will not necessarily understand it any better. The echoes from other writers are here truly organic, and the poems are not personal reflections garnished with choice morsels from other men's books—they are a cut from the joint of English poetry, and Eliot has wielded the knife. He has become wholly and effortlessly aware "of the mind of Europe—the mind of his own country—a mind which [a writer] learns in time to be much more important than his own private mind." Of all living poets, he has the strongest historical sense, which is "nearly indispensable to anyone who would continue to be a poet beyond his twenty-fifth year." Some of his early work has been reproached, and justly, for its too heavy load of erudition; it may be true that "a poet ought to know as much as will not encroach upon his necessary receptivity and necessary laziness," but one cannot quite forgive those early explanatory notes—a poem should no more need them than a string quartet does. The notes were necessary before, but are no longer. The gazetteer will tell anyone who is interested that East Coker is a village of 1360 acres in Somerset, with a population of 798, and that Burnt Norton is not to be found on a map (he will probably conclude that the poet has named it after the Harvard critic who shares his name); but neither this knowledge, nor a familiarity with Nicholas Ferrar's community at Little Gidding (acr. 724, pop. 39—and you really do "turn behind the pig-sty" when you make the pilgrimage to that remote and lovely spot, "to kneel where prayer has been valid") nor its connection with Charles I, is necessary for purely literary appreciation of the poems. If such facts as these, and many others, are known, they merely add extra and extra-literary enjoyment.

The handling of the symbolism throughout the *Quartets* is superb. Eliot has reached the stage when he can quote freely from other writings of his own as well as other people's ("human kind cannot bear very much reality" had already been said by his Becket); the corridor ("Gerontion"), the rose garden ("Ash-Wednesday"), the shaft of sunlight (*Murder in the Cathedral*), the heard laughter of children ("New Hampshire")—all these were used again in that fine and underrated play *The Family Reunion*, and all of them occur more than once in these latest poems. To them are now added the figure of the dance, and the pattern (already important in *Murder in the Cathedral*). The various meters and stanza forms throughout the poem are, with the possible exception of the second section of "The Dry Salvages," handled in a masterly way. There remains that special characteristic of Eliot's verse, his continual protestations of inarticulateness. "Prufrock" exclaimed nearly thirty years ago "It is impossible to say just what I mean," and the poet has been repeating the same thing, on and off, ever since—he says it, very beautifully and with a skillful variety of phrasing that carries its own denial, several times in these *Quartets*. It is becoming increasingly less true; the conversation that was once, indeed, "so nicely restricted to What Precisely and If and Perhaps and But" has lately assumed a lovely lucidity. And it is difficult to see how his almost Trollopian use of the propria persona is artistically justified, or what place there is for such phrases as "I have said before" and "You say I am repeating something I have said before. I shall say again" in the work of one who believes (how rightly!) that "the progress of an artist is a continual self sacrifice, a continual extinction of personality," and has himself triumphantly achieved the classical manner of writing that "is not a turning loose of emotion, but an escape from personality."

It never does to ignore the quotations at the head of his poems; the two fragments from Heraclitus printed at the beginning of this book, pre-Christian words with their profoundly Christian significance, form a fitting introduction to these four magnificent poems—to "Burnt Norton" with its faultless opening and concluding sections about Time, and its resolute pursuit of the *via negationis* to reach the "still point of the turning world" (the Grecian urn has here become a Chinese jar); to "East Coker" with its brilliant use of a typographical device to gain a particular poetical effect, its strong and thoroughly characteristic chthonic sense, and the lovely section about humility and the need for "waiting on" God; to "The Dry Salvages" with its admirable opening passage about the River (a new note in Eliot's verse is heard here) and the further preoccupation with "the unattended moment" that alone brings perfect reconciliation; and to "Little Gidding," certainly the finest poem of the four, with its Dantesque second section, its further handling of the themes of renunciation and the intersections of Time and Timeless, above all perhaps the moving refrain from the thirteenth *Shewing* of Julian of Norwich, in which Our Lord tells her that "synne is behovabil, but al shal be wel and al shal be wel and al manner of thyng shal be wele." These nine-hundred-odd lines ask for constant re-reading, not so much because of their "difficulties" (which are not really considerable) as because of the astonishing richness of their poetic content, and for a proper appreciation of their technical achievements. They are a true part of the English poetic tradition. They provide, also, the theme of a mediation, in which the intellectual and emotional elements are admirably balanced and mutually fortified, upon the mystery of the Incarnation.

Checklist of Additional Reviews

*"Mr. Eliot's Confession." *Times Literary Supplement*, no. 2014 (14 September 1940).

*W. H. Mellers. "Cats in Air-Pumps (or Poets in 1940)." *Scrutiny* 9 (December 1940), 298–300. ["East Coker"]

James Johnson Sweeney. "'East Coker': A Reading." *Southern Review* 6 (Spring 1941), 771–91.

Andrews Wanning. "Criticism and Principles: Poetry of the Quarter." *Southern Review* 6 (Spring 1941), 796–98. ["Burnt Norton"]

**Ethel M. Stephenson. "T. S. Eliot and the Lay Reader" I, *Poetry Review* 32 (October 1941), 289–94. ["Burnt Norton"]

*"Mr. T. S. Eliot's Progress. Search for Tradition. From Revolution to Orthodoxy." *Times Literary Supplement* 40, no. 2075 (8 November 1941), 554–58.

*Helen Gardner. "The Recent Poetry of T. S. Eliot." *New Writing and Daylight* (London: Hogarth Press, 1942), 84–86. ["The Dry Salvages"]

*Dilys Powell. "T. S. Eliot." *Britain Today* 69 (January 1942), 25–26.

*Frank Prince. "Some Recent Books." *Dublin Review* 210 (January 1942), 92–94.

Rolfe Humphries. "Salvation from Sand in Salt." *Poetry: A Magazine of Verse* 59 (March 1942), 338–39. ["The Dry Salvages"]

**Ethel M. Stephenson. "T. S. Eliot and the Lay Reader" II, *Poetry Review* 33 (March–April 1942), 80–83. ["East Coker"]

Philip Wheelwright. "The Burnt Norton Trilogy." *Chimera* 1, no. 2 (Autumn 1942), 7–18.

*"Midwinter Spring." *Times Literary Supplement*, December, 1942.

*Desmond MacCarthy. "A Religious Poem." *Times Literary Supplement*, 19 December 1942, p. 622.

**John Waller. "An Old Man and a Young Maiden." *Poetry Review* 31 (1943), 431–35.

*Melville Chaning-Pearce. "Little Gidding." *Nineteenth Century* 133 (February 1943), 74–78.

*Irene Brown. "Correspondence. Mr. Eliot, Mr. Orwell and Miss Raine." *Poetry* 2, no. 9 (February–March 1943), 61.

*James Kirkup. "Eliot." *Poetry* 2, no. 9 (February–March 1943), 52–55. ["Little Gidding"]

*Charles Williams. "A Dialogue on Mr. Eliot's Poem." *Dublin Review* 212 (April 1943), 114–22.

A. D. Emmart. "Mr. Eliot's *Four Quartets.*" *Baltimore Evening-Sun*, 8 May 1943, p. 4.

W. E. Garrison. "The Cult of the Irrational." *Christian Century* 60 (19 May 1943), 609–10.

Louise Bogan. "Verse." *New Yorker* 19 (22 May 1943), 72–74.

Lee Varley. "T. S. Eliot's *Four Quartets.*" *Springfield Republican* [Massachusetts], 23 May 1943, p. 7e.

Pearl Strachan. "The World of Poetry." *Christian Science Monitor Weekly Magazine*, 29 May 1943, p. 11.

"At the Still Point." *Time* 41, pt. 2 (7 June 1943), 96, 98, 101.

*Melvin Lasky. "On T. S. Eliot's New Poetry." *New Leader*, 19 June 1943, p. 3.

*R. N. Higinbotham. "Objections to a Review of 'Little Gidding.'" *Scrutiny* 11 (Summer 1943), 259–61. [Response to Harding's review reprinted in this volume, pp. 465–67.]

*F. R. Leavis. "Reflections on the Above." *Scrutiny* 11 (Summer 1943), 261–67. [Response to Harding's review and Higinbotham's objection to it]

Babette Deutsch. "The Enduring Music of the Past." *New York Herald Tribune Books*, 18 July 1943, p. 6.

Raymond Holden. "The Dark Night of the Soul." *Saturday Review of Literature* 26 (24 July 1943), 11.

Theodore Maynard. "Review of *Four Quartets*." *Catholic World* 157 (August 1943), 553–54.

Josephine Nichols Hughes. "The Unfamiliar Name." *America* 69 (28 August 1943), 577–78.

Francis X. Connelly. *Spirit* 10 (January 1944), 185–87.

*John Shand. "Around 'Little Gidding.'" *Nineteenth Century* 136 (September 1944), 120–32.

*Edwin Muir. "Later Poetry of T. S. Eliot." *Britain Today* 105 (January 1945), 37–38.

*Richard Lea. "T. S. Eliot's *Four Quartets*." *Adelphi* 21 (July–September 1945), 186–87.

*J. Henry Bodgener. "Spiritual Life and Literary Trends." *London Quarterly and Holborn Review* 170 (July 1945), 321–27.

*David Paul. "Views and Reviews: Structure in Some Modern Poets." *New English Weekly* 27 (26 July 1945), 131–32.

NOTES TOWARDS THE DEFINITION OF CULTURE
1948, 1949

Notes towards
the Definition of Culture

by

T. S. ELIOT

DEFINITION: 1. The setting of bounds ;
limitation (rare) - 1483
  —*Oxford English Dictionary*

FABER AND FABER LIMITED
24 Russell Square
London

*George Orwell. "Culture and Classes." *Observer*, 28 November 1948, p. 4.

In *Notes Towards the Definition of Culture*, Mr. T. S. Eliot argues that a truly civilized society needs a class system as part of its basis. He is, of course, only speaking negatively. He does not claim that there is any method by which a high civilization can be created. He maintains merely that such a civilization is not likely to flourish in the absence of certain conditions, of which class distinctions are one.

This opens up a gloomy prospect, for on the one hand it is almost certain that class distinctions of the old kind are moribund, and on the other hand Mr. Eliot has at the least a strong *prima facie* case.

The essence of his argument is that the highest levels of culture have been gained only by small groups of people—either social groups or regional groups—who have been able to perfect their traditions over long periods of time. The most important of all cultural influences is the family, and family loyalty is strongest when the majority of people take it for granted to go through life at the social level at which they were born. Moreover, not having any precedents to go upon, we do not know what a classless society would be like. We know only that, since functions would still have to be diversified, classes would have to be replaced by "élites," a term Mr. Eliot borrows with evident distaste from the late Karl Mannheim. The élites will plan, organize and administer: whether they can become the guardians and transmitters of culture, as certain social classes have been in the past, Mr. Eliot doubts, perhaps justifiably.

As always, Mr. Eliot insists that tradition does not mean worship of the past; on the contrary, a tradition is alive only while it is growing. A class can preserve a culture because it is itself an organic and changing thing. But here, curiously enough, Mr. Eliot misses what might have been the strongest argument in his case. This is, that a classless society directed by élites may ossify very rapidly, simply because its rulers are able to choose their successors, and will always tend to choose people resembling themselves.

[. . .]

Mr. Eliot [. . .] argue[s] that even the antagonism between classes can have fruitful results for society as a whole. This again is probably true. Yet one continues to have, throughout his book, the feeling that there is something wrong, and that he himself is aware of it. The fact that class privilege, like slavery, has somehow ceased to be defensible. It conflicts with certain moral assumptions which Mr. Eliot appears to share, although intellectually he may be in disagreement with them.

All through the book his attitude is noticeably defensive. When class distinctions were vigorously believed in, it was not thought necessary to reconcile them either with social justice or with efficiency. The superiority of the ruling classes was held to be self-evident, and in any case the existing order was what God had ordained. The mute inglorious Milton was a sad case, but not remediable on this side of the grave.

This, however, is by no means what Mr. Eliot is saying. He would like, he says, to see in existence both classes *and* élites. It should be normal for the average human being to go through life at his pre-destined social level, but on the other hand, the right man must be able to find his way into the right job. In saying this he seems almost to give away his whole case. For if class

499

distinctions are desirable in themselves, then wastage of talent, or inefficiency in high places, are comparatively unimportant. The social misfit, instead of being directed upwards or downwards, should learn to be contented in his own station.

Mr. Eliot does not say this: indeed, very few people in our time would say it. It would seem morally offensive. Probably, therefore, Mr. Eliot does not believe in class distinctions as our grandfathers believed in them. His approval of them is only negative. That is to say, he cannot see how any civilization worth having can survive in a society where the differences arising from social background or geographical origin have been ironed out.

It is difficult to make any positive answer to this. To all appearances the old social distinctions are everywhere disappearing, because their economic basis is being destroyed. Possibly new classes are appearing, or possibly we are within sight of a genuinely classless society, which Mr. Eliot assumes would be a cultureless society. He may be right, but at some points his pessimism seems to be exaggerated. "We can assert with some confidence," he says, "that our own period is one of decline; that the standards of culture are lower than they were fifty years ago; and that the evidence of this decline is visible in every department of human activity."

This seems true when one thinks of Hollywood films or the atomic bomb, but less true if one thinks of the clothes and architecture of 1898, or what life was like at that date for an unemployed laborer in the East End of London. In any case, as Mr. Eliot himself admits at the start, we cannot reverse the present trend by conscious action. Cultures are not manufactured, they grow of their own accord. Is it too much to hope that the classless society will secrete a culture of its own? And before writing off our own age as irrevocably damned, is it not worth remembering that Matthew Arnold and Swift and Shakespeare—to carry the story back only three centuries—were all equally certain that they lived in a period of decline?

---

*C. H. Sisson. "What Is Culture?" New English Weekly 34 (2 December 1948), 91–92.

[. . .]

The *Notes Towards the Definition of Culture*, the appearance of which is the occasion of the present notice, is, in a sense, a synthesis of various interests which have been exhibited in Mr. Eliot's earlier writings in prose. Characteristically, he tells us, in the first lines of his introduction, of some purposes he had *not* in mind in writing the book. He did not, he tells us, intend to outline a social or political philosophy, nor to make the book merely a vehicle for his observations on a number of topics. His aim was "to help to define a word, the word *culture*." In short, he is concerned to make the thing look as little like a synthesis, and as much like an analysis, as possible. In the course of the book he does the things he disclaims the intention of doing, and several other things as well. But the words of the Introduction serve to warn us that Mr. Eliot is here airing only such of his views on social and political philosophy as are relevant to the definition of culture, and no one, therefore, should suppose after reading this book that he has more than partial indications of Mr. Eliot's views on these matters. The book goes beyond its nominal subject matter only in the sense that it is impossible to talk sociology without talking several other things at the same time.

In the first chapter [. . .], Mr. Eliot endeavors "to distinguish and relate," the uses of the word which differ according to whether one has in mind "the development of an *individual*, of a *group* or *class*, or of a *whole society*." "It is part of my thesis," he says, "that the culture of the individual is dependent upon the culture of a group or class, and that the culture of the group or class is dependent upon the culture of the whole society to which that group or that class belongs. Therefore it is the culture of the society that is fundamental." Mr. Eliot then goes on to "try to expose the essential relation of culture to religion," and here he comes to a point which is original in more senses than one, and somewhat abstruse. He wishes to "make clear the limitation of the word *relation* as an expression of this 'relation.'" Mr. Eliot conceives "culture and religion as being, when each term is taken in the right context, different aspects of the same thing." Therefore neither can culture be preserved or developed in the absence of the religion, nor religion preserved and maintained without reckoning with culture. But, if there is question here of the unity of religion and culture, there is no question of their identity. Hence "aesthetic sensibility must be extended into spiritual perception, and spiritual perception must be extended into aesthetic sensibility and disciplined taste." It is true that Mr. Eliot speaks as if religious standards and aesthetic standards were ideally identical; or, to report him more accurately, as if to judge by either of these standards "should come in the end to the same thing," but he is careful to add that that "end" is one "at which no individual can arrive." The whole of the passage from which this is taken must be studied in Mr. Eliot's [. . .] own words and not merely in summary, comment or even quotation. It is, I think, the central point of the book, and, incidentally, it is the point at which Mr. Eliot's prose exhibits the maximum of suppleness, passion and refinement. In these pages Mr. Eliot seems to be struggling to express the perception which is the basis of all his subsequent ratiocination, and the writing shows at moments almost an excess of its own essential quality, just as a paragraph of Sir Thomas Browne may seem, even when the intensity of the writing is at its greatest, pleasurably over-burdened with its own very different self.

After explaining his theory of religion and culture Mr. Eliot goes on to discuss three of the conditions for culture. "The first of these," he says,

> is organic (not merely planned but growing) structure, such as will foster the hereditary transmission of culture within a culture: and this requires the persistence of social classes. The second is the necessity that a culture should be analysable, geographically, into local cultures: this raises the problem of "regionalism." The third is the balance of unity and diversity in religion—that is, universality of doctrine with a particularity of cult and devotion.

The first two are conditions that were evidently likely to strike a man whose political philosophy was of the kind to which Mr. Eliot's was supposed to belong, but it would be unfortunate if readers who do not share the views that they imagine to be his were thereby distracted from a careful study of the relevance of the persistence of social classes and regional differentiation to the persistence of culture. [. . .]

It is the later chapters of this book, I think, and particularly the notes on education, which are likely to receive most immediate attention from the public at large. There would be no great harm in this, if the people were thereafter and thereby coaxed into a consideration of the more fundamental matters with which the book starts. That may not always happen, however, for Mr. Eliot's remarks on education are not only of great intrinsic interest but of great emotive force. There are several wholesome but unpopular truths in this final chapter, and it is unfortunate that Mr. Eliot's presentation of them has in it an element which is bound to alienate certain readers more than the truths themselves would do. Mr. Eliot's long residence in this country has not, one might guess, enabled him to see the country's social structures otherwise than as an outsider. The result is, one suspects, that he has an unduly simplified notion of what constitutes the governing classes, and perhaps attributes undue weight and value to the upper and upper middle classes. [. . .] In a note to the *Idea of a Christian Society* which is of special interest to the reader of the present book, Mr. Eliot says: "Britain will presumably continue to be governed by the same mercantile and financial class which, with a continual change of personnel, has been increasingly important from the fifteenth century." That was hardly perspicacious, even for 1939, and a man of much less remarkable gifts, born and brought up in this country, would have avoided such a presumption. A similar defect of social perception marks some of the comments on education in this chapter. It is difficult, in the context of present society in England, to attach much meaning to being "educated above the level of those whose social habits and tastes one has inherited," at any rate in the cases where the education has had any appreciable effect on the subject. And it is a pity that, in discussing the case against equality of opportunity in education, Mr. Eliot has, as it were, looked at the problem from the top side only and spoken of the educated being unpleasant, or merely too numerous, and not con-

cerned himself with the lot of the underdog, who would be deprived of his natural protagonist in the person of the man of lively wits who remains in the subordinate classes. One wonders, too, what Mr. Eliot considers constitute advantages of birth in present-day England. The idea is not a simple one at any time; one might always ask whether a high degree of literacy in several consecutive generations may not deprive the heir of those generations of more than it gives him.

Without any major questions of principle being settled, or even more widely agreed upon, much that is done in this country might be better done if certain assumptions were less lightly made. One might recommend this book to politicians, but for the fact that politicians are rarely of an age or temper to be persuaded to abandon their assumptions. To Mr. Eliot's ordinary public, recommendation of any of his books is superfluous, but one may say that this one has a special interest for those who follow the elusive line of this paper. It is, by the way, inscribed to Philip Mairet.

*E. M. Forster. "The Three T. S. Eliots." *Listener* 41 (20 January 1949), 111.

There is T. S. Eliot who is a poet, and there are also two Mr. Eliots who write criticism. The poet does not enter into the volume under review; his great achievement lies elsewhere, and it has been awarded the highest possible honors, both in this country and abroad.

The critic—or rather critics—do enter. They dominate the scene, and although they never contradict one another there is a difference between them which must be noted. They differ according to the audiences they address. Most of the book is addressed to sophisticated and highly educated people, and it is, on the whole, not satisfactory. At the end of it, three broadcasts are printed; these were intended for popular audiences and they are, on the whole, a success. It would seem that when Mr. Eliot is wishing to instruct, his prose remains lucid, considerate, and assured; his excellent handbook on Dante is an example of this. When on the other hand he is writing for people who may answer him back, he becomes wary and loads his sentences with qualifications and precautions which make them heavy going. The very title of the book is ominous. It is not about culture nor about a definition of culture, nor does it even offer notes on a definition. It offers "notes towards the definition." By its caution and astuteness the title forestalls many possible objections. But what cumbersome English!

The broadcasts were intended for a German-speaking audience, and were translated into German for that purpose. In the first of them, Mr. Eliot speaks of the unity of European culture, and ascribes the richness of English to our continental connection. In the second, he describes the break-up of European culture during the last twenty years, and refers to the *Criterion*, the admirable review which he once edited. The third broadcast is the least satisfactory, because he advances in it towards a definition of culture, and then retires without making it clear where he has been. Culture is connected with the family if we interpret the family rightly. It is also connected—in certain circumstances—with much else. It is assuredly connected with Christianity. Here we reach firmer ground. We feel—and he would wish us to feel—that his religious faith is more important to him than anything else, and that art and literature

are only valid in their relation to it. The relation may be negative: "only a Christian culture could have produced Voltaire and Nietzsche." But as far as Europe is concerned, the relation must exist. Where there is not Christianity there is nothing. And it has to be Christianity of an approved type: Mr. Eliot grows increasingly theological. Smartly over the knuckles does he rap a certain book called *The Churches Survey Their Task*. They surveyed it wrongly. The rap occurs in the main body of the work. Here we may pursue, in greater detail and with superior caution, the ideas exposed in the broadcasts. There is much that is subtle and profound, much that is provocative, and we are bound to admit at the end that culture is even more important than we guessed. Unfortunately she has not become more accessible. Through the criss-cross of reservations and postulates we can scarcely catch sight of her, or see where she is going.

The book is prefaced by a quotation from Lord Acton: "I think our studies ought to be all but purposeless." The quotation does not seem appropriate in view of Mr. Eliot's purposeful interest in polemical Christianity. Acton, too, was a deeply religious man. But he was also a convinced liberal, and Mr. Eliot, for all his many-sidedness, cannot be described as that.

---

*Christopher Dawson. "Mr. T. S. Eliot on the Meaning of Culture." *Month* 1, n.s. (March 1949), 151–57.

It is eighty years ago since Matthew Arnold first took up the cudgels in defense of culture against the Philistines as represented by John Bright and Frederic Harrison and the *Daily Telegraph*. At that date the very word was unfamiliar, and when John Bright described it as a "smattering of two dead languages" he was probably expressing the views of the average Englishman. Today the situation has entirely changed. The word is not only accepted; it has been adopted by the planners and the politicians, and has become part of the international language or jargon of propaganda and ideological controversy. Consequently when Mr. Eliot comes forward in defense of culture, his first task is to rescue the word from the bad company into which it has fallen, to define its proper limits and to restore its intellectual respectability and integrity. [. . .]

Mr. Eliot is no longer using the word in Matthew Arnold's sense. For while the latter was concerned only to maintain and extend its traditional classical sense as the harmonious development of human nature by the cultivation of the mind, the former has adopted the modern sociological concept of culture as a way of life common to a particular people and based on a social tradition which is embodied in its institutions, its literature and its art.

[. . .]

The value of Mr. Eliot's approach may be seen by the way in which it directs our attention to those great primary elements of culture—family, region and religion—which tend to be ignored equally by the socialist advocates of a planned society, on the one hand, and by the surviving champions of the liberal ideal of free individual culture on the other.

He does not, however, deal as fully with the social function of the family as we might have expected, since his chapter on the organic structure of culture is almost entirely concerned with the question of classes and elites. Unfortunately contemporary opinion on this subject has been so deeply affected by the economic individualism of the nineteenth century and by the Marxian ideology of class war that it is now almost impossible to restore the sociological concept of class as Mr. Eliot sees it and as it existed in the past. For even the nineteenth-century terminology of "upper," "middle" and "lower" was already economic rather than sociological in character.

[. . .]

Mr. Eliot is concerned above all with the problem of social tradition—i.e. the maintenance and transmission of the standards of culture. This, he argues, is the function of the class, rather than the elite, for "it is the function of the class as a whole to preserve and communicate standards of *manners*—which are a vital element in group culture." At this point Mr. Eliot comes into sharp collision with the dominant ideologies not only of Marxian socialism but of his own democratic world. For the equalitarian traditions of the American and the French Revolutions have always been profoundly hostile to the idea of an organic class structure; and though American society has traveled a long way from the agrarian democracy of the early nineteenth century, it has always accepted the atomic conception of society which Mr. Eliot condemns; so that the millionaires, at any rate in theory, represent an economic elite with no uniform social background rather than a governing class or an economic aristocracy. [. . .]

Nevertheless the problem is a serious one which at least deserves serious discussion. We are too apt to believe that everything would go well with the world if only we could enforce common standards by universal economic planning and some form of political world organization, and we ignore the tremendous dangers which threaten man's spiritual freedom under the impersonal tyranny of a mechanized order in which the individual is considered merely as one among the hundred million or five hundred million units which compose the modern promiscuous mass society. [. . .]

Religion, not social differentiation, is the real safeguard of spiritual freedom, since it alone brings man into relation with a higher order of reality than the world of politics or even of culture and establishes the human soul on eternal foundations. This, however, does not mean that religion is alien from or indifferent to culture. No one could put the case for the unity of religion and culture more strongly than Mr. Eliot does. In fact he argues that if a culture is the way of life of a whole people, then a Christian people, which seeks to be wholly Christian and Christian all the time, must inevitably aspire to the identification of religion and culture. In other words, a culture is the incarnation of a religion: they are not two different things which may be related to one another, but different aspects of the same thing: one common life, viewed at different levels or in reference to different ends.

If this view is carried to its logical conclusion, it leads us into considerable difficulties, as Mr. Eliot himself admits. "To reflect that from one point of view religion is culture," he writes,

> and from another point of view culture is religion, can be very disturbing. To ask whether the people have not a religion already, in which Derby Day and the dog track play their parts, is embarrassing; so is the suggestion that part of the religion of the higher ecclesiastic is gaiters and the Athenaeum. It is inconvenient for Christians to find that as Christians they do not believe enough, and that on the other hand they, with everyone else, believe in too

many things: yet this is a consequence of reflecting, that bishops are a part of English culture, and that horses and dogs are a part of English religion.

Yet, in spite of these paradoxical consequences Mr. Eliot remains convinced that religion and culture are inseparable and that the traditional conception of a *relation* between religion and culture as two distinct realities is fundamentally erroneous and unacceptable. Yet I believe that the idea of such a relation is inseparable from the traditional Christian conception of religion and that the paradoxes that are inherent in his view are gratuitous difficulties which are due to ignoring the necessary transcendence of the religious factor.

[. . .]

Certainly religion is the great creative force in culture and almost every historic culture has been inspired and informed by some great religion. Nevertheless Religion and Culture remain essentially distinct from one another in idea, and the more religious a religion is the more does it tend to assert its "*otherness*" and its transcendence of the limits of culture. This ultimate dualism is most strongly marked in Christianity which has always placed its center of gravity outside the present world, so that the Christian way of life is seen as that of a stranger and an exile who looks home towards the eternal city in which alone his true citizenship is to be found. [. . .]

[T]his introduction of a higher spiritual principle into man's life—this denial of the self-sufficiency and self-centeredness of human life is no more opposed to the development of culture than it is to the freedom of the personality. On the contrary, the widening of man's spiritual horizon, which results from the Christian view of the world, also widens the field of culture, just as the personality of the individual is deepened and exalted by the consciousness of his spiritual destiny.

No one understands this better than Mr. Eliot, who has done so much to restore to our generation a consciousness of the high tradition of Christian culture. Indeed, his own poetic achievement is a most striking example of the way in which the Christian view of reality has enriched and deepened the inner life of our own contemporary culture. And what is here achieved in the unique personal form of poetic creation may be realized also at every level of the social process in the common life of the people as a whole. Everywhere man's way of life is capable of being guided and informed by the spirit of religious faith. But, however completely a culture may seem to be dominated by religion, there remains a fundamental dualism between the order of culture which is part of the order of nature and the principle of faith which transcends the natural order and finds its center outside the world of man.

[. . .]

W. H. Auden.
"Port and Nuts with the Eliots."
New Yorker 25 (23 April 1949), 92–97.

Like most important writers, Mr. T. S. Eliot is not a single figure but a household. This household has, I think, at least three permanent residents. First, there is the archdeacon, who believes in and practices order, discipline, and good manners, social and intellectual, with a thoroughly Anglican distaste for evangelical excess:

his conversation, so nicely
Restricted to What Precisely
And If and Perhaps and But.

And no wonder, for the poor gentleman is condemned to be domiciled with a figure of a very different stamp, a violent and passionate old peasant grandmother, who has witnessed murder, rape, pogroms, famine, flood, fire, everything; who has looked into the abyss and, unless restrained, would scream the house down:

Reflected in my golden eye
The dullard knows that he is mad.
Tell me if I am not glad!

Last, as if this state of affairs were not difficult enough, there is a young boy who likes to play slightly malicious practical jokes. The too earnest guest, who has come to interview the Reverend, is startled and bewildered by finding an apple-pie bed or being handed an explosive cigar.

From its rather formidable title, it is evident that Mr. Eliot's latest essay, *Notes Towards the Definition of Culture*, is officially from the pen of the archdeacon, who is diffident about his powers but determined to do his social duty even under very unpropitious circumstances [. . .].

With a proper caution and a schoolmaster's conscientiousness, the archdeacon begins by defining the various senses in which the word "culture" is used: to mean (1) the conscious self-cultivation of the individual, his attempt to raise himself out of the average mass to the level of the élite; (2) the ways of believing, thinking, and feeling of the particular group within society to which an individual belongs; and (3) the still less conscious way of life of society as a whole.

There are always two cultural problems: cultural innovation, i.e., how to change a culture for the better, however "good" may be defined; and cultural transmission, i.e., how to transmit what is valuable in a culture from one generation to the next. It is to the second problem that Mr. Eliot addresses himself—and rightly, most people, I think, will agree, for in the unstatic and unstable societies of our age, transmission, or cultural memory, is the major problem. Starting from the premise that no culture has appeared or evolved except together with a religion, whichever may be the agent that produces the other, he states and develops the thesis that the transmission of any culture depends on three conditions: (1) the persistence of social classes; (2) the diversity of local or regional cultures within a larger cultural unit; (3) the diversity of religious cult and devotion within a large universality of religious doctrine. The premise is, I think, undeniable, even by the most violent atheist, for the word "religion" simply means that which is binding, the beliefs or habits of conduct that the conscience of an individual or a society tells him he should affirm, even at the cost of his life (and nobody has a personal identity without such). . . . Nor will anyone quarrel, I think, with Mr. Eliot's contention that in a civilized society religion and culture, though interdependent—"bishops are a part of English culture, and horses and dogs are a part of English religion"—are not and should not be identical; e.g., it is only in a barbarous society that to drive on the right or to eat boiled cabbage or to listen to the music of Elgar would be regarded not as matters of habit or convenience or taste but as matters of ultimate significance. This, however, involves the conclusion that the religion of a civilized society is distinguished by the existence of dogma as separate from mythology and cult.

[. . .]

However, it is not Mr. Eliot's views on religion that are going to get him into hot water with a great many people but his approval of hereditary classes and his doubts about universal education, for here the archdeacon is from time to time replaced by the boyish practical joker, whose favorite sport is teasing the Whigs, particularly if they happen to be Americans.

[. . .]

The value of Mr. Eliot's book is not the conclusions he reaches, most of which are debatable, but the questions he raises. For instance, how has culture been transmitted in the past? If the methods of the past are no longer possible, how can it be transmitted now? Mr. Eliot is only partly right, I think, in asserting that in the past the role of transmission was played by a class or by classes. For many centuries, it was transmitted by the Church; i.e., by an institution with a hereditary status whose members could be drawn from any social class. In England, it was only during the last two centuries or so that the responsibility for culture passed to social classes, first to the landed aristocracy, and then, when they became stockholders without responsibility, to the professional classes—the clergy, the doctors, the lawyers, etc. And even then it was certain institutions—the greater universities, the cathedral closes—that were really responsible. [. . .]

The American problem has been unique. Jefferson and Hamilton read no different from Europeans; then, between 1830 and 1870, say, there emerged a culture that was definitely non-European, but also entirely Anglo-Saxon; after that, in a sense, America had to begin all over again. It was perhaps unfortunate that, with the exception of the Germans of '48 and the Jews who came to escape persecution, the stimulus to immigration from Europe during the nineteenth century was so simply poverty, for this meant that of, for instance, the Irish and Italians who came, few were conscious bearers of their native culture and few had many memories they wished to preserve. This, and the absence of any one dominant church, has placed almost the whole cultural burden on the school, which has had to struggle along as best it could, with all too little help from even the family. It is a very encouraging sign that social groups within American society—the labor unions, for instance—are beginning to go into education instead of leaving it all to the state. [. . .]

Further, the more the total task of education can be shared among different groups, the smaller the educational unit can be. It is almost impossible for education organized on a mass scale not to imitate the methods that work so well in the mass production of goods.

The greatest blessing that could descend on higher education in this country would be not the erection of more class barriers but the removal of one; namely, the distinction drawn between those who have attended college and those who have not. As long as employers demand a degree for jobs to which a degree is irrelevant, the colleges will be swamped by students who have no disinterested love of knowledge, and teachers, particularly in the humanities, aware of the students' economic need to pass examinations, will lower their standards to let them.

So one could go on chatting and wrangling with the archdeacon all evening. [. . .]

The talk has been stimulating, the port excellent. Do go on. I am not questioning the usefulness . . .

[. . .]

The conversation trails off into silence. Whig? Tory? All flesh is grass. Culture? The grass withereth. One realizes that one is no longer reading lucid prose or following an argument; one has ceased trying to understand or explain anything; one is listening to the song of the third Eliot, a voice in Ramah, weeping, that will not be comforted.

R. P. Blackmur.
"T. S. Eliot on Culture."
Nation 168 (23 April 1949), 475–76.

The American reviews which I have seen of T. S. Eliot's *Notes Towards the Definition of Culture* have conspicuously and I think outrageously misunderstood both Eliot's intentions and the context of thought and feeling in which he wrote, I cannot set these reviewers right—I am not sure I can be right about Eliot myself—but it should be at least possible to make out that Eliot is not a snob in his feelings and that his thought is genuine: it touches the actual world while reminding us of the oldest form of the ideal world.

As to his feelings, what matters is that always, when the time comes, Eliot is great-spirited. His magnanimity is the rhythm—something deeper and more moving than what he says—that makes him memorable. What other Christian of our time would so often require, not conformity or conversion, but the active help of the atheist and the agnostic? Who else so practices his belief in "dining with the Opposition"? Who else, with such evident warrant of sincerity, insists that to liquidate the enemy is a crime against culture as well as against religion? He might share Santayana's argument that the Gospel reason for loving one's enemy is that God loves him; but he puts it well enough for himself: "Fortunate is the man who, at the right moment, meets the right friend; fortunate also the man who at the right moment meets the right enemy. . . . One needs the enemy . . . The universality of irritation is the best assurance of peace."

As for his thought—and the feeling is there with the thought—what matters is

508

that in these essays on culture he is making a great plea for the individual, not for the superior individual or for the inferior individual in a superior position, but for the human individual himself, whatever his talent or position may be. That is the very strong personal theme of the book: the search for the recovery of individual life from mass or collective life, and for the renewal of private life. He makes his effort along lines which are meant to reduce the scope and raise the value of public life. No doubt he runs counter to his time, believing his time to be a backwash or eddy in the main stream; and beyond a doubt also he is trying to persuade us to a task difficult at any time.

To Eliot the individual is the hardest thing to be, and it takes permanent and continuous effort. He knows a man may be an individual only among other men. No one could be individual in a wholly strange society, or in a society that was wholly a crowd. Nor, again, could individuals survive in a society governed by a rigid order, or by an order asserted and developed by any single part of the mind. The individual requires rather conversation with his own kind and with other kinds; he requires, in his own society, to be developed out of what came before him and to develop, if he can, what will come after him. Otherwise there will be nothing individual in him, only what can be atomized, so that he could never enjoy, whether in great affairs or in personal intimacy, either a silly joke or a contented silence, which are right rules for both.

It is such individuals and such a society (society: the fellowship of individuals) that Eliot wants; he wants the culture which will make them possible; and for that culture he is willing to pay the cost— the cost that is everything, the cost that has always been paid except when substitutes or bankruptcy made the event. The cost Eliot is willing to pay for culture is that of a prestige society—a society capable of creating prestige for its values, where the greater the prestige, the greater the manifestation of value, both at the upper and the lower levels of society, and where the classes with the greatest prestige (not the greatest power) have the function of carrying on what as individuals they may not possess, the possibility of the highest form of these values.

Is not prestige, the possession of presence by attribution, the public proof *and* the inner assurance of the private, individual life? Prestige is the saturated atmosphere between personalities which is felt as consideration. The *moving* quality in a private or a public relationship is prestige. We force upon each man his function, but there is with each function the gift of the prestige of the function. Think of family, the love affair, the law, parliament, the church. Think, above all, when reading Eliot, of the church and of the religion under the church. What is religion but the cultivation of the force which is the source of all prestige? We practice forms, each time praying they may be filled; certainly we do not always know with what. It is the same whether in "church" or in "society," in religion or in culture.

Here is the important part of Eliot's position. For him it depends only on your point of view whether you say religion develops out of culture or culture develops out of religion. He will not identify religion with culture, and he will distinguish when he must between culture and religion; and he knows that there is more at work in a mind than either culture or religion. There is terror for us all in the form his recognition takes. We are not unified, he says, we are not pure, our behavior has something to do with our belief, and we live also on the level where these cannot be distinguished. It is very disconcerting, he says, to play on this reflection. "It gives an importance to our most trivial pursuits, to the occupation of our every minute, which we cannot contemplate long without horror or nightmare."

What Eliot *ventures* to say himself— and it is a very real venture, the venture of what all his later poetry is up to—is that culture is the *incarnation* of the religion of a people; incarnation, bodying forth; the attempt of the ultimate real to become actual. Something of this sort is what, from a secular point view, Roger Sessions meant by saying that music makes great gestures of the spirit. Perhaps, in Eliot's context, culture has to do with the relation between the spiritual and material organization in a society, as felt and carried by individuals. Perhaps, for him, it is religion alone which communicates the forces that keep life going in the individual; something very different from either identification or relation, something very like *incarnation*. It is a poet's thought, not an educator's, but it is thought.

Being a poet's thought, it is dramatic. The degree and kind of incarnation, will vary from region to region, group to group, individual to individual, without impairments of what is being incarnated. Loyalties will vary, politics contrast, unity is far off. So there must be neither excess of unity nor excess of division; uniformity is death, and orthodoxy must develop out of conflict with fresh heresies. There must be both the constant struggle between the centrifugal and the centripetal for the sake of balance, and an unremitting effort to be individuals in whom alone the balance can be reached.

This is a friendly account of Eliot's attempt to define culture as the incarnation of the religion of a people. His definition seems to me to touch life and also to renew life: it is, in the poetic sense, a partial act of incarnation; and it seems to me that it is altogether under this head that

we ought to accept, to quarrel with, or to discount Eliot's particular deductions about education and politics and elites: that there ought not to be too much of any of these, and that the intellect does not know enough about any of them to decide how much is enough.

As for myself, I discount more than I quarrel, and quarrel more than I accept, as one ought to in any conversation concerned with developing orthodoxy, whether Christian or otherwise human. I am not a politician and have no wish to nose out ideas, as Eliot says, only when they have begun to stink. But I rather think I should like to agree when Eliot says, early in the book: "To judge a work of art by artistic or by religious standards, to judge a religion by religious or artistic standards should come in the end to the same thing: though it is an end at which no individual can arrive." I agree, because this is at heart the direction in which Eliot works.

---

*Hermann Peschmann. *Adelphi* 25 (July–September 1949), 331–32.

[. . .]

Mr. Eliot is conservative in the exact sense in which all his prose writing from "Tradition and the Individual Talent" (1917) to *The Idea of a Christian Society* (1939) is conservative: and all valuable writing about culture must be of this nature. For, as Mr. Eliot insists, "culture" is a residual and accumulative thing, partly built, but, in the main, unconsciously growing out of the beliefs, traditions, occupation and achievements of a particular people, in a given locality, over a period of time: "You cannot put on a new culture ready made. You must wait for the grass to grow to feed the sheep to give the wool out of which your new coat will be made."

Culture is the way of life of a whole people interacting for their common benefit. An endeavor to impose uniformity of culture—and we do not need to look only at the Totalitarian countries for this, but a little nearer home—can only be a leveling down where, as Browning says in a rather different context, "A common greyness silvers everything."

"We need variety in unity," Mr. Eliot reminds us, "not the unity of organization, but the unity of nature." And this is where, and why, he is hierarchic. He sees three levels of culture: that of the individual; that of the group (the smallest group is the family) or class of which the individual is a member; that of the society of which the group or class is a component. It is culture in its widest [sense] with which he is ultimately concerned—the culture of a society; but his thesis is that that can flourish only if it does so at different levels in different strata, in groups and individuals, and with some accentuation of regional characteristics. And ultimately the culture of a society is to be *related to*, but never to be *identified with*, the religion of that society, "the culture being, essentially, the incarnation of the religion of a people." Many pages of thought go to the exposition of these distinctions, and to the meaning of "related."

After a brief introductory survey, Mr. Eliot deals with the three senses of culture—in individual, group, and society; defends the necessary stratification of society and expounds his doctrine of an elite—a word not tainted here with the implications of snobbery it too often has. He then passes on to consider sub-cultures (again not a term of derogation) of region, sect, and cult. There follow notes on politics and on education in which he shows how the greater (the culture of the society) must comprehend the least (politics or education) and not vice versa as is widely the case today. In the course of this he subjects our conceptions of education to a searching analysis. The book concludes with the English text of three wise and luminous broadcast talks to Germany, [. . .] "The Unity of European Culture."

The whole work is written with a rare humility implicit in the very tentativeness of its title, and recurrent throughout its pages. [. . .] [H]is conviction of the rightness of his beliefs is tempered with courteous consideration for those of others; not arrogance, but humble certitude is the keynote of his approach to his subject, the magnitude of which he never for a moment underestimates. [. . .]

Richard M. Weaver. "Culture and Reconstruction." *Sewanee Review* 57 (Autumn 1949), 714–18.

It is a historical truth that institutions do not produce their great apologias until they are on the point of passing away. In the days of their vigor, their value and perdurance are assumed; and it is only when that value is challenged and their existence becomes a matter of question that we are stirred to prepare a logical defense of them. This unhappy recollection is prompted by the appearance of T. S. Eliot's *Notes towards the Definition of Culture.* Mr. Eliot's view is somber, and he is not unaware that he may be defining a thing which, for our time, is moribund. "We can assert with some confidence that our own period is one of decline; that the standards of culture are lower than they were fifty years ago; and that the evidences of this decline are visible in every department of human activity." It therefore seems to him not unreasonable to anticipate "a period, of some duration, of which it is possible to say that it will have *no* culture."

Perhaps the surest sign that modern culture is in a critical state is the number of things which are today mistaken for culture; and I imagine that Mr. Eliot's work will have value chiefly as a corrective of popular misconceptions. The list of these is worth noting.

First of all, culture does not consist of a set of manners and attitudes which are the property of those at the top of the social and economic structure. On the contrary, any healthy culture is to be found diffused throughout the entire structure, and the author feels that in the end we are driven to locate it "in the pattern of society as a whole." Culture requires the persistence of classes, but it is not a class possession. It is equally wrong to suppose that the modern hypostatization Education is synonymous with culture. It appears rather that in spreading that abstraction we are lowering our standards and giving up the study of those things through which real culture is transmitted. Education of the modern kind is a defensive response to a disintegrating society; we have no evidence that it can improve culture, though we have evidence that it can "adulterate and degrade it." [. . .]

Thus far the definition proceeds through a series of eliminations, and we expect next a look at the positive nature of culture itself. Here naturally the author moves with caution. I believe that his best thought appears in what I should term the principle of counterpoise. It explains the proportion of space he has given to a defense of regionalism and of religious diversity, and allows us to see the grounds on which he embraces the unpopular principle of the class society.

The principle of counterpoise is probably best seen in relation to the latter. [. . .] [A] class structure is necessary, along with other patterns, because cultures need forces that offset each other. "One needs the enemy." A nation whose enthusiasms and antagonisms are counterpoised at home is less likely to go looking abroad for a fight, and culture demands periods of real peace. It is precisely when these internal differences are made to disappear in favor of an enforced solidarity that the world begins to scent an aggressor. In this sense *culture* and *Kultur* are seen to be opposed conceptions. "A nation which has gradations of class seems to me, other things being equal, likely to be more tolerant and pacific than one which is not so organized." The same principle applies to differences of religious sect and cult. The opponent, or the counterweight, helps one to define himself. A "world" culture, or a national culture, is richer for tolerating local cultures, if indeed it does not find its very existence in the relations between these.

Mr. Eliot has so many valuable things to say about the services of regionalism to a culture that one wishes he had drawn examples from the United States, where regionalists have had an uphill battle against nationalizing and centralizing tendencies, and where the right to regionalism may well be decided for the whole world, considering the prestige of the American leviathan. He points out quite properly that the champions of local traditions are often most fiercely opposed by others among their own people. Sometimes this occurs because the defenders make out an absurd case; but it occurs more often, I should say, because the compatriots have found that they can do profitable business with the national or general culture which is swallowing the region. In any event, one of Mr. Eliot's most illuminating remarks is that to have a culture a people needs not merely enough to eat, but also "a proper and particular *cuisine*." In our own country, it should have been recognized, corn bread or blueberry pie is more indicative of culture than is a multimillion-dollar art gallery which is the creation of some philanthropist.

This is virtually the extent of the definition. [. . .] [H]e stops with calling it "that which makes life worth living" and "the unconscious background of all our planning." [. . .]

The book as a whole seems directed at the bureaucratic delusion that everything is an administrative problem. If culture begins to flag, there must be a revision of administrative procedure, or the invention of new administrative machinery, to "save" it. Certainly it is no small achievement to expose the dilemmas which lie in wait for those who would reform culture by applying political catchwords.

The steps toward a definition of culture then are a series of corrections to keep an age which has confused virtually everything else from confusing culture with something material or mechanical. We realize that in the realm of contemporary politics words like "peace," "justice," and "democracy" are sometimes made to do duty for their logical opposites. The same thing could happen to "culture," and, within limits, has already begun to happen. If Mr. Eliot succeeds in saving the word from such perversion, he will have performed another important work of rescue and clarification.

Checklist of Additional Reviews

*Goronwy Rees. "Modest Proposal." *Spectator* 181, no. 6282 (19 November 1948), 666.
*Fyfe Hamilton. "Analysis of Culture." *John O'London's Weekly*, 21 January 1949, p. 49.
*G. H. Bantock. "Mr. Eliot and Education." *Scrutiny* 16 (March 1949), 64–70.
*Charlotte Young. "The Definition of Culture." *Adam* 17 (March 1949), 20.
Charles Poore. "Books of the Times." *New York Times*, 3 March 1949, p. 23.
Irwin Edman. "T. S. Eliot's Sociology." *New York Times Book Review*, 6 March 1949, pp. 3, 22.
Douglas Bush. "No Small Program." *Virginia Quarterly Review* 25 (Spring 1949), 287–90.
Max Lerner. "Towards a Definition of T. S. Eliot." *National Review* 120 (9 May 1949), 22–23.
Henry Rago. "T. S. Eliot on Culture." *Commonweal* 50 (13 May 1949), 122–25.
William Barrett. "Aristocracy and/or Christianity." *Kenyon Review* 11 (Summer 1949), 489–96.
Hugh Kenner. "Mr. Eliot's New Book." *Hudson Review* 2 (Summer 1949), 289–94.
Herbert Read. "Mr. Eliot's New Book." *Hudson Review* 2 (Summer 1949), 285–89.
Robert Gorham Davis. "Culture, Religion, and Mr. Eliot." *Partisan Review* 16 (July 1949), 750–53.
*George Catlin. "T. S. Eliot and the Moral Issue." *Saturday Review* 32 (2 July 1949), 7–8, 36–38.

E. Haldeman-Julius. "Eliot and the Critics." *American Freeman* 2126 (November 1949), 9.

*Brian Simon. "The Defence of Culture." *Communist Review* 4 (December 1949), 763–68.

Cleanth Brooks. "The Crisis in Culture." *Harvard Alumni Bulletin* 52 (1950), 768–72.

H. B. Acton. "Discussion: Religion, Culture, and Class." *Ethics* 60 (January 1950), 120–30.

*L. A. Cormican. "Mr. Eliot and Social Biology." *Scrutiny* 17 (Spring 1950), 2–13.

Robert Maynard Hutchins. "T. S. Eliot on Education." *Measure* 1 (Winter 1950), 1–8.

H. O. Pappe. "Some Notes on Mr. Eliot's Culture." *Landfall* [New Zealand] 4 (September 1950), 230–43.

THE COCKTAIL PARTY
1949, 1950

THE
COCKTAIL PARTY

a comedy by

T. S. ELIOT

FABER AND FABER LTD
24 Russell Square
London

*Desmond Shaw-Taylor.
"The Edinburgh
Festival—I."
New Statesman 38
(3 September 1949), 243.

[. . .]

The Cocktail Party, unlike Mr. Eliot's two earlier plays, is on the surface a specimen of contemporary dramatic style, as it is understood in Shaftesbury Avenue. The curtain rises on the usual stylish flat, with a white telephone, a Marie Laurencin, and a group of rather exasperated people determined to make the party go. The host, we begin to perceive, is also anxious to make the party go—in another sense; but when at last they depart, he persuades one of them to stay, a stranger to whom he can blurt out the embarrassing truth which he has tried to conceal from the rest: his wife has left him, and the guests we have seen are merely those who couldn't be reached and put off. A first-rate situation, and what follows is better still. The hitherto obscure and taciturn guest comes to life with a bang, takes command of the situation, and pours out a stream of sardonic and paradoxical home-truths to the egotistical husband; finally, [. . .] he bursts into song. The spirit of early Shaw hovers deliciously in the air; the wit sparkles and we begin to feel pleasantly sure that everything will be turned inside out and upside down in the second act.

So it is. The obscure guest is revealed as the eminent Sir Henry Harcourt-Reilly, of Harley Street; the two most tiresome of the guests turn out to be his assistants, almost his spies. The party-givers (the husband who is incapable of loving, and the wife who can never inspire love) are shown the truth about themselves, and persuaded to make the best of it. Making the best of it, says Sir Henry (and here for the first time we detect the accents of the lay preacher), making the best of a bad job is what we all have to do—all except the very few who are potential saints. One of these also comes to his consulting room: a girl who has just seen the bottom fall out of her ideal of romantic love. It is she who chooses the *via crucis* which leads from Sir Henry's mysterious "sanatorium" to literal crucifixion, accompanied by revolting details, at the hands of fanatical natives. When the news reaches another cocktail party, two years after the first, everyone shudders, except Sir Henry, who smiles his inscrutable smile. It was an issue which he had more or less foreseen.

No less inscrutable must be the author's smile. He has written a dazzling light comedy which is also a tract for the times; and the audience, who lap up the surface cream, don't know what to make of the depths, while suspecting that they must be more interesting than milk. Will the author help them? Only, a very, very little. When Sir Henry, accustomed to pronounce a priest-like benediction on his departing patients, remarks, "I do not understand what I myself am saying," a slight ripple of mirth went round the audience. Pressed by one of the characters for an explanation of his philosophy, he quotes Shelley:

> Ere Babylon was dust,
> The Magus Zoroaster, my dead child,
> Met his own image walking in the
> garden,
> That apparition, sole of men, he saw.

In short, know yourself; choose; come to terms with your insignificance, or—if you happen to be one of the saintly few—face the full consequences of your choice.

If the moral, as I attempt to put it, sounds rather thin and milky, it is doubtless my fault—one which deeper

517

acquaintance with this fascinating play might mend. But there is something about it which chills me: perhaps the lack of delight in the rich variety of human nature. Mr. Eliot's characters are admirably amusing puppets, he manipulates them as cunningly as the magician in *Petrouchka*, but, like the host of his own party, he seems incapable of love: of warmth towards the particular, as opposed to a diffused benevolence. The muddy adorable substance of life as it is lived seems curiously far from this fragile community, and I find something faintly repellent in the quiet smiles and antiseptic wisdom of Sir Henry and his two pals. Considered as moral teachers and "guardians" (a key-word of the play), they suggest a group of infinitely superior Buchmanite leaders, out of the Upper Sixth instead of the usual Lower Fourth; but considered simply and solely as theatrical figures they are superb, just as the whole play is a superbly contrived conversation piece—lively, often cynical, sometimes profound. The verse is perceptible only as a gentle rhythmic pulse, and the language is almost that of life except for the substitution of "was not" for "wasn't," etc., which gives a pleasant stiffening to the dialogue. [. . .]

Robert Speaight. "The Cocktail Party." Tablet 194 (3 September 1949), 154–55.

The Cocktail Party, presented last week at the Edinburgh Festival, is the most advanced and original point yet reached in Mr. Eliot's dramatic writing. Yet of his three plays this one will surely prove the most accessible to the ordinary playgoer. *Murder in the Cathedral* presupposed a certain familiarity with Christian dogma and liturgy, and a readiness to accept a poetry which never concealed its metrical diversity. In *The Family Reunion* the Greek Eumenides were made the messengers of grace; and although *The Family Reunion* marked a long step forward in theatrical technique, and although Mr. Eliot had discovered a verse form suitable for a contemporary subject and setting, the play moved a little stiffly and its climax of conversion was not dramatically realized. It was the actor rather than the dramatist, who had to sharpen the play to its point in the great dialogue between Agatha and Harry. But in *The Cocktail Party* there is little impediment for anyone who is not tone-deaf to the supernatural. It is a profound and subtle play, with multiple layers of meaning and an intricate symbolism. But the poetry, more loquative than the poetry of *The Family Reunion*, is precise and lucid; and the design is clear.

In the play's center are four people whose lives have become entangled. Edward, a middle-aging barrister, whose wife, Lavinia, has just left him, and who has for some time been in love with Celia; Peter, his friend, who is also in love with Celia; Celia, who loves Edward; and Lavinia, who loves Peter but knows herself to be unloved by him. It is a familiar mixture, but it is not the mixture as before. Around this central group are two friends, Julia, a gray-haired, good-natured society chatterbox, with Alex, a bright young man about town, and a third figure, unidentified at first, whom they have introduced to the Cocktail Party which opens the play. This is a well-known psychiatrist, Sir Henry Harcourt-Reilly, and his purpose is to set these frustrated lives in order. In the first act the pattern of personal relationships unfolds itself. In the second, Lavinia returns to a husband who surprisingly wants to take her back, although he has not yet learned to love her; and Celia says good-bye to a lover whom she had thought to marry but has now mysteriously outgrown. In the third act the scene shifts to Sir Henry's consulting-room. The psychiatrist, whom both Edward and Lavinia have been persuaded to see, neither of them knowing that he is their unidentified friend of the Cocktail Party, confronts husband and wife with each other and sends them back, not to the ecstasies and illusions of romantic love, but to what is still "in a world of lunacy, violence, stupidity, greed . . . a good life." From now on they will be

> . . . contented with the morning that
>   separates
> And with the evening that brings
>   together
> For the casual talk before the fire
> Two people who know they do not
>   understand each other,
> Breeding children whom they do not
>   understand
> And who will never understand them.

The scene that follows is the finest passage in the play. Celia comes in and we presently realize that here is a soul capable of subsisting on the glaciers of the spiritual life. Though she does not yet know it herself, she is a contemplative. This development has been subtly prepared for us, in her previous scene with Edward. At a loss to explain her own reaction at his desire to have Lavinia back—she is humiliated but surprised at her capacity to survive humiliation—she is aware of a state of mind for which Edward was not mainly responsible. "It no longer seems worth while to speak to anyone."

Now, confronted with the surgery of a consulting-room which is also a confessional, she can articulate her sense of sin. This is not a remorse for anything she has done, not a conventional consciousness of immorality, it is a sense, rather, "of emptiness, of failure / Towards someone, or something, outside myself; / And I feel I must . . . atone." She is coming, also, to a new understanding of love—"a vibration of delight / Without desire, for desire is fulfilled / In the delight of loving." And so Sir Henry sends her to the Special Sanatorium, which is reserved for those who, by suffering greatly themselves, can teach others that without suffering there is neither salvation nor significance. Celia is on the threshold of the intolerable discovery—that only sanctity makes sense. Supported by the "faith that issues from despair," she does not even know where she is going.

> The destination cannot be described;
> You will know very little until you get
>   there;
> You will journey blind. But the way
>   leads towards possession
> Of what you have sought for in the
>   wrong place.

For Celia, who is preeminently a lover, there can be no turning back. "I couldn't give anyone the kind of love—/ I wish I could!—which belongs to *that* life." Her nuptials are to be elsewhere; and as she goes, Sir Henry with Alex and Julia, who have contrived all these consultations and listened to them from the next room, pour out three glasses of sherry, and, breaking for the first time into formal verse, implore protection on her journey.

In the fourth act Edward and Lavinia are giving another a cocktail party. Among the guests are Sir Henry and Julia; Alex, returned from Africa, where he had been sitting on a Royal Commission; and Peter, arrived from Hollywood, where he has made good as a script writer, and eager to claim Celia as the film actress which he believes her to be. Then Alex explains that he cannot have Celia—because Celia is dead. She had joined a nursing order of nuns and been crucified by natives in a village which Alex had visited. He had seen her body decomposed and devoured by ants. This revelation, so dreadful and so uplifting, is achieved with extraordinary skill. The rattling of glasses and banter of conversation is suddenly arrested— and we are not embarrassed. Here, as elsewhere, Mr. Eliot is helped by his actors; no one puts a foot or an inflection wrong. The play ends with Sir Henry explaining why Celia's death had been a happy one, and with him, Julia and Alex, going off to another party.

The play is a masterpiece of theatrical contrivance. In the first act the trivial interventions of Julia and Alex, which seem an interruption of serious emotional business, prepare us for their critical intervention later. (Perhaps the Guardian Angels, whom they so amusingly symbolize, are more familiar than we guess.) The dramatist focuses his light, first upon Edward, who is our old friend J. Alfred Prufrock, and then upon Celia, who is already living the experience of the *Four Quartets*. Thus the play resumes, in its unstressed fashion, the long journey that Mr. Eliot has traveled. The loneliness of Gerontion is in Edward's definition of his dilemma:

> Hell is oneself,
> Hell is alone, the other figures in it
> Merely projections. There is nothing
>   to escape from
> And nothing to escape to. One is
>   always alone.

This is the other side of the Sartrian image which was dramatized in *Huis Clos*. The Lenten reminders of *Ash-Wednesday* are in Sir Henry's parting words to the reconciled couple: "Go in peace. And work out your salvation with diligence." Just as the realism and humility of the *Quartets* are

in his subsequent observation: "The best of a bad job is all any of us make of it—/ Except of course, the saints."

The gesture with which Mr. Alec Guinness took out his watch on these last words was perhaps the most imaginative moment in a magnificent performance. Sir Henry might so easily have become an ethical bore, sugaring his pills with whimsy. But with Mr. Guinness we are worlds away from ethics; this is the confessional and the choice is between the loss of personality and the love of God. Miss Irene Worth suggested, in a moving and vibrant study, the whole of Celia's capacity for sacred and profane love; Miss Ursula Jeans, with no sacrifice of natural charm, made Lavinia naturally unlovable, but yet made us realize, in the last act, how grace was doing its work; Mr. Robert Flemyng, young in years for Edward, gave us the authentic sag of middle age and a twinge of the Existentialist agony; and Miss Cathleen Nesbitt conducted Julia with both judgment and wit along the realistic and symbolic levels. This superb ensemble of English acting was so well directed by Mr. Martin Browne that you didn't notice it. But then Mr. Browne has been Mr. Eliot's theatrical *éminence grise* since the days of *Murder in the Cathedral*—and earlier. Author, actors and audience should be grateful that he has assisted into life a play which is among the rare masterpieces of the modern stage.

*Donald Bain. "The Cocktail Party." Nine 2 (January 1950), 16–22.

"A plot of contemporary people, such as the men and women we know, in the usual clothes that they wear today, in the same perplexities, conflicts, and misunderstandings that we and our acquaintances get involved in, and uttering no lines that are not relevant to the situation, the mood, and the dramatic action." This extract from Mr. Eliot's Presidential Address to the Poet's Guild, published contemporaneously with the Edinburgh production, explains the intention of *The Cocktail Party*.

[. . .]

The Cocktail Party is a play on two planes. And the first is that of artificial social comedy. As it were Prufrock on Pinero, with two sets of lovers and a circle to be squared; or at least so it seems for the first half of the play. But on the other plane *The Cocktail Party* is a justification of the ways of God to man in the high symbolic vein: the "Guardians" control our destiny, hell lies about us in our infancy, and God is not mocked. But if the intention is spiritual the framework is social.

The curtain goes up on a party. The sort of cocktail party where people know each other well enough not to be polite, and yet are too egotistical to be aware of each other as anything more than conversational buffers. The characters have stilted, oddly associative names—Mr. Chamberlayne, Miss Coplestone, Mrs. Shuttlethwaite, Peter Quilpe. Edward Chamberlayne is giving the party and not apparently making it a success. Later we learn that his wife, Lavinia, has just left him, forgetting to warn him about the party. As he is the sort of man who still believes that the final humiliation is to appear ridiculous, he pretends that nothing untoward has happened. He attempts to entertain two inquisitive friends of the family, his mistress, his wife's lover, and an elderly gentleman whom nobody seems to know. Mr. Eliot we feel is loose in the

Waugh country and practicing Cowardice with mellifluous glee.

The guests chatter on: "Lady Klootz was very lovely, once upon a time / Before she lost her teeth, and before she had three husbands . . ." and Mr. Eliot indulges his fascination with names. [. . .] This aptitude has for some time been suppressed but now it reemerges and the phalanx is augmented. Delia Verinder and her third brother—"They had to find an island for him / Where there were no bats . . ." [. . .] but more interesting than all of these is that imposing relative of the late Mr. Bunbury, Lavinia's aunt, who suffers from a mysterious illness in the depths of Essex and is the cause of numerous confusing telegrams.

It seems necessary to draw attention to these characteristics because the Edinburgh commentators tended to overlook the genuine humor of the play. Certainly at the eight festival performances the high-pitched intellectual giggle was frequently drowned by the full-throated roar one expects at a performance of *Harvey*. The hints dropped by Aunt Ivy and the Hon. Arthur Piper have come to fruition.

But the comedy is never allowed to become overloaded, and as soon as the party breaks up the main theme emerges. The Unidentified Guest remains behind and Edward Chamberlayne indulges in "the luxury / Of an intimate disclosure to a stranger" and then finds to his discomfort

... that to approach the stranger
Is to invite the unexpected, release a
    new force,
Or let the genie out of the bottle.
It is to start a train of events
Beyond your control ...

His guest describes the position of the man whose wife has left him—

Finding your life becoming cosier and
cosier
Without the consistent critic, the
patient misunderstander
Arranging life a little better than you
like it,
Preferring not quite the same friends
as yourself,
Or making your friends like her better
than you;

and then proceeds to persuade him that
when the clock stops thus in the dark,
"You're suddenly reduced to the status of
an object." [...] Eventually Edward grudg-
ingly admits that he wants his wife back,
because "I must find out who she is, to find
out who I am."

It is a short scene, and the information, in the second act, that the Unidentified Guest is not a visitor from an astral
plane, but Sir Henry Harcourt-Reilly, a
Harley Street psychiatrist, amplifies it in
retrospect. But Eliot only uses psychiatry
as the simplest method of putting spiritual
cross-examination on the modern stage.
He has not attempted to write a play about
psychoanalysis.

"All cases are unique and very similar to others," is only one aspect of Sir
Henry's attitude to his patients. When he
leaves Edward in the first act after drinking
a considerable amount of gin and water he
breaks into song: "Toory-ooly toory-iley, /
What's the matter with One-Eyed Riley."
When he dismisses his patients from his
consulting room his final injunction to
them is "Go in peace. And work out your
salvation with diligence." And finally it
appears that he is one of the three superior beings known as "Guardians." These
three, Sir Henry, Julia Shuttlethwaite, and
Alexander MacColgie Gibbs, the ubiquitous civil servant, combine the normal and
the vaguely supernatural in the manner of
the characters of Charles Williams. And

it is through the activities of these three,
rather than through the benefits of psycho-
analysis, that the solution of each personal
problem is reached.

As the play continues the intention
becomes clearer; on one side the benev-
olent Guardians, sufficiently human and
yet mysterious; on the other the four
distracted mortals overburdened by the
world and their own conscience. And by
the end of the play each in his own
way has worked out his salvation. Peter
Quilpe, the young man who loved Celia
and was Lavinia's lover, finds it by getting
a job for which he was fitted and making a success of it. Celia Coplestone, who
loved Edward, finds it by being "directed"
to Kinkanja, where "It would seem that
she must have been crucified / Very near
an anthill. [. . .]" In fact her salvation
is to become a saint. And Edward and
Lavinia having been "stripped naked to
their souls" and discovered "A man who
finds himself incapable of loving / And a
woman who finds that no man can love
her," achieve their salvation together by a
deeper understanding and sympathy.

But while each is led to the moment of
choice by the Guardians, the choice itself
is left to the individual. Mr. Eliot does
not concern himself with "the insuperably,
innocently dull," but the others, he insists,
must choose, if they are to avoid

                        . . .The final desolation
Of solitude in the phantasmal world
Of imagination, shuffling memories
    and desires.

And the second act describes the moment
of choice in the most sustained writing of
the play. For Edward and Lavinia it means
a return to "The stale food mouldering in
the larder / The stale thoughts mouldering in their minds," a recognition that they
"must make the best of a bad job." For
them the solution would seem to be in the

words of "East Coker." "The only wisdom we can hope to acquire / Is the wisdom of humility: humility is endless." [. . .] Mr. Eliot spares neither of the participants in the state of marriage before he allows them to make their choice. [. . .] But in the long duologue that follows between the psychiatrist who is, at another level, a Guardian, and the girl who is soon on the human level to become a saint, he gives a less bitter version of the married state.

[. . .]

The solution for Edward and Lavinia is to accept humility. "Don't strangle each other with knotted memories," Sir Henry tells them. For Celia it is more difficult; she must accept her vocation for a life of service leading to death. [. . .] The long scene with Sir Henry where she makes her choice, is the most remarkable and moving statement of the modern spiritual dilemma in the whole play.

The Cocktail Party may be altered before it comes to London. Already it has been cut and reshaped in rehearsal in a way in which the earlier plays were not. The combination between author and actor has been sympathetic on both sides. But as it stands the play is a significant advance for the English stage. The verse is eminently suited for the actor, and avoids the obscurity of some of *The Family Reunion* [. . .]. There is none of the absorption of character in antiphonal chorus that mark the climaxes of the earlier days. Only once at the end of the second act the Guardians join in a form of incantation reminiscent of the ceremony of the birthday cake at the end of *The Family Reunion*. And in the absence of chorus the characters gain in solidity. The women no longer discuss Michelangelo but themselves. Lavinia and Celia, the wife and the mistress, have a validity as women which was only achieved in *The Family Reunion*

by Lady Monchensey and possibly by that restless shivering painted shadow, Harry's dead wife. Agatha, the austere High Priestess, is followed by Julia, the social busybody. Peter Quilpe is a completely normal young man, gauche and ebullient in the right proportions. And Edward, the central figure of the play, is not dedicated to atonement from the beginning in the manner of Harry Monchensey. There are no Eumenides for him, aware though he is of "the python. The octopus." Edward is pompous, sensual, miserable; in fact supremely ordinary. The torment for him is not in an overcrowded desert, jostled by ghosts, but in his own "indomitable spirit of mediocrity." [. . .]

Only in its physical atmosphere does *The Cocktail Party* fall below *The Family Reunion*. The sense of the seasons that are part of Wishwood, "the ache in the moving root," are lacking in the Chamberlaynes' flat. This is in part due to the cosmopolitan background [. . .]. But Mr. Eliot's evocations of the mood of London have been so successful in the past that it is surprising that he now makes no attempt to paint in the weather in the streets.

The Cocktail Party is important not only as part of the Eliot canon, but as a significant advance in poetic drama. When Auden and his followers tried to break away from the main tradition with plays such as *The Dog Beneath the Skin* and *Out of the Picture*, it seemed that they were to be the forerunners of a new school. [. . .] But looking back across the distance of the war their plays seem as clumsy as *Armageddon*. They confused the expression with the reality and fatally sacrificed character for situation. The Group Theatre of the thirties has remained barren—a modern School of Night. But in *The Cocktail Party* Mr. Eliot elaborates the lesson of *The Family Reunion*. He shows that it is possible to write a play in verse within the framework of the modern stage without sacrificing the validity of either poetry or drama.

[. . .]

Brooks Atkinson. "T. S. Eliot's Party." *New York Times*, 29 January 1950, sec. 2, p. 1.

Since T. S. Eliot has written *The Cocktail Party* with great moral earnestness it deserves thoughtful consideration by everyone devoted to the art of theatre. Even those who dislike it or are puzzled by it cannot remain impervious to its underlying strength. It is a contribution to the art of the stage by a man of talent and aspiration. For Mr. Eliot is very earnest about two fundamental things: Poetic style in the modern drama and the sickness of the soul in contemporary life. He has to be judged both as a literary craftsman and a moral prophet.

For a number of years he has been interested in restoring poetic drama to the modern stage. Being a modest man, he believes that the burden of proof is as much on the poet as on the audience; and he believes that modern poets must prove that poetic drama can deal with contemporary subjects which are usually expressed in prose. Several months ago, he made a speech before the Poets' Theatre Guild in London that might serve as a preface to *The Cocktail Party*.

In the purely narrative portions of the drama "the verse should be unnoticeable; the audience should not be conscious of the difference from prose," he said. "Here the purpose of the verse should be to operate upon the auditor unconsciously so that he shall think and feel in the rhythms imposed by the poet without being aware of what these rhythms are doing. All the time these rhythms should be preparing the audience for the moments of intensity when the emotion of the character in the play may be supposed to lift him from his ordinary discourse until the audience feels not that the actors are speaking verse, but that the characters of the play have been lifted up into poetry."

To judge by other statements in this speech, Mr. Eliot regards *The Cocktail Party* as something of an experiment in technique and esthetics. If I may offer myself as a guinea pig in the experiment, the effect of the writing in *The Cocktail Party* is precisely as Mr. Eliot had planned it. At the opening performance I was not aware that the play was written in verse until the climactic passages which begin early in the second act and reach their peak in the last scene. Most of the dialogue sounds like prose—uncommonly precise prose but prose nevertheless. But, as a matter of fact, almost every line of dialogue is written in the form of verse, including the first remarks by Alex at the cocktail party.

If a play to be offered as a contribution to the poetic drama I am not sure that Mr. Eliot's modest and reticent style is sufficiently exhilarating for the purpose. His verse has subtleties of nuance that are lacking in most prose. But it is less effective theatre speech than Sean O'Casey's lyric prose which gives us the underhum of poetry. And even in the moments of intensity Mr. Eliot's verse seems to me to be aridly poetic—intellectualized, attenuated, narrow in range, thin in emotion.

As dramatic poetry, it is less vivid than the work of Robinson Jeffers who writes in fiery imagery that stimulates the mind and awakens the emotions. It seems to me that Mr. Eliot's verse in this play derives from a sanctimonious attitude toward life rather than from the superior spiritual vitality of a poet.

Mr. Eliot is a moral philosopher. *The Cocktail Party* is a morality play. Although the characters might have come out of a Noel Coward comedy and although Mr. Eliot has a wry sense of humor about their foibles in the first act, he is really concerned with their souls. He is not so much speculating about as prescribing their destinies. His principal characters are Edward and Lavinia Chamberlayne, a fashionable husband and wife who loathe each other; Celia Coplestone, who is Lavinia's friend and Edward's mistress, and Sir Henry Harcourt-Reilly, a fashionable psychiatrist who is literally a man of science but serves as a religious oracle. He doubtless represents Mr. Eliot's point of view.

The three pivotal characters are spiritually ill; they describe their sickness as various forms of a nervous breakdown. The Chamberlaynes and Celia go separately to Sir Henry for treatment and advice. Up to this point *The Cocktail Party* is a conventional and entertainingly sardonic drawing room drama. But it begins to have mystic overtones as soon as it enters Sir Henry's Harley Street consultation room. Through the medium of Sir Henry's diagnoses, Mr. Eliot starts arranging the destinies of the principal characters.

Since Edward and Lavinia are ordinary worldly people he finds a worldly solution to their problems. He removes their illusions about themselves and each other, and they are able to live a pleasant worldly life together. That is a good life, in Sir Henry's opinion.

But there is also a higher life that requires "the kind of faith that issues from despair"—the life of selfless dedication. Acting as spiritual counselor, Sir Henry rather mysteriously offers that way of life to Celia, who takes it. She joins a religious order, goes to a plague-ridden heathen island to nurse the natives and is crucified

in a native rebellion. At a second meeting of the characters two years later, the Chamberlaynes and their friends hear the news of her crucifixion. They are horrified by it, but Sir Henry persuades them to regard it as a triumphant destiny.

Although the externals of the play remain realistic in terms of a drawing room and fashionable people, *The Cocktail Party* has thus become a play of religious salvation. The psychiatrist has become a priest and Celia a pilgrim. Some of the minor characters have acquired the functions of angels and archangels. Since the background of the play has not altered, Mr. Eliot's change of emphasis is a little puzzling, and a theatregoer has to ask a few rude questions.

By what authority does Sir Henry, the bland and omniscient psychiatrist, arrange the destinies of other people with so much assurance? By what right does he recommend the low road to the Chamberlaynes but the high road to Celia, who up to this point, appears to be made of the same stuff as the Chamberlaynes. If the frame of reference is still a London drawing room, why is Celia's crucifixion at the hands of the savages a triumphant destiny rather than a harrowing disaster? Who decides these things?

Although the word "God" never appears in the play, God is obviously uppermost in Mr. Eliot's mind, and Mr. Eliot makes these godlike decisions for his characters. But, speaking for myself, I am unable to accept Mr. Eliot on these terms—perhaps merely because his poetry is not exalting enough to make the transition from worldly things to things that are sublime.

Whatever its merits may eventually turn out to be, *The Cocktail Party* is a remarkably provocative play—a fascinating experiment in the suitability of poetic drama to modern themes and in the religious interpretation of modern life. But to me, it is insufficiently poetic. It needs more eloquence, passion and imaginative courage. Mr. Eliot is writing about things that cannot be adequately expressed in the earthbound, cerebral style he has deliberately chosen for his experiment.

[. . .]

Howard Barnes.
"Eliot Brings Poetry to the Stage."
New York Herald Tribune, 29 January 1950, sec. 5, p. 1.

The problem of restoring poetic drama to its rightful place in the theater has concerned one of the greatest writers of our time. T. S. Eliot has met it squarely and eloquently in his new verse play, *The Cocktail Party*. Employing a variety of metrical forms which frequently have the sound of prosaic chit-chat, he has composed a stern and illuminating commentary on modern life which challenges the perception and imagination of the beholder at every point.

The Cocktail Party is a far cry from *Murder in the Cathedral*. That earlier play by the Nobel Prize winner took refuge in the past; it made much of a chorus and the conventional accouterments associated with the Elizabethan and Jacobean periods of vaulting, cadenced theater. Eliot has set himself a new goal in his play at Henry Miller's theater. By his own admission he now believes that the poet–playwright's chief function is to examine the present day and curb his verse to the dictates of theatrical communication. It is

encouraging to find that he has succeeded so brilliantly in his task.

There is a want in *The Cocktail Party*, unfortunately, for all the wisdom and humor that have been lavished on most of the scenes. The examination of a sick society and the reaffirmation of faith in a contemporary world gathers so much emotional momentum that it becomes unresolved in a dull and mystical climax.

His thesis is as simple as it is symbolic. The work centers very clearly on a cocktail party in London, where an eccentric lawyer is forced into patent lies about the fact that his wife is not present. (She has left him that morning, forgetting to cancel the party.) There is an uninvited guest, who tarries after the others, and who confounds the stuffy barrister by seeming to have a special insight into his life. The stranger later turns out to be a psychiatrist, but to Eliot, of course, he is also a high priest.

Eliot makes much of this man's resolution of a broken marriage and the tangential tragedies which are concerned with it. The scene in the psychiatrist's office, when the healer of souls confronts husband and wife with their particular inadequacies and adulteries, has imponderable overtones. After listening to the husband's diagnosis of his own illness, the doctor tells him, "I learn a good deal by merely observing you, / . . . / And taking note of what you do not say."

There is no way for a reviewer to communicate the poetic grandeur of this drama which signalizes the season. Eliot has been repetitious in his prosody, but he has rarely failed to make a passage of his dialogue electric. In the final scene there is a letdown from genuine emotion, as the somber tale is told of the crucifixion of the husband's former mistress next to an ant hill while serving the heathen in a nursing order in an outpost of the British Empire known as Kinkanja. This immolation, one suspects, is the author's essential thesis, but it throws his play into considerable confusion.

For faith and drama are at odds in *The Cocktail Party*. During most of two lengthy acts, the work would have one believe that a hapless marriage in a sick society was all-important. The psychiatrist, or priest, restores some sort of equilibrium to the relationship of husband and wife, but there is a grave lack of catharsis in the ministrations. What is welcome, rich and effective in this production is the beautifully modulated metrical designs which Eliot has conceived for what he believes may be a renaissance of poetic drama.

[. . .]

William Carlos Williams. "'It's About Your Life and Mine, Darling.'" *New York Post*, 12 March 1950, p. 18.

The Cocktail Party is a very thrilling play, which in the reading moved me deeply. The lines begin with capitals so that you see at once that it is all intended as verse. Those who hear the play and have not read it will not know that. I think definitely though that they will feel it to be verse—without knowing and without offense. To me this would be a very considerable achievement on the part of Mr. Eliot.

Verse by its arrangement of [words] attempts to do something above the literal meaning [. . .]. It attempts to erect a structure of meaning that raises the literal meaning to moral heights, a moral that goes back to the state itself—if we knew.

I don't think that Mr. Eliot's lines quite do that. It is a bare sort of verse, verse cut down to pure numbers, to pure counting on a very elementary basis. I must say though that I don't know what other kind of verse could have been used to the purpose. It fits the very simple story, the very plain everyday sort of story that Mr. Eliot has chosen for his effects; a quadrangular affair of husband and wife with their complementary partners in illicit love.

The whole parade of events, very quiet events, that make up the play is illumined by revelations of the character of a girl named Celia as she goes calmly to her destruction—which casts a sunset glow over all the final scenes. I think this is, on or off the stage, Mr. Eliot's most moving character. As the tremendous emotional climax approaches you might expect the verse to quicken and gain an increased closeness of emotional texture. It doesn't.

As a matter of fact this reticence enhances the tragic effect. The poet has kept a close rein on the texture of the verse quite as ordinary speech would have it. This is in the English character and in character too with the later Eliot. He has come down to his audience with humility and, I believe, success.

The cocktail party, on the stage, with which the play begins and ends, not the same cocktail party but a cocktail party B.C. and A.D., you might say, is, darling, your life and mine. And there are two ways out—and it was very kind of Mr. Eliot to have provided them—the way of the Chamberlaynes and Celia's way. Without Celia and her heroism (a strange new note in Mr. Eliot's poems), the day-to-day solution by homely honesty could not have emerged quite as brilliantly as it did. But it was kind, I repeat, for Mr. Eliot to offer the poor married ones an escape also.

The final toast is to Lavinia's Aunt, invented by Edward, the husband, for his own convenience—the imagination, the lie, the poem itself that occasionally serves to waken us from a sleep troubled by violent dreams.

I shall say no more, I do not want to spoil the fun.

Joseph Wood Krutch. "T. S. Eliot on Broadway." *New York Herald Tribune Book Review*, 19 March 1950, p. 7.

The reputation of T. S. Eliot is imposing enough to make the critic—let alone a mere reviewer—just a little self-conscious. In the case of the present play, moreover, there is an additional difficulty, for the danger of taking parts of it too seriously is as great as the danger of not taking them seriously enough.

[. . .]

Details aside, there is, however, little doubt about what Mr. Eliot is saying, and saying with great seriousness. [. . .] The moral seems to be something like this: unhappiness, discontent, the sense of being lost in one's world may be cured in either one of two ways. One may learn either to accept the world or to reject it. For most people only the first is possible; for a few only the second.

Some of Eliot's admirers may be somewhat surprised at how tolerant he seems to be of the worldly. "Neither way," says the psychoanalyst, "is better / Both ways are necessary." But then he goes on. "It is also necessary /To make a choice between them," and that is the crux. The real failures, the really guilty, perhaps, are those who believe themselves too good for the world and yet will not renounce it; those who believe that there is some middle way; that what the world requires is not good enough for them even though they themselves are not good enough for anything else. The rewards (or penalties) of either way are predictable. Choose the one and you run at least the risk of martyrdom. Choose the other and the most you can expect is to give good cocktail parties. [. . .]

Concerning this general meaning there can be, I think, little dispute. Most will also agree that the play is fascinating to read as well as to see on the stage. It is written in verse so easy most of the time that it is only barely above the level of prose. [. . .] Much of the dialogue turns around the subject of "personality" or the "persona" in the theological sense of the term and there are two scenes which are especially fine: the one in which Celia is led to realize that she is by nature a saint and the very funny, satirical one in which Alex, apparently a sort of trouble shooter for the Foreign Office, describes what are generally called "conditions" in the remote colony of Kinkanja where the pagan natives consider the monkeys sacred, where the Christian natives eat them, and where the foreign agitators convince the heathen that the slaughter of the animals has put a curse on them. Alex has "drawn up an interim report" which will be published in a year or two. "Meanwhile the monkeys multiply."

Dispute, or at least discussion, seems to center around the question of the meaning of certain "symbols," even around the question of whether they are symbols at all. [. . .] Are the psychoanalyst and his two secret colleagues, Alex and Julia, the apparently idle old lady, Guardian Angels or are they the Holy Trinity—Julia representing the Holy Ghost because her tendency to turn up everywhere is the earthly equivalent of omnipresence, and Alex being the symbol of Jesus because his insistence that he can knock out a meal no matter how little there is in the kitchen is actually a reference to the miracle of the loaves and fishes? Julia remarks that her spectacles have only one lens and the psychoanalyst not only wears a monocle but sings a comic song in which he refers to himself as "one-eyed Riley." Does this have something to do with the three-fold vision, and if so, where is the representative of the third eye?

Meanwhile the play is on Broadway the big hit which the author must have had the outside hope that it would be. Some of the spectators are there no doubt to pay tribute to the most imposing of contemporary literary reputations; some, no doubt, simply out of the curiosity which is finally aroused by even an esoteric reputation which has lasted as long as Eliot's. But the majority are probably merely enjoying a play which can be enjoyed in a relatively simple fashion. Mr. Eliot has said that he regarded it as only a beginning from which a genuinely popular poetic drama might take its rise after it had first met the popular audience on its own ground. Certainly *The Cocktail Party* is wonderfully promising from that point of view. It introduces a genuinely new note into writing for the contemporary theater.

Stephen Spender.
"After *The Cocktail Party*."
New York Times Book Review, 19 March 1950, pp. 7, 20.

As I looked for my glasses, the place where I had left them suddenly flashed across my mind, to the accompaniment of the words "In that moment of illumination / When you suddenly remember where you left your spectacles." Which shows how Eliot's *Cocktail Party* rhythms and his imaginative striking of metaphysical matches get under your skin.

In 1926 and 1927 there appeared in *The Criterion* two fragments of *Sweeney Agonistes,* to my mind the most exciting of Eliot's experiments in poetic drama until *The Cocktail Party*. Those fragments were written in a meter macabre yet gay, above all, oddly catchy, which *The Cocktail Party* recalls [. . .].

It is a sophisticated, jazzy style, with a rather sinister undertow tugging at its three stresses which stand out in each line like posts in a swirling muddy stream. It can beat on the mind barbarically like a tom-tom to suggest the lights and shadows of intelligence and passion behind a social gathering. Within this rhythm, lightened with macabrely amusing anecdotes and with some extremely funny lines, Eliot insidiously leads you on until he has laid bare the soul of Celia in pursuit of her own death by crucifixion, and layer after layer of the unhappy marriage of Edward and Lavinia Chamberlayne, to a center which is understanding of one another and mutual considerateness, if not love.

So in going back to *Sweeney Agonistes* he has taken a great step forward and solved several of the problems raised by the intervening plays. These tended to be monologues against the background of a chorus, and the plots were weak because the purpose of the chief character in *Murder in the Cathedral* and *The Family Reunion* was to impose a moral on the audience. In his new play, Eliot has broken down the monologue, and created out of a skillful arrangement of fragmentary sketches, a picture, all in flickering light and shade, of a group of people.

Among other things, *The Cocktail Party* is a first-rate comedy of manners. Here it owes at least as much to the American as to the English scene. In fact, in reading it I found myself repeatedly thinking that the party was not in London but New York. There are signs here of Eliot's returning to his American roots.

Most important of all, Eliot at least approaches a solution to the main objection to poetic drama for the past hundred years: that poetry, while able to create memorable human symbols, cannot convincingly depict subtle psychological character. Now the one great invention of the modern theatre is the portrayal of "real"-seeming persons on the stage. We have become so used to this that without it a play seems archaic. Too often the poetic drama has been poetic at the expense of providing precisely the complex characterization which we are most interested to see on the stage.

By using very little imagery, by his language which is so idiomatic that one accepts his rhythm as that of ordinary speech with an insistent beat pulsing though it (which explains why the lines about finding my spectacles came into my mind), Eliot really does portray real-seeming characters. He cuts down his poetic effects to the minimum, and then finally rewards us with most beautiful poetry. This arises out of the intensity of the dramatic situation, and is as natural as the "flat" passages: he writes poetry when poetry is the most natural way of saying things (and there are such moments).

[. . .]

Where does *The Cocktail Party* leave Eliot as a dramatist? The theme is a recapitulation of his preoccupations of the past twenty-four years, from the nihilism of *Sweeney Agonistes* to the faith of *Four Quartets*. Personal faith has been discovered, social faith seems irrelevant. Celia goes into society on her mission, socially absurd, which saves herself. His characters are alone with themselves, alone when with one another, alone with God. Yet after all, man is a social being, and the wonderful truth of Eliot's vision is a curiously one-sided truth. Eliot last took a good look at society in *The Waste Land*. Perhaps [. . .] one day he will dramatize a call into the world less quixotic than that of Celia.

---

*"Entertainment and Reality." *Times Literary Supplement*, no. 2513 (31 March 1950), 198.

If it were no more than an academic experiment in verse drama, *The Cocktail Party*, simply by virtue of its technical accomplishment, would demand attention alike from Mr. Eliot's fellow experimentalists and from all who are convinced that the present theatrical forms badly need to be refreshed with a new kind of energy. But the comedy, to judge from its reception at the Edinburgh Festival and in New York, succeeds on the stage; and to win just this kind of success is the main object of the experiment.

It seeks to show in practice how well founded is the theory that verse can deal with the dramatic material that is of most immediate interest to the ordinary playgoing public. The appeal is not to a small circle of initiates, but to the main body of theatrical pleasure-seekers who hold very reasonably that the primary business of dramatic entertainments is to entertain. It has yet to be known what the verdict of London will be, but potential patrons—many of whom will scarcely trouble to read the text—may be assured that the author has in this instance shown as much respect for what Shaftesbury Avenue is supposed to want as for his own sense of reality.

The characters are the men and women of drawing-room comedy. To that convention belong all the perplexities, conflicts and misunderstandings in which they are involved. The cocktail party chatter, light, easy, amusing, is gaily decorated with the sprightly extravagances that make in the theatre an effect of wit. The action moves from first to last with smoothness and speed, and at least two of the three acts have a continuing tension. It is true that the reality to which the characters ultimately conform is the author's own and may not win anything like general acceptance, may indeed excite the active hostility of those who have a more affectionate regard for the vagaries of human character than Mr. Eliot permits himself. But then the validity of Mr. Eliot's spiritual conviction is always open to debate. To debate it in connection with *The Cocktail Party* is to cloud a question of more moment to the theatre: does the comedy issue its idiosyncratic challenge in good dramatic terms?

It is relevant to the dramatic values of the piece to point out that by the end of the second act the main crises have been virtually resolved. The third act is no more than an epilogue describing how the persons involved in the crises have fared. When the husband and wife—he a man who finds himself incapable of loving, she a woman who finds that no man can love her—have been brought to accept their limitations, they have made their dramatic choice. They have faced the reality of their own littleness and, abandoning their fixed attitudes, have agreed to regard the common sense of isolation not as a reason for loathing each other but as the bond which holds them together. Their decision

to make the best of a bad job is dramatic; what in practice they make of it is not of much dramatic importance. So it is with the heroine, a cocktail-drinking girl who has the courage to face her own truth. The scene in which she bares her spiritual misgivings and strivings in the Harley Street consulting room is superbly charged with energy. Tension is controlled by verse which makes its transitions between the prosaic and the poetic with unfaltering certainty and the utmost smoothness. It is perhaps the finest scene in modern poetic drama. Celia Coplestone chooses the hard, the terrifying way to fulfillment, and having made the choice, she becomes a character fulfilled. The third act reports that she has died a martyr in the most horrible way imaginable, but the fact adds nothing, dramatically speaking, to our knowledge of her as a woman capable of making the hard choice. Mr. Eliot uses the third act to moralize the crises which have been resolved and also to deepen the shadows of a world behind the world which have flickered disturbingly through the comedy. The Chamberlaynes are shown in process of working out salvation according to their limited means, and Celia's death is represented by the doctor who has helped her to make the choice which led to it as the happiest of deaths, that of a saint. "She did not suffer as ordinary people suffer?" asks Edward Chamberlayne, clutching at easy comfort. "She suffered all that we suffer in fear and pain and loathing," replies Sir Henry Harcourt-Reilly. "She paid the highest price in suffering. That is part of the design." By these means Mr. Eliot keeps interest alive through the third act, but the play would be structurally stronger if more were made of Peter Quilpe, a young film producer who stands spiritually midway between the mediocrities and the saints. He finds his own path to salvation, but it is a dimly, even perfunctorily lighted path, and the chiaroscuro of the act could certainly afford him a few more lamps.

Mr. Eliot has incurred easy smiles by saying that the verse he uses in this play need not be recognized as verse. Stage performance has made his meaning clear. The purpose of the verse is not to paint scenery in the Elizabethan way, nor to make verbal patterns, nor to create emotions in excess of the matter under discussion, but to give the dialogue the finest possible precision and intensity. It avoids specifically poetic language, but it is, even during the prosaic passages of the dialogue, preparing the ear of the auditor for scenes which have by imperceptible transitions reached a pitch of intensity needing the compression of verse to sustain them. The auditor need not notice the versification. He is meant only to be aware of the higher charge of energy which has entered the scene by means of the versification.

[. . .]

William Barrett. "Dry Land, Dry Martini." *Partisan Review* 17 (April 1950), 354–59.

Among the many questions raised by T. S. Eliot's *The Cocktail Party*, the first and most immediate would seem to be how far we can separate, even provisionally, the play and its success from the author and his fame. The audience did not appear to wish such separation, for one sensed in its enthusiasm a certain self-congratulation that it was able to enjoy what it felt it *ought* to enjoy, and had feared, coming to the theater, it might not be able to enjoy. The critics simply made this response articulate: some were enthusiastic by the stan-

dards of Broadway; nearly all were pleased with themselves that they were not bored by what they had been told in advance was a play in verse; some seemed to veil their real dissatisfaction with the play for fear of self-exposure in attacking so great a name. I labor these points at the start because I have found, in talking with people who have seen the play, a very curious ambiguity in its reception: on the one hand, the play seems to have been carried to a critical and commercial success by the author's name, but on the other hand seems to be finally approved of by the standards of Broadway, which are hardly those of Eliot. For my own part, I am unable to separate the play from its author; the standards that Eliot's other work invokes and often satisfies, and measuring by such standards I find *The Cocktail Party* a disappointing work: thin and unconvincing as drama and weak as poetry—perhaps the weakest poetry that Eliot has yet written.

The play, and very largely because of its success, does throw a new light upon Eliot's old problem, his lifelong obsession with the possibility of restoring the poetic drama to the modern stage. *Murder in the Cathedral* was produced here by the WPA,[1] *The Family Reunion*, so far as I know, only by little theater groups, while *The Cocktail Party* is now a Broadway hit! Eliot would seem then to have solved his problem, at least for practical purposes; but the question is whether he has not succeeded by so sugar-coating his pill that very little of poetic substance remains: whether, in short, he has so compromised with the formal convention of verse in accordance with which poetic drama ought to be written that the audience is never shocked from its habitual habits of listening and can receive this play as merely another version of the drawing-room comedy. "*Isn't it wonderful!*" a friend said to me as we left the theater,

"*It's poetry but you would never know it.*" I am simple-minded enough to think that this must be a very ambiguous compliment for the author, even though he seems to have calculated some such effect, according to his own explanation of the theory behind the play. He argues that the audience should be unaware of the fact that it is hearing poetry, except in rare moments of intensity when the character seems "lifted into poetry." [. . .] This [. . .] strategy sounds good, but does *The Cocktail Party* really lift its actors at any point to that level of intense or moving speech where the poetry is no longer hidden but open? [. . .] In his earlier fragment *Sweeney Agonistes* Eliot had not sought to transmute the formal convention of verse into something hardly distinguishable from prose, but had in fact insisted upon the convention that makes this work, fragmentary as it is, his greatest achievement as a dramatic poet. A whole play in the style of *Sweeney* would have been a much more considerable step toward the revival of poetic drama, but I doubt that such a play would ever reach Broadway, for it would demand an audience ready to accept a formal and stylized theater; and years ago Eliot himself in his "Dialogue on Dramatic Poetry" announced through one of the interlocutors that the search for a poetic drama valid for our time must be carried forward by small experimental theaters. But the question of the audience aside, what we would like to recall is Eliot's own repeated emphasis in his earlier critical writings that poetic drama to be valid must insist upon its convention, the form and stylization implicit in verse, and that the error of William Archer and the realistic theater was to believe that only the convention of prose was valid. *The Cocktail Party* seems to parallel a tendency apparent in recent years in the production of Shakespeare, where the passages of blank verse are made to sound more "natural"—i.e.,

acceptable to the audience—by being spoken as if they were prose, or at most some vaguely rhythmic free verse.

The present play demands comparison with *Sweeney Agonistes* on other grounds, for both deal, though in different ways, with the sheer overwhelming fact of human banality: in *Sweeney* the crudity of the lower orders, here the tedious chatter of the middle classes. The opening scenes attempt in fact to rework the same device of repetition that had been so successfully banal in the earlier work, but they do not do so well here because they lack the formal definiteness, the bare strident saxophone note, of *Sweeney*. [. . .] To this general cocktail atmosphere Eliot adds some typically modern ingredients: the strained marriage of the Chamberlaynes, the separate affairs of husband and wife (*mélange adultère de tous*), the running away of the wife, and then the entrance of the modern tinker of broken marriages, the psychiatrist. (All these carefully calculated elements show a cunning intelligence at work, and it is not generally deficient of literary intelligence, but of creative vitality, that we complain of this play.) Against the background of these banal furnishings Eliot wishes, of course, to develop his own Christian themes, but right there the difficulties of incongruity begin [. . .]. Eliot has set a formidable problem: How to make the possibility of the saint meaningful against the backdrop of cocktail chatter? The saint appears here in the person of a young woman Celia Coplestone, who, when her affair with Edward Chamberlayne breaks off, becomes a missionary and is finally crucified by the natives of a remote island. [. . .]

In a certain sense all these difficulties of incongruity are concentrated in the character of Harcourt-Reilly, who as pyschiatrist and priest seems to be somehow functioning simultaneously on both the natural and supernatural levels.

As a psychiatrist he performs the quite unbelievable feat of bringing the estranged Chamberlaynes together by explaining that they are perfectly suited to each other since the wife is unlovable and the husband is incapable of loving. Chamberlayne, when he hears this, is on the edge of a nervous breakdown, and it strikes me that the only possible effect of these words would be to drive him off the deep end. I was surprised that some of the critics found the thought of the play difficult and obscure, when it is in fact simple and obvious: we must, Eliot is saying, either make the best of a bad job—bear with resignation the limitations and frustrations of daily life—or follow the path of the saints; there are no other alternatives. [. . .] One can have a pretty vivid sense of the horrors of marriage, as well as of the final isolation in which we are all imprisoned, but still one gags at these lines as representing the ultimate possibilities for human love. [. . .] The question is not so much that of understanding but of opening oneself in love to another person; human kind, as Eliot puts it, may not be able to bear very much reality, but even the Chamberlaynes of this world are capable of more than he allows them. Here we must remember that Eliot, the last great product of the Puritan mind, has never shown in his poetry any real belief in the possibility of human love. The moment of love is presented always as the moment of withdrawal and renunciation, the awful daring of a moment's surrender, one of "the things that other people have desired"; and consequently the beauty of the world is never present in the fullness of joy, but always with that painful clutch at the heart as at something taken away, lost, uncapturable. No doubt, resignation is necessary to get through life at all, and Freud himself stated that the aim of analytic therapy was to enable the neurotic to bear the sufferings inevitable in human life; but this is only half the picture, for the work of the analyst may also be to liberate the patient for the positive joys that life can hold, even perhaps for the possibility of love, and if the neurotic were told that he is to be resigned only for resignation's sake, it is very unlikely that he would have the strength to go on.

I was surprised to read that one critic found in the play the gaiety that Stendhal recommends for all art, for it seems to me that at bottom the world of *The Cocktail Party* is the same empty world of *Prufrock*, except that 37 years ago Eliot did not disguise his contempt for this emptiness. So I feel at the heart of this play some immense *tricherie*, or at least self-deception, for I can't believe that Eliot takes the Chamberlaynes as seriously as he pretends to. Here again, comparison with *Sweeney Agonistes* becomes instructive, for in this earlier fragment Eliot fully released all his hatred of human life and really enjoyed himself in the raucous company of Doris, Sweeney, Klipstein, and Krumpacker—in comparison with whose vulgar vitality the characters at the cocktail party are genteel skeletons. As a writer Eliot has never really given us God's plenty: the qualities of his genius are not robustness and richness, but precision, terseness, and intensity; and the shadow which haunts these qualities is a certain tendency to thinness and brittleness that here in *The Cocktail Party* has at last caught up with him.

The public reception of this play points toward the larger problem (that we can only mention briefly here) arising from Eliot's present position in the world of letters: the embarrassing and delicate situation of the master at the height of his fame and influence at the very moment when his creative powers and energy appear to be at their lowest ebb. Many years ago now, it seems, we were undergraduates, and Eliot's name was a secret and holy conspiracy among us against our teachers of English literature and the tastes they

534

taught. Since then we have seen his influence spread abroad, and his figure become entrenched in the academy itself; this influence has been immensely valuable, and it is hard to imagine what we might be without it; but every influence is exclusive in some directions, and so we have seen this one too become in time stiff and rigid, and finally lend itself to academicism. It would be, of course, unfair to blame a man for all the things done in his name, but the character of this influence, the doors of experience it closes, must be pointed out, for we have, if we are to go on living, to make way always for a new future. Perhaps every new literary generation has to begin by killing its father.

Note

1. Works Projects Administration (WPA): a former agency of the U.S. government, created in 1935 by executive order of President Franklin D. Roosevelt to provide work for the unemployed. Among other things, it sponsored many arts and theatre projects.

*Bonamy Dobrée. "Books and Writers." *Spectator* 184, no. 6356 (21 April 1950), 541.

Mr. Eliot is, from all appearance, one of that class of poets who work from the "meaning" or intuition to the symbol, what he has called "the objective correlative," rather than from the spectacle of life to an "imitation" so shaped that some meaning will emerge from it, some attitude be induced. It is for this reason, one supposes, that his chief technical difficulty would seem to be the fusing together of the various planes of reality, which must co-exist to some degree in any play, and which with him is a major problem, as it must be with any playwright whose work is at the same time original and highly complex. The problem did not trouble the Elizabethans, who, living in a pre-scientific age, were prepared to accept the simultaneous presentation of various planes (as, say, in *The Tempest*): but it did trouble Ibsen, as it does M. Sartre. To some extent the re-handling of an old myth is a solution, as so many French playwrights including M. Anouilh have found, and as Mr. Eliot did when he flirted with one in *The Family Reunion*: but here, in his new play, though his Furies have become Eumenides, or Guardians, they are not ghostly characters, but, at the same time as Guardians, men and women living in the world. Strange vessels of the spirit indeed, to whom we shall return.

His other technical problems Mr. Eliot seems finally to have resolved. He never had much difficulty over dramatic movement; the sense of it is in his blood: it shaped *The Waste Land* and gave form to *Four Quartets*: but to translate this into stage terms was none the less an operation needing experience, and Mr. Eliot stumbled a little in *Murder in the Cathedral*; but afterwards there was no hitch. His medium of speech was not so easily attained: too heavily rhythmed in *Sweeney*, uncertain and wavering in *The Rock*, it was nearly right in *The Family Reunion*, though there it occasionally swung off into a lyrical movement which in the setting was a little disturbing, though by itself, in the study, enchanting. Now, we feel secure, Mr. Eliot has achieved his mastery: he has worked out a form of speech suitable for an actor to say, and actor-proof, cadenced enough to enable the stresses to tell, flexible enough to be either portentous or light; and while it is a universal medium it yet carries his own individual rhythms. A third problem, still not quite solved, perhaps, is how to get the important universalizing statements made by the characters. The chorus simply will not do today, as others together with Mr. Eliot have discovered: it was cunningly disguised in *The Family Reunion*: but here, though perhaps vestigial traces remain in the libation scene at the end of the second act, the effect is more that of ritual utterance among the Guardians than of a chorus. Indeed the Guardians throughout carry the *sententiae*; but in so far as they are ordinary people living in the everyday humdrum world, they do not draw undue attention to the fact that they are doing so. Here and there, however, they seem a little self-conscious about it.

A comedy? What you think of that label will depend upon your idea of comedy. In so far as comedy is concerned with man's relation to man, the goings-on of the Chamberlayne–Quilpe group are certainly comic, indeed at moments brilliant comedy with all the classical implications of the word: but in so far as tragedy deals with man's relation to God, then the other group, and certainly Celia Coplestone, belong to the world of tragedy. [. . .] All, of course, depends on the attitude the play finally induces in you, in which particular world you feel involved, and what you think the play is really about.

And it is here, perhaps, that Mr. Eliot has not quite conquered his medium: though he himself, it would seem, can now move with perfect freedom within the form, it is not quite clear in what direction he is expecting us to move. There are, perhaps, too many meanings, and we may come away regarding the play either as a comedy within a thin outer shell of tragedy, or as a tragedy within a thick casing of comedy. And the trouble, I think, is that there are moments when we do not know what plane of reality we are supposed to be on: we sometimes feel that

we are being offered two or three planes at one time in one person, especially at the transitions. [. . .] There are, we may say, four planes. First, the amoral one of Sweeney: the conversation of the first few moments might come directly from *Sweeney Agonistes*; then, when the yet undiscovered Reilly after some witty cynicisms says "But let me tell you, that to approach the stranger / Is to invite the unexpected, release a new force . . ." we are on the plane of Agatha in *The Family Reunion*, the moral one. Later, when first Peter and then Celia speak of the nature of reality, we are on a metaphysical plane; finally, with the Guardians in session as Guardians, on a transcendental one. And the main "meaning" of the play seems to be dual—moral and transcendental.

Yet the statement in either case is that every individual must find that place in life which suits him: it is the old conception of degree in the chain of being, combined with a Stoic acceptance. [. . .] Each and every person is offered a choice and must make one, though it is not very illuminating to be told that "the right choice is the choice you cannot but make," though indeed a sense of destiny runs faintly through the play. Celia, predestined as we are later told, made a choice based on "the kind of faith that issues from despair." [. . .] [T]here are so many fascinating themes in *The Cocktail Party*, the play is so rich, so amazingly complex, that each person will gain from it what he can, or put in it what he must: for, as Mr. Eliot himself has said, in a poem of any complexity the poet himself is not aware of all the possible meanings.

[. . .] The play is a disturbing experience, and certainly nobody will lay the book down—and it is to be suspected that nobody will come away from seeing the play—without feeling that somewhere some barb has pierced beneath the skin. If he does not feel that, he had better begin looking into himself: or perhaps, on reflection, he had better not.

Frederick Morgan. "Notes on the Theatre." *Hudson Review* 3 (Summer 1950), 289–93.

[. . .]

Any effort to redeem the contemporary theater from its degraded naturalism is to be welcomed, and Eliot's is perhaps the most important now being made in our language. The problem of giving the drama a supernatural dimension, like that of adapting to it a suitable poetic diction, is today a very difficult one. The playwright may assume a world, removed in time or place from our own, in which the supernatural is taken as actually present, interfusing the natural world, an inseparable part of the *donnée*. [. . .]

Eliot's new strategy, [. . .] the reverse of that of *Murder in the Cathedral*, [. . .] centers the action on characters representative of the modern, secular world. The key to the method is to be found in the well-known sentences from his introduction to Pascal's *Pensées*:

> The Christian thinker [. . .] proceeds by rejection and elimination. He finds the world to be so and so; he finds its character inexplicable by any non-religious theory; among religions he finds Christianity, and Catholic Christianity, to account most satisfactorily for the world and especially for the moral world within; and thus [. . .] he finds himself inexorably committed to the dogma of the Incarnation.

The method of *The Cocktail Party*, like that of *Murder in the Cathedral*, is the method of demonstration, but it is a demonstration that uses our modern world as a starting-point, and proceeds from it, by means of reason and self-knowledge, into faith. It is also the method of parable, by means of which stock characters take on significance in terms of a new dimension of reference. [. . .] It is deeply concerned with the possibility of mystical experience within the contemporary context; but it is the possibility that is dramatized, not the experience itself. The realm of transcendent experience remains off-stage; it is assumed, referred to more or less indirectly; what goes on on the stage points to it. The possibility is explored in no vague fashion, but with an almost mechanical precision; and the conventions of the parlor-drama are the machinery which the playwright has seen fit to use. And here he has shown considerable dramatic tact: in the persons of the Guardians, for example, who are fixed as figures in the parlor-drama before their full significance is more than hinted at, and in the verse itself, which is established from the start as "right" for the play and is capable of whatever degree of tension may be required. [. . .] What we have, through most of the play, is entire economy and precision, profundity of analysis, and almost incredible "rightness" and brilliance of expression. If the method also imposes certain limitations—dryness, intellectuality, restriction of possibilities in the natural world—yet, given Eliot's talents and the present condition of the theater, the method was necessary if the play was to be written at all.

Taken on its own terms, *The Cocktail Party* is a fine play and a very considerable artistic success. The exposition in the first act is masterful; the consulting-room scene, in which the Chamberlaynes and Celia make their fateful decisions, is probably one of the high spots of the modern theater. The last scene, on the other hand, is the least successful, and seems to have proved a stumbling-block to many. It is centered on the account given by Alex, the civil servant, of Celia's martyrdom at the hands of the natives of "Kinkanja," and on the effect of this announcement on the other characters. Alex performs the function of messenger, describing at length the off-stage apotheosis of the hero. There is some limp writing (the only limp writing of the play) toward the beginning of the scene, when Alex, prior to his revelation, is giving a preliminary description of Kinkanja, and also in the conversation attending Peter Quilpe's return. It is as if the playwright, after the unravelment of the consulting-room scene, had not quite known, "two years later," how to take hold. Matters improve in the latter half of the scene, and the verse regains its vitality; but, on the whole, it is doubtful whether this last scene comes off dramatically at all, and whether *The Cocktail Party* must not be added to the long list of very good plays with unsuccessful endings. By comparison to the immediacy with which the initial situation is presented and worked out, the entire business of Kinkanja and of Celia's martyrdom seems remote and unreal. It is not that we disbelieve that such a thing could have happened, but that, in dramatic terms, it has not happened. Consequently, the attempts made by the other characters to grasp the full significance of the event seem excessively contrived and mechanical. The last scene would seem to represent a departure from drama into an on-the-whole distinguished, but undramatic sort of summation, and as such to be a comparative failure. And it seems likely that this failure is due to the playwright's having attempted something very difficult and very important that lay beyond the scope of his method.

It is interesting that in the interview with *World Review* reported by William Arrowsmith, Eliot should refer to the necessity for turning away from the Theater of Ideas to the Theater of Character. For it seems to me that Eliot has emerged as a very distinguished dramatist whose work displays the typical excellences and suffers the typical limitations of a theater of ideas. Be that as it may, he is almost the only person writing in English for the theater in whose work we can find life, significance, and hope for the future; in *The Cocktail Party* he has at last written a play that as a theater piece is entirely performable, and that will probably make a permanent addition to dramatic literature.

[. . .]

Hilton Kramer.
"T. S. Eliot in New York (Notes on the End of Something)."
Western Review 14 (Summer 1950), 303–05.

When we find the proper face of T. S. Eliot on the cover of *Time* and read therein that he is receiving an income of $1600 a week from the success of *The Cocktail Party* on Broadway, surely we must feel a sense of change, we must feel that the end of something has occurred even if we cannot immediately determine what it is. And this success of Eliot's combines itself with certain other recent events to mark, somehow, a boundary.

Is it true, as William Carlos Williams wrote in his review of *The Cocktail Party* [*New York Post*, 12 March, reprinted in this volume pp. 527–28], that Eliot has

538

here come down to his audience? If so it would be one more symptom to note. And if Dr. Williams is right in this point, it is significant indeed since in most other ways *The Cocktail Party* does not represent an Eliot changed from him we knew. Only the New York drama critics were surprised to find the play first-rate comedy; anyone who knew Eliot's work previous to the play would have been prepared by his earlier display of satiric and sardonic wit. What has always been an integral part of Eliot's art—an accuracy of social observation combined with a satiric vision of the modern world—is in this play concentrated into a genre. And the thematic dialectic which provides the conflict of this drama continues the dialectic which has always prevailed in various emphases throughout Eliot's writing. The dialectic consists of seeing, on the one hand, the experience of the modern world as desolate and modern society itself as resting on values which are precarious and improper; and on the other hand, of seeing this desolate present in contrast to heroic values of the past, values symbolized and dramatized by the heroic figures of classical literatures and religions, values now represented in their isolation by "an occupation for the saint." It would be difficult to discover any important work by Eliot which does not draw upon some area of this dialectic.

The Cocktail Party represents a kind of consolidation of these themes into an artistic statement more direct than we are used to finding in Eliot's art, and in this sense Dr. Williams is doubtless correct in observing that Eliot has here come down to his audience. The inadequate social world is dramatized, as it must be on a stage, by a small company of persons, now involved in rather uninspired love affairs and unsuccessful marriage and now, as always, utterly alone. (Eliot's method in *The Waste Land* for avoiding the general

statement and concentrating on the specific scene has wonderfully prepared him for this play.) In one of the small company the heroic note is sounded, Celia Coplestone giving herself over triumphantly to the "occupation for the saint." Thus, Celia continues the voice which utters the saintly last lines of "What the Thunder Said" and which reaches fuller expression in "Ash-Wednesday," the *Quartets* and the other more recent writings.

The voice of Eliot which is most familiar to us, however, and perhaps the one which we best understand is represented by the partners in a loveless marriage, Edward and Lavinia Chamberlayne, and by Peter Quilpe, a writer gone Hollywood—these take their places in the company of Prufrock, the Lady, Mr. Apollinax and the bourgeois characters of "Gerontion" and *The Waste Land*. The images of contemporary London, which in the earlier poetry dramatized a modern Inferno, are amplified in *The Cocktail Party* with the Chamberlaynes caught in the eternal whirlwind of their inability to love and be loved and with Peter Quilpe finally succeeding in a vocation which consists of reproducing in Hollywood what is already in decay in England.

Sir Henry Harcourt-Reilly, whom the duped New York drama critics all interpreted as a literal psychoanalyst (psychoanalysis is treated chiefly in parody), functions as the agent through whom the characters achieve freedom; that is, he is the agent of choice, and freedom functions only as the freedom to accept and to fulfill the consequences of choice. Thus, Celia's choice is tragic in its implications and in its moral earnestness, and she is somewhat of a tragic heroine in accepting and fulfilling the consequences of a deeply significant choice.

The major symbol of the consequence of choice, however, is the cocktail party which represents the Chamberlaynes' (and, in a sense, the audience's) decision to return to the somewhat tiresome modern world—after all, we are told, the best of a bad job is all any of us can do, except the saints. Thus, the dialectic is drawn again in the consequences of choice: the cocktail party and the crucifixion.

[. . .]

Checklist of Additional Reviews

Bert McCord. "To Produce New Eliot Play." *New York Herald Tribune*, 2 August 1949, p. 10.

*R. P. M. G. "Première of T. S. Eliot's Play: *The Cocktail Party* at Edinburgh." *Daily Telegraph and Morning Post*, 22 August 1949, p. 6.

*W. A. Darlington. "Fine Play by T. S. Eliot." *Daily Telegraph and Morning Post*, 23 August 1949, p. 5.

*"The Festival, *The Cocktail Party*: New T. S. Eliot Play." *Scotsman*, 23 August 1949, p. 6.

*Review of *The Cocktail Party*. *Aberdeen Press*, 23 August 1949, [page no. missing].

*I. H. "Mr. T. S. Eliot's New Play." *Manchester Guardian*, 23 August 1949, p. 3.

*Cecil Wilson. "Festival Play was Eliot's Little Joke." *Daily Mail*, 23 August 1949, p. 3.

*A. V. Cookman. [*The Cocktail Party*]. *Times*, 24 August 1949, [page no. unknown].

*"The Edinburgh Festival: *The Cocktail Party*." *Times*, 24 August 1949, p. 8.

*"T. S. Eliot Discusses His New Play." *Glasgow Herald*, 27 August 1949, p. 4.

*Alan Dent. "Accent in Edinburgh." *News-Chronicle*, 27 August 1949, p. 4.

*Ivor Brown. Review of *The Cocktail Party*. *Observer*, 28 August 1949, [page no. unknown].

*Mary Carson. Review of *The Cocktail Party*. *Glasgow Herald*, 31 August 1949, [page no. unknown].

*Kenneth J. Robinson. "Contemporary Arts: The Theatre." *Spectator* 183, no. 6323 (2 September 1949), 294.

"New Play in Edinburgh." *Time* 54 (5 September 1949), 58.

*John Courtney Trewin. "Symbols and Saints." *Illustrated London News* 125 (10 September 1949), 388.

W. A. Darlington. "London Letter: Edinburgh Festival Has Two New Plays." *New York Times*, 11 September 1949, p. 2x.

Harold Hobson. "Opera, Ballets, Orchestras, Eliot's *The Cocktail Party*." *Christian Science Monitor*, 17 September 1949, p. 8.

"*The Cocktail Party*: Poet Uses Worldly Scene for a Christian Comedy." *Life* 27 (26 September 1949), 18, 20, 23.

Peter Russell. "A Note on T. S. Eliot's New Play." *Nine* 1 (October 1949), 28–29.

Louis Calta. "New T. S. Eliot Play to Bow in January." *New York Times*, 15 October 1949, p. 11.

*Iain Hamilton. "Reflections on *The Cocktail Party*." *World Review* 9 (November 1949), 19–22.

Sam Zolotow. "Miller Importing Cast for Comedy." *New York Times*, 30 November 1949, p. 35.

*Vivienne Koch. "Programme Notes on *The Cocktail Party*." *Poetry Quarterly* 2 (Winter 1949), 248–51.

*A. V. Cookman. "The Verse Play." *The Year's Work in the Theatre 1949–1950* (London: Longmans, Green, 1950), 24–28.

George Jean Nathan. "*The Cocktail Party*." *The Theatre Book of the Year: 1949–50* (New York: Knopf, 1950), 197–203.

*"American Production of Mr. Eliot's Play." *Times*, 5 January 1950, p. 4.

"Eliot Play Raises Issue." *New York Times*, 6 January 1950, p. 24.

*Harold Hobson. "Eliot." *Sun Times*, 8 January 1950, p. 2.

"A Play by a Poet." *Cue*, 14 January 1950, p. 12.

"New English Favorite in T. S. Eliot's *Cocktail Party*." *Brooklyn Eagle*, 22 January 1950, p. 27.

Brooks Atkinson. "At the Theatre." *New York Times*, 23 January 1950, p. 17.

Howard Barnes. "Modern Morality Play." *New York Herald Tribune*, 23 January 1950, p. 12.

John Chapman. "*Cocktail Party* a Masterpiece: Cast Gives Superb Performance." *New York Daily News*, 23 January 1950, p. 39.

Robert Coleman. "Eliot's Fine 'Cocktail Party' Goes Right to the Head." *New York Daily Mirror*, 23 January 1950, p. 20.

Rowland Field. "Cocktail Party." *Newark Evening News*, 23 January 1950, p. 12.

Robert Garland. "*The Cocktail Party*: There's Nothing Like It in Today's Theatre." *Journal American* [New York], 23 January 1950, p. 8.

William Hawkins. "T. S. Eliot Analyzes *The Cocktail Party*." *New York World-Telegram*, 23 January 1950, p. 16.

Arthur Pollock. "Eliot's *The Cocktail Party* Engrossing and Skillful." *Daily Compass* [New York], 23 January 1950, p. 18.

Louis Shaeffer. "T. S. Eliot's *The Cocktail Party*." *Brooklyn Eagle*, 23 January 1950, p. 6.

Richard Watts Jr. "The Theatre Event of the Season." *New York Post*, 23 January 1950, p. 32.

Ethel Colby. "*The Cocktail Party*." *New York Journal of Commerce*, 24 January 1950, p. 15.

"T. S. Eliot's Play Tops a Full Week." *Cue*, 28 January 1950, p. 18.

Wolcott Gibbs. "Eliot and Others." *New Yorker* 25 (28 January 1950), 47–48.

Margaret Marshall. "Drama." *Nation* 170 (28 January 1950), 94–95.

Howard Barnes. "Eliot Brings Poetry to the Stage." *New York Herald Tribune*, 29 January 1950, p. 12.

Arthur Pollock. "*Cocktail Party* and Green Hills Far Away." *Sunday Compass* [New York], 29 January 1950, magazine sec., p. 18.

"New Plays." *Newsweek* 35 (30 January 1950), 66.

"New Plays in Manhattan. *The Cocktail Party*." *Time* 55 (30 January 1950), 37.

Kappo Phelan. "The Stage." *Commonweal* 51 (3 February 1950), 463.

*"Poetry and Theatre." *Times Literary Supplement*, no. 2505 (3 February 1950), 73.

*John Mason Brown. "Honorable Intentions." *Saturday Review* 33 (4 February 1950), 28–30. [Reprinted in *Still Seeing Things* (New York: McGraw-Hill, 1950), 167–74]

*William Rose Benét. "*The Cocktail Party*." *Saturday Review* 33 (11 February 1950), 48.

Eliot Norton. "Most Remarkable Broadway Hit is *The Cocktail Party*." *Boston Sunday Post*, 12 February 1950, p. 31.

Geoffrey Parsons. "Solving Some of Eliot's Riddles." *New York Herald Tribune*, 12 February 1950, sec. 5, p. 1.

"Screw-eyed Success." *Time* 55 (13 February 1950), 52.

Harold Clurman. "Theatre: Cocktail Poetry." *New Republic* 122 (13 February 1950), 30.

Philip Burnham. "Communications: *The Cocktail Party*." *Commonweal* 51 (17 February 1950), 507–08. [A reply to Phelan's review of 3 February]

John J. Fox. "Communications: *The Cocktail Party*." *Commonweal* 51 (17 February 1950), 508.

Harold Hobson. "The Paradoxical Public." *Christian Science Monitor*, 25 February 1950, magazine sec., p. 10.

*Chard Powers Smith. "*The Cocktail Party*." *Saturday Review* 33 (25 February 1950), 23.

Maurice Zolotow. "Psychoanalyzing the Doctor." *New York Times*, 26 February 1950, sec. 2, p. 3.

Euphemia van Rensselaer Wyatt. *Catholic World* 170 (March 1950), 466–67.

"'Cocktail Party' for London?" *New York Times*, 2 March 1950, p. 32.

"Reflections, Mr. Eliot." *Time* 55 (6 March 1950), 22–26.

Lewis Gannett. "Books and Things." *New York Herald Tribune*, 10 March 1950, p. 17.

Charles Poore. "Books of the *Times*." *New York Times*, 16 March 1950, p. 29.

M. C. Blackman. "*The Cocktail Party*." *New Yorker* 26 (18 March 1950), 110.

Elinor Hughes. "Eliot's *The Cocktail Party* Is Fascinating and Controversial." *Boston Herald*, 19 March 1950, p. 6c.

*E. M. Forster. "Mr. Eliot's 'Comedy.'" *Listener* 43 (23 March 1950), 533.

H. C. G. [Harold Gardiner]. "Hors-d'oeuvre for the 'Party.'" *America* 82 (25 March 1950), 725.

Harold Hobson. "Poetic Drama Ascendant." *Christian Science Monitor*, 25 March 1950, p. 4.

Thomas G. V. O'Connell. "T. S. Eliot's *The Cocktail Party*." *America* 82 (25 March 1950), 724–25.

Robert Peel. "A Poetic Exploration of Man's Spiritual Loneliness." *Christian Science Monitor*, 25 March 1950, magazine sec., p. 7.

M. C. Blackman. "Middlebrow Enjoys *The Cocktail Party* Too." *New York Herald Tribune*, 26 March 1950, sec. 5, p. 3.

Geoffrey Dutton. "London Letter: A Measure for a Cocktail." *Meanjin* 9 (Spring 1950), 204–06.

*John Peter. "Sin and Soda." *Scrutiny* 17 (Spring 1950), 61–66.

Elizabeth Vassilieff. "Piers to Cocktails." *Meanjin* 9 (Spring 1950), 193–203.

Henry Popkin. "Theatre Letter." *Kenyon Review* 12 (Spring 1950), 337–39.

"The New Plays." *Theatre Arts* 34 (April 1950), 8, 10.

"*The Cocktail Party*." *Vogue* 115 (April 1950), 122–23.

Henry Sherek. "On Giving a Cocktail Party." *Theatre Arts* 34 (April 1950), 24–26.

James Thurber. "*What* Cocktail Party?" *New Yorker* 26 (1 April 1950), 26–29.

"From the Drama Mailbag." *New York Times*, 2 April 1950, sec. 2, p. 2x.

"Pulitzer Prize Next?" *New York Times*, 6 April 1950, 33.

"8 Perry Awards Go to *South Pacific*, . . . T. S. Eliot's *Cocktail Party* Captures 'Tony'." *New York Times*, 10 April 1950, p. 14.

Foster Hailey. "An Interview with T. S. Eliot." *New York Times*, 16 April 1950, sec. 2, pp. 1, 3.

"The Laurels." *Time* 55 (17 April 1950), 80.

*Richard Murphy. "*The Cocktail Party.*" *Spectator* 184, no. 6357 (28 April 1950), 569.

*Harold Hobson. "New Theatre: *The Cocktail Party.*" *Times*, May 1950 [exact date uncertain], p. 2.

W. Motter Inge. "Bookshelf." *Theatre Arts* 34 (May 1950), 8–9.

George Jean Nathan. "The Theatre: Clinical Notes." *American Mercury* 70 (May 1950), 557–58.

*"New Theatre. *The Cocktail Party.*" *Times*, 4 May 1950, p. 2.

"T. S. Eliot's Comedy Unveiled in London." *New York Times*, 4 May 1950, p. 33.

*John Barber. "T. S. Eliot's 'Party' Witty, Brutal . . . Valuable." *Daily Express*, 4 May 1950, [page no. unknown].

*Beverley Baxter. "I'm Not Drinking." *Evening Standard*, 5 May 1950, [page no. unknown].

George Miles. "*The Cocktail Party.*" *Commonweal* 52 (5 May 1950), 106–08.

*Stephen Williams. "Why Call It Poetic?" *Evening News*, 5 May 1950, [page no. unknown].

*John Drummond. "After the Party." *Sunday Chronicle*, 6 May 1950, p. 4.

*"Stage." *Reynolds News*, 7 May 1950, [page no. unknown].

*"Theatre." *Sunday Dispatch*, 7 May 1950, [page no. unknown].

*Ivor Brown. "Gin and Falernian." *Observer*, 7 May 1950.

Claudia Cassidy. "Broadway Salutes Drama as an Enigmatic Masterpiece." *Chicago Tribune*, 7 May 1950, [page no. unknown].

*Alan Dent. "Fly in the Ointment." *News-Chronicle*, 7 May 1950, p. 4.

*Harold Hobson. "Mr. Eliot's Play." *Sun Times*, 7 May 1950, p. 4.

Helen Ormsbee. "Irene Worth's Roundabout Trip to a Cocktail Party." *New York Herald Tribune*, 7 May 1950, sec. 5, p. 3.

John Courtney Trewin. "*The Cocktail Party* Opens in London." *New York Times*, 7 May 1950, sec. 2, p. 2x.

Charles E. Whiting. "'Cocktail' as Hit Baffles Eliot." *Daily Compass* [New York], 9 May 1950, [page no. unknown].

*Eric Keown. "At the Play." *Punch* 218 (10 May 1950), 524.

*Peter Fleming. "Contemporary Arts. Theatre." *Spectator* 184, no. 6359 (12 May 1950), 694.

*Philip Hope-Wallace. "Theatre: *The Cocktail Party.*" *Time and Tide* 31 (13 May 1950), 466.

*T. C. Worsley. "The Second Cocktail Party." *New Statesman* 39 (13 May 1950), 543.

"Eliot Says the Play Is to Entertain." *New York Herald Tribune*, 14 May 1950, sec. 5, p. 2.

Stephen Longstreet. "Shaggy Grandfathers Sire Strong Breed." *Daily News* [Los Angeles], 20 May 1950, p. 17.

*John Courtney Trewin. "Wine and Water." *Illustrated London News* 216 (20 May 1950), 792.

Harold Hobson. "*The Cocktail Party.*" *Christian Science Monitor Magazine*, 27 May 1950, p. 6.

William Arrowsmith. "Notes on English Verse Drama." *Hudson Review* 3 (Summer 1950), 203–16.

Ray C. B. Brown. "Alcoholic Allegory." *Voices* (Summer 1950–51), 33–40.

*Robert Speaight. "Sartre and Eliot." *Drama* 17 (Summer 1950), 15–17.

Lionel Trilling. "Wordsworth and the Iron Time." *Kenyon Review* 12 (Summer 1950), 493–94.

*Heidi Heimann. "A God in Three Disguises." *World Review*, June 1950, pp. 66–69.

Howard Taubman. "Records: *Cocktail Party*." *New York Herald Tribune*, 11 June 1950, [page no. unknown].

*Irwin Edman. "Incantations by Eliot." *Saturday Review* 33 (24 June 1950), 56–57.

*Wilbur Dwight Dunkel. "T. S. Eliot's Quest for Certitude." *Theology* 7 (July 1950), 228–36.

Eric Johns. "Creating a T. S. Eliot Role." *Theatre World*, 46, no. 306 (July 1950), 27, 34.

*T. R. Fyvel. "Letter from London." *New Leader*, 22 July 1950, pp. 16–17.

*"Sagittarius" [pseudonym]. "Nightingale among the Sweenies." *New Statesman* 40 (29 July 1950), 118.

Rowland Field. "Along Broadway: *The Cocktail Party* is Heady Fare, Affecting Audiences in Various Ways." *Newark Evening News*, 31 July 1950, p. 12.

*John Minchip White. "What a Party!" *Poetry* 19 (August 1950), 24–27.

*"Writing for the Theatre." *Times Literary Supplement* 2534 (25 August 1950), viii.

William Arrowsmith. "Notes on English Verse Drama II: *The Cocktail Party*." *Hudson Review* 3 (Autumn 1950), 411–30.

Leo Hamalian. "Mr. Eliot's Saturday Evening Service." *Accent* 10 (Autumn 1950), 195–206.

Robert Heywood. "Everybody's Cocktail Party." *Renascence* 3 (Autumn 1950), 28–30.

John J. McLaughlin. "A Daring Metaphysic: *The Cocktail Party*." *Renascence* 3 (Autumn 1950), 15–28.

Hermann Peschmann. "*The Cocktail Party*: Some Links between the Poems and Plays of T. S. Eliot." *Wind* 7 (Autumn 1950), 53–58.

John Pick. "A Note on *The Cocktail Party*." *Renascence* 3 (Autumn 1950), 30–32.

C. J. Vincent. "A Modern Pilgrim's Progress." *Queen's Quarterly* 57 (Autumn 1950), 346–52.

Sandra Wool. "Weston Revisited." *Accent* 10 (Autumn 1950), 207–12.

William Henry Beyer. "The State of the Theatre: Seasonal High Lights." *School and Society* 72 (16 September 1950), 180–82.

W. K. Wimsatt, Jr. "Eliot's Comedy." *Sewanee Review* 58 (October 1950), 666–78.

"The Theatre: By Slow Stages to a Sand Bar." *New Yorker* 26 (7 October 1950), 51–52.

"People: The Calloused Hand." *Time* 56 (23 October 1950), 42.

"$2,800 Awarded T. S. Eliot. He Wins *London Sunday Times*' Prize for *The Cocktail Party*." *New York Times*, 6 November 1950, p. 33.

*Charles Poore. "From 'Ol' Man River' to T. S. Eliot." *Christian Science Monitor*, 11 November 1950, p. 8.

"T. S. Eliot's *The Cocktail Party* Has a Single Performance at the Teatro Agiuleon in Mexico City." *New York Times*, 16 November 1950, p. 39.

*John Middleton Murry. "Mr. Eliot's Cocktail Party." *Fortnightly* 168, no. 1008, n.s. (December 1950), 391–98.

Lewis Funke. "News and Gossip of the Rialto: Interview." *New York Times*, 17 December 1950, sec. 2, p. 3x.

"The Year in Books." *Time* 56 (18 December 1950), 107.

*Stephen Spender. "On *The Cocktail Party*." *The Year's Work in Literature, 1950* (London: Longmans, Green, 1951), 17–23.

THE CONFIDENTIAL CLERK
1954

THE

CONFIDENTIAL CLERK

A PLAY

by

T. S. ELIOT

FABER AND FABER LTD
24 Russell Square
London

*Henry Hewes.
"T. S. Eliot—Confidential Playwright."
Saturday Review 36
(29 August 1953), 26–28.

T. S. Eliot, whose unquestioned merit as a poet, playwright, and essayist has been officially recognized by Her Majesty with an O.M. (Order of Merit), is this week unveiling his fourth full-length play in eighteen years. Titled *The Confidential Clerk*, it opens at the Edinburgh Festival, moves on to Newcastle, and finally arrives in London in mid-September. A fortnight before embarking for Caledonia the distinguished writer granted me an hour-and-a-half interview—an extremely thoughtful dispensation, for in addition to the normal stress that every playwright must face in the crucial rehearsal period Mr. Eliot was continuing to punch the clock three days a week at the publishing offices of Faber and Faber, Ltd.

"Now let's see," he began, shoving his hands deep in his pockets and bowing his head a bit, "I mustn't say too much about this play, as I want the audience to make up its own mind. If I say I intended such-and-such, then people will feel they have to find just that in it. But, really, if a play is any good it ought to have a great deal in it that its author doesn't completely understand."

Although *The Confidential Clerk*'s director, Martin Browne, has publicly announced that the play is "a modern comedy lighter in tone than any of his previous plays," the playwright even refuses to define it as either comedy or tragedy. "Since no one is murdered or dies violently in *The Confidential Clerk*, I am letting the audience call it what they like. It can be regarded as either."

On this subject Mr. Eliot, who regards himself as neither a pessimist nor an optimist, maintains that his *Murder in the Cathedral* (1935) is a comedy; *The Family Reunion* (1939) neither, due to his own error in construction which came about when he concluded with the tragic death of one character but indicated at the same time an indefinite progress of the hero; and *The Cocktail Party* (1949) a comedy, because the heroine, Celia, dies heroically in the service of something. "There is no feeling of waste in Celia, and you must always [feel] waste in a tragedy. A real tragic character is capable of a successful life in the best sense, but misses it when fortune smacks him in the face."

While the playwright refuses to label his new play, he does say that it is the same general type as *The Cocktail Party*, but with two improvements. "In *The Cocktail Party* only four of the seven characters are characters in the true sense. The psychiatrist and his two assistants are outside the action of the play. They interfere, but there is no character development in these three. They just perform a job. I think that the audience may have been mystified by this. So, in *The Confidential Clerk* all seven in the cast are characters in their own right with none being outside the action."

The second change is an even more important one. Readers may remember that many of the critics complained that the last act of *The Cocktail Party* was not a true last act but an epilogue. "It was a necessary epilogue, but these critics were right in the sense that the dramatic action was all over," admits the bespectacled poet ungrudgingly. "In my new play I've tried to keep things happening right up to the end."

In addition, there is no drinking and no psychiatry in *The Confidential Clerk*. "To tell you the truth I think the psychiatry had a lot to with the success of *The Cocktail Party*. It made it very fashionable."

The plot of the new play—and Mr. Eliot is a bit reluctant to reveal too much of it—begins with a rich English financier, Sir Claude Mulhammer, who, in choosing a new clerk to succeed his old confidential clerk who is retiring, selects a young man whom he believes to be his own illegitimate son. Sir Claude's wife, who does not know this chapter of her husband's past, had before her own marriage a child of her own and she comes to the conclusion that the new clerk is *her* missing illegitimate son. The situation is further complicated by the introduction of a young woman who turns out to be Sir Claude's illegitimate daughter.

Although these plot outlines suggest that the play was inspired by Euripides's *Ion*, Mr. Eliot won't commit himself definitely on the point. All he will say is: "The ideas for all this came to me out of a classical story, just as *The Cocktail Party* started out with my wondering about *Alcestis*. I was interested in what happened at the point Euripides leaves off. What was it going to be like when the wife is brought back from the dead? After all, it isn't the same as losing her on a shopping expedition. Then I added Reilly to get Heracles in the triangle. And after that the other characters developed. Celia, at first, was brought in just to throw light on the relationship between the man and his wife, but later became much more important."

[. . .]

Mr. Eliot is not disclosing the source of *The Confidential Clerk* for a good reason. "Why I don't let this very small cat out of the bag," he says, "is that if you say that such-and-such a parallel exists it will lead people up the garden path." What the poet means is that playwriting should not be like watchmaking, where you follow a carefully worked out procedure of fitting pieces together. "Whatever the source," he goes on, "the author

should let the play grow inside him. In that way he puts some not completely understood parts of himself into the play." This theory also applies to character-drawing and leads to Mr. Eliot's assertion that "to make a character alive there ought to be more in him than can be contained in the author's analysis of him."

Attempting to make *The Confidential Clerk* alive, Mr. Eliot avoided starting with an ethical problem and giving it a setting. Rather he began with a serious situation, namely that of a young clerk who finds that being claimed by two different sets of parents is more embarrassing than being claimed by none. With this the author felt he could explore the fundamental truth of parent–child relationships. "I was more concerned with getting the reactions of the people to each other right than I was with the deductions to be drawn from these reactions," he says with a degree of earnestness that belies any criticism of over-intellectualism that might be lodged against him.

If the poet does have a private temptation that he indulges, it is in the matter of selecting names for his characters. He is a great admirer of Conan Doyle, Sir Walter Scott, and Dickens for their skill in this respect, and very disappointed in Henry James for his often coming up with surprisingly poor cognomens. "I name my characters right after I have written the first description of them. I try to let a name come to mind that will fit the character without being able to give a reason for it. But it's damn hard to invent names that don't exist. In *The Cocktail Party* I thought I had an original name in MacColgie Gibbs, but one of these people who are always analyzing my work discovered that Gibbs is an English toothpaste and Colgate an American one. In *The Confidential Clerk* I thought up an original name for one of the characters, a man whom I called Kaghan. A year later I picked up a newspaper to find that Mr. Kaghan is one of those unfortunate officials being investigated by Mr. Cohn and Mr. Schine." Incidentally, Mr. Eliot as a former American citizen feels no sense of disgrace about the Cohn–Schine affair. "It would be silly to identify a few low-comic figures with a whole nation," he states.

As for the verse technique in *The Confidential Clerk*, it is approximately the same as *The Cocktail Party*. That is an attempt to find a rhythm close to contemporary speech with the stresses where we would naturally put them. To do this the poet uses a varying length of line with a varying number of syllables and a series of irregular stresses. This doesn't affect the rhythm any more than it does in music where the composer can vary the number and length of notes within any one bar. Mr. Eliot's unrhymed lines are characterized by a caesura and three stresses, one stress on one side of a caesura and two on the other. "Auden says I have four stresses and he may be right. All I know is that when a line sounds wrong to me, which is the only time I think about the meter, I go back and use the three-stress test." At this point Mr. Eliot took a brief caesura to fill and light what appeared to be a well-used corncob pipe.

"This kind of verse is damned difficult for the actor," he continued, "because he has to study each line by itself. He cannot speak the verse as if it were prose, and he must not let the rhythm lead him to speaking it monotonously." Fortunately, the producer, Henry Sherek, has signed a cast that includes such experienced performers as Denholm Elliott, Alan Webb, Isabel Jeans, Margaret Leighton, Paul Rogers, Alison Leggatt, and Peter Jones, and the playwright seemed quite happy about the way rehearsals were progressing.

He is also happy about resuming his collaboration with Martin Browne, who as a director has stimulated much of the rewriting that has been done on the script. "You know, when I write a play now I write a first draft with the main object of merely completing it. Then I find that I have to do most of my rewriting on my first act. You can't really know what the beginning should be like until you get to the end. If your third act is good you have a standpoint from which to review the rest of the play. But a good first act sometimes makes it more difficult to write a good second and third act. I found that out with *The Family Reunion*. It's the same with criticism, I think. When I first started writing reviews Desmond MacCarthy told me that when he finally finished a review he usually went back and found he didn't need the first paragraph. I've found that to be generally true too. The first paragraph is just for the purpose of getting yourself warmed up."

Another weakness that Mr. Eliot finds in his first drafts is a tendency to write too many dialogues and to make too many scenes. "Originally the first act of *The Confidential Clerk* was in three scenes, and Martin Browne asked me to cut it down. So I sacrificed some amusing but superfluous passages and removed a lot of inessential background and material in an effort to concentrate the play a little more—the way Ibsen used to do as well. With great labor I put it all in two scenes, but neither of us was satisfied with the result. I had arrived at that moment of despair when I thought I just couldn't do anything more to it. But of course you can always do more, and I eventually was able to get Act I into its present single scene."

However, the rewriting did not stop the final draft. "When you hear the actors start speaking your lines things come to light that you hadn't realized. Something that is self-evident to the author may not be to other people. Sometimes you find that one phase of a scene is too long or too short in relation to the whole and you have to cut down in one place and expand in another. So far in *The Confidential Clerk* most of the changes have been mechanical ones such as changing the means whereby one character becomes aware of another who is approaching."

While Mr. Eliot has no false modesty and obviously believes he is a pretty good poet, it should be evident from the above that he has the good human judgment to enter the theatre with the humility that can come only from knowing what it is to master a craft. As he says, "The poet has a hell of lot to learn in the theatre. You can't get along with good verse and bad theatrical technique." Since *The Cocktail Party* brought him a reported $150,000 in royalties, we can possibly assume that his theatrical technique is fast approaching a state of adequacy.

---

*T. C. Worsley.
"The Confidential Clerk."
New Statesman 46
(5 September 1953), 256.*

With *The Confidential Clerk*, Mr. Eliot has done it again. By this I do not mean that he has merely repeated the success of *The Cocktail Party*; he is not the kind of writer to repeat his successes. Each work is for him (and consequently for us) an exploration, and initially, if I understand what he has written about his own methods, an exploration in technique. *The Confidential Clerk* explores new territory and uses methods in some ways quite different from anything that has gone before, and yet it is able to rivet the attention of ordinary theatre audiences who could not—and should not—be expected to be interested in questions of technique. An audience

judges by results, and though this play is, I believe, very imperfect, Mr. Eliot has now reached a stage where the authority with which he puts his questions imposes itself absolutely.

From the very opening of the play we feel we are on sure ground. Yet it is a very odd sort of sure ground, this of Mr. Eliot's. It is by no means the conventional sure ground of problems posed and solutions neatly found for them. On the contrary, we are never quite sure what the problems really are; and as for the solutions, they none of them seem to fit us at all. Why then we should be content to follow so fumbling and faltering a guide is a mystery. But so it is. His authority is such that he compels us along.

Our exploration is of Sir Claude Mulhammer's curiously assorted household. Sir Claude himself has inherited a financial business from his father; he runs it successfully enough but is at heart an artist *manqué*. Then there is his wife, Lady Elizabeth, a scatterbrained woman interested in fake religions. There is an ambiguous young woman whom the faithful old confidential clerk pronounces "flighty"; and she is engaged to a successful young protégé of Sir Claude's, B. Kaghan. Finally there is yet another protégé, Mr. Colby Simpkins, a young musician *manqué* who is in training as confidential clerk in Eggerson's place. The clue to the plot is not with the rather Gilbertian revelations of paternal and maternal mix-ups. It is not a question of who we are, but of what we choose to be. We must, it is suggested, follow in our father's footsteps. Young Colby, of doubtful origins, failed organist but with a talent for finance, can choose one of several fathers who offer themselves to guide his footsteps. Which shall he choose to be saved? The theme is decorated with several variations ranging from the poignant to the farcical. For all of them are, or have been, faced with related choices, and they are only reminded that once they have chosen "we all of us have to adapt ourselves to the wish that is granted."

What is new in the play is that for the first time Mr. Eliot approaches, in his own devious way, the question of human relationships. We are not yet dealing with people in the Ibsenite or the novelist's sense, and the fact that the characters are not people in this sense makes for a certain confusion. But the human interest is there, and it gives us a first act which fairly bristles with the possibilities of development. It gives us too, to start the second, a scene of great tenderness, a love scene—or rather a scene which beautifully embodies the reaching out towards a first shy contact between two young people. Technically, too, Mr. Eliot has succeeded with his last act which, even if emotionally it may leave us baffled, is, with its family conference and its *deus ex machina*, dramatically effective and flowers out of what has gone before.

Yet, amusing, fascinating, oddly disturbing as *The Confidential Clerk* is, I cannot help feeling that in approaching the question of human relationships Mr. Eliot set himself more problems than he had anticipated. His present compromise is uneasy. If his characters are to have relationships which interest us, they must become less spiritual types and more people—at least so long as Mr. Eliot, for his own reasons, insists on suppressing the verse. Nor can the people be in any important relation with each other so long as the action is on the level of the absurd. It is all very well to try to reassure us by founding the plot on classical myth. That doesn't put right the confusion of modes. The comic exaggerations of the plot don't fit the terms of contemporary life—or at least they are not made to fit with these particular people and their particular problems. Quite a different form of make-believe is needed for each set. We

can perfectly accept a changeling found in a hand-bag, if we are introduced to it in the fantasy of comedy. But we would be hard put to it to take seriously the spiritual problems of such a changeling, or feel solemn over the announcement that it was to read for Holy Orders.

[. . .]

Mr. Eliot has now carried his principles about the kind of verse appropriate to modern verse drama to their logical conclusion. The controlling beat, which could still be faintly heard in *The Cocktail Party*, is no longer audible at all. It is the abrogation of this control that is, I think, largely responsible for the confusion. Surely he has now reached the point he was aiming at, when "he can dare to make more liberal use of poetry."

Philip Mairet. *"The Confidential Clerk." New Republic* 129 (21 September 1953), 17–18.

If T. S. Eliot's new play, *The Confidential Clerk*, can be placed in a category, it is an essay in the higher melodrama. Can it be that a poet, tired of being told that his drama lacked theatrical construction, determined at last to show what he *could* do? True, this piece is in the same tragicomic vein as the last. But in *The Cocktail Party* the theme was the subjective effects of secret love affairs upon individuals. The present play deals with the offspring of such liaisons, and with the delayed effects upon their parents. It points a social, not a transcendent, moral. The plot hinges upon no less than three cases of bastardy that have occurred in the same family about a quarter of a century before the curtain rises. Anyone, a critic may retort, could make a plot out of such a packet of mysterious origins. Perhaps; though not one as ingenious as Eliot has contrived, nor fraught with as much *meaning*. The drawback of having to deal with such a wildly improbable complication as he has presupposed lies not so much in its artificiality as in keeping his comedy of manners too near the verge of melodrama. Three acts of continuous "discovery scenes" of long lost parents and children is a stiff dose. The deserved celebrity of the previous play may cast an invidious shadow over this one. But comparisons are odious; this is rich entertainment, and a tract for the times.

Sir Claude Mulhammer is a successful financier, the son of a financial genius, but is childless by a wife who is a lady in her own right. Both have sons by former lovers, and Sir Claude is scheming to induce his wife to adopt his son, of whose existence he has not told her. She knows, however, about his illegitimate daughter by another mistress of much less cherished memory; and he knows that his Lady Elizabeth had a son, of whom she had lost track in infancy, ever since her lover died in Africa. Sir Claude's confidential clerk, who is retiring, is to be replaced by the illegitimate son, Colby, as an initiation into his father's household and profession. The hope is that Lady Elizabeth will acquire a maternal interest in this highly presentable and well-educated young man. She does so with a vengeance. A veiled remark of Colby's about his foster-mother's name and address leads her to believe, too precipitately, that he is *her* son; and she and her husband are contending for the parenthood of the boy until the final *dénouement*.

The play exploits all the possibilities of this situation, which is further complicated by the presence of Lucasta, the illicit daughter. Sir Claude hopes to see her married to a young financial colleague, the bumptious Kaghan, who had good foster-parents and is not in the least sensitive about his foundling origin. An intimate understanding begins to develop between Colby and Lucasta, cut short by a violent misunderstanding as soon as she confides in him the secret of her birth. There is no lack of plot and counterplot; if anything rather too much; there is wit enough, too, and very genial comedy in the character of the old confidential clerk. But the sustaining interest is in the psychology of the filial and parental relationships. No doubt the author is concerned to show, to a generation visibly in danger of emotional disintegration, how essential and fundamental are the bonds between parent and child; but he does this without resort to any of the more obviously evil consequences. None of the illegitimates develop badly; there is no delinquency on their part, nor hatred on the part of the parents. On the contrary, the parents suffer from frustrated desire for the children they once disowned; and suffer most of all when they discover that all their efforts for the good of their secret progeny have failed to repair the broken bond. This cannot be a one-way relation, as Colby points out to his father. As Ibsen said of another relationship, you may patch a fiddle but you can't mend a bell.

What about the poetry? No one will recognize it as verse until he sees it in print. There, I suspect, he may have the experience of finding it easier to read than prose. It is a logical continuation on the way Eliot's verse has been going since he took to play-writing. In *The Cocktail Party* there were still some few purple patches which everyone knew were poetry; in this piece there are none. All the same, this is a master's use of the everyday vernacular. When the characters explain what is in the depths of their minds—which they have to do rather often—the subtlety comes over with consummate clarity.

[. . .]

---

*Russell Kirk. "Two Plays of Resignation." *Month* 10 (October 1953), 223–25.

At the Edinburgh Festival, two new plays suffused with a religious spirit were performed—although neither of them was exhortatory: Mr. T. S. Eliot's *The Confidential Clerk* and Mr. George Scott-Moncrieff's *Fotheringhay*. In form, *The Confidential Clerk* is a comedy; *Fotheringhay*, a history. Neither play aspires to the state of tragedy; yet both are written in sorrow, and both produce, in different ways, a catharsis.

The sinister suggestions latent in Mr. Eliot's title are not realized: for the confidential clerk is simply a man of business, and all the characters are people ordinary enough, with the partial exception of Colby, the new clerk. Their ordinariness, indeed, is the cause of their unhappiness, and provides the play with its principal theme: the prison of Self. Sir Claude Mulhammer the financier, and his flighty wife Lady Elizabeth, and his protégés Lucasta Angel and Colby, and B. Kaghan the rising young broker, do not understand one another, or themselves, or even from whence they came. The younger people know that they were born out of wedlock, but apprehend little enough else about their world. Sir Claude, in the first act, declares that his principle of action is always to assume that he understands

nothing about any man he meets, but that the other man sees into *him* thoroughly; yet even this premise betrays Mulhammer in the end, until he cries, with his eyes shut, "Is Colby coming back?"—knowing now that even the presumed existence of his own son had been an illusion for twenty-five years.

These people, the wrack of broken families, specimens of a generation without certitudes or continuity with the past are involved in the very oldest of dramatic plots—mistaken identity, the missing son, and the comedy of errors. Mr. Eliot revives these devices ingeniously, doubtless with some pleasure in his anachronisms; and, perhaps consciously, he has written whole speeches that could have been the work of Wilde, and others that could have been Shaw's, and others Ibsen's. Lady Elizabeth, with her "mind study," her Swiss clinics, and her intuitions, would have done credit to Wilde; the bond between Lucasta and Colby, broken by Colby's discovery that they may be brother and sister, has a Shavian touch; while through all three acts, somberly, the echo of *The Wild Duck* whispers that the truth we seek about ourselves may be our undoing. When all is over, Colby and Lucasta and Kaghan, at least, do know who they are, and in some degree realize their end in life, but they accept the discovery of their true nature with resignation, rather than relief; and upon them all, though most heavily upon Sir Claude Mulhammer, descends a consciousness of the vanity of human wishes.

Everyone in the play (except, perhaps, old Eggerson, the retiring clerk, with his wife and garden and simple virtues) is haunted by a terrifying loneliness and a regret for talents frustrated. Even accomplishment in the arts (Mulhammer would have liked to be an accomplished potter, and Colby a great organist and composer) generally is baffled by the spirit of our age, Mr. Eliot seems to suggest. These people are what Burke called the flies of a summer, unable to link with dead generations or those yet unborn, without memories or high hope. They are seeking for continuity, status, faith; and, beyond all these (though only Colby, perhaps, knows this) some assurance that their lives *matter*, and that the barriers which separate every man from his fellows are transcended by a Reality more than human.

In structure, *The Confidential Clerk* is close to *The Importance of Being Earnest*, even to the revelations in the last act by the old nurse (or rather, here, Mrs. Guzzard, the foster-mother); and it is possible to laugh at certain lines and certain characters. Yet the man who sees *The Confidential Clerk* laughs only like Democritus, at the pathos of all earthly things, for in its essence this play is sad, profoundly sad, as sad as *The Waste Land*. In the second act, especially, occur lines of great tenderness and pathos, as when Lucasta comes to believe that she understands Colby and herself, and is on the brink of self-realization—and this is overwhelmed, in the next instant, by disillusion, or rather illusion of a different sort. Throughout the play, Mr. Eliot treats these people with a noble mercy and sympathy; they become lovable, indeed, all of them. From Sir Claude to Mrs. Guzzard, they are men and women of kindly natures, honest inclination, and generous hearts. But, being human, they are heir to all the imperfections of the spirit and the flesh; thus they cannot escape the rootlessness of their time, nor the sense of talents run to waste, nor the prison of Self. They do not know themselves or the nature of being.

Lucasta thinks that Colby is different from all the rest of them, for he can withdraw from their midst into his garden of the imagination, a sanctuary from the material world of desolation; but Colby himself knows better: his garden of the mind is as lonely as the real world without. If Colby had conviction of an abiding reality that transcends the wasteland—why, then, indeed, he never would be solitary in his realm of imagination, for "God would walk in my garden." Lacking this faith, however, the man is left melancholy and unnerved, deprived of love, and scarcely caring who his parents may be. We see him, near the end of the third act, groping toward a churchly vocation; yet only Eggerson, the practical old clerk, has come close to understanding Colby. Lucasta, turning back to Kaghan for some sense of affection and belonging, thinks that Colby needs no human company, being secure in the citadel of self-knowledge; she does not know how like a citadel is to a prison.

Although successful as a dramatic production, *The Confidential Clerk* will be remembered more for its occasional lines of melancholy beauty and its penetration into the recesses of Self than as a neat and close-knit play; nor is it, I am inclined to believe, likely to be considered one of Mr. Eliot's principal works. Yet I am not sure of this last: this is a play which touches most movingly upon the sources of longing and the need for enduring love, and so bears the mark of a man of genius.

[. . .]

*Richard Findlater. "The Camouflaged Drama." *Twentieth Century* (October 1953), 311–16.

Mr. T. S. Eliot's new play *The Confidential Clerk*—first staged at the Edinburgh

Festival this August, four years after the production of *The Cocktail Party*—seems likely to be even more successful at the box-office than its predecessor, and its prosperity may be fostered by the playgoer's sense of Mr. Eliot's condescension in being so persistently straightforward. No libations here, or all-knowing Strangers; no sermons on salvation, and propaganda for the saints; [. . .] indeed, *The Confidential Clerk* was hailed in Edinburgh [. . .] with relief, surprise and delight as an unmistakable farce. The names of Robertson Hare and Lady Bracknell have been freely invoked by critics, and comparisons have been made with Wilde and Labiche, rather than with the *Ion* of Euripides, to which the author has acknowledged his debt. Where *The Cocktail Party* made its home in the shell of a modern comedy of manners, *The Confidential Clerk* masquerades as a kind of Aldwych farce; the formalized plot is resolutely thick, where that of *The Cocktail Party* was precariously thin; the characters have theatrical substance, and the situations are sprung with deliberate precision and mounting absurdity; the note of portentous piety, hitherto inseparable from Mr. Eliot's plays, is virtually inaudible; and the verse is even more dexterously presented as eloquently colloquial prose. In the theatre it is notably well acted, and provides very good entertainment. But we expect more of England's leading dramatist: has he more to give?

Like *The Cocktail Party*, the new play is written on different levels of attention, and it seeks what Eliot once described, in an essay on Marston, as "a kind of doubleness in the action, as if it took place on two planes at once." There is, indeed, "an under-pattern, less manifest than the theatrical one" (I quote from the same essay), and beneath the comedy about the parentage of bastards lies a drama about the fatherhood of God. So,

at least, it seemed to one observer of the play in Edinburgh; although this underlying meaning may well be one of which—as Eliot said of Marston—the author was not fully aware. Eliot indeed has, as it were, exalted this unconsciousness as a principle of dramaturgy, and in his public statements he has emphasized, with studied detachment, that his plays are larger than his own intentions. He said of *The Cocktail Party*, in 1949:

> Whatever the play's message is, it is as much a matter of what message the audience finds in it as what message I put in it, and if there is nothing more in the play than what I was aware of meaning, then it must be a pretty thin piece of work;

and he made a similar disclaimer of responsibility for the contents of *The Confidential Clerk*. One of the results is the temptation, in the theatre, to multiply the ambiguities of the plot. The consciousness that all around them lie immensities of experience—surely Mr. Eliot is meaning more than *that!*—gives a crossword puzzle fever to intellectual playgoers, who snap up clues with hungry solemnity all through this crypto-farce. Such a guessing game seems to be one inevitable effect of his methods. Mr. Eliot, in fact, has plenty to give besides entertainment; but it is debatable whether he has chosen the right disguise.

[. . .]

It is notable that the density of the farcical plot emphasizes still more clearly Eliot's concern with the *pattern* in human lives, the mysterious operations of destiny which bring the soul to a moment of choice, "Greek tragedy is the tragedy of necessity," W. H. Auden has written, "Christian tragedy is the tragedy of possibility." *The Confidential Clerk* which, like all of Eliot's plays, is a religious drama, is a tragi-comedy of choice: all of his characters choose their destiny in the moment of crisis. The most significant choice, perhaps, is that of Colby (in whom we may find echoes of Celia in *The Cocktail Party*): Mrs. Guzzard, who appears in the last act as an alarming fairy godmother, asks Colby whose son he would wish to be—Sir Claude's, or the son of a "dead, obscure man." Colby rejects Sir Claude, and thus chooses his own inheritance: he must, like Lord Monchensey and Celia Coplestone, work out his own salvation.

[. . .]

The Confidential Clerk is also concerned, like *The Cocktail Party*, with vocation and salvation, but these themes are implied or disguised in the action.

[. . .]

The plot involves, too, a discussion of make-believe and reality, in the lives of Sir Claude and Lady Elizabeth; of art as a substitute for religion (Sir Claude's ceramics in a private room); of the acceptance of the human condition and the incomprehensibility of other people (Sir Claude's own empirical philosophy, which is turned against himself); the drama of human responsibility; and, of course, the questions of paternity, heredity and fatherhood in God—for what, ultimately, do all these topsy-turvy relationships—whose reality is questioned with a Pirandellian confusion—matter, besides the fact that, as Lady Elizabeth reminds us, "we are nearer to God than anyone"? "There can be no relation of father and son / Unless it works both ways," Colby announces. Here, as elsewhere in *The Confidential Clerk*, the author releases—consciously or unconsciously—vast and disturbing suggestions, beyond the literal statement of the text.

There are densities of meaning, then, in Mr. Eliot's new play which entitle it to some consideration not only as a money-making farce, but as a religious drama. [. . .] But it is already obvious, I think, that *The Confidential Clerk* may be ranked as another brilliant failure, another experimental stage in Mr. Eliot's progress towards the creation of a great contemporary play. For although the play is designed with laborious cunning as an intricate theatrical machine, which works on two levels at once, the author ultimately fails to resolve the action on both its planes; and once again he fails to achieve the emotional unification of the play's meaning, the direct illumination of experience with the intensity of high drama. Eliot's elaborate mystification, justified here by the pretext of the farce, is designed to energize and universalize the play's action inside the naturalist convention, but it does not work *in the theatre* with the necessary light and heat of effective poetic drama. Writing of Massinger, Mr. Eliot said thirty years ago: "The poetic drama must have an emotional unity, let the emotion be whatever you like. It must have a dominant tone; and if this be strong enough, the most heterogeneous emotions may be made to reinforce it." What *The Confidential Clerk* lacks in the last resort is precisely this "emotional unity"—achieved for example, in *Murder in the Cathedral*, within a very different dramatic convention.

Yet it goes without saying, I think, that Mr. Eliot's failure is of considerably greater importance to the future of the English drama than the easier successes of other, luckier dramatists who can touch the audiences' hearts without destroying their preconceived ideas. Slowly and deliberately, he has created a new kind of theatrical language which, as he shows in *The Confidential Clerk*, has a flexible, anonymous and lightly hypnotic power; and in the search for a dramatic convention to express the complexity of contemporary experience he has moved away from the trappings of the Chorus, rhetorical and lyrical interpolations, and the direct intervention of the author, leaving behind him a trail of abandoned poetic properties. He has found, and held, an audience in the "commercial" theatre, and by disguising his subjects as carefully as he disguises his verse, he has tried to solve the problems of the lack of moral, aesthetic and social conventions that can be shared by a contemporary audience. Beginning in revolt against the naturalism of the proscenium stage, he has returned to work inside its limitations, seeking to give them depth and intensity, fashioning his Trojan Horses under the sponsorship of Mr. Henry Sherek. In this process *The Confidential Clerk* marks a further state, and at the same time illustrates the dangers of his method.

"It seems to me," Mr. Eliot said in 1949, with the magisterial diffidence of a reluctant oracle, "that we should turn away from the Theatre of Ideas to the Theatre of Character. The essential poetic play should be made with human beings rather than with ideas." Moreover, he has made it clear that "the essential poetic play" should sound as if it were written in prose: "a present-day audience, which realizes that it is listening to a play in verse, cannot be expected to have the right attitude to what I am trying to do." To adjust the attitudes of such an audience, therefore, the essential poetic play must be accommodated inside the picture-frame stage, the naturalist prose drama, and the unholy trade of modern show business. "If the poetic drama is to reconquer its place, it must, in my opinion, enter into overt competition with prose drama," Mr. Eliot has said, and it is with this competitive spirit, for one, that he was imbued in writing *The Cocktail Party* and *The Confidential Clerk*. In such a contest, he has decided, the best chance of success is to impersonate one's opponent, and his two post-war plays may thus be regarded as ingenious experiments in theatrical camouflage, in which a religious drama is presented to the secular groundlings of today under an increasingly heavy disguise.

Yet the failure of *The Confidential Clerk*, it seems to me, illustrates the dangers of this disguise, most of all the danger that it may be only too successful. Has the camouflage proved too much for the poetic competitor? Is Mr. Eliot's victory a Pyrrhic one?

> I have before my eyes [he says] a kind of mirage of the perfection of the verse drama, which would be a design of human action and of words, such as to present at once the two aspects of dramatic and of musical order . . . To go as far in this direction as it is possible to go, without losing contact with the ordinary everyday world with which drama must come to terms, seems to me the proper aim of dramatic poetry.

With this mirage before him, is he content to leave a large part of his audience unaware that they have watched anything but a melodramatic farce? How far can he afford to go on compromising with "the ordinary everyday world"? I am reminded of Sir Claude's declaration in *The Confidential Clerk*: "if you haven't the strength to impose your own terms / Upon Life, you must accept the terms it offers you." It is time for Mr. Eliot to impose his own terms upon the theatre he has conquered from within.

Burke Wilkinson. "A Most Serious Comedy by Eliot." *New York Times*, 7 February 1954, sec. 2, pp. 1, 3.

T. S. Eliot's *The Confidential Clerk* has just completed its two-week tour here. Capital-ites came in droves, and remained to give the two rounds of polite applause which is the equivalent of an ovation in this cau-tious city. On the eve of Broadway—with a New Haven opening and a Boston inter-lude safely behind him—Elliott Martin Browne, the director, was in the mood to discuss the special problems and fascina-tions of staging this most serious of come-dies. You might call Mr. Browne Mr. Eliot's nuncio, for his credentials as spokesman for the pontiff of modern poets are impres-sive.

Their close association goes back to 1930. He has directed all the five plays that Eliot has written, beginning with *The Rock* (1934), a religious pageant play "in a structure borrowed from a C. B. Cochran revue." [. . .]

One Man's Opinion

Did Mr. Browne care to make a compari-son between the new play and *The Cock-tail Party*?

"It is better," was the prompt reply. "Better because the things he sets out to say are all said *in* the lives of the characters, characters involved in dramatic action. There are no onlookers—no Alex or Julia or Reilly. Even Eggerson, the clerk himself, is involved by his final-curtain acquisition of Colby as his spiritual son."

Henzie Raeburn, Browne's lively actress wife, had something to add: "The audience is involved, too, caught up, dynamically implicated. Whether pro or con they seem to feel an extraordinary necessity to explain."

[. . .]

Could Mr. Browne give any clue as to Mr. Eliot's feeling about the essence of his play, beneath the smooth veneer of comedy? Mr. Browne became deeply earnest, more than ever emissary of a higher authority. The best way to be seri-ous today, he thought, is through the medium of a comedy.

The Message

The Wildean, two-dimensional plot serves notice early of its own absurdity, but in this "high-comedy" style the audience can still become aware of each character as a human being. It also gives a certain lee-way over and above the two-dimensional reality of the characters, and it is in this area that Eliot is able to embed his deeper message of man's adjustment to his lot—resignation almost—and his closeness to God in the discovery of that lot.

"When I first talked to Eliot," Browne remarked, pursuing this theme, "he said to me 'Eggerson is the only *developed* Chris-tian in the play.' I think, to Eliot, Egger-son is the catalyst. He is the man who cul-tivates his own garden, who is at peace with himself and his God. Everything else becomes soluble in his warmth. And Colby becomes his son in spirit in the end."

Mr. Browne's method of directing Eliot's intricate blend of surface nonsense, with its deeply serious interludes was, first of all, to get the cast in a circle and to read aloud over and over for three or four days "to get the Eliot verse rhythms into their subconscious, to lift them out of realism into the special climate of poetry." Then, by stage business of the most explicit kind, the aura of realism could be supplied to the poetry. This, it seems, is mainly a matter of what Mr. Browne calls "modulations"— transitions, changes of pace. He cited, as an example, Lady Elizabeth's long, musing speech ending with "we are nearer to God than anyone" and her sudden swift question to Colby at its end, "Where did you live as a child?"

[. . .]

Would Mr. Browne care to comment on Mr. Eliot at rehearsal?

Steady Improvement

"He has become more and more facile with the years. When we did *The Family Reunion* in 1939 he was still not familiar enough with the medium to adjust. Even now he will not improvise. The pattern of his plays is too complex for that, a geometric, almost Celtic using and re-using of patterns. But if he is convinced that a point has not been properly made, he will go away and bring something back in a day or two. He worked with us a lot in the rehearsals of *The Confidential Clerk* and during the two weeks of the Edinburgh Festival where we opened. But now the actual text is, of course, set and he would be wary of change. At rehearsal he is very quiet, although he can be passionate enough in private. He will never say, 'you can't alter' or 'I won't.' He is a craftsman who wants to perfect his craft, and the most discreet of authors of course as well."

Mrs. Browne, who had remained out of the conversation much of the time, remarked vehemently, "He has good manners in the bone."

In Washington the reaction to the play has been mixed. Scholars say the Trinitarian meaning is obvious enough: Act I is the Father, Act II, the Son, and Act III,

the Holy Ghost. But a noted correspondent remarked that "it is far worse than *The Cocktail Party*. In that one he was only fooling the public. In this, he's fooling himself."

Is Colby a latter-day Christ? Sir Claude a slightly disillusioned Divinity? Lucasta a Mary Magdalene?

These are questions that New York will contemplate and deliberate. For one prediction can be made with assurance: Mr. Eliot's latest adventure in play-making will not be greeted with indifference.

*Helen Gardner.
New Statesman 47
(20 March 1954), 373–74.

Mr. Eliot's first attempt to write a popular comedy was naturally an experiment, retaining certain elements from his earlier work. *The Cocktail Party* was a blend of two traditions: the tradition of the comedy of manners, whose subject is the love-game, and the tradition of romantic comedy, in which the fortunes of the characters are manipulated by more or less supernatural powers. The whole conception of the Guardians—comic Eumenides, at first regarded as nuisances, at the end recognized as "kindly ones"—looked back to *The Family Reunion*. It was as if those awkward shapes, whose intrusion into the drawing-room Mr. Eliot has himself mocked, and Agatha, the stern monitress, had insisted on being present, although in comic disguise. In subject, too, *The Family Reunion* and *The Cocktail Party* are closely related. *The Cocktail Party* is the story of a marriage that breaks down and then comes right, as *The Family Reunion* is the story of marriage with a tragic issue. [. . .]

559

With *The Confidential Clerk* a break has been made. The "Eumenides" and the martyr have been left behind. The goddess in the machine, Mrs. Guzzard, holds the role of Pallas Athene; but she is not that wise virgin, nor any other. She is firmly rooted in her suburb, Teddington [. . .], the widow of Herbert Guzzard, an organist. She is mother, yet not mother, of Colby Simpkins, not in any mystical or symbolical sense, but because, though she was his mother after the flesh, she preferred to be his aunt. Mr. Eggerson, the "wise one" of this play, does not burst out with cryptic little runes, pour libations to the gods of the hearth in his hot milk, or circle around a birthday cake—and he is mercifully unaware that he is wise. The lonely figure is still here, the person who is "different." But the desert to which Colby retreats is a comfortable one. [. . .]

The rather uneasy blend of the comedy of manners with a kind of divine comedy has given way to another kind of comedy, something nearer to the comedy of humors. Sir Claude, with his dreams of himself as a potter, and his talk about being "obedient to the facts," when it is clear that he has the utmost difficulty in recognizing a fact at all, much more in obeying it; Lady Elizabeth, with her belief in her unconventionality and her search into any fashionable form of wisdom; Lucasta, with her "tough blonde" act; B. Kaghan, with his "commonness"—these are [. . .] characters [from a comedy of humors], jolted by twists and turns of the improbable plot into acknowledgment of their true natures. *The Confidential Clerk* has a unity which Mr. Eliot has not achieved before in a play. No single one of the characters has a monopoly of wisdom or virtue, and no character exists simply to be despised [. . .]. Each in his or her own way has glimpses of the truth and each is capable of suffering, because capable of love. The plot has an obvious source in the

Ion of Euripides, a fountain-head of Greek romance, and of the comedy of Menander and his Roman imitators, and Mr. Eliot has followed good precedent in his adaptation. As Shakespeare doubled the twins of his source in *The Comedy of Errors* to make the fun faster, so, for the one foundling of the *Ion*, Mr. Eliot has provided three. The element of fantasy, necessary if comedy is to rise above being a mere transcript of daily life and reach towards general truth, is not, as in *The Cocktail Party*, imposed on a particular story by the addition of extraneous characters. It is the plot itself.

The Confidential Clerk differs from Mr. Eliot's earlier plays in having a weak and untheatrical beginning, but a strong third act and a splendid final curtain. Always before he excelled in exposition and failed in his *dénouement*. Here, in the last act, with revelation piled on revelation, is a real theatrical climax. The slow exposition is the price that has been paid for the complications of the plot and the classically restricted cast. It is a serious blemish in a play which aims at being theatrical. But, apart from this defect, the play seems to me, both on the stage and in reading, an advance dramatically on its predecessor.

The subject of *The Cocktail Party* was freedom and destiny, our narrow area of choice. The subject of *The Confidential Clerk* is related; but the plot turns less upon choice than upon the acceptance of choices made long ago and not necessarily made by ourselves. The "Know thyself" of *The Cocktail Party* is seen here to involve knowing other people. Mrs. Guzzard chose to be her son's aunt, not his mother. Lady Elizabeth chose not to be a mother, except in wish. Sir Claude chose to be a patron rather than a father: to be in "a kind of fiduciary relationship" to his daughter, and to keep a son in cold storage, as it were, until he was ready for him. Colby, the central figure, is the object of other people's choices and wishes. Personable, intelligent, well-behaved, he is the ideal son, ready-made, off the peg. At the beginning he is trying to adapt himself to what he believes to be the facts. At the close, asked what he wishes, he declares that he wants what he has had: to have no father and no mother in this life. The only true father he can have is a father who died before he was born, who did not refuse him the knowledge of a father's love, because he was not there to give it. His music is not to be like Sir Claude's love of his pots. He is not content for it to be a hobby. The knowledge of who his father was confirms him in his knowledge that his music is something in his very being, a key to his nature. His mother must "rest in peace"; he has never known a mother and cannot in any true sense know one now. Colby's "difference" is something that has been imposed upon him, which he has made and will make a source of strength.

[. . .]

In *The Cocktail Party* the divine broke into the pattern of human lives in the form of the heroic, and the heroic is, as Von Hügel said, the most easily recognizable manifestation of the supernatural. It is not difficult to respond with admiration to the mystic's search for union and the martyr's absolute rejection of what this life has to offer. But to be asked to find a test of the values by which we live in Mr. Eggerson, pottering about in his garden in Joshua Park, performing commissions for Mrs. E. at the draper's, and finding everyone has a heart of gold, is another matter. Mr. Eggerson never opens his mouth without a cliché. The "monuments of unageing intellect" are, one imagines, quite meaningless to him. His reading is the evening paper, and I don't like to think what pictures adorn his lounge or what tasteful vases stand upon its what-nots.

For a poet to place such a character at the spiritual center of his play is the strongest possible indication that "the poetry does not matter." What the author has to say here is said in the whole design of his plot, in the behavior of all the characters to each other. The play stands or falls by our acceptance of the characters and not by any particular scenes or passages of deep significance or high poetic beauty. This is not to say that the play is not finely written, and that those characters who properly can do so do not express themselves with an exquisite precision. But whatever message the play holds is diffused over the whole.

As I see the play, judgment of Mr. Eliot's achievement must depend on our judgment of his characterization, on whether we believe in his characters and whether we care about them. The queer family party we are left with at the end, Sir Claude, Lady Elizabeth, Lucasta and B. Kaghan, both convince the imagination, I think, and touch the heart. The difficulty lies in Colby and Mr. Eggerson. For Colby has very little character and Mr. Eggerson perhaps too much. [. . .] I can think of only one English writer who has succeeded beyond question in presenting the kind of goodness which Eggerson is intended to embody, Jane Austen in Miss Bates. But the novel can do things which the stage cannot do, and *vice versa*. The theatre exaggerates, and in the glare of the footlights Eggerson may come out as too little a person and too much a character part. In these two roles Mr. Eliot has asked a great deal of his actors.

All the same, the gulf that in Mr. Eliot's earlier plays separated the heroes from their fellows does not yawn in *The Confidential Clerk*. In *The Family Reunion* Harry and Agatha hardly seemed to belong to the same species as the uncles and aunts of the chorus. Even in *The Cocktail Party*, where different ways of

561

salvation were shown, the death of Celia and the domestic felicity of Edward and Lavinia were too far apart for either to seem true; each infected the other with a kind of unreality. The obscurely faithful Eggerson is a better touchstone in the world of comedy than the romantically conceived Celia, presenting, quite unconsciously, a stronger challenge to our conception of the good life.

Checklist of Additional Reviews

W. A. Darlington. "New Eliot Comedy Cheered by Scots." *New York Times*, 26 August 1953, p. 10.

Louis Calta. "Sherek May Stage Eliot Play Here." *New York Times*, 29 August 1953, p. 10.

Ivor Brown. [*The Confidential Clerk*]. *New York Herald Tribune*, 30 August 1953, [page no. unknown].

W. A. Darlington. [*The Confidential Clerk*]. *New York Times*, 30 August 1953, [page no. unknown].

*Harold Hobson. "Mr. Eliot in the Saddles." *Sunday Times*, 30 August 1953, p. 4.

"*The Confidential Clerk*." *Variety*, 2 September 1953, [page no. unknown].

*Henry Donald. "Edinburgh Festival." *Spectator* 191 (4 September 1953), 238.

*[*The Confidential Clerk*]. *Illustrated London News* 223 (5 September 1953), 353.

"*The Confidential Clerk*." *New York Times Magazine* 6 (6 September 1953), 36–37.

*Henry Hewes. "A Bang and a Whimper." *Saturday Review* 36 (12 September 1953), 44–46.

*J. G. Weightman. "Edinburgh, Elsinore and Chelsea." *Twentieth Century*, October 1953, pp. 306–08.

Mollie Panter-Downes. "Letter from London." *New Yorker* 29 (10 October 1953), 110–11.

Ian Crawford. "More Mirth Than Mysticism." *Theatre Arts* 37 (November 1953), 81–82.

Bonamy Dobrée. "*The Confidential Clerk*." *Sewanee Review* 62 (January 1954), 117–31.

"*The Confidential Clerk*." *Variety*, 13 January 1954, [page no. unknown].

T. S. Matthews. "T. S. Eliot Turns to Comedy." *Life* 36 (1 February 1954), 56–58.

Harvey Breit. "An Unconfidential Close-Up of T. S. Eliot." *New York Times Magazine*, 7 February 1954, pp. 16, 24–25.

Brooks Atkinson. "First Night at the Theater. Comedy by T. S. Eliot with Ina Claire, Claude Rains and Joan Greenwood." *New York Times*, 12 February 1954, p. 22.

John Chapman. "T. S. Eliot's *The Confidential Clerk*. A Stimulating, Enjoyable Comedy." *Daily News* [New York], 12 February 1954, [page no. unknown].

Robert Coleman. "Eliot's *Confidential Clerk* is Superlative Theatre." *Daily Mirror* [New York], 12 February 1954, [page no. unknown].

William Hawkins. "Comedy, Pathos Mix in *Confidential Clerk*." *New York World-Telegram and Sun*, 12 February 1954, [page no. unknown].

Sam Hynes. "Religion in the West End." *Commonweal* 59 (12 February 1954), 475–76.

Walter F. Kerr. "*The Confidential Clerk*." *New York Herald Tribune*, 12 February 1954, [page no. unknown].

John McClain. "Rewarding Drama: Appreciation of Play Takes Hard

Work." *Journal American* [New York], 12 February 1954, [page no. unknown].

Richard Watts Jr. "T. S. Eliot's *Confidential Clerk*." *New York Post*, 12 February 1954, [page no. unknown].

John Beaufort. "*The Confidential Clerk* on Broadway." *Christian Science Monitor*, 20 February 1954, p. 16.

Wolcott Gibbs. "The Importance of Being Eliot." *New Yorker* 30 (20 February 1954), 62, 64–65.

"Drama Mailbag. Reactions to Critic's Review of Play by T. S. Eliot." *New York Times*, 21 February 1954, sec. 2, p. 3.

"T. S. Eliot on Life and Its Paradoxes." *New York Times Magazine*, 21 February 1954, p. 16.

Brooks Atkinson. "T. S. Eliot's 'Clerk.'" *New York Times*, 21 February 1954, sec. 2, p. 1.

Walter F. Kerr. "T. S. Eliot Strolls in the Same Garden." *New York Herald Tribune*, 21 February 1954, sec. 4, p. 7.

"*The Confidential Clerk*." *Time* 63 (22 February 1954), 80, 83.

"First Night: *The Confidential Clerk*." *Newsweek* 43 (22 February 1954), 94.

Eric Bentley. "Old Possum at Play." *New Republic* 130 (22 February 1954), 22.

*John Mason Brown. "Not with a Bang." *Saturday Review* 37 (27 February 1954), 26–28.

Harold Clurman. "Theatre." *Nation* 178 (27 February 1954), 184–87.

[Letters regarding *The Confidential Clerk*]. *New York Times*, 28 February 1954, sec. 2, p. 2.

*Nicholas Brooke. "*The Confidential Clerk*: A Theatrical Review." *Durham University Journal*, March 1954, pp. 66–70.

*Nicholas Mosley. "Mr. Eliot's *Confidential Clerk*: The Importance of Being Amusing." *European* 13 (March 1954), 38–44.

"People are Talking About . . ." *Vogue* 123 (1 March 1954), 130–31.

"Eliot and Hepburn." *New York Times Magazine* 6 (14 March 1954), 6.

Richard Hayes. *Commonweal* 59 (19 March 1954), 599–600.

*Anthony Hartley. "The Drama and Mr. Eliot." *Spectator* 192, no. 6561 (26 March 1954), 364–65.

"*The Confidential Clerk*." *Theatre Arts* 38 (April 1954), 22–25.

Spencer Brown. "T. S. Eliot's Latest Poetic Drama." *Commentary* 17 (April 1954), 367–72.

Saul Bellow. "Pleasure and Pains of Playgoing." *Partisan Review* 21 (May–June 1954), 312–15.

George Spelvin. "Confidentially, *Clerk* Had 'em Confused." *Theatre Arts* 38 (May 1954), 77, 91.

William Arrowsmith. "Menander and Milk Wood." *Hudson Review* 7 (Summer 1954), 291–96.

William Becker. "Broadway: Classics and Imports." *Hudson Review* 7 (Summer 1954), 269–71.

Francis Fergusson. "On the Edge of Broadway." *Sewanee Review* 67 (Summer 1954), 475–78.

Eric Bentley. "Theatre." *New Republic* 131 (9 August 1954), 22.

Mary Hivnor. "Theatre Letter." *Kenyon Review* 16 (Autumn 1954), 463–65.

William S. Weedon. "Mr. Eliot's Voices." *Virginia Quarterly Review* 20 (Autumn 1954), 610–13.

Hugh Kenner. "Possum by Gaslight." *Poetry* 85 (October 1954), 47–54.

THE ELDER STATESMAN
1959

THE
ELDER STATESMAN

A PLAY

by

T. S. ELIOT

FABER AND FABER LTD
24 Russell Square
London

"Love and Mr. Eliot."
Time 72 (8 September 1958), 43–44.

On opening night at the Edinburgh Festival last week, the author (who will be 70 this month) sat in the audience holding hands with his 31-year-old wife, his former secretary whom he married a year and a half ago. That scene offered a clue to the proceedings onstage. More than any of his previous plays or most of his poems, T. S. Eliot's *The Elder Statesman* extols love. Compared to *The Cocktail Party* and *The Confidential Clerk*—intellectual avocados spiky with Greek myth and Christian mysticism—Eliot's latest seems as simple as the peach that Prufrock was once afraid to eat.

The play's theme: dishonesty toward oneself is the worst policy. The play's hero: Lord Claverton, an aged, retired Cabinet minister who idly fingers the empty pages of his once-crowded engagement book. Two unwelcome visitors from the past destroy the sand castle of his memories—precarious memories of what was essentially bogus success. Visitor No. 1 is a moneyed spiv from Central America who shared in a disreputable episode of Claverton's youth. Visitor No. 2 is Maisie Moutjoy (now respectably renamed Mrs. Carghill), a onetime chorus girl whom the young Claverton seduced; in true Victorian melodramatic fashion. Claverton's father had squelched her breach-of-promise suit with cash. Now she accuses her former lover of having posed as a man of the world during their affair, just as he has since posed as an elder statesman: "You'll still be playing a part in your obituary, whoever writes it."

Trying to salvage the one good thing left to him—his daughter Monica's love—Claverton tells her the truth about himself and finds that "if a man has one person . . . / To whom he is willing to confess everything—/ [. . .] / Then he loves that person, and his love will save him." As a serene Claverton goes off to die under a beech tree—faintly echoing Sophocles' *Oedipus at Colonus*—he wears his fate like a royal robe: "I feel at peace now. / It is the peace that ensues upon contrition / When contrition ensues upon knowledge of the truth."

In the past Eliot seems to have agreed with Sartre that hell is other people; now he introduces the novel idea (for him) that heaven may be other people too. For this beaming Mr. Eliot, British critics had mostly middle-drawer adjectives—"entertaining," "touching," "his most human"—while the London *Observer's* Kenneth Tynan crashed through with "banal." U.S. audiences may have a chance to judge for themselves before long. The play is scheduled to move to London later this month, but at week's end Producer Henry Sherek was mulling "most flattering offers" to transport *The Elder Statesman* direct from Edinburgh to Broadway.

*Henry Hewes.
"T. S. Eliot at Seventy" and "Eliot on Eliot: 'I Feel Younger than I did at 60.'"
Saturday Review 41 (13 September 1958), 30–32.

To those who think of T. S. Eliot as clever, cynical, despairing, and enigmatic, his newest play—*The Elder Statesman*—will seem disappointingly simple and much too full of the milk of human kindness. And to any sophisticated playgoer the "official" opening of it at the Edinburgh Festival may have seemed a static and conventional production.

Indeed, the most conventional and dated scene comes right at the beginning when we are treated to a love proposal to a young lady named Monica by her very correct suitor, Charles. But just at the moment when we look at our program to see if perhaps we have wandered into the wrong play, there comes a line which suggests that something more than romance is intended. Monica says, "We must keep our private world private to ourselves, learn the path of transition out into the public world and back again to ours." This line relates the love duet to Monica's father, the just-retired Lord Claverton, who has lost this path of transition. Furthermore, because he is fatally ill he is being forced to retire from the public world. He faces this enforced idleness cheerfully "With no desire to act, yet a loathing of inaction, / A fear of the vacuum, and no desire to fill it."

Lord Claverton is deeply troubled as, accompanied by his daughter, he enters a convalescent home called Badgley Court. Softly in a Hamlet-like soliloquy he asks,

What is this self inside us, this silent observer,
Severe and speechless critic, who can terrorise us
And urge us on to futile activity,
And in the end, judge us still more severely
For the errors into which his own reproaches drove us?

And now these errors, embodied as people, return to haunt him. The first is an unsavory companion of his college days who remembers the night he ran over a man on the road and did not stop. The companion has changed his name to Gomez and gone off to prosper through shady dealings in Central America. But he too faces a lonely old age and needs to renew his acquaintance with Lord Claverton, because Lord Claverton is the only one who knows all the unpleasant facts about him, and yet cannot judge him because Gomez also knows about him. Next there is a rich widow, who turns out to be the former showgirl, Maisie Mountjoy. Maisie once had a brief affair with Lord Claverton, but was bought off by his father. She too wants to rehash the details of this incomplete first love. Finally, Lord Claverton's ne'er-do-well son Michael appears. He has lost his job and wants his father to stake him to a partnership abroad, something in "import and export / With an opportunity of profits both ways." He wants to be something on his own account, not a prolongation of his father's existence. After furiously upbraiding Michael, the ludicrousness of Lord Claverton's position is made apparent as he says:

What I want to escape from
Is myself, is the past. But what a coward I am,
To talk of escaping! And what a hypocrite!
A few minutes ago I was pleading with Michael
Not to try to escape from his own past failures:
I said I knew from experience. Do I understand the meaning
Of the lesson I would teach? Come, I'll start to learn again.
Michael and I shall go to school together
[. . . . .]
And suffer the same humiliations
At the hands of the same master.

In Act III Lord Claverton does learn. He states: "If a man has one person, just

568

one in his life, / To whom he is willing to confess everything—/ [. . .] / Then he loves that person, and his love will save him."

Thus he is able to confess to his daughter. "It's impossible to be quite honest with your child / [. . .] / To one's child one can't reveal oneself / While she is a child. And by the time she's grown / You've woven such a web of fiction about you!"

The tragedy of non-communication between parent and child manifests itself in Michael going off to Central America with the corrupt Gomez, and Eliot is realistic enough to allow this to happen. However, Claverton receives his son's unwelcome decision with surprising and new-found compassion. He tells Michael:

I shall never repudiate you
Though you repudiate me. I see now
  clearly
The many many mistakes I have made
My whole life through . . .
I see that your mother and I, in our
  failure
To understand each other, both
  misunderstood you.

In this magnanimous spirit Lord Claverton goes off to die in tranquility under a beech tree. He has, ironically, found peace at Badgley Court.

The play is Greek in its inspiration. Lord Claverton and Monica loosely parallel Oedipus and Antigone in Sophocles' *Oedipus at Colonus*. Past states are announced and analyzed. And the lessons are summed up for the audience.

[. . .]

Eliot on Eliot: An Interview

EDINBURGH

Despite the fact that his seventieth birthday is only days away, T. S. Eliot seems heartier, more unworried, and more unafraid of the world than he did when interviewed by this writer five years ago.[1] This phenomenon he attributes to his recent marriage (his second) to his former secretary.

"Love reciprocated is always rejuvenating," he says, leaning forward in his armchair. "Before my marriage I was getting older. Now I feel younger at seventy than I did at sixty. Any man if he is alone becomes more aware of being lonely as he ages. An experience like mine makes all the more difference because of its contrast with the past."

Mr. Eliot confesses that when he was young he thought of fifty as the age at which a writer goes downhill, and fully expected to be completely finished by seventy. However, he claims not to be conscious of any diminution of his mental faculties and is, in fact, planning to write one more verse play, and some literary or social criticism in prose.

"I'm curious," he adds, "to see if I shan't also want to write a few more poems in a rather different style. I feel I reached the end of something with the *Four Quartets*, and that anything new will have to be expressed in a different idiom."

This experience of reaching an end and making a new beginning has happened several times in his career as a poet. It happened after "The Hollow Men," which he no longer likes very much because it represents a period of extreme depression about his future work. It happened again after "Ash-Wednesday," when it took the commissioning of *The Rock* to get him restarted.

Mr. Eliot tends to enjoy his more recent work because it is closer to the man he now is. He believes that the one work with which he is most satisfied is the last of the *Four Quartets*. However, he experiences less dissatisfaction on rereading his earlier poems than his prose work.

"The poems permanently represent the best that I could do when I wrote them. But I judge my prose as if I'd written it yesterday and now disagreed with some of what it said."

When asked whether he would still write his famous prophecy, ("This is the way the world ends / Not with a bang but a whimper"), Mr. Eliot admits he would not. One reason is that while the association of the H-bomb is irrelevant to it, it would today come to everyone's mind. Another is that he is not sure the world will end with either. People whose houses were bombed have told him they don't remember hearing anything.

The original meaning, he explains, "was a subjective dissatisfaction with the pettiness of life. When one is young, the expression of that mood is simply an effusion of one's individual situation."

While this might seem to link him with today's angry young men, he prefers not to think so. Mr. Eliot feels that, like Rudyard Kipling, who spent his early years in another country, he has a special feeling for England. On the other hand, he believes that his poetry belongs more in the American current than it does in the British.

As for his plays, the poet who likes to be liberated from both the past and the future rates them in the inverse order in which he wrote them. When asked if he now reads himself in the title role of *The Elder Statesman*, he has this to say: "There are three ingredients in all one's characters: (1) observation of other people, (2) pure invention, and (3) something of oneself which includes what Yeats calls the anti-self. But I find that the character is most effective when one is least conscious of putting oneself into it."

While the word God is never mentioned in *The Elder Statesman*, the leading character finds confession to those he loves the road to salvation and peaceful death, and thus echoes Mr. Eliot's personal attitude about death and eternity, which is the ordinary Catholic one. He does not believe we can really grasp the concept of the timeless, although he himself has had intuitive flashes which he's hinted at in the *Quartets*. He feels these will only be communicable to those who have had similar flashes.

"Death is not oblivion," he says. "People who believe that are not afraid of death, they are only afraid of dying." Mr. Eliot cannot understand people feeling religious hope without feeling also a religious fear of what their fate may be.

"For the Christian," he explains, "there is that perpetual living in paradox. You must lose your life in order to save it. One has to be otherworldly and yet deeply responsible for the affairs of this world. One must preserve a capacity for enjoying the things of this world such as love and affection."

Also implied in *The Elder Statesman* is the pressure on any famous man to be what other people think him to be, to become the servant of the myth that surrounds him. Mr. Eliot knows this influence well through the kind of cult a great many of his admirers make about him. His formula for avoiding it is constant struggle against it, plus a sense of humor with which to see one's own absurdity.

"At seventy I laugh at myself more than I did when I was young," he says, "and conversely I am less and less worried about making a fool of myself."

Notes

1. *Saturday Review* 36 (29 August 1953), 26–28. This interview, part of a review of *The Confidential Clerk*, is included in this volume, pp. 547–50.

*Helen Gardner.
"The 'Aged Eagle' Spreads His Wings. A 70th Birthday Talk with T. S. Eliot."
Sunday Times, 21 September 1958, p. 8.

When the Literary Editor of *The Sunday Times* told me that Mr. Eliot had consented to be interviewed on the occasion of his seventieth birthday and asked me whether I was willing to be the interviewer, I imagined it would be a rather formal session. I saw myself sitting with a pad on my knees, and Mr. Eliot, perhaps at his desk in his room at Faber's, giving possibly rather cryptic answers to my prepared questions.

But instead Mr. and Mrs. Eliot invited me to lunch, and after a long and happy conversation on travel—Mrs. Eliot has just paid her first visit to the United States—on poets, poetry and the theatre, questions which I had long wanted to ask him arose naturally over coffee and brandy, and he talked freely about his own work with the simplicity and seriousness of someone who cares more for the things which he has tried to do than for his own success.

Although T. S. Eliot is the most famous of living poets and the greatest living man of letters, he is still essentially the poet who has never been content to repeat himself, who has always "fared forward," trying to find the right way to say the thing which he wants to say now.

'Bursts of Poetry'

I asked him whether, looking back on his life, he was conscious of any sharp division in his poetry between his early and his late style, and, if so, where it came. He said that he thought people had exaggerated the difference between the poetry which he wrote before he became a Christian and the poetry he wrote after. He himself felt that his poetry had come in bursts, as it were. He always had the feeling after a period of poetic activity that he had come to the end and would never write anything more, and then "something started him off again."

After he had written the early poems, ending with "Prufrock," he came to Europe, became interested in philosophy and did not feel any urge to write poetry. Then he began to write little poems in French for amusement, and "that," he said "got me going again and led to poems like 'The Hippopotamus.'" Pound's encouragement and the reading he was doing in the minor Elizabethan dramatists led to "Gerontion" and *The Waste Land*. "They go together," he said, and came out of a blend of personal feeling, experience and new reading.

A Late Developer

"I think," he added in parentheses, "I was very slow in maturing and took a long time to grow up." I asked him how this fitted with his describing himself as "an aged eagle" in "Ash-Wednesday," and he laughed and said, "Well, isn't that the kind of exaggeration which goes with immaturity, seeing oneself as older than one is?"

As for poets who had influenced him, Dante was there from the beginning. He first read Dante in 1911. Some poets who one admired one couldn't learn from: they were too idiosyncratic and could only be parodied. Hopkins was an instance, as far as he was concerned. One learned, he thought, from those who had done the kind of thing one wanted to do oneself and from the "great masters of the common style," perfectionists like Dryden.

Although one was writing a very different kind of poetry, one could feel "Dryden would not have let that line pass." He thought that of all his poems "Little Gidding" was the most satisfying in this way. It best stood the test of intellectual analysis. It said precisely what it meant.

Test of Reason

We had a pleasant short excursus then on famous lines which did *not* mean what they appeared to say, and he said he had often thought of making a little collection of well-known lines which do not "stand the test of reason."

He thought he had learned more from writers of the second rank than from the masters: more from the minor Elizabethans than from Shakespeare, and more from Laforgue than from Baudelaire. "One appreciates the greatest writers too late to be influenced by them," he said. "To be mature enough to appreciate Racine is to be too old to be influenced." As for Shakespeare—"Oh, it takes a lifetime to grow up to Shakespeare."

Asked whether he would agree that *Four Quartets* was his greatest poem, he said that he thought that he would, although it was in a way a byproduct of his interest in the theatre and of circumstances. "Burnt Norton" began from "bits leftover from *Murder in the Cathedral*" which he thought too good to waste. They "got mixed up" with the beginning of *Alice in Wonderland* and a visit to the garden of an empty house on a holiday in the Cotswolds.

Then he wrote *The Family Reunion* and was "depressed by its defects of structure"; but the war made it impossible to write another play and so he thought of writing a second poem, in the mood and style of "Burnt Norton" on another place. It was while he was writing "East Coker" that he realized that there should be four poems.

I asked him whether he thought he would write any more poems, or whether he thought of himself as wholly absorbed by plays. He said he thought he very well might, but that he did not at the moment see what they would be like. They would have to be new poems in a new idiom. For a short space we allowed ourselves to be depressed by the thought of the later Browning and the later Swinburne.

One Social Class

As a writer for the stage, he envied dramatists of an earlier age who knew what was expected of them by the public. A modern dramatist could not rely on a public educated in a dramatic convention. He had been blamed for writing about people of one social class; but he could only write about the kind of people he had met, and he owned that his experience was limited: "I have never met a murderer." I asked him how important the Greek myths behind his plays were and he said, "Oh, they are something to start from. Greek drama is full of situations, and I need a situation to begin from; but once the play has got going, the 'source' is not very important."

In *The Family Reunion*, he was concerned with the possibility of translating myth on to the modern stage; but not in *The Cocktail Party*. What interested him in the *Alcestis* was the question, "What would be the relation of the wife who returned from the dead to her husband?" The play began with the trio, husband, wife and savior (Heracles). Celia was an addition; the married couple were in the center. As for *The Confidential Clerk*, what had stirred him in the *Ion* was "the poetry of the natural celibate, the temple servant, the boy Ion" but "I am afraid," he added, "I didn't manage to make that clear. The love-scene between Colby and Lucasta was not meant to be a real love-scene, but a scene of illusion on both sides.

The other man was the right man for her and Colby was a natural solitary." I said that I thought the notion of celibacy being "natural" to some was not a very congenial idea today, and he laughed and said, "Oh dear, no. It is taken for granted that a celibate is either a pervert or thwarted."

The New Play

He thought that the critics who had called *The Elder Statesman* his most human play were probably right, but added, speaking of the two earlier comedies, that the rather Pauline conception of marriage attributed to him had not been what he intended. He had meant to suggest different ways for different people rather than to represent marriage as a "second-best."

He was willing to talk very much about young poets. "I am, after all, a publisher," he said. But he thought that the young poet today had more chance of a sympathetic hearing than he and his contemporaries had had, and was less likely to be called "a literary Bolshevik." On the other hand the financial situation was worse. The cost of publication was so much greater and the public which bought poetry had not expanded to meet the rise in the cost of production.

He owned to pride, as well he might, in his record as a publisher of poetry, and said of the Faber poets of the thirties that he thought, although he disagreed with their politics, that they were the best poets of their generation. He also felt proud of his editorship of *The Criterion*, particularly because it had made contacts between writers in this country and writers in France, Germany and Italy.

Gratitude

It was getting late by now and I thought it would be an abuse of hospitality to go on any longer and engage Mr. Eliot in discussion of his work as critic of literature and critic of society. He has made for himself a unique position in English life and thought; but he is primarily a great poet, and it was his poetry which I wanted to talk to him about.

I felt as I talked with him and his wife in their home what I am sure thousands of people all over the world will be feeling on Friday, his seventieth birthday: gratitude, reverence and affection. Throughout a long life, in a period of intellectual and moral confusion, Mr. Eliot has striven to know himself and his world and to set down "the thing as it was." He has wrestled with words and with meanings, and we are the beneficiaries of his struggle. Countless people, of whom I am one, have learned from him some first steps in the difficult art of sincerity. That one has often disagreed with him, is unimportant. What matters is the continuous effort to be truthful and for this we give him our thanks and revere him. Our good wishes to him on his birthday are given a peculiar warmth and sweetness by the fact that it is not only to him, but to him and his wife, that we wish all happiness.

Derek Stanford. "Mr. Eliot's New Play." *Contemporary Review* 194 (October 1958), 199–201.

[Reprinted and expanded in *Queen's Quarterly* 65 (Winter 1959), 682–89]

We are told that Sophocles sat down to write *Oedipus at Colonus* at the age of 80.

Mr. T. S. Eliot, who was 70 this September, has based his play on the Greek theme, and we could wish him endowed with the gift of productiveness for at least ten more years. A new serenity, a new peace, and a powerful declaration of the spirit of love inform this septuagenarian work. Yeats, as he himself said, "withered into truth," while Eliot, who appeared to believe that severity solely was the path to perfection, seems at length to have realized the momentous meaning inherent in the phrase "Ripeness is all." For years now, in this author's writing, we have seen the losing fight which Eros has put up against a narrowly conceived Agape. "Love," one felt Mr. Eliot was saying, "is either illusion or renunciation," and the grim marriage-lore of *The Cocktail Party* (How to treat your wife though you cannot endure her) was hardly a concession to the world which gives and takes in terms of the flesh. *The Elder Statesman* revises this conflict. Of course, renunciation is still in the picture; but Eros and Agape are brought into balance, and this equilibrium is a lovely thing. One might call this drama a hint on holy dying, adding the postscript that it is also a counsel on loving and a praise of right living. Those who are old must seek to depart in peace: those who are young to enter peace through love—it would be in some such formula as this that the "message" of the play might be summarized.

[. . .]

Here is a play, like *The Tempest*, which closes with a kind of autumnal promise. Claverton, his daughter, and her lover have succeeded in plucking the fruits of self-knowledge. With the golden apple in their hand, each can go their appointed way: the older man serenely into the dark, the lovers happily into life together. As to the theatrical success of the piece one may admit to certain reservations. Dramatic critics who do not share Mr. Eliot's religious point-of-view often fault his drama for what is really an ideological difference of opinion. [. . .] None the less, as staged at Edinburgh, *The Elder Statesman* clearly had imperfections. With Claverton under medical sentence of death Mr. Eliot has scored a success. Monica, his daughter, is a tender live creature, quiveringly alert to love. Gomez and Mrs. Carghill (the ghosts from Claverton's past) remain, however, *good ideas for characters* rather than convincingly realized persons. Claverton's son is stereotyped, not a distinct individual; while Charles Hemington, Monica's lover, is a sorry cardboard cut-out, a pin-stripe young prig.

[. . .]

At a press conference, Mr. Eliot stated that he thought a writer's religious view of life should color his work without being evident in so many explicit statements. This, maybe, is another way of saying that if *The Elder Statesman* is a didactic work, what it teaches is not specific doctrine. The Christian *over-tones* in this drama are fewer than in any of the previous plays. (Nor is there much reason for believing that Claverton, after his contrition and confession, dies in a profession of the Faith. It is true that he speaks metaphorically of himself and his son "side by side, at little desks" and suffering "the same humiliations / At the hands of the same master." But the "master" here may be "experience" in a general way rather than "Divine Providence." In Act One Claverton talks of his remaining years and death to come as a "vacuum"—an agnostic manner of describing his position, and intellectually—though not emotionally—there is no exact reversal of this.) But if the over-tones are absent, the Christian under-tones are in abundance. *Caritas*, in all its vast plenitude of meaning—this is what the drama luminously expresses. To some of us it has seemed that Eliot's genius needed humanizing along the path of sympathy, mercy, and forgiveness. To be both deeply humane and religious is, for certain minds, an herculean task. In *The Elder Statesman* many may feel that this difficult symbiosis has been achieved. The otherworldly aspect of our make-up rejoices over Claverton's hard-won "happy death" while the portion of our nature turned outwards to Creation delights in the relationship of the young lovers. This late touching vision of youthful love in an aging author is an endearing thing. The world of "the hollow men," terminating with a whimper, now regenerates itself with a kiss.

---

*J. G. Weightman. "After Edinburgh." *Twentieth Century* 164 (October 1958), 342–44.

Although T. S. Eliot's new verse play, *The Elder Statesman*, is not explicitly Christian, the flavor is much the same as that of *The Cocktail Party* and *The Confidential Clerk*. The first two acts make very good theatre and contain some slivers of bleak poetry; the third strikes me as an almost complete failure, contrived and moralizing. If anything, this play is more clearly a *pièce à thèse* than the other two, the lesson being that if you want to live and die happy, you ought to be honest with yourself. Lord Claverton, the elder statesman, has lived a lie all his life. During his wild youth at Oxford, he ran over an old man but did not stop, not wishing it to be known that there were two women in the car with him. After leaving Oxford, he got himself involved in a breach of promise action with a musical comedy actress whom, in a sense, he genuinely loved. The memory of these two early misdeeds has festered within him and prevented him from being anything more than a near-success. His peerage symbolizes his acceptance of outward show instead of inner truth. His conventionally suitable wife has long been dead. He is at loggerheads with his son, who has hated growing up in his shadow. He is now ill and living in retirement with his daughter, an intelligent girl who cherishes him. It is at this point that two ghosts from his past come to plague him: a friend of his student days, a scholarship-boy whom he corrupted and who witnessed the motor-car incident, and the ex-actress, now a wealthy widow. Under their taunts he comes to realize his mistakes, and finds peace before death.

Mr. Eliot has always been good at expressing negative emotion. This play conveys an immense fatigue with life, tempered in some degree by an apparently new discovery, embodied in the daughter and her fiancé, of the experience of shared love. At first, it looks as if this contrast is going to give a unique interest to the work. But as the action unfolds, the play, instead of thickening, seems to become thinner and, as often happens with *pièces-à-thèse*, the implied attitude turns out to be rather at variance with the explicit moral. Lord Claverton, [. . .] who is made up to look exactly like the present Prime Minister, achieves some progress toward spiritual enlightenment, but not as much as Mr. Eliot seems to suggest. Mr. Eliot castigates him, yet all the time surrounds him with a rather unjustified aura of sympathy. If I may be allowed to moralize in reply, from the fourth row of the stalls, I should say that it is not enough to confess one's sins and so slough off paralyzing guilt. The final test is to realize that other people actually exist, in the way one exists oneself; this, I take it, is the true meaning of "love thy neighbor as thyself." Mr. Eliot himself said as much in *The Family Reunion*: "We must try to penetrate the other private worlds / Of make-believe and fear. To rest in our own suffering / Is evasion of suffering." Lord Claverton should realize that the ex-musical comedy star and his old student friend, now a rather shady South American millionaire, are just as important, spiritually, as he is. They are, as it happens, the two most interesting characters and, had Shakespeare been holding the pen, they would have run away with the action. It is true that in the first half of the play Mr. Eliot gives them a promising subtlety. The ex-scholarship boy has not come back to blackmail Claverton, but to recapture a sense of identity through talking to the only surviving witness of his past. The feather-brained musical comedy star remembers the early love-affair as the one important experience of her life. But in the third act, this reality is taken away from them, and they are represented as vindictive schemers, anxious to revenge themselves on Claverton by helping his son to emigrate to South America. The daughter and her priggish fiancé insult them, with Mr. Eliot's obvious approval. Claverton, having confessed his mistakes, is now able to dismiss these "ghosts" from his mind and die happy. Surely, in the very act of condemning egotistical self-deception, Mr. Eliot is showing himself to be morally snobbish. To put it crudely, he saves the phoney lord at the expense of the uncultured types, so that he is really repeating the misdeed from which the whole action is supposed to have started.

The play is quite fascinating in its pattern of confessions and inhibitions. It could have been written fifty years ago.

There is a bell-rope, and a butler who brings in the tea-tray, and not a single reference to the contemporary world. When Claverton confesses that he was once the musical comedy star's lover, the fiancé takes the daughter's arm with a look of concern, as if she will be distressed by this revelation. Yet there are faintly Shavian bursts of outspokenness, although Mr. Eliot has always affected to despise Shaw. Strangest of all is Mr. Eliot's feeling for the vitality of the vulgar which gives life to the first two acts and yet is so fiercely repressed in the third.

---

*Nona Balakian. "Affirmation and Love in Eliot." *New Leader* 42 (11 May 1959), 20–21.

"It is my experience," T. S. Eliot remarked in his 1940 lecture on Yeats, "that toward middle age, a man has three choices: to stop writing altogether, to repeat himself . . . or . . . to adapt himself to middle age and find a different way of working." To do the last, he went on, means "experiencing new emotions appropriate to one's age . . . and in which the feelings of youth are integrated."

The "different way of working" for Eliot since his own middle years has been the theater. In the 24 years since his *Murder in the Cathedral*, he has enriched the meager repertory of modern poetic drama with plays which, though similar in theme, have shown progression and a capacity to integrate all stages of his experience. At the age of 70, he has written a new work which, if remote from the Eliot of *Prufrock* and the *Four Quartets* [. . .], unmistakably derives from the Eliot of the early and middle years.

"The new emotion" he has experienced—love, earthly love—appropriate at any age, is particularly right for him now, in the light of his recent, happy marriage. It can be no mere coincidence that this most serene work of the elder poet is dedicated to his wife [. . .].

Indeed, Eliot has confessed to a new hopefulness and calm since his marriage. To his erstwhile defeatist question, "Why should the agèd eagle stretch its wings?" Eliot finds it possible in *The Elder Statesman* to offer as positive an answer as he has yet dared to give—and this time in *secular* terms, which should pose no difficulties for modern audiences. In the reading, it seems the inevitable coda to the evolving Divine Comedy of modern life which Eliot's work as a whole suggests.

Eliot's plays, all written since his conversion to Anglicanism in the late '20s, have depicted life as a delusive ritual of appearances in which the essential struggle is the liberation of the authentic self. Because his religious and psychological insights have converged, his meaning, even in such obviously religious plays as *Murder in the Cathedral*, has never been simply doctrinaire. By identifying the religious concepts of contrition and purgation with psychoanalytical process involving the social Persona and the real Self that lies below it, he has found a new moral approach to character.

What has distinguished his heroes in the past has been their capacity and willingness to suffer in the hope of finding the elusive meaning of their existence. Stripped of their masks, and vulnerable before their fate, they have accepted the ultimate consequence: renunciation of their social being and ordinary human relationships. To suggest their susceptibility to intangible truths, Eliot has not hesitated to use unrealistic devices such as Tempters, ghosts and divine confessors in disguise. Mainly through the mystical overtones of his poetry, he has persuaded us that these are of another order of human beings.

The fact that *The Elder Statesman* is bare of such devices is indicative that the demand on the hero has greatly lessened. In Lord Claverton, the central character, the play has a considerably modified Eliot hero: an aging public figure, condemned by ill health to retire, Claverton has only a brief stop to make in his "purgatory" before he is released from the burden of his "guilt." In a lifetime of riding on the high tide of success, he has never been troubled by his conscience, and it is only awakened on the eve of his retirement when by accident he meets two figures from his remote past who remind him of moral failures in his youth. One, a former Oxford classmate now turned into a cynical Central American businessman, draws a likely parallel between his own fraudulent life and the statesman's; the other, an aging musical comedy star, recalling how he had callously jilted her, pricks his ego by observing: "The difference between being an elder statesman / And posing successfully as an elder statesman / Is practically negligible. And you look the part."

But Claverton does not sense his counterfeit image until he is also confronted by his son, Michael, who protests that as the son of a famous father he has been denied the right of realizing himself. In the midst of advising Michael not to run away from his past failures, Claverton has a sudden illumination about himself, and growing humble, asks: "Do I understand the meaning / Of the lesson I would teach?" Turning to his daughter, Monica, he adds: "Is it too late for me?"

Apparently it is not too late. For in the next act, having confessed all his transgressions to Monica, Claverton has the courage and insight to acknowledge himself "a broken-down actor" who has never loved anyone. Yes, he has loved Monica, "but there's the impediment: / It's impossible to be quite honest with your child." "How could I be sure that she would love the actor / If she saw him, off the stage, without his costume and makeup?"

[. . .]

Only in the realization of Monica's steadfast love can he finally accept himself. There is potential pathos in his lines: "If a man has one person, just one in his life / To whom he is willing to confess everything . . . / Then he loves that person and his love will save him."

In this concept of love as a catalyst in self-realization, Eliot has come a long way from *The Cocktail Party*, where one encountered at every turn the counterfeit faces which lovers create to meet their own needs.

Although the religious implication in this new insight is muted, the play unmistakably suggests the *Paradiso* episode of the poet's *Divine Comedy*. For here, without strife or suffering, and in the presence of a loving, forgiving person, the penitent finds both freedom and bliss.

It is, perhaps, in the nature of a *Paradiso* to lack drama. But what adds to the static quality of the play is a central character who is too abstractly conceived to be anything more than a mouthpiece for the poet. And in the absence of his "special language," Eliot's leaning toward Victorian plotting is unhappily emphasized. But as philosophy it marks a turning-point. From the questioning which began with "Ash-Wednesday," Eliot has moved on to an affirmation which is essentially Dantesque.

*Hugh Kenner.
"For Other Voices."
Poetry 95 (October 1959),
36–40.

Mr. Eliot admits no actor to his intimacy. That is one meaning of the marked change that pervades his verse when he writes for the stage. His poems, he has nearly told us, he conceives in some psychic center where the obscure phatic sensations of his own voice take their origin. When you are writing such poetry, "The way it sounds when you read it to yourself is the test," and the sensation of reading to yourself what you have written is permeated by the way it feels to be speaking: larynx, lips, and nameless intimate zones of feeling, all affirming, urging, intertexturing their modulations of a fluid of sound, in a prolonged ritual courtship of the silence which at last closes round the utterance. "Revive for a moment a broken Coriolanus . . ." Not the least of the pleasures such a line implies is the pleasure of uttering it.

Shakespeare wrote plays in the same way; that is why he never lacks willing actors to singe their wings in his flame. He makes thrilling speaking; and often, difficult hearing. But Eliot's plays reverse the premise not only of Shakespeare's plays but of Eliot's poetry: they exist not to be spoken but to be heard. It is true that others besides the author will experiment with the sensations of enunciating "Gerontion" or *The Waste Land*, but that is *per accidens*. But that stage verse shall be spoken by other people is the essential condition of its existence. And Mr. Eliot's way of distinguishing and identifying his characters seems inseparable from a reluctance to allow any of them access to the central pleasure of enunciating Eliotic verse. "In a play," he has said, "you write for other voices, and you do not know whose voices they will be"; a truth, but one which did not intimidate Shakespeare, whose central act of sympathy was always with the actor. Eliot is careful to keep his sympathies on this side of the footlights; he writes (at least after *Murder in the Cathedral*) on behalf of the audience, whose experience of the play is likely to be not merely more comprehensive than that of anyone on stage, but profounder.

[. . .]

At the heart of each of the postwar plays lies a problem analogous with this disquieting freedom enjoyed by the actors. Some mystery to which no one possesses the whole key condemns everyone on stage to state with explicit candor very little at a time. No obfuscation can be blamed on the language they employ. It is the clearest verse ever written, and every discernible poetic means assists to make it clearer. Parallelisms explicate the structure of long speeches, diamond-like precisions of diction clinch shorter ones. A metric, not of recurrences but of groupings, adjusts salient words to one another. Novelty of metaphor is eschewed; symbols are absent; epithets do not astonish but inform. The language of these plays is upper-middle-class English colloquial speech, raised from badinage to system. We have only to listen for five minutes to the admirable English cast speaking *The Cocktail Party* on the Decca recordings to see how intimate is the phrasing of the verse with that of English talk: its run has nothing in common with the deliberate unemphatic phrasing of any spoken American. It is not 'prosaic'; its system of communicating is unlike that of prose, which appeals to shared meanings and agreed areas of understanding. The verse of *The Elder Statesman*, like the language of Euclid, is coolly adequate to anything that requires saying. Spoken prose is never quite adequate to what it is saying: hence its ritual of unfinished sentences, gesturing hands, meeting eyes.

The Elder Statesman begins with badinage modulating into a love scene:

MONICA: How did this come,
      Charles? It crept so softly
On silent feet, and stood behind my
      back
Quietly, a long time, a long long time
Before I felt its presence. . . .

Before long the world of the lovers offsets the loveless world of Monica's father, *The Elder Statesman*, whose speech (we are to listen, not doze between rhetorical thrills) has a kind of bloodless adequacy because he is a ghost:

Perhaps I've never really enjoyed living
As much as most people. At least, as
      they seem to do,
Without knowing that they enjoy it.
      Whereas I've often known
That I didn't enjoy it.

That is the way Lord Claverton talks. It is "poetry" by no definition but this one, that it embodies the exact meaning that requires embodying, at this point in this fable.

[. . .]

This extraordinary explicitness isn't making a point of throwing cards on the table, or dramatizing its own candor; it is simply a function of the language Eliot gives characters to speak in the most matter-of-fact way. Mrs. Carghill neither *wields* this talk nor is subsumed by it; she utters it and is detached from it. A Lear, a Cassius, an Antony, by being preternaturally articulate becomes a function of the capacity of the English language for expressiveness: an upwelling: an overflow: anything, in fact, but an embodiment of human privacy articulating what it chooses to articulate. One cannot conceive of a silent Othello, and Cordelia's silences are a mode of speech; but Lord Claverton and Mrs. Carghill have their reticences and their blighted areas.

The tension of *The Elder Statesman*, in fact, is located in the very idea of human privacy. It is a tension between privacies of two sorts: the sort which withholds itself behind a rôle and one day withers into a ghost—

> If I've been looking at this engagement
>   book, to-day,
> Not over breakfast, but before tea,
> It's the empty pages that I've been
>   fingering –
> The first empty pages since I entered
>   Parliament.

—and the blessed sort which can give itself into communion with another person precisely because it *is* a privacy, a self, a serene personal entity, this and not an interfering determination to make its existence felt. "I've been freed," Lord Claverton sums up a few minutes before the end of the play,

> . . . from the self that pretends to be
>   someone;
> And in becoming no one, I begin to
>   live.
> It is worth while dying, to find out
>   what life is.

Then the lovers, Charles and Monica, close the play as they opened it.

[. . .]

The play's form is as simple as medi-aeval music: a precarious compromise between something as sparely intimate as *At the Hawk's Well* and the innocent pretensions of a formal theatre. The actors who can combine the authority and self-effacement it demands are to be found, one supposes, in some ideal world not very

different from ours but less avid of brilliance. The work will never attract Mr. Elia Kazan. Mr. Eliot can be forgiven if he doesn't much care. He has written, perhaps under the illusion that he was serving a theatre that exists, the most intimate of his works, so much so that the lyric dedication of the book to his wife is perfectly in keeping. That drama is the most personal of forms is one way of stating this play's theme. As Lord Claverton was able to enter into reality only through others, through a daughter he had hitherto tried to keep to himself, a son he had constrained, and a former lover he had allowed to be bought off, so his poet is set free from the lyric flame by writing for other voices, not knowing whose voices they will be.

Bonamy Dobrée. "The London Stage." *Sewanee Review* 67 (Winter 1959), 109–15.

What most critics of Mr. Eliot's plays seem to ignore is that he is writing a new kind of drama. Whereas most plays appeal to the passions—pity, terror, the glamor of love—or to the intellect, or would stir our zeal for political reform, his plays are based on an appeal to the conscience, or the consciousness of self. Here is this person, he says in effect, guilty of this or that; how far are you, dear spectator, in the like case? Our response comes from a different center. That is why some people do not applaud his plays; nobody likes to be made to think about his weakness, his failures, or his sins. Not that many of us have committed crimes: but then crimes, as we are told in this play, are in relation to the law, sins in relation to the sinner. To be sure, plays *about* conscience are not lacking; we need only think of *Hamlet*, or of *Julius Caesar*, or, for that matter, the Oedipus plays. *The Elder Statesman*, indeed, has a close relation to these last; there is a possible accidental murder, a mortifying sexual business, which worry Lord Claverton's conscience, and a final reconciliation as at Colonus, a kind of redemption. *Oedipus at Colonus* is only a shadowy background, "a starting-point," to use Eliot's own phrase for what he owes the classical drama; the background does not obtrude. But in all the plays about conscience, from Sophocles to Ibsen, we are detached spectators. We sympathize with the struggling character, we perhaps enter into his difficulties, his agonies. Here, however, we are forced to ask ourselves: "Have I never run away from myself? Have I never tried to blot out incidents from my past?"

[. . .]

All of us, no doubt, in one degree or another, try to evade the actuality that is ourselves. "The great business of his life (Dr. Johnson said) was to escape from himself," so Boswell informs us. But what in a play makes a commonplace theme into a universal one is the power with which it is driven home, how far it is thrown into relief against the whiffling activity, or the pompous pretensions, of everyday life. It is through the gradual revelation of Lord Claverton to himself that Mr. Eliot makes the theme tell. Little by little we hear of Claverton's terror of being alone, and his equal need for privacy; of his loneliness, as he conceives it, his isolation. Isolation? [. . .] Little by little Claverton comes to a realization of this covering-up process, which began with a dissatisfaction with himself that made him always seek justification. There is general comment upon the worst failures, that of men who have to pretend to themselves that their failures are successes. He forces himself to admit, "What I want to escape from / Is myself": but you can't escape from your own failures. As the play progresses, and he has every shred of self-respect torn from him, he seems to grow in stature because at last he faces himself. He can even take blows with equanimity. When Mrs. Carghill goes over their broken love-affair, she says that her friend (a mysterious, worldly-shrewd Effie) has told her, "That man is hollow . . . / Or did she say yellow?"; he hardly flinches. It is all part of the accusation he is leveling at himself.

How far his failures haunt him is revealed in the intensely dramatic scene where his son Michael turns upon him and rends him for trying to distort his life. The young man wants to go abroad, to work out his own destiny as an individual, and not dwindle to being the son of a distinguished figure. Why does he want to go abroad? his father asks him. Has he been guilty of manslaughter? Oh no, Michael tells him; he's far too good a driver for that! Has he got into a mess with a woman? "I'm not such a fool / As to get myself involved in a breach of promise suit." He accuses him of wanting to escape from himself, from his failure in England, the irony of the imputations escaping Michael. [. . .]

If the first two acts are dramatic enough in their surprises, the play in the last, moving scene becomes contemplative rather than dramatic, unity being maintained by the thread of comedy, not always ironic, which Mr. Eliot skillfully weaves into the basic sadness surrounding the man we now know to be dying, and who comes to know it himself, not without relief. "It is worth while dying, to find out what life is." At the end he achieves tremendous dignity. When he tells Monica and Charles that he is going to confess, he asks Charles if there is nothing in his life he would wish to hide, some meanness, cowardice, or even occasion for ridicule? Here, of course, he touches all of us. "We are the hollow men / We are the stuffed men" just as much as he is. [. . .] [H]e comes to realize that he has never yet been able to confess because he has passed his life without love, even for his wife [. . .]. And does Monica love him, the real him, or only an idol, the part he plays, the sham he has built up? She responds beautifully; her love for Charles has given her understanding: and Claverton's love also enlarges itself. From being selfish and possessive—though, as he says, we must always respect love whenever we meet it, however selfish it may be—it becomes generous; he gladly gives Monica to Charles, and she comes to love her father with a more real love now that she sees him for what he really is. Love, in fact, is the resolution of the whole play, which at the end is suffused with an ethos that is a curious dovetailing of the Christian ethos with that of the Perennial Philosophy. "I am only a beginner in the practice of loving," the stricken man says, but "that is something." He professes love even for his son, in a passage that comes perilously near the sentimental. Yet his extraordinary new dignity asserts itself as he withdraws to meditate under the beech tree, a place which has become to him a kind of holy spot.

This has been called, and is now advertised on the posters as being, "Mr. Eliot's most human play." This may be because of the delicacy with which he treats the young lovers, but one ventures to think that it is judged to be such because of its greater clarity. Not that the story is plainer than in, say, *The Confidential Clerk*, but that the phrasing is absolutely sure throughout. There is never a word wasted. It is, no doubt, written in some form of verse (the text is not yet to hand), though only once or twice does it have the rhythm or

intensity of poetry; but then, verse on the stage is no more than the most effective form of speech for an actor to utter. The structure of the play too is beautifully balanced, dramatic structure being the way in which the emotions are induced in the spectator to produce a final result. There is no dominant crisis, either in the action or emotionally; there is a kind of inexorable movement from the beginning. It might be accounted to fail dramatically as a whole, though not in detail. Yet, after all, one judges a play by the mood in which one leaves the theatre. Has the katharsis (or whatever you like to call it) appropriate to the kind of play been achieved? Has it enlarged the bounds of one's sympathy with or understanding of other people? or in this case, has it brought about any kind of revelation of one's self to one's self? Judged by such standards, *The Elder Statesman* is Mr. Eliot's best play of the peculiar individual kind he has set himself to fashion, enduring a popular form with a deeper meaning.

Best, of course, within its particular context, and measured by the degree to which the dramatist has succeeded in doing what he set out to do, provided always that the "matter" was worth dramatization. It has been complained, and so far as that goes the young couple in the play urge it upon Claverton, that to let conscience over errors prey upon one to the extent depicted, is morbid; errors moreover that have produced no harm. [. . .] Morbid? Maybe. But without conscience no civilized community is possible; and it is the business of the dramatist to isolate and underline certain characteristics in human behavior. The play lacks, perhaps, the pitying humanity of *Murder in the Cathedral*; no characters emerge so starkly and yet so subtly as Agatha and Lady Monchensey in *The Family Reunion*; and so on with the other plays. But from all the previous plays the spectator, I do not say the reader, emerges with a certain puzzledom. All draw their response from the individual conscience, in varying degrees; but the moral problem posed does not seem to find its solution completely in the action of the characters, or if it does, it is based on premises not all can accept. There is loss and gain; but it would seem, immediately after seeing it, that although something has been lost from the giddier roundabouts of the earlier plays, more has been gained on the simpler swings of the present one.

[. . .]

Checklist of Additional Reviews

*"Mr. Eliot's Most Human Play." *Times*, 26 August 1958, p. 11.
*Philip Hope-Wallace. "T. S. Eliot's New Play: *The Elder Statesman*." *Manchester Guardian*, 27 August 1958, [page no. unknown].
*T. C. Worsley. "Mr. Eliot at Colonus." *New Statesman* 56 (30 August 1958), 245–46.
W. A. Darlington. "By T. S. Eliot." *New York Times*, 31 August 1958, sec. 2, p. 3.
*Kenneth Tynan. [*The Elder Statesman*]. *Observer*, 31 August 1958, [page no. unknown].
*Christopher Salmon and Leslie Paul. "Two Views of Mr. Eliot's New Play." *Listener* 60 (4 September 1958), 340–41.
*Alan Brien. "The Invisible Dramatist." *Spectator*, 5 September 1958, pp. 305–06.
Harold Hobson. "T. S. Eliot's *The Elder Statesman*." *Christian Science Monitor*, 6 September 1958, p. 4.
"The Elder Statesman." *Variety*, 19 September 1958, [page no. unknown].
*"London Opening of an Eliot Play." *Times*, 26 September 1958, [page no. unknown].
W. Macqueen Pope. "O'Neill, Eliot Represented on West End." *Morning Telegraph* [New York], 9 October 1958, [page no. unknown].
*Caryl Brahms. "*The Elder Statesman*." *Plays and Players* 6 (November 1958), 11.
Dorothy Livesay. "London Notes." *Canadian Forum* 38 (November 1958), 171–72.
Gerald Weales. "*The Elder Statesman*." *Kenyon Review* 21 (1959), 473–78.
John R. Willingham. "*The Elder Statesman*." *Books Abroad* 33 (1959), 410.
Denis Donoghue. "Eliot in Fair Colonus: *The Elder Statesman*." *Studies: An Irish Quarterly Review* 48 (Spring 1959), 49–58.
*"Thespis: Theatre Notes." *English* 12 (Spring 1959), 139–40.
*Frank Kermode. "What Became of Sweeney?" *Spectator* 202 (10 April 1959), 513.
*Barbara Everett. "*The Elder Statesman*." *Critical Quarterly* 1 (Summer 1959), 163–64, 166.
Leonard Unger. "Deceptively Simple—and Too Simple." *Virginia Quarterly Review* 35 (Summer 1959), 501–04.

Index

British and Irish journals are identified by an asterisk (∗); journals published in both the United States and the United Kingdom by two asterisks (∗∗).

Bach, Johann Sebastian 282, 325
Bacon, Francis 200
Bain, Donald 520–24
Balakian, Nona 576–78
Baltimore Evening Sun 23, 495
Balzac, Honoré de 13
Bantock, G. H. 513
Barber, C. L. 409
Barber, John 543
Barker, George 233, 358
Barnes, Howard 348, 526–27, 541
Barnes, T. R. 348
Barrett, William xxxvi, 513, 532–35
Barrymore, Ethel xxxv
Baudelaire, Charles 85, 124, 141, 149, 150,
    158, 162, 165, 184, 189, 195, 198, 207,
    209, 210, 218, 221, 285, 294, 356, 368,
    433, 572
  L'Art Romantique 221
  Curiosités aesthétiques 221
  Les Fleurs du Mal 356
  "*La Mort*" 184
  Journaux Intimes 221
Baxter, Beverly 543
Bazan, Don César de 79
Beardsley, Aubrey 373
Beaufort, John 563
Becker, William 563
Beethoven, Ludwig von 114, 442, 461, 470,
    480, 485
Beevers, John 294
Belgion, Montgomery xxviii, 253–54,
    280–81
Bell, Bernard Iddings 425
Bell, Clive xviii, xxiv, 34–36, 90, 91, 112–14
Bellow, Saul 563
Benchley, Robert 349
Benda, Julien 162
Benét, William Rose 120, 185–86, 316, 541
Bennett, Arnold 113
Bennett, Joan 240–41
Bentley, Eric 563
Berdyayev, Nikolai 488
Bergson, Henri 488
Bettany, F. G. 54, 72
Beyer, William Henry 544
Bhagavadgita 469, 474, 481
Bible, The Authorized Version 177
Binsse, Harry Lorin 425
Binyon, Lawrence 153
Birrell, Augustine 72
Birrell, Francis 178–79, 316
Bishop, Virginia Curry 425
Bixler, J. S. 425
Black, Ivan 375
Blackfriars 269, 309, 409, 425, 459–61
Blackman, M. C. 542

Blackmur, R[ichard] P. xxvii, xxxv, 222–24,
    273–75, 375, 425, 508–10
  The Expanse of Greatness 425
Blake, William 26, 33, 58, 61, 62, 64, 65–66,
    145, 195, 198, 199, 209, 219, 225, 240,
    443
Blast xiv, xvii, 10, 42
Blok, Aleksandr A. 264
Blum, Walter Cornelius 73
Boccaccio, Giovanni 177
  The Pearl 177
Bodgener, J. Henry 496
Bodkin, Maud xxxi, 386–88
Bogan, Louise 348, 409, 495
Boie, Mildred 375
Boileau, Nicholas 198
Bonnard, Pierre 34
Booklist 23
Bookman 46–47, 72, 146, 174, 192, 225,
    294
Books Abroad 583
Bossuet, Jacques-Benine 161
Boston Evening Transcript 22, 409, 425
Boston Herald 38, 119, 542
Boston Sunday Post 541
Boswell, James 581
Bradbrook, M[uriel] C[lara] xxxiii, 443–46,
    462–64
Bradley, F[rancis] H[erbert] 118, 150, 151,
    157, 158, 162, 172, 210, 368
  Appearance and Reality 118
Brahms, Caryl 583
Braithwaite, W. S. 22
Bramhall, John 151, 157, 158, 161, 162, 165,
    184, 202, 207, 220, 223
  Just Vindication of the English Church 161
Braque, Georges xviii, 34
Brégy, Katherine 397–99
Breit, Harvey 562
Brémond, Abbé 237, 239, 247
Brentford, Viscount 221
Brickell, Herschel 269
Bridges, Robert S. 24
  "The Necessity of Poetry" 24
Bridson, D. G. xxviii, 229–30, 251–53, 316
Brien, Alan 583
Bright, John 504
Brightman, Edgar Sheffield 425
Britain Today 495, 496
British Weekly 409
Bronowski, Jacob xxv, 149
Brooke, Nicholas 563
Brooke, Rupert 358
Brooklyn Eagle 348, 374, 541
Brooks, Cleanth xxvii, xxxviii, 254–56,
    390–91, 514
Brooks, Van Wyck 471

588

589

Eliot, T. S., prose: books
  After Strange Gods xiv, xxvii, xxviii–xxix,
    272–95, 312, 313, 314, 416, 417
  Dante xxv, 167–73
  Essays Ancient and Modern 357, 365
  For Lancelot Andrewes xxv–xxvi, 171–72,
    173, 182, 196, 213, 217, 219, 254, 258,
    280, 287, 357, 417
  Homage to John Dryden 122–26, 154, 155,
    163, 184, 196, 218, 220, 222–23, 357
  The Idea of a Christian Society xxxiv,
    412–25, 502, 510
  Notes Towards the Definition of Culture
    xxxiv–xxxv, 498–514
  The Sacred Wood xiii, xvii, xviii, xix–xx,
    xxviii, 52–73, 82, 87, 105, 114, 143, 145,
    150, 153, 155, 156–57, 158, 163–64,
    171, 172, 196, 206, 218, 219, 220, 239,
    254, 256, 263, 312, 314, 357
  Selected Essays xxvi, xxvii, xxviii, 194–226,
    252
  The Use of Poetry and the Use of Criticism
    xxvi, xxvii–xxviii, xxix, 236–69, 285, 359
  Projected [unwritten] books: *The School of
    Donne*, *The Outline of Royalism*, *The
    Principles of Modern Heresy* 149, 158
Eliot, Valerie Fletcher xxxvii, 567, 569, 571,
  573
Elizabeth I 161
Elizabeth II 547
Elliott, Denholm 549
Elyot, Simon 439
Elyot, Sir Thomas 439, 473
  [*The Boke Named the*] *Governour* 439, 473
Emmart, A. D. 495
Encyclopedia Britannica 473
Engel, A. Lehman 342
Engels, Friedrich 370
English 583
English Review xvii, 15–16, 23, 72,
  269
English-Speaking World 409
English Studies 73, 146, 438–39
Epistle of the Privy Council [Anon.] 478
Ethics 514
Euclid 579
Euripides 82, 195, 404, 548, 555, 560, 572
  Alcestis 548, 572
  Ion 548, 555, 560, 572
European 563
Evening News 543
Evening Standard 543
Everett, Barbara 583
Every, Brother George 295, 424
Everyman [journal] 294, 316
Everyman [play] 199, 326, 344
Ezekiel [Old Testament] 85, 115, 187

Fabre, Jean Henri 266
Faure, Elie 92
Fausset, Andrew Robert 221
Fénelon, Archbishop of Canterbury 149
Fenolloso, Ernest F. 266
Fergusson, Francis 156–58, 256–58, 409,
  563
Fernandez, Ramon 171, 172
Ferrar, Nicholas 459, 468, 472, 491
Field, Rowland 541, 544
Findlater, Richard xxxvi, 554–57
Firbank, Ronald 358
Fitts, Dudley 185
Fitzgerald, Edward 31
Fitzgerald, F[rancis] Scott 80, 287
Flaubert, Gustave 58
Flecker, James Elroy 358
Fleming, Peter 543
Flemyng, Robert 520
Fletcher, John 61, 114
  The Faithful Shepherdess 114
Fletcher, John Gould 483–85
  Elegies 484
  Symphonies 484
Flint, F[rank] S[tuart] xix, 53, 54, 55
Foerster, Norman 201, 203
  American Criticism 201
Fogerty, Elsie 300
Ford, Ford Madox [Ford Madox Hueffer] 23
Ford, John 220
Forster, E[dward] M[organ] xxxiv, 453, 542
Fortnightly 544
Forum 120
Forum and Century 349
Fox, Arthur W. 375
Fox, John J. 542
France, Anatole 109
Frank, Waldo 208–12, 256, 258, 422, 423,
  424
  Chart for Rough Water 422
Franklin, Benjamin 423
  Poor Richard's Almanac 423
Frazer, Sir James xxi, 83, 85, 100, 115, 116,
  368, 407
  The Golden Bough 83, 85, 116, 407
Freeman [United States] xix, xxiii, 44–46,
  61–64, 93–95, 97
Freeman [Ireland] 120
Freeman, John 126
Frere, John Hookham 229
Freud, Sigmund 62, 79, 456, 534
Friend 295
Friesz, Othon 34
Frobenius, Leo 266
Frost, Robert 16, 379
Froude, James Anthony 85, 368
Fugitive 90–91

590

Funke, Lewis 544
Fyvel, T. R. 544

Gabriel, Gilbert W. 348
Galilei, Galileo 418
Gallup, Donald C. 409, 425
Gannett, Lewis 542
G[ardiner], H[arold] C. 542
Gardner, Helen xxxvii, xxxviii, 495, 559–62, 571–73
Garland, Robert 348, 541
Garnett, David 133
Garrett, John 409
Garrison, W. E. 203–04, 495
Gary, Franklin 171–73
Gautier, Théophile 362
Gay, John 133
    The Beggar's Opera 133
Gaye, Phoebe Fenwick 380–81
Géraldy, Paul 14
Gerstäcker, Friedrich 439
    Germelshausen 439
Gibbs, Wolcott 541, 563
Gibson, W[ilfred] W[ilson] 9
Gidlow, Elsa 120
Gilbert, Sir William S. 550
Gilmore, William 374
*Glasgow Herald 225, 540
Goethe, Johann Wolfgang von 92, 145, 253, 263, 264, 435
    Faust 92
    Gelassenheit 435
Gohdes, Clarence 269
Goldring, Douglas xix, 53
Goldsmith, Oliver 85, 92, 111
Goodman, Paul 481–83
Gorman, Herbert S. 120
Gorman, William J. 192
Gosse, Edmund 123
Gourmont, Rémy de 62–63, 68, 70, 88, 155, 222
Grant, Duncan 90
Grant, Michael xxxviii, xli
    T. S. Eliot: The Critical Heritage xxxviii, xli
*Granta 225, 269, 295
Graves, Robert xxxvi
Gray, Thomas 114, 125, 126, 187, 211
    "Elegy Written in a Country Churchyard" 211
Gregory, Horace xxix, xxxi, 192, 284–87, 339–40, 349, 403–06, 471–73
Guinness, Sir Alec 520

HD [Hilda Doolittle] 36, 404
Hailey, Foster 542
Haldeman-Julius, E. 514
Hamalian, Leo 544

Hamilton, Alexander 507
Hamilton, Fyfe 513
Hamilton, Ian 540
Handbook of Birds of Eastern North America 118
Hannay, A. H. 72
Harding, D. W. xxix, xxxiii, 244–45, 307–08, 370–73, 417–20, 447, 448–49, 450, 451, 465–67
Hardy, Thomas 91, 140, 182, 275, 279, 281, 289, 292, 364
    "Barbara of the House of Grebe" 281
    "Surview" 279
Harrison, Frederic 504
Hart, Henry G. 120
Hartley, Anthony 563
Hartley, Marsden 22
Harvard Advocate xiv
Harvard Alumni Bulletin 514
Harvard Progressive 425
Häusermann, H. W. 438–39
Hawkins, Ann 349
Hawkins, Desmond xxxi–xxxii, 269, 399–401
Hawkins, William 541, 562
Hawthorne, Nathaniel 142, 328
    Notebooks 142
Hayakawa, S. I. xxix, 287–91
Haydn, Franz Joseph 434, 492
Hayes, Richard 563
Hayward, John 348, 374
Hazlitt, Henry xxvii, 200–02
Hazlitt, William 201
Heard, Gerald 177–78
Hedley, Bishop John Cuthbert 479
    Prayer and Contemplation 479
Hegel, Georg Friedrich Wilhelm 488
Heimann, Heidi 543
Heller, Otto 120
Hemingway, Ernest 286, 287
Henley, William Ernest 10, 11
    London Voluntaries 10
Heppenstall, Rayner 269
Heraclitus 471, 481, 488, 490, 494
Herbert, Sir A[lan] P[atrick] 453
Herbert, George 207, 446, 468
Herrick, Robert 441
Hewes, Henry xxxvii, 547–50, 562, 567–70
Heywood, Robert 544
Heywood, Thomas 220
Higinbotham, R. N. 495
Hillyer, Robert xxvii, 224–25
Hitler, Adolf 345, 423
Hivnor, Mary 563
Hobbes, Thomas 151, 161, 162, 202, 206, 220
Hobson, Harold 540, 541, 542, 543, 562, 583
Hodgson, Ralph 358

Lightning Source UK Ltd.
Milton Keynes UK
UKHW022104220822
407649UK00006B/1295